KUPERARD

2007

The ORIGINAL

Pets Welcome

50th Edition! Summer

Including our Guide to Pet Friendly Pubs

and Holidays with Horses

NEW French Holiday section

Taking your pet to France – all you need to know

For Contents see page 3

Index of towns/ counties see back of guide

Contents

EDITORIAL SECTION 2-70
FOREWORD 5
PETS PICTURES 40

DONATE £1 TO PETS' CHARITY 53
TOURIST BOARD RATINGS 72, 306, 346
READER'S OFFER VOUCHERS 407

FRANCE 21

ENGLAND

BUCKINGHAMSHIRE 75
CAMBRIDGESHIRE 76
CHESHIRE 76
CORNWALL 77
ISLES OF SCILLY 114
CUMBRIA 115
DERBYSHIRE 141
DEVON 145
DORSET 188
DURHAM 202
GLOUCESTERSHIRE 204
HAMPSHIRE 210
HEREFORDSHIRE 214
ISLE OF WIGHT 217
KENT 222
LANCASHIRE 224
LEICESTERSHIRE & RUTLAND 227
LINCOLNSHIRE 228
NORFOLK 230
NORTHUMBERLAND 244
NOTTINGHAMSHIRE 248
OXFORDSHIRE 249
SHROPSHIRE 251
SOMERSET 254
STAFFORDSHIRE 264
SUFFOLK 265
SURREY 272
EAST SUSSEX 273
WEST SUSSEX 278
WARWICKSHIRE 280
WILTSHIRE 282
WORCESTERSHIRE 282
EAST YORKSHIRE 286
NORTH YORKSHIRE 288
WEST YORKSHIRE 303

SCOTLAND

ABERDEEN, BANFF & MORAY 308
ARGYLL & BUTE 310
AYRSHIRE & ARRAN 317
BORDERS 318
DUMFRIES & GALLOWAY 320
DUNBARTONSHIRE 323
EDINBURGH & LOTHIANS 323
FIFE 324
HIGHLANDS 325
LANARKSHIRE 337
PERTH & KINROSS 338
SCOTTISH ISLANDS 343

WALES

ANGLESEY & GWYNEDD 349
NORTH WALES 357
CARMARTHENSHIRE 365
CEREDIGION 367
PEMBROKESHIRE 370
POWYS 378
SOUTH WALES 382

IRELAND 384

NARROWBOAT HOLIDAYS 384

HOLIDAYS WITH HORSES 385

GUIDE TO PET FRIENDLY PUBS 390

INDEX OF TOWNS & COUNTIES 424

ISBN 978-1-85055-395-3

Typeset by FHG Guides Ltd, Paisley.
Printed and bound in Singapore by Imago.

Distribution. Book Trade: ORCA Book Services, Stanley House,
3 Fleets Lane, Poole, Dorset BH15 3AJ
(Tel: 01202 665432; Fax: 01202 666219)
e-mail: mail@orcabookservices.co.uk
Published by FHG Guides Ltd., Abbey Mill Business Centre,
Seedhill, Paisley PA1 ITJ (Tel: 0141-887 0428 Fax: 0141-889 7204).
e-mail: admin@fhguides.co.uk

Pets Welcome! is published by FHG Guides Ltd,
part of Kuperard Group.

Cover design: FHG Guides
Cover Pictures: With thanks to
Clive Hockley, Dunstable.
Gary Baxter, Fleet.
Elaine Brooks, Leeds.
Mrs Cullimore, Fareham
Thanks to Philip Walker for photographs on page 359.

All the advertisers in **PETS WELCOME!** have an entry in the appropriate classified section and each classified entry may carry one or more of the following symbols:

- 🐕 This symbol indicates that pets are welcome free of charge.
- **£** The £ indicates that a charge is made for pets. We quote the amount where possible, either per night or per week.
- **pw!** This symbol shows that the establishment has some special provision for pets; perhaps an exercise facility or some special feeding or accommodation arrangements.
- ⌂ Indicates separate pets' accommodation.

PLEASE NOTE that all the advertisers in **PETS WELCOME!** extend a welcome to pets and their owners but they may attach conditions. The interests of other guests have to be considered and it is usually assumed that pets will be well trained, obedient and under the control of their owner.

Foreword

We know just how important your dog is to you and your family, and in this edition of **Pets Welcome!**, we have put together a collection of quality properties where you and your pet will be warmly welcomed. Choose from self-catering cottages and flats, caravans, hotels and B&Bs. All of our advertisers go out of their way to ensure that the whole family feel at home, and many are dog owners themselves and have a real understanding and affection for pets.

A little common sense and consideration will ensure that our proprietors continue to welcome pets and responsible owners in the future. You should discourage your pet from jumping up on furniture or people, and also remember that muddy paws and sandy coats are not always welcome indoors. Dogs should never be left unattended, especially in a strange environment - a lonely or unhappy pet is likely to get into mischief.

Most of our entries are of long standing and are tried and tested favourites with animal lovers. However as publishers we do not inspect the accommodation advertised in Pets Welcome! and an entry does not imply our recommendation. Some proprietors offer fuller facilities for pets than others, and in the classified entry which we give each advertiser we try to indicate by symbols whether or not there are any special facilities and if additional charges are involved. However, we suggest that you raise any queries or particular requirements when you make enquiries and bookings.

If you have any problems or complaints, please raise them on the spot with the owner or his representative in the first place. We will follow up complaints if necessary, but we regret that we cannot act as intermediaries nor can we accept responsibility for details of accommodation and/or services described here. Happily, serious complaints are few. Finally, if you have to cancel or postpone a holiday booking, please give as much notice as possible. This courtesy will be appreciated and it could save later difficulties.

Boarding your Pet (Page 13), Preparing your Dogs and Cats for Travel Abroad (Page 16), Readers' Offer Vouchers (Page 407), Holidays with Horses (Page 385), and The Guide to Pet Friendly Pubs (Page 390) are now regular features, and on page 36 you will find some useful information on keeping your pet happy in warm weather. Our latest selection of Pets Pictures starts on page 39.

Those who like to venture further afield will find a selection of holiday properties in France – see pages 21-36, and we have included some practical advice about the Pets Travel Scheme to ensure that you are fully prepared.

We would be happy to receive readers' suggestions on any other useful features. Please also let us know if you have had any unusual or humorous experiences with your pet on holiday. This always makes interesting reading! And we hope that you will mention **Pets Welcome!** when you make your holiday inquiries or bookings.

Anne Cuthbertson, **Editor**

Around the magnificent coast of Wales
Pembrokeshire, Cardigan Bay, Snowdonia, Anglesey, Lleyn Peninsula, Borders
Choose from over 200 Quality Cottages
Pets Welcome Free
A small specialist agency with 40 years experience letting quality cottages.
Enjoy unashamed luxury in traditional Welsh Cottages. Situated near safe sandy beaches and in the heart of Wales — famed for scenery, walks, wild flowers, birds, badgers and foxes.
Pets welcome FREE at most of our properties
Leonard Rees, Quality Cottages, Cerbid, Solva, Haverfordwest, Pembrokeshire. SA62 6YE
Telephone: (01348) 837871 for our FREE Colour Brochure
QUALITY COTTAGES CERBID
www.qualitycottages.co.uk
100s of pictures of quality cottages and beautiful Wales

Before you go anywhere,
take a trip to
Pets at Home.
Whatever your pet needs, cruise down to Pets at Home. With a comprehensive range of quality food, treats, toys and bedding, we've everything a pet could ask for every day of the year. And when it's holiday time, there's even a fantastic choice of accessories for pets on the move, including pet carriers, H2O 'to go' water bottles, portable travel bowls, toothbrushes, travel blankets and more. Plus, if it's travel tips you're looking for, we can offer all the expert advice you need to ensure a smooth journey. Wherever you're heading, head for Pets at Home first.
pets
at home
For details of your nearest store, simply call 0800 328 8255 or visit our website www.petsathome.com

See Advertisement under Perthshire, St. Fillans

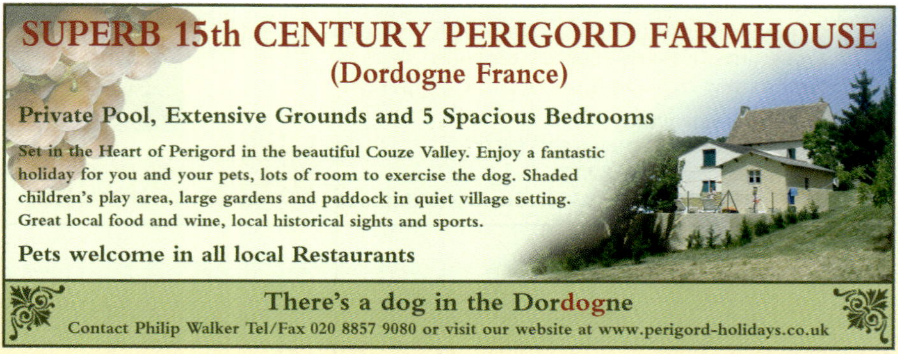

Since the advent of the pet's passport scheme more and more owners are opting to take their 'best friend' on holiday to other countries. With that in mind, we have included in this edition of Pets Welcome a small selection of **holiday properties in France.** You will find full details of each property, plus some very useful practical information and a brief description of the regions. Enjoy your stay.

See page 21 for full selection.

The Winalot Approved Dog Friendly Awards

Dog friendly places to stay, play, go, eat or drink around the UK, as well as dog friendly services, shops and celebrities.

Overall Winner:
Ickworth Hotel, Bury St Edmunds, Suffolk

Category winner Most Dog Friendly place to EAT & DRINK:
Hollybush Inn, Denford, Staffordshire

For more information and a list of Category Winners see PAGES 390-391
Or visit **www.winalot-dog.co.uk** to read all about nominations and winners.

Boarding Your Pet

by Ken Oultram

Blue Grass Animal Hotel

THE remarkable growth of travel and tourism has provided satellite industries like **Animal Boarding Establishments (ABE)** with year-round financial benefits, though ABE owners will reveal they were never entirely dependent on the holiday-maker. For this is very much a service industry in its own right; greatly appreciated by, for example, pet owners who may be moving house...entering hospital...taking a work assignment abroad...having the builders in...throwing a fireworks party...coping with a bitch in season or, perhaps, a cat recuperating from surgery. As looking after pets is an awesome responsibility and a job for the professional, is it reasonable to expect a neighbour or pet-sitter to take this on?

Staff at an ABE must be alert for blood, constipation, diarrhoea, lethargy, coughing, fleas, incontinence, sneezing, worms and vomit! It is taken for granted that an ABE will accept the allergic, the arthritic, the diabetic, the epileptic, the hyper-active and the neurotic...and administer pills, drops and injections. Most of all they will be expected to guarantee the safe-keeping of your pet during your absence. Postmen may claim they face the risk of dog bites, but try opening the kennel door of an outsize hound with a 30 inch neck and two cute rows of flashing stained teeth.

Early advance booking at an ABE for your pet's boarding card is now essential as the equation of 5,000 kennels/catteries to cope with a potential 11 million UK dogs and cats simply doesn't balance and, at peak times, you'll discover there's no room at the inn.

All ABEs are inspected annually by an officer from the Environmental Health Department of the Local Authority which issues a licence to operate. It is illegal to run an ABE without a licence and this must be displayed for all to see (usually in the reception area).

Some general guidelines:

- A brochure indicates a professional approach. Ring round requesting these.
- Do NOT book if the ABE will not permit you to inspect the facilities. On arrival ask to see the exercise area for dogs (leaving dogs to their own devices all day in outside runs is NOT exercise). In catteries check that sneeze barriers are installed.
- If vaccinations are not necessary do NOT book; especially if dogs are not required to be vaccinated against kennel cough.
- Ask if the ABE's insurance covers your pet's stay; otherwise a nasty vet's bill could be awaiting your return.
- Many pet owners have more than one dog or cat. Look for family-sized units and check heating facilities (after all, our winters are twice the duration of our summers...and the ABE staff need to be kept warm too!)
- Check that your pet will not come into contact with another client's pet.
- On arrival – your ears, eyes and nose will tell all! You are looking for cleanliness, contented boarders and an experienced, caring staff. If apprehensive ask if you may send someone to visit your pet during its stay. You could also try your pet for a day (or a night) prior to the planned lengthy stay.
- If your pet is taken ill, ensure that the ABE is advised whether to call its own veterinarian or your own. Leave a contact number.
- If the ABE does not stock your pet's favourite food, offer to supply this, though there may not be any discount off your bill by doing so.
- Ask if a grooming service is offered. Some ABEs do. Others provide a collection and delivery service.

Finally, the time has surely come for an exhaustive, independent survey of British kennels and catteries with a one-to-four star ratings assessment. Perhaps one of the major motoring organisations should attempt this.... after all, 99% of ABE clients arrive on four wheels.

For free advice and addresses
call the Animal Boarding Advisory Bureau on 01606 891303
or the Feline Advisory Bureau on 0870 742 2278 during office hours.
You may even wish to recommend your own
Animal Boarding Establishment.

12 Months FREE Petback Protection

Missing Pets Bureau

It's easy to say it'll never happen. But hundreds of pets go missing in the UK **every day** and in unfamiliar surroundings, pets on holiday can be hard to find.
Give your pet extra security with a **free** identification and reunification service.

Protection

You get a unique pet ID tag linked to a 24-hour freephone number for people to call if they find your pet. There's also a 24-hour hotline for you to call if your pet goes missing, and a unique serial number to protect your identity.

Action

The team works day and night. They will send you a pet recovery action sheet. Place your pet's details on the national Missing Pets Register. And contact all the major animal charities on your behalf.

Response

Chances are your pet will have been located before you even know it has gone. That's how fast Missing Pets Bureau works.

Give your pet the security of Petback protection today

Call freephone 0800 0198 123

Email: pets@missingpetsbureau.com

Web: www.missingpetsbureau.com

Preparing your Dogs and Cats for travel abroad

How can my pet travel? Because of stringent requirements, dogs and cats travelling under the so-called pet passport scheme cannot make last minute reservations; in general, six-month advance planning is required. Veterinarians must implant a microchip in the animal, inoculate it against rabies, have a laboratory recognized by the Department for Environment, Food and Rural Affairs (DEFRA) confirm by blood sample that the vaccine is active, and issue a PETS certificate. Certificates are valid from six months after obtaining the blood sample results until the date of the animal's next rabies booster shot. (Dogs and cats resident in Britain whose blood sample was drawn before Feb 29, 2000 are exempt from this six month rule). Dogs and cats must also be treated against ticks and tapeworms no less than 24 nor more than 48 hours before check-in (when the animal enters carrier's custody). Animals travelling by air are placed in containers bearing an official seal (the number of which is also inscribed on the PETS certificate) to ensure animals are not exposed to disease en route. Sealing requirements do not apply to Cyprus or Malta. Owners must also sign a certificate attesting that the animal has not been outside participating territories in the last six months. Travellers are cautioned that Britain will enforce its rules rigorously.

Your pet must be injected with a harmless identification ISO (International Standards Organisation) approved microchip. This chip will be read by a handheld scanning device.

From and back to the UK.

Ask your vet to implant an ISO (International Standards Organisation) approved microchip - then to vaccinate against rabies recording the batch number of the vaccine on a veterinary certificate together with the microchip number.

Approximately 30 days later your vet should take a blood sample and send it to one of the DEFRA approved laboratories to check that the vaccine has provided the correct level of protection.

Your vet will then issue you with a certificate confirming all the above – in the UK this is called The Pet Travel Scheme Re-Entry Certificate. It is valid for the life of the rabies vaccine, so keep your rabies vaccine up to date and a new certificate will be issued without the need for further blood tests.

Six months from the taking of a successful blood test you will be able to enter or re-enter the UK from Western Europe and 28 other countries including Australia, Japan and Singapore.

Pets must be treated for ticks and for the echinococcus parasite by a qualified vet who will record this on an official UK certificate not less than 24 hours and not more than 48 hours before entry into the UK. We are trying to secure changes in this very awkward timetable, which is being rigidly enforced.

On entering the UK you must therefore have two official certificates; one for the microchip, rabies vaccine and blood test; the second for treatment against ticks and parasites. You will also have to sign a residence declaration form - provided by the travel operator who is carrying out the checking. It simply confirms that the pet has not been outside the approved countries in the previous six months.

From Europe to the UK

As above, you must microchip your pet, vaccinate against rabies and approximately 30 days later your vet will take a blood test sending it to one of the laboratories from the list of those approved by MAFF. SIX MONTHS after a successful blood test your pet will be allowed to travel to the UK providing it has been treated against ticks and worms.

Costs:

- Microchip: Should be in the region of £25.00
- Vaccine: Varies according to vet but again approximately £30.00
- Blood test: We know that the blood testing laboratory at Weybridge (VLA) charge £49.50 per test.

Therefore anything in addition is that levied by the vet. Providing the rabies vaccination is kept up to date the blood test will not have to be repeated. Should there be a break between rabies vaccines a further blood test would have to be taken and then a period of 6 months allowed before re-entry to the UK would be permitted.

Therefore: Microchip and blood-test are one-off costs but the rabies vaccination is a yearly or 2 yearly cost depending on the vaccine used.

More information can be obtained from

Department of Environment, Food and Rural Affairs PETS
website: www.defra.gov.uk/animalh/quarantine/index.htm

Scottish Executive Environment and Rural Affairs Department
website: www.scotland.gov.uk/AHWP

PETS Helpline:
0870 241 1710 (Monday to Friday – 08.30 to 17.00 UK time)
E-mail:
pets.helpline@defra.gsi.gov.uk (enclose your postal address and daytime telephone number)

Current ports of entry are Dover (from Calais by ferry), Portsmouth (from Caen, Cherbourg, Le Havre or St Malo by ferry) and Folkestone (from Calais or Cheriton by Eurotunnel). London Heathrow is the authorised port-of-entry for : British Midland Airlines from Amsterdam-Schiphol, Brussels, Madrid, Palma Majorca, and Paris (Paris for guide dogs only); Finnair from Helsinki; and Lufthansa from Frankfurt.

The laboratories approved by MAFF for blood testing:

Veterinary Laboratory Agency New Haw, Addlestone Surrey KT15 3NB UNITED KINGDOM	Tel: (+44) 01932 357 840 Fax:(+44) 01 932 357 239 Costs: £49.50
BioBest Pentlands Science Park Bush Loan Penicuik Midlothian EH26 0PZ SCOTLAND	Tel: (+44) 0131 445 6101 Fax: (+44) 0131 445 6102 Costs: £32.50
Agence Francaise De Securite Sanitaire des Aliments Nancy Domaine de Pixerecourt BP9 F-54220 Maizeville FRANCE	Tel: (+33) 3 83 298950 Fax:(+33) 3 83 298959 Costs: 425ff = approx £42
National Veterinary Institute Commission of Diagnosites Section of Diagnostic Department of Virology S -75189 Uppsala SWEDEN	Tel: (+46) 1867 4000 Fax:(+46) 1867 4467 Costs: 500K=approx £40
Danish Veterinary Institute for Virus Research Lindholm DK-4771 Kalvehave DENMARK	Tel: (+45) 72 34 60 00 Fax:(+45) 72 34 79 01 Costs: 252K=approx £25
National Veterinary and Food Research Institute Mustialankatu 3 FI - 00790 Helsinki FINLAND	Tel: (+35) 20 77 24 576 Fax:(+35) 20 77 24 363 Costs: 396.50 Fmark = approx £26.00
Institut fur Virologie Frankfurter Strasse 107 D35392 Giessen GERMANY	Tel: (+49) 641 99 38350 Fax: (+49) 641 99 38359 Costs: 72.60DM= approx £25

Dept. for Equine, Pets and Vaccine Control Virology Unit Federal Institute for the Control of Viral Infection in Animals Robert-Koch-Gasse 17 A-2340 Modling AUSTRIA	Tel: (+43) 2236 46 640 909 Fax:(+43) 2236 46 640 941	Costs: 600 schillings= approx £30
Instituto Zooproftilattico Sperimentale delle Venezie Via Romea 14/A 1-35020 Legnaro ITALY	Tel: (+39) 4980 84 259 Fax:(+39) 4988 30 530	Costs: price unknown
Laboratorio central de veterinaria de Santa Fe Camino del Jau s/n E-18320 Santa Fe (Granada) SPAIN	Tel: (+34) 958 44 03 75 Fax:(+34) 958 44 12 00	Costs: price unknown
Institute Pasteur of Brussels 642, Rue-Engeland-Straat B 1180 Brussels BELGIUM	Tel: (+32) 2 373 32 56 Fax:(+32) 2 373 33 86	Costs: 1,500BF- approx £25
Institute of Veterinary Virology Schweizerische Tollwutzentrale Langgass-Strasse 122 CH-3012 Bern SWITZERLAND	Tel: (+41) 31 631 2378 Fax:(+41) 31 631 2534	Costs: 96.75 SF= approx £40

What we musn't forget?

✔ Medicine, if needed ✔ Toys ✔ Health certificates ✔ Food and drink dishes

✔ The dog's basket or blanket – it is extremely important that your dog has something to make him feel at home ✔ A thermometer

✔A bell to hang around the dog's collar ✔ A can opener if you have canned food

✔ A deodorant for the hotel room ✔ Paper towels ✔ Brushes to brush your dog

✔ A towel to dry the dog in case of rain or when you get back to the hotel room

HOLIDAYS IN FRANCE
For you and your pets

Since the advent of the pet's passport scheme more and more owners are opting to take their 'best friend' on holiday to other countries.

With that in mind, we have included in this edition of **Pets Welcome!** a small selection of holiday properties in France.

You will find full details of each property, plus some very useful practical information and a brief description of the regions.

Enjoy your stay!

The Pet Passport Scheme

The Extended Pet Holiday • with thanks to Philip Walker

Earlier this year I was in my local vet's surgery in France when he asked me to come into the surgery and translate for two English ladies who wanted their dog treated for the return journey the following day. Unfortunately their friends who live in France had advised them that the passport expires after three years. Indeed for French residents this is the case, but they were UK residents and the UK passport expires after two years. They were mortified to learn that their dog would either have to receive a new Rabies vaccine and stay with their friends for six months in France, put the dog in quarantine for six months in Calais or destroy the dog.

The Pet Passport scheme has been running for a number of years now and many of us pet owners have found it a valuable addition to our holidays. What better way to reward your best friend than a trip across the Channel, letting them enjoy a proper holiday with the family. Our German Shepherd, Max, has made over thirty trips on Euro Star and has become a well loved visitor in our village in the Dordogne. We often see many families with their dogs and cats queuing in "Pet Passport" control on our return trip through the Calais terminal, but oh dear, not a single trip goes by without our standing behind some poor pet owner in tears because their pet is not able to make the crossing that evening.

The sad thing is that by the time you reach the terminal in Calais it's far too late to rectify the problem. The French staff, who are marvellous, are often heard explaining to disbelieving Brits, "sorry madam, but your dog must remain in Calais" or "it is the UK Government who insist on this, we cannot change the rules".

There are a number of absolutes that all pet owners must be familiar with.

The UK Pet Passport expires after two years and must be renewed before expiry. Just to confuse matters the French version expires after three years and the Belgian passport after one year

With the first passport your pet cannot re-enter the UK until six months after the date the original blood sample was tested. You can leave the UK before this date but not return until six months has expired.

Before your return you must visit a registered vet and make sure your animals tick & worming has been carried out

The key timing is your arrival in the UK. You must visit a vet at least 24 hours before making the crossing back into the UK. You have only a further 24-hour period to enter the UK or you will have to visit a vet again and complete the process once more. In other words you cannot return to the UK more than 48 hours after visiting the vet.

After administering the treatment the vet must sign and stamp your pet's passport. No stamp or signature, no crossing.

The trade name of the product used must be clearly listed in the passport, if not, **no crossing**.

The vet must mark clearly the date and time when the treatment was administered. No date or time, no crossing. Both must be clearly stated for each product.

Always, always check the details put in the passport before leaving the vet's surgery. I almost made this mistake in June this year. I only thought to check the details at 6.55 pm, they close at 7.00 pm, and to my horror one of the times was blank. After a frantic phone call the vet agreed to wait an extra 15 minutes and added in the time mentioned at the beginning.

As for the two ladies, they chose the first option and according to my vet have now been reunited with their dog and have taken him back to the UK. He was forced to have a very extended holiday.

AQUITAINE

This region of wide open spaces includes Europe's largest forest and offers a long list of outdoor activities. There are many quality golf courses which makes this France's leading region for golfers. For those interested in the past, there are a number of prehistoric sites and a fascinating variety of artefacts. Visitors should make a point of seeing the many cave paintings and engravings found in the Dordogne Valley. Enjoy the bustling towns, peaceful countryside and villages, and sample the fine wines of Bordeaux and the gastronomic specialties of the region, which include Foie Gras and truffles.

Bayac (Dordogne)

Old village in the picturesque Couze Valley within easy reach of all of Dordogne's historic sites. Lots of forest walks. Bayac has restaurants, tobacconist and bar, and there are also restaurants and shops in many other nearby villages.

PERIGORD FARMHOUSE, DORDOGNE. Superb 15th century farmhouse, set in the beautiful Couze Valley. 5 bedrooms, private pool, extensive grounds. Large gardens, shaded children's play area. Pets welcome in all local restaurants. [pw!] Contact MR PHILIP WALKER:(Tel & Fax: 020 8857 9080).
website: www.perigord-holidays.co.uk

Le Bugue (Dordogne)

The pretty town of Le Bugue provides an excellent range of shops, including supermarkets, banks, chemists, post office and English-speaking doctor. There is a colourful and busy market every Tuesday, offering a wide selection of local produce, poultry, meats, pates and cheeses. Further afield you can visit prehistoric caves, some with world-famous cave drawings.

SOUTH DORDOGNE. Three period cottages with fenced pool on 65-acre estate with fishing lake. Sleep 2/6. Great countryside for walking. Local English-speaking vet. Contact Mike/Lindy Crowcroft 0033 (0) 553 03 23 20 (summer); 020 8340 2027 (winter). []
e-mail: mikecrowcroft@onetel.com website: www.lessarrazinies.com

St Marcel du Perigord (Dordogne)

St Marcel is situated off the D32, 12 miles from Bergerac and 6 miles from St Alvere. There is a good restaurant and bar in the village. The nearest large town is Lalinde, 7 miles, which has one of the prettiest markets in the area. Market day is Thursday.

LE MANOIR DE ST MARCEL. 5 high quality, attractively restored and well equipped properties, sleep 2-12. Resident owners. You will appreciate a warm welcome from fellow animal lovers. Our vet speaks English and can help with formalities. Tel: 020 7617 7115 (UK), +33(0)5 53 61 06 17 (France).
e-mail: reservations@LeManoir.org website: www.LeManoir.org

AUVERGNE

Lying in the heart of France only an hour from Lyon or three hours from Paris the Auvergne region has a volcanic terrain with a natural beauty and dramatic landscapes. The area is ideal for sporting activities, including skiing, golfing, hiking and hang-gliding, and for the watersports enthusiast, there are excellent opportunities for canoeing, fishing, swimming and sailing.

Gîtes du Château de Coisse ❖ Auvergne

Situated in a small hamlet in the heart of the Livradois Forez Regional Park, get away from the stress and grind of daily life in this tranquil, beautiful part of France.

★★ **2 person gîte** is on the ground floor of this recently converted 18th century barn.

★★★ **6 person gîte** forms the first and second floors and has its own south-facing terrace.

Both have been carefully restored to keep many original features but are also modern, fully equipped and child/pet friendly.

Fiona & Graham Sheldon, Gîtes du Château de Coisse, 63220 Arlanc, France • Tel: 04 73 95 00 45

e-mail: fiandgra@chateaudecoisse.com • www.chateaudecoisse.com

Coisse (Puy-de-Dôme)

Tiny village in the rolling hills of Monts du Livradois, an area of outstanding natural beauty. Town of Arlanc, 2km away, has all amenities.

FIONA & GRAHAM SHELDON, GITES DU CHATEAU DE COISSE, 63220 ARLANC (04 73 95 00 45)
Two restored gîtes in this tranquil, beautiful part of France. 2 star/2 person gîte on ground floor of 18th century barn. 3 star/ 6 person gîte on first and second floors with its own south-facing terrace. Child/pet friendly.[🐕]
e-mail: fiandgra@chateaudecoisse.com website: www.chateaudecoisse.com

Note

All the information in this guide is given in good faith in the belief that it is correct. However, the publishers cannot guarantee the facts given in these pages, neither are they responsible for changes in ownership or facilities that may take place after the date of going to press.

Readers should always satisfy themselves that the facilities they require are available and that the terms, if quoted, still apply.

BRITTANY

This is a region steeped in tradition, and has maintained its Celtic traditions throughout the centuries. Mont Saint-Michel is reputed to be Brittany's best-known attraction. The beautiful bay of the Gulf of Morbihan is dotted with dozens of little islands, and you can visit fairy tale woods in the Ille aux Moines. Inland is the medieval forest of Merlin the Magician, where it is said that the Knights of the Round Table searched for the Holy Grail. The coast is a great attraction for tourists, who enjoy such activities as wind surfing, water skiing and underwater diving and, as you would expect, there is a wonderful variety of seafood available, including lobsters, oysters salmon and trout.

Malestroit (Morbihan)

This beautiful medieval town located on the river Oust has shops, restaurants, bars and banks. The Museum of the Resistance to the Second World War is located in nearby St Marcel.

DOGSWELCOME.FR. Looking for a comfortable cottage for your holiday in Brittany? We have several specially selected cottages sleeping two, four, six and eight people. Prices from £120 pw. Contact Nicola Harrington (01342 322272). [Pets £15 per week].
E-mail: nicola@dogswelcome.fr www.dogswelcome.fr

LANGUEDOC-ROUSSILLON

The region has a widely varying landscape from mountains and plateaux, to moorlands and coastal plains. The coast is a blend of resorts such as Cap d'Agde and Port Camargue, and old villages and fishing ports. Good beaches offer a variety of watersports and there are many golf courses throughout the region. There are health spas and nature reserves as well as good fishing, cycling and riding, and the area is ideal for walkers. In winter there are good cross-country ski routes and excellent skiing. Markets can be found in towns and villages from early spring until late autumn, and festivals, fetes and concerts can all be enjoyed.

The area is noted for its seafood, including oysters and anchovies, and Sete, the largest Mediterranean fishing port on the coast of France has many excellent fish restaurants. Strong Mediterranean flavours dominate the local dishes, with rich game or beef stews, and, of course, the famed Cassoulet. Other regional specialities include olives, fruit, honey, full fruity red wines and delicious dessert wines.

Your Own Private Domaine **Two lovely houses with large pool and tennis court**

In a beautiful elevated position overlooking the medieval village of Montagnac, Domaine de l'Hortevieille, a former wine-making property is set in 10 acres of fields, gardens and orchards with its own large, secure pool and tennis court.Two individually designed spacious houses are available for rental - each one well equipped with washing machine, dishwasher, microwave, fridge/freezer, television, DVD player and mini hi-fi. Each has its own private furnished terrace with barbecue facilities. Horse riding is available and mountain bikes are provided for you to explore the beautiful adjacent countryside.

The property is ideally suited for a tranquil summer holiday by the pool or on the beach or if you prefer a more active break in or out of season there are endless possibilities to get to know this rich and historic area. Whatever your interests - wine, good food, golf, fishing, antiques, history, the list is endless - the Domaine's English owners are on hand to help you enjoy your stay to the full.

Weekly rental rates from €500 or £370 to €1800 or £1350 inclusive of maid service, bed linen and towels and a welcome pack when you arrive. **For more information or to make a booking contact Malcolm or Alyson at hortevieille@wanadoo.fr or telephone 00 33 467 24 13 98.**

Montagnac (Herault)

Montagnac is within easy reach of Beziers and Montpellier and only a few kilometres from the A75 motorway. The nearest beach is about 10 minutes' drive away. The village centre has been recently renovated and there is a good selection of shops including bakers, general stores and butcher, as well as two bars – one of which serves snacks.

DOMAINE DE L'HORTEVIEILLE, MONTAGNAC. Two spacious houses, each well equipped, with private terrace and BBQ. Horse riding and mountain bikes available. English owners on hand to help you enjoy your stay to the full. Contact Malcolm or Alyson (00 33 467 24 13 98).
e-mail: hortevieille@wanadoo.fr

Vernet-les-Bains (Pyrenees-Orientales) *See Advertisment on opposite page*

This is a mountain village, peaceful and tranquil, situated between the ski resorts and the Mediterranean and long known for its hot water spring and thermal spa. Local facilities include shops, restaurants, cafes, sports centre and casino. Excellent opportunities exist for leisure activities such as walking, cycling and fishing.

LE VILLAGE CATALAN, VERNET-LES-BAINS. Self-catering holidays for pet owners. Plenty of space and lots to see and do. (France 0033(0)4 6805 6571; UK FREEPHONE 0800 652 1255)
e-mail: info@petbreaks.com website: www.petbreaks.com

Petbreaks.com

There is no need to leave your best friend behind, when you go on holiday in France!

Your pet is welcome here in Le Village Catalan in the South of France, where we offer 1, 2 and 3-bedroomed self-catering holiday homes. You will be glad you brought your pet when you discover great nature walks, the refreshing streams and rock pools, the pure mountain air, and the happiness of the animal sensing the call of the wild...

Self-catering in the Mediterranean Pyrenees is ideal for pet owners, there is plenty of space, and lots to see and do for everyone. Our houses are split-level, and the bedrooms downstairs stay cool even in the hot season. When you book a holiday property to include your pet, we provide: A welcome snack, a food bowl and water bowl, bags to collect and properly dispose of the droppings, and information on suitable walks with water and shade. And if you need any help or advice, we are experienced pet-owners and founders of Rescue3.org

Rental prices start at £240 per week for a cottage up to £1595 for a large villa with private pool and a 2 acre fenced garden.

Le Village Catalan
F-66820 Vernet-les-Bains
France 0033(0)4 6805 6571
UK Freephone 0800 652 1255
Email: info@ petbreaks.com
www.petbreaks.com

LIMOUSIN

The Limousin region, situated in the centre of France, offers visitors a peaceful and traditional way of life. This is a charming and historic land of hills and valleys, forests and plains, rivers and picturesque ancient cities. The region takes its name from the Capital Limoges, which is renowned for its exquisite enamel and porcelain. This pleasant town has many parks and gardens, and the old quarter with its narrow medieval streets and houses is worth a visit. There are many opportunities to enjoy swimming, sailing, canoeing and water skiing on the numerous rivers and lakes, and there are several golf courses throughout the region. There is good riding country in the south and many riding establishments catering for all standards of rider. Here you will find the National Stud and racecourse at Arnac-Pompadour. There are many fairs and markets in towns and villages on various days of the week, and you can enjoy pates and foie gras, and perhaps even sample the local speciality, an excellent potato pie made with smoked ham and herbs.

Upper Dordogne Valley • Limousine • Corrèze • Near Argentat

Character Cottage, sleeps 2

On the edge of a picturesque village. One bedroom with en suite shower room.

Low Season £140
Mid Season £160
High Season £190
15% off second week booked

Kitchen/diner. Sitting room. Terrace and sun deck. Walk from cottage into amazing countryside.

See other cottages and B&B on www.argentat.co.uk. Contact Jim Mallows e-mail: au-pont@wanadoo.fr

Argentat (Coreze)

This delightful market town is an ideal holiday destination offering peace and quiet, and beautiful scenery. Excellent food and wine can be enjoyed in attractive riverside restaurants and other good eating places. There is a wide variety of cultural and sporting activities to enjoy, and many shows and exhibitions take place during the summer.

UPPER DORDOGNE VALLEY. Character Cottage, sleeps two.On the edge of a picturesque village. One bedroom with en suite shower room. Kitchen/diner. Sitting room. Terrace and sun deck. Walk from cottage into amazing countryside. Contact JIM MALLOWS for details
e-mail: au-pont@wanadoo.fr website: www.argentat.co.uk

Readers are requested to mention this FHG guidebook when seeking accommodation

Le Chant d'Oiseau, Estivals

Situated in a hamlet on borders of Corrèze, Lot and Dordogne, four oak-timbered gites provide perfect relaxation in tranquil countryside.
• Fully equipped kitchen with microwave, dishwasher and washing machine • French doors to patio with barbecue and garden furniture.
• Pool with alarm • Bed linen • Baby furniture available • Pets welcome.

Close to many attractions of the region, with horse riding, cycling, canoeing, walking, golf and tennis easily available.

Readily connected by motorway, rail (inc. motorail) and regional airports.

Contact Robin or Loraine Cornish • Tel: 00 33 5 55 85 31 28
e-mail: robin.cornish@wanadoo.fr • www.lechantdoiseau.com

Estivals (Haute Vienne)

The village is centrally located for visiting many places of interest including attractive prehistoric and medieval sites and interesting cave formations. Brive la Gaillarde, 16km south west offers a viriety of supermarkets and shops, and the nearby village of Cressensac has a mini-market and bakery.

LE CHANT D'OISEAU, ESTIVALS. Four oak-timbered gites provide perfect relaxation in tranquil countryside. Fully equipped kitchen with microwave, dishwasher and washing machine. Bed linen. Pets welcome. Close to many attractions, with horse riding, cycling, canoeing, walking, golf and tennis easily available. Contact ROBIN OR LORAINE CORNISH (00 33 5 55 85 31 28
e-mail: robin.cornish@wanadoo.fr website: www.lechantdoiseau.com

LOWER NORMANDY

The region of Normandy, with its lush countryside and a coastline warmed by the Gulf Stream, has long been a favourite destination with holidaymakers. There are many resorts and seaside towns and, inland, magnificent forests, tranquil streams and the many orchards which are indicative of this fruit producing region. There are many delights to discover such as the picturesque harbour of Honfleur, the Bayeux Tapestry and William the Conquerors birthplace. Normandy promises many gastronomic delights, from seafood and duck, to cream, cheeses and the famous Calvados. Why not explore the 'Cider Road' and the 'Cheese Road', or simply relax on a horse drawn carriage ride.

La Ferté-Macé (Orne)

Small town with a range of shops and restaurants. Beach offers water sports, fishing and supervised swimming. 10km from the spa town of Bagnoles-de-l'Orne with good shopping, sports facilities, casino and golf.

JOHN AND CHRIS GIBSON, LA DETOURBE, BEAUVAIN, 61600 LA FERTE-MACE, ORNE. (0033 (0) 2 33 30 12 68; Fax: 0033 (0) 2 33 30 12 70). A stone longère set in two acres of beautiful grounds, with a barn conversion providing two gites. Ideal location for enjoying the peace and tranquillity within the Normandy regional park. [🐕]
e-mail: johnandchrisg@wanadoo.fr www.normandy-gites.co.uk

Please note

All the information in this book is given in good faith in the belief that it is correct. However, the publishers cannot guarantee the facts given in these pages, neither are they responsible for changes in policy, ownership or terms that may take place after the date of going to press. Readers should always satisfy themselves that the facilities they require are available and that the terms, if quoted, still apply.

Le Gast (Calvados)

Small hamlet in a peaceful setting. Easy driving distance to beach and close to many famous attractions. 10km from market town of Villedieu-les-Poeles with restaurants and bars and 35km from the resort town of Granville with Dior Museum.

LA PETITE MAISON A LA DENILLIERE. Gite finished to exceptional standard with beautiful artwork, lovely rugs and antiques. Amidst beautiful countryside just outside the small village of Le Gast. Central for touring Normandy's historic sites. Sleeps up to 4. Pets and responsible owners welcome. Contact owners on (0871 717 4235 or 0033 2 31 66 94 59).
e-mail: info@french-holidaygite.co.uk website: www.french-holidaygite.co.uk

St Malo de la Lande (Manche)

Small village 70km from Mont St Michel with its famous Abbey, shops and museums; 40km from D-Day beaches.

MME. MOIRA NICOLAY, NORMANDY COTTAGES, The Barn, 50200 St Malo de la Lande (00 33 2 33 47 91 38; Fax: 00 33 2 33 45 02 12) A selection of lovely holiday homes in sunny Normandy, in the small village of St Malo de la Lande. Each property is well equipped with all modern appliances. Sleep 2 to 7 people. [🐕]
e-mail: hello@normandycottages.net www.normandycottages.net

WESTERN LOIRE

This region, with its pleasing warm climate, has long been a favourite holiday destination. The visitor is spoilt for choice as lush countryside, vineyards, long sandy beaches and salt marshes vie for attention with fascinating cities, sleepy villages, ancient buildings and castles with stunning artwork, and cultural festivals galore. The famous 24-hour race is held at Le Mans-Laval, and there are facilities throughout the region for a huge variety of sporting activities, both land and water based. The countryside is easily explored by bicycle or on foot, or you may prefer to spend a day cruising on the tranquil waterways. Explore the Loire Valley vineyards, and enjoy the delicious and famous wines of the area with fresh fruit and vegetables, game, wild mushrooms and generous platters of seafood from the region's rivers and the sea.

Fonteney le Comte (Vendée)

A town of art and history with elegant squares and gardens. Nôtre Dame church and the Vendée museum are worth a visit. Numerous festivals and events take place throughout the year..

LES AUGERELLES, VENDEE/CHARENTES BORDER. 3 Bed house (sleeps 7/9) and 1 bed gite (sleeps 2/4). Well equipped and recently refurbished. Swimming pool. Heating for off season. Quiet hamlet with market town nearby. Managed by family members resident in the region. Contact: JANET & JOHN NUTHALL (01249 443458) [🐕]

e-mail: jnuthall@aol.com website: www.vendee-gites.co.uk/lesaugerelles.htm

Symbols

🐕 Indicates that pets are welcome free of charge.

£ Indicates that a charge is made for pets: nightly or weekly.

pw! Shows some special provision for pets; exercise facility, feeding or accommodation arrangement.

⌂ Indicates separate pets accommodation.

For many of us enjoying a country holiday also means taking our dogs on scenic walks, or for a journey in the car - often in warm weather, and at these times they may need a little extra care and attention. The following tips could make your pet's life on hot days considerably more comfortable:

WATER!

A normal 20kg dog will drink about one and a half pints of water a day. In the heat this can increase by 200 to 300%. Water should always be available. Make sure you take plenty for your pet, as well for yourself when out walking and in the car. Stabilising non-spill water bowls are great for travel, while handy inflatable bowls are ideal for stowing in your knapsack. You can even buy water bottles that your dog can carry.

SHADE

Encourage your dog to favour shady, cool spots when you stop for a rest - rather than sunbathe with the rest of the family!

CAR

NEVER leave your dog in the car unattended. Placing a dog in the back of any car even with an open rear window is undesirable and may be fatal. Remember - even a car parked in shade in the morning when it's cool could reach over 100 degrees very quickly as the sun moves. Heat stroke can occur within minutes.

EXERCISE

Plan your walk so you avoid strenuous exercise during the hottest part of the day. Some dogs like to paddle or swim - if there is no water around and your dog seems uncomfortably hot, seek a shady spot and provide water.

HEALTH

A dog's heat loss system is dependent on overall health. If your dog is fit, supple and active then walking will be a pleasurable experience, however, if there is any indication of heart or respiratory problems arising, controlled exercise in the cool is recommended. Veterinary advice should be sought if problems persist during heat stressful times.

HEAT STROKE

This is an emergency and potentially life threatening situation. If in doubt take the following action, then seek advice. A chilled dog is better than an overheated one.

- Cease any form of exercise.
- Move the dog into a cool place.
- Sponge the dog with cold water - all over, avoiding water round the mouth or
- Do not offer food or fluids until evident recovery.
- Seek veterinary advice if in doubt.

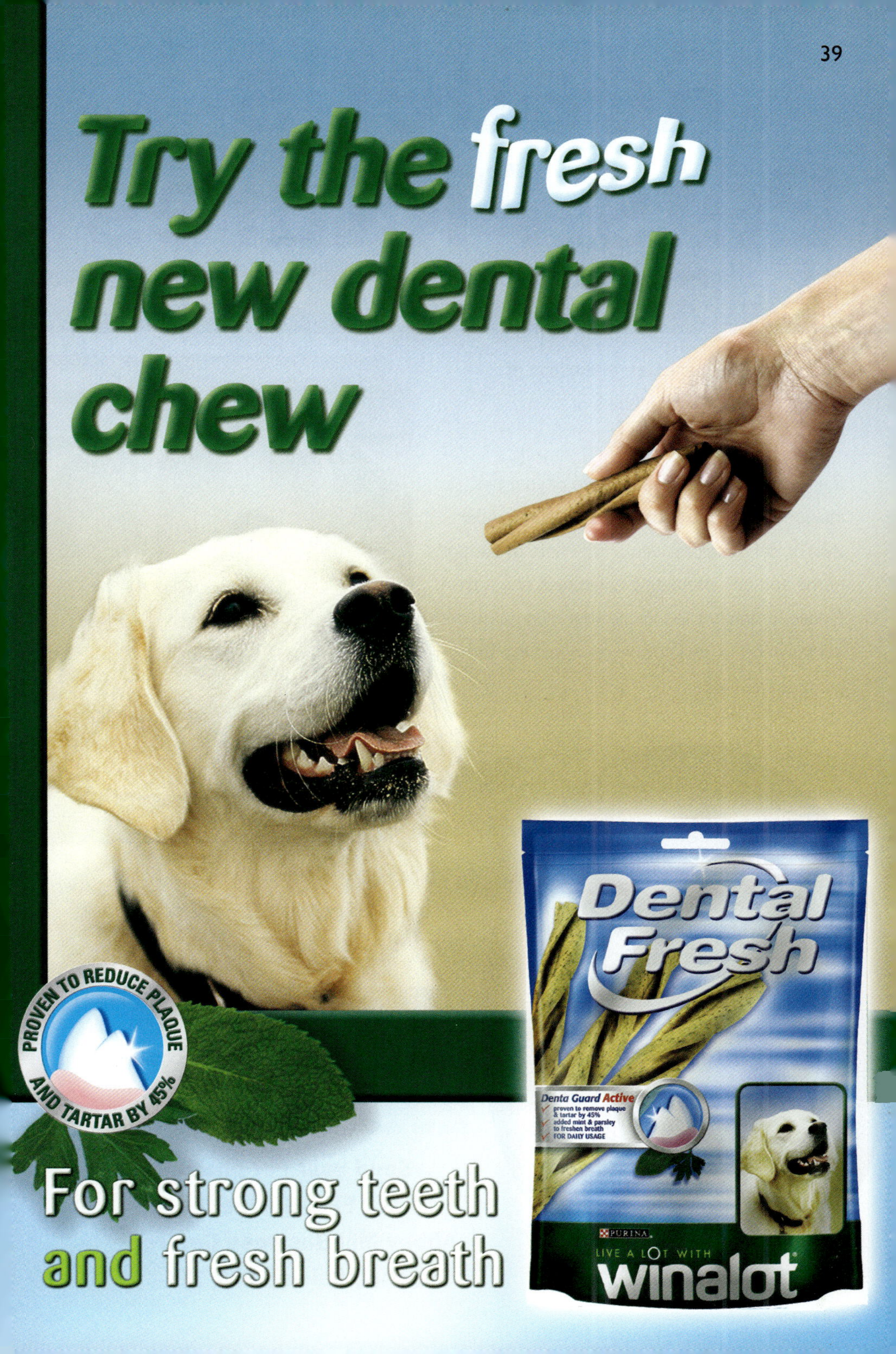
Try the fresh
new dental
chew
PROVEN TO REDUCE PLAQUE
AND TARTAR BY 45%
For strong teeth
and fresh breath
Dental
Fresh
Denta Guard Active
proven to remove plaque & tartar by 45%
added mint & parsley to freshen breath
FOR DAILY USAGE
PURINA
LIVE A LOT WITH
winalot

Reader's Pets Pictures

Send us your favourite Pet Photo!

On the following pages are a selection of Pets photos sent in by readers of

Pets Welcome!

If you would like to have a photo of your pet included in the next edition (published in April 2007), send it along with a brief note of the pet's name and any interesting anecdotes about them. Please remember to include your own name and address and let us know if you would like the pictures returned.

We will be happy to receive prints, transparencies or pictures on disk or by e-mail to **admin@fhguides.co.uk**

All pictures should be forwarded by the end of January 2007. Thanks to everyone who sent in pictures of their pets and regret that we were unable to include all of them.

See the following pages for this year's selection

Send your Pet photo to:
FHG Guides,
Abbey Mill Business Centre,
Seedhill, Paisley PA1 1TJ

Chablis
and friends
From Mrs Steadman, Dunstable

Pasco is having a "wheely" good time.
From Mrs Wendy Halling of Bedford

I'm sure I saw a mouse, says **Troy**
From Mrs Thomson of Barrhead

LUCY – just having a little rest
Sent by Mrs K J Dolphin of Birmingham

Reader's Pets Pictures

Vhen's dinner, I'm starving?
asks **Murphy**
Sent by Mrs Black
from Erskine

Tigger gives **Pooh Bear** a bedtime cuddle
From Gary Baxter of Fleet, Hampshire

Pooh Bear and **Mishka** share a serious moment
From Gary Baxter, Fleet, Hampshire

Pooh Bear enjoys the Joke
Sent by Gary Baxter, Fleet, Hampshire

Reader's Pets Pictures

Gemma-Kelly, Oban and **Jack** wait to welcome guests
From E. Walker-Parker of Inverness-shire

I'm not just a pretty face, I can fly too says **Pooh Bear**
Sent by Gary Baxter, Fleet, Hampshire

Where did they hide the TV? wonders **Boustead**
From Mrs Jones of Lytham

This is a nice spot, bring on the picnic says **Chablis**
From Mrs Steadman, Dunstable

Islay really looks up to her friend **Mel**
From Mrs Gorman of Cambuslang

What a motley crew!
Sent by Julie Davis of Houghton Regis

Reader's Pets Pictures

Jade Princess – walking in an Autumn Wonderland
Sent by Clive Hockley of Dunstable

Bet you can't beat me says **Rory**
Sent by Richard Duggan, Isle of Wight

Fred gets cleaned up for his holidays
Sent by Yvonne Baker of Wolverhampton

Well, what are you all waiting for, lets get into the sea? says **Brooke**
Sent by Mrs Paisley from Paisley

Yassko and **Cerys** take time out for a nice cool drink
From Mrs Halling of Bedford

Did someone mention a tent? Ask **Yassko** and **Cerys**
Sent by Mrs Halling of Bedford

Look what we've found shout **Yassko** and **Cerys**
Sent by Mrs Halling of Bedford

Reader's Pet Pictures

Something smells fishy thinks **Katie**
Sent by Mrs Thomson of Louth

Spike and his friends stop for a bite to eat
From Kate and Owen of Hitchin, Herts

Mum says I can.......
so there!!!
Says **Angus**
From B. Young of Blackburn

Feline fine!

Corky settles down to watch his favourite programme
From Kate and Owen of Hitchin, Herts

I spy with my little eyes says **Corky** Williams
Sent by Kate and Owen of Hitchin, Herts

Pepper has found a nice shady spot
Sent by Miss Docherty of Barrhead

Pepper admires the garden
From Miss Docherty of Barrhead

Reader's Pet Pictures

Sparky takes time out to relax in the sun
From Mrs Clements of Paisley

Tibby keeps a lookout
Sent by Miss Docherty of Barrhead

Sparky always remembers to wash before meals
Sent by Mrs Clements of Paisley

I suppose it's time to get up thinks **Sparky**
From Mrs Clements of Paisley

Troy's a sleepy boy
Sent by Mrs Thomson of Lenzie

Reader's Pets Pictures

Has anyone seen my ball, asks **Brooke**
Sent by Mrs J Paisley, of Paisley

Jade Princess – in action
From Clive Hockley of Dunstable

Benbo goes duck hunting
Sent by Tony Keen of Woking, Surrey

Try to get my best side, says **Isla**
From Erin Gorman of Paisley

DogsTrust
the new name for the NCDL

DogsTrust: A Dog is For Life

Are you thinking of going on holiday in the UK with your dog?

If so, the Dogs Trust has a free factsheet which will be of particular interest.

"Safe travel and happy holidays with your hound in the UK"

For this and any other of our free Dogs Trust factsheets please contact us at:

Dogs Trust,
17 Wakley St. London EC1V 7RQ.
Tel: 020 7837 0006
Website: www.dogstrust.org.uk
or e-mail us, info@dogstrust.org.uk

Last year Dogs Trust cared for over 11,500 stray and abandoned dogs at our network of 15 Rehoming Centres.
So if you are looking for a companion for your dog or you have a friend who might like a dog, just contact your nearest Dogs Trust Rehoming Centre.

We care for around 1,600 dogs on any given day, so we are sure we will be able to find your perfect partner. The Dogs Trust never destroys a healthy dog.
For details of our Sponsor-a-Dog scheme please call 020 7837 0006
or visit www.sponsoradog.org.uk

Dogs Trust Rehoming Centres

ENGLAND

Dogs Trust Canterbury
01227 792 505

Dogs Trust Darlington
01325 333 114

Dogs Trust Evesham
01386 830 613

Dogs Trust Ilfracombe
01271 812 709

Dogs Trust Kenilworth
01926 484 398

Dogs Trust Leeds
01132 613 194

Dogs Trust Merseyside
0151 480 0660

Dogs Trust Newbury
01488 658 391

Dogs Trust Roden
01952 770 225

Dogs Trust Salisbury
01980 629 634

Dogs Trust Shoreham
01273 452 576

Dogs Trust Snetterton
01953 498 377

WALES

Dogs Trust Bridgend
01656 725 219

SCOTLAND

Dogs Trust West Calder
01506 873 459

NORTHERN IRELAND

Dogs Trust Ballymena
028 2565 2977

Registered Charity No. 227523

Donate £1 to your favourite Pets Charity

FHG has agreed to donate £1 from the price of this Pets Welcome! Guide to EITHER the Royal Society For The Prevention of Cruelty to Animals, Dogs Trust, The Kennel Club Charitable Trust or the Scottish Society for the Prevention of Cruelty to Animals

RSPCA

THE KENNEL CLUB CHARITABLE TRUST
Making a difference for dogs

DogsTrust
the new name for the NCDL

SCOTTISH SPCA
Living for the day when ANIMAL CRUELTY STOPS

To allow the Charity of your choice to receive this donation simply complete the slip below and return to FHG at

FHG Guides Ltd
Abbey Mill Business Centre
Seedhill
Paisley PA1 1TJ

Closing date 26th October 2007

Note: Original forms only please, do not send photocopies.

✂- -

Please donate £1 from the price of this Pets Welcome! guide to:

RSPCA ☐ **DOGS TRUST** ☐ **SSPCA** ☐ **CHARITABLE TRUST** ☐

Name ....

Address...

....Postcode ....

Date...

FHG
KUPERARD

FHG Guides may send readers details of discount offers for our holiday guides.
If you do not wish to receive this information please tick here ☐
Your details will not be passed on to any other organisation.

IF YOU LOVE DOGS YOU'LL LOVE YOUR DOG

A dog-friendly walk in... North Yorkshire

This exhilarating walk takes you along the glorious high-level coastline between Robin Hood's Bay and Hawsker.

Robin Hood's Bay to Hawsker

From the lovely village of Robin Hood's Bay, walk the Heritage Coast to enjoy the spectacular seascape. Then make your return along the old railway track. Leave yourself time to explore the village and call at one of its many quaint tea shops or inns. **By Mary Welsh.**

The quaint houses of the village.

The picturesque village of Robin Hood's Bay.

Fact file

Distance: 7.4km/ 4½ miles.
Time: 3 hours.
Map: Explorer OL 27.
Start/Parking: Car park by the old railway station at the top of the hill into Robin Hood's Bay; grid ref: 950055.
Terrain: Easy walking with very few ascents or descents.
Nearest town: Whitby.
Refreshments: Good choice in the village.
Public toilets: In car park.
Public transport: Contact Traveline, tel. 0870 608 2608.
Stiles: Four.
Suitable for: For the whole family and all dogs.

These walks have been reproduced from Your Dog Magazine, Britain's best-selling dog magazine. Available from all good newsagents from the seventh of every month. Your Dog is priced at £3.10 and is packed with practical advice on every aspect of caring for and enjoying your pet. For more information, contact the editorial department on tel. 01780 766199; for subscription details contact tel. 01858 438854.

The crescent-shaped rock formations that you'll see on this walk.

1 From the car park by the old railway station, high above the bay, cross the road and take the grassy track leading north, signposted Cleveland Way. It passes several houses and then goes through dense blackberry bushes crowding the cliff top. Head on into Rocket Field. Sit on the second bench seat and enjoy the splendid view of the fishing village.

2 Go on from here along the distinct stiled and gated cliff-top path for two miles. At the signpost, turn left for Hawsker and walk ahead to join a metalled track through the caravans of a holiday park, where the dog must be on the lead. Follow the footpath signs, right and then left. Then bear left and walk downhill to cross Oakham Beck and continue on a short way to join the old railway track.

3 Turn left and begin to walk the easy, hedged way to pass through the quiet rural countryside, where your dog can have more freedom and enjoy lots of interesting smells. From here you might spot old quarries and spoil heaps where alum was once loaded on to the trains. The railway track brings you back to the old station car park.

A dog-friendly walk in... Leicestershire

Sailing is a popular pastime on the lakes.

This walk allows you to explore the pleasant countryside of Leicestershire, a county with plenty of open spaces and waterways to enjoy.

Watermead Country Park

Hidden away in the Soar Valley, five miles north of Leicester, is Watermead Country Park, a green oasis which is a haven for all kinds of wildlife. It is a most beautiful stretch of countryside with the River Soar and Grand Union Canal running through it. Depending how you feel on the day there is a shorter version of the walk around the first half of the park. **By Paul and Sandy Biggs.**

A platform with statues depicting a scene from Shakespeare's King Lear can be seen on a lake during this walk.

1 Head for the information board at King Lear's Lake and turn right to join the gravelled path around the edge of the lake. Pass the platform with the King Lear statues to reach a bridge across the River Soar.

2 Cross, turn left and join a grassy path ahead. Keep to this path to find a metal swing gate. Go through and follow the path to a picnic area by another lake. Turn left on to another path between two smaller lakes then ignore the path off to the nature reserve and bird hides. Continue ahead and you will reach a junction of paths at an information board. For the shorter walk turn left here, and follow the path between two lakes, to reach the River Soar at Thurmaston Lock (point 6 of the walk). For the main walk, turn right towards Meadow Lane car park, then left just before a gate for the car park. This path now passes through a wooded area then rejoins the River Soar touching on the edge of Birstall village.

3 Continue by the river to cross over a white bridge to reach Birstall Lock. Cross, turn right and follow the riverside path ahead. Cross the long footbridge over the weir to rejoin the riverside path ahead as far as the high bank for Watermead Way (a road).

4 Turn left, walk along the obvious path with the lake left to cross a bridge. Continue ahead where at the top of some steps you will encounter a mammoth! Go down the grassy hill to the car park then, with a lake to your left, head for a group of industrial buildings.

5 At the buildings turn left along a track then immediately right at a public footpath signpost. A narrow path passes alongside Raynsway Marina for 300 metres to a group of steps. A pleasant water meadow path crosses several fields to reach Thurmaston Lock, where the shorter walk joins.

6 Cross the lock bridge then follow on and turn left across another bridge. Continue by the river taking a grassy path to a long footbridge across a weir. Cross the concrete bridge over the River Soar and return into the park with the Grand Union Canal and hedge now on your right. You now rejoin the path that circles King Lear's Lake and follow it round to the top of the lake to return to the car park.

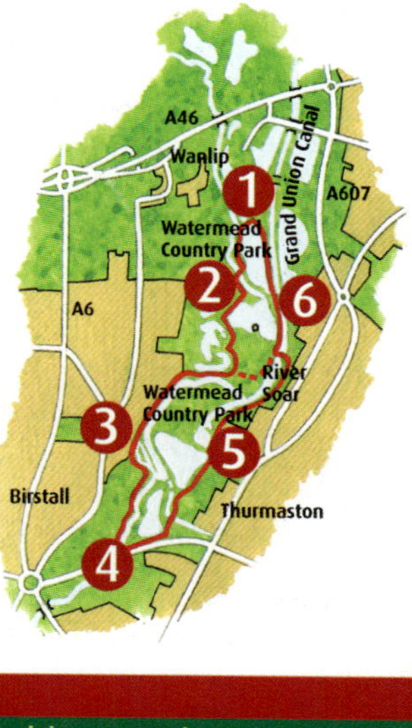

Fact file

Distance: 6.4km/ 4 miles with shorter walk of 2.8km/ 1.7 miles.
Time: Allow up to two hours for main walk and one hour for short walk.
Maps: OS Explorer 246 and OS Explorer 233.
Start/parking: Watermead Country Park, north entrance, Wanlip; grid ref: SK606106. Car park next to King Lear's Lake (£1 fee).
Terrain: Flat walking along gravelled paths and grassy tracks. Much of the north part of the park is suitable for wheelchair users.
Nearest town: Leicester.
Refreshments: None en route — take your own.
Public toilets: In Watermead Country Park North by King Lear's Lake.
Public transport: Contact Traveline East Midlands, tel. 0870 608 2608.
Stiles: Seven.
Suitable for: All the family and all dogs.

A dog-friendly walk along...

The Fife Coastal

Your dog could have a romp on Port Laing beach.

Although this path starts close to Edinburgh and ends close to busy Dundee, much of the route is through wild and spectacular natural landscapes.

Fife Coastal Path

The Fife Coastal Path is approximately 135km long and is excellently waymarked. This walk takes you along from its very beginning at North Queensferry, near the magnificent Forth Rail Bridge. Whatever time of the year you walk the path, there is always something interesting to see. In winter many wading birds are attracted to the waters and in spring and summer the paths are lined with a wealth of flowers. **By Mary Welsh.**

The Forth Rail Bridge as viewed from Carlingnose Point.

ath

You and your dogs should enjoy exploring this route.

Your Dog Magazine is available from all good newsagents. For more information, contact the editorial department on tel. 01780 766199.

1 Follow the signpost directions from the Battery Road car park, or from Dalmeny Station, from below the Forth Rail Bridge, to the southern start of the coastal path in front of the 1816 Waterloo Well, constructed in the shape of Napoleon's hat, North Queensferry. As you climb the paved way look for the coastal path logos set into the wall, on the left, just before you pass below the rail bridge.

2 Follow the old road up to the disused quarries of Carlingnose, now a wildlife reserve. This is a lovely quiet area, where dogs will find interesting smells. Pause here to watch the fulmars fly into their nests on the many ledges of rock. Take care as you move to the edge of the cliffs to enjoy the wonderful views up the Forth. Look for the islands out in the estuary. In earlier times they had fortresses built on them and then later, during plague times, they were used as places of quarantine. Three hundred million years ago they were volcanoes. As the islands have no predators on them they support large numbers of nesting birds.

3 Descend the path to join a narrow road and follow it until you can wind round to a small beach — Port Laing, where dogs can have a wonderful romp. Then return to the little road. From here you may wish to return by road (very dull for the dog) by winding uphill and then turning left to descend under a rail bridge and continue to the start or return by the same route, climbing up on the headland to enjoy all those views you missed on the way out. There is another choice too — to continue on the waymarked coastal path, say to Inverkeithing, and make use of public transport for your return.

Fact file

Distance: 3.4km/2 miles.
Time: 1 to 2 hours.
Map: The Fife Coastal Path.
Start/parking: Battery Road car park directly below the Forth Rail Bridge, where there is an orientation panel and signs for the start of the Fife Coastal Path.
Terrain: Steady climb and descent from Carlingnose Headland on unmade path.
Nearest town: Edinburgh.
Refreshments: Corus Hotel, North Queensferry, located immediately on the north shore of the Forth Road Bridge.
Public toilets: Near car parking area under rail bridge.
Public transport: Contact Traveline, tel. 0870 608 2608 or visit www.traveline.org.uk
Stiles: None.
Suitable for: All. For information on the Fife Coastal Path visit www.fifecoastandcountrysidetrust.co.uk or contact tel. 01333 592591.

A dog-friendly walk in...

Kent

Secluded Botany Bay at the end of the walk is popular with visitors. Dogs are allowed on the beach and water is available from the kiosk.

With its secret bays, lofty cliffs and views of the Channel, the stretch of Kent coast between Margate and Dover is great for exploring on foot.

Kingsgate

Discover a quiet corner of the Kent coast which provided the inspiration for one of the world's most popular and enduring adventure thrillers — 'The Thirty-nine Steps' by John Buchan. Away from the sea the walk visits the pretty village of Reading Street, before heading for popular Botany Bay. **By Nick Channer.**

Kent is famous for its sweeping white cliffs.

Kingsgate Castle on the cliff top.

1 From the car park at Joss Bay follow the cliff-top path with the sea on your left. Join Cliff Promenade and further on reach the top of the private staircase leading down to the beach. Turn right after a few steps into Anns Road. On the corner is St Cuby. In Buchan's story this is Trafalgar Lodge where the spies are based. Pass a house on the left, appropriately called The Thirty-nine Steps, and make for the T-junction. There is a postbox here.

2 Turn right and follow North Foreland Avenue. Turn left at the junction towards the lighthouse. Pass it and then swing right at the gate. Join the footpath and follow it round the perimeter of the lighthouse grounds, making for a gate in a brick-and-flint wall. Go straight ahead on the obvious path cutting across farmland; over to your right you can glimpse Kingsgate Castle. Continue on a concrete track and veer right when you reach a farm, following the waymarked path to the road.

3 Turn left and walk along to Reading Street. Turn right at the sign for St Andrew's church. Keep ahead alongside the White Swan pub and go straight on at the crossroads into Reading Street Road. Pass some allotments on the left and avoid a path on the left. Continue for about 90 metres and then turn right to join a path through a field. Keep ahead between fencing on the far side of the field and cross the road by the Nineteenth Hole pub into Percy Avenue, following the sign for Botany Bay.

4 Walk down the road and eventually round to the right into Marine Drive. Botany Bay is seen to the left. Pass the Fayreness Hotel on the right and follow the cliff-top path with good views out to sea. Soon you reach the Captain Digby pub. Turn left at the road, pass the entrance to Kingsgate Castle and look for the North Foreland Lighthouse up on the hill. Walk along to the junction with Elmwood Avenue and return to the car park at Joss Bay.

Your Dog Magazine is available from all good newsagents. For more information, contact the editorial department on tel. 01780 766199.

Fact file

Distance: 7.2km/ 4½ miles.
Time: 2 hours.
Map: Explorer 150.
Start/parking: Car park at Joss Bay; grid ref: 397701.
Terrain: Cliff-top paths, roads, field tracks.
Nearest town: Broadstairs.
Refreshments: There are cafés and pubs at regular intervals.
Public toilets: Joss Bay and Botany Bay.
Public transport: Contact Traveline on tel. 0870 608 2608.
Stiles: None.
Suitable for: All.

A dog-friendly walk in...

The Lake District

There is a rich and varied landscape in the Lake District.

This walk will take you into the beautiful and often dramatic countryside of the Cumbrian Lake District.

Ulverston

This walk takes you to a striking south Lakeland landmark and then continues over high-level countryside. It returns through deciduous woodland and then the lower slopes of Hoad Hill from where there are some very pleasing views. **By Mary Welsh.**

You can see Hoad Monument from the town of Ulverston.

1 From the car park, with the dog on the lead, walk down Mill Street. Wind left at the end, cross Soutergate and turn left into Church Walk. Continue to the end of the road to pass through the ornate gates of St Mary's Church. Do not walk the track that leads to the church door but continue on the reinforced track that passes through the churchyard. Walk on along the continuing high-walled way to take, on the left, another tall-walled way. At the top, cross Belmont Road and head on up the short track opposite to go through the wrought iron kissing gate (the first of several) on to a reinforced path climbing steadily up a pasture. If there are no sheep the dog can have his first taste of freedom.

2 Go through the next kissing gate to continue on the good path through the high pasture. Where the track ends go on up over grass, keeping beside the boundary on your right. Carry on up to walk a glorious walled path and, at its end, go through a gate and stroll on up with a wall to your right. Head on parallel with the wall as it winds right, soon to join a good track heading in the direction of the monument that stands on Hoad Hill. Pass through a kissing gate beside a farm gate, across the track, and follow the rising way. Continue where it winds right and climbs again to the foot of the monument.

3 Return down the same way and wind left to go through the kissing gate, again. Then leave the track and bear right over grassy slopes, gradually winding half-left to come beside a long wall on your right. Follow the wall steadily upwards until you reach a kissing gate. Beyond, strike half-right, steadily dropping diagonally down the slope, to come close to the corner of two walls. As you descend be careful because it can be boggy. Descend by the wall, now on your left, to climb a stile over the cross wall ahead. Drop down the slope beside a hawthorn hedge on your left. There are sometimes cattle here and, if so, dogs should be on leads. Where there is a large break in the hedgerow, move left to cross a small stream and then go on descending beside the wall, left.

4 At the bottom of the slope ignore a stranded stile. Descend the rough banking carefully to join a wide track and turn right. Walk on through pleasing woodland. Emerge from the trees on to a wide terraced path, with views down to Newland hamlet. Continue on this track and then descend steadily, winding right to come to the side of the A590, where dogs must be on the lead.

5 Turn right and walk the pavement for 275m to take a gate on the right. This gives access to a reinforced path that climbs gently away from the busy road, to pass below Hoad's rock face. Remain on the excellent path, with the monument high above you. Carry on the high-level way to come to a gate. Go ahead along Ladies Walk and on past the church, now on your right. Walk on ahead along Church Walk to reach the mini roundabout. Cross with care to take the second right to return to the Gill car park.

These walks have been reproduced from Your Dog Magazine, Britain's best-selling dog magazine. Available from all good newsagents from the seventh of every month. Your Dog is priced at £3.10 and is packed with practical advice on every aspect of caring for and enjoying your pet. For more information, contact the editorial department on tel. 01780 766199; for subscription details contact tel. 01858 438854.

Fact file

Distance: 5.2km/ 3¾ miles.
Time: 2½ hours.
Maps: Explorer OL 6 and 7.
Start/parking: The Gill car park on the west side of Ulverston; grid ref: 286785.
Terrain: Good paths and tracks generally. One damp patch, one pathless pasture, one little awkward slope.
Nearest towns: Barrow, Ulverston, Kendal.
Refreshments: Spoilt for choice in Ulverston.
Public toilets: Beside car park.
Public transport: Good bus service. For information contact tel. Traveline on 0870 608 2608.
Stiles: One.
Suitable for: All the family.

A dog-friendly walk by...

The Firth of Clyd

As the Clyde opens out, away from the hustle and bustle of Glasgow, there is attractive countryside and an interesting coastline to explore on this walk.

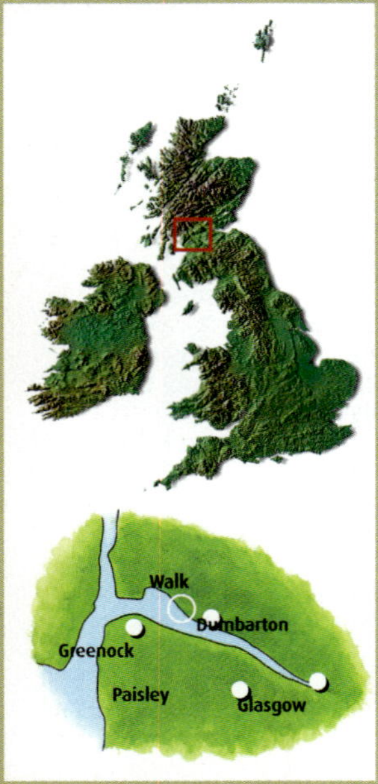

Ardmore Point

This delightful short walk is ideal for a sunny evening and also for a brisk winter's walk. All the family including the dog will enjoy it as you stroll along the path with views over the blue waters of the Clyde. By Mary Welsh.

The Lodge at the start of the walk.

The path runs close to the shore along the walk.

A railway line runs close to the route of this walk.

1 From the parking area walk on along the narrow road and at the smart white cottage, The Lodge, join a good track to the left of the dwelling; go on along this, with pastures — the haunt of skylarks — to the right and the blue waters of the Clyde to the left. Here you might spot waders on the shore. Soon you can look across to the right over more pastures to Ardmore House on the side of the little Hill of Ardmore. Wind on round the excellent path and look inland to see a clump of wild cherry trees, not often seen in Scotland. This is a great path for a walk and there are lots of interesting smells for your pet to investigate.

2 Stroll past conglomerate rock on the beach and then large plates of sandstone. Go on to pass through gorse bushes; the colour and perfume of the blossom is delightful. Look across the estuary to see the town of Gourock and then follow the path as it continues along the edge of the shore, with freedom for the dog. From here you have an attractive view of the Hill of Ardmore framed with mixed deciduous trees, skirted by birch and pussy willow, and hemmed with gorse.

3 Carry on past patches of yellow iris and as the path winds east look left into the bay. If the tide is out you might spot an old fish yair, a permanent funnel-mouthed fish trap. Pause here to look north to see Helensburgh at the entrance to Gare Loch. Saunter on through a tunnel of gorse and then follow the path as it winds out into pasture at the head of the bay, a tiny pocket of the Clyde.

4 Here take a path on the right, newly constructed and fenced, that takes you back to The Lodge. Walk along the road to collect your vehicle.

Fact file

Distance: 3.5km/ 2¼ miles.
Time: 1½ hours.
Maps: OS Explorer 347, Landranger 63.
Start/parking: Park south of Ardmore Farm; grid ref: 323787. This is reached by following the A814 from Dumbarton, through Cardross and then Geilston. Once past the signs for Cardross Cemetery and Crematorium carry on for 500m to turn left immediately beyond a cottage. Drive on to cross the railway line and park overlooking the Firth of Clyde.
Terrain: Very easy walking.
Nearest towns: Helensburgh, Dumbarton and Glasgow.
Refreshments: Plenty of choice at Helensburgh and Cardross.
Toilets: None.
Public transport: For information contact Traveline Scotland, tel. 0870 608 2608.
Stiles: None.
Suitable for: All.

A dog-friendly walk in... Lancashire

The Leeds-Liverpool Canal at Parbold.

This county has splendid walking country with vast stretches of moorland to tempt walkers, and their dogs, on to the heights.

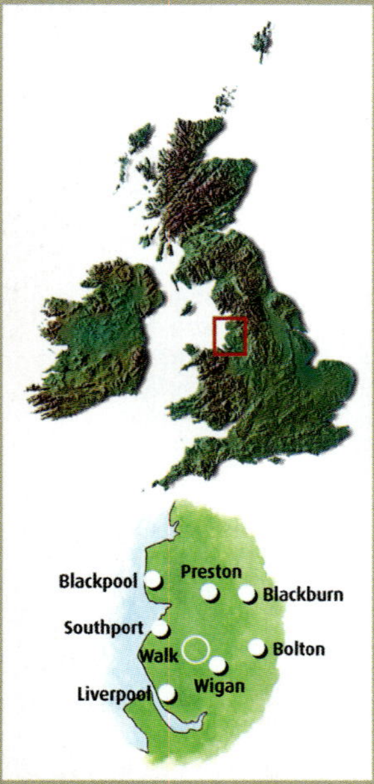

Parbold

This walk starts along the Leeds-Liverpool Canal but soon leaves it and climbs gently, passing through fertile pastures. The route returns along the canal side from Appley Bridge to Parbold, a delightful stretch of towpath. **By Mary Welsh.**

The canal as it heads towards Parbold.

1 Cross Parbold Bridge and descend left to join the towpath, with the waterway to your left. Walk on with a view, left, of the church. Go on to pass under the A5209 road bridge and carry on until you can cross the canal by the picturesque cobbled bridge, no 39.

2 Carry on along the shady lane to reach a T-junction. Cross, and bear slightly right, to take a stile, on the left, to a path that runs beside the fence of the last of a row of houses. Soon the path climbs up into pastures. Then go on up to climb a stile on to the busy A5209; put the dog on the lead.

3 Cross and drop down left, on the pavement, to take a signposted footpath just beyond the bus stop. Ignore a path that drops left and go straight ahead through woodland. Cross a little stream and then continue on a gently climbing path. Emerge from the trees by a stile and stride on the waymarked track, beside a field to your right and a tree-lined gully to your left. At the end of the trees, follow the wide track as it winds right, cutting the pasture in two, to a stile. Once over, walk on up the lane. As you near Bowling Green House Farm bear right along its access track to join the road.

4 Where the road turns left and there is a footpath sign, turn sharp right to walk a hedged green lane, with vast pastures on either side. Pass two small copses on your left and, at a Y-junction of grassy trods, take the left branch to go on past a small pool surrounded by alders. Walk on towards woodland and bear left alongside its edge. Cross two stiles and continue on down through the woodland, where you cross a footbridge and bear left and carry on along a wet area. Then climb a stile out of the trees and walk on, with a wall to the left. Follow the path as it winds round the far edge of the large field to join a lay-by on the A5209.

5 Turn right and join the road. Remain on the pavement for a few metres, then cross, opposite to a board welcoming you to Fairy Glen. Just off the A-road, turn left to take a stepped path that drops down beside the brook on your left. Go down the easy path, with the brook now on your right. Don't cross the next footbridge but descend steps that take you below huge tree-clad sandstone crags. Then cross the next footbridge. Walk on a slightly raised path, with a stream on either side. Ignore the steps down to your right and climb gently left to a track, where you turn right to leave the glen.

6 After 50m, take the stile on the left, hidden by a hedge and just before a gate to a farm. Go along the footpath with a hedge on your right. Go through a gap in the hedge ahead, cross a lane and climb the steps opposite. Walk ahead to another stile and then across the middle of a field to a lane. Here turn right for 20m and then take the footpath, left, to continue along a grassy way, in the same general direction, to Appley Lane North, where you turn right. Descend the B-road. Cross the bridge over the railway and press on over canal bridge no 42.

7 Beyond, drop down right to the towpath. Go ahead past some cottages on your left and continue out into the rolling Lancashire countryside. Dawdle past a canal lock with deciduous woodland on the opposite bank. Stride on along the pleasing towpath, passing under and beside bridges until you reach Parbold. Climb a slope to join the road and turn right to return to the place where you have parked.

Fact file

Distance: 9.5km/ 6 miles.
Time: 2 – 3 hours.
Map: Explorer 285.
Start/parking: Small parking area on the north-west side of Parbold canal bridge, no 37, grid ref: 494105.
Terrain: Easy walking all the way. A gently rising path takes you up on to Parbold Hill. The towpath is a joy to walk. Some road walking.
Nearest towns: Burscough, Standish.
Refreshments: Tea shop: 'Yours is the Earth'; pubs: The Windmill Inn and The Railway Inn, Parbold.
Public toilets: None en route. Ask for key to toilets in waiting room at the railway station. Both pubs allow people to use their toilets.
Public transport: For travel enquiries contact Traveline, tel. 0870 608 2608.
Suitable for: All.

FHG
KUPERARD

Your guides to Good Holidays 2007

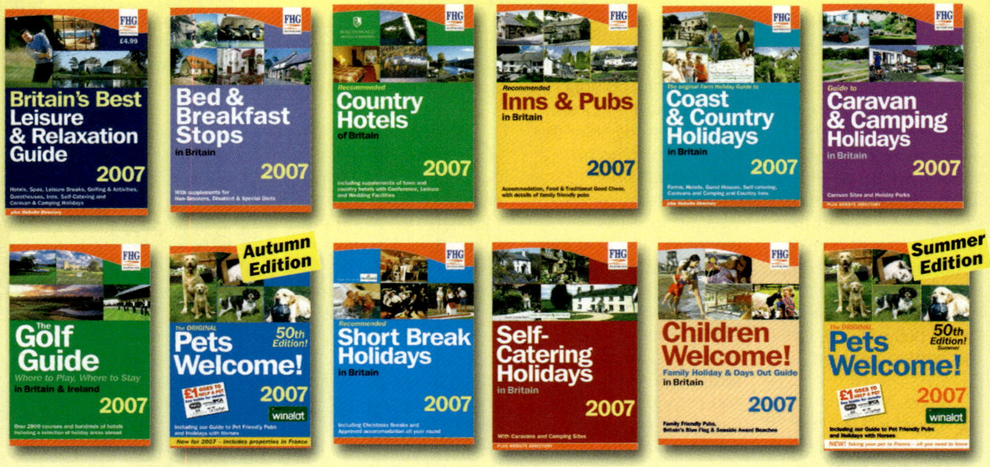

BRITAIN'S BEST LEISURE & RELAXATION GUIDE user-friendly guide to all kinds of holidays **£4.99**

BED & BREAKFAST STOPS ever more popular independent guide with over 1000 entries **£7.99**

Recommended COUNTRY HOTELS a quality selection of Britain's best Country Houses and Hotels **£7.99**

Recommended INNS & PUBS accommodation, food and traditional good cheer **£7.99**

COAST & COUNTRY HOLIDAYS holidays for all the family, from traditional farm houses to inns, guesthouses and small hotels **£7.99**

CARAVAN & CAMPING HOLIDAYS covers every type of caravan and camping facility **£7.99**

THE GOLF GUIDE Where to Play / Where to Staya detailed list covering virtually every club and course in the UK with hotels and other accommodation nearby – recommended by golfers, to golfers **£9.99**

PETS WELCOME! the pet world's version of the ultimate hotel guide, over 1000 properties where pets and their owners are made welcome **£8.99**

Recommended SHORT BREAK HOLIDAYS approved accommodation all year round for short breaks **£7.99**

SELF CATERING HOLIDAYS perhaps the widest selection of self-catering accommodation **£7.99**

CHILDREN WELCOME! Family Holiday and Days Out guide **£7.99**

Available from bookshops or larger newsagents

FHG GUIDES LTD Abbey Mill Business Centre, Seedhill, Paisley, Renfrewshire PAI ITJ

www.holidayguides.com

The best-selling series of UK Holiday Guides

England

otos: Biggin Hall, Buxton, Derbyshire

Stone House Hotel, Hawes, North Yorkshire

Holmdene Farm, Beeston, Norfolk

Ratings & Awards

For the first time ever the AA, VisitBritain, VisitScotland, and the Wales Tourist Board will use a single method of assessing and rating serviced accommodation. Irrespective of which organisation inspects an establishment the rating awarded will be the same, using a common set of standards, giving a clear guide of what to expect. The RAC is no longer operating an Hotel inspection and accreditation business.

Accommodation Standards: Star Grading Scheme

Using a scale of 1-5 stars the objective quality ratings give a clear indication of accommodation standard, cleanliness, ambience, hospitality, service and food, This shows the full range of standards suitable for every budget and preference, and allows visitors to distinguish between the quality of accommodation and facilities on offer in different establishments.All types of board and self-catering accommodation are covered, including hotels, B & Bs, holiday parks, campus accommodation, hostels, caravans and camping, and boats.

The more stars, the higher level of quality

★★★★★
exceptional quality, with a degree of luxury

★★★★
excellent standard throughout

★★★
very good level of quality and comfort

★★
good quality, well presented and well run

★
acceptable quality; simple, practical, no frills

VisitBritain and the regional tourist boards, **enjoyEngland.com, VisitScotland** and **VisitWales,** and **the AA** have full details of the grading system on their websites

enjoy**England**.com

★★★★ FARMHOUSE

Scottish Tourist Board ★★★ HOTEL

visit**Scotland**.com

visit**Wales**.com

Bwrdd Croeso Cymru Wales Tourist Board GWESTY ★★★ HOTEL

AA ★★★ Guest Accommodation

the AA .com

National Accessible Scheme

If you have particular mobility, visual or hearing needs, look out for the National Accessible Scheme. You can be confident of finding accommodation or attractions that meet your needs by looking for the following symbols.

Typically suitable for a person with sufficient mobility to climb a flight of steps but would benefit from fixtures and fittings to aid balance

Typically suitable for a person with restricted walking ability and for those that may need to use a wheelchair some of the time and can negotiate a maximum of three steps

Typically suitable for a person who depends on the use of a wheelchair and transfers unaided to and from the wheelchair in a seated position. This person may be an independent traveller

Typically suitable for a person who depends on the use of a wheelchair in a seated position. This person also requires personal or mechanical assistance (eg carer, hoist).

THE FOUR SEASONS HOTEL, ST FILLANS PH6 2NF (01764 685333). Ideal holiday venue for pets and their owners. Spectacular Highland scenery, walking, fishing, watersports. Wonderful food. Full details on request. STB ★★★ Hotel, AA ★★★ and 2 Red Rosettes, Which? Hotel Guide, Johansens, Best Loved Hotels. [🐕]
e-mail: sham@thefourseasonshotel.co.uk website: www.thefourseasonshotel.co.uk

THE INDEPENDENT TRAVELLER, FORD COTTAGE, THORVERTON, EXETER EX5 5NT (01392 860807 Fax: 01392 860552). For a wide choice of cottages and apartments throughout England, Scotland & the Isles. Pets welcome in many properties. Quality Cottages in coastal, country and mountain location. Property finding service.
e-mail: help@gowithit.co.uk website: www.gowithit.co.uk

DALES HOLIDAY COTTAGES. Over 500 personally inspected cottages in sublime locations throughout Northern Britain, for couples, groups and families. Full of character, near great walks and country pubs, just right for pets. Call 0870 909 9500 or visit our website.
website: www.dalesholcot.com

HOSEASONS. Tailwagging holidays at over 200 locations where your pet is as welcome as you are. Pine lodges surrounded by picturesque countryside. Or seaside holiday parks with miles of coastline to explore. Mid-week and weekend short breaks available. Many open all year round. Call for your free brochure on 0870 900 9011 Quote H0031 or book on-line.
website: www.hoseasons.co.uk

MR P.W. REES, "QUALITY COTTAGES', CERBID, SOLVA, HAVERFORDWEST, PEMBROKESHIRE SA62 6YE (01348 837871). Cottages set in all coastal areas, unashamed luxury, highest residential standards. Dishwashers, microwaves, washing machines. Log fires. Linen supplied. Pets welcome. [pw! 🐕]
website: www.qualitycottages.co.uk

Go BLUE RIBAND for quality inexpensive self-catering holidays where your dog is welcome – choice of locations all in the borough of Great Yarmouth. Detached 3 bedroom bungalows, seafront bungalows, detached Sea-Dell chalets and modern sea front caravans. Free colour brochure: DON WITHERIDGE, BLUE RIBAND HOUSE, PARKLANDS, HEMSBY, GREAT YARMOUTH NR29 4HA (01493 730445). [pw! First pet free when booking through Pets Welcome!, 2nd pet £10 per week].
website: www.BlueRibandHolidays.co.uk

COTTAGE IN THE COUNTRY COTTAGE HOLIDAYS (0870 027 5930). Lovely locations with superb walks in some of England's most picturesque countryside. We'll do our best to find the right place for you to call 'home'!
e-mail: enquiries@cottageinthecountry.co.uk website: www.cottageinthecountry.co.uk

Readers are requested to mention this FHG publication when seeking accommodation

HOSEASONS. Tailwagging holidays at over 200 locations where your pet is as welcome as you are. Pine lodges surrounded by picturesque countryside. Or seaside holiday parks with miles of coastline to explore. Mid-week and weekend short breaks available. Many open all year round. Call for your free brochure on 0870 900 9011 Quote H0031 or book on-line.
website: www.hoseasons.co.uk

WELCOME. Pets deserve holidays too, and most welcome properties accept pets, which always go free! If you holiday with your pet between October and the end of March you'll get £25 off. Call for a 2007 brochure. (0870 192 0848).
website: www.welcome2007.co.uk

CAMPING & CARAVANNING CLUB (0845 130 7632). Visit one of our award-winning UK Club Sites. Our sites have dog walking areas for you and your dog to explore. A friendly welcome will be given to you and your pet on our sites, joining is great value for money. QUOTE REF NO 0716
website: www.campingandcaravanningclub.co.uk

BUCKINGHAMSHIRE

Chesham, Milton Keynes

Chesham

Town on south side of Chiltern Hills. Ideal walking area.

PAT & GEORGE ORME, 49 LOWNDES AVENUE, CHESHAM HP5 2HH (01494 792647). B&B in detached house, 10 minutes from the Underground. Private bathroom, tea/coffee, TV. Good walking country - Chiltern Hills three minutes. ETC ◆◆◆ [🐕]
e-mail: bbormelowndes@tiscali.co.uk

Milton Keynes

Purpose-built new city, home to the Open University. Midway between London, Birmingham, Leicester, Oxford and Cambridge.

SWAN REVIVED HOTEL, HIGH STREET, NEWPORT PAGNELL, MILTON KEYNES MK16 8AR (01908 610565; Fax: 01908 210995). Delightful 16thC former coaching inn, extensively modernised to provide 40 comfortable guest rooms, two bars, à la carte restaurant, meeting rooms and banqueting facilities. Pets very welcome. [🐕]
e-mail: info@swanrevived.co.uk website: www.swanrevived.co.uk

CAMBRIDGESHIRE

Ely

Magnificent Norman Cathedral dating from 1083. Ideal base for touring the fen country of East Anglia.

MRS C. H. BENNETT, STOCKYARD FARM, WISBECH ROAD, WELNEY PE14 9RQ (01354 610433; Fax: 01354 610422). Comfortable converted farmhouse, rurally situated between Ely and Wisbech. Conservatory breakfast room, TV lounge. Free range produce. Miles of riverside walks. No smoking. B&B from £20. [pw!]

CHESHIRE

Balterley, Chester

Balterley

Small village two miles west of Audley.

MR & MRS HOLLINS, BALTERLEY GREEN FARM, DEANS LANE, BALTERLEY, NEAR CREWE CW2 5QJ (01270 820214). 145-acre farm in quiet and peaceful surroundings. Within easy reach of Junction 16 on the M6. Bed and Breakfast from £25pp. Also cottage for self-catering. Caravans and tents welcome. [pw! Pets £2 per night]

Chester

Former Roman city on the River Dee, with well-preserved walls and beautiful 14th century Cathedral. Liverpool 25 miles

THE EATON HOTEL, CITY ROAD, CHESTER CH1 3AE (01244 320840; Fax: 0870 6221691). Ideally located for you and your dog, in the heart of Chester, with parking, and bordering the Shropshire Union Canal towpath. []
website: www.eatonhotelchester.co.uk

Useful Guidance for Guests and Hosts

Every year literally thousands of holidays, short breaks and overnight stops are arranged through our guides, the vast majority without any problems at all. In a handful of cases, however, difficulties do arise about bookings, which often could have been prevented from the outset.

It is important to remember that when accommodation has been booked, both parties – guests and hosts – have entered into a form of contract. We hope that the following points will provide helpful guidance.

Guests

- **When enquiring about accommodation, be as precise as possible. Give exact dates, numbers in your party and the ages of any children.**
- **State the number and type of rooms wanted and also what catering you require – bed and breakfast, full board etc. Make sure that the position about evening meals is clear – and about pets, reductions for children or any other special points.**
- **Read our reviews carefully to ensure that the proprietors you are going to contact can supply what you want. Ask for a letter confirming all arrangements, if possible.**
- **If you have to cancel, do so as soon as possible. Proprietors do have the right to retain deposits and under certain circumstances to charge for cancelled holidays if adequate notice is not given and they cannot re-let the accommodation.**

Hosts

- **Give details about your facilities and about any special conditions. Explain your deposit system clearly and arrangements for cancellations, charges etc. and whether or not your terms include VAT.**
- **If for any reason you are unable to fulfil an agreed booking without adequate notice, you may be under an obligation to arrange suitable alternative accommodation or to make some form of compensation.**

Pet-Friendly

Pubs, Inns & Hotels

on pages 390-405

Please note that these establishments may not feature in the main section of this book

St Breward,
Bodmin, Cornwall
PL30 4LZ
Tel: 01208 850277 / 850617
Fax: 01208 850915

Penrose Burden Holiday Cottages

Set in an area of outstanding natural beauty, sits 'Penrose Burden' surrounded by its 250 acres with breathtaking views overlooking the protected Camel Valley, on the edge of Bodmin Moor. Penrose Burden is a settlement of attractive stone cottages, varying in size, catering for two to seven persons, that have been beautifully converted into holiday homes. Also nestling beside Wenford Bridge are two riverside character cottages, idyllic for the free estate salmon and trout fishing!

NEW IN 2002: "TOAD HALL" a creative concept for today's open-plan living. All bedrooms en suite, enjoy 'patio dining' perched among stunning views, in your own grounds. With the ever-changing seasons, this all year round accommodation is geared to meet all seasonal requirements, including wood burners. All accommodation is suitable for disabled guests.

Paradise for dogs and their owners! Situated midway between north and south coasts, easy access to the new 'Eden Project', 'The Lost Gardens' and 'National Trust' properties. Why not walk or cycle the 'Camel Trail' and end up at "Rick Stein's"? Our 'Patsy' provides delicious home-cooked Cornish food, and will have a meal waiting on your arrival, at your request. Penrose Burden has received much acclaim including being featured on television and in the national press!

www.penroseburden.co.uk

Close to The Eden Project

A self-catering holiday to relax and unwind

An idyllic Cornish hamlet of picturesque stone cottages and quiet riverside lodges set amidst a glorious 30-acre estate. Gardens, wildlife, fishing, friendly farm animals, safe play areas, 4-posters, log burners, BBQs. Pub/Restaurant, indoor pool, pony trekking and moorland walks from the village. Sandy beaches, Eden Project, Rock and Padstow nearby. Well behaved dogs very welcome. Open all year. **Coombe Mill, St Breward, Bodmin PL30 4LZ**

01208 850344 • www.coombemill.com • mail@coombemill.com

Coombe Mill

Darrynane Cottages

Darrynane, St Breward, Bodmin Moor PL30 4LZ

Tel/Fax: 01208 850885 * www.darrynane.com * enquiries@darrynane.co.uk

3 detached cottages all with private, gated gardens. Situated in a unique moorland valley, with oak woods, waterfalls and the river. The cottages provide a homely base for walking, relaxing or touring Cornwall. Woodburning stoves, four-poster beds. Open all year.

HENWOOD BARNS HOLIDAY COTTAGES

Three stone barns set around original courtyard on the edge of Bodmin Moor, with stunning views. Tranquil, village location, horse riding two minutes' walk. Woodburning stoves; sleep 2/5; within easy reach of North Cornwall and Devon.

HENWOOD, LISKEARD PL14 5BP • 01579 363576/07956 864263

e-mail: henwoodbarns@tiscali.co.uk • www.henwoodbarns.co.uk

FREE or REDUCED RATE entry to Holiday Visits and Attractions – see our READERS' OFFER VOUCHERS on pages 407-423

Atlantic Coast • Near Boscastle • 01840 250289

Country bungalow sleeping 2-6, heating; microwave; colour TV. Near the spectacular coastal path and sandy beaches. Beautiful scenery, walking distance to the local inn and store. Just off the old A39 and central to most tourist attractions. Spring and autumn £190 - £250. Pets welcome. **Mrs Prout.**

Sunrise offers something special... service with a smile, stylish en suite bedrooms, superb breakfasts and ideal location, close to beaches, shops, cafes and restaurants. An ideal place to stay at any time of the year. Beautifully refurbished Victorian house providing stylish and comfortable four diamond accommodation, moments' walk from dog friendly beach and downs.
Excellent breakfast menu, including vegetarian. Special diets catered for. B&B from £27

Lesley Sharratt, Sunrise, 6 Burn View, Bude EX23 8BY
Tel: 01288 353214 • Fax: 01288 359911
e-mail: sunriseguest@btconnect.com • www.sunrise-bude.co.uk

WILLOW VALLEY HOLIDAY PARK

Dyehouse Bush, Bude EX23 9LB • Tel: 01288 353104

Four wooden lodges equipped to high standard. Each has 2 bedrooms, sofa bed in lounge, colour TV, bathroom, fully equipped kitchen. Two miles from town and sandy surfing beaches. Brochure on request. Open February to December. www.willowvalley.co.uk • willowvalley@talk21.com

RAC SELECTED SITE

Hedley Wood Caravan & Camping Park

Bridgerule (Near Bude), Holsworthy, Devon EX22 7ED
Tel: 01288 381404 • Fax: 01288 382011

16 acre woodland family-run site with outstanding views, where you can enjoy a totally relaxing holiday with a laid-back atmosphere, sheltered and open camping areas. Just 10 minutes' drive from the beaches, golf courses, riding stables and shops.

On site facilities include: Children's Adventure Areas, Bar, Clubroom, Shop, Laundry, Meals and all amenities. Free Hot Showers/Water. **Nice dogs/pets are very welcome. Daily kennelling facility. Dog walks/nature trail.**

Static caravans for hire. Caravan storage available. **Open all year.**

Visit our website: www.hedleywood.co.uk or write or phone for comprehensive brochure

LISTED SITE

Wringford Down **Family-friendly hotel set in 4 acres of Cornish countryside**

Located on the Rame peninsula in an Area of Outstanding Natural Beauty with tiny Cornish fishing villages, dramatic cliff top walks and secluded sandy bays.

Great facilities for all ages: • Family suites • Ball pool, bouncy castle • Bar & restaurant • Tennis court • Pool & table tennis • Covered, heated pool • Childcare on-site • Shetland ponies & other animals • Indoor & outdoor play areas **• Tel: 01752 822287 • www.cornwallholidays.co.uk**

Self-contained apartments set in an 18th Century listed farmhouse, in two acres of grounds on the beautiful Rame peninsula, enjoy stunning views and wonderful sunsets, coastal walks, birdwatching, fishing and surfing. Whitsand Bay, picturesque Cawsand, Kingsand close by. Pets welcome. B&B and Short Breaks available.

e-mail: MelBandJaneB@aol.com • www.ramebarton.co.uk
JANE BEANEY, RAME BARTON, RAME, CAWSAND PL10 1LG (01752 822789).

FHG Guides

publish a large range of well-known accommodation guides.
We will be happy to send you details or you can use the order form at the back of this book.

Give your pet the holiday it deserves

Crackington Haven, Bude, Cornwall

Quality Cornish Cottages sleeping from 1 to 8, at a price you can afford.
Situated in peaceful wooded valley leading to the beach.
Perfect location for walking, touring or just relaxing.
14 acres of fields/woodlands to exercise your dog.

Website: www.mineshop.co.uk

or phone Charlie or Jane on **01840 230338**

We are proud that all our properties are inspected by, and featured in,

The Good Holiday Cottage Guide

Five 18th Century converted barns, beamed ceilings, log fires and secluded rural setting. Ideal touring base. Five miles to coast at Crackington Haven. Sleep 2/6. Pets welcome. Open all year. From £80 short breaks, £145 per week. **ETC ★★★**.

Lorraine Harrison, Trenannick Cottages, Warbstow,
Launceston, Cornwall PL15 8RP • Tel: 01566 781443
e-mail: trenannick-1@tiscali.co.uk • www.trenannickcottages.co.uk

Crantock Bay Hotel a very special place, all year round...

Crantock Bay Hotel is superbly located for a holiday with your dogs. Our gardens lead direct to the Cornish coastal path and within 10 minutes walk of the 'dogs welcome' beaches of Polly Joke and Crantock Bay. Facilities include: comfortable bedrooms - many with sea views, a quality restaurant, indoor pool, Jacuzzi, gym and tennis court. NEW 'Thalgo' Beauty Treatment Rooms.

Crantock Bay Hotel
West Pentire, Crantock, Cornwall TR8 5SE

Tel: (01637) 830229 Fax: (01637) 831111
Email: stay@crantockbayhotel.co.uk
www.crantockbayhotel.co.uk

Please mention PETS WELCOME! when making enquiries about accommodation featured in these pages

Cusgarne (near Truro)

Sleeps 2. A cosy, clean, detached dwelling within grounds of Saffron Meadow. In a quiet hamlet five miles west of Truro. Own enclosed garden, secluded and surrounded by wooded pastureland. Bedroom (double bed) with twin vanity unit. Fully tiled shower/WC and L.B. Comprehensively equipped kitchen/diner. Compact TV room. Storage room. Hot water galore and gas included. Metered electricity. Your own ample parking space.Inn, good food, a short walk. Central to Truro, Falmouth and North and South Coast. £170 - £280 per week. Up to 10 years return bookings.

Joyce and George Clench, Saffron Meadow, Cusgarne, Truro TR4 8RW Tel: 01872 863171

Penquite Country Cottages

Duloe, Near Liskeard PL14 4QG

Four spacious and comfortable one-bedroom barn conversions for couples, or just one. Set in tranquil surroundings and enjoying outstanding views, Penquite offers real peace and quiet. Woodland walks from your front door, and within easy distance of the moors and coast, we are well situated for all that Cornwall has to offer. Fully equipped; heating, electricity, bedding and towels all included.

Well behaved dogs most welcome. No children.

Please contact Martin and Wendy Welch for further information/brochure on 01503 220260 or e-mail: stay@penquitecountrycottages.co.uk
See us at www.penquitecountrycottages.co.uk

Penmorvah Manor Hotel and Courtyard Cottages

Falmouth, Cornwall TR11 5ED

- 3 Star Country House Hotel and Self Catering Courtyard Cottages
- Situated in 6 acres of mature gardens and woodland
- Ideal for visiting Cornwall's superb gardens
- Close to Falmouth and Coastal Paths • Well-behaved dogs welcome
- Ground floor bedrooms for easy pet access • Ample car parking

Tel: 01326 250277 • Fax: 01326 250509
e-mail: reception@penmorvah.co.uk
website: www.penmorvah.co.uk

Creekside Cottages

offer a fine selection of individual water's edge, village and rural cottages, sleeping from 2-10, situated around the creeks of the Carrick Roads, near Falmouth, South Cornwall. Set in enchanting and picturesque positions, with many of the cottages offering panoramic creek views. Perfect locations for family holidays, all close to superb beaches, extensive sailing and boating facilities, Cornish gardens and excellent walks. The majority of the cottages are available throughout the year, and all offer peaceful, comfortable and fully equipped accommodation; most have open fires. Dogs welcome.

Just come and relax

For a colour brochure please phone 01326 375972
www.creeksidecottages.co.uk

CREEKSIDE HOLIDAY HOUSES

Spacious houses sleep 2/4/6/8. Peaceful, picturesque water's edge hamlet. Boating facilities. Use of boat. Own quay, beach. Secluded gardens. Near Pandora Inn. Friday bookings. Dogs welcome.

PETER WATSON, CREEKSIDE HOLIDAY HOUSES, RESTRONGUET, FALMOUTH TR11 5ST • 01326 372722
www.creeksideholidayhouses.co.uk

www.foweyvacations.com
tel: 01726 814263
sarahfurniss@aol.com

Near Fowey

LANCROW BARN is set amidst its own large, spacious garden, with exceptional countryside views and the coast beyond. Located close to the coast and towns of Fowey and Lostwithiel, also The Eden Project.

There are three double bedrooms, all with en suite bath or shower room. Upstairs there is a spectacular sitting room with wonderful views in every direction, and a spacious, well equipped kitchen. The decor and furnishings are of an extremely high standard, with every comfort and convenience. Pets welcome.

The Old Ferry Inn

Why not bring your dog for its well deserved holiday to the family-run Old Ferry Inn, close to the edge of the beautiful River Fowey. There are many varied walks from country and riverside to breathtaking views along the Cornwall Coastal Path. The 400-year-old hotel has an excellent à la carte restaurant for evening meals and a comprehensive bar menu for lunch and evening. The Inn has 12 letting rooms with tea and coffee making facilities, colour TV and telephone, most rooms being en suite, some with views of the Fowey river.

Prices are from £60-£85 per night for two people sharing.

Bodinnick-by-Fowey PL23 1LX
Tel: (01726) 870237 • Fax: (01726) 870116
www.oldferryinn.com • e-mail: royce972@aol.com

Two apartments, sleeping 2-4 persons. Sea views, large garden and private parking. 600 yards from beach, harbour and shops. Superb coastal walks. Open all year. VisitCornwall Southwest Tourism Member. VisitBritain ★★★

MRS S. PIKE, TREGILLAN, TREWOLLOCK LANE, GORRAN HAVEN, ST AUSTELL PL26 6NT • 01726 842452
e-mail: tregillanapartment@tiscali.co.uk
www.tregillanapartments.co.uk

BOSCREGE
CARAVAN & CAMPING PARK

★ Special out of season offers
★ Award winning quiet family park close to local beaches and attractions with no bar or clubs
★ Free showers ★ Microwave facilities
★ Games room ★ Child's play area
★ Laundry ★ Pets welcome

For Brochure Telephone:
01736 762231
www.caravanparkcornwall.com
enquiries@caravanparkcornwall.com

Lower Dutson Farm, Launceston PL15 9SP • Tel: 01566 776456

Guests may enjoy the pretty walks down to the River Tamar and along its bank which borders our fields and meander by the lake. Ideal stay for visiting National Trust properties, Dartmoor, Bodmin Moor and the beaches and harbours of Devon and Cornwall. Well-equipped cottage with field to the rear.
e-mail: holidays@farm-cottage.co.uk • www.farm-cottage.co.uk

Hopsland Cottages, Commonmoor, Liskeard PL14 6EJ
Tel & Fax: 01579 344480. A beautiful barn on our farm which has been converted into 3 well-equipped self-catering cottages, which sleep between 4 and 6 persons. Beautiful views and very peaceful. Own exercise fields for dogs, or just 150 yards from Bodmin Moor, with miles of open space. Many ancient monuments to visit.
www.hopslandholidays.co.uk • e-mail: hopslandholidays@aol.com

Hayloft Courtyard Cottages, Menheniot, Liskeard A warm welcome and Cornish Cream Tea await your arrival at our family-run cottages. Lovingly converted from original stone barns and equipped to a high standard with many home-from-home comforts including beautiful new jacuzzi bathrooms in most cottages. An excellent touring base - only a short drive to Looe and Polperro. The Coastal Path, moors and dog-friendly beaches are all nearby. Restaurant on-site offering popular meal delivery service. Children's play area. Short breaks available.
www.hayloftcourtyardcottages.com Michele & Steve Hore • 01503 240879 • e-mail: courtyardcottage@btconnect.com

Butterdon Mill Holiday Homes

Idyllic rural site set in 2.5 acres of mature gardens. Two-bedroom detached bungalows sleeping up to six. Games barn and children's play areas. Ideal for touring coasts and moors of Cornwall and Devon. Located 3 miles from Liskeard, 8 miles from Looe. Discounts for Senior Citizens/couples Sept to June. PETS WELCOME. Brochure available.
Butterdon Mill Holiday Homes, Merrymeet, Liskeard, Cornwall PL14 3LS
Tel: 01579 342636 **e-mail: butterdonmill@btconnect.com**

CUTKIVE WOOD HOLIDAY LODGES

Nestling in the heart of a peaceful and lovely family-owned country estate, there are six well-equipped cedar-clad lodges. Set on the edge of bluebell woods with wonderful rural views, you can relax and enjoy yourself in this tranquil and idyllic setting. Ideally situated to enjoy year-round holidays. You can help to feed the animals, milk the goats, explore the woods and fields. Big play area. So much to see and do - including memorable beaches, wonderful coasts, walk the moors, theme attractions, historic gems and the Eden Project. Dogs welcome. Short breaks. Open all year.

southwesttourism inspected and approved by the regional tourist board for the south west of England

St Ive, Liskeard, Cornwall PL14 3ND • Tel: 01579 362216
www.cutkivewood.co.uk • holidays@cutkivewood.co.uk

MEMBER VisitCornwall southwesttourism

FHG Guides

publish a large range of well-known accommodation guides.
We will be happy to send you details or you can use the order form at the back of this book.

FHG K·U·P·E·R·A·R·D

Caradon Country Cottages

in magnificent countryside between Bodmin Moor and Looe. Ideal for exploring Devon and Cornwall, Eden Project, coast and countryside. Central heating and log burners for cosy Winter Breaks. 5-acre grounds. Every comfort for you and your pets.

e-mail: celia@caradoncottages.co.uk
East Taphouse, Liskeard, Cornwall PL14 4NH

Mullion Holiday Park

Weststar HOLIDAY PARKS

An award winning holiday park near Helston, in an area of outstanding natural beauty. Dogs most welcome!

Call: 0870 444 0080 book online: www.weststarholidays.co.uk/pw

Quote: WP

• Mount View Hotel •

A family-run pub with comfortable accommodation, situated 100 yards from Mount's Bay in Longrock village. Three en suite rooms and two with shared bathroom. Breakfast in dining room, lunch and dinner available. Dogs welcome by arrangement. Prices from £20 pppn.

Longrock, Penzance, Cornwall TR20 8JJ • Tel: 01736 710416

Fox Valley Cottages

Lanlawren, Trenewan, Looe PL13 2PZ

Set in beautiful countryside
For a peaceful and relaxing holiday

A warm welcome from Andy & Linda, who are two of the partners who live on site.
• Indoor heated pool, spa and sauna • Cleaned to a high standard, warm, comfortable and well equipped • Log fires for those cosy winter nights • A field where your dog can have a good run around • Just three miles from Polperro, with country and coastal walks nearby • We are open all year round, including Christmas. • Short breaks, long weekends or midweek breaks out of season.

Tel: 01726 870115 • e-mail: lanlawrenfarm@lycos.com • www.foxvalleycottages.co.uk

TALLAND CARAVAN PARK

Talland Bay, Looe, Cornwall PL13 2JA

A small family site situated in secluded Talland Bay between Looe and Polperro and adjacent to the Coastal Heritage Path. We have a wide range of fully equipped caravans with both two or three beds. The camping area overlooks the bay with direct access down to the shore. The site has a shop, licensed bar with bar meals and takeaways, laundry, play area and swimming pool. An ideal site for families and as a touring centre

Pets are welcome, with coastal walks at your doorstep.

Telephone: (01503) 272715 **www.tallandcaravanpark.co.uk**

Looe Bay Holiday Park

Weststar HOLIDAY PARKS

An award winning holiday park near Looe, in a stunning location close to stunning sandy beaches and superb attractions. Dogs most welcome!

Call: 0870 444 0080 book online: www.weststarholidays.co.uk/pw

Quote: WP

CARDWEN FARM, PELYNT, LOOE PL13 2LU

Bed and Breakfast in 17th century Grade II Listed farmhouse. En suite rooms. Pelynt, with pub and restaurant, half a mile, Looe and Polperro four miles, Eden project under 10 miles away. Coastal Path nearby. Self-catering also available.

MRS KEILTHY - 01503 220213

E-MAIL: CARDWENFARM@FREENET.CO.UK • WWW.CARDWENFARM.COM

Secluded traditional cottages set in the grounds of a country estate minutes from Looe and the coast.

- Private gardens and grounds
- Log fires and generous heating
- Delicious optional home-cooked food delivery
- Coastal path, woodland and moor walking nearby
- Well-behaved dogs welcome
- Open all year, winter short breaks

www.trenantcottages.com

e-mail: Liz@holiday-cottage.com Tel: 01503 263639

Valleybrook

Peakswater, Lansallos, Looe, Cornwall PL13 2QE

Peaceful 9 acre country site, with 6 superb lodges and 2 delightful cottages. 3 miles from coast, Eden Project 11 miles

- All accommodation dog friendly - 2 dogs maximum
- Individual fenced gardens
- Dog friendly local pubs
- Dog walk and off lead dog paddock on site
- Many dog friendly beaches
- Day kennelling nearby
- Short Breaks available
- Open All year

Contact Denise, Keith & Brian Holder

www.valleybrookholidays.co.uk **01503 220493**

COLDRINNICK COTTAGES Duloe, Near Looe PL14 4QF

Coldrinnick Cottages are attractively converted barns, set in their own large secure, secluded garden on a working dairy farm. Outstanding views, woodland walks to west Looe valley, close to moors and coast. Excellent locality for walking and relaxing. Well Meadow sleeps 2 people, Wagon sleeps 2/4 and Rose 2/6. Heating, electricity, bed linen etc all inclusive. An ideal place for families and dogs alike.

For a brochure or any information please contact: ***Bill and Kaye Chapman on 01503 220251***

www.cornishcottage.net ETC ★★★★

Looking for holiday accommodation?

for details of hundreds of properties throughout the UK visit:

www.holidayguides.com

WRINGWORTHY COTTAGES
LOOE

Our 8 traditional stone cottages are set amongst unspoilt Cornish hills in 4 acres of space. Wringworthy is minutes from Looe with its stunning coastal path and sandy beaches. Walks from our door; dog-friendly beaches within a short drive. The perfect base to explore the delights of Cornwall and Devon – hidden gardens, Eden, Bodmin Moor, NT and more.

Sleeping 2-8, each cottage layout is unique but all are fully equipped with fridges, washing machines, DVD/video, microwaves, linen, towels etc. You can't help but relax at Wringworthy – outdoor heated pool, games barn, BBQ areas, lawns, outdoor games and friendly farm animals. Safe fun for children and wide open spaces for everyone.

Whether you take a short break or longer our heated cottages and warm welcome await you all year round.

Green Acorn Award holders for sustainable tourism and commitment to the environment.

Tel: 01503 240685 www.wringworthy.co.uk pets@wringworthy.co.uk

Talehay Holiday Cottages
Pelynt, Near Looe PL13 2LT
A Quiet Haven in the Countryside near the sea

Cosy, traditional cottages with many original features retained provide superb holiday accommodation on 17C non-working farmstead. Set in 4 acres of unspoilt countryside offering peace and tranquillity with breathtaking coastal and country walks on your doorstep. This is an ideal location for dogs and their owners alike. C.T.B. approved. Close to the Eden Project.

Tel: Mr & Mrs Dennett: 01503 220252

E-mail: infobookings@talehay.co.uk Website: www.talehay.co.uk

TREMAINE GREEN
for MEMORABLE HOLIDAYS

"A beautiful private hamlet" of 11 traditional cosy Cornish craftsmen's cottages between **Looe** and **Polperro.** Clean, comfortable and well equipped, with a warm friendly atmosphere, for pets with 2 to 8 people. Set in award-winning grounds, only 12 miles from the **Eden Project** with country and coastal walks nearby. Pets £18 pw; owners from £118.

• Towels, Linen, Electric & Hot Water included • Dishwashers in larger cottages • Launderette • Kid's Play Area • Games Room • Tennis Court • TV/DVDs • Cots & Highchairs • Pubs & Restaurants in easy walking distance • Activities Area

Mr & Mrs J Spreckley, Tremaine Green Country Cottages, Pelynt, Near Looe, Cornwall PL13 2LT
Web: www.tremainegreen.co.uk • e-mail: stay@tremainegreen.co.uk • Tel: (01503) 220333

POLPERRO CORNWALL

Spectacularly situated holiday cottages in picturesque Cornish fishing village.
Sleeping from 2 to 8 persons - £175 to £575 per cottage per week.

With terraced gardens and fabulous outlook over harbour, encompassing 15 mile sea views. Private parking, two minutes shops, beach, quay and National Trust cliff walks. Open all year. Children and pets most welcome. All cottages are fully furnished and equipped to include a colour television, microwave, electric oven, refrigerator, duvets and pillows. **Graham Wright, Guardian House, Liskeard PL14 6AD**

01579 344080

Cornish Dream

"For those who enjoy the comfort of a high quality hotel but prefer the freedom of a cottage"
...The Good Holiday Cottage Guide

Idyllic 18th Century 5 Star Country Cottages for romantics and animal lovers, near the sea in the beautiful Looe River valley.
Your own delightful private garden with roses around the door and breathtaking views.
Exclusively furnished, antiques, crackling log fires, candlelit meals, four-posters, crisp white linen.
Riding, heated swimming pool & tennis court. Wonderful walks from your cottage gate. Open all year.
Golf, fishing, sea, coastal walks all nearby. Pets are welcome.

English Tourism Council ★★★★★ SELF CATERING

Tel: 01503 262730

www.cornishdreamcottages.co.uk

Badham Farm, St Keyne, Liskeard PL14 4RW • 01579 343572
www.badhamfarm.co.uk • e-mail: badhamfarm@yahoo.co.uk

Farmhouse and farm buildings converted to a high standard. Sleep 2-10. All well furnished/equipped; prices include electricity, bed linen and towels. Most have a garden. Tennis, putting, children's play area, fishing lake, animal paddock, games room with pool and table tennis. Separate bar. Laundry. Barbecue.
Well behaved dogs welcome (not in high season). Prices from £120 per week.

★★★★ SELF CATERING

Paul & Barbie Higgins
Trewith, Duloe, near Liskeard
Cornwall PL14 4PR

TREWITH HOLIDAY COTTAGES

Self Catering Accommodation Open All Year

Tel: 01503 262184
mobile: 07968 262184

Situated in a superb elevated position of outstanding natural beauty. Just 1 1/2 miles from Looe. Choice of 4 refurbished cottages with 1-3 bedrooms. Fully-equipped and tastefully furnished with full central heating. Use of laundry room. Peaceful location with delightful walks. Many beaches, coves, fishing, shopping close by in Looe. Because of ponds young children need supervision. Well behaved dogs welcome.

E-mail: holiday-cottages@trewith.freeserve.co.uk
www.trewith.freeserve.co.uk

A useful index of towns/counties appears on pages 424-429

St Anthony – Helford River

www.StAnthony.co.uk

Enchanting creekside cottages in a timeless and tranquil hamlet. Springtime bluebell woods and hedgerows banked with primroses, reflections of multi-coloured sails off sandy beaches, the solitary blue flash of a Kingfisher in autumn, smoke grey herons and shining white egrets standing patiently by the shoreline all evoke the atmosphere of this truly beautiful corner of Cornwall.

- Stunning coastal and riverside walks
- Great country inns and local food
- Warm and comfortable with cosy log fires
- Our own sailing dinghies and fishing boats
- Moorings and easy launching
- National Trust and private gardens nearby
- Short breaks, open all year including Christmas

St Anthony Holidays, Manaccan, Helston, Cornwall TR12 6JW
Tel: 01326 231 357 • e-mail: info@stanthony.co.uk

THE GODOLPHIN ARMS

West End, Marazion, Cornwall TR17 0EN

Perched on the edge of the sand, facing St Michael's Mount. Recently refurbished, The Godolphin arms has 10 individually designed en suite bedrooms, most with breathtaking sea views. Fresh local seafood served in restaurant. Relaxing, comfortable bar and terraced beer garden. Perfect for exploring coast and coves.

01736 710202

email: enquiries@godolphinarms.co.uk
www.godolphinarms.co.uk

AA ★★
Highly Commended in Cornwall Tourism Awards "Pub of the Year" and "Hotel of the Year"

Blue Bay HOTEL

Trenance, Mawgan Porth, Cornwall TR8 4DA
hotel@bluebaycornwall.co.uk
www.bluebaycornwall.co.uk

- Beautifully situated in tranquil location, panoramic sea views. Close to beach, coastal path and lovely valley walks.
- Licensed family hotel, highly commended for our service, friendly atmosphere and home cooking.
- Dogs welcome, may sleep with you, and are allowed on the beach all year.
- TV lounge, board games, cards, library available for guests' use.
- Family, double, single rooms, most en suite, majority ground floor. Colour TV.
- BB&EM from £237 per week.

SPECIAL BREAKS
Four nights for the price of *three*
FREE colour brochure

James & Pippa McLuskie:
01637 860324

Kilbol Country House Hotel & Cottages **Polmassick, Mevagissey PL26 6HA**
'Perfect Peace in Hidden Cornwall' A small, cottage-style country hotel set in 5-acre grounds. Dating back to the 16th century, it has been fully refurbished and offers 8 rooms, as well as two self-catering cottages. Two miles from the Lost Gardens of Heligan and Mevagissey, and close to the Eden Project. Outdoor swimming pool, riverside walk, wooded area. No children under 12 years in the hotel. Pets welcome. **Tel: 01726 842481 • e-mail: Hotel@kilbol-hotel.co.uk • www.kilbol-hotel.co.uk**

Traditional cottage, sleeps two to five. Linen, towels, electricity supplied. Beach one mile. Large garden. Central for touring/walking. Near Heligan Gardens and Eden Project. Pets welcome.

MRS M.R. BULLED, MENAGWINS, GORRAN, MEVAGISSEY PL26 6HP • 01726 843517

POLVELLAN HOLIDAY FLAT • • • MOUSEHOLE
Fully furnished, self contained flat with full sea view at the entrance to the unspoiled fishing village of Mousehole. Pets are welcome at no charge. Fully equipped kitchen. Sleeps 2. For details contact:
Mr A. G. Wright, 164 Portland Road, Selston, Notts NG16 6AN
01773 775347 • alang23@hotmail.com

Retorrick Mill *St Mawgan, Newquay TR8 4BH*
Tel: 01637 860460

Set in 11 acres, self-catering Retorrick Mill has two cottages and six chalets, all very well equipped. Peace and tranquillity, within easy reach of everything. Pets including horses very welcome. For a brochure or further assistance contact Chris Williams.

www.retorrickmill.co.uk

Dewolf Guest House **100 Henver Road, Newquay TR7 3BL**
The amenities of Newquay are close at hand, Porth Beach only a short walk from the Guest House. Single, Double or Family rooms including two Chalets situated in the rear garden, ideal for pets. All rooms non-smoking with en suite facilities, colour TV and tea/coffee making facilities. B&B from £22 per person. Licensed. Off-road car parking available. Special breaks available. Suitable for M1 Disabled. Open all year. NATC Approved. AA ★★★★
Tel: 01637 874746 • e-mail: holidays@dewolfguesthouse.com • www.dewolfguesthouse.com

QUARRYFIELD Caravan & Camping Park, Crantock, Near Newquay.
Superbly situated overlooking beautiful Crantock Bay and the River Gannel estuary, park with fully equipped modern caravans for hire, and separate level camping field. Bar, pool, children's play area.
Contact: MRS WINN, TRETHERRAS, NEWQUAY, CORNWALL TR7 2RE
Tel & Fax: 01637 872792

Free or reduced rate entry to
Holiday Visits and Attractions – see our
READERS' OFFER VOUCHERS on pages 407-423

Trethiggey Touring Park
Quintrell Downs, Newquay TR8 4QR

Our friendly, family-run park is just minutes by car from Newquay's famous surf beaches and 15 miles from the amazing Eden Project. Beautifully landscaped, the park has panoramic countryside views and is ideal for touring caravans, tents and campervans. We also have luxury holiday homes for hire. Facilities include shop, off-licence, free showers, electric hook-ups, laundry, children's play area, TV/games room, fishing and take-away food in summer.

Open from March 1st to January 1st including Christmas and New Year. Short Breaks available. Off season rallies welcome.

For more information phone 01637 877672 or see our website:
www.Trethiggey.co.uk • e-mail: enquiries@trethiggey.co.uk

Raintree House Holidays

A range of well equipped houses and bungalows near Trevose Golf Club, sandy beaches, scenic walks.

Mrs Watts, "Whistlers", Treyarnon Bay, Padstow PL28 8JR
Tel: 01841 520228

e-mail: gill@raintreehouse.co.uk ***www.raintreehouse.co.uk***

Large elegant Victorian Guesthouse in peaceful location close to seafront, town centre and gardens. Spacious en suite rooms, some with sea views. All with colour TV and tea/coffee making facilities.

Real fires and fully centrally heated. Unrestricted parking. Delicious breakfast choices. Ideal location for beaches, SW coastal path, Scilly Isles. Open all year. Please contact HELEN CAHALANE. ETC ◆◆◆◆

GLENCREE HOUSE, 2 MENNAYE ROAD, PENZANCE TR18 4NG • 01736 362026

e-mail: stay@glencreehouse.co.uk
www.glencreehouse.co.uk

• *Lamorna Cove, Cornwall* • *Bal-Red Bungalow* •

Well equipped bungalow sleeping four (one double, one twin). Situated near harbour, with cliff walks close by. Linen and towels supplied. Colour TV incl. Sky channels. DVD & CD player. Parking. Metered electricity (£1 coins). Well behaved pets by arrangement. Open all year.

Enquiries: **Miss S. Daniel, Sarah's Cottage, Lamorna, Penzance TR19 6XJ • 01736 731227**

TORWOOD HOUSE HOTEL 01736 360063
ALEXANDRA ROAD, PENZANCE TR18 4LZ

Torwood is a small, family-run hotel, situated in a beautiful tree-lined avenue 500 metres from the seafront. All rooms en suite, with TV/DVD, tea/coffee makers and radios. Dinner available on request.
For further details telephone LYNDA SOWERBY
e-mail: Lyndasowerby@aol.com • www.torwoodhousehotel.co.uk

Near Perranporth

Greenmeadow Cottages

Highly praised luxury cottages. Sleep 6. Superbly clean, comfortable and spacious. Open all year. Short Breaks out of season. Pets welcome in two of the cottages. Non-smoking available. Ample off-road parking.

For brochure and bookings

Tel: 01872 540483

Step onto The Coastal Path...

Escape the pressures of life. Relax! explore the Cornish Coast from Green Door Cottages in Port Gaverne.

8 comfortable, restored 18th Century cottages set around a sheltered court-yard, plus 2 prestigious apartments with panoramic sea views beside a picturesque cove, directly on the Coastal path, less than half a mile from Port Isaac.

An ideal location for your holiday and short breaks. Well behaved dogs are very welcome.

Call now for a brochure on:
01208 880293

Green Door Cottages
PORT GAVERNE
email: enquiries@greendoorcottages.co.uk
web: www.greendoorcottages.co.uk

CHIMNEYS

Port Gaverne, Port Isaac, Cornwall PL29 3SQ Tel & Fax: 01208 880254

A charming 18th Century Cottage just 10 metres from the beach making it a wonderful venue for pets and their owners. Four bedrooms, two bathrooms, lounge, dining room and kitchen. Good size garden. Close to Eden Project, many golf courses & the Camel Trail.

Brochure available from **Mrs Holmes.**

GULLROCK COTTAGES

Port Gaverne Port Isaac North Cornwall

Personal attention from resident owner ensures your home from home comfort in a tranquil setting just yards from the sea at bygone Port Gaverne.

Tel: Malcolm Lee (01208) 880106 • e-mail: gullrock@ukonline.co.uk

PORTHLEVEN • *Kernow Cottages*

Fishermen's cottages. Harbour, bay or country views. 3 minutes to beach, coast path, harbourside eating places. Open fires. Pets welcome. **Tel: 01209 860410**

FHG Guides

publish a large range of well-known accommodation guides.
We will be happy to send you details or you can use the order form at the back of this book.

FHG
K·U·P·E·R·A·R·D

The Garden House near Port Isaac, Cornwall

Brand new for 06 season. Secure garden for dogs (1 large or 2 small maximum). Doggy shower. Lovely far-reaching view across open countryside. Very warm and cosy for all year round. Full central heating, electricity, bed linen and towels included. One bedroom with twin or double. Lounge/kitchen/dining and shower room all fully equipped to very high standards. Central location in small quiet hamlet near Michaelstow and within 8 miles of Port Isaac, Boscastle, Tintagel, Polzeath, Rock, Wadebridge, Bodmin Moor and Camel Trail. From £160 pw.

Contact David & Jenny Oldham. 01208 850529
Trevella, Treveighan, St Teath, Cornwall PL30 3JN
email. david.trevella@btconnect.com www.trevellacornwall.co.uk

THE CORNISH ARMS Pendoggett, Port Isaac PL30 3HH

Tel: 01208 880263 • Fax: 01208 880335 • www.cornisharms.com

A delightful 16th century coaching inn just one mile from the coast. Whilst retaining the character of a traditional coaching inn, The Cornish Arms offers all modern amenities in every bedroom. The daily specials board features locally caught seafood and an extensive range of other dishes.

LONG CROSS HOTEL & VICTORIAN GARDENS

TRELIGHTS, PORT ISAAC PL29 3TF • www.portisaac.com

Stay in one of Cornwall's most unusual hotels. Set in our own magnificent gardens in an Area of Outstanding Natural Beauty, and visited by thousands of garden lovers every year. Restaurant, Bar and Terraces with panoramic views. Spacious, newly refurbished, en suite rooms. Children's adventure play area.

Tel: 01208 880243 • e-mail: longcross@portisaac.com

This renowned 17th century inn is situated in an unspoilt fishing cove on the rugged North Coast of Cornwall. The beach is just 50 yards from the front door and the Coastal Path offers miles of breathtaking scenery. For a relaxing break with a friendly atmosphere you need look no further. Golf, fishing, sailing and riding are all nearby.

Pets welcome in the Inn and Self-catering accommodation available.

Port Gaverne Hotel Near Port Isaac, Cornwall PL29 3SQ Tel: 01208 880244 Fax: 01208 880151

Friesian Valley Cottages

For Colour Brochure Telephone 01209 890901

Luxury Cottages in peaceful rural hamlet on Atlantic coast between Newquay and St Ives, surrounded by fields, beautiful sandy beaches and National Trust Coastal Path.

£130 to £620 per week.

Terms quoted in this publication may be subject to increase if rises in costs necessitate

The Rosevine Hotel

Porthcurnick Beach, Portscatho, Nr St Mawes, Cornwall TR2 5EW
Tel: 01872 580206 • Fax: 01872 580230
e-mail: info@rosevine.co.uk
website: www.rosevine.co.uk

The newest luxury hotel in Cornwall

• De luxe bedrooms and suites • Award-winning cuisine
• Beautiful sub-tropical gardens facing directly over the safe, sandy beach fronting the National Trust coastline
• Warm heated indoor pool & jacuzzi
• Children and pets most welcome

AA ★★★ 80% BRITAIN'S BEST HOTELS

WHITSAND BAY SELF-CATERING

12 cottages sleeping 4-10, all with sea views and situated by an 18-hole clifftop golf course.

Children and pet-friendly

01579 345688
www.whitsandbayselfcatering.co.uk

Jasmine and Two Ways, Praa Sands, Near Penzance

Well appointed bungalows. One chalet-bungalow sleeps 8+ in 4 bedrooms. Lovely peaceful countryside with very large garden, not overlooked. 2 miles inland. One three bedroomed, sleeps 6+, overlooking sea, with large garden. Beach 5 mins. Both fully equipped. Dogs very welcome. **MRS JANE LAITY, CHYRASE FARM, GOLDSITHNEY, PENZANCE TR20 9JD • TEL: 01736 763301**

Blue Hills TOURING PARK

Cross Coombe, Trevellas, St Agnes, Cornwall TR5 0XP

Set in a beautiful rural position close to a coastal footpath, a small site with good toilets. A pleasant location for exploring nearby coves, beaches and villages.
2-acre site with 30 touring pitches
01872 552999 • loo@zoom.co.uk
www.bluehillscamping.co.uk

- Caravan Holiday Homes
- Touring & Camping
- Families & Couples
- Pets Welcome
- Exclusive leisure facility:
- Gym, Sauna & Steamroom
- Shop/Off-licence
- Laundry room • Games room
- Children's play area
- Multi-service hook-ups
- Satellite TV in all units
- No club, bar or disco

Chiverton Park

Set in the heart of Cornish countryside, yet only a short distance from superb beaches, this spacious, well-run park offers peace and relaxation in a delightful rural setting. Holiday homes are fully equipped (except linen, which may be hired)

Chiverton Park, Blackwater, Truro TR4 8HS • 01872 560667
info@chivertonpark.co.uk • www.chivertonpark.co.uk

BEACON
Country House Hotel

Set in a quiet and beautiful area just outside the village of St Agnes, the hotel has fabulous views over the surrounding countryside and coastline. All the luxurious bedrooms are en suite and equipped to the highest standards, the majority benefiting from the wonderful views. A relaxed and rewarding stay is guaranteed at

The Beacon Country House Hotel.

Pets stay free • Open all year • Non-smoking throughout

ETC/AA ★★

For brochure write or phone: 01872 552318
The Beacon Country House Hotel
Goonvrea Road, St Agnes, Cornwall TR5 0NW
e-mail: info@beaconhotel.co.uk www.beaconhotel.co.uk

wooded valleys coast paths doggy beaches log fires

Driftwood Spars
HOTEL
THE ONLY HOTEL AT THE COVE

Character 17thC hotel of contrasts that compliment...

...dark mysterious bars, light airy bedrooms, both with a nautical theme, stunning sea views, sizzling log fires, massive beams & breakfasts.

OPEN ALL YEAR
PETS £3 PER NIGHT
AMPLE PARKING

And now, a brand new Seafood Restaurant with alfresco balconies and locally sourced ingredients.

Trevaunance Cove,
St Agnes, Cornwall TR5 0RT
01872 552428
www.driftwoodspars.com

AA ♦♦♦♦ Guest Accommodation

microbrewery on site serious walkies start here...

PENKERRIS

Penkerris **Penwinnick Road, St Agnes TR5 0PA**
Tel & Fax: 01872 552262 *Dorothy Gill-Carey*

Creeper-clad B&B/guest house with lawned garden. A home from home offering real food, comfortable bedrooms. Ample parking. Three sandy beaches and dramatic cliff walks (½ mile). Central for touring. Bed and Breakfast from £20.00 to £30.00 pppn. Open all year. **ETC ★★ Guest House**

e-mail: info@penkerris.co.uk • www.penkerris.co.uk

FHG Guides

publish a large range of well-known accommodation guides.
We will be happy to send you details or you can use the order form at the back of this book.

FHG
K·U·P·E·R·A·R·D

BOSINVER HOLIDAY COTTAGES

Self-catering Establishment of the Year 2006 • Cornwall Tourism Awards

Nestling in a hidden valley near the sea, the Eden Project and Lost Gardens of Heligan, our small farm has friendly animals and ponies. Choose from our 16th Century thatched farmhouse or cottages privately set in their own gardens surrounded by wildflower meadows. Wander down to the fishing lake or village pub, swim in the pool, play tennis, or relax and listen to the birdsong. No pets during Summer school holidays please.

Brochure from: Mrs Pat Smith, Bosinver Farm, Trelowth, St Austell, Cornwall PL26 7DT • Tel: 01726 72128
e-mail: reception@bosinver.co.uk • www.bosinver.co.uk

HOLIDAY COTTAGE - *ST BREWARD*

Warm and lovely cottage sleeping four in great comfort and utter peace. Log fires, large garden with stream. Glorious walking. Available all year. Terms from £200 to £490 per week, depending on season.

Dogs welcome, £10 per week. St Breward is a picturesque village high on Bodmin Moor and within easy reach of both coasts. Situated four miles from the A30. **Sleeps 4/5.**

For further details please contact:
Mrs Paddy Powell (01208 850186)
website: www.vacation-cornwall.co.uk

The Links Holiday Flats

Lelant, St Ives, Cornwall TR26 3HY

Magnificent location alongside and overlooking West Cornwall Golf Course, Hayle Estuary and St Ives Bay. Both flats have lovely views. Wonderful spot for walking. We are five minutes from the beach and dogs are allowed there all year round. Two well-equipped flats which are open all year.

Your hosts are Bob and Jacky Pontefract • Phone or fax 01736 753326

SANDBANK HOLIDAYS

St Ives Bay, Hayle, Cornwall TR27 5BL
www.sandbank-holidays.co.uk

High quality Apartments and Bungalows for 2-6 persons. Peaceful garden setting close to miles of sandy beach, acres of grassy dunes and SW Coastal Path. Dogs Welcome. Fully equipped for your self-catering holiday. Heated, Colour TV, Microwave etc. Spotlessly clean. All major debit and credit cards accepted. **Tel: 01736 752594**

Sea Pink **Near St Mawes, South Cornwall.** Nestling in a picturesque setting overlooking the little bay of St Just-in-Roseland, Sea Pink is ideally located for exploring the coast and attractions. Recently refurbished, there is a spacious lounge, dining area opening on to sun terrace and lawned garden; three bedrooms (one en suite). **Contact Judy Juniper • Tel: 01872 863553**
e-mail: cottageinfo@btconnect.com • www.luxury-holiday-cottages.com

Dalswinton

A Victorian stone-built house standing in 10 acres of gardens and meadowland in the glorious Vale of Lanherne, midway between Padstow and Newquay. Overlooking the village of St Mawgan, with views to the sea at Mawgan Porth, Dalswinton offers a warm welcome, friendly atmosphere, and great food prepared with fresh local produce.

We are totally non-smoking, and are not suitable for children under 16.

- Dogs free of charge and allowed everywhere except the restaurant
- 8 acres of private meadowland for dog exercise
- Dog-friendly beach 1.5 miles
- Bed & Breakfast from £39.00 per person per night
- Weekly rates available. Special offers Oct//Mar/Apr.
- Heated outdoor pool (in season). Car parking
- All rooms en suite, with tea/coffee making facilities, colour TV and radio
- Residents' bar, and restaurant serving breakfast and 3-course dinner
- Self-catering Garden Lodge (sleeps 3 adults)
- Easy access to Newquay Airport, Padstow and the Eden Project

★★★★ GUEST ACCOMMODATION

Proprietors: Stuart and Sal Hope
Dalswinton House, St Mawgan-in-Pydar, Cornwall TR8 4EZ
Tel: 01637 860385
Visit us at www.dalswinton.com e-mail: dalswintonhouse@tiscali.co.uk

Comfortable end of terrace cottage in picturesque and friendly village. Enclosed garden and parking. Ideal location for exploring all Cornwall. Short Breaks and brochure available. Contact:

MRS R REEVES, POLSTRAUL, TREWALDER, DELABOLE PL33 9ET
Tel & Fax: 01840 213120 • e-mail: a.p.reeves@homecall.co.uk
www.maymear.co.uk

Comfortable, well equipped wing of farmhouse, set in a beautiful valley on the edge of Bodmin Moor. Sky TV and central heating. Dogs welcome, use of kennels, exercise field. Excellent walks and dog friendly beaches nearby. Eden Project 10 miles, Padstow 12 miles.

Trewithian Farm, St Wenn PL30 5PH 01208 895181
www.cornwall-online.co.uk/trewithianfarm

Comfortable, well-equipped, centrally heated cottages sleeping two. Ideal for touring, walking and relaxing. Close to Coastal Path and village amenities. Private parking. Ring for brochure. Pets Free.

SANDY AND DAVE WILSON, SALUTATIONS, ATLANTIC ROAD, TINTAGEL PL34 0DE • 01840 770287
e-mail: sandyanddave@tinyworld.co.uk • www.salutationstintagel.co.uk

Treloan Coastal Farm Holidays, Treloan Lane, Portscatho TR2 5EF

Traditional 1930's working farm on coastal footpath. Open all year. Sea views. Access to three coves (local beaches accept pets). Self-catering mobile homes, touring, camping and camping barn. Shire horses, Jersey milking cows/calves and hens/chicks. Experience farm practices: horse ploughing, harvesting, steam tractor, threshing, milking, feeding, egg collecting. Close to shops, pubs, etc. Half an hour from Truro, Eden Project.

01872 580899/580989 • e-mail: enquiries@coastalfarmholidays.co.uk • www.coastalfarmholidays.co.uk

Two comfortable, well-equipped cottages set in an Area of Outstanding Natural Beauty, each with its own charming garden. Individually furnished with co-ordinating furnishings. Full central heating and double glazed. Microwave, colour TV and video, telephone, washing machine, fridge and all bed linen. We also offer use of our boat during your stay, All these included in the price. Pets are welcome. Beautiful woodland walks for you to stroll through. Perfect for fishing and bird watching.

Tel: 01326 319417
e-mail: jean@kingharry.net

King Harry Ferry Cottages

High Quality Cottages to Let near Truro

www.kingharry-info.co.uk

TRENONA FARM

Ruan High Lanes, Truro, Cornwall TR2 5JS

Enjoy a relaxing stay on this mixed farm, on the unspoilt Roseland Peninsula midway between Truro and the Eden Project at St Austell.

B&B in the Victorian farmhouse in double/family rooms, either en suite or with private bathroom.

Self-catering in two renovated barns, each sleeping 6, both well equipped and furnished. Ample parking with room for boats and trailers.

Pets welcome by arrangement. Wheelchair access.

Tel: 01872 501339 • e-mail:info@trenonafarmholidays.co.uk • www.trenonafarmholidays.co.uk

CLASSY COTTAGES – Spectacular cottages feet from beach. Isolated residence on coast, isolated garden cottage. Open log fires. Dog-friendly beaches. Access to indoor swimming pool, gym and tennis courts. Local pubs serving good food, and allowing dogs. Contact FIONA & MARTIN NICOLLE (07000 423000). [pw! Pets £12 per week]
e-mail: nicolle@classycottages.co.uk website: www.classycottages.co.uk

TRENCREEK FARM COUNTRY HOLIDAY PARK, HEWAS WATER, ST AUSTELL (01726 882540). Pet-friendly holidays in Cornwall. Luxury lodge, caravan and bungalow accommodation. Motorhome, tourer and tent pitches. Fishing lakes, farm animals, swimming pool and hot tubs. Call for your FREE brochure. ETC ★★★, David Bellamy Silver Award.
website: www.surfbayholidays.co.uk

TOAD HALL COTTAGES (01548 853089). Over 250 outstanding waterside and rural properties in truly beautiful locations in Devon, Cornwall and Exmoor. Call for our highly acclaimed brochure. Pets welcome.
e-mail: thc@toadhallcottages.com website: www.toadhallcottages.com

WESTSTAR HOLIDAY PARKS, CORNWALL, DORSET AND HAMPSHIRE (0870 444 0080). Award-winning holiday parks with superb all weather facilities and fantastic live entertainment. Blue Flag Beaches, coastal walks, great visitor attractions. Pet-friendly holiday homes, designated dog-walking areas. Quote WP ETC ★★★★ David Bellamy Gold Conservation Award. [pw! Pets £35 per week].
website: www.weststarholidays.co.uk/pw

A fine selection of Self-catering and similar Cottages on both coasts of Cornwall and on Scilly. Pets welcome in many cottages. Free colour brochure from: CORNISH TRADITIONAL COTTAGES, BLISLAND, BODMIN PL30 4HS (01208 821666; Fax: 01208 821766). [Pets £16 per week]
website: www.corncott.com

WEST CORNWALL COTTAGE HOLIDAYS, WEST CORNWALL (01736 368575). Coastal and country cottages, town houses and apartments. Pets with well behaved owners welcome in many of our properties. [Charge for pets.]
website: www.westcornwallcottageholidays.com

Bodmin

Quaint county town of Cornwall, standing steeply on the edge of Bodmin Moor. Pretty market town and touring centre. Plymouth 31 miles, Newquay 20, Wadebridge 7.

PENROSE BURDEN, ST BREWARD, BODMIN PL30 4LZ (01208 850277 & 850617; Fax: 01208 850915). Holiday Care Award Winning Cottages featured on TV. Open all year. Outstanding views over wooded valley. Free Salmon and Trout fishing. Daily meal service. Superb walking area. Dogs welcome, wheelchair accessible. [Pets £15 per week]
website: www.penroseburden.co.uk

Terms quoted in this publication may be subject to increase if rises in costs necessitate

COOMBE MILL, ST BREWARD, BODMIN PL30 4LZ (01208 850344). An idyllic Cornish hamlet of quiet riverside cottages set amidst a glorious 30 acre estate. Gardens, friendly farm animals, tractor rides, play areas, wildlife, fishing lakes and river fishing. Four-posters, log burners, BBQs, home cooking and groceries delivered. Well behaved dogs welcome [pw! Pets £20 per week].
e-mail: mail@coombemill.com website: www.coombemill.com

Bodmin Moor

Superb walking area attaining a height of 1375 feet at Brown Willy, the highest point in Cornwall.

DARRYNANE COTTAGES, DARRYNANE, ST BREWARD, BODMIN MOOR PL30 4LZ (Tel & Fax: 01208 850885). Absolutely fabulous detached cottages. Set in private gated gardens. Unique moorland valley setting. Waterfalls, woods, river. Woodburning stoves, four-poster beds, Eden Project and Camel Trail close by. ETC ★★★ [Pets £10 per week]
e-mail: enquiries@darrynane.co.uk website:www.darrynane.com

HENWOOD BARNS HOLIDAY COTTAGES, HENWOOD, LISKEARD PL14 5BP (01579 363576/07956 864263). Three stone barns set around original courtyard on the edge of Bodmin Moor, with stunning views. Tranquil, village location, horse riding two minutes' walk. Woodburning stoves; sleep 2/5; within easy reach of North Cornwall and Devon. [Pets £15 per week]
e-mail: henwoodbarns@tiscali.co.uk website: www.henwoodbarns.co.uk

Boscastle

Picturesque village in tiny harbour, with rocky beach, some sand, and fine scenery. Tintagel 4 miles.

ATLANTIC COAST, NEAR BOSCASTLE. Country bungalow sleeping 2-6, heating; microwave; TV. Near sandy beaches, spectacular coastal path. Beautiful scenery, walking distance local Inn and store. Just off A39 and central to most tourist attractions. Spring and Autumn £190-£250. Pets welcome. MRS PROUT (01840 250289). **[🐕]**

Bude

Popular seaside resort overlooking a wide bay of golden sand and flanked by spectacular cliffs. Ideal for surfing; sea water swimming pool for safe bathing.

LESLEY SHARRATT, SUNRISE, 6 BURN VIEW, BUDE EX23 8BY (01288 353214; Fax: 01288 359911). Beautifully refurbished Victorian house providing stylish and comfortable accommodation, moments' walk from dog friendly beach and downs. Excellent breakfast menu, including vegetarian. B&B from £27. **[🐕]**
e-mail: sunriseguest@btconnect.com website: www.sunrise-bude.co.uk

WILLOW VALLEY HOLIDAY PARK, BUSH, BUDE EX23 9LB (01288 353104). Two bedroom lodges equipped to high standard. Colour TV, bathroom, fully equipped kitchen. Two miles from beach and town. Brochure on request. [Pets £10 per week]
e-mail: willowvalley@talk21.com website: www.willowvalley.co.uk

IVYLEAF BARTON HOLIDAY COTTAGES, NEAR BUDE EX23 9LD. Six cottages sleeping 2-8 in converted stone barns, some with spectacular coastal views. Comfortable, well-equipped with all modern conveniences. Laundry. Tennis court. Certain cottages welcome pets. Contact: ROBERT B BARRETT (01288 321237 or 07771 908108; Fax: 01288 321937). [Pets £16 per week].
e-mail: info@ivyleafbarton.co.uk website: www.ivyleafbarton.co.uk

Cawsand

Village adjoining Kingsand on Cawsand Bay, which stretches from Picklecombe Pt in the north to Penlee Pt in the south.

WRINGFORD DOWN HOTEL, CAWSAND PL10 1LE (01752 822287). Family-friendly hotel with fully licensed bar. Set in four acres just outside Kingsand and Cawsand. Great facilities for all ages. Write or phone for brochure. [🐕]
website: www.cornwallholidays.co.uk

Readers are requested to mention this guidebook when making enquiries about accommodation.

JANE BEANEY, RAME BARTON, RAME, CAWSAND PL10 1LG (01752 822789). Self-contained apartments set in two acres of grounds on the beautiful Rame peninsula, enjoy stunning views and wonderful sunsets, coastal walks, birdwatching, fishing and surfing. Whitsand Bay, picturesque Cawsand, Kingsand close by. B&B and Short Breaks available. Pets welcome. [🐕]
e-mail: MelBandJaneB@aol.com website: www.ramebarton.co.uk

Crackington Haven

Small coastal village in North Cornwall set amidst fine cliff scenery. Small sandy beach, Launceston 18 miles, Bude 10, Camelford 10.

MINESHOP, CRACKINGTON HAVEN, BUDE EX23 0NR. Cornish Character Cottages, sleep 1 to 8, in tranquil location. Footpath leads through fields/woods to beach/pub. Excellent walking, breathtaking scenery. Open all year. Proud to be inspected and featured in The Good Holiday Cottage Guide. For more details phone CHARLIE or JANE (01840 230338). [£15 per pet per week.]
e-mail: info@mineshop.co.uk website: www.mineshop.co.uk

Five 18th century converted barns, beamed ceilings, log fires and secluded rural setting. Ideal touring base. Five miles to coast at Crackington Haven. Sleep 2/6. Pets welcome. Open all year. From £80 short breaks, £145 per week. ETC ★★★. APPLY: LORRAINE HARRISON, TRENANNICK COTTAGES, WARBSTOW, LAUNCESTON PL15 8RP (01566 781443). [pw! Pets £10 per stay]
e-mail: trenannick–1@tiscali.co.uk website: www.trenannickcottages.co.uk

Crantock

Village near the coast 2miles/3 km SW of Newquay across the River Gannel

CRANTOCK BAY HOTEL, WEST PENTIRE, CRANTOCK TR8 5SE (01637 830229; Fax: 01637 831111). Superbly located for a holiday with your dogs; beach 10 minutes' walk. Comfortable bedrooms, quality restaurant, indoor pool, tennis etc. AA ★★★ [Pets £5 per night]
e-mail: stay@crantockbayhotel.co.uk website: www.crantockbayhotel.co.uk

Cusgarne (near Truro)

Located four miles east of Redruth.

CUSGARNE (NEAR TRURO), JOYCE & GEORGE CLENCH, SAFFRON MEADOW, CUSGARNE, TRURO TR4 8RW (01872 863171). A cosy, single storey, clean, detached dwelling within grounds of Saffron Meadow. Own enclosed garden, secluded and surrounded by wooded pastureland, five miles west of Truro. [Pets £10 per week]

Duloe

Village 4 miles south of Liskeard.

MARTIN AND WENDY WELCH, PENQUITE COUNTRY COTTAGES, DULOE, NEAR LISKEARD PL14 4QG (01503 220260). Four spacious one-bedroom barn conversions within easy reach of coast and moors. Well behaved dogs most welcome. No children.[Pets £15 per week]
e-mail:stay@penquitecountrycottages.co.uk website: www.penquitecountrycottages.co.uk

Falmouth

Well-known port and resort on Fal estuary, ideal for boating, sailing and fishing; safe bathing from sandy beaches. Of interest is Pendennis Castle (18th century). Newquay 26, Penzance 26, Truro 11.

PENMORVAH MANOR HOTEL & COURTYARD COTTAGES, BUDOCK WATER, NEAR FALMOUTH TR11 5ED (01326 250277; Fax: 01326 250509). Situated in 6 acres of mature gardens and woodland. Ideal for visiting Cornwall's superb gardens.Close to Falmouth and Coastal Paths. Well behaved dogs welcome. AA ★★★ Hotel, ETC ★★★★ Self-catering. [Pets £7.50 per night.]
e-mail: reception@penmorvah.co.uk website: www.penmorvah.co.uk

CREEKSIDE COTTAGES offer a fine selection of individual water's edge, village and rural cottages, sleeping from 2-10. All offer peaceful, comfortable and fully equipped accommodation. Just come and relax. For a colour brochure phone 01326 375972. [Pets £20 per week]
website: www.creeksidecottages.co.uk

PETER WATSON, CREEKSIDE HOLIDAY HOUSES, RESTRONGUET, FALMOUTH TR11 5ST (01326 372722). Spacious houses sleep 2/4/6/8. Peaceful, picturesque water's edge hamlet. Boating facilities. Use of boat. Own quay, beach. Secluded gardens. Near Pandora Inn. Friday bookings. Dogs welcome. [Pets £15 per week]
website: www.creeksideholidayhouses.co.uk

SELF-CATERING BUNGALOW. Sleeps 6. Walking distance of harbour and town. Dogs welcome. Low Season. £210 to £270; High Season £300 to £425. ETC ★★★. Apply MRS J.A. SIMMONS, 215A PERRY STREET, BILLERICAY, ESSEX CM12 0NZ (01277 654425). [Pets £10 per week]

Fowey

Historic town, now a busy harbour, Regatta and Carnival Week in August.

LANCROW BARN, NEAR FOWEY (01726 814263). In own spacious garden, near coast, Fowey, Lostwithiel, Eden Project. Three double en suite bedrooms, sitting room, well equipped kitchen; decor and furnishings of very high standard. [Pets £25 per week].
e-mail: sarahfurniss@aol.com website: www.foweyvacations.com

OLD FERRY INN, BODINNICK-BY-FOWEY PL23 1LX (01726 870237; Fax: 01726 870116). Family-run Inn, ideal for many varied walks. Excellent à la carte restaurant; bar meals available. Comfortable bedrooms with colour TV and tea/coffee. Rate £60-£85 per night for two people sharing. ETC ◆◆◆◆ [Pets £3 per night per pet]
e-mail: royce972@aol.com website: www.oldferryinn.com

Gorran Haven

Coastal village 3 miles from Mevagissey

MRS S. PIKE, TREGILLAN, TREWOLLOCK LANE, GORRAN HAVEN, ST AUSTELL PL26 6NT (01726 842452). Two apartments, sleeping 2-4 persons. Sea views, large garden and private parking. 600 yards from beach, harbour and shops. Superb coastal walks. Open all year. VisitCornwall Southwest Tourism Member. VisitBritain ★★★ [Pets £4 per night, £25 per week]
e-mail: tregillanapartment@tiscali.co.uk website: www.tregillanapartments.co.uk

Helston

Ancient Stannary town and excellent touring centre, noted for the annual "Furry Dance". Nearby is Looe Pool, separated from the sea by a bar. Truro 17 miles, St Ives 15, Redruth 11, Falmouth & Penzance 12.

BOSCREGE CAMPING & CARAVAN PARK, ASHTON, HELSTON TR13 9TG. (Tel & Fax: 01736 762231) Award-winning, quiet, rural family park close to beaches and attractions. Colour brochure available. Pets welcome. ETC ★★★★, AA THREE PENNANTS. [🐕]
e-mail: enquiries@caravanparkcornwall.com website: www.caravanparkcornwall.com

Launceston

On A30 about 1 mile from Cornwall/Devon border. The "Ancient Capital" and acknowledged as "The Gateway to Cornwall".

SWALLOWS & MEADOW COTTAGE. Well equipped cottages with field to the rear. Riverside walks. TV lounge and kitchen. Centrally located for visiting NT houses and gardens, Dartmoor, Bodmin Moor, beaches and harbours. Pets welcome by arrangement. ETC ★★★. Contact: LOWER DUTSON FARM, LAUNCESTON PL15 9SP (01566 776456).
e-mail: holidays@farm-cottage.co.uk website: www.farm-cottage.co.uk

Liskeard

Pleasant market town and good centre for exploring East Cornwall. Bodmin Moor and the quaint fishing villages of Looe and Polperro are near at hand. Plymouth 19 miles, St Austell 19 miles, Launceston 16, Fowey (via ferry) 15, Bodmin 13, Looe 9.

LINDA & NEIL HOSKEN, HOPSLAND HOLIDAYS, HOPSLAND COMMONMOOR, LISKEARD, CORNWALL PL14 6EJ (Tel & Fax: 01579 344480). Hi, I'm Ki, an adorable border collie. Come and stay with your pets at my converted barn cottages. Fully equipped. Own field to exercise in or 150 yards from open moorland. ETC ★★★★ [pw!]
e-mail: hopslandholidays@aol.com website: www.hopslandholidays.co.uk

MICHELE & STEVE HORE, HAYLOFT COURTYARD COTTAGES, MENHENIOT, LISKEARD (01503 240879). Family-run cottages with many home-from-home comforts including jacuzzi bathrooms in most cottages. Excellent touring base. Restaurant on-site and meal delivery service. Children's play area. ETC ★★★★ [Pets £20 per week].
e-mail: courtyardcottage@btconnect.com website: www.hayloftcourtyardcottages.com

BUTTERDON MILL HOLIDAY HOMES, MERRYMEET, LISKEARD PL14 3LS (01579 342636) Two-bedroom detached bungalows on idyllic rural site. Sleep up to six. Games barn; children's play areas. Ideal for touring coasts & moors. Discounts for Senior Citizens/couples Sept to June. Brochure available. [ ]
e-mail: butterdonmill@btconnect.com

CUTKIVE WOOD HOLIDAY LODGES, ST IVE, LISKEARD PL14 3ND (01579 362216). Six well-equipped cedar-clad lodges on country estate with wonderful views. Great for children, dogs welcome. Ideal for coasts, beaches, moors etc. Short breaks. Open all year. [pw! Pets £10 per week]
e-mail: holidays@cutkivewood.co.uk website: www.cutkivewood.co.uk

CELIA HUTCHINSON, CARADON COUNTRY COTTAGES, EAST TAPHOUSE, NEAR LISKEARD PL14 4NH (Tel & Fax: 01579 320355). Luxury cottages in the heart of the Cornish countryside. Ideal centre for exploring Devon and Cornwall, coast and moor and Eden Project. Meadow and paddock (enclosed). Central heating and log burners for cosy off-season breaks. [pw! Pets £10 per week.]
e-mail: celia@caradoncottages.co.uk website: www.caradoncottages.co.uk

Lizard

The most southerly point in England, with fine coastal scenery and secluded coves. Sandy beach at Housel Bay. Truro 28 miles, Helston 11.

MULLION HOLIDAY PARK, WESTSTAR HOLIDAYS (0870 444 0080). Award-winning holiday park near Helston in an Area of Outstanding Natural Beauty, close to safe sandy beaches. Dogs welcome! Quote WP. ETC ★★★★ [pw! Pets £35 per week]
website: www.weststarholidays.co.uk/pw

GALLEN-TREATH GUEST HOUSE, PORTHALLOW TR12 6PL (Tel & Fax: 01326 280400). Spectacular coastal views, comfortable en suite rooms, hearty meals and a warm welcome await. Close to coastal path, diving, gardens and more. AA ◆◆◆ [pw! Pets £1 per night]
e-mail: gallentreath@btclick.com

Longrock

Hamlet to the east of Penzance. Submerged forest to the east.

MRS DOREEN CAPPER, MOUNT VIEW HOTEL, LONGROCK, PENZANCE TR20 8JJ (01736 710416) A family-run pub with comfortable accommodation, situated 100 yards from Mount's Bay in Longrock village. Three en suite rooms and two with shared bathroom. Breakfast in dining room, lunch and dinner available. Dogs welcome by arrangement. Prices from £20 pppn. [ ]

Readers are requested to mention this FHG publication when seeking accommodation

Looe

Twin towns linked by a bridge over the River Looe. Capital of the shark fishing industry; nearby Monkey Sanctuary is well worth a visit.

FOX VALLEY COTTAGES, LANLAWREN, TRENEWAN, LOOE PL13 2PZ (01726 870115). Set in beautiful countryside, just three miles from Polperro. Indoor heated pool and spa. Open all year round. Field for dogs to run around. Contact ANDY & LINDA for details. [pw! Pets £15 per week]
e-mail: lanlawrenfarm@lycos.com website: www.foxvalleycottages.co.uk

TALLAND CARAVAN PARK, TALLAND BAY, LOOE PL13 2JA (01503 272715). Fully equipped two and three bedroom caravans. Direct access to coastal path and beach. Shop, clubroom, laundry, play area and swimming pool. Short Breaks off-season. Pets welcome. [Pets £1.50 per night camping, £30 per week static caravan, pw!]
www.tallandFuk

LOOE BAY HOLIDAY PARK, WESTSTAR HOLIDAYS (0870 444 0080). Award-winning holiday park near Looe in an Area of Outstanding Natural Beauty, close to safe sandy beaches. Dogs welcome! Quote WP ETC ★★★★ David Bellamy Conservation Award. [pw! Pets £35 per week].
website: www.weststarholidays.co.uk/pw

MRS KEILTHY, CARDWEN FARM, PELYNT, LOOE PL13 2LU (01503 220213). Bed and Breakfast in 17th century Grade II Listed farmhouse. Looe and Polperro four miles, Eden Project under 10 miles. Coastal Path nearby. Self-catering also available. [🐕]
e-mail: cardwenfarm@freenet.co.uk website: www.cardwenfarm.com

TRENANT PARK COTTAGES (01503 263639). Secluded traditional cottages in grounds of country estate. Private gardens and grounds. Optional home-cooked food delivery. Open all year, winter short breaks. Well behaved dogs welcome. [Pets £15 per week].
e-mail: Liz@holiday-cottage.com website: www.trenantcottages.com

VALLEYBROOK, PEAKSWATER, LANSALLOS, LOOE PL13 2QE. Peaceful nine acre site with six superb lodges and two delightful cottages, all dog friendly. Individual fenced gardens, dog walks, dog friendly beaches nearby. Short breaks. Open all year. 2 dogs max. ETC ★★/★★★/★★★★. Contact DENISE, KEITH or BRIAN HOLDER (01503 220493).
website: www.valleybrookholidays.co.uk

COLDRINNICK COTTAGES, DULOE, NEAR LOOE. Attractively converted barns set in large secluded gardens. Excellent locality for walking and relaxing. Sleeps 2/6 people. Ideal place for families and dogs alike. ETC ★★★★. For a brochure contact BILL AND KAYE CHAPMAN, COLDRINNICK FARM, DULOE, LISKEARD PL14 4QF (01503 220251). [Pets £15 per week, pw!]
website: www.cornishcottage.net

WRINGWORTHY COTTAGES, LOOE (01503 240685). 8 traditional stone cottages set in 4 peaceful acres offer you and your pet space for the perfect break. A friendly welcome awaits in our fully equipped, centrally heated cottages, sleeping 2-8. Linen included, walks from our door and more! ETC ★★★★, Green Acorn Award. [First pet free, additional pets £18 per week]
e-mail: pets@wringworthy.co.uk website: www.wringworthy.co.uk

NEIL AND THERESA DENNETT, TALEHAY HOLIDAY COTTAGES, PELYNT, NEAR LOOE PL13 2LT (Tel & Fax: 01503 220252). Cosy, traditional cottages set in four acres of unspoilt countryside offering peace and tranquillity. Breathtaking coastal and country walks. An ideal location for dogs and their owners. Non-smoking. Close to the Eden Project. C.T.B. approved. ETC ★★★★ [Pets £3 per night, £15 per week]
e-mail: infobookings@talehay.co.uk website: www.talehay.co.uk

TREMAINE GREEN COUNTRY COTTAGES, PELYNT, NEAR LOOE PL13 2LT (01503 220333). A beautiful hamlet of 11 award-winning traditional cosy craftsmen's cottages. Clean, comfortable and well equipped. Set in award-winning grounds with country/coastal walks and The Eden Project nearby. [pw! Pets £18 per week]
e-mail: stay@tremainegreen.co.uk website: www.tremainegreen.co.uk

NEAR LOOE. In picturesque Cornish fishing village of Polperro, one of the finest on the South Cornish coast, spectacularly situated holiday cottages sleeping from two to eight persons at a charge of £175 to £575 per cottage per week. With terraced gardens and fabulous outlook over harbour encompassing 15 mile sea views. Excellent selection of quality restaurants and olde worlde pubs nearby, and on offer delicious pasties and locally made ice-cream. Private parking, two minutes shops, beach, quay and National Trust cliff walks. Open all year, children and pets most welcome. All cottages are fully furnished and equipped, to include a colour television, microwave, electric oven, refrigerator, duvets and pillows. GRAHAM WRIGHT, GUARDIAN HOUSE, LISKEARD, CORNWALL PL14 6AD (01579 344080). [🐕]

Idyllic 18th century country cottages for romantics and animal lovers. Looe three miles. Wonderful walks from your gate. Cottages warm and cosy in winter. Personal attention and colour brochure from: B. WRIGHT, TREWORGEY COTTAGES, DULOE, LISKEARD PL14 4PP (01503 262730). VisitBritain ★★★★★ Quality Assurance Scheme. [Pets £20.50 per week.]
website: www.cornishdreamcottages.co.uk

BADHAM FARM, ST KEYNE, LISKEARD PL14 4RW (01579 343572). Farmhouse and farm buildings converted to a high standard. Sleep 2-10. All well furnished/equipped; prices include electricity, bed linen and towels. Well behaved dogs welcome (not in high season). Prices from £120 per week. ETC ★★★★ [Pets £4 per night, £20 per week].
e-mail: badhamfarm@yahoo.co.uk website: www.badhamfarm.co.uk

MRS BARBIE HIGGINS, TREWITH HOLIDAY COTTAGES, TREWITH, DULOE PL14 4PR (01503 262184; mobile: 07968 262184). Four refurbished cottages in peaceful location with panoramic views near Looe. Fully equipped, 1-3 bedrooms, tastefully furnished. Full central heating. Well behaved dogs welcome. [Pets from £14 per week]
e-mail: holiday-cottages@trewith.freeserve.co.uk website: www.trewith.freeserve.co.uk

O. SLAUGHTER, TREFANNY HILL, DULOE, NEAR LISKEARD PL14 4QF (01503 220622). Nestling on a south-facing hillside, near coast. Delicious food. Heated pool, tennis, badminton, lake, shire horses. Enchanting 70 acre estate with bluebell wood, walking and wildlife.
e-mail: enq@trefanny.co.uk website: www.trefanny.co.uk

Manaccan

Village 7 miles east of Helston.

Enchanting creekside cottages in a timeless and tranquil hamlet. Stunning coastal and riverside walks, country inns, local food, warm and comfortable with cosy log fires. Boat hire, moorings. Short breaks. Open all year. ST ANTHONY HOLIDAYS, MANACCAN, HELSTON TR12 6JW (01326 231 357). [Pets £3 per night, £21 per week].
e-mail: info@stanthony.co.uk website: www.StAnthony.co.uk

Marazion

Quaint little village, possibly the oldest town in Britain. Good beach and splendid fishing, sailing waters.

THE GODOLPHIN ARMS, WEST END, MARAZION TR17 0EN (01736 710202) Perched on the edge of the sand, facing St Michael's Mount. Ten individually designed en suite bedrooms, most with breathtaking sea views. Relaxing, bar and restaurant. Perfect for exploring coast and coves. AA★★
e-mail: enquiries@godolphinarms.co.uk website: www.godolphinarms.co.uk

Mawgan Porth

Modern village on small sandy bay. Good surfing. Inland stretches the beautiful Vale of Lanherne. Rock formation of Bedruthan Steps is nearby. Newquay 6 miles west.

BLUE BAY HOTEL, TRENANCE, MAWGAN PORTH TR8 4DA (01637 860324). Small licensed Hotel. Close to beach and coastal path. Two good golf courses nearby. Good English cooking. Rooms with tea making facilities, colour TV, most ground floor/en suite. [pw! Pets £1 per night]
e-mail: hotel@bluebaycornwall.co.uk website: www.bluebaycornwall.co.uk

Mevagissey

Central for touring and walking. Eden project nearby.

KILBOL COUNTRY HOUSE HOTEL & COTTAGES, POLMASSICK, MEVAGISSEY PL26 6HA (01726 842481). 'Perfect Peace in Hidden Cornwall'. Small country hotel set in 5-acre grounds, two miles from the coast. Eight rooms, and two self-catering cottages. Outdoor swimming pool, riverside walk. No children under 12 years in hotel. [pw! Pets £10 per week].
e-mail: Hotel@kilbol-hotel.co.uk website: www.kilbol-hotel.co.uk

MRS M.R. BULLED, MENAGWINS, GORRAN, MEVAGISSEY PL26 6HP (01726 843517). Traditional cottage, sleeps two to five. Linen, towels, electricity supplied. Beach one mile. Large garden. Central for touring/walking. Near Eden Project and Heligan Gardens. Pets welcome. [🐕]

Mousehole

Picturesque fishing village with sand and shingle beach. Penzance 3 miles.

POLVELLAN HOLIDAY FLAT. In Mousehole, a quaint and unspoilt fishing village, a fully equipped self-catering flat with full sea views. Sleeps two. Microwave, cooker, fridge, TV, all bedding and towels provided. Open all year. Apply: MR A.G. WRIGHT, 164 PORTLAND ROAD, SELSTON, NOTTINGHAM NG16 6AN (01773 775347) [🐕]
e-mail: alang23@hotmail.com

Newquay

Popular family holiday resort surrounded by miles of golden beaches. Semi-tropical gardens, zoo and museum. Ideal for exploring all of Cornwall.

RETORRICK MILL, ST MAWGAN, NEWQUAY TR8 4BH (01637 860460). Set in 11 acres, self-catering Retorrick Mill has two cottages and six chalets, all very well equipped. Pets including horses very welcome. For a brochure or further assistance contact Chris Williams.
website: www.retorrickmill.co.uk

MRS DEWOLFREYS, DEWOLF GUEST HOUSE, 100 HENVER ROAD, NEWQUAY TR7 3BL (01637 874746). Single, double or family rooms, two chalets in rear garden. All rooms non-smoking with en suite facilities, colour TV and tea/coffee making facilities. Ideal for pets. AA ★★★★[🐕]
e-mail: holidays@dewolfguesthouse.com website: www.dewolfguesthouse.com

QUARRYFIELD CARAVAN & CAMPING PARK, CRANTOCK, NEWQUAY. Fully equipped modern caravans overlooking beautiful Crantock Bay. Separate camping field. Bar, pool, children's play area. Contact: MRS WINN, TRETHERRAS, NEWQUAY TR7 2RE (Tel & Fax: 01637 872792). [Pets £1.50 per night (camping only); £10 per week camping, £20 per week in caravan]

TRETHIGGEY TOURING PARK, QUINTRELL DOWNS, NEWQUAY TR8 4QR (01637 877672). Friendly, family-run park minutes from surfing beaches. Touring caravans, tent and campervans welcome. Luxury holiday homes for hire. Shop, off-licence, free showers, electric hook-ups, laundry, children's play area, TV/games room, fishing and take-away food in summer. ETC ★★★★
e-mail: enquiries@trethiggey.co.uk website: www.Trethiggey.co.uk

Padstow

Bright little resort with pretty harbour on Camel estuary. Extensive sands. Nearby is Elizabethan Prideaux Place. Newquay 15 miles, Wadebridge 8.

RAINTREE HOUSE HOLIDAYS, WHISTLERS, TREYARNON BAY, PADSTOW PL28 8JR (01841 520228). We have a varied selection of accommodation. Small or large, houses and apartments, some by the sea. All in easy reach of our lovely beaches. Please write or phone for brochure. [🐕]
e-mail: gill@raintreehouse.co.uk website: www.raintreehouse.co.uk

FREE or REDUCED RATE entry to Holiday Visits and Attractions
– see our READERS' OFFER VOUCHERS on pages 407-423

Tintagel

Attractively situated amidst fine cliff scenery; small rocky beach. Famous for associations with King Arthur, whose ruined castle on Tintagel Head is of interest. Bude 19 miles, Camelford 6.

SANDY AND DAVE WILSON, SALUTATIONS, ATLANTIC ROAD, TINTAGEL PL34 0DE (01840 770287). Comfortable, well-equipped, centrally heated cottages sleeping two. Ideal for touring, walking and relaxing. Close to Coastal Path and village amenities. Private parking. Ring for brochure. Pets Free. []
e-mail: sandyanddave@tinyworld.co.uk website: www.salutationstintagel.co.uk

Truro

Bustling Cathedral City with something for everyone. Museum and Art Gallery with interesting shop and cafe is well worth a visit.

TRELOAN COASTAL FARM HOLIDAYS, TRELOAN LANE, PORTSCATHO TR2 5EG (01872 580899/ 580989). Traditional working farm on coastal footpath. Open all year. Sea views. Experience farm practices. Close to shops, pubs, etc. [Pets £1 each per night, £12 each per week in mobile homes].
e-mail: enquiries@coastalfarmholidays.co.uk website: www.coastalfarmholidays.co.uk

KING HARRY FERRY COTTAGES, FEOCK, TRURO TR3 6QJ (01326 319417). Two comfortable well equipped cottages in own charming gardens. Pets welcome. Beautiful woodland walks. Perfect for fishing and bird watching. []
e-mail: jean@kingharry.net website: www.kingharry-info.co.uk

MRS PAMELA CARBIS, TRENONA FARM, RUAN HIGH LANES, TRURO TR2 5JS (01872 501339). Enjoy a relaxing stay on the unspoilt Roseland Peninsula between Truro and St Austell. Self-catering in two renovated barns, B&B in Victorian farmhouse. Children and pets welcome. Brochure available. [Pets £5 per stay,]
e-mail: info@trenonafarmholidays.co.uk website: www.trenonafarmholidays.co.uk

THE VALLEY (01872 862194). A secluded hamlet of contemporary cottages in a tranquil country valley. Beautiful gardens and woodland walks, ideal for dogs. Relax in luxury, with leisure facilities, and experience exquisite cuisine in the stylish Cafe Azur. ETC ★★★★★
website: www.the-valley.co.uk

Wadebridge

Town on River Camel, 6 miles north-west of Bodmin

Three barn converted luxury cottage-style self catering homes near Wadebridge. Found along a leafy drive, with wonderful views, beside the lazy twisting Camel River with its "Trail" for walking and cycling. CORNWALL TOURISM AWARDS 2002 - Self Catering Establishment of the Year - "Highly Commended". Sleep 2-7 plus cot. Two dogs per cottage welcome. GARY NEWMAN, COLESENT COTTAGES, ST TUDY, WADEBRIDGE, CORNWALL PL30 4QX (Tel & Fax: 01208 850112). [pw!]
e-mail: enquires@colesent.co.uk website: www.colesent.co.uk

ISLES OF SCILLY

St Mary's

Largest of group of granite islands and islets off Cornish Coast. Terminus for air and sea services from mainland. Main income from flower-growing. Seabirds, dolphins and seals abound.

MRS PAMELA MUMFORD, SALLAKEE FARM, ST MARY'S TR21 0NZ (01720 422391). Self-catering farm cottage, available all year round. Sleeps 5. Woodburner. Near beach and coastal paths. Pets welcome. Write or phone for details. ETC ★★★

FREE or REDUCED RATE entry to Holiday Visits and Attractions – see our READERS' OFFER VOUCHERS on pages 407-423

Holiday Homes Allonby

If it's peace and quiet you yearn for, you'll find few better places than the Cumbrian coastal village of Allonby which offers easy access to the Lake District as well as Carlisle. Three holiday homes available for let - **Solway Villa** (sleeps 10), **Iona Cottage** (sleeps 4) and **West View** (sleeps 5). All are situated in the centre of the village, within easy walking distance of all amenities and, best of all, just a stone's throw away from the beach.

For more details, or to book, contact Mrs D. Hetherington, East House, Allonby CA15 6QF
Tel : (01900) 881264 or (01900) 881549

015394 32330
www.smallwoodhotel.co.uk

smallwood house hotel

Compston Road, Ambleside, Cumbria. LA22 9DJ

..where quality and the customer come first

En-suite rooms • Car parking • Leisure Club Membership

IVY HOUSE HOTEL & RESTAURANT

Hawkshead, Near Ambleside, Cumbria LA22 0HS
Telephone: 015394 36204 • Website: www.ivyhousehotel.com

Family-run Listed Georgian hotel, full of great charm and character, 11 en suite bedrooms with colour television and equipped with hot drink trays.

Contact Rob or Julia Treeby for Brochure.

RAC Dining Award

'Rest awhile in style'

Quality B&B. Tranquil settings in the heart of the village. Own grounds. Car park. All en suite. Kettle, clock/radio, TV, fridge, CD and video players. Heated indoor pool, sauna, hot tub, sun lounge and rooftop terrace. Special breaks. Friendly service where pets are welcome. **www.oldvicarageambleside.co.uk**

Contact Ian, Helen or Liana
The Old Vicarage
Vicarage Road
Ambleside LA22 9DH
Tel: 015394 33364

AMBLESIDE •••• 2 LOWFIELD, OLD LAKE ROAD

Ground floor garden flat half a mile from town centre; sleeps 4. Lounge/diningroom, kitchen, bathroom/WC, two bedrooms, one with en suite shower. Linen supplied. Children and pets welcome. Parking for one car. Bookings Saturday to Saturday. Terms from £140 to £240 per week.

Contact: MR P. F. QUARMBY, 3 LOWFIELD, OLD LAKE ROAD, AMBLESIDE LA22 0DH
Tel & Fax: 015394 32326 •••••• e-mail: paulfquarmby@aol.com

Kirkstone Foot

*****AMBLESIDE****

Superior Cottage & Apartment Complex, set in peaceful gardens adjoining the Lakeland Fells & Village centre. Luxury Bathrooms & Fully Fitted Kitchens

ETC FOUR & FIVE STAR RATING
AMONGST THE BEST IN BRITAIN
PETS WELCOME IN MANY UNITS

Brochures & Reservations Tel: 015394 32232
Kirkstone Pass Road, Ambleside, Cumbria LA22 9EH
e-mail: enquiries@kirkstonefoot.co.uk
website: www.kirkstonefoot.co.uk

Greenhowe Caravan Park

Great Langdale, English Lakeland.

Welcome Host

English Tourism Council ★★★★ Caravan Park

BH&HPA David Bellamy Conservation Award Silver

An English Tourism Council Rose award park

Greenhowe is a permanent Caravan Park with Self Contained Holiday Accommodation. Subject to availability Holiday Homes may be rented for short or long periods from 1st March until mid-November. The Park is situated in the heart of the Lake District some half a mile from Dungeon Ghyll at the foot of the Langdale Pikes. It is an ideal centre for Climbing, Fell Walking, Riding, Swimming, or just a lazy holiday.

Please ask about Short Breaks.

Greenhowe Caravan Park
Great Langdale, Ambleside
Cumbria LA22 9JU

For free colour brochure

Telephone: (015394) 37231
Fax: (015394) 37464
Freephone: 0800 0717231
www.greenhowe.com

Betty Fold, Hawkshead Hill, Ambleside LA22 0PS
e-mail: csalisbury@bettyfold.fsnet.co.uk • website: www.bettyfold.co.uk
Situated near Hawkshead and Tarn Hows, large country house in spacious grounds in the heart of Lake District National Park. Betty Fold offers self-catering accommodation in ground floor apartment with private entrance, sleeps 4. One double en suite and one small twin with bathroom and colour TV. Open-plan kitchen/livingroom with electric cooker, fridge, microwave. Terms inclusive of heat, light, power, bed linen and towels.

Lyndale GUEST HOUSE Lake Road, Ambleside LA22 0DN
015394 34244 • www.lyndale-guesthouse.co.uk
Nestled midway between Lake Windermere and Ambleside village, with superb views of Loughrigg Fell and the Langdales beyond. Excellent base for walking, touring, or just relaxing.

Scalebeck Holiday Cottages **Scalebeck, Great Asby, Appleby CA16 6TF • 01768 351006**
e-mail: mail@scalebeckholidaycottages.com **ETC ★★★★**

Comfortable and well-equipped self-catering accommodation in the tranquil Eden Valley, central for the Lakes, Yorkshire Dales, Northumberland and Scottish Borders.
Sleep 2/5 • Ground floor bedrooms • Public telephone • Games room.
Table tennis/pool table • No smoking • Pets welcome • BBQ/Patio area

Brook House Cottage Holidays - Delightful cottages in attractive hamlet near Keswick (sleep 2-10). Excellent food at village pub. Ideally for Skiddaw, Bassenthwaite Lake, Keswick and Cockermouth. See virtual tour website.
Bassenthwaite Hall Farm - excellent value for money farmhouse B&B . Good Cumbrian breakfast with healthy options.
Near Keswick, Cumbria CA12 4QP • Tel & Fax: 017687 76393
www.holidaycottageslakedistrict.co.uk • www.bedandbreakfast-lakedistrict.co.uk • e-mail: stay@amtrafford.co.uk

Skiddaw View Holiday Park
Quality self-catering accommodation in the Northern Lakes.
Cottage, Caravan or Timber Lodge.
Handy for Keswick, Cockermouth etc. 4-acre pet walking field.
Call us on 016973 20919 or log on to www.skiddawview.co.uk
Bookings taken 9am-9pm seven days a week

English Tourism Council ★★★★ HOLIDAY PARK

English Tourism Council ★★ HOTEL

MARY MOUNT HOTEL Set in 4½ acres of gardens and woodlands on the shores of Derwentwater. 2½ miles from Keswick in picturesque Borrowdale. Superb walking and touring. All rooms en suite with colour TV and tea/coffee making facilities. Licensed. *Brochure on request.* **BORROWDALE, NEAR KESWICK CA12 5UU**
017687 77223 • e-mail: mawdsley1@aol.com • www.marymounthotel.co.uk

FHG
K·U·P·E·R·A·R·D

Visit the FHG website
www.holidayguides.com
for details of the wide choice of accommodation featured in the full range of FHG titles

Farlam Hall Hotel Brampton, Cumbria CA8 2NG
Tel: 016977 46234 • Fax: 016977 46683

Standing in four acres of gardens, with its own lake, Farlam Hall has that indefinable quality that makes a stay here something really special. Fine quality cuisine, individually decorated and well-equipped guest rooms. Ideal touring centre for the Lakes, Borders & Hadrian's Wall.

e-mail: farlam@relaischateaux.com • www.farlamhall.co.uk

Two well-equipped cottages and two caravans in excellent walking area. Wildlife/birdwatchers paradise. Private fishing lake. Ancient woodlands, quiet, relaxing, warm welcome. Established 1968. ETC ★★★

J. JACKSON, THORNTHWAITE FARM, WOODLAND HALL, WOODLAND, BROUGHTON-IN-FURNESS LA20 6DF
Tel & Fax: 01229 716340 • e-mail: info@lakedistrictcottages.co.uk

Woodend Bothy • between the Eskdale and Duddon Valleys

Woodend is remote and surrounded by hills and moorland with views towards Scafell Pike. The bothy is a self-contained building offering cosy accommodation for two. Steps lead to the combined lounge / dining / kitchen area and stairs lead down to the bedroom which has stone walls and exposed beams and an en suite bathroom.

Short breaks available out of season. Visit our website at www.woodendhouse.co.uk or phone 019467 23277

NEW HOUSE FARM

BUTTERMERE/LORTON VALLEY, COCKERMOUTH, CUMBRIA CA13 9UU
web: www.newhouse-farm.co.uk • e-mail: hazel@newhouse-farm.co.uk

Tel: 01900 85404
Fax: 01900 85478
(See Map 5 Ref C3)

SITUATED IN THE QUIETEST AND MOST BEAUTIFUL PART OF THE LAKES, NEW HOUSE FARM HAS 15 ACRES OF OPEN FIELDS, PONDS, STREAMS AND WOODS WHICH GUESTS AND DOGS MAY WANDER AROUND AT LEISURE AND THERE IS EASY ACCESS TO NEARBY LAKES AND FELLS. THERE ARE FIVE LUXURIOUS EN SUITE BEDROOMS, ALL WITH SPECTACULAR VIEWS, AN ELEGANT DINING ROOM AND THREE SITTING ROOMS, ALL WITH OPEN FIRES. GOOD FOOD. WELCOMING HOSTS.

BED & BREAKFAST FROM £71, DINNER, BED & BREAKFAST FROM £92.

Good Hotel Guide | Which? Hotel Guide | **AA ★★★★★**

"THE LORTON VALE — A PLACE FOR ALL SEASONS"

NEW PALLYARDS, HETHERSGILL, CARLISLE CA6 6HZ • 01228 577308

One modern bungalow, 3/4 bedrooms, sleeps 8. Two lovely cottages on farm. Bed and Breakfast, Half Board. En suite double/family, twin/single rooms. Disabled welcome. Won the National Award for the Best Breakfast in Britain and have been filmed for BBC TV. **ETC ◆◆◆◆ / ETC ★★★★**

B&B from £25.00, Dinner £14.00 • DB&B weekly rate £170.00 - £180.00.
Self Catering £150.00 - £672.00
e-mail: newpallyards@btinternet.com • www.4starsc.co.uk

GRAHAM ARMS HOTEL

Longtown, Near Carlisle, Cumbria CA6 5SE

A warm welcome awaits at this 180-year-old former Coaching Inn. Situated six miles from the M6 (J44) and Gretna Green, The Graham Arms makes an ideal overnight stop or perfect touring base for the Scottish Borders, English Lakes, Hadrian's Wall and much more. 16 comfortable en suite bedrooms, including four-poster and family rooms with TV, radio etc. Meals and snacks served throughout the day. Friendly 'local's bar' and new 'Sports bar' serving real ale, extra cold lagers, cocktails and a fine selection of malt whiskies. Secure courtyard parking for cars, cycles and motorcycles. Beautiful woodland and riverside walks. Pets welcome with well behaved owners!

Visit our website on www.grahamarms.com • Tel: 01228 791213 • Fax: 01228 794110

Email: office@grahamarms.com • Website: www.grahamarms.com

Bed and full traditional breakfast £32– £36. Special rates for weekend and midweek breaks. AA ★★

Seven cottages sleeping 2-6. Set behind a large Georgian house set in parkland on the side of Hamps Fell. Beautiful garden, great walks.
Pets and children welcome. Open all year. Please telephone for details.

Contact: MR M. AINSCOUGH, LONGLANDS AT CARTMEL, CARTMEL LA11 6HG • 015395 36475 • Fax: 015395 36172
e-mail: longlands@cartmel.com • www.cartmel.com

The Derwent Lodge

Embleton, Near Bassenthwaite, Cockermouth CA13 9YA • Tel: 017687 76606

A warm welcome awaits you and your pet at the Derwent Lodge. Choose from luxury self-catering apartments or our en suite hotel rooms or suites. Light snacks and meals served daily in our cosy lounge bar or licensed restaurant. Ideally located for touring the Western Lake District and coast. Private car park and adjoining field for exercising dogs!

For a full colour brochure or further information please call **017687 76606**

NEW for August 2007 INDOOR POOL AND FITNESS SUITE
www.derwentlodge.co.uk • email: derwent_lodge@yahoo.co.uk

016973 22420

THE MANOR HOUSE, OUGHTERSIDE, ASPATRIA, CUMBRIA CA7 2PT

e-mail: richardandjudy@themanorhouse.net • www.themanorhouse.net

Our lovely manor farmhouse dates from the 18th century, retaining many original features and several acres of land. Spacious en suite rooms, tea/coffee making facilities, TV and lots of little extras. Peaceful surroundings, easy access to the Western Lakes and Solway Coast. All pets and children welcome. Bed & Breakfast from £25. Evening meals by arrangement.
Inspection Commended.

Rose Cottage

Lorton Road, Cockermouth CA13 9DX

Family-run guest house on the outskirts of Cockermouth. Warm, friendly atmosphere. Ample off-road parking. All rooms en suite with colour TV, tea/coffee, central heating and all have double glazing.

Pets most welcome in the house (excluding dining room), and there are short walks nearby. Ideal base for visiting both Lakes and coast.

Tel & Fax: 01900 822189 website: www.rosecottageguest.co.uk

Waterhead Hotel Coniston LA21 8AJ

Situated alongside Coniston Water, with lawns running down to the shore, The Waterhead Hotel makes a perfect retreat. •22 en suite bedrooms • Mountain View Restaurant • Sunday Carvery • Lounge bar with Lake views • Open to Non-residents • Non-Smoking • Ideal base for outdoor activities, also lake cruises and historic houses (Beatrix Potter, John Ruskin).

Tel: 015394 41244 • Fax: 015394 41193 • www.classic-hotels.net

BROCKLEBANK GROUND HOLIDAY COTTAGES

TORVER, CONISTON LA21 8BS

Three luxury cottages in a quiet rural setting, sleeping 2,4 & 7. Excellent walking from the door. Dog friendly pubs 600 yards. Short breaks available. Prices from £275. ETC ★★★★

info@brocklebankground.com • www.brocklebankground.com

The Coppermines & Coniston Lakes Cottages

★★★ to ★★★★

70 unique Lakeland cottages for 2-30 of quality and character in stunning mountain scenery. Log fires, exposed beams. Weekends and Short Breaks.

Book online: www.coppermines.co.uk

015394 41765 **Pets very welcome!**

Fisherground Farm, Eskdale, Cumbria

Fisherground is a lovely traditional hill farm, with a stone cottage and three pine lodges, sharing an acre of orchard. Ideal for walkers, nature lovers, dogs and children, we offer space, freedom, peace and tranquillity. We have a games room, a raft pool and an adventure playground. Good pubs nearby serve excellent bar meals.

Ian & Jennifer Hall, Orchard House, Applethwaite, Keswick, Cumbria CA12 4PN

01768 73175 • e-mail: holidays@fisherground.co.uk • www.fisherground.co.uk

Publisher's note

While every effort is made to ensure accuracy, we regret that FHG Guides cannot accept responsibility for errors, misrepresentations or omissions in our entries or any consequences thereof. Prices in particular should be checked.

We will follow up complaints but cannot act as arbiters or agents for either party.

THE BOOT INN

Boot, Eskdale, Cumbria CA19 1TG • Tel: 019467 23224
e-mail: enquiries@bootinn.co.uk • www.bootinn.co.uk

Situated in this stunning valley close to amazing walks, including Scafell, Harter and Gable. Both you and your well-behaved dog can stay in one of our nine en suite bedrooms. We offer excellent home-produced food served in the bar, restaurant or conservatory, where you can enjoy one of our fine real ales and plan your next day's assault. Dogs are most welcome to be in the bar with you for lunch and dinner. *Special Breaks available all year. Call for a brochure.* ***(formerly The Burnmoor Inn)***

BIRKHOW COTTAGE, ESKDALE

Situated in the village of Eskdale, with stunning views of the Lake District fells, Birkhow Cottage is in beautiful order throughout, offering peaceful accommodation for up to six people. With its coal fire and comfortable surroundings, Birkhow is the perfect place to return to after a day walking in the hills.

CONTACT SALLY: 017687 76836, sally@hollinhead.co.uk

Hampsfell House Hotel In two acres of private grounds, just a few minutes' walk from the town centre. The nine en suite bedrooms are well appointed and include one ground floor bedroom. Relax in the traditionally decorated lounges and then enjoy the best of fresh Cumbrian produce in the elegant dining room, where fine wines complement the table d'hôte menus. Grange-over-Sands makes an ideal base for exploring the Lake District. From £35 per night. *AA ★★*

Hampsfell Road, Grange-over-Sands LA11 6BG • Tel: 015395 32567
www.hampsfellhouse.co.uk • enquiries@hampsfellhouse.co.uk

THE GRASMERE HOTEL

BROADGATE, GRASMERE LA22 9TA

A delightful 13 bedroomed Victorian Country House Hotel, quietly situated in the village, with ample parking and a licensed lounge. All bedrooms recently refurbished, and all are en suite. Single rooms available. Beautiful award-winning restaurant overlooking large secluded gardens, river and surrounding hills. Superb four-course dinners and carefully chosen wine list. Non Smoking throughout.

Special breaks throughout the year.

Tel & Fax: 015394 35277
website: www.grasmerehotel.co.uk
e-mail: enquiries@grasmerehotel.co.uk

LAKE VIEW COUNTRY HOUSE & SELF-CATERING APARTMENTS

GRASMERE LA22 9TD • 015394 35384/35167

Luxury B&B or 3 Star Self-Catering accommodation in unrivalled location near to village yet secluded with wonderful views and lakeshore access. All B&B rooms en suite, some with whirlpool baths. Ground floor accommodation available. No smoking. Featured in "Which?" Good B&B Guide.

Midweek Breaks available in B&B • Winter Short Breaks available in S/C accommodation.

Lakeland Hideaways Cottages

Cottages in and around Hawkshead – Great walks and lakes for swimming, dog friendly pubs, open fires to lie in front of... owners will enjoy it too!

Tel: 015394 42435 • www.lakeland-hideaways.co.uk

Hideaways, The Square, Hawkshead LA22 0NZ

THE KINGS ARMS HOTEL

Hawkshead, Ambleside, Cumbria LA22 0NZ
015394 36372 • www.kingsarmshawkshead.co.uk

Join us for a relaxing stay amidst the green hills and dales of Lakeland, and we will be delighted to offer you good food, homely comfort and warm hospitality in historic surroundings. We hope to see you soon!

- SELF-CATERING COTTAGES ALSO AVAILABLE -

Sawrey House

Quality Country House Hotel; stunning lake views in peaceful surroundings; superb location for walking, fishing, water sports, riding and touring. Open Christmas and New Year.

AA ◆◆◆◆◆

❧ Beautiful En Suite Rooms ❧ Excellent Cuisine ❧ Elegant Lounge and Bar ❧ Midweek Special Breaks ❧ AA Red Rosette ❧ Log Fire ❧ Non-smoking Hotel ❧ Pets most welcome ❧ **website: www.sawreyhouse.com**

Sawrey House Country Hotel & Restaurant, Near Sawrey, Hawkshead, Cumbria LA22 0LF
Telephone: 015394 36387 Facsimile: 015394 36010

Mirefoot Cottages • Self-catering in the Lake District

5 Star, pet friendly, self-catering cottages in a superb rural location in the Lake District National Park. Both cottages sleep 2. Fully equipped with TV (Freeview), DVD, WiFi, gas central heating. Tennis court, private parking.

Mirefoot Cottages, Mirefoot, Kendal, Cumbria LA8 9AB
Tel: 01539 720015 • E-mail: booking@mirefoot.co.uk • www.mirefoot.co.uk

RUSSELL FARM Burton-in-Kendal, Carnforth, Lancs LA6 1NN

Tel: 01524 781334 • email: miktaylor@farming.co.uk

Bed, Breakfast and Evening Meal offered • Ideal centre for touring Lakes and Yorkshire Dales, or as a stopover for Scotland or the South • Good food, friendly atmosphere on working dairy farm • Modernised farmhouse • Guests' own lounge • **Contact Anne Taylor for details.**

Stonecross Manor Hotel **Milnthorpe Road, Kendal, Cumbria LA9 5HP**

Established in 1857 as an orphanage, Stonecross Manor Hotel offers easy access to town, ample car parking, local cuisine, conference and banquet facilities, indoor swimming pool and fourposter bedrooms.

Tel: 01539 733559 Fax: 01539 736386 Email:info@stonecrossmanor.co.uk www.stonecrossmanor.co.uk

Ian & Jennifer Hall, Orchard House, Applethwaite, Keswick, Cumbria CA12 4PN • 017687 73175

Orchard House Holidays
Applethwaite, Keswick

Two lovely detached houses with stunning views, sleeping 8-12. Each has two reception rooms, fully equipped kitchen, 2/3 bathrooms and a large private garden. Keswick and Lake Derwentwater are just two miles away, with every land and water activity available, yet Applethwaite is a sleepy little hamlet. Pets welcome and free; lots of walks from the doorstep.

e-mail: holidays@fisherground.co.uk
www.orchardhouseholidays.com

CRAGSIDE A quiet, comfortable guest house with beautiful views of the surrounding fells yet close to the centre of Keswick. All rooms are en suite, tastefully decorated and centrally heated and have clock radio, colour TV and tea/coffee making facilities. Rest assured you will have a comfortable and relaxed stay with us. Bed and Breakfast from £22.50. £140 per week. Children of all ages welcome.

AA ♦♦♦♦

PETS WELCOME 39 Blencathra Street, Keswick CA12 4HX

Tel & Fax: 017687 73344 • wayne-alison@cragside39blencathra.fsnet.co.uk • www.SmoothHound.co.uk/hotels/cragside

Traditional Lakeland hotel with friendly atmosphere. Home cooking, cosy bar, comfortable lounge and some riverside rooms. Winter and Summer discount rates. Brochure and Tariff available.

AA ★

ROYAL OAK HOTEL, BORROWDALE, KESWICK CA12 5XB
017687 77214 • e-mail: info@royaloakhotel.co.uk
www.royaloakhotel.co.uk

Midtown Cottages, High Lorton

These two cottages have both been awarded four stars and are electrically centrally heated for all year round use. Built around a courtyard area, they are 'upside down' – the bedrooms (one double, one twin) being downstairs with the lounge, dining area and small but well equipped kitchen with dishwasher and freezer upstairs to make the most of the views over the fells. Whilst the two cottages are not absolutely identical, they are both furnished to the same high standard. They are both non-smoking, but pets are very welcome. Cot & high chair available if required. Lorton lies at the northern end of Lorton Vale, a beautiful valley which runs from Cockermouth in the west to Buttermere in the east. The river Cocker runs the full length of the valley, and at the end of the 18th century its fast flowing streams that flow down from the fells, through the village were used as the motive power for flour and linen mills. Some of these mill buildings survive today, having later been used by the Jennings family as their brewery. The 'Yew Tree Hall', now the village hall, was once the brewery malt house. Jennings ales are still brewed in nearby Cockermouth.

Complete weeks £465(High Season), £395 (Mid Season), £270 (Low Season). Short breaks from £180

Please contact: Mr & Mrs M. Burrell • Tel: +44(0) 1264 710165
e-mail: info@midtown-cottages.com • website: www.midtown-cottages.com

COLEDALE INN

ETC ♦♦♦

Braithwaite, Near Keswick, Cumbria CA12 5TN Tel: 017687 78272

A friendly, family-run Victorian Inn in a peaceful hillside position above Braithwaite, and ideally situated for touring and walking. All bedrooms are warm and spacious, with en suite shower room and colour television. Children are welcome, as are pets. Home-cooked meals, and real ales. Open all year. **website: www.coledale-inn.co.uk**

Portinscale, Keswick, Cumbria CA12 5RH

Set within its own garden with private car parking, in the picturesque village of Portinscale near the shores of Lake Derwentwater within walking distance of the market town of Keswick. Ideally situated for exploring all parts of the Lakes. Offering comfort, friendly service, these being the essential qualities provided by the resident proprietor. A well-stocked bar offering draught beers; comfortable lounge and elegant dining room where a four course dinner can be enjoyed with a varied selection of wines. All rooms en suite with tea and coffee making facilities, colour TV, telephone.

DB&B from £52, Winter Rates Available (Special Breaks).

Brochure on request, contact Joe or Audrey on 017687 72344
e-mail: stay@rickerbygrange.co.uk • www.rickerbygrange.co.uk

RAC ♦♦♦♦ SPARKLING DIAMOND AWARD & WARM WELCOME AWARD

AA/ETC ♦♦♦♦

Woodside

Ideally situated away from the busy town centre yet only a short walk down the C2C bridle path to the town. The property has been extensively refurbished and has larger than average rooms with good-sized en suites. Being a family-run establishment you are guaranteed a friendly reception. After a good night's sleep you will be ready for a hearty English breakfast together with cereal, fruit and yoghurt. Dogs welcome by arrangement. B&B from £28.

Ann & Norman Pretswell, Woodside, Penrith Road, Keswick CA12 4LJ • 017687 73522
www.woodsideguesthouse.co.uk

KESWICK COTTAGES

Tel: 017687 78555

8 Beechcroft, Braithwaite, Keswick Cumbria CA12 5TH

Superb selection of cottages and apartments in and around Keswick. All of our properties are well maintained and thoroughly clean. From a one bedroom cottage to a four bedroom house we have something for everyone. Children and pets welcome. Contact us for a free colour brochure.

e-mail: info@keswickcottages.co.uk • www.keswickcottages.co.uk

Overwater Hall

Hosts: Stephen Bore
Adrian & Angela Hyde

Overwater, Ireby, Near Keswick,
Cumbria CA7 1HH
Tel: 017687 76566
e-mail: welcome@overwaterhall.co.uk
www.overwaterhall.co.uk

Our elegant, family-run Country House Hotel offers you the best in traditional comforts, award-winning food and friendly hospitality. Peacefully secluded yet within only a short drive of the popular centres of the Lake District, this is the ideal place for a real break.

Dogs genuinely welcome in your room, in one of the lounges and in our 18 acres of grounds.

Special four night breaks available all year from £560.00 per room, inclusive of Dinner and Breakfast.

Please telephone us for a brochure, or refer to our website for further information.

01768776065

Email:info@lakelandcottages.co.uk

www.lakelandcottages.co.uk

LAKELAND
Cottage Holidays

Self-catering cottages for you and your pets in and around Keswick and beautiful Borrowdale

Janet and Peter, 1 Friars Ground, Kirkby-in-Furness LA17 7YB

"Sunset Cottage" is a spacious self-catering 17th century two/three bedroomed character cottage with a large enclosed garden. Original features include inglenook fireplace with logburning stove, oak beams, flagstone floor and oak panelling. Panoramic views over sea/mountains; ideal for walking and birdwatching. Coniston/Windermere 30 minutes. Non-smoking. Terms from £150. Open all year. Debit/credit cards accepted.

e-mail: enquiries@southlakes-cottages.com • www.southlakes-cottages.com

A warm welcome awaits you at **ULLATHORNS**, a working farm situated in the unspoilt Lune Valley. The farmhouse is dated 1617, and 'Ullathorn' is a Viking name for ' place where wolves lie'. One family/twin/double and one double, both en suite, with TV and drink making facilities. Hearty breakfast served. Ample car parking.An ideal touring base for Lakes and Dales or as a stopover point as situated between M6 junctions. Non-smoking. B&B from £24 (based on two sharing) with reductions for children. Short break offers. **VisitBritain** ◆◆◆◆ Brochure from:
Pauline Bainbridge, Ullathorns Farm, Middleton, Kirkby Lonsdale LA6 2LZ
Tel: 015242 76214 • e-mail: pauline@ullathorns.co.uk • www.ullathorns.co.uk

The Snooty Fox Kirkby Lonsdale

The Snooty Fox is a newly refurbished Jacobean Inn, offering 9 en suite rooms, award-winning restaurant and lounge bar. Situated in the heart of the market town of Kirkby Lonsdale and boasting fine cask ales and log fires, The Snooty Fox is the perfect base from which to explore both the Lake District and Yorkshire Dales.

Tel: 01524 271308 • www.thesnootyfoxhotel.co.uk

Cocklake House

MALLERSTANG CA17 4JT • 017683 72080

Charming, High Pennine Country House B&B in unique position above Pendragon Castle in Upper Mallerstang Dale offering good food and exceptional comfort to a small number of guests. Two double rooms with large private bathrooms. Three acres riverside grounds. Dogs welcome.

www.grizedale-lodge.com

Grizedale Lodge **Hawkshead, Ambleside LA22 0QL**

Set in the heart of Grizedale Forest National Park, in a beautiful location, and within easy reach of Beatrix Potter country, Windermere and Coniston. All rooms en suite, some with four-posters. Central heating. Residents' licence. Open all year, from £30pppn.

Tel 015394 36532 • Fax: 015394 36572 • enquiries@grizedale-lodge.com

BOWNESS LAKELAND HOLIDAYS

Traditional Lakeland cottages, well-equipped and furnished to a high standard, set in Bowness-on-Windermere and the surrounding scenic South Lakes. Ideal setting from which to explore the Lake District. Pets welcome in many properties. Brochure available. Winter Short Breaks. Contact: **131 RADCLIFFE NEW ROAD, WHITEFIELD, MANCHESTER M45 7RP • 0161 796 3896 • Fax: 0161 272 1841**

e-mail: info@bownesslakelandholidays.co.uk • www.bownesslakelandholidays.co.uk

Felldyke Cottage Holidays • "a warm and friendly welcome"

Visiting the Western Lakes? Then why not stay in this lovely 19th century cottage. Sleeps 4, short breaks can be arranged. Pets are welcome. Open all year, for you to enjoy the Lake District in all its guises.

Mrs A. Wilson • 01946 861151 • dockraynook@talk21.com

www.felldykecottageholidays.co.uk VB ★★★★

Some of the loveliest cottages in the Lake District with stunning scenery on their doorsteps are ready to welcome you and your pets. Prices vary. Please visit our website.

ETC ★★★ - ★★★★★

e-mail: enquiries@wheelwrights.com
www.wheelwrights.com

WHEELWRIGHTS

**HOLIDAY COTTAGES,
ELTERWATER,
NEAR AMBLESIDE LA22 9HS
Tel: 015394 38305
Fax: 015394 37618**

Book with this advert and claim a FREE Bottle of house wine at dinner.

THE BRITANNIA INN

Elterwater, Langdale, Cumbria LA22 9HP

Tel: 015394 37210

A 500 year-old quintessential Lakeland Inn nestled in the centre of the picturesque village of Elterwater amidst the imposing fells of the Langdale Valley. Comfortable, newly refurbished en suite double and twin-bedded rooms. Dogs welcome. Enquire about our Winter Mid-Week Special Offer of three nights B&B for the price of two. Relax in the oak-beamed Bars or Dining Room whilst sampling local real ales and dishes from our extensive menu of fresh, home-cooked food using lots of Cumbrian produce.

www.britinn.co.uk • e-mail: info@britinn.co.uk

HIGHFOLD COTTAGE • LITTLE LANGDALE

Very comfortable Lakeland cottage, ideally situated for walking and touring. Superb mountain views. Sleeps 5. Personally maintained. Pets welcome. Weekly £220–£450. **MRS C.E. BLAIR, 8 THE GLEBE, CHAPEL STILE, AMBLESIDE LA22 9JT • 015394 37686 • www.highfoldcottage.co.uk**

Tanglewood Caravan Park

CAUSEWAY HEAD, SILLOTH-ON-SOLWAY, CUMBRIA CA7 4PE

Tanglewood is a family-run park on the fringes of the Lake District National Park. It is tree-sheltered and situated one mile inland from the small port of Silloth on the Solway Firth, with a beautiful view of the Galloway Hills. Large modern holiday homes are available from March to January, with car parking beside each home. Fully equipped except for bed linen, with end bedroom, panel heaters in both bedrooms and the bathroom, electric lighting, hot and cold water, toilet, shower, gas fire, fridge and colour TV, all of which are included in the tariff. Touring pitches also available with electric hook-ups and water/drainage facilities, etc. Play area. Licensed lounge with adjoining children's play room. Pets welcome free but must be kept under control at all times. Full colour brochure available.

AA ★★★ **TEL: 016973 31253**

e-mail: tanglewoodcaravanpark@hotmail.com

website: www.tanglewoodcaravanpark.co.uk

MR & MRS BURNETT, FELL VIEW HOLIDAYS, FELL VIEW, GLENRIDDING, PENRITH CA11 0PJ • Tel & Fax: 017684 82342 • Evenings 01768 867420

Sleep 2-6. Our comfortable well-equipped cottages/apartments have only a field between them and the lake, and have magnificent views of the mountains. Our gardens and grounds are full of birds and flowers which everyone can enjoy. From £220 per week, short breaks from £165. Pets free.

e-mail: enquiries@fellviewholidays.com • www.fellviewholidays.com

Land Ends Cabins, Watermillock, Near Ullswater CA11 0NB

Tel: 017684 86438 • Only one mile from Ullswater, our four detached log cabins have a peaceful fellside location in 25-acre grounds with two pretty lakes. Ducks, moorhens, red squirrels and wonderful birdlife. Doggy heaven! Sleep 2-5. **e-mail: infolandends@btinternet.com • www.landends.co.uk**

★★★ SELF CATERING

Readers are requested to mention this guidebook when making enquiries about accommodation.

Pet-Friendly
Pubs, Inns & Hotels

on pages 390-405

Please note that these establishments may not feature in the main section of this book

LONSDALE HOUSE HOTEL

11 Daltongate, Ulverston, Cumbria LA12 7BD

LONSDALE HOUSE HOTEL – situated right in the heart of Ulverston (South Lakes festival town). Offering friendly service, great food and comfortable accommodation. Dogs are most welcome, provided they are accompanied by well-behaved owners, and can stay in the rooms. A short walk from the hotel, on the edge of the National Park overlooking Ulverston, is Sir John Barrow's Monument on Hoad Hill. A popular place for walking with superb views of the Lake District peaks and panoramic view of Morecambe Bay. There are also some good walks along the bay coast a short drive from the hotel. Lonsdale House Hotel is an excellent base to explore the Lake District, being only 15 minutes from Lake Windermere and about 30 minutes from Windermere Village, Coniston and Cartmel.

Phone **01229 582598** for a brochure and find out about our Special Breaks.
www.lonsdalehousehotel.co.uk

WATERMILL INN, INGS, NEAR STAVELEY, KENDAL LA8 9PY
01539 821309 • Fax: 01539 822309. Shelly and friends (Dogs) welcome you to the award-winning Inn. 16 real ales. Cosy fires, en suite rooms, excellent bar meals. Doggie water and biscuits served in the bar. Good doorstep dog walking.
e-mail: all@watermillinn.co.uk • www.watermillinn.co.uk

Langdale Chase Hotel **Windermere LA23 1LW**

Magnificent country house hotel with over six acres of beautifully landscaped grounds sloping to the edge of Lake Windermere. Panoramic views of lake and fells, log fires, excellent food, and friendly, professional staff all ensure a memorable stay.

015394 32201 **www.langdalechase.co.uk**

The Famous Wild Boar

Nestled within the beautiful Gilpin Valley, unwind in tranquil and secluded surroundings in a former Coaching Inn, set within its own private 72-acres of woodland perfect for walking your dogs. Excellent restaurant with quality food with an emphasis on local produce complemented by real ales and highly commended wine list. Relax in the choice of cosy rooms and suites all available with our pets welcome policy. Windermere Golf Club is on our doorstep along with free membership of the Leisure Club at our sister hotel, the Low Wood.

Tel: 08458 504 604 • E-mail: wildboar@elhmail.co.uk • Website: www.elh.co.uk

RECOMMENDED COTTAGE HOLIDAYS. 1st choice for dream cottages at very competitive prices in all holiday regions of beautiful Britain. Pets welcome. All properties inspected. Free brochure - call 01751 475547.
website: www.recommended-cottages.co.uk

DALES HOLIDAY COTTAGES. Beauty in every direction you walk, all within view of outstanding cottages, barns and houses that are personally inspected and cater for everyone from couples and families to pet lovers and groups of friends. Call 0870 909 9505 or visit our website.
website: www.dalesholcot.com/cumbria

Allonby

Village on the Solway Firth, 5 miles north-east of Maryport.

HOLIDAY HOMES IN ALLONBY. Three well equipped houses available, one with four bedrooms and two with two bedrooms. Gas, electric, linen and towels included. Centre of village. Excellent value. Near beach. Contact: MRS D HETHERINGTON, EAST HOUSE, ALLONBY, MARYPORT CA15 6QF (01900 881264 or 01900 881549).

Ambleside

Popular centre for exploring Lake District at northern end of Lake Windermere. Picturesque Stock Ghyll waterfall nearby, lovely walks. Associations with Wordsworth. Penrith 30 miles, Keswick 17, Windermere 5.

SMALLWOOD HOUSE HOTEL, COMPSTON ROAD, AMBLESIDE LA22 9DJ (015394 32330). Where quality and the customer come first. En suite rooms, car parking, leisure club membership. ETC ◆◆◆◆ [Pets £3 per night]
website: www.smallwoodhotel.co.uk

IVY HOUSE HOTEL AND RESTAURANT, HAWKSHEAD, NEAR AMBLESIDE LA22 0HS (015394 36204). Family-run listed Georgian hotel. 11 en suite bedrooms with colour TV and equipped with hot drinks trays. No charge for dogs. Children most welcome. Write or telephone Rob or Julia Treeby for brochure. ETC ◆◆◆◆, RAC Dining Award. [🐕]
website: www.ivyhousehotel.com

THE OLD VICARAGE, VICARAGE ROAD, AMBLESIDE LA22 9DH (015394 33364). 'Rest a while in style'. Quality B&B set in tranquil wooded grounds in the heart of the village. Car park. All rooms en suite. Kettle, clock/radio, TV. Heated indoor pool, sauna, hot tub, sun lounge and rooftop terrace. Special breaks. Friendly service where your pets are welcome. Telephone IAN OR HELEN BURT. [🐕]
website: www.oldvicarageambleside.co.uk

2 LOWFIELD, OLD LAKE ROAD, AMBLESIDE. Ground floor garden flat half a mile from town centre; sleeps 4. Lounge/diningroom, kitchen, bathroom/WC, two bedrooms, one with en suite shower. Linen supplied. Children and pets welcome. Parking. Terms from £140 to £240 per week. Contact: MR P. F. QUARMBY, 3 LOWFIELD, OLD LAKE ROAD, AMBLESIDE LA22 0DH (Tel & Fax: 015394 32326) [🐕]
e-mail: paulfquarmby@aol.com

KIRKSTONE FOOT, KIRKSTONE PASS ROAD, AMBLESIDE LA22 9EH (015394 32232; Fax: 015394 32805). Superior cottage and apartment complex, set in peaceful gardens, adjoining the Lakeland fells and village centre. Open all year. ETC ★★★★/★★★★★ [pw! Pets £3.00 per night.]
e-mail: enquiries@kirkstonefoot.co.uk website: www.kirkstonefoot.co.uk

GREENHOWE CARAVAN PARK, GREAT LANGDALE, AMBLESIDE LA22 9JU (015394 37231; Fax: 015394 37464; Freephone: 0800 0717231). Permanent Caravan Park with Self Contained Holiday Accommodation. An ideal centre for Climbing, Fell Walking, Riding, Swimming, or just a lazy holiday. ETC ★★★★ [Pets £6 per night, £30 per week]
website: www.greenhowe.com

BETTY FOLD, HAWKSHEAD HILL, AMBLESIDE LA22 0PS (015394 36611). Ground floor apartment sleeping four. Private entrance. Set in peaceful and spacious grounds, ideal for walkers and families with pets. Open all year. [pw! Pets £2 per night.]
e-mail: csalisbury@bettyfold.fsnet.co.uk website: www.bettyfold.co.uk

LYNDALE GUEST HOUSE LAKE ROAD, AMBLESIDE LA22 0DN (015394 34244) Nestled midway between Lake Windermere and Ambleside village, with superb views of Loughrigg Fell and the Langdales beyond. Excellent base for walking, touring, or just relaxing. [🐕]
website: www.lyndale-guesthouse.co.uk

Appleby-in-Westmorland

Located in the Eden Valley, ideal for walking, riding, fishing and cycling. Annual events include The Gypsy Horse Fair and the Jazz Festival.

KEITH AND DIANE BUDDING, SCALEBECK HOLIDAY COTTAGES, SCALEBECK, GREAT ASBY, APPLEBY CA16 6TF (01768 351006; Fax: 01768 353532). Comfortable and well-equipped self-catering accommodation in the tranquil and picturesque Eden Valley. Sleep 2/5. No smoking. ETC ★★★★ [pw! £20 per week]
e-mail: mail@scalebeckholidaycottages.com

Bassenthwaite

Village on Bassenthwaite Lake with traces of Norse and Roman settlements.

BROOK HOUSE COTTAGE HOLIDAYS, NEAR KESWICK CA12 4QP (Tel & Fax: 017687 76393). Delightful cottages in attractive hamlet near Keswick (sleep 2-10). Excellent food at village pub. Ideally for Skiddaw, Bassenthwaite Lake, Keswick and Cockermouth. Farmhouse B&B also available.
e-mail: stay@amtrafford.co.uk website: www.holidaycottageslakedistrict.co.uk
www.bedandbreakfast-lakedistrict.co.uk

SKIDDAW VIEW HOLIDAY HOME PARK, BOTHEL, NEAR BASSENTHWAITE CA7 2JG (016973 20919). Quality lodge, cottage and holiday home accommodation for 2-5 in peaceful, relaxing surroundings. Please telephone for brochure and prices. ETC ★★★★ [pw!🐕]
e-mail: office@skiddawview.com website: www.skiddawview.co.uk

Borrowdale

Scenic valley of River Derwent, splendid walking and climbing country.

MARY MOUNT HOTEL, BORROWDALE, NEAR KESWICK CA12 5UU (017687 77223). Set in 4½ acres of gardens and woodlands on the shores of Derwentwater. 2½ miles from Keswick in picturesque Borrowdale. Superb walking and touring. All rooms en suite with colour TV and tea/coffee making facilities. Licensed. Brochure on request. ETC ★★ [pw! £6.50 per 2/3 nights , £10 per week.]
e-mail: mawdsley1@aol.com website: www.marymounthotel.co.uk

Symbols

🐕 Indicates that pets are welcome free of charge.

£ Indicates that a charge is made for pets: nightly or weekly.

pw! Shows some special provision for pets; exercise facility, feeding or accommodation arrangement.

⌂ Indicates separate pets accommodation.

Brampton

Market town with cobbled streets. Octagonal Moat Hall with exterior staircases and iron stocks.

FARLAM HALL HOTEL, BRAMPTON, CUMBRIA CA8 2NG (016977 46234; Fax: 016977 46683). Standing in four acres of gardens, with its own lake, Farlam Hall offers fine quality cuisine and individually decorated guest rooms. Ideal touring centre for the Lakes, Borders and Hadrian's Wall. AA Three Stars Inspectors' Choice and Two Rosettes, Relais & Chateaux. [🐕]
e-mail: farlam@relaischateaux.com website: www.farlamhall.co.uk

Broughton-in-Furness

Village 8 miles NW of Ulverston.

J. JACKSON, THORNTHWAITE FARM, WOODLAND HALL, WOODLAND, BROUGHTON-IN-FURNESS LA20 6DF (Tel & Fax: 01229 716340). Two well-equipped cottages and two caravans in excellent walking area. Wildlife/birdwatchers paradise. Private fishing lake. Ancient woodlands, quiet, relaxing, warm welcome. Established 1968. ETC ★★★ [Pets £15 per week]
e-mail: info@lakedistrictcottages.co.uk website: www.lakedistrictcottages.co.uk

PAUL SANFORD, WOODEND BOTHY, WOODEND, ULPHA, BROUGHTON-IN-FURNESS LA20 6DY (019467 23277). Woodend is a self-contained building offering cosy accommodation for two between the Eskdale and Duddon Valleys. Stone walls and exposed beams and an en suite bathroom. Short breaks available out of season.
website: www.woodendhouse.co.uk1

Buttermere

Between lake of same name and Crummock Water. Magnificent scenery. Of special note is Sour Milk Ghyll waterfall and steep and impressive Honister Pass. Keswick 15 miles, Cockermouth 10.

NEW HOUSE FARM, BUTTERMERE/LORTON VALLEY, COCKERMOUTH CA13 9UU (01900 85404; Fax: 01900 85478). New House Farm has 15 acres of fields, woods, streams and ponds which guests and dogs can wander around. Luxurious en suite accommodation and fine traditional food. Off season breaks. AA ★★★★★. [Pets £6 per night]
e-mail: hazel@newhouse-farm.co.uk website: www.newhouse-farm.co.uk

Carlisle

Important Border city and former Roman station on River Eden. Castle is of historic interest, also Tullie House Museum and Art Gallery. Good sports facilities inc. football and racecourse. Kendal 45 miles, Dumfries 33, Penrith 18.

NEW PALLYARDS, HETHERSGILL, CARLISLE CA6 6HZ (01228 577308). Relax and see beautiful North Cumbria and the Borders. Self-catering accommodation in one Bungalow, 3/4 bedrooms; two lovely Cottages on farm. Also Bed and Breakfast or Half Board – en suite rooms. ETC ◆◆◆◆/★★★★ [Pets from £10 per week]
e-mail: newpallyards@btinternet.com website: www.4starsc.co.uk

GRAHAM ARMS HOTEL, ENGLISH STREET, LONGTOWN, CARLISLE CA6 5SE (01228 791213; Fax: 01228 794110). 16 bedrooms en suite, including four-poster and family rooms, all with tea/coffee facilities, TV and radio. Secure courtyard locked overnight. Pets welcome with well-behaved owners. AA ★★ [🐕]
e-mail: office@grahamarms.com website: www.grahamarms.com

Cartmel

Village 4 miles south of Newby Bridge.

RATHER SPECIAL COTTAGES. Seven cottages sleeping 2-6. Set behind a large Georgian house set in parkland on the side of Hamps Fell. Beautiful garden, great walks. Pets and children welcome. Open all year. Please telephone for details. ETC ★★★★. Contact: MR M. AINSCOUGH, LONGLANDS AT CARTMEL, CARTMEL LA11 6HG (015395 36475; Fax: 015395 36172). [🐕]
e-mail: longlands@cartmel.com website: www.cartmel.com

Terms quoted in this publication may be subject to increase if rises in costs necessitate

Cockermouth

Market town and popular touring centre for Lake District and quiet Cumbrian coast. On Rivers Derwent and Cocker. Penrith 30 miles, Carlisle 26, Whitehaven 14, Keswick 12.

THE DERWENT LODGE, EMBLETON, NEAR BASSENTHWAITE, COCKERMOUTH CA13 9YA (017687 76606). A warm welcome awaits you and your pet. Choose from luxury self-catering apartments or en suite hotel rooms/suites. New for August 2007 indoor pool and fitness suite. Ideal for touring Western Lakes and coast.
info@derwent_lodge@yahoo.co.uk website: www.derwentlodge.co.uk

THE MANOR HOUSE, OUGHTERSIDE, ASPATRIA, CUMBRIA CA7 2PT (016973 22420). 18th century manor farmhouse retaining many original features and several acres of land. Spacious en suite rooms, tea/coffee making facilities, TV and lots of little extras. All pets and children welcome. Inspection Commended. [🐕]
e-mail: richardandjudy@themanorhouse.net website: www.themanorhouse.net

ROSE COTTAGE GUEST HOUSE, LORTON ROAD, COCKERMOUTH CA13 9DX (Tel & Fax: 01900 822189). Family-run guest house on the outskirts of Cockermouth. Warm, friendly atmosphere. Parking. All rooms en suite with colour TV, tea/coffee, central heating. Pets welcome. Ideal base for visiting both Lakes and coast. ETC ◆◆◆◆ [🐕]
website: www.rosecottageguest.co.uk

Coniston

Village 8 miles south-west of Ambleside, dominated by Old Man of Coniston (2635ft).

WATERHEAD HOTEL, CONISTON LA21 8AJ (015394 41244; Fax: 015394 41193). Situated alongside Coniston Water, The Waterhead Hotel makes a perfect retreat. 22 en suite bedrooms, Mountain View Restaurant, lounge bar with views across the Lake. Non smoking. Ideal base for outdoor activities, also lake cruises and historic houses. [Pets £5.00 per night, £20 per week].
website: www.classic-hotels.net

BROCKLEBANK GROUND HOLIDAY COTTAGES, TORVER, CONISTON LA21 8BS (015394 49588). Three luxury cottages in a quiet rural setting, sleeping 2,4 & 7. Excellent walking from the door. Dog-friendly pubs 600 yards. Short breaks available. Prices from £275. ETC ★★★★. [🐕]
website: www.brocklebankground.com

THE COPPERMINES AND CONISTON LAKES COTTAGES (015394 41765). Unique Lakeland cottages for 2 – 30 of quality and character in stunning mountain scenery. Log fires, exposed beams. Pets welcome! ★★★ - ★★★★ Book online. [Pets £25 per stay]
website: www.coppermines.co.uk

LAKELAND HOUSE, TILBERTHWAITE AVENUE, CONISTON LA21 8ED (015394 41303). Village centre guest house, hearty breakfasts, from £23 per person. Two self-catering cottages also available, sleeping two to six - one with lake views, one with four-poster. [Pets £10 per week]
e-mail: info@lakelandhouse.co.uk website: www.lakelandhouse.co.uk

Crosthwaite

Hamlet 4 miles west of Kendal

DAMSON DENE HOTEL, CROSTHWAITE LA8 8JE (015395 68676). Tranquil location only 10 minutes from Lake Windermere. Best Lakes Breaks from £139 per person for 3 nights. [🐕 pw!]
e-mail: info@damsondene.co.uk website: www.bestlakesbreaks.co.uk

Eskdale

Lakeless valley, noted for waterfalls and ascended by a light-gauge railway. Tremendous views. Roman fort. Keswick 35 miles, Broughton-in-Furness 10 miles.

FISHERGROUND FARM, ESKDALE. Traditional hill farm, with a stone cottage and three pine lodges, ideal for walkers, nature lovers, dogs and children. Games room, raft pool and adventure playground. Good pubs nearby. IAN & JENNIFER HALL, ORCHARD HOUSE, APPLETHWAITE, KESWICK CA12 4PN (017687 73175)
e-mail: holidays@fisherground.co.uk website: www.fisherground.co.uk

THE BOOT INN (FORMERLY THE BURNMOOR INN), BOOT, ESKDALE CA19 1TG (019467 23224). Nine en suite bedrooms. Dogs welcome to be in the bar with you for lunch and dinner. We do not make a charge for well behaved dogs. Special breaks available all year. Call for a brochure. [🐕]
e-mail: enquiries@bootinn.co.uk website:www.bootinn.co.uk

BIRKHOW COTTAGE, ESKDALE. Sleeps 6. Stunning views of the Lake District fells. Peaceful accommodation with coal fire and comfortable surroundings. A perfect place to return to after a day walking in the hills. Contact: SALLY (017687 76836).
e-mail: sally@hollinhead.co.uk

Grange-over-Sands

Charming Edwardian resort set between Lake District Fells and Morecambe Bay.

HAMPSFELL HOUSE HOTEL, HAMPSFELL ROAD, GRANGE-OVER-SANDS LA11 6BG (015395 32567). In two acres of private grounds, just a few minutes' walk from the town centre. The nine en suite bedrooms are well appointed. Enjoy the best of fresh Cumbrian produce in the elegant dining room. From £35pppn. Ideal base for exploring the Lake District. AA ★★ [Pets £3 per night].
enquiries@hampsfellhouse.co.uk website: www.hampsfellhouse.co.uk

Grasmere

Village famous for Wordsworth associations; the poet lived in Dove Cottage (preserved as it was), and is buried in the churchyard. Museum has manuscripts and relics.

GRASMERE HOTEL, BROADGATE, GRASMERE LA22 9TA (015394 35277). Charming 13 bedroomed Country House Hotel, with ample parking and a licensed lounge. All rooms recently refurbished with en suite facilities. Award-winning restaurant overlooking gardens, river and surrounding hills. Special breaks throughout the year. AA/ETC ★★ Silver Award.[Pets £5 per stay].
e-mail: enquiries@grasmerehotel.co.uk website: www.grasmerehotel.co.uk

LAKE VIEW COUNTRY HOUSE & SELF-CATERING APARTMENTS, GRASMERE LA22 9TD (015394 35384/35167). Luxury B&B or 3 Star Self-Catering accommodation in unrivalled location near to village yet secluded with wonderful views and lakeshore access. All B&B rooms en suite, some with whirlpool baths. Ground floor accommodation available. No smoking. Featured in "Which?" Good B&B Guide.

Hawkshead

Quaint village in Lake District between Coniston Water and Windermere. The 16th century Church and Grammar School, which Wordsworth attended, are of interest. Ambleside 5 miles.

HIDEAWAYS, THE SQUARE, HAWKSHEAD LA22 0NZ (015394 42435). Cottages in and around Hawkshead. Great walks and lakes for swimming, dog friendly pubs, open fires to lie in front of... owners will enjoy it too. [Pets £15 per week].
e-mail: bookings@lakeland-hideaways.co.uk website: www.lakeland-hideaways.co.uk

THE KINGS ARMS HOTEL, HAWKSHEAD, AMBLESIDE LA22 0NZ (015394 36372). Join us for a relaxing stay amidst the green hills and dales of Lakeland, and we will be delighted to offer you good food, homely comfort and warm hospitality in historic surroundings. We hope to see you soon! Self-catering cottages also available.[🐕, pets £20 per week s/c]
website: www.kingsarmshawkshead.co.uk

SAWREY HOUSE COUNTRY HOTEL & RESTAURANT, NEAR SAWREY, HAWKSHEAD LA22 0LF (015394 36387; Fax: 015394 36010). Quality family-run hotel in three acres of peaceful gardens with magnificent views across Esthwaite Water. Excellent food, warm friendly atmosphere. Lounge, bar. Pets welcome. Non-smoking. AA Red Rosette for food. AA ◆◆◆◆◆. [Pets £10 per night.]
website: www.sawreyhouse.com

Ireby

A peaceful and uncrowded village just outside The Lake District National Park. Wigton 7 miles, Carlisle 18 miles.

2 MOOT HALL, IREBY CA7 1DU. (01423 360759; Mobile: 07774420996) Lovely cottage, part of 16th century Moot Hall in unspoilt village; delightful walks in Uldale Fells and northern Lake District. Sleeps 4. Linens/fuel/electricity included in weekly charge of £250 to £360. Open all year. Reductions for PAT, Assistance and Rescue Dogs. [🐕]
e-mail: david.boyes1@virgin.net

Kendal

Market town and popular centre for touring the Lake District. Of historic interest is the Norman castle, birthplace of Catherine Parr. Penrith 25 miles, Lancaster 22, Ambleside 13.

MIREFOOT COTTAGES, MIREFOOT, KENDAL, CUMBRIA LA8 9AB (Tel: 01539 720015). 5 Star, pet friendly, self-catering cottages in a superb rural location in the Lake District National Park. Both cottages sleep 2. Fully equipped with TV (Freeview), DVD, WiFi, gas central heating. Tennis court, private parking. VB ★★★★★ [🐕]
e-mail: booking@mirefoot.co.uk website: www.mirefoot.co.uk

ANNE TAYLOR, RUSSELL FARM, BURTON-IN-KENDAL, CARNFORTH, LANCS. LA6 1NN (01524 781334). Bed, Breakfast and Evening Meal offered. Ideal centre for touring Lakes and Yorkshire Dales. Good food, friendly atmosphere on working dairy farm. Modernised farmhouse. Guests' own lounge. [🐕]
e-mail: miktaylor@farming.co.uk

STONECROSS MANOR HOTEL, MILNTHORPE ROAD, KENDAL LA9 5HP (01539 733559; Fax: 01539 736386). Stonecross Manor offers easy access to town, ample parking, local cuisine, conference and banquet facilities, indoor swimming pool, and four-poster bedrooms. [Pets £15 per night].
e-mail: info@stonecrossmanor.co.uk website: www.stonecrossmanor.co.uk

MRS HELEN JONES, PRIMROSE COTTAGE, ORTON ROAD, TEBAY CA10 3TL (015396 24791). Adjacent M6 J38 (10 miles north of Kendal). Excellent rural location for North Lakes and Yorkshire Dales. Superb facilities include jacuzzi bath, king and four-poster beds. One acre garden. Also self-contained ground floor flat and 3 self-catering bungalows for disabled guests plus pets. Pets welcome, very friendly. National Accessible Scheme Level II. ETC ◆◆◆◆ [🐕]
e-mail: info@primrosecottagecumbria.co.uk website: www.primrosecottagecumbria.co.uk

RIVERSIDE HOTEL, BEEZON ROAD, KENDAL LA9 6EL (015397 34861). Lovely riverside location. Best Lakes Breaks from £139 per person for 3 nights. [🐕 pw!]
e-mail: info@riversidekendal.co.uk website: www.bestlakesbreaks.co.uk

Keswick

Famous Lake District resort at north end of Derwentwater with Pencil Museum and Cars of the Stars Motor Museum. Carlisle 30 miles, Ambleside 17, Cockermouth 12.

ORCHARD HOUSE HOLIDAYS, APPLETHWAITE, KESWICK. Two lovely detached houses , sleeping 8-12. Each has fully equipped kitchen, 2/3 bathrooms and a large private garden. Pets welcome and free; lots of walks from the doorstep. IAN & JENNIFER HALL, ORCHARD HOUSE, APPLETHWAITE, KESWICK CA12 4PN (017687 73175) [🐕]
e-mail: holidays@fisherground.co.uk website: www.orchardhouseholidays.co.uk

CRAGSIDE GUEST HOUSE, 39 BLENCATHRA STREET, KESWICK CA12 4HX (Tel & Fax: 017687 73344). Quiet, comfortable guest house close to the centre of Keswick. All rooms en suite, tastefully decorated, centrally heated and have clock radio, colour TV and tea/coffee making facilities. AA ◆◆◆◆ [🐕]
e-mail: wayne-alison@cragside39blencathra.fsnet.co.uk
website: www.SmoothHound.co.uk/hotels/cragside

ROYAL OAK HOTEL, BORROWDALE, KESWICK CA12 5XB (017687 77214). Traditional Lakeland hotel with friendly atmosphere. Home cooking, cosy bar, comfortable lounge and some riverside rooms. Winter and Summer discount rates. Brochure and Tariff available. AA ★ Hotel. [🐕]
e-mail: info@royaloakhotel.co.uk website: www.royaloakhotel.co.uk

MIDTOWN COTTAGES, HIGH LORTON. Two well equipped cottages, both with central heating, furnished to a high standard. All cottages have dishwashers & freezers. Overlooking Fells, at north end of Lorton Vale. Pets welcome. Non- smoking. For details contact MR & MRS BURRELL (01264 710165). ETC ★★★★ [🐕]
e-mail: info@midtown-cottages.com website: www.midtown-cottages.com

COLEDALE INN, BRAITHWAITE, NEAR KESWICK CA12 5TN (017687 78272). Friendly, family-run Victorian Inn in peaceful situation. Warm and spacious en suite bedrooms with TV. Children and pets welcome. Open all year. ETC ◆◆◆ [🐕]
website: www.coledale-inn.co.uk

RICKERBY GRANGE, PORTINSCALE, KESWICK CA12 5RH (017687 72344). Delightfully situated in quiet village. Licensed. Imaginative home-cooked food, attractively served. Open all year. ETC/AA ◆◆◆◆ RAC ◆◆◆◆ Sparkling Diamond Award. [Pets £2.50 per night, £15 per week]
e-mail: stay@rickerbygrange.co.uk website: www.rickerbygrange.co.uk

WOODSIDE, PENRITH ROAD, KESWICK CA12 4LJ (017687 73522). Friendly family-run establishment. All our rooms are en suite. We have ample private parking and large gardens. Non-smoking. Dogs welcome. [🐕]
website: www.woodsideguesthouse.co.uk

KESWICK COTTAGES, 8 BEECHCROFT, BRAITHWAITE, KESWICK CA12 5TH (017687 78555). Cottages and apartments in and around Keswick. Properties are well maintained and clean. From a one bedroom cottage to a four bedroom house. Children and pets welcome. [Pets £10 per week]
e-mail: info@keswickcottages.co.uk website: www.keswickcottages.co.uk

OVERWATER HALL, OVERWATER, NEAR IREBY, KESWICK CA7 1HH (017687 76566). Elegant Country House Hotel in spacious grounds. Dogs very welcome in your room. 4 night mid-week breaks from £560 per room, inclusive of Dinner and Breakfast. Mini breaks also available all year. Award-winning restaurant. See also advertisement on page 125 [pw! 🐕]
e-mail: welcome@overwaterhall.co.uk website: www.overwaterhall.co.uk

Warm, comfortable houses and cottages in Keswick and beautiful Borrowdale, welcoming your dog. Inspected and quality graded. LAKELAND COTTAGE HOLIDAYS, KESWICK CA12 4QX (017687 76065; Fax: 017687 76869). [Pets £15 per week]
e-mail: info@lakelandcottages.co.uk website: www.lakelandcottages.co.uk

DERWENT WATER MARINA, PORTINSCALE, KESWICK CA12 5RF Lakeside self-catering apartments. Three apartments sleep 2 plus folding bed for occasional use, one apartment sleeps 6. Superb views over the lake and fells. Includes TV, heating and bed linen. Non-smoking. Watersports and boat hire available on site. (017687 72912) for brochure. [🐕]
website: www.derwentwatermarina.co.uk

LOW BRIERY HOLIDAYS (017687 72044). A peaceful and scenic riverside location just outside Keswick. A choice of cottages, timber lodges and holiday caravans to suit all budgets. ETC ★★★★ [Pets £10 per week]
website: www.keswick.uk.com

Kirkby-in-Furness

Small coastal village (A595). 10 minutes to Ulverston, Lakes within easy reach. Ideal base for walking and touring.

JANET AND PETER, 1 FRIARS GROUND, KIRKBY-IN-FURNESS LA17 7YB (01229 889601). "Sunset Cottage", self-catering 17th century two/three bedroom character cottage with garden. Original features. Panoramic views over sea/mountains; Coniston/Windermere 30 minutes. Non-smoking. Open all year. VisitBritain ★★★★ [Pets £15 per pet]
e-mail: enquiries@southlakes-cottages.com website: www.southlakes-cottages.com

Kirkby Lonsdale

Georgian buildings and quaint cottages. Riverside walks from medieval Devil's Bridge.

MRS PAULINE BAINBRIDGE, ULLATHORNS FARM, MIDDLETON, KIRKBY LONSDALE LA6 2LZ (015242 76214). 17th Century farmhouse on a working farm situated in the Lune Valley. B&B from £24. Children and well-behaved pets welcome. Non-smoking. Brochure available. VisitBritain ◆◆◆◆ [🐕]
e-mail: pauline@ullathorns.co.uk website: www.ullathorns.co.uk

THE SNOOTY FOX, KIRKBY LONSDALE (01524 271308). A newly refurbished Jacobean Inn, offering 9 en suite rooms, award-winning restaurant and lounge bar, the perfect base from which to explore both the Lake District and Yorkshire Dales. AA/RAC/ETC ★★ [🐕]
website: www.thesnootyfoxhotel.co.uk

Kirkby Stephen

5 miles south on B6259 Kirkby Stephen to Hawes road.

COCKLAKE HOUSE, MALLERSTANG CA17 4JT (017683 72080). Charming, High Pennine Country House B&B in unique position above Pendragon Castle in Upper Mallerstang Dale offering good food and exceptional comfort to a small number of guests. Two double rooms with large private bathrooms. Three acres riverside grounds. Dogs welcome. [🐕]

Kirkoswald

Village in the Cumbrian hills, lying north west of the Lake District. Ideal for touring. Penrith 7 miles.

SECLUDED COTTAGES WITH PRIVATE FISHING, KIRKOSWALD CA10 1EU (24 hour brochure line 01768 898711, manned most Saturdays). Quality cottages, clean, well equipped and maintained. Centrally located for Lakes, Pennines, Hadrian's Wall, Borderland. Enjoy the Good Life in comfort. Pets' paradise. Guests' coarse fishing. Bookings/enquiries 01768 898711. ETC ★★★ [pw! £2.50 per pet per night, £14 per week].
e-mail: info@crossfieldcottages.co.uk website: www.crossfieldcottages.co.uk

Lake District

North-west corner of England between A6/M6 and the Cumbrian Coast. Fells. valleys and 16 lakes, the largest being Lake Windermere.

GRIZEDALE LODGE, HAWKSHEAD, AMBLESIDE LA22 0QL (015394 36532; Fax: 015394 36572). In the heart of Grizedale Forest National Park, within easy reach of Windermere, Coniston, Beatrix Potter country and other attractions. All rooms en suite, some with four-posters. Open all year.
e-mail: enquiries@grizedale-lodge.com website: www.grizedale-lodge.com

BOWNESS LAKELAND HOLIDAYS. Traditional Lakeland cottages set in Bowness-on-Windermere and the surrounding scenic South Lakes. Pets welcome in many properties. Brochure available. Winter Short Breaks. Contact: 131 RADCLIFFE NEW ROAD, WHITEFIELD, MANCHESTER M45 7RP (0161 796 3896; Fax: 0161 272 1841). [Pets £20 per week.]
e-mail: info@bownesslakelandholidays.co.uk website: www.bownesslakelandholidays.co.u

Lamplugh

Hamlet 7 miles south of Cockermouth.

FELLDYKE COTTAGE HOLIDAYS, LAMPLUGH. Visiting the Western Lakes? Then why not stay in this lovely 19th century cottage. Sleeps 4, short breaks can be arranged. Pets are welcome. Open all year. Contact MRS A. WILSON (01946 861151). VB ★★★★ [pw! 🐕]
e-mail: dockraynook@talk21.com website: www.felldykecottageholidays.co.uk

Langdale

Dramatic valley area to the west of Ambleside, in the very heart of the National Park.

WHEELWRIGHTS HOLIDAY COTTAGES, ELTERWATER, NEAR AMBLESIDE LA22 9HS (015394 38305; Fax: 015394 37618). Some of the loveliest cottages in the Lake District with stunning scenery on their doorsteps are ready to welcome you and your pets. Prices vary. Please visit our website. ETC ★★★ - ★★★★★ [🐕]
e-mail: enquiries@wheelwrights.com website: www.wheelwrights.com

Terms quoted in this publication may be subject to increase if rises in costs necessitate

THE BRITANNIA INN, ELTERWATER, AMBLESIDE LA22 9HP (015394 37210; Fax: 015396 78075). 500-year-old traditional lakeland inn. Extensive, home-cooked menu, real ales, cosy bars, log fires. Newly refurbished, non-smoking en suite accommodation. Well-behaved pets welcome. ETC ★★★ [🐕]
e-mail: info@britinn.co.uk website: www.britinn.co.uk

Little Langdale

Hamlet 2 miles west of Skelwith Bridge. To west is Little Langdale Tarn, a small lake.

HIGHFOLD COTTAGE, LITTLE LANGDALE. Very comfortable Lakeland cottage, ideally situated for walking and touring. Superb mountain views. Sleeps 5. Personally maintained. Pets welcome. Weekly £220–£450. ETC ★★★. MRS C.E. BLAIR, 8 THE GLEBE, CHAPEL STILE, AMBLESIDE LA22 9JT (015394 37686). [🐕]
website: www.highfoldcottage.co.uk

Newby Bridge

Village at southern end of Lake Windermere, 8 miles from Ulverston

NEWBY BRIDGE HOTEL, NEWBY BRIDGE LA12 8NA (015395 31222). Overlooking the southern shores of Lake Windermere. Best Lakes Breaks from £139 per person for 3 nights. [🐕 pw!]
e-mail: info@newbybridgehotel.co.uk website: www.bestlakesbreaks.co.uk

Penrith

Market town and centre for touring Lake District. Of interest are 14th century castle, Gloucester Arms (1477) and Tudor House. Excellent sporting facilities. Windermere 27 miles, Keswick 18.

CARROCK COTTAGES. Four recently renovated, award-winning, stone-built cottages set on the fringe of the Lakeland Fells. Games room, spa facilities. Home cooked meals service. Ideal for fell walking. Excellent restaurants nearby. A warm welcome guaranteed. ETC ★★★★★ Contact MALCOLM OR GILLIAN (01768 484111; Fax: 01768 488850). [Pets £20 per week each].
e-mail: info@carrockcottages.co.uk website: www.carrockcottages.co.uk

Ravenstonedale

Conservation village in the Eden Valley, 5 miles from Kirkby Stephen.

THE BLACK SWAN HOTEL, RAVENSTONEDALE, KIRKBY STEPHEN CA17 4NG (015396 23204). A welcoming hotel and village inn, perfect for touring the Lakes and Yorkshire Dales. Riverside garden, own 9-hole golf course. 10 en suite bedrooms, excellent home-cooked food, wines and ales. [🐕 pw!]
enquiries@blackswanhotel.com website: www.blackswanhotel.com

Silloth-on-Solway

Solway Firth resort with harbour and fine sandy beach. Mountain views. Golf, fishing. Penrith 33 miles, Carlisle 23, Cockermouth 17.

MR AND MRS M.C. BOWMAN, TANGLEWOOD CARAVAN PARK, CAUSEWAY HEAD, SILLOTH CA7 4PE (016973 31253). Friendly country site, excellent toilet and laundry facilities. Tourers welcome or hire a luxury caravan. Open 1st March - January 31st. Telephone or e-mail for a brochure. AA *THREE PENNANTS.* [🐕]
e-mail: tanglewoodcaravanpark@hotmail.com website: www.tanglewoodcaravanpark.co.u

Ullswater

Lake stretching for 7 miles with attractive Lakeside walks.

MR & MRS BURNETT, (FELL VIEW HOLIDAYS), FELL VIEW, GLENRIDDING, PENRITH CA11 0PJ (Tel & Fax: 017684 82342; Evenings 01768 867420). Sleep 2-6. Our comfortable well-equipped cottages/apartments have only a field between them and the lake; magnificent views. Our gardens and grounds are full of birds and flowers. ETC ★★★★ [🐕 pw!]
e-mail: enquiries@fellviewholidays.com website: www.fellviewholidays.com

LAND ENDS CABINS, WATERMILLOCK, NEAR ULLSWATER CA11 0NB (017684 86438). Only one mile from Ullswater, our four detached log cabins have a peaceful fellside location in 25-acre grounds with two pretty lakes. Doggy heaven! Sleep 2-5. ETC ★★★ [🐕]
e-mail: infolandends@btinternet.com website: www.landends.co.uk

Ulverston

Old town and port with cobbled streets and market square. Laurel and Hardy Museum worth a visit.

LONSDALE HOUSE HOTEL, 11 DALTONGATE, ULVERSTON LA12 7BD (01229 582598). Situated in the heart of Ulverston. Friendly service, great food and comfortable accommodation. Pets welcome. Brochure available. [Pets £5 per night]
website: www.lonsdalehousehotel.co.uk

Wasdale

Hamlet 1 mile north east of Wast Water

THE BRIDGE INN, SANTON BRIDGE, HOLMROOK CA19 1UX (019467 26221; Fax: 019467 26026). Award-winning country inn providing good food and accommodation. 18 bedrooms, most en suite. Ideal for exploring the Western Lakes and fells. Well behaved dogs welcome.
e-mail: info@santonbridgeinn.com website: www.santonbridgeinn.com

Windermere

Famous resort on lake of same name, the largest in England. Magnificent scenery. Car ferry from Bowness, one mile distant. Kendal 9 miles.

WATERMILL INN & BREWERY, INGS, NEAR STAVELEY, KENDAL LA8 9PY (01539 821309; Fax: 01539 822309). Shelly and friends (Dogs) welcome you to the award-winning Inn. 16 real ales. Cosy fires, en suite rooms, excellent bar meals. Doggie water and biscuits served in the bar. Good doorstep dog walking. ETC ◆◆◆. [Pets £3 per night (includes donation to Dogs' Trust].
e-mail: all@watermillinn.co.uk website: www.watermillinn.co.uk

THE FAMOUS WILD BOAR (08458 504 604). Nestled in the beautiful Gilpin Valley, former coaching Inn set within its own private 72 acres of woodland. Excellent restaurant with local produce and real ales. Windermere Golf Club and Leisure Club nearby. [Pets £15.00 per night.]
e-mail: wildboar@elhmail.co.uk website: www.elh.co.uk

Hundreds of self-catering holiday homes in a variety of wonderful locations, all well equipped and managed by our caring staff. Pets welcome. Free leisure club membership. For brochure, contact: LAKELOVERS, BELMONT HOUSE, LAKE ROAD, BOWNESS-ON-WINDERMERE LA23 3BJ. (015394 88855; Fax: 015394 88857). ETC ★★★ - ★★★★★ [Pets £15.00 per week.]
e-mail: bookings@lakelovers.co.uk website: www.lakelovers.co.uk

LOW SPRINGWOOD HOTEL, THORNBARROW ROAD, WINDERMERE LA23 2DF (015394 46383). Millie and Lottie (Boxers) would like to welcome you to their peaceful Hotel in its own secluded gardens. Lovely views of Lakes and Fells. All rooms en suite with colour TV etc. Some four-posters. Brochure available. [🐕 pw!]

LANGDALE CHASE HOTEL, WINDERMERE LA23 1LW (015394 32201). Magnificent country house hotel with grounds sloping to the edge of Lake Windermere. Panoramic views, log fires, excellent food and friendly professional staff all ensure a memorable stay. [🐕]
e-mail: sales@langdalechase.co.uk website: www.langdalechase.co.uk

Symbols

🐕 Indicates that pets are welcome free of charge.

£ Indicates that a charge is made for pets: nightly or weekly.

pw! Shows some special provision for pets; exercise facility, feeding or accommodation arrangement.

⌂ Indicates separate pets accommodation.

Bring The Whole Family

Get off on the right foot whether you are a walker, climber potholer, sportsman . . . enjoy a relaxing holiday visiting the many country houses in the Derbyshire Dales and Peaks, one of the most beautiful settings in Britain

- **Choose from over 200 quality self catering properties**
- **Pets welcome in many**

Peak Cottages .com

....the friendly local service

0114 262 0777

Ashbourne

DOG & PARTRIDGE

· COUNTRY INN ·

AA ★★

English Tourism Council ★★ HOTEL

Swinscoe, Ashbourne DE6 2HS

Mary and Martin Stelfox welcome you to a family-run 17th century Inn and Motel set in five acres, five miles from Alton Towers and close to Dovedale and Ashbourne. We specialise in family breaks, and special diets and vegetarians are catered for. All rooms have private bathrooms, colour TV, direct-dial telephone, tea-making facilities and baby listening service. Ideal for touring Stoke Potteries, Derbyshire Dales and Staffordshire Moorlands. Open Christmas and New Year.

'Staffs Good Food Winners 2003/2004'.

Restaurant open all day, non-residents welcome

PETS REALLY WELCOME • special dog-friendly rooms, good walks in all directions, dog-walking service, dogs can join you for meals in the bar.

e-mail: info@dogandpartridge.co.uk • Tel: 01335 343183

www.dogandpartridge.co.uk

THROWLEY HALL FARM • ILAM, ASHBOURNE DE6 2BB (01538 308202/308243)

Self-catering accommodation in farmhouse for up to 12 and cottages for five and seven people (**ETC ★★★★**). Also Bed and Breakfast in farmhouse (**ETC ◆◆◆◆**). Central heating, en suite rooms. No Smoking. TV, tea/coffee facilities in rooms. Children and pets welcome. Near Alton Towers and stately homes.

THE DEVONSHIRE ARMS, PEAK FOREST, NEAR BUXTON SK17 8EJ (01298 23875) Situated in a village location in the heart of the Peak District. All rooms en suite with tea/coffee and colour TV. Meals served every day. Excellent walking area. ETC ◆◆◆ [🐕]
website: www.devarms.com

Peak District National Park

A green and unspoilt area at the southern end of the Pennines, covering 555 square miles.

WHEELDON TREES FARM, EARL STERNDALE, BUXTON SK17 0AA (Tel & Fax: 01298 83219). Sleep 2-6. 18th century barn conversion offers seven cosy self-catering holiday cottages. Laundry and games room. ETC ★★★★ [🐕]

BIGGIN HALL, PEAK PARK (01298 84451). Close Dove Dale. 17th century hall sympathetically restored. Bathrooms en suite, log fires, C/H comfort, warmth and quiet. Fresh home cooking. Beautiful uncrowded footpaths. Brochure on request. ETC ★★
website: www.bigginhall.co.uk

Note

All the information in this guide is given in good faith in the belief that it is correct. However, the publishers cannot guarantee the facts given in these pages, neither are they responsible for changes in ownership or facilities that may take place after the date of going to press. Readers should always satisfy themselves that the facilities they require are available and that the terms, if quoted, still apply.

PORT LIGHT
Hotel, Restaurant & Inn

As featured in Times, Guardian, Mail, Telegraph, Express, Dogs Today, Your Dog and many pet-friendly internet sites

- Luxury en suite rooms, easy access onto the gardens
- Close to secluded sandy cove (dogs permitted) 20 minutes' walk
- No charge for pets which are most welcome throughout the hotel
- Recognised for outstanding food and service
- Outstanding reputation for superb home-cooked fayre specialising in fresh sea food
- Set alongside the famous National Trust Salcombe to Hope Cove coastal walk
- Fully licensed bar - log burner - real ale
- Winner 2004 "Dogs Trust" Best Pet Hotel in England
- Large free car park ◆ Open Christmas & New Year ◆ Self-catering cottages

A totally unique location, set amidst acres of National Trust coastal countryside with panoramic views towards Cornwall, Dartmoor and France.

Important advice: always check to ensure other so-called 'pet-friendly' hotels really are! Talk to us to find out more.

Doggies' Heaven, Walkers' Paradise, Romantics' Dream

WE ARE REALLY, TOTALLY PET-FRIENDLY

Bolberry Down, Malborough, Near Salcombe, South Devon TQ7 3DY
e-mail: info@portlight.co.uk • website: www.portlight.co.uk
Tel: (01548) 561384 or (07970) 859992 • Sean & Hazel Hassall

❖ Bolberry Farm Cottages ❖

Bolberry, Near Salcombe, Devon TQ7 3DY

Luxury two and three bedroom barn conversion cottages
• Private gardens • Shared orchard • Views across valley • Gas, coal, open fires
• Parking • Finished to a very high standard • Linen and towels included
• Central heating • Close to coastal path and pet-friendly beaches • No charge for pets
• Dog wash • Short Breaks out of season • Discount on meals taken at our Hotel nearby – Port Light Hotel • Credit/Debit cards accepted

Tel: 01548 561384 • e-mail: info@bolberryfarmcottages.co.uk • www.bolberryfarmcottages.co.uk

Hazel & Sean Hassall • *The Pet Holiday Specialist* •

Recommended COTTAGES Low Prices

1st Choice

Selected cottages throughout Devon, Southern England, Cotswolds, East Anglia, Cornwall and Somerset

Pets Welcome • Low prices

free brochure 01751 475 547

recommended-cottages.co.uk

Farm & Cottage HOLIDAYS

holidaycottages.co.uk
01237 479698

freedom of choice

Enjoy the freedom and the beauty of this delightful corner of South West England with over 750 of the finest holiday cottages throughout Cornwall, Devon, Somerset and Dorset. All situated in superb coastal & rural locations. The perfect holiday is yours to choose!

• Log Cabins • Luxury Riverside Apartments • Fisherman's Cottages • Barn Conversions

Ashburton

ETC ★★★ - ★★★★

Mrs Angela Bell
Wooder Manor, Widecombe in the Moor, Near Ashburton TQ13 7TR
Tel & Fax: (01364) 621391
website: www.woodermanor.com
e-mail: angela@woodermanor.com

Cottages and converted coach house on 170-acre working family farm nestled in the picturesque valley of Widecombe, surrounded by unspoilt woodland moors and granite tors. Half-a-mile from village with post office, general stores, two good pubs (dogs welcome) and National Trust Information Centre. Excellent centre for touring Devon with a variety of places to visit and exploring Dartmoor by foot or on horseback. Accommodation is clean and well-equipped with colour TV, central heating, laundry room. Children welcome. Large gardens and courtyard for easy parking. Open all year, so take advantage of off-season reduced rates. Short Breaks available. Two properties suitable for disabled visitors. Colour Brochure.

Parkers Farm Cottages

Come and stay on a real 400-acre farm in South Devon

FARM COTTAGES • STATIC CARAVANS

Friendly, family-run self-catering complex with cottages and static caravans surrounded by beautiful countryside. 12 miles from the sea and close to Dartmoor National Park. Perfect for children and pets, with farm animals and plenty of space to roam. Large area to walk your dogs. Laundry, bar and restaurant. Good discounts for couples. A warm welcome awaits you.

How to find us from Exeter: Take A38 to Plymouth. When you see the sign "26 miles Plymouth", take the second left at Alston Cross signposted Woodland - Denbury. Continue past Parkers Farm Holiday Park, cottages on right hand side part way up hill

PETS WELCOME

British Farm Tourist Award, AA Four Pennants, 2006 Gold Award for Quality and Service, Silver David Bellamy Conservation Award, Practical Caravan 2004 Top 100 Parks, Rose Award 2005. ETC ★★★★

THE ROCKERY, CATON, ASHBURTON, DEVON TQ13 7LH • Tel: 01364 653008 • Fax: 01364 652915
e-mail: parkerscottages@btconnect.com • website: www.parkersfarm.co.uk

Parkers Farm Holiday Park

Come and stay on a real 400-acre farm in South Devon

STATIC CARAVANS • TOURING SITE

Friendly, family-run touring site and static caravans situated in unspoilt countryside. Two fully tiled modern shower blocks; electric hook-ups. Large dog walking areas with spectacular views across Dartmoor National Park; 12 miles to coast. Shop, bar and restaurant (main season), dogs welcome in Oak Room. Short Breaks available.

How to find us from Exeter: Take A38 to Plymouth. When you see the sign "26 miles Plymouth", take the second left at Alston Cross signposted Woodland - Denbury

British Farm Tourist Award, AA Four Pennants, 2006 Gold Award for Quality and Service, Silver David Bellamy Conservation Award, Practical Caravan 2007 Top 100 Parks, Rose Award 2005. ETC ★★★★

PETS WELCOME

HIGHER MEAD FARM, ASHBURTON, DEVON TQ13 7LJ

Tel: 01364 654869 • Fax: 01364 654004

e-mail: parkersfarm@btconnect.com • website: www.parkersfarm.co.uk

Ashwater, North Devon EX21 5DF

Tel: 01409 211224 • Fax: 01409 211634

BLAGDON MANOR
HOTEL & RESTAURANT

AA ★★

Liz and Steve, along with our two Chocolate Labradors, Nutmeg and Cassia, look forward to welcoming you to Blagdon Manor.

Restaurant: Enjoy excellent cuisine using locally sourced produce. Dinner available every night for residents.

Accommodation: 7 en suite bedrooms

Panoramic views of the Devon countryside and Dartmoor. Beautifully restored Grade II Listed building. Enjoy a peaceful location halfway between Dartmoor and Exmoor and only 20 minutes from the North Cornish coast at Bude.

3 acres of gardens and 17 acres of fields. Children over the age of 12 and dogs are welcome. Double/twin rooms £125.00 per night, based on two sharing. Single occupancy £85.00. Dogs £5.00 per night.

e-mail: stay@blagdon.com

www.blagdon.com

Lea Hill

MEMBURY, NEAR AXMINSTER EX13 7AQ

Tranquil location • Wonderful scenery • Close to World Heritage Coast. Eight acres of grounds and gardens • Comfortable self-catering cottages with own gardens. • Luxuriously appointed B&B rooms.

e-mail: reception@leahill.co.uk • www.leahill.co.uk • 01404 881881

Lilac Cottage

Smallridge, Axminster. Detached cottage, carefully renovated, retaining the inglenook fireplace, oak beams, floors and doors. Oil-fired central heating, colour TV, fully-equipped all-electric kitchen. Furnished to a high standard, sleeps six plus cot. Children and pets are welcome. Walled garden and garage. The villages and surrounding countryside are beautiful on the borders of Devon, Dorset, and Somerset. Many seaside towns within 10 miles – Lyme Regis, Charmouth and Seaton. Contact: **Mrs J.M. Stuart, 2 Sandford House, Kingsclere RG20 4PA • Tel & Fax: 01635 291942 • e-mail: joanna.sb@free.fr**

Lower Hearson Farm, Swimbridge, Barnstaple EX32 0QH

A former dairy farm set in 13 acres of gardens, field and woodland, perfect for a relaxing holiday. Our five holiday cottages are surrounded by two acres of gardens making this a safe place for children. 20 minutes from the coast and 5 miles from Barnstaple, Lower Hearson is an ideal base for exploring North Devon with lots of attractions for both children and adults within easy reach. Riding stables, fishing lakes and golf are all close at hand. Good base for the Exmoor National Park and the Tarka Trail. Within the grounds we have an outdoor covered, heated swimming pool, a children's play area, sandpit, trampoline and a games room. ***Well behaved dogs are welcome.***

Tel: 01271 830702 • www.hearsoncottagesdevon.co.uk

North Devon & Exmoor

Enjoy Exmoor's rugged natural beauty and spectacular coastline, together with Marwood Hill and RHS Rosemoor. This charming former rectory offers quiet comfort, long views and Aga-based cookery, all set in 8 acres. Ground floor rooms available. Well-behaved dog owners welcome. Also two-person self-catering cottage.

English Tourism Council ♦♦♦♦♦ GUEST ACCOMMODATION

Bracken House Hotel

Bratton Fleming EX31 4TG

Pets Welcome Free of Charge

Tel: 01598 710320 or visit www.brackenhousehotel.co.uk

Welcome to North Hill – deep in the rolling hills of Devon, a truly pastoral retreat.

17th century farm buildings, sympathetically converted into cottages sleeping 2-6, with exposed beams, wood stoves and central heating. Set in 9 acres of pastures and gardens with a children's play area. Facilities include: indoor heated swimming pool, sauna, all weather tennis court and games room.

This area of North Devon offers some of the finest beaches in the country and the National Park of Exmoor offers thousands of acres of moorland to explore.

Terms from £210 to £800

Carol Ann and Adrian Black, North Hill, Shirwell, Barnstaple EX31 4LG

Tel: 01271 850611 or 07005 850413 • Fax: 07005 850423 • Mobile: 07834 806434 • www.north-hill.co.uk

Please note

All the information in this book is given in good faith in the belief that it is correct. However, the publishers cannot guarantee the facts given in these pages, neither are they responsible for changes in policy, ownership or terms that may take place after the date of going to press. Readers should always satisfy themselves that the facilities they require are available and that the terms, if quoted, still apply.

YOUR PET STAYS FREE

ETC ★★★

Sandy Cove Hotel stands in 20 acres of cliff, coast and garden. The Hotel Restaurant overlooks the sea and cliffs with spectacular views of the bay. Mini-breaks are available as well as special weekly rates, all of which offer a five-course meal including seafood platters with lobster, smoked salmon and steak. Every Saturday there is a Swedish Smorgasbord and Carvery followed by dancing till late. All bedrooms have colour TV, telephone, teamaking and are en suite. There is an unique indoor swimming pool with rolling back sides to enjoy the sun, as well as a whirlpool, sauna, steam-room and fitness area with gym equipment.

Please return this advertisement to qualify for "Pets Stay Free" offer.
Children have free accommodation sharing parents' room.
Children under 5 years completely free, including meals.

You'll love the special atmosphere of Sandy Cove, why not find us on our website at www.sandycove-hotel.co.uk or ring to request a brochure

SANDY COVE
HOTEL

Combe Martin Bay,
Devon EX34 9SR
Tel: 01271 882243
01271 882888

Mead Barn Cottages
Welcombe, Devon

ETC ★★★Graded Quality Self-Catering Cottages.
Peace and tranquillity in stunning Devon countryside.
Choose from two, three or four bedrooms.
Comfortable, well equipped – home from home.
Robert & Lisa Ireton: **Tel: 01288 331 721**
E-mail: holidays@meadbarns.com
www.meadbarns.com

Waterside Cottage Bideford, Devon

Waterside Cottage is a pretty cottage right on the tidal River Torridge with glorious unrestricted views over the river and with moorings for a boat. Back garden wall is on the riverside, and from the garden and cottage you can watch boats coming or going, or fish. Enclosed garden with garden furniture.

• Two bedrooms • Private parking • Dog welcome • On the Coastal Path – ideal for walking.

SAE please for colour brochure with details of this and other seafront cottages to P.W. Barnes, 140 Bay View Road, Bideford EX39 1BJ or telephone 01237 473801 for prices and vacancies, or visit our website www.seabirdcottages.co.uk

The Pines at Eastleigh

A Georgian country house set in 7 hilltop acres with magnificent views over the Torridge estuary to Lundy Island. Log-fires, king-size beds, garden room bar with library, maps and a warm welcome await our guests.

Breakfasts use home produced and prize-winning locally sourced ingredients.

There are ground floor rooms set around the courtyard garden with easy access. All rooms are en suite and have teletext television, well-stocked hospitality tray with tea and coffee making facilities, telephones and hairdryers.

Selected by the AA as "One of Britain's Best in 2007."

Bed & Breakfast from £40.
Self-catering from £317 for 4. No Smoking.

www.thepinesateastleigh.co.uk
e-mail: pirrie@thepinesateastleigh.co.uk

Hotel & Cottages
Eastleigh, Near Bideford,
North Devon EX39 4PA
Tel: 01271 860561

AA ◆◆◆◆

Bigbury-on-Sea, near Kingsbridge, convenient for Salcombe and Dartmouth

8 berth mobile home on private site. Fully equipped including linen, gas and electricity. Peaceful, quiet, beautiful views. Area of outstanding beauty, also National Trust area which has to be seen to be believed. Excellent walks on fields, footpaths and sandy beaches. Five minutes to shop and Post Office. Dog-friendly pubs. Brochure on request. Prices from £245 per week. Reductions for 2 persons.

Holwell Farm, St Ann's Chapel, Bigbury-on-Sea, Near Kingsbridge TQ7 4HQ

MOUNT FOLLY FARM

Cliff top position, with outstanding views of Bigbury Bay. Spacious, self catering wing of farmhouse, attractively furnished. Farm adjoins golf course and River Avon. Lovely coastal walks, ideal centre for South Hams and Dartmoor. No smoking.

Always a warm welcome, pets too!

MRS J. TUCKER, BIGBURY-ON-SEA, KINGSBRIDGE TQ7 4AR (01548 810267).
e-mail: chris.cathy@goosemoose.com • www.bigburyholidays.co.uk ETC ★★★

Lake House Cottages and B&B
Lake Villa, Bradworthy, Devon EX22 7SQ

North Devon/Cornwall Border

Four cosy, well equipped, character cottages sleeping 2 to 5/6 in peaceful countryside. Large gardens and tennis court. Half-a-mile from village. Ideal for exploring coast and moors, Eden Project and Rosemoor. Also two en suite B&B rooms with balcony.

Brochure: Peter & Lesley Lewin on 01409 241962 • e-mail: info@lakevilla.co.uk • www.lakevilla.co.uk

A HAVEN OF PEACE AND TRANQUILLITY

at Little Comfort Farm, Braunton, North Devon ETC★★★

Five spacious self-catering cottages with secluded gardens on organic family farm. Just minutes from golden sandy beaches where dogs are allowed. Well stocked coarse fishing lake. Private 1½km walk. Wood fires for cosy winter breaks. Pets very welcome.

Tel: 01271 812 414 • info@littlecomfortfarm.co.uk • www.littlecomfortfarm.co.uk

Woodlands Guest House

Parkham Road, Brixham, South Devon TQ5 9BU

Overlooking the beautiful Brixham Harbour and Torbay - The English Riviera.

Dogs most welcome – free of charge • Your dogs sleep with you in your bedroom • Near dog-friendly parks and beaches • Bedrooms en suite • All bedrooms with colour TV, tea/coffee making facilities, mini-fridge etc. • Fantastic panoramic views over Brixham, Harbour, Marina, the Sea and Torbay • Ideal holiday base from which to explore Glorious South Devon • Car park within grounds and unrestricted on-road parking outside.

BED & 4-COURSE BREAKFAST WITH CHOICE OF MENU - EN SUITE ROOMS - ONE NIGHT FROM ONLY £23 TO £32 PER PERSON INCLUSIVE - REDUCTIONS FOR LONGER STAYS. PHONE 01803 852040 PAUL OR RITA POPE FOR FREE COLOUR BROCHURE.

e-mail: woodlandsbrixham@btinternet.com • www.dogfriendlyguesthouse.co.uk

Brixham
HOLIDAY PARK

English Tourism Council ★★★★ HOLIDAY PARK

Friendly, comfortable, family-run park offering all you could want from a holiday. Relax under the palm trees, laze by the superb indoor swimming pool, enjoy a drink or meal at the club.

Choose from apartments, chalets in a lawned setting, all fully furnished and equipped – pets welcome in many.

150 yards from beach • 10 minutes' walk from Brixham Harbour • Free Club membership with entertainment • Comfortable bar with meals and takeaway service • Shop and Launderette • Special off-season breaks

BROCHURE HOTLINE

01803 853324

wwww.brixhamholidaypark.co.uk

enquiries@brixhamholpk.fsnet.co.uk

An English Tourism Council Rose award park

Fishcombe Cove, Brixham, South Devon TQ5 8RB

British Holiday & Home Parks Association

FHG Guides

publish a large range of well-known accommodation guides.

We will be happy to send you details or you can use the order form at the back of this book.

FHG K·U·P·E·R·A·R·D

DEVONCOURT HOLIDAY FLATS

BERRYHEAD ROAD, BRIXHAM, DEVON TQ5 9AB

Devoncourt is a development of 24 self-contained flats, occupying one of the finest positions in Torbay, with unsurpassed views. At night the lights of Torbay are like a fairyland to be enjoyed from your very own balcony.

EACH FLAT HAS:

- Heating
- Sea Views over Torbay
- Private balcony
- Own front door
- Separate bathroom and toilet
- Separate bedroom
- Bed-settee in lounge
- Lounge sea views over Marina
- Kitchenette - all electric
- Private car park
- Opposite beach
- Colour television
- Overlooks lifeboat
- Short walk to town centre
- Double glazing
- Open all year
- Mini Breaks October to April

Tel: 01803 853748
(or 07050 853748 after office hours)
website: www.devoncourt.info

West Banbury Farm Cottages...where relaxation is a way of life

Come to West Banbury and you'll discover a rural haven where you can unwind and relax. We are in Broadwoodwidger, West Devon, ideally located for exploring Devon and Cornwall. We have ten charming cottages, all spacious and very comfortable, set around two courtyards with stunning views to Dartmoor. The cottages sleep 2 to 8 and dogs are welcome in all of them. We also have a large indoor pool, sauna, games room, children's play area, 9-hole pitch & putt and a grass tennis court. Roadford Lake is only 1 mile away. Short breaks are available.

For more information call **Amanda** on **01566 784946**

www.westbanbury.co.uk

SNAPDOWN FARM CARAVANS **Chittlehamholt, Umberleigh, North Devon EX37 9PF (01769) 540708**

6 ONLY – 6 berth CARAVANS with all facilities in beautiful, peaceful, unspoilt country setting - down our quiet lane, on the farm, lots of lovely places to visit nearby . Each with outside seats and picnic table. Field and woodland walks, abundant wildlife, help feed and milk the goats. Easy reach sea and moors. Well behaved pets welcome.£120 to £315 per caravan per week inc. gas and electricity in caravans. **Illustrated brochure available. (Discount for couples early/late season.)**

FREE or REDUCED RATE entry to Holiday Visits and Attractions
– see our READERS' OFFER VOUCHERS on pages 407-423

Bungalow set well back from the main road into town. One en suite double bedroom, use of large comfortable lounge. Good base for seeing Devon, plenty of places to walk dogs. B&B from £25 per person per night. Dogs welcome FREE of charge.

Tel: 01626 852172

S & G Harrison Crawford, Linden Lea, Parade, Chudleigh TQ13 0JG

Northcott Barton Farm Cottage

Beautifully equipped, spotlessly clean three bedroom cottage with large enclosed garden. A walker's and country lover's ideal: for a couple seeking peace and quiet or a family holiday. Very special rates for low season holidays, couples and short breaks. Near golf, riding, Tarka trail and R.H.S. Rosemoor. Character, comfort, beams, log fire, *"Perfick"*. Pets Welcome, no charge.

For availability please contact Sandra Gay,
Northcott Barton, Ashreigney, Chulmleigh, Devon EX18 7PR
Tel/Fax: 01769 520259
e-mail: sandra@northcottbarton.co.uk
web: www.northcottbarton.co.uk

Modern bungalow in the heart of Mid Devon. Spacious garden and patio. Comfortable accommodation with tea/coffee making facilities, with TV in bedroom and lounge. Bedrooms en suite or with private bathroom. Walking distance to the New Inn, Coleford. Dartmoor and Exmoor a short drive away. Children and pets welcome. Open all year. Ample parking. Smoking accepted. *Terms from £22pp B&B.*

Pearl Hockridge, The Oyster, Colebrooke, Crediton EX17 5JQ

Graded ★★★★

MANLEIGH HOLIDAY PARK

COMBE MARTIN EX34 0NS (01271 883353)

Quiet family-run site set in beautiful countryside near village, beaches, rocky coves and Exmoor. Chalets and caravans tastefully sited on side of Combe Martin valley. Swimming pool, children's play area, laundry. Dog walk. Wine Bar serving delicious home-made food.

Colour Brochure: Lynne & Craig Davey
www.manleighpark.co.uk

Watermouth Cove Cottages, Watermouth, near Combe Martin EX34 9SJ • Tel: 0870 241 3168

Beautiful cottages, most with four-poster and log fire, set in grounds of Watermouth Castle, 200 yards from the harbour/coastal path. Pets welcome all year.

e-mail: stay@coastalvalleyhideaways.co.uk • www.coastalvalleyhideaways.co.uk

FOREST GLADE Caravan & Camping Park

A small country estate surrounded by forest in which deer roam. Situated in an area of outstanding natural beauty.

Large, flat, sheltered camping/touring pitches Modern facilities building, luxury 2/6 berth full service holiday homes, also self contained flat for 2 persons. Forest walks with dog.

CULLOMPTON
DEVON
EX15 2DT

COLOUR BROCHURE ON REQUEST
Tel: (01404) 841381 (Evgs to 8pm)

Fax: (01404) 841593 • www.forest-glade.co.uk • email: enquiries@forest-glade.co.uk

Peaceful woodland setting next to the River Walkham in the Dartmoor National Park. Ideally placed to explore the beauty of Devon. Purpose - built lodges available all year round, sleeping 2-7, tastefully blending into the surroundings. Interior specification and furnishings to a high standard - including fully-fitted kitchen with oven, microwave and dishwasher.

• 3 golf courses a short drive away. • Easy walk to village and shops • Scenic walks. • Fishing • Dogs accepted • Horse riding nearby • Small, select touring area for caravans, tents and motor caravans • Launderette • On A386 Plymouth-Tavistock road.

For Free Brochure:

Dept PW, Dartmoor Country Holidays, Magpie Leisure Park, Horrabridge, Yelverton, Devon PL20 7RY. Tel:01822 852651 or visit our website: www.dartmoorcountryholidays.co.uk

DARTMOOR COUNTRY HOLIDAYS
MAGPIE LEISURE PARK

GET AWAY FROM IT ALL

Escape from life's pressures to relax and unwind in the comfort of:

The Cherrybrook Hotel

AA ♦♦♦♦ Guest Accommodation

Dartmoor Tourist Association Member

We are in the middle of the Dartmoor National Park, so while you are here, you can walk, cycle or ride on the open moor, and enjoy the breathtaking scenery, or use us as a base to explore this amazingly beautiful part of South West England. In the evenings, enjoy an aperitif in the bar, followed by our delicious, award-winning, home-made food.

And don't forget - your dog is welcome too!

For more information telephone Anne or Roy Daniels on 01822 880260

Cherrybrook Hotel, Two Bridges, Yelverton, Devon PL20 6SP

e-mail: info@cherrybrookhotel.co.uk • www.cherrybrookhotel.co.uk

TWO BRIDGES HOTEL

Two Bridges, Princetown, Dartmoor PL20 6SW • Tel: 01822 890581 • Fax: 01822 892306

Both Dartmoor and Two Bridges offer total escapism. To enter the Two Bridges is like stepping back in time. Sink back into the leather chairs around the blazing log fires, with the gleam of copper and brass. The well appointed Tors Restaurant serves the very finest West Country cuisine. For that extra special occasion treat yourself to one of our Premier bedrooms with four-poster bed and jacuzzi bath. A warm welcome awaits all our guests. **ETC/AA ★★**

www.warm-welcome-hotels.co.uk
e-mail: enquiries@warm-welcome-hotels.co.uk

Where else would your dog rather walk?

Walk straight from the hotel... for miles, then relax with our traditional country house hospitality, where dogs are genuinely welcomed. Indulge in our AA Rosetted restaurant with local produce and hearty breakfasts. Country pursuits such as fishing and riding, or golf, and garden or historic house visits are all within easy reach. Tranquillity abounds.
No charge for well-behaved dogs.

01822 890403

AA/VisitBritain ★★

Silver
SILVER AWARD

PRINCE HALL *Hotel*

Dartmoor, Devon PL20 6SA
e-mail: bosun@princehall.co.uk • www.princehall.co.uk

The Rosemont

Greenbank Terrace, Yelverton PL20 6DR
01822 852175 • e-mail: office@therosemont.co.uk • www.therosemont.co.uk

Large Victorian house overlooking the green at Yelverton, just yards from lovely open moorland. All rooms en suite, all with TV and tea/coffee making facilities. Good pubs and restaurants within village. Non-smoking throughout. Credit cards accepted. B&B from £28. ETC/AA ★★★★

LYDFORD HOUSE, LYDFORD, OKEHAMPTON, DARTMOOR EX20 4AU
TEL: 01822 820347; Fax: 01822 820539

Family-run Country House with a relaxed, friendly atmosphere, set within 8 acres of delightful grounds surrounded by the spectacular scenery of Dartmoor National Park,near to Lydford Gorge. Nine beautifully appointed spacious rooms plus self-catering. "La Cascata" in-house exclusive Italian restaurant, cycle hire, licensed tearooms, award-winning local restaurants. Pets welcome, your horse comes free.
e-mail: info@lydfordhouse.com • www.lydfordhouse.com

The Edgemoor Country House Hotel

Haytor Road, Lowerdown Cross, Bovey Tracey, Devon TQ13 9LE • 01626 832466

Charming RAC ★★★ Country House Hotel in peaceful wooded setting adjacent Dartmoor National Park. Many lovely walks close by. All rooms en suite. Excellent food. Dogs (with well-behaved owners) welcome. For more information, photographs, current menus and general information about the area see our website :
www.edgemoor.co.uk or e-mail: reservations@edgemoor.co.uk

Readers are requested to mention this guidebook when making enquiries about accommodation.

Watermill Cottages

Six stone cottages on the banks of a small river in a peaceful secluded valley a mile inland from Slapton Sands. Wonderful valley walks and freedom for children to explore. Close to dog friendly beaches, pubs and great coastal walks. Home cooking available, log fires and enclosed gardens. Winter breaks from £95.

Hansel, Dartmouth, South Devon TQ6 0LN
website: www.watermillcottages.co.uk

For our colour brochure call 01803 770 219 or e-mail: graham@hanselpg.freeserve.co.uk

Torcross Apartments

Situated directly on the beach in the unspoilt countryside of the South Hams between the blue waters of Start Bay and the Slapton Ley Nature Reserve. Seven miles to Dartmouth. Half-price breaks. Central heating. Ground floor apartments and lift to all floors. In-house bar and restaurant; private car park. Lovely walks on coastal path. New Beauty treatment salon including infrared sauna/steam room.

Brochure with pleasure or visit our **website** on **www.torcross.com**

Torcross, South Devon TQ7 2TQ Tel: 01548 580206 • Fax: 01548 580996
e-mail: enquiries@torcross.com

THE OLD BAKEHOUSE • Tel & Fax: 01803 834585

Mrs S.R. Ridalls, 7 Broadstone, Dartmouth TQ6 9NR

Character cottages with beams and old stone fireplaces, one with four-poster bed.
In conservation area, 2 minutes from historic town centre and river.
Blackpool Sands 15 minute drive. Free parking. Open all year. Autumn/Winter/Spring breaks

www.oldbakehousedartmouth.co.uk • e-mail: ridallsleisure@aol.com

Green Tourism SILVER

English Tourism Council ★★★ SELF CATERING

DARTSIDE *Holidays*

Apartments at Dartmouth, Devon

Comfortable holiday apartments with private balconies – superb river and harbour views. Sailing, boating, fishing, coastal walks within easy reach. Available all year round with colour TV, linen and parking.

Phone for FREE colour brochure

RIVERSIDE COURT, SOUTH EMBANKMENT, DARTMOUTH TQ6 9BH
Tel: 01803 832093 • Fax: 01803 835135 • www.dartsideholidays.com

Station Lodge, Doddiscombsleigh, Exeter

Comfortably furnished apartment In the beautiful Teign River valley. Excellent location for exploring Devon's moors, coasts and villages. Kitchen, lounge/diner, en suite bedroom with double bed. Private garden, extensive grounds. Pubs, shops and walks nearby, golf, fishing, horseriding, tennis and swimming pools within 10 miles. Central heating. Colour TV. All linen provided. Parking. Non-smokers only. Well behaved dogs welcome. From £180 per week. For further details contact:

Ian West, Station House, Doddiscombsleigh, Exeter EX6 7PW • Tel & Fax: 01647 253104
e-mail: enquiries@station-lodge.co.uk • www.station-lodge.co.uk

THE ROYAL OAK INN

Dunsford, Near Exeter EX6 7DA
Tel: 01647 252256

Enjoy a friendly welcome in our traditional Country Pub in the picturesque thatched village of Dunsford. Quiet en suite bedrooms are available in the tastefully converted cob barn. Ideal base for touring Dartmoor, Exeter and the coast, and the beautiful Teign Valley. Real Ale and home-made meals are served.

Well-behaved children and dogs are welcome

Regular dog Kizzy • Resident dog Connie

Please ring Mark or Judy Harrison for further details.

RYDON FARM

WOODBURY, EXETER EX5 1LB Tel & Fax: 01395 232341

16th Century Devon Longhouse on working dairy farm. Bedrooms with private or en suite bathrooms, hairdryers, tea/coffee facilities. Romantic 4-poster. Open all year. From £29 to £40.

AA ♦♦♦♦

Bussells Farm, Huxham, Exeter EX5 4EN • Lucy & Andy Hines • Tel 01392 841238

Set in the picturesque Exe Valley, seven luxury barn conversion cottages with access to thirty acres of farmland. Sleep 6/7. Excellent coarse fishing lakes (securely fenced). Outdoor heated swimming pool (May to September), adventure playground and indoor games room. Sandy beaches, Dartmoor and Exmoor within easy reach. 4 miles Exeter. Open all year. ETC ★★★★

e-mail bussellsfarm@aol.com • www.bussellsfarm.co.uk

THE LORD HALDON COUNTRY HOUSE HOTEL

THE LORD HALDON Privately Owned Country Hotel

The Lord Haldon Country House Hotel is the perfect venue for a quiet get-away break with your beloved pet. Acres of private grounds, mile of driveway for exercise and animals are welcome in guests' bedrooms by arrangement.The hotel stands in its own grounds, four miles south west of Exeter, set 400 feet above sea level in the Haldon Hills. The hotel is AA*** recognised with two Red Rosettes for its restaurant, which is open seven days a week. There is also an intimate Lounge Bar which serves bar food. For further information about how you can enjoy the finest part of Devon, please telephone for a free hotel brochure, or visit our website: **www.lordhaldonhotel.co.uk**

Dunchideock, Near Exeter
Devon EX6 7YF
Tel: 01392 832483
Fax: 01392 833765
e-mail: enquiries@lordhaldonhotel.co.uk

AA ★★★

THE SPIRIT OF EXMOOR Riding holidays for adults

Exhilarating riding across miles of untamed moorland in small groups. Fit, friendly, forward going, well schooled horses. Non-riders and own horses and pets welcome. Accommodation in secluded, comfortable, 17th century farmhouse or cosy en suite lodges. Delicious home-cooked cuisine; vegetarians welcome. Horse whispering courses. 70% repeat booking says it all.

Please phone Stephany Pettinger for a colour brochure or more information.

stephany@spiritofexmoor.fsnet.co.uk www.spiritofexmoor.com

Twitchen Farm

Comfort for country lovers in Exmoor National Park. All rooms en suite with TV. Meals prepared with local and some organic produce. Stabling £50 per week. Dogs no charge. B&B £26–£36, DB&B £46–£56 ETC ♦♦♦♦

Jaye Jones & Helen Asher, Twitchen Farm, Challacombe, Barnstaple EX31 4TT

Telephone 01598 763568 • e-mail: holidays@twitchen.co.uk • www.twitchen.co.uk

• WELCOMBE-IN •

Welcombe Cross, Hartland, Devon EX39 6HD

Telephone: 01288 331130; mobile: 07714 664547

Comfortable ground floor guest rooms. Pet-friendly, non-smoking. Great breakfasts, local produce, packed lunches, evening meals. Stunning coastal North Devon. Plenty to entertain everyone. **www.welcombe-in.co.uk**

THE FOREST INN

Hexworthy, Dartmoor PL20 6SD

A haven for walkers, riders, fishermen, canoeists or anyone just looking for an opportunity to enjoy the natural beauty of Dartmoor. We specialise in homemade food using local produce wherever possible. With the emphasis on Devon beers and ciders, you have the opportunity to quench your thirst after the efforts of the day with a drink at the bar or relaxing on the chesterfields in the lounge area, complete with log fire for winter evenings.

Tel: 01364 631211 • Fax: 01364 631515 • e-mail: info@theforestinn.co.uk

Tinney Waters

Coarse Fishing Holidays • Self Catering • Bed & Breakfast • No closed Season

Beautiful setting where you will be able to enjoy peace and tranquillity in the heart of rural Devon. Lots of non-fishing activities.

Telephone: 01409 271362 • www.tinneywaters.co.uk

HOPE BARTON BARNS

Tel: 01548 561393
www.hopebarton.co.uk

Open All Year

Nestling in its own valley close to the sandy cove, Hope Barton Barns is an exclusive group of 17 stone barns in two courtyards and 3 luxury apartments in the converted farmhouse. Heated indoor pool, sauna, gym, lounge bar, tennis court, trout lake and a children's play barn. We have 35 acres of pastures and streams with sheep, goats, pigs, chickens, ducks and rabbits. Superbly furnished and fully equipped, each cottage is unique, and vary from a studio to four bedrooms, sleeping 2 to 10. Farmhouse meals. Ample parking. Golf, sailing and coastal walking nearby. A perfect setting for family summer holidays, walking in Spring/Autumn or just a "get away from it all" break. Free-range children and well behaved dogs welcome. For full colour brochure please contact: ***Mrs & Mrs M. Pope.***

Hope Cove - Near Salcombe - South Devon - TQ7 3HT

Note

All the information in this guide is given in good faith in the belief that it is correct. However, the publishers cannot guarantee the facts given in these pages, neither are they responsible for changes in ownership or facilities that may take place after the date of going to press.

Readers should always satisfy themselves that the facilities they require are available and that the terms, if quoted, still apply.

LEAD YOUR MASTER AND MISTRESS TO HERE!

St Brannocks House

Hi! I'm Sam the daxi and my friends can come and stay here free. Look forward to seeing you. I've got:

- ★ Brilliant walks, Exmoor and beaches nearby
- ★ A lovely relaxing home which is open all year
- ★ A level walk to the nearby town shops & harbour
- ★ Great food, cosy Bar and comfy lounge
- ★ A mistress who likes us - and children too
- ★ A large dog-carriage park

enjoyEngland.com ★★ HOTEL

Phone or write to Barbara Clarke
St Brannocks Road, Ilfracombe EX34 8EQ
email: barbara@stbrannockshotel.co.uk
www.stbrannockshotel.co.uk

Tel/Fax: 01271 863873

The Foxhunters Inn **West Down, Near Ilfracombe EX34 8NU**

300 year-old coaching Inn conveniently situated for beaches and country walks. Serving good local food. En suite accommodation. Pets allowed in bar areas and beer garden, may stay in accommodation by prior arrangement. Water bowls provided.

Tel: 01271 863757 • Fax: 01271 879313 • www.foxhuntersinn.co.uk

Varley House, Chambercombe Park, Ilfracombe EX34 9QW

Tel: 01271 863927 • Fax: 01271 879299 • e-mail: info@varleyhouse.co.uk • www.varleyhouse.co.uk

Built at the turn of the 20th century for returning officers from the Boer War, Varley generates a feeling of warmth and relaxation, combined with an enviable position overlooking Hillsborough Nature Reserve. Winding paths lead to the Harbour and several secluded coves. Our attractive, spacious, fully en suite bedrooms all have colour TV, central heating, generous beverage tray, hairdryer and clock radio alarm. Superb food, beautiful surroundings and that special friendly atmosphere so essential to a relaxing holiday. Cosy separate bar. Car Park. Children over 5 years of age. Dogs by arrangement. B&B from £29 per person. Weekly from £182 per person. Dinner available. 4 courses £15.95, 2 courses £11.95. NON-SMOKING

beachdown

Relax in a setting so peaceful, you can actually hear the silence! Comfortable and unpretentious. Your pets more than welcome.

Comfortable, fully-equipped, detached cedarwood chalets, most with small enclosed garden for your pet. Car parking alongside. Just 150 yards away from the beach and the South West Coastal Path. We are situated within the beautiful South Hams area of South Devon. Just a 10 minute walk from Burgh Island. Open all year round.

• SHORT BREAKS AVAILABLE •

Call Nigel/Gareth for a brochure on 01548 810089 or visit our website for more details.

Challaborough Bay, Kingsbridge, South Devon TQ7 4JB • Tel: 01548 810089
e-mail: petswelcome@beachdown.co.uk • www.beachdown.co.uk

Please mention this advert when booking and your pets can come free of charge.

'So quiet and peaceful, Ben (our dog). loved the open space'

Perfect location for dogs and their owners.
Six stone cottages with gardens and country views.
Wildlife nature trail for 'walkies' on site.
Dog-friendly beaches and pubs nearby.
Woodburners and Spa Baths.
• Short Breaks off season • Open all Year

For more information, prices and availability, please visit our website:
www.dittiscombe.co.uk

Colour Brochure: tel 01548 521272
Dittiscombe Holiday Cottages, Slapton
Near Kingsbridge, South Devon TQ7 2QF

COLLACOTT FARM

Quality Country Cottages

Eight delightful country cottages sleeping 2-12 set around a large cobbled courtyard, amidst twenty acres of tranquil Devon countryside. All are well equipped with wood-burning stove, dishwashers, heating, bed linen, and their own individual patio and garden. A tennis court, heated swimming pool, games room, children's play area, trampoline room and BHS approved riding centre makes Collacott an ideal holiday for the whole family.

Collacott Farm, King's Nympton,
Umberleigh, North Devon EX37 9TP
Telephone: S.Molton 01769 572491
website: www.collacott.co.uk
e-mail: info@collacott.co.uk

British Horse Society
Approved Riding Establishment

Rudge Farm

House built in the 14th Century. Listed as of special historical and architectural interest. Set in beautiful grounds with pond, orchard and woods. Trout fishing and almost 200 acres to wander in. Much wildlife and perfect for watching buzzards and badgers. House very tastefully furnished and fully equipped. Will sleep up to 8. No charge for dogs, linen or fuel. David and Marion Mills look forward to meeting you. **Send for our brochure.**

LAPFORD • CREDITON • DEVON • EX17 6NG
TEL: 01363 83268

Lynmouth, Exmoor

Bath & Tors

Prices from £35.00 pppn

Bath Hotel AA ★★

Prices from £53.00 pppn

Tors Hotel AA ★★★

Off Season discounts available. Great views of harbour. Quality rooms and service. Ideal for moors. Pets Welcome.

01598 752238 www.torslynmouth.co.uk 01598 753236

Two apartments within a family-run guesthouse sleeping two or three persons.

Our ground floor apartment comprises double bedroom, lounge, kitchen and bathroom with own entrance and private courtyard garden.

The second apartment, on the first floor is larger with two bedrooms, shower room, lounge with screened kitchen and dining area, with views over the gardens and surrounding Exmoor countryside.

Set within the National Park the spectacular Southwest Coastal Path and Lynton and Lynmouth are within easy reach, all offering excellent walks for you and your dogs. All hotel amenities available on your return.

Moorlands

Where countryside and comfort combine

Woody Bay, Devon EX31 4RA
www.moorlandshotel.co.uk
Tel: 01598 763224

COUNTISBURY LODGE HOTEL

Countisbury Hill, Lynmouth EX35 6NB

www.countisburylodge.co.uk

AA ♦♦♦♦ Guest Accommodation

A former Victorian vicarage with magnificent views over the Lyn Valley and sea. Extremely quiet and peaceful yet within 5 minutes' walk of the picturesque village of Lynmouth. Licensed bar. All our bedrooms are centrally heated and en suite. Private parking. Pets welcome free of charge.

❖ **ALSO SELF CATERING COTTAGE AND APARTMENT AVAILABLE** ❖

Brochure/Tariff with pleasure from Pat & Paul Young (01598 752388)

Self-contained holiday accommodation at

LYNTON AND LYNMOUTH RAILWAY STATION

Ideal for four in two bedrooms (cot available). Sitting room. Bathroom and separate WC. Kitchen/dining room. Children and pets welcome. £150 to £220 per week.

W. PRYOR, STATION HOUSE, LYNTON, DEVON EX35 6LB • Tel: (01598) 752275 or 752381 • Fax: (01598) 752475

Jim and Susan Bingham,
New Mill Farm, Barbrook,
Lynton, North Devon EX35 6JR
Tel: (01598) 753341
e-mail: info@outovercott.co.uk

EXMOOR VALLEY

English Tourism Council ★★★★ SELF CATERING

Two delightful genuine modernised XVII Century Cottages by a stream on a 100-acre farm with "ABRS Approved" Riding Stables. Also a Bungalow with fenced garden and panoramic views of Exmoor. All have modernised kitchens, central heating, colour television and video, washing machine, tumble dryers, dishwasher and microwave. Linen available if required. Thoroughly inspected before arrival. Pets welcome at £15 each weekly. Safe for children and pets to play. Horse riding over Exmoor from our own A.B.R.S. Approved stables. Free fishing.

We offer weekend and midweek breaks throughout the year.

Please ask for a brochure.

www.outovercott.co.uk

Doone Valley Holidays

One visit is never enough

CLOUD FARM is set amidst the idyllic beauty and tranquillity of Exmoor's legendary valley, and offers year-round 'away from it all' holidays, weekend and short breaks unlike any other. Pets and horses welcome. **VisitBritain ★★★★**

Comfortable, cosy S/C cottages sleeping up to 8

- Camping - excellent facilities all on site
- Touring - perfect base to explore Exmoor
- Walking - valleys and moors on the doorstep
- Wildlife - a nature lovers' paradise
- Riding - all levels catered for
- Riverside recreation
- Shop and off-licence
- Tearoom and gardens

www.doonevalleyholidays.co.uk • www.doonevalleytrekking.co.uk

Colin & Jill Harman, Cloud Farm, Oare, Lynton, North Devon EX35 6NU
Tel: 01598 741234 • Fax: 01598 741154 • e-mail: doonevalleyholidays@hotmail.com

Situated on the South West Coastal Path with wonderful views, and delicious home cooking, the North Cliff is an ideal base for discovering Exmoor and the North Devon Coast. We welcome pets, children and groups.

Self-catering flat, sleeps 6, also available.

The North Cliff Hotel

North Walk, Lynton, North Devon EX35 6HJ
Tel: 01598 752357
e-mail: holidays@northcliffhotel.co.uk
www.northcliffhotel.co.uk

THE SMUGGLERS

Situated in the pretty village of Mortehoe, The Smugglers offers luxury accommodation from twin rooms to family suites. Treat yourselves and your pets to beautiful coastal walks and golden beaches, before you sample our delicious home-cooked meals, real ales and warm, year round hospitality.

The Smugglers Rest Inn, North Morte Road, Mortehoe, N. Devon EX34 7DR • Tel/Fax: 01271 870891
info@smugglersmortehoe.co.uk • www.smugglersmortehoe.co.uk

DOGS WELCOME FREE

Quality en suite accommodation in small, friendly hotel magnificently situated on cliff-side above secluded cove with spectacular sea views. Superb food, well-stocked licensed bar lounge. TV and tea-making facilities in all rooms. ***Please write or telephone for full details.***

Lundy House Hotel

Mortehoe, North Devon EX34 7DZ • Tel: 01271 870372
E-mail: info@lundyhousehotel.co.uk • Website: www.lundyhousehotel.co.uk

CRAB COTTAGE, NOSS MAYO, SOUTH DEVON www.crab-cottage.co.uk
• Charming fisherman's cottage, 50 yards from the quay on the River Yealm • Watch the boats on the river from the cottage gardens and window seats • Delightful, quiet village in an area of outstanding natural beauty • Fantastic walks, beaches and dog-friendly pubs on the doorstep • Walk across to village shops in Newton Ferrers at low tide • Close to the South Devon Coastal Path • Sleeps 5 Phone 01425 471372 for a brochure

• NORTHLAKE •

EXETER ROAD, OKEHAMPTON EX20 1QH

A warm welcome awaits at this friendly bed and breakfast with views across Dartmoor. Superbly sited for walking, cycling, riding and touring. Day kennelling available. **Tel: 01837 53100**
e-mail: pamjeffery@northlakedevon.co.uk www.northlakedevon.co.uk

Cat lovers' paradise in charming 16th century farmhouse set in lovely Otter Valley. Two acres of beautiful gardens with pond and stream. All rooms en suite, TV and Teasmaids. Pets welcome free of charge. Plenty of dog walking space. Brochure available. Terms from: B&B £25pppn.

FLUXTON FARM, Ottery St Mary, Devon EX11 1RJ
Tel: 01404 812818 • www.fluxtonfarm.co.uk

SOUTH DEVON • NEAR TORBAY

6 and 8 berth caravans new in 2007 and other 4 and 6 berths to let. All with toilets and showers. All with electricity, colour TV and fridges. Dogs on lead welcome.

Tourist Board graded park ★★★★.

Launderette, shop and payphone. Also separate area for tourers, motor caravans and tents with modern toilet/shower block with family rooms. Electric hook-ups and hard standings.

J. & E. BALL, Dept PW, Higher Well Farm Holiday Park
Stoke Gabriel, Totnes, S. Devon TQ9 6RN Tel: 01803 782289

AMBER HOUSE HOTEL

6 Roundham Road, Paignton, Devon TQ4 6EZ • Tel: 01803 558372

- Family-run Hotel. * Overlooks Goodrington Sands.
- All en suite. * Ground floor rooms. * Non-smoking.
- Good food; special diets catered for. * Large car park.
- Well-behaved dogs welcome. * Walkers welcome.
- Park and all year round dog-friendly beach 5 minutes' walk.
- We pride ourselves on our high standards.

Contact: **Christine Clark & Lloyd Hastie.**

e-mail: enquiries@amberhousehotel.co.uk
www.amberhousehotel.co.uk

Give your pets a holiday at
Churchwood Valley

Eleven times David Bellamy Gold Award Winner
Gold in Green Grading Scheme

Relax in one of our comfortable log cabins, set in a peaceful wooded valley near the beach. Wonderful walks in woods and along the coast. Abundance of birds and wildlife. Up to two pets per cabin.

Open April to January including special Christmas and New Year Breaks.

Wembury Bay, Near Plymouth

churchwoodvalley@btconnect.com
www.churchwoodvalley.com

Tel: 01752 862382

The Cranbourne

278/282 Citadel Road,
The Hoe, Plymouth PL1 2PZ
Tel: 01752 263858/661400/224646
Fax: 01752 263858

• Equidistant City Centre and Hoe Promenade • All bedrooms beautifully decorated, heated, with colour TV, tea/coffee facilities • $^3/_4$ mile Ferry Terminal • Keys for access at all times • Licensed Bar • Pets by prior arrangement (No charge) • Large secure car park

Under the personal supervision of The Williams Family

E-mail: cran.hotel@virgin.net • www.cranbournehotel.co.uk

PORT LIGHT Hotel, Restaurant & Inn

As featured in Times, Guardian, Mail, Telegraph, Express, Dogs Today, Your Dog and many pet-friendly internet sites

- Luxury en suite rooms, easy access onto the gardens • Close to secluded sandy cove (dogs permitted) 20 minutes' walk • No charge for pets which are most welcome throughout the hotel. • Outstanding reputation for superb home-cooked fayre specialising in fresh sea food • Set alongside the famous National Trust Salcombe to Hope Cove coastal walk • Fully licensed bar – log burner – real ale
- Winner 2004 "Dogs Trust" Best Pet Hotel in England • Large free car park
- Open Christmas & New Year • Self-catering cottages

Doggies' Heaven, Walkers' Paradise, Romantics' Dream
WE ARE REALLY, TOTALLY PET-FRIENDLY

Important advice: always check to ensure other so-called 'pet-friendly' hotels really are! Talk to us to find out more.

Bolberry Down, Malborough, Near Salcombe, South Devon TQ7 3DY
e-mail: info@portlight.co.uk • website: www.portlight.co.uk
Tel: (01548) 561384 or (07970) 859992 • Sean & Hazel Hassall

A totally unique location, set amidst acres of National Trust coastal countryside with panoramic views towards Cornwall, Dartmoor and France.

❖ Bolberry Farm Cottages ❖

Bolberry, Near Salcombe, Devon TQ7 3DY

Luxury two and three bedroom barn conversion cottages

- Private gardens • Shared orchard • Views across valley
- Gas, coal, open fires • Parking • Finished to a very high standard
- Linen and towels included • Central heating
- Close to coastal path and pet-friendly beaches • No charge for pets • Dog wash • Short Breaks out of season
- Discount on meals taken at our Hotel nearby – Port Light Hotel • Credit/Debit cards accepted

Tel: 01548 561384 • e-mail: info@bolberryfarmcottages.co.uk
www.bolberryfarmcottages.co.uk • Hazel & Sean Hassall

❖ The Pet Holiday Specialist ❖

★★★★★ SELF CATERING

Sand Pebbles

Hope Cove, near Salcombe and Kingsbridge.
Family-run guesthouse, 250 metres from delightful sandy beaches and coastal walks.
4 Star Guest Accommodation
Excellent comfort and service. Pets welcome!

T. 01548 56 16 73

www.sandpebbles.co.uk

★★★★ GUEST ACCOMMODATION

Axevale Caravan Park

Colyford Road, Seaton EX12 2DF • Tel: 0800 0688816

English Tourism Council ★★★★ HOLIDAY PARK

A quiet, family-run park with 68 modern and luxury caravans for hire. The park overlooks the delightful River Axe Valley, and is just a 10 minute walk from the town with its wonderfully long, award-winning beach. Children will love our extensive play area, with its sand pit, paddling pool, swings and slide. Laundry facilities are provided and there is a wide selection of goods on sale in the park shop which is open every day. All of our caravans have a shower, toilet, fridge and TV with digital channels. Also, with no clubhouse, a relaxing atmosphere is ensured. Prices from £80 per week; reductions for three or fewer persons early/late season.

www.axevale.co.uk

Boswell Farm

Boswell Farm, Sidford, EX10 0PP

ETC ★★★★

Tel: 01395 514162

Website: www.boswell-farm.co.uk

Email: dillon@boswell-farm.co.uk

17th Century Farmhouse with seven individual cottages, beautifully converted from period farm buildings, each with its own enclosed, flower-filled cottage garden.

Cradled in 45 acres of peaceful valley amid glorious Devon countryside. Abundant wildlife. Art Studio facilities in restored historical Victorian building with stunning views. All weather tennis court, trout pond. Idyllic walks in Area of Outstanding Natural Beauty, two miles from beach and World Heritage Coastline.

14th Century Inn and amenities within walking distance. Open all year. ETC ★★★★

ETC ★★★★

LEIGH FARM SELF-CATERING HOLIDAYS

WESTON, SIDMOUTH, DEVON EX10 0PH

Cottage & Bungalows 150 yards from National Trust Valley leading to Coastal Path and beach. Lovely cliff-top walks and level walks around nearby Donkey Sanctuary fields.

Contact: Geoff & Gill Davis • Tel: 01395 516065 • Fax: 01395 579582

e-mail: leigh.farm@virgin.net • www.streets-ahead.com/leighfarm

TAVISTOCK - EDGE OF DARTMOOR

Comfortably furnished studio cottage five miles from the market town of Tavistock. Ideal for two. Private walled garden. Pets welcome. Private parking, free coal for open fire. All linen provided. Wonderful walking, riding, fishing country with excellent local pubs. Terms £195 per week.

Higher Quither, Milton Abbot, Tavistock, Devon PL19 0PZ

Contact: Mrs P.G.C. Quinton • Tel: 01822 860284.

Cutaway Cottage • Thurlestone, Kingsbridge TQ7 3NF

Self-catering cottage within fenced garden in the middle of the village, on private road. • 5 minutes to pub and shop. • 20 minutes to beaches and sea • Ideal for children, dog walkers & bird watchers.

Phone Pat on 01548 560688

FHG Guides

publish a large range of well-known accommodation guides. We will be happy to send you details or you can use the order form at the back of this book.

FHG
K·U·P·E·R·A·R·D

Superior Quality Self-catering Accommodation

NEWHOUSE FARM COTTAGES

Eight beautifully converted, well equipped, Grade II Listed stone barns, with a choice of accommodation ranging from a one-bedroom cottage with four-poster bed through to our spacious five-bedroom barn sleeping 10.

Take a stroll through 23 acres of flower-filled meadows and woodland, or simply relax in our heated indoor swimming pool and games room.

For long or short breaks and more information, please call us on 01884 860266 or visit our website at www.newhousecottages.com

Newhouse Farm, Witheridge, Tiverton, Devon EX16 8QB

The Downs Hotel

A warm welcome awaits you from resident proprietor Stuart Lewton and family. Totally non-smoking. All rooms en suite with tea/coffee making, colour TV, telephone. Sea view and balcony rooms available. Excellent breakfast. Dogs welcome.

ETC ★★★ Babbacombe Downs Road, Torquay TQ1 3LN • Tel: 01803 328543

www.downshotel.co.uk • e-mail: manager@downshotel.co.uk

Red House Hotel and Maxton Lodge

The best of both worlds!...

- ★ *Indoor and Outdoor Swimming Pools* ★ *Spa Pool*
- ★ *Licensed Restaurant* ★ *Gym*
- ★ *Beauty Salon* ★ *Sauna*
- ★ *Launderette* ★ *Solarium*
- ★ *Indoor Recreation Room*

We've joined together the friendly service and facilities of the 2 star Red House Hotel for those wanting a traditional hotel atmosphere, with the privacy and freedom of Maxton Lodge's 24 self-contained holiday apartments. Two styles of accommodation sharing the same conveniently located grounds and superb range of facilities, so whether you're a working conference delegate or a fun loving family you'll find a style to suit you.

AA ★★

Red House Hotel, Rousdown Road, Chelston, Torquay TQ2 6PB
Tel: (01803) 607811
Fax: (01803) 605357
E-mail: Stay@redhouse-hotel.co.uk
Web: www.redhouse-hotel.co.uk

★★ HOTEL ★★★ SELF CATERING

Fuchsia Cottage • wing of 15th century farmhouse sleeping 4 + cot.

Beaches at Westward Ho! and Instow 20 minutes' drive. Dogs welcome.
Bed linen, towels, electricity & heating incl. Open all year.
Short Breaks October - May. No smoking. VisitBritain ★★★

Mr & Mrs Blake, Higher Hollamoor Farm, Frithelstock Stone, Torrington EX38 8LF • Tel: 01805 601330 • www.hollamoor.co.uk

SEA TROUT INN

Staverton, Near Totnes, Devon TQ9 6PA
Tel: 01803 762274 • Fax: 01803 762506
www.seatroutinn.com

AA — ★★ HOTEL

Hidden away in the tranquil Dart Valley, the inn dates back to to the 15th century, and until thirty or so years ago was known as the Church House. It has has two attractive bars with oak beams, log fires, brasses and prize specimens of fish in showcases. With an excellent selection of cask-conditioned ales and a wide range of wines, spirits and especially, malt whiskies, relaxation is easy. You can choose to dine in the attractive restaurant, or in the more informal lounge bars. Delightful bedrooms await the overnight guest; all have private bathroom, central heating, colour television, and direct-dial telephone. Permits for trout, sea trout and salmon fishing are available from the Inn, the unofficial headquarters of the Dart Angling Association. For a real taste of rural Devon in the heart of an Area of Outstanding Natural Beauty, the Sea Trout has it all!

❖ WEST PUSEHILL FARM COTTAGES ❖

Nestling within the Kenwith Valley, our cottages are set along the beautiful North Devon Coast.

◆ 10 cottages, converted from farm buildings built from traditional local stone in 1854. ◆ 40 ft heated outdoor pool set amongst secluded, sheltered lawns. ◆ Perfectly situated to explore coast and countryside. ◆ Many "award winning" attractions close by. ◆ Pets and children welcome. ◆ Resident proprietors. ◆ Open all year. ◆ Walks, Golf, Riding & Fishing nearby.

West Pusehill Farm, Westward Ho!, North Devon EX39 5AH
Tel: 01237 475638/474622 ◆ www.wpfcottages.co.uk

CHICHESTER HOUSE HOLIDAY APARTMENTS

Quiet, relaxing, fully furnished apartments. Opposite Barricane Shell Beach – central seafront position with outstanding sea and coastal views.

Watch the sun go down into the sea from your own balcony.

• Open all year • Free parking • Pets by arrangement.

SAE to resident proprietor, Joyce Bagnall.

Off-peak reductions. Short Break details on request.

The Esplanade, Woolacombe EX34 7DJ
Tel: 01271 870761

Sunnymeade • Tel: 01271 863668

• Friendly, comfortable Country Hotel • Lovely countryside views • Centrally placed close to Woolacombe's dog-friendly beach, Ilfracombe and Exmoor • Off-season special breaks • 4 ground floor bedrooms • Deaf accessible BSL signed • Award-winning home-cooked food • Pets welcome – dogs are free • Lots of lovely walks from the front door

www.sunnymeade.co.uk • Fax: 01271 866061

SUNNYMEADE COUNTRY HOTEL
DEAN CROSS, WEST DOWN, DEVON EX34 8NT

First floor flat overlooking Barricane beach where dogs permitted, (10 minute walk). Sea views, garden. Colour TV/video. Fridge/freezer, washer/dryer. Microwave. C.H. included early/late season. Open all year. Sleeps 5 + cot. Rates from £200-£500. Pets welcome. Resident proprietor.

MRS VIVIEN LAWRENCE, COVE COTTAGE, SHARP ROCK, MORTEHOE, WOOLACOMBE EX34 7EA • 01271 870403) • e-mail: vlawrence05@aol.com

English Tourism Council ★★ SELF CATERING

EUROPA PARK

Beach Road, Woolacombe
Devon EX34 7AN
Bookings: 01271 871425

Camping & Touring: beautiful landscaped camping and touring pitches, all overlooking Woolacombe Bay. Electric/All Service available.

Site Accommodation: Surf lodges, bungalows, static caravans and surf cabins. Sleep 4-9

Facilities: restaurant, clubhouse, indoor pool, sauna, launderette, shop. • Special Area for young people and large groups • Open all year • Early booking discounts.

e-mail: holidays@europapark.co.uk **www.europapark.co.uk**

PORT LIGHT, BOLBERRY DOWN, MALBOROUGH, NEAR SALCOMBE TQ7 3DY (01548 561384 or 07970 859992). A totally unique location set amidst acres of National Trust coastline. Luxury en suite rooms. Superb home-cooked fare, specialising in local seafood. Licensed bar. Pets welcome throughout the hotel. Short Breaks throughout the year. Self-catering cottages also available. Contact: Sean and Hazel Hassall. [ ]
e-mail: info@portlight.co.uk website: www.portlight.co.uk

TOAD HALL COTTAGES (01548 853089). Over 250 outstanding waterside and rural properties in truly beautiful locations in Devon, Cornwall and Exmoor. Call for our highly acclaimed brochure. Pets welcome.
e-mail: thc@toadhallcottages.com website: www.toadhallcottages.com

HELPFUL HOLIDAYS (01647 433535). Wonderful variety of cottages all over the West Country. Ideal for countryside rambles. Many welcome pets.
website: www.helpfulholidays.co.uk

HOLIDAY HOMES & COTTAGES S.W, 365A TORQUAY ROAD, PAIGNTON TQ3 2BT (01803 663650; Fax: 01803 664037). Hundreds of Self-Catering Holiday Cottages, Houses, Bungalows, Apartments, Chalets and Caravans in Devon and Cornwall. Please write or phone for free colour brochure.
e-mail: holcotts@aol.com website: www.swcottages.co.uk

MARSDENS COTTAGE HOLIDAYS, DEPT 14, 2 THE SQUARE, BRAUNTON EX33 2JB (01271 813777; Fax: 01271 813664). Over 300 Visit Britain inspected holiday cottages on North Devon's National Trust coastline and Exmoor. Pets welcome at over half our cottages at £15 per week. Online availability and booking.
e-mail: holidays@marsdens.co.uk website: www.marsdens.co.uk

NORTH DEVON HOLIDAY HOMES, 19 CROSS STREET, BARNSTAPLE EX31 1BD (01271 376322; Fax: 01271 346544). Free colour guide to the best value pet friendly cottages around Exmoor and Devon's National Trust Coast. [Pets £12 per week.]
e-mail: info@northdevonholidays.co.uk website: www.northdevonholidays.co.uk

RECOMMENDED COTTAGE HOLIDAYS. 1st choice for dream cottages at very competitive prices in all holiday regions of beautiful Britain. Pets welcome. All properties inspected. Free brochure - call 01751 475547.
website: www.recommended-cottages.co.uk

FARM & COTTAGE HOLIDAYS (01237 479698). Over 750 of the finest selection of holiday cottages throughout Devon, Cornwall, Dorset and Somerset in superb rural and coastal locations.
website: www.holidaycottages.co.uk

Ashburton

Delightful little town on southern fringe of Dartmoor. Centrally placed for touring and the Torbay resorts. Plymouth 24 miles, Exeter 20, Kingsbridge 20, Tavistock 20, Teignmouth 14, Torquay 14, Totnes 8, Newton Abbot 7.

MRS A. BELL, WOODER MANOR, WIDECOMBE IN THE MOOR, NEAR ASHBURTON TQ13 7TR (Tel & Fax: 01364 621391). Cottages nestled in picturesque valley. Surrounded by unspoilt woodland and moors. Clean and well equipped, colour TV, central heating, laundry room. Two properties suitable for disabled visitors. Colour brochure available. ETC ★★★ to ★★★★ [pw! £15 per week for first dog]
e-mail: angela@woodermanor.com website: www.woodermanor.com

PARKERS FARM COTTAGES, THE ROCKERY, CATON, ASHBURTON, NEWTON ABBOT TQ13 7LH (Tel: 01364 653008; Fax: 01364 652915). Farm Cottages and Static Caravans to let surrounded by beautiful countryside. Perfect for children and pets. Central for touring; 12 miles Torquay. ETC ★★★★, AA Four Pennants. [pw! Pets £17 per week]
e-mail: parkerscottages@btconnect.com website: www.parkersfarm.co.uk

PARKERS FARM HOLIDAY PARK, HIGHER MEAD FARM, ASHBURTON TQ13 7LJ (01364 654869; Fax: 01364 654004). Static caravans to let, also level touring site with two toilet/shower blocks and electric hook-ups. Central for touring; 12 miles Torquay. ETC ★★★★, AA Four Pennants. [pw! Pets £1.20 per night touring, £17 per week]
e-mail: parkersfarm@btconnect.com website: www.parkersfarm.co.uk

Ashwater

Village 6 miles south-east of Holsworthy.

BLAGDON MANOR HOTEL AND RESTAURANT, ASHWATER, NORTH DEVON EX21 5DF (01409 211224 Fax: 01409 211634) Beautifully restored Grade II Listed building in peaceful location 20 minutes from Bude. 7 en suite bedrooms, three-acre gardens. No children under 12 years. AA ★★, 2 Rosettes. [pw! Dogs £5 per night]
email: stay@blagdon.com website: www.blagdon.com

Axminster

Small friendly market town, full of old world charm, set in the beautiful Axe Valley. Excellent centre for touring Devon, Somerset and Dorset. 5 miles from coast.

LEA HILL, MEMBURY, NEAR AXMINSTER EX13 7AQ (01404 881881). Tranquil location. Wonderful scenery. Close to World Heritage Coast. Eight acres of grounds and gardens. Comfortable self-catering cottages with own garden. Luxuriously appointed B&B rooms. [pw! Pets £10.00 per week]
e-mail: reception@leahill.co.uk website: www.leahill.co.uk

LILAC COTTAGE. Detached cottage, furnished to a high standard, sleeps six plus cot. Children and pets are welcome. Walled garden and garage. On borders of Devon, Dorset, and Somerset; many seaside towns within 10 miles. Contact: MRS J.M. STUART, 2 SANDFORD HOUSE, KINGSCLERE RG20 4PA (Tel & Fax: 01635 291942)
e-mail: joanna.sb@free.fr

Barnstaple

Market town at head of River Taw estuary, 34 miles north west of Exeter.

LOWER HEARSON FARM, SWIMBRIDGE, BARNSTAPLE EX32 0QH (01271 830702). Five holiday cottages on former dairy farm, five miles from Barnstaple. Ideal base for exploring North Devon. Outdoor pool, children's play area. Well behaved dogs welcome. [Pets £15 per week].
website: www.hearsoncottagesdevon.co.uk

BRACKEN HOUSE HOTEL, BRATTON FLEMING EX31 4TG (01598 710320). Enjoy Exmoor's rugged natural beauty and spectacular coastline at this charming former rectory, Quiet comfort, long views and Aga-based cookery, all set in 8 acres. Ground floor rooms available. Well-behaved dog owners welcome. Also Self-catering cottage. ETC ◆◆◆◆◆. [🐕]
website: www.brackenhousehotel.co.uk

NORTH HILL COTTAGES, NORTH HILL, SHIRWELL, BARNSTAPLE EX31 4LG (01271 850611 OR 07005 850413; mobile: 07834 806434; Fax: 07005 850423). Sleep 2-6. 17th century farm buildings, sympathetically converted into cottages. Indoor heated swimming pool, sauna, all weather tennis court and games room. [Pets £20 per week]
website: www.north-hill.co.uk

Berrynarbor

This peaceful village overlooking the beautiful Sterridge valley has a 17th century pub and even older church, and is half-a-mile from the coast road between Combe Martin and Ilfracombe.

SANDY COVE HOTEL, BERRYNARBOR EX34 9SR (01271 882243 or 882888). Hotel set amidst acres of gardens and woods. Heated swimming pool. Children and pets welcome. A la carte restaurant. All rooms en suite with colour TV, tea-making. Free colour brochure on application. ETC ★★★ [🐕 one dog]
website: www.sandycove-hotel.co.uk

Bideford

Neat port village overlooking the beautiful Sterridge Valley has a 17th century pub and even older church, and is half-a-mile from the coast road between Combe Martin and Ilfracombe.

ROBERT & LISA IRETON, MEAD BARN COTTAGES, WELCOMBE, NEAR BIDEFORD EX39 6HQ (01288 331721). Peace and tranquillity in stunning Devon countryside. Comfortable, well equipped cottages. Choose from two, three or four bedrooms. Lots to do. Children and up to two dogs welcomed. [Pets £20 per week] ETC ★★★
e-mail: holidays@meadbarns.com website: www.meadbarns.com

WATERSIDE COTTAGE, BIDEFORD. Pretty cottage right on riverside with moorings for boat. Two bedrooms. Enclosed garden. Private parking. Dog welcome. For details of this and other seafront cottages contact P.W. BARNES, 140 BAY VIEW ROAD, BIDEFORD EX39 1BJ (01237 473801).
website: www.seabirdcottages.co.uk

THE PINES AT EASTLEIGH, NEAR BIDEFORD EX39 4PA (01271 860561). Luxury B&B and cottages. Log-fires, king-size beds, garden room bar with library, maps and a warm welcome await our guests. Children welcome. B&B from £40; Cottages from £317 for 4 persons. No smoking. AA ◆◆◆◆ [pw! 🐕]
e-mail: pirrie@thepinesateastleigh.co.uk website: www.thepinesateastleigh.co.uk

Bigbury-on-Sea

A scattered village overlooking superb coastal scenery and wide expanses of sand.

SOUTH DEVON, BIGBURY-ON-SEA. Kingsbridge, Salcombe and Dartmouth area. 8-berth mobile home on private site, fully equipped including linen, gas and electricity. Peaceful, quiet, beautiful views. Excellent walks. Five minutes to shop and Post Office. Dog-friendly pubs. Brochure on request. Terms £245, reductions for 2 persons. Contact MRS CAROL HEXT, HOLWELL FARM, ST ANN'S CHAPEL, BIGBURY-ON-SEA, NEAR KINGSBRIDGE TQ7 4HQ (01548 810251). [Pets £5 per night, £20 per week].

MRS J. TUCKER, MOUNT FOLLY FARM, BIGBURY-ON-SEA, KINGSBRIDGE TQ7 4AR (01548 810267). Cliff top position, with outstanding views of Bigbury Bay. Spacious, self-catering wing of farmhouse, attractively furnished. Farm adjoins golf course and River Avon. Lovely coastal walks, ideal centre for South Hams and Dartmoor. No smoking. Always a warm welcome, pets too! ETC ★★★.[pw! Pets £15 per week]
e-mail: chris.cathy@goosemoose.com website: www.bigburyholidays.co.uk

Dartmoor

365 square miles of National Park with spectacular unspoiled scenery, fringed by picturesque villages.

DARTMOOR COUNTRY HOLIDAYS, MAGPIE LEISURE PARK, DEPT PW, BEDFORD BRIDGE, HORRABRIDGE, YELVERTON PL20 7RY (01822 852651). Purpose-built pine lodges in peaceful woodland setting. Sleep 2-7. Furnished to very high standard (microwave, dishwasher etc). Easy walk to village and shops. Launderette. Dogs permitted. [🐕]
website: www.dartmoorcountryholidays.co.uk

CHERRYBROOK HOTEL, TWO BRIDGES, YELVERTON PL20 6SP (01822 880260). In the middle of Dartmoor National Park with seven comfortable en suite bedrooms. Award-winning, excellent quality, home-made food. See our website for details, tariff and sample menu. AA ◆◆◆◆ [🐕]
e-mail: info@cherrybrookhotel.co.uk website: www.cherrybrookhotel.co.uk

TWO BRIDGES HOTEL, TWO BRIDGES, DARTMOOR PL20 6SW (01822 890581; Fax: 01822 892306). Famous Olde World riverside Inn. Centre Dartmoor. Log fires, very comfortable, friendly, excellent food. Ideal walking, touring, fishing, riding, golf. Warning – Addictive. ETC/AA ★★[🐕]
e-mail: enquiries@warm-welcome-hotels.co.uk website: www.warm-welcome-hotels.co.uk

PRINCE HALL HOTEL, DARTMOOR PL20 6SA (01822 890403). Small, friendly, relaxed country house hotel with glorious views onto open moorland. Walks in all directions. Nine en suite bedrooms. Log fires. Gourmet cooking. Excellent wine list. Fishing, riding, golf nearby. Three-Day Break from £100pppn. AA/VisitBritain ★★, AA Rosette for food. [🐕]
e-mail: bosun@princehall.co.uk website: www.princehall.co.uk

THE ROSEMONT, GREENBANK TERRACE, YELVERTON PL20 6DR (01822 852175). Large Victorian house overlooking the green at Yelverton, just yards from lovely open moorland. All rooms en suite, all with TV and tea/coffee making facilities. Non-smoking throughout. B&B from £28 ETC/AA ★★★★[🐕]
e-mail: office@therosemont.co.uk website: www.therosemont.co.uk

STEVE AND LORY JENDEN, LYDFORD HOUSE, LYDFORD, OKEHAMPTON EX20 4AU (01822 820347; Fax: 01822 820539). Family-run Country House with a relaxed, friendly atmosphere, surrounded by the spectacular scenery of Dartmoor National Park, near to Lydford Gorge. Set within 8 acres of delightful grounds. Nine beautifully appointed spacious rooms plus self catering. "La Cascata" in-house exclusive Italian restaurant, cycle hire, licensed tearooms, award-winning local restaurants, ETC ◆◆◆◆ [pw! Pets £5 per night, horses free.]
e-mail: info@lydfordhouse.com website: www.lydfordhouse.com

THE EDGEMOOR COUNTRY HOUSE HOTEL, HAYTOR ROAD, LOWERDOWN CROSS, BOVEY TRACEY TQ13 9LE (01626 832466; Fax: 01626 834760). Country House Hotel in peaceful wooded setting adjacent Dartmoor National Park. Many lovely walks close by. All rooms en suite. Dogs welcome. See our website for further details. RAC ★★★, Rosettes for Excellent Food [pw! 🐕]
e-mail: reservations@edgemoor.co.uk website: www.edgemoor.co.uk

DEVONSHIRE INN, STICKLEPATH, OKEHAMPTON EX20 2NW (01837 840626). A real country pub! Out the back door past the water wheels, cross the river by ford or footbridge and up through the woods onto the north edge of Dartmoor proper. Dogs and horses always welcome, fed and watered. 1994 Winner National Beta Petfood Golden Bowl Competition for most dog-friendly pub!

Dartmouth

Historic port and resort on the estuary of the River Dart, with sandy coves and pleasure boat trips up the river. Car ferry to Kingswear.

PAM & GRAHAM SPITTLE, WATERMILL COTTAGES, HANSEL, DARTMOUTH TQ6 0LN (01803 770219). Sleep 3-6. Comfortable, well equipped old stone cottages in peaceful riverside setting. Wonderful walks in and around our idyllic valley near dog friendly Slapton Sands and coastal path. Wood fires. Winter breaks from £95. Brochure available. [Pets £15 per week]
e-mail: graham@hanselpg.freeserve.co.uk website: www.watermillcottages.co.uk

Readers are requested to mention this FHG publication when seeking accommodation

TORCROSS APARTMENTS, SLAPTON SANDS, TORCROSS VILLAGE, NEAR KINGSBRIDGE, SOUTH DEVON TQ7 2TQ (01548 580206; Fax: 01548 580996). Fully equipped self-catering apartments with lovely lake and sea views. Resident owners and spotlessly clean. New beauty treatment salon. Half-price Breaks. Private car park. [Pets £15 to £40 per week]
e-mail: enquiries@torcross.com website: www.torcross.com

MRS S.R. RIDALLS, THE OLD BAKEHOUSE, 7 BROADSTONE, DARTMOUTH TQ6 9NR (Tel & Fax: 01803 834585). Four cottages (one with four-poster bed). Sleep 2–6. Near river, shops, restaurants. Blackpool Sands 15 minutes' drive. TV, video, linen free. Open all year. Free parking. Green Tourism Silver Award. ETC ★★★ [🐕]
e-mail: ridallsleisure@aol.com website: www.oldbakehousedartmouth.co.uk

DARTSIDE HOLIDAYS, RIVERSIDE COURT, SOUTH EMBANKMENT, DARTMOUTH TQ6 9BH (01803 832093; Fax: 01803 835135). Comfortable holiday apartments with private balconies and superb river and harbour views. Available all year with colour TV, linen and parking. Free Colour Brochure on request. [Pets £30 per week.]
website: www.dartsideholidays.com

Doddiscombsleigh

Village 6 miles south west of Exeter.

STATION LODGE, DODDISCOMBSLEIGH, EXETER (Tel & Fax: 01647 253104). Comfortably furnished apartment for two people in beautiful Teign River valley. Excellent location for exploring Dartmoor. From £180 per week. For further details contact: IAN WEST, STATION HOUSE, DODDISCOMBSLEIGH, EXETER EX6 7PW. [pw! 🐕]
e-mail: enquiries@station-lodge.co.uk website: www.station-lodge.co.uk

Dunsford

Attractive village in upper Teign valley with Dartmoor to the west. Plymouth 35 miles, Okehampton 16, Newton Abbot 13, Crediton 9, Exeter 8.

ROYAL OAK INN, DUNSFORD, NEAR EXETER EX6 7DA (01647 252256). Welcome to our Victorian country inn with real ales and home-made food. All en suite rooms are in a 300-year-old converted barn. Well behaved children and dogs welcome. [🐕]

Exeter

Chief city of the South-West with a cathedral and university. Ample shopping, sports and leisure facilities.

MRS SALLY GLANVILL, RYDON FARM, WOODBURY, EXETER EX5 1LB (Tel & Fax: 01395 232341). 16th Century Devon Longhouse on working dairy farm. Bedrooms with private or en suite bathrooms, hairdryers, tea/coffee facilities. Romantic 4-poster. Open all year. From £29 to £40. ETC/AA ◆◆◆◆. [🐕]

LUCY & ANDY HINES, BUSSELLS FARM COTTAGES, BUSSELLS FARM, HUXHAM, EXETER EX5 4EN (01392 841238). Seven luxury barn conversion cottages, sleep 6/7. Coarse fishing lakes (securely fenced). Outdoor heated swimming pool (May to September), adventure playground and indoor games room. Open all year. ETC ★★★★ [🐕]
e-mail bussellsfarm@aol.com website: www.bussellsfarm.co.uk

THE LORD HALDON COUNTRY HOUSE HOTEL, DUNCHIDEOCK, NEAR EXETER EX6 7YF (01392 832483, Fax: 01392 833765). Extensive gardens amid miles of rolling Devon countryside. ETC ★★★, AA ★★★ and 2 Rosettes. [Pets £5 per night.]
e-mail: enquiries@lordhaldonhotel.co.uk website: www.lordhaldonhotel.co.uk

Symbols

🐕 Indicates that pets are welcome free of charge.
£ Indicates that a charge is made for pets: nightly or weekly.
pw! Shows some special provision for pets; exercise facility, feeding or accommodation arrangement.
⌂ Indicates separate pets accommodation.

Exmoor

265 square miles of unspoiled heather moorland with deep wooded valleys and rivers, ideal for a walking, pony trekking or fishing holiday

THE SPIRIT OF EXMOOR - RIDING HOLIDAYS FOR ADULTS (01598 753318). Accommodation in secluded, comfortable 17th century farmhouse or cosy en suite lodges. Delicious home-cooked cuisine, vegetarians welcome. Non-riders, own horses and pets welcome. Horse whispering courses. Telephone STEPHANY PETTINGER for colour brochure or more information.
e-mail: stephany@spiritofexmoor.fsnet.co.uk website: www.spiritofexmoor.com

JAYE JONES AND HELEN ASHER, TWITCHEN FARM, CHALLACOMBE, BARNSTAPLE EX31 4TT (01598 763568). Comfort for country lovers in Exmoor National Park. All rooms en suite with TV. Meals prepared with local and some organic produce. Stabling £50 per week. B&B £26–£36, DB&B £46–£56. ETC ◆◆◆◆ [🐕, ⌂]
e-mail: holidays@twitchen.co.uk website: www.twitchen.co.uk

Hartland

Village 4 miles west of Clovelly.

WELCOMBE-IN, WELCOMBE CROSS (A39), HARTLAND EX39 6HD (01288 331130; mobile: 07714 664547). Comfortable ground floor guest rooms. Pet-friendly, non-smoking. Great breakfasts, local produce, packed lunches, evening meals. Stunning coastal North Devon. Plenty to entertain everyone. Small charge for pets.
website: www.welcombe-in.co.uk

Hexworthy

Hamlet on Dartmoor 7 miles west of Ashburton.

THE FOREST INN, HEXWORTHY, DARTMOOR PL20 6SD (01364 631211; Fax: 01364 631515). A haven for walkers, riders, fishermen, canoeists or anyone just looking for an opportunity to enjoy the natural beauty of Dartmoor. Restaurant using local produce wherever possible; extensive range of snacks; Devon beers and ciders. ETC ★★★ [🐕]
e-mail: info@theforestinn.co.uk

Holsworthy

Town 9 miles east of Bude.

TINNEY WATERS, PYWORTHY. Self-catering. Three beautiful lakes - carp, tench, bream. No day tickets, no close season. Ideal for birdwatching. Contact: J. MASON (01409 271362).
e-mail: jeffmason@freenetname.co.uk website: www.tinneywaters.co.uk

TAMARSTONE FARM, PANCRASWEEK, HOLSWORTHY EX22 7JT (01288 381734). Peacefully situated by river-bordered meadows and woodlands on the Devon/Cornwall border. Three bedroom cottage sleeping seven, and basically equipped static caravan sleeping two adults and two children. [pw! Pets £15 per week]
e-mail: pets@tamarstone.co.uk website: www.tamarstone.co.uk

HEDLEY WOOD CARAVAN & CAMPING PARK, BRIDGERULE, (NR BUDE), HOLSWORTHY EX22 7ED (01288 381404). 16 acre woodland family-run site; children's adventure areas, bar, clubroom, shop, laundry, meals & all amenities. Static caravans for hire, Caravan Storage available. Dog walk nature trail. See main advertisement under Bude. [pw! 🐕]
website: www.hedleywood.co.uk

Hope Cove

Attractive fishing village, flat sandy beach and safe bathing. Fine views towards Rame Head; cliffs. Kingsbridge 6 miles.

HOPE BARTON BARNS, HOPE COVE, NEAR SALCOMBE TQ7 3HT (01548 561393). 17 stone barns in two courtyards and three luxury apartments in farmhouse. Farmhouse meals. Free range children and well behaved dogs welcome. For full colour brochure please contact: Mr & Mrs M. Pope. [pw! Pets £20 per week]
website: www.hopebarton.co.uk

Ilfracombe

This popular seaside resort clusters round a busy harbour. The surrounding area is ideal for coastal walks.

ST BRANNOCKS HOUSE, ST BRANNOCKS ROAD, ILFRACOMBE EX34 8EQ (Tel & Fax: 01271 863873). Lovely relaxing home with level walk to shops and harbour. Brilliant walks, Exmoor and beaches nearby. Great food, cosy bar, comfy lounge. Children and dogs welcome. Open all year. EnjoyEngland.com ★★ [🐕]
e-mail: barbara@stbrannockshotel.co.uk website: www.stbrannockshotel.co.uk

THE FOXHUNTERS INN, WEST DOWN, NEAR ILFRACOMBE EX34 8NU (01271 863757; Fax: 01271 879313). 300 year-old coaching Inn conveniently situated for beaches and country walks. En suite accommodation. Pets welcome by prior arrangement.
website: www.foxhuntersinn.co.uk

VARLEY HOUSE, CHAMBERCOMBE PARK, ILFRACOMBE EX34 9QW (01271 863927; Fax: 01271 879299). Relax with your dog, fabulous walks nearby. Fully en suite non-smoking rooms with lots of thoughtful extras. Superb food, beautiful surroundings. Bar. Car Park. Children welcome over five years. ETC ◆◆◆◆ AA ★★★★ Selected Award. [🐕] WE WANT YOU TO WANT TO RETURN.
e-mail: info@varleyhouse.co.uk website: www.varleyhouse.co.uk

WIDMOUTH FARM, NEAR ILFRACOMBE EX34 9RX (01271 863743). Comfortable, well equipped cottages in 35 acres of gardens, pasture, woodland and private beach. Wonderful scenery. Ideal for birdwatching, painting, sea fishing & golf. Dogs welcome. ETC ★★★. [pw! Pets £20 per week].
e-mail: holiday@widmouthfarmcottages.co.uk website: www.widmouthfarmcottages.co.uk

Instow

On estuaries of Taw and Torridge, very popular with boating enthusiasts. Barnstaple 6 miles, Bideford 3.

BEACH COTTAGE, INSTOW. Two seafront cottages with extensive beach and sea views. Sleep 5. Enclosed garden, own parking. Central heating, colour TV, coastal walks. Dog welcome. For colour brochure send SAE to Mrs P. I. BARNES, 140 BAY VIEW ROAD, NORTHAM, BIDEFORD EX39 1BJ (01237 473801). [Dog £10 per week]
website: www.seabirdcottages.co.uk

Kingsbridge

Pleasant town at head of picturesque Kingsbridge estuary. Centre for South Hams district with its lush scenery and quiet coves.

MRS B. KELLY, BLACKWELL PARK, LODDISWELL, KINGSBRIDGE TQ7 4EA (01548 821230). 17th century Farmhouse, five miles from Kingsbridge. Ideal centre for Dartmoor, Plymouth, Torbay, Dartmouth and many beaches. Some bedrooms en suite. Bed and Breakfast. Evening meal optional. Dogsitting. Pets welcome free of charge. [pw! 🐕]

BEACHDOWN, CHALLABOROUGH BAY, KINGSBRIDGE TQ7 4JB. Comfortable, fully-equipped chalets on private, level and secluded site in beautiful South Hams. 150 yards from beach and South West Coastal Path. Contact: NIGEL or GARETH (01548 810089). [pw! Pets £15.00 per week].
e-mail: petswelcome@beachdown.co.uk website: www.beachdown.co.uk

DITTISCOMBE HOLIDAY COTTAGES, SLAPTON, NEAR KINGSBRIDGE, SOUTH DEVON TQ7 2QF (01548 521272). Nature trail and 20 acres of open space. Perfect holiday location for dogs and owners. All cottages have gardens and and views of surrounding valley. ETC ★★★★. [Pets £16 per week]
e-mail: info@dittiscombe.co.uk website: www.dittiscombe.co.uk

HOLLOWCOMBE COTTAGE, START POINT, KINGSBRIDGE. Country cottage with secluded garden. One mile to beautiful Lannacombe and Mattiscombe beaches. Excellent coastal walks. Ideally situated to explore South Devon. Sleeps up to 12. JUDY FOSS, DOWN FARM, START POINT, KINGSBRIDGE TQ7 2NQ (01548 511234). [Pets £15 per week]
email: judy@downfarm.co.uk website: www.downfarm.co.uk

King's Nympton

3 miles north of Chulmleigh. Winner of CPRE Award for Devon Village of the year 1999.

COLLACOTT FARM, KING'S NYMPTON, UMBERLEIGH, NORTH DEVON EX37 9TP (01769 572491). Eight Country Cottages sleeping from 2 to 12 in rural area; lovely views, private patios and gardens. Well furnished and equipped. Heated pool, tennis court, BHS approved riding school. Laundry room. Open all year. [pw!, Pets £3 per night, £20 per week]
e-mail: info@collacott.co.uk website: www.collacott.co.uk

Lapford

Village 5 miles south east of Chumleigh.

DAVID & MARION MILLS, RUDGE FARM, LAPFORD, CREDITON EX17 6NG (01363 83268). Set in beautiful grounds with pond, orchard and woods. Trout fishing and almost 200 acres to wander in. House very tastefully furnished and fully equipped (sleeps 8). No charge for dogs, linen or fuel. Send for brochure. [🐕]

Lynmouth/Exmoor

Small resort with Harbour at foot of cliff below Lynton, on Lynmouth Bay.

BATH HOTEL, TORS HOTEL, LYNMOUTH, EXMOOR, NORTH DEVON EX35 6EL (01598 752238). Great views of harbour. Quality rooms and service. Ideal for moors. Pets welcome. Off-season discounts available. [🐕]
website: www.torslynmouth.co.uk

Lynton/Lynmouth

Picturesque twin villages joined by a unique cliff railway (vertical height 500 ft). Lynmouth has a quaint harbour and Lynton enjoys superb views over the rugged coastline.

MOORLANDS. Where countryside and comfort combine. Two self-contained apartments within a family-run guesthouse, within the Exmoor National Park. Hotel amenities available for guests' use. Contact: MR I. CORDEROY, MOORLANDS, WOODY BAY, PARRACOMBE, NEAR LYNTON, DEVON EX31 4RA (01598 763224). ETC ◆◆◆◆ [🐕]
website: www.moorlandshotel.co.uk

COUNTISBURY LODGE HOTEL, COUNTISBURY HILL, LYNMOUTH EX35 6NB (01598 752388). Former Victorian vicarage, peacefully secluded yet only 5 minutes to Lynmouth village. En suite rooms, central heating. Ideal for birdwatching and moors. Parking. Short Breaks. Also available S/C cottage and apartment. AA ◆◆◆◆ [🐕]
website: www.countisburylodge.co.uk

MRS W. PRYOR, STATION HOUSE, LYNTON EX35 6LB (01598 752275/752381; Fax: 01598 752475). Holiday accommodation situated in the former narrow gauge railway station closed in 1935, overlooking the West Lyn Valley. Centrally placed for Doone Valley and Exmoor. Parking available. £150 - £220 per week. [🐕]

JIM AND SUSAN BINGHAM, NEW MILL FARM, BARBROOK, LYNTON EX35 6JR (01598 753341). Exmoor Valley. Two delightful genuine modernised XVII century cottages by stream on 100-acre farm with A.B.R.S. Approved riding stables. Free fishing. ETC ★★★★. [pw! Pets £15 per week.]
e-mail: info@outovercott.co.uk website: www.outovercott.co.uk

FREE or REDUCED RATE entry to Holiday Visits and Attractions – see our READERS' OFFER VOUCHERS on pages 407-423

DOONE VALLEY HOLIDAYS. Comfortable self catering cottages sleeping up to 8. Perfect touring base to explore Exmoor. Camping facilities on-site. Riverside location, shop, off-licence, tearoom and gardens. Horse riding holidays with grazing and stabling. Contact: COLIN & JILL HARMAN, CLOUD FARM, OARE, LYNTON EX35 6NU (01598 741234; Fax: 01598 741154). VisitBritain ★★★★ [Pets £12 per week].
e-mail: doonevalleyholidays@hotmail.com website: www.doonevalleyholidays.co.uk www.doonevalleytrekking.co.uk

THE NORTH CLIFF HOTEL, NORTH WALK, LYNTON EX35 6HJ (01598 752357). On the South West Coastal Path, the North Cliff is an ideal base for discovering Exmoor and the North Devon Coast. Delicious home cooking. We welcome pets, children and groups. Self-catering flat, sleeps 6, also available. [Pets £3 per night].
e-mail: holidays@northcliffhotel.co.uk website: www.northcliffhotel.co.uk

Mortehoe

Adjoining Woolacombe with cliffs and wide sands. Interesting rock scenery beyond Morte Point. Barnstaple 15 miles.

THE SMUGGLERS REST INN, NORTH MORTE ROAD, MORTEHOE EX34 7DR (Tel & Fax: 01271 870891). In the pretty village of Mortehoe. The Smugglers offers luxury accommodation from twin rooms to family suites. En suite rooms, satellite TV, full English breakfast, licensed bar, beer garden, home-cooked meals. Well trained pets welcome. [Pets £5 per week].
e-mail: info@smugglersmortehoe.co.uk website: www.smugglersmortehoe.co.uk

LUNDY HOUSE HOTEL, MORTEHOE, NORTH DEVON EX34 7DZ (01271 870372). Quality en suite accommodation in small, friendly hotel. Superb food, licensed bar lounge, restaurant. TV & tea-making facilities in all rooms. Write or phone for full details. [🐕]
e-mail: info@lundyhousehotel.co.uk website: www.lundyhousehotel.co.uk

Noss Mayo

Village 3 miles south west of Yealmpton, on south side of creek running into River Yealm estuary, opposite Newton Ferrers.

CRAB COTTAGE, NOSS MAYO. Charming fisherman's cottage, 50 yards from the quay. Fantastic walks, beaches and dog-friendly pubs on the doorstep. Close to the South Devon Coastal Path. Sleeps 5. Phone 01425 471372 for a brochure. [£15 per pet, per week]
website: www.crab-cottage.co.uk

Okehampton

Market town on edge of Dartmoor.

MRS PAM JEFFERY, NORTHLAKE, EXETER ROAD, OKEHAMPTON EX20 1QH (01837 53100). A warm welcome awaits at this friendly bed and breakfast with views across Dartmoor. Superbly sited for walking, cycling, riding and touring. Day kennelling available. [🐕] [pw!]
e-mail: pamjeffery@northlakedevon.co.uk website: www.northlakedevon.co.uk

Ottery St Mary

Pleasant little town in East Devon, within easy reach of the sea. Many interesting little buildings including 11th century parish church. Birthplace of poet Coleridge.

MRS A. FORTH, FLUXTON FARM, OTTERY ST MARY EX11 1RJ (01404 812818). Charming 16th Century farmhouse. B&B from £25. Peace and quiet. Cat lovers' paradise. Masses of dog walks. AA ◆◆ [🐕 pw!]
website: www.fluxtonfarm.co.uk

Paignton

Popular family resort on Torbay with long, safe sandy beaches and small harbour. Exeter 25 miles, Newton Abbott 9, Torquay 3.

J. AND E. BALL, DEPARTMENT P.W., HIGHER WELL FARM HOLIDAY PARK, STOKE GABRIEL, TOTNES TQ9 6RN (01803 782289). Within 4 miles Torbay beaches and 1 mile of River Dart. Central for touring. Dogs on leads. Tourist Board Graded Park ★★★★. [pw! Pets £2 per night, £15 per week in statics, free in tents and tourers]

CHRISTINE CLARK & LLOYD HASTIE, AMBER HOUSE HOTEL, 6 ROUNDHAM ROAD, PAIGNTON TQ4 6EZ (01803 558372). Family-run hotel. All en suite; ground floor rooms. Good food. Highly recommended. Non-smoking. A warm welcome assured to pets and their families.
e-mail: enquiries@amberhousehotel.co.uk website: www.amberhousehotel.co.uk

Plymouth

Historic port and resort, impressively rebuilt after severe war damage. Large naval docks at Devonport. Beach of pebble and sand.

CHURCHWOOD VALLEY, WEMBURY BAY, NEAR PLYMOUTH PL9 0DZ (01752 862382). Relax in one of our comfortable log cabins, set in a peaceful wooded valley near the beach. Enjoy wonderful walks in woods and along the coast. Abundance of birds and wildlife. Up to two pets per cabin. [Pets £5 per week each]
e-mail: churchwoodvalley@btconnect.com website: www.churchwoodvalley.com

THE CRANBOURNE, 278/282 CITADEL ROAD, THE HOE, PLYMOUTH PL1 2PZ (01752 263858/ 661400/224646; Fax: 01752 263858). Convenient for Ferry Terminal and City Centre. All bedrooms with colour TV and tea/coffee. Licensed bar. Keys provided for access at all times. Under personal supervision. Pets by arrangement. AA/VisitBritain ★★★ [🐕]
e-mail: cran.hotel@virgin.net website: www.cranbournehotel.co.uk

Salcombe

Fishing and sailing centre in sheltered position. Fine beaches and coastal walks nearby.

PORT LIGHT, BOLBERRY DOWN, MALBOROUGH, NEAR SALCOMBE TQ7 3DY (01548 561384 or 07970 859992). A totally unique location set amidst acres of National Trust coastline. Luxury en suite rooms. Superb home-cooked fare, specialising in local seafood. Licensed bar. Pets welcome throughout the hotel. Short Breaks throughout the year. Contact: Sean and Hazel Hassall. [🐕]
e-mail: info@portlight.co.uk website: www.portlight.co.uk

BOLBERRY FARM COTTAGES, BOLBERRY, NEAR SALCOMBE, DEVON TQ7 3DY (01548 561384). HAZEL AND SEAN HASSALL. Luxury Barn conversion cottages. Private gardens. Close to coastal path and pet-friendly beaches. Dog wash. Short Breaks out of season. The Pets Holiday Specialist. ETC ★★★★★ [🐕]
e-mail: info@bolberryfarmcottages.co.uk website: www.bolberryfarmcottages.co.uk

SAND PEBBLES HOTEL, HOPE COVE, NEAR KINGSBRIDGE TQ7 3HF (01548 561673). Family-run guesthouse 250 metres from delightful sandy beaches and coastal walks. Relaxing breakfast restaurant. Excellent comfort and service. Pets welcome! VisitBritain ★★★★. [Pets £4 per night]
website: www.sandpebbles.co.uk

Seaton

Bright East Devon resort near Axe estuary. Shingle beach and chalk cliffs; good bathing, many lovely walks in vicinity. Exeter 23 miles, Sidmouth 11.

MILKBERE HOLIDAYS, 3 FORE STREET, SEATON EX12 2LE (01297 22925 – brochure/01297 20729 – bookings). Attractive self-catering Cottages, Bungalows, Apartments. Coast and Country on Devon/Dorset border. Free colour brochure. Pets welcome. Online availability and booking. VisitBritain Inspected. [Pets £20 per week].
e-mail: info@milkberehols.com website: www.milkberehols.com

Terms quoted in this publication may be subject to increase if rises in costs necessitate

AXEVALE CARAVAN PARK, COLYFORD ROAD, SEATON EX12 2DF (0800 0688816). A quiet, family-run park with 68 modern and luxury caravans for hire. Laundry facilities, park shop. All caravans have a shower, toilet, fridge and TV. Relaxing atmosphere. ETC ★★★★ [Pets £10 per week]
website: www.axevale.co.uk

Sidmouth

Sheltered resort, winner of many awards for its floral displays. Good sands at Jacob's Ladder beach.

BOSWELL FARM COTTAGES, SIDFORD, SIDMOUTH EX10 0PP (Tel: 01395 514162) 17th century farmhouse with seven individual cottages, beautifully converted from period farm buildings, each with its own enclosed, flower-filled cottage garden. Facilities available - art studio, tennis court and trout pond. Idyllic walks in Area of Outstanding Natural Beauty, two miles from beach and World Heritage coastline. ETC ★★★★ [pw! Pets £21 per week.]
e-mail: dillon@boswell-farm.co.uk website: www.boswell-farm.co.uk

LEIGH FARM SELF-CATERING HOLIDAYS, WESTON, SIDMOUTH EX10 0PH. Cottage & Bungalows 150 yards from National Trust Valley leading to Coastal Path and beach. Lovely cliff top walks and level walks around nearby Donkey Sanctuary fields. ETC ★★★★ Contact: Geoff & Gill Davis (01395 516065; Fax: 01395 579582). [pw! Pets £18 per week]
e-mail: leigh.farm@virgin.net website: www.streets-ahead.com/leighfarm

Tavistock

Birthplace of Sir Francis Drake and site of a fine ruined Benedictine Abbey. On edge of Dartmoor, 13 miles north of Plymouth

MRS P.G.C. QUINTON, HIGHER QUITHER, MILTON ABBOT, TAVISTOCK PL19 0PZ (01822 860284). Modern self-contained barn conversion. Own private garden. Terms from £195 inc. linen, coal and logs. Electricity metered. [pw!]

Thurlestone

Village resort above the cliffs to the north of Bolt Tail, 4 miles west of Kingsbridge.

CUTAWAY COTTAGE, THURLESTONE, KINGSBRIDGE TQ7 3NF. Self-catering cottage within a fenced garden in the middle of the village. Private road, 5 minutes to pub & shop, 20 minutes to beaches & sea, Ideal for children, dog walkers & bird watchers. Phone PAT on 01548 560688 [ ]

Tiverton

Market town on River Exe, 12 miles north of Exeter.

NEWHOUSE FARM COTTAGES, WITHERIDGE, TIVERTON EX16 8QB (01884 860266). Eight well equipped Grade II Listed stone barns, with accommodation ranging from a one bedroom cottage to a five bedroom barn. 23 acre grounds, heated indoor pool and games room.
website: www.newhousecottages.com

Torquay

Popular resort on the English Riviera with a wide range of attractions and entertainments. Yachting and watersports centre with 10 superb beaches and coves.

THE DOWNS HOTEL, BABBACOMBE DOWNS ROAD, TORQUAY TQ1 3LN (01803 328543). A warm welcome awaits you from resident proprietor Stuart Lewton and family. Totally non-smoking. All rooms en suite with tea/coffee making, colour TV, telephone. Sea view and balcony rooms available. ETC ★★★ [Pets £5 per night].
e-mail: manager@downshotel.co.uk website: www.downshotel.co.uk

RED HOUSE HOTEL AND MAXTON LODGE HOLIDAY APARTMENTS, ROUSDOWN ROAD, CHELSTON, TORQUAY TQ2 6PB (01803 607811; Fax: 01803 605357). Choose either the friendly service and facilities of a hotel or the privacy and freedom of self-catering apartments. The best of both worlds! AA/ETC ★★ Hotel & ★★★ Self-catering. [in flats; £3 per night in hotel]
e-mail: stay@redhouse-hotel.co.uk website: www.redhouse-hotel.co.uk

Torrington

Pleasant market town on River Torridge. Good centre for moors and sea. Exeter 36 miles, Okehampton 20, Barnstaple 12, Bideford 7.

Wing of 15th century farmhouse sleeping 4 + cot. Beaches 20 minutes' drive. Well-behaved dogs welcome. Bed linen, towels, fuel and heating incl. Open all year. Short Breaks. No smoking. VisitBritain ★★★ MR & MRS BLAKE, HIGHER HOLLAMOOR FARM, FRITHELSTOCK STONE, TORRINGTON EX38 8LF (01805 601330). [Pets £15 per week].
website: www.hollamoor.co.uk

RICH AND DIANA JONES, STOWFORD LODGE, LANGTREE, GREAT TORRINGTON EX38 8NU (01805 601540). Sleep 4/6. Picturesque and peaceful. Four delightful cottages set within 6 acres of private land with heated indoor pool. Magnificent countryside. Convenient North Devon coast and moors. Phone for brochure. VisitBritain ★★★ [Pets £15 per week, pw!]
e-mail: enq@stowfordlodge.co.uk website: www.stowfordlodge.co.uk

Totnes

Town at tidal estuary of River Dart, 7 miles west of Torquay

SEA TROUT INN, STAVERTON, NEAR TOTNES TQ9 6PA (01803 762274; Fax: 01803 762506). Hidden away in the tranquil Dart Valley but conveniently placed for Dartmoor, Torbay and the South Devon coast. Delightful cottage- style bedrooms, two traditional English bars and elegant restaurant. ETC ★★
website: www.seatroutinn.com

Westward Ho!

An excellent resort with 3 miles of golden sands, amusements, pubs, clubs and restaurants. 2 miles north west of Bideford.

WEST PUSEHILL FARM COTTAGES, WEST PUSEHILL FARM, WESTWARD HO!, NORTH DEVON EX39 5AH (01237 475638/474622). Nestling within the Kenwith Valley, 10 cottages with heated outdoor pool. Perfectly situated to explore coast and countryside. Many attractions close by. Pets and children welcome. Open all year. [Pets £20 per week].
website: www.wpfcottages.co.uk

Witheridge

Unspoilt farming village situated on Two Moors Way. South Molton 10 miles, Tiverton and Dulverton 12 miles.

MAGGIES COTTAGE. On Two Moors Way between Dartmoor and Exmoor, easy driving distance Devon beaches. Two bedrooms, lounge with exposed beams, inglenook; new kitchen; bath and electric shower. Available all year. Contact: MRS PEGLER (00 351 251 648107). [Pets £20 per week].
e-mail: magsinmoncao@hotmail.com website: www.maggiescottage.co.uk

Woolacombe

Favourite resort with long, wide stretches of sand. Barnstaple 15 miles, Ilfracombe 6.

MRS JOYCE BAGNALL, CHICHESTER HOUSE, THE ESPLANADE, WOOLACOMBE EX34 7DJ (01271 870761). Holiday apartments on sea front. Fully furnished, sea and coastal views. Watch the sun go down from your balcony. Open all year. SAE Resident Proprietor. [Pets £12 per week, pw!]

SUNNYMEADE COUNTRY HOTEL, WEST DOWN, NEAR WOOLACOMBE EX34 8NT (01271 863668; Fax: 01271 866061). Small country hotel set in beautiful countryside. A few minutes away from Ilfracombe, Exmoor and Woolacombe's Blue Flag Beach. 10 en suite rooms, 4 on the ground floor. Deaf accessible. Pets welcome – dogs are free. [🐕 pw!]
website: www.sunnymeade.co.uk

MRS VIVIEN LAWRENCE, COVE COTTAGE, SHARP ROCK, MORTEHOE, WOOLACOMBE EX34 7EA (01271 870403). First floor flat overlooking Barricane beach where dogs permitted, (10 minute walk) Sea views, garden. Well equipped. C.H. included early/late season. Open all year. Sleeps 5 + cot. Resident proprietor. Terms £200-£500. ETC ★★ [Pets £1 per night].
e-mail: vlawrence05@aol.com

EUROPA PARK, BEACH ROAD, WOOLACOMBE (01271 871425). Static caravans, chalets, camping, surf lodges and surf cabins. Full facilities. Pets welcome. Indoor heated swimming pool, sauna, 24-hour shop. AA *THREE PENNANTS.*
e-mail: holidays@europapark.co.uk website: www.europapark.co.uk

Yelverton

Small town on western edge of Dartmoor, Tavistock 5 miles..

BROOK TOR, SAMPFORD SPINEY, YELVERTON PL20 7QX (01822 853668). Everything a dog could wish for plus peaceful and relaxing bed and breakfast for you. Wonderful moorland walks near to historic Tavistock, Plymouth and Cornwall. Contact: BRIAN AND ROSIE KEHOE. [🐕]

Dorset Coastal Cottages

www.dorsetcoastalcottages.com

Tel: 0800 9804070

Carefully selected, traditional cottages in or near villages within ten miles of Dorset's spectacular World Heritage Coast. Many are thatched and have open fires or logburners.

Over half of our cottages welcome dogs.

Full weeks or Short Breaks all year round.

Rents include linen/towels and electricity/gas etc.

Blandford, Bournemouth

THE ANVIL INN

Salisbury Road, Pimperne, Blandford, Dorset DT11 8UQ

Tel: 01258 453431/480182

A long, low thatched building set in a tiny village deep in the Dorset countryside – what could be more English? This typical Old English hostelry offering good old-fashioned English hospitality, a full à la carte menu with mouthwatering desserts in the charming beamed restaurant with log fire,together with specials of the day and light bites menu in the two bars. All bedrooms with private facilities. Ample parking. **From £65 single, £90 double/twin.**

e-mail: theanvil.inn@btconnect.com

website: www.anvilhotel.co.uk

BOURNEMOUTH HOLIDAY APARTMENTS

16 Florence Road, Bournemouth BH5 1HF • Tel: 01202 304925

Modern well-equipped flats close to sea and shops. Sleep up to ten persons. Car parking. Children and pets welcome. Phone for brochure or e-mail.

website: www.selfcateringbournemouth.co.uk

Langtry Manor

The Country House Hotel in Bournemouth

Built by Edward VII as a Lovenest for Lillie Langtry. A rare gem of a hotel where the building, food, service and history blend to form something quite exceptional. Four posters, Jacuzzi's, complimentary leisure club and award-winning restaurant. Midweek and weekend breaks. As featured on BBC Holiday Show. Pets welcome by arrangement.

"Best Hotel in Bournemouth" - The Guardian

Derby Road, East Cliff, Bournemouth BH1 3QB

Tel: (01202) 553887 www.langtrymanor.com

FREE or REDUCED RATE entry to Holiday Visits and Attractions

– see our READERS' OFFER VOUCHERS on pages 407-423

Guests enjoying the lounge

THE *REALLY* DOG-FRIENDLY PLACE
WHITE TOPPS

Small, friendly and catering only for guests with dogs. In a nice quiet position close to lovely walks on the beach (dogs allowed) and Hengistbury Head. Plus the New Forest isn't far away. There's no charge for pets, of course and the proprietor, MARJORIE TITCHEN, just loves dogs.

- DOG(S) ESSENTIAL - ANY SIZE, ANY NUMBER, ANYWHERE
- GROUND FLOOR ROOM FOR ELDERLY DOGS
- ADULTS ONLY (14yrs +)
- GENEROUS HOME COOKING
- VEGETARIANS WELCOME
- NOT SUITABLE FOR DISABLED
- CAR PARKING

WRITE (SAE APPRECIATED) OR PHONE FOR FACT SHEET.

WHITE TOPPS, 45 CHURCH ROAD, SOUTHBOURNE, BOURNEMOUTH, DORSET BH6 4BB
TEL: 01202 428868

e-mail: thedoghotel@aol.com • www.whitetopps.co.uk
IF YOU DON'T LOVE DOGS YOU WON'T LIKE WHITE TOPPS

Alum Dene Hotel

2 Burnaby Road, Alum Chine, Bournemouth BH4 8JF Tel: 01202 764011

Renowned for good old fashioned hospitality and friendly service. Come and be spoilt at our licensed hotel. All rooms en suite, colour TV. Some have sea views. 200 metres sea. Parking. Christmas House party. No charge for pets.

Southbourne Grove Hotel,

96 Southbourne Road, Southbourne, Bournemouth BH6 3QQ Tel: 01202 420503; Fax: 01202 421953

Friendly, family-run hotel with beautiful garden and ample guest parking. Close to beach and shops. Excellent food served in spacious restaurant. En suites, four-poster suite, ground floor rooms (one suitable for partially disabled) and large family bedrooms - all with colour TV and tea/coffee making facilities. Senior Citizen and Child discounts. Dogs welcome free of charge. B&B from £22 per night, from £122 per week.

HOLIDAY FLATS AND FLATLETS 07788 952394

• A SHORT WALK TO GOLDEN SANDY BEACHES • MOST WITH PRIVATE BATHROOMS • CLEANLINESS AND COMFORT ASSURED • LAUNDRY ROOM • FREE PRIVATE PARKING • DOGS WELCOME • COLOUR TV IN ALL UNITS • NO VAT CHARGED •

CONTACT: M. DE KMENT, 4 CECIL ROAD, BOURNEMOUTH BH5 1DU

THE VINE HOTEL

22 Southern Road, Southbourne
Bournemouth BH6 3SR
Telephone: 01202 428309 •www.vinehotel.co.uk

A small, family, award-winning non smoking Hotel only three hundred yards from dog-friendly beach and shops. All rooms en suite; tea/coffee making facilities and colour TV. Residential licence with attractive bar. Full central heating. Forecourt parking. Open all year.

Pets Welcome – Free of Charge. FHG Diploma South West Tourism ◆◆◆

FROGMORE FARM
CHIDEOCK, BRIDPORT DT6 6HT

Enjoy Bed and Breakfast on a 90-acre grazing farm set in beautiful West Dorset, overlooking Lyme Bay. En suite shower rooms available. Cosy TV lounge with wood fire; guests' dining room, tea making facilities. Children and dogs welcome. OR CHOOSE our lovely self catering Cottage, sleeps 5. Fully equipped, bed linen supplied; lounge with woodburner and colour TV. Car essential. Open all year. Brochure and terms free on request.

Apply Mrs S. Norman • Tel: 01308 456159

'DOG DAYS IN DORSET' • DOGS ARE MOST WELCOME AND COME FREE

Wonderful tail-wagging walks from a peaceful small holiday bungalow park (one & two bedrooms). Just a short stroll from the beach on the beautiful Jurassic coast. Our guests may bring more than one dog. For **SHORT BREAKS** and **WEEKLY SUMMER HOLIDAYS**

Telephone today for Information Pack and Prices 01308 421 521
Golden Acre Holiday Bungalows, Eype, Bridport, Dorset DT6 6AL • www.golden-acre.com

✦ EYPE HOUSE CARAVAN & CAMPING PARK ✦

Small, quiet family-run park lying on the Heritage Coastal Path, 200 yards from the beach.

Static vans for hire from £190 to £430, tent pitches (all terraced with sea views) £10 to £17 for four people. Sorry, no touring caravans. **Children and dogs welcome.**

Eype, Bridport DT6 6AL • web: www.eypehouse.co.uk • Tel: 01308 424903

Lancombes House ~ Holiday Cottages

ETC ★★★

Four superbly converted cottages, each with its own sitting-out area, barbecue and garden furniture. Some have fenced gardens. Spacious open plan living areas, most with wood burning stoves. Deep in the heart of Hardy country, this is a delightful area to explore whether on foot or horseback. There are many things to do and pets and children are very welcome. Prices start at £120 for mini-breaks; open all the year round.

Lancombes House, West Milton, Bridport DT6 3TN
Tel: 01308 485375 • website: www.lancombes-house.co.uk

Tamarisk Farm Beach Road, West Bexington, Dorchester DT2 9DF

On slope overlooking Chesil beach, four large (**Mimosa is for wheelchair disabled Cat 1, M3; Granary Lodge is disabled-friendly, M1**) and two small COTTAGES (ETC 3/4 Stars), each standing in own fenced garden. Sleep 4/7. Part of organic farm with arable, sheep, cattle, horses, market garden (organic vegetables, meat and wholemeal flour available) and conservation. Good centre for touring, sightseeing, glorious walks by the sea and inland. Lovely place for dogs. Very quiet. Sea views. Terms from £250-£995.

Mrs Josephine Pearse • Tel: 01308 897784 * e-mail: holidays@tamariskfarm.com • www.tamariskfarm.com

MANOR FARM HOLIDAY CENTRE

Charmouth, Bridport, Dorset DT6 6QL (01297) 560226

Two and three bedroomed houses, Luxury caravans. All units for four to six people. Children and pets welcome. Swimming pool and children's pool. Licensed bar with family room. Shop. Launderette. Children's play area. Ten minutes' walk to safe sand and shingle beach. Many fine walks locally. Golf, riding, tennis, fishing and boating all nearby. **SAE TO MR. F. LOOSMORE FOR COLOUR BROCHURE.**

The Queen's Armes Hotel

The Street, Charmouth, Dorset DT6 6QF Telephone 01297 560339

Phillip and Carole Mapstone

www.queensarmeshotel.co.uk

Former coaching inn built around 1500, oak beams and panelling.
Log fires; 10 unique bedrooms, all en suite.
Guest lounge, licensed bar and dining room. Vegetarians and Vegans catered for.
An abundance of National Trust land, footpaths and Heritage coastline. Dogs welcome.

ETC 4 Star Guest Accommodation **Non Smoking**

NEW FOREST - Country Holiday Chalet on small, quiet, secluded woodland park, situated within the National Park. Sleeps four. Fenced private garden. Dogs welcome. Car parking. £175 to £350 per week. Write enclosing SAE or telephone:

Mrs L.M Bowling, Owlpen Caravans Ltd, Owlpen, 148 Burley Road, Bransgore, Near Christchurch, Dorset BH23 8DB Tel: 01425 672875 • Mobile: 07860 547391 • www.owlpen-caravans.co.uk

GREYGLES Melcombe Bingham, Near Dorchester. Enjoy rural peace in this spacious, well-equipped stone house on the edge of a friendly village, just 10 miles from Dorchester. It comfortably sleeps up to seven in four bedrooms (one on the ground floor). • Sitting room with open fire • Dining room • Kitchen with Aga, dishwasher etc • Garden with patio and Wendy house • Heating, electricity, linen and towels incl. • Short breaks available • No smoking • Ideal for exploring Dorset and the Jurassic Coast

Booking: Tel: 020 8969 4830 • Fax: 020 8960 0069 • e-mail: enquiry@greygles.co.uk

P. SOMMERFELD, 22 TIVERTON ROAD, LONDON NW10 3HL

Charming cottage with enclosed garden. Lounge/dining room, study/bedroom, two bedrooms, well-equipped kitchen, two bathrooms. Pub nearby. Non-smokers only. Good touring centre.

Apply: **MRS WILLIS, 46 FLEET STREET, BEAMINSTER DORSET DT8 3EH • Tel: 01308 863868**
e-mail: nickywillis@tesco.net

THE STABLES, Hyde Crook, Frampton DT2 9NW • 01300 320075

Comfortable country house developed around a 1935 cottage overlooking the valley of Frampton. Set in the heart of Thomas Hardy country, we enjoy uninterrupted views of open countryside. Off-road parking and 20 acres of ground with wild life, ducks, sheep and horses. Guest accommodation is contained in a separate wing of the house. All rooms double glazed with central heating. Terms from £46 per room. We specialise in pet friendly facilities for dogs and horses.

e-mail: coba.stables@tiscali.co.uk • www.framptondorset.com

ETC ◆◆◆◆ SILVER AWARD

CHURCHVIEW GUEST HOUSE

Winterbourne Abbas, Dorchester, Dorset DT2 9LS Tel/Fax: 01305 889296

Our 17th century Guest House, noted for warm hospitality, delicious breakfasts and evening meals, makes an ideal base for touring beautiful West Dorset. Our character bedrooms are comfortable and well-appointed. Meals, served in our beautiful dining room, feature local produce, with relaxation provided by two attractive lounges and licensed bar. Hosts, Jane and Michael Deller, are pleased to give every assistance, with local information to ensure a memorable stay. Short breaks available. Non-smoking.

Terms: Bed and Breakfast: £30 – £38; Dinner, Bed and Breakfast: £46 – £57.

e-mail: stay@churchview.co.uk • www.churchview.co.uk

WESTOVER FARM COTTAGES

In an area of outstanding beauty, Wootton Fitzpaine epitomizes picturesque West Dorset. Within walking distance of sea. 4 beautiful cottages sleep 6/7 with large secluded gardens. Car parking. Logs available, Linen supplied, 3 bedrooms. £190-£750. Pets welcome.

Wootton Fitzpaine, Near Lyme Regis, Dorset DT6 6NE

Brochure: Jon Snook & Debby Snook • 01297 560451/561395

e-mail: wfcottages@aol.com *www.westoverfarmcottages.co.uk* *ETC★★★/★★★★*

LITTLE HEWISH BARN. For a relaxing long or short break. Five-Star accommodation in the heart of rural Dorset. Fully equipped, with no hidden extras; organic arrival pack included. Children and pets welcome. Truly a home from home. Please call for a full information pack.

Little Hewish Barn, Milton Abbas, Blandford Forum, Dorset DT11 0DP

Tel: 01258 881235 • e-mail: alex@littlehewish.co.uk

Sandford Holiday Park

Weststar HOLIDAY PARKS

An award winning holiday park near Poole, in a beautiful woodland setting and close to stunning sandy beaches. Dogs most welcome!

Call: 0870 444 0080 book online: www.weststarholidays.co.uk/pw

Quote: WP

THREE HORSESHOES Powerstock, Dorset DT6 3TF

01308 485328 • www.threehorseshoesinn.com

Dogs and families welcome

'The Shoes' is a Victorian inn tucked away in a peaceful part of West Dorset. Dogs are welcome in the three spacious double en suite guest rooms. The Inn boasts a great reputation for excellent cuisine. Light lunches are available daily with an à la carte menu for the evening. Combine this with an expansive fine wine list, log fires in the winter and sunsets over the valley from the terraced garden in the summer and you have an enjoyable evening awaiting you.

Folke Manor Farm Cottages • Four comfortable, spacious cottages in converted barns. • Sleep 4-8.• Peaceful location, outstanding views, walking. • Near Sherborne • **Folke Manor Farm, Sherborne DT9 5HP**
John & Carol Perrett • 01963 210731 • Open all year

Please mention PETS WELCOME! when making enquiries about accommodation featured in these pages

Self-Catering Barn Cottages

White Horse Farm

ETC ★★★/★★★★

Comfortable, well-equipped barn conversions, set in 2 acres of paddock, duck-pond and gardens in beautiful Hardy countryside. Surrounded by all rural pursuits and within easy reach of several tourist attractions. 100 yards from inn serving good food and local ales. We have all-year-round appeal and are friendly, helpful hosts.

Middlemarsh, Sherborne, Dorset DT9 5QN • 01963 210222

Visit our website: www.whitehorsefarm.co.uk e-mail: enquiries@whitehorsefarm.co.uk

"Welcome to one of the most beautiful places in England. I can't take credit for the glorious views and the beaches. But I am proud to provide a comfortable and relaxing hotel with good food and attentive but informal service, to give you the break you deserve."

Andrew Purkis

Manor House Hotel, Studland, Dorset, BH19 3AU • T - 01929 450288 • W - www.themanorhousehotel.com • E - themanorhousehotel@lineone.net

DORSET COTTAGE HOLIDAYS

PETS GO FREE. Self-catering cottages, town houses, bungalows and apartments. All within 10 miles of Heritage Coastline and sandy beaches. Excellent walking in idyllic countryside. Short breaks from £80, weekly from £135 (per cottage). Open all year.

Free brochure tel: 01929 553443

e-mail: enq@dhcottages.co.uk • www.dhcottages.co.uk

◆◆◆◆

THE LIMES HOTEL

A warm welcome awaits all dogs – and their owners – at the Limes Hotel, only a few hundred yards from wonderful coastal walks and beach, surrounded by the unspoilt Purbeck Hills. En suite rooms with colour TV and hospitality trays. Pets come free!

• Car Park • Families Welcome •

• Open all Year for Bed and Breakfast •

48 Park Road, Swanage, Dorset BH19 2AE

Tel: 01929 422664

info@limeshotel.net

www.limeshotel.net

SWANAGE BAY VIEW HOLIDAY PARK

4/5/6 BERTH FULL MAINS CARAVANS

COMFORTABLE AND WELL EQUIPPED

*Colour TV * Launderette * Sea Views * Parking space * Pets welcome*
* Fully licensed club with entertainment. * Indoor swimming pool*

EASTER – OCTOBER, REDUCED TERMS EARLY/LATE HOLIDAYS

SAE: M. Stockley, 17 Moor Road, Swanage, Dorset BH19 1RG • Tel: 01929 424154

TOLPUDDLE HALL Tolpuddle, Near Dorchester DT2 7EW

An historic house in village centre in an Area of Outstanding Natural Beauty, not far from the coast. • Two double, one family, one twin and two single bedrooms; two en suite, all with TV • Full English breakfast • Tea/coffee making • TV sitting room • Pets welcome except high season • Open all year except Christmas • From £20pp sharing, £27.50 single. Weekly rate available.

Dormer Cottage

In the midst of 'Hardy Country', a secluded cottage, sleeping 5, converted from a former barn and forming part of the ex Dower House of Hyde Estate. All linen provided. Golf, pony-trekking, riding nearby. Pets and children most welcome. Ideal for a quiet holiday far from the madding crowd.

SAE please for terms and further particulars from Mrs M.J.M Constantinides

"Woodlands", Hyde, Near Wareham BH20 7NT • Tel: 01929 471239

Cromwell House Hotel

Lulworth Cove, Dorset

Catriona and Alistair Miller welcome guests to their comfortable family-run hotel, set in secluded gardens with spectacular sea views. Situated 200 yards from Lulworth Cove, with direct access to the Jurassic Coast. A heated swimming pool is available for guests' use from May to October. Accommodation is in 20 en suite bedrooms, with TV, direct-dial telephone, and tea/coffee making facilities; most have spectacular sea views. There is disabled access and a room suitable for disabled guests. Self-catering flat available. Restaurant, bar wine list.

B&B from £40. Two nights DB&B (fully en suite) from £114 per person. Off-peak mid week breaks all year except Christmas.

Cromwell House Hotel, Lulworth Cove, Dorset BH20 5RJ

Tel: 01929 400253/400332 • Fax: 01929 400566

ETC/AA/RAC ★★

Note

All the information in this guide is given in good faith in the belief that it is correct. However, the publishers cannot guarantee the facts given in these pages, neither are they responsible for changes in ownership or facilities that may take place after the date of going to press. Readers should always satisfy themselves that the facilities they require are available and that the terms, if quoted, still apply.

DORSET COASTAL COTTAGES (0800 9804070). Carefully selected, traditional cottages in or near villages within ten miles of World Heritage Coast. Many are thatched; open fires or logburners; over half welcome dogs. Available all year.
website: www.dorsetcoastalcottages.com

Blandford

Handsome Georgian town that rose from the ashes of the 1731 fire; rebuilt with chequered brick and stone. Also known as Blandford Forum.

ANVIL INN & RESTAURANT, PIMPERNE, BLANDFORD DT11 8UQ (01258 453431/480182). A typical Old English hostelry offering good old-fashioned English hospitality. Full à la carte menu with mouthwatering desserts in the charming restaurant with log fire, delicious desserts, bar meals, specials board. All bedrooms with private facilities. Ample parking. ETC/AA/RAC ◆◆◆◆ [Pets £5 per night]
e-mail: theanvilinn@btconnect.com website: www.anvilhotel.co.uk

Symbols

- 🐕 Indicates that pets are welcome free of charge.
- £ Indicates that a charge is made for pets: nightly or weekly.
- **pw!** Shows some special provision for pets; exercise facility, feeding or accommodation arrangement.
- ⌂ Indicates separate pets accommodation.

Bournemouth

One of Britain's premier holiday resorts with miles of golden sand, excellent shopping and leisure facilities. Lively entertainments include Festival of Lights at the beginning of September.

MIKE AND LYN LAMBERT, 16 FLORENCE ROAD, BOURNEMOUTH BH5 1HF (01202 304925). Modern Holiday Apartments sleeping up to ten persons, close to sea and shops. Clean, well-equipped flats. Car park. Phoneor e-mail for brochure. [Pets from £35 per week]
website: www.selfcateringbournemouth.co.uk

LANGTRY MANOR, DERBY ROAD, EAST CLIFF, BOURNEMOUTH BH1 3QB (01202 553887). A rare gem of a hotel where the building, food, service and history blend to form something quite exceptional. Midweek and weekend breaks. Pets welcome by arrangement. [🐕]
website: www.langtrymanor.com

BILL AND MARJORIE TITCHEN, WHITE TOPPS HOTEL, 45 CHURCH ROAD, SOUTHBOURNE, BOURNEMOUTH BH6 4BB (01202 428868). Situated in quiet position close to lovely walks and beach. Dogs essential. Free parking. [🐕 pw!]
e-mail: thedoghotel@aol.com website: www.whitetopps.co.uk

ALUM DENE HOTEL, 2 BURNABY ROAD, ALUM CHINE, BOURNEMOUTH BH4 8JF (01202 764011) Renowned for good old fashioned hospitality and friendly service. Come and be spoilt at our licensed hotel. All rooms en suite, colour TV. Some have sea views. 200 metres sea. Parking. Christmas House party. No charge for pets. [🐕]

SOUTHBOURNE GROVE HOTEL, 96 SOUTHBOURNE ROAD, SOUTHBOURNE, BOURNEMOUTH BH6 3QQ (01202 420503; Fax: 01202 421953). Friendly, family-run hotel with beautiful garden and ample guest parking. Close to beach and shops. Excellent food served in spacious restaurant. En suite, four-poster suite, ground floor and large family rooms available, all with colour TV and tea/coffee facilities. B&B from £22 per night, £122 per week. [🐕]

HOLIDAY FLATS AND FLATLETS a short walk to golden, sandy beaches. Most with private bathrooms. Cleanliness and comfort assured. Dogs welcome. Contact: M DE KMENT, 4 CECIL ROAD, BOURNEMOUTH BH5 1DU (07788 952394). [Pets £25 per week]

ANNE & RICHARD REYNOLDS, THE VINE HOTEL, 22 SOUTHERN ROAD, SOUTHBOURNE, BOURNEMOUTH BH6 3SR (01202 428309). A small, family, award-winning non-smoking Hotel only three hundred yards from dog-friendly beach and shops. All rooms en suite with tea/coffee making facilities and colour TV. Residential licence with attractive bar. Full central heating. Forecourt parking. Open all year. FHG Diploma, South West Tourism ◆◆◆ [🐕]
website: www.vinehotel.co.uk

Self-contained two-bedroom apartments in quiet avenue, one minute from clean, sandy beaches and five minutes from shops. Sleeps 2-6. Includes linen. Fully equipped kitchen, cooker, fridge/freezer, microwave, colour TV, washing machine, tumble dryer. Toilet and shower. Central heating. Parking. Terms from £200. Contact: MRS HAMMOND, STOURCLIFFE COURT, 56 STOURCLIFFE AVENUE, SOUTHBOURNE, BOURNEMOUTH BH6 3PX (01202 420698). [Pets £2 per night, £10 weekly]

Bridport

Market town of Saxon origin noted for rope and net making. Harbour at West Bay has sheer cliffs rising from the beach

MRS S. NORMAN, FROGMORE FARM, CHIDEOCK, BRIDPORT DT6 6HT (01308 456159). The choice is yours - Bed and Breakfast in charming farmhouse, OR self-catering Cottage equipped for five, pets welcome. Brochure and terms free on request. [1st dog free, 2nd dog £3 per night, £15 per week]

GOLDEN ACRE, EYPE, NEAR BRIDPORT DT6 6AL (01308 421521). Private peaceful park. Close to beach. Chalet bungalows (1 or 2 bedrooms), sleep 2-4. Wonderful walks, on the Jurassic Coast. Pets free, house-trained owners welcome! [🐕]

EYPE HOUSE CARAVAN & CAMPING PARK, EYPE, BRIDPORT DT6 6AL (01308 424903) Small, quiet family-run park lying on the Heritage Coastal Path, 200 yards from the beach. Static vans for hire from £190 to £430, tent pitches (all terraced with sea views) £10.00 to £17.00 for four people. Sorry, no tourers. Children and dogs welcome. [Pets £3 per night, £15 per week.]

Sherborne

Town with abbey and two castles, one of which was built by Sir Walter Raleigh with lakes and gardens by Capability Brown.

FOLKE MANOR FARM COTTAGES. Four comfortable, spacious cottages in converted barns. Sleep 4-8. Peaceful location, outstanding views, walking. Near Sherborne. Open all year. JOHN & CAROL PERRETT, FOLKE MANOR FARM, SHERBORNE DT9 5HP (01963 21073).

WHITE HORSE FARM, MIDDLEMARSH, SHERBORNE DT9 5QN. The Willows sleeps 4-6; Toad Hall sleeps 4; Badger's sleeps 2; Ratty's sleeps 2/4; Moley's sleeps 2. Character self-catering holiday cottages in rural location. Well-equipped and comfortable. TV, video, free films. 2 acres of paddock, garden and duck pond. Inn 100 yards. ETC ★★★/★★★★. AUDREY & STUART WINTERBOTTOM (01963 210222) [pw!]
e-mail: enquiries@whitehorsefarm.co.uk website: www.whitehorsefarm.co.uk

Studland Bay

Unspoilt seaside village at south western end of Poole Bay, 3 miles north of Swanage.

THE MANOR HOUSE HOTEL, STUDLAND BAY BH19 3AU (01929 450288; Fax: 01929 452255). National Trust hotel set in 20 acres on cliffs overlooking Studland Bay. Superb food and accommodation. Log fires and four-posters.Tennis, horse-riding, golf and walking. [Pets £3.50]
e-mail: themanorhousehotel@lineone.net website: www.themanorhousehotel.com

THE KNOLL HOUSE, STUDLAND BH19 3AW (01929 450450). Country house hotel within National Trust reserve. Golden beach. 100 acre grounds. Family suites of connecting rooms, six lounges. Tennis, golf, swimming, games rooms, health spa. See our Full Page Advertisement under Studland Bay.
e-mail: info@knollhouse.co.uk website: www.knollhouse.co.uk

Swanage

Traditional family holiday resort set in a sheltered bay ideal for water sports. Good base for a walking holiday.

DORSET COTTAGE HOLIDAYS. Self-catering cottages, town houses, bungalows and apartments. All within 10 miles of Heritage Coastline and sandy beaches. Excellent walking in idyllic countryside. Short breaks from £80, weekly from £135 (per cottage). Open all year. Free brochure tel: 01929 553443. [ ]
e-mail: enq@dhcottages.co.uk website: www.dhcottages.co.uk

LIMES HOTEL, 48 PARK ROAD, SWANAGE BH19 2AE (01929 422664). Small friendly Hotel. En suite rooms, TV, tea/coffee making facilities. Children and pets welcome. Credit cards accepted. ETC◆◆◆◆ [ ]
e-mail: info@limeshotel.net website: www.limeshotel.net

MRS M. STOCKLEY, SWANAGE BAY VIEW HOLIDAY PARK, 17 MOOR ROAD, SWANAGE BH19 1RG (01929 424154). 4/5/6-berth Caravans. Pets welcome. Easter to October. Colour TV. Shop. Parking space. Rose Award Park [ ]

Tolpuddle

Village 4 miles west of Bere Regis, famous for "Tolpuddle Martyrs".

TOLPUDDLE HALL TOLPUDDLE, NEAR DORCHESTER DT2 7EW (01305 848986). Historic house in an Area of Outstanding Natural Beauty, not far from the coast. Two double, one family, one twin and two single bedrooms; two en suite, all with TV. Pets welcome except high season. Open all year except Christmas. From £20pp sharing, £27.50 single.

Wareham

Picturesque riverside town almost surrounded by earthworks, considered pre-Roman. Nature reserves of great beauty nearby. Weymouth 19 miles, Bournemouth 14, Swanage 10, Poole 6.

DORMER COTTAGE, WOODLANDS AT HYDE, NEAR WAREHAM BH20 7NT (01929 471239). In the midst of Hardy Country, secluded cottage. All linen provided. Golf, pony trekking, riding nearby. Children and pets welcome. Beds ready made. [ ]

CATRIONA AND ALISTAIR MILLER, CROMWELL HOUSE HOTEL, LULWORTH COVE BH20 5RJ (01929 400253/400332; Fax: 01929 400566). Comfortable family-run hotel, set in secluded gardens with spectacular sea views. Heated swimming pool, 20 en suite bedrooms. Restaurant, bar wine list. Self-catering. Disabled access. ETC/AA/RAC ★★. [🐕]

West Bexington

Seaside village with pebble beach. Chesil beach stretches eastwards. Nearby is Abbotsbury with its Benedictine Abbey and famous Swannery. Dorchester 13 miles, Weymouth 13, Bridport 6.

GORSELANDS CARAVAN PARK, DEPT PW, WEST BEXINGTON-ON-SEA DT2 9DJ (01308 897232; Fax: 01308 897239). Holiday Park. Fully serviced and equipped 4/6 berth caravans. Shop and launderette on site. Glorious sea views. Good country and seaside walks. One mile to beach. Holiday apartments with sea views and private garden. Pets most welcome. Colour brochure on request. ETC ★★★★, David Bellamy Silver Award. [🐕]
e-mail: info@gorselands.co.uk website: www.gorselands.co.uk

Weymouth

Set in a beautiful bay with fine beaches and a picturesque 17th century harbour, Weymouth has a wide range of entertainment and leisure facilities.

GLENTHORNE, CASTLE COVE, 15 OLD CASTLE ROAD, WEYMOUTH DT4 8QB (01305 777281; Mobile: 07831 751526). Secluded beachfront B&B in elegant Victorian villa and well equipped apartments with panoramic sea views of Olympic sailing area. Extensive gardens, heated pool, play areas, dog friendly beach, coastal path. Parking. Contact OLIVIA NURRISH. [pw! 🐕]
e-mail: info@glenthorne-holidays.co.uk website: www.glenthorne-holidays.co.uk

Bishop Auckland

Town on right bank of River Wear, 9 miles south-west of Durham. Castle, of varying dates, residence of the Bishop of Durham.

ALISON & KEITH TALLENTIRE, LOW LANDS FARM, LOW LANDS, COCKFIELD, BISHOP AUCKLAND DL13 5AW (01388 718251; mobile: 07745 067754). Two self-catering cottages on a working livestock farm. Each sleeps up to 4, plus cot. Prices from £150-£340. Call for a brochure. Pets and children most welcome. ETC ★★★★ ETC CATEGORY 3 DISABLED ACCESSIBILITY (one cottage). [Pets £10 per week]

e-mail: info@farmholidaysuk.com website: www.farmholidaysuk.co

Castleside

A suburb 2 miles south-west of Consett.

MELITA & DAVID TURNER, BEE COTTAGE FARMHOUSE, CASTLESIDE, CONSETT DH8 9HW (01207 508224). Charming farmhouse with stunning views. You will be most welcome. Ideal for Newcastle, Durham, Beamish etc. Bed and Breakfast; dinner available, licensed. Great for pets. ETC ◆◆◆◆ [pw! 🐕]

e-mail: welcome@beecottagefarmhouse.freeserve.co.uk website: www.beecottage.co.uk

Teesdale

Admin district of the County of Durham. Ideal area for all outdoor .

FROG HALL COTTAGE (Tel & Fax: 01833 622215). Traditional cottage, magnificent views. Rare flora and fauna near Nature Reserve on award-winning environmental farm. Sheep and cows peer over your garden wall. Guided walks arranged.[ ]
e-mail: kath.herdship@btinternet.com website: www.herdship.co.uk

Waterhouses

6 miles west of Durham.

MRS P. A. BOOTH, IVESLEY EQUESTRIAN CENTRE, IVESLEY, WATERHOUSES, DURHAM DH7 9HB (0191 373 4324; Fax: 0191 373 4757). Beautifully furnished comfortable country house set in 220 acres in Durham but very quiet and rural. Excellent dog exercising facilities. En suite bedrooms. Excellent food. Licensed. Fully equipped Equestrian Centre adjacent. [Pets £2 per night].
e-mail: ivesley@msn.com website: www.ridingholidays-ivesley.co.uk

Weardale

A designated Area of Outstanding Natural Beauty, 10 miles from the market town of Alston.

NEWFIELD HOUSE AND RAINWALKER HOUSE WEARDALE, NORTH PENNINES (01207 504828). Area of Outstanding Natural Beauty. Super holiday cottages, sleep 5/6. Ideal base for touring Lakes etc. Log burners, Aga, Sky/DVD. From £155-£450 per week all inclusive.
website: www.cottageguide.co.uk/rainwalker

HARTWELL FARM COTTAGES **Ready Token, Near Bibury, Cirencester GL7 5SY**
Two traditionally built cottages with far reaching views, on the southern edge of the Cotswolds. Both are fully equipped to a high standard, with heating and woodburning stoves; large private enclosed gardens. Stabling for horses; tennis court. Ideal for touring and horse riding. Glorious walks, excellent pubs. Children and well-behaved dogs welcome. Sleep 3-4/4-5. • **Contact: Caroline Mann: Tel: 01285 740210**
E-mail: ec.mann@btinternet.com • www.selfcateringcotswolds.com

THE CHESTER HOUSE HOTEL

VICTORIA STREET,
BOURTON-ON-THE-WATER,
GLOUCESTERSHIRE GL54 2BU

TEL: 01451 820286 • FAX 01451 820471
e-mail: info@chesterhousehotel.com
www.chesterhousehotel.com

Chester House Hotel
AND BAR

Bourton-on-the-Water - The Venice of the Cotswolds. A haven of peace and comfort tucked away in a quiet backwater of this famous village.

STRATHSPEY AA ◆◆◆

Lansdowne, Bourton-on-the-Water GL54 2AR
Tastefully furnished bedrooms with TV, refreshment tray, hairdryer, clock radio. Pleasant tranquil garden. Five minutes' walk from centre of village. Open all year. Terms from £24 pppn. Pets welcome by prior arrangement.
Tel: 01451 810321 • mobile: 07889 491993
e-mail: bookings@strathspey.org.uk **www.strathspey.org.uk**

Rose's Cottage **Broadwell, Cotswolds** ETC ★★★★

Delightful country cottage in Broadwell, tastefully decorated and furnished. It is heated by storage radiators and electric log effect burner. On the ground floor is a well-equipped kitchen with hob, oven, microwave, washer-dryer and fridge. Lounge has TV, comfortable furniture. Bedroom and a large bathroom upstairs. Small patio. Next door to owners' house. Close to family pub. Good walking area. Welcome provisions, linen and towels provided.

Tel: 01451 830007

*** Tariff: low £260, mid £290 and high £330 ***

Attention All Dog Lovers! www.doggybreaks.co.uk

Romantic 18th century Coach House in the heart of the beautiful Cotswolds. Close to 600 acres of NT common. Sleeps 4 + 2 children. Beams, woodburners. Outdoor heated swimming pool and bubbling hot tub. Hillside garden and 20 acres of woodland. Free private kennel facilities (optional). Breaks £125-£615. Brochure: **Ros Smith, The Old Coach House, Edgecombe House, Toadsmoor, Brimscombe, Stroud GL5 2UE • Tel: 01453 883147**

Please note

All the information in this book is given in good faith in the belief that it is correct. However, the publishers cannot guarantee the facts given in these pages, neither are they responsible for changes in policy, ownership or terms that may take place after the date of going to press. Readers should always satisfy themselves that the facilities they require are available and that the terms, if quoted, still apply.

Fairford, Forest of Dean, Meysey Hampton, Nailsworth

ETC ★★

The Bull Hotel

The Market Place, Fairford, Gloucestershire GL7 4AA

Tel: 01285 712535/712217 • Fax: 01285 713782

e-mail: info@thebullhotelfairford.co.uk

website: www.thebullhotelfairford.co.uk

AA ★★

15th century family-run coaching inn. Ideal for touring Cotswolds. A la carte restaurant situated in original stables. Ideal for conferences and weddings. 1½ miles private fishing on River Coln. The hotel has a choice of 22 fully equipped bedrooms with sloping roofs and oak beams. Four-poster beds available. There are good golf courses, squash and tennis courts, sailing facilities within easy reach of the hotel. 1½ miles of private fishing on River Coln. Situated in the South Cotswolds. **Tariff: £49.50 - £89.50**

DRYSLADE FARM

ENGLISH BICKNOR, COLEFORD GL16 7PA

Tel & Fax: 01594 860259

AA ★★★★

www.drysladefarm.co.uk

Daphne and Phil warmly welcome you and your dogs for B&B at at their 18th century farmhouse on family working farm. Situated in Royal Forest of Dean and close to Symonds Yat with ample walking. Excellent breakfast. Terms from £26- £35.

The Speech House

Coleford, Forest of Dean GL16 7EL

Tel: 01594 822607 • Fax: 01594 823658

A friendly Hotel set in the heart of the Forest of Dean, perfect for walking dogs. Almost completely enveloped by trees, the Speech House is the perfect place to get away from it all. The hotel has 37 bedrooms, all of which are en suite, plus a Beauty Salon. The hotel has several four-poster beds and was built by King Charles II as a Hunting Lodge. Courtyard ground floor rooms are available. Pets are welcome. **AA/RAC ★★★**

E-mail: relax@thespeechhouse.co.uk • Website: www.thespeechhouse.co.uk

THE MASONS ARMS

28 High Street, Meysey Hampton, Near Cirencester, Gloucs GL7 5JT

Tel & Fax: 01285 850164

Set beside the village green, the Masons Arms dates from the 17th century and lies on the southern fringe of the Cotswolds. Here is an opportunity to enjoy excellent food and drink in delightful surroundings. The menu is an intriguing blend of imaginative starters and home-cooked traditional fare, whilst the daily 'specials' make interesting reading. Comfortable, individually decorated rooms all have en suite facilities, heating, remote-control colour television and tea and coffee tray.

e-mail: jane@themasonsarms.freeserve.co.uk • www.SmoothHound.co.uk/hotels/mason

The Laurels at Inchbrook

The Laurels at Inchbrook, Nailsworth GL5 5HA

Tel: 01453 834021• Fax: 01453 835190

e-mail: laurelsinchbrook@tiscali.co.uk• www.laurelsinchbrook.co.uk

A comfortable, rambling house, cottage and garden set beside the Inch Brook and adjoining fields. Lovely secluded garden, with badgers and bats: the stream is an otter route, and many birds come to visit us. Pets are most welcome, there are dozens of splendid walks and the National Trust's Woodchester Park is on our doorstep.

Nailsworth, a fashionable Cotswold town and a centre for excellence when it comes to eating out, is just under a mile away. Ideally placed for exploring the West Country, Bath and Forest of Dean as well as the Cotswolds, our house is perfect for groups and family gatherings. Brochure on request. Self-catering facilities may be available at certain times of the year.

B&B from £25 per person. Rooms: 2 double, 2 twin, 2 family, 1 ground floor accessible - all rooms en suite. No smoking. Children and pets welcome. Never closed.

THE SPEECH HOUSE, COLEFORD, FOREST OF DEAN GL16 7EL (01594 822607; Fax: 01594 823658). A friendly Hotel set in the heart of the Forest of Dean. The perfect place to get away from it all. 37 en suite bedrooms. Lavish restaurant. Beauty suite. AA/RAC ★★★ [Pets £10 per stay]
e-mail: relax@thespeechhouse.co.uk website: www.thespeechhouse.co.uk

OLD BREWERY HOUSE, BREWERY YARD, REDBROOK ON WYE, MONMOUTHSHIRE NP25 4LU (01600 713819). Welcoming en suite accommodation with courtyard garden and private parking. Scenic riverside and off-road walks. Two village pubs serve meals. B&B £75 per room per night. 10% discount for 2 or more nights. Dogs free. WTB ★★★★ [🐕]
e-mail: enquiries@oldbreweryhouse.com website: www.oldbreweryhouse.com

Meysey Hampton

Award-winning village 6 miles east of Cirencester, 12 miles north west of Swindon.

THE MASONS ARMS, 28 HIGH STREET, MEYSEY HAMPTON, NEAR CIRENCESTER GL7 5JT (Tel & Fax: 01285 850164). 17th century inn beside village green. Excellent food and drink with daily 'specials'; comfortable bedrooms with en suite facilities, TV. tea/coffee. AA/ETC ◆◆◆
e-mail: jane@themasonsarms.freeserve.co.uk
website: www.SmoothHound.co.uk/hotels/mason

Nailsworth

Hilly town 4 miles south of Stroud

THE LAURELS, INCHBROOK, NAILSWORTH GL5 5HA (01453 834021; Fax: 01453 835190). A lovely rambling house, cottage and secluded garden where dogs and their owners are encouraged to relax and enjoy. Ideally situated for touring all parts of the Cotswolds and West Country; splendid walks. Brochure. [🐕]
e-mail: laurelsinchbrook@tiscali.co.uk website: www.laurelsinchbrook.co.uk

Newnham-on-Severn

Town on right bank on River Severn, 10 miles south-west of Gloucester.

SWAN HOUSE GUEST HOUSE, HIGH STREET, NEWNHAM-ON-SEVERN GL14 1BY (01594 516504). 17th century Grade II Listed house, tastefully furnished and decorated, near Forest of Dean. All rooms en suite. Choice of delicious breakfasts using fresh local produce. Garden for relaxing. On bus routes. Children and pets welcome. AA ◆◆◆◆ [Pets £8 per stay].
e-mail: stay@swanhousenewnham.co.uk website: www.swanhousenewnham.co.uk

Painswick

Beautiful little Cotswold town with characteristic stone-built houses.

MISS E. COLLETT, HAMBUTTS MYND, EDGE ROAD, PAINSWICK GL6 6UP (01452 812352; Fax: 01452 813862). Bed and Breakfast in an old Converted Corn Mill. Very quiet with superb views. Three minutes to the centre of the village. Central heating. One double room, one twin, one single, all with TV. From £30 to £55 per night per room, 10% discount for 4 nights or more. ALL ROOMS EN SUITE. RAC/TBC ◆◆◆. [🐕]
e-mail: ewarland@aol.com

Stow-on-the-Wold

Charming Cotswold hill-top market town with several old inns and interesting buildings. Birmingham 45 miles, Gloucester 26, Stratford-upon-Avon 21, Cheltenham 18, Chipping Norton 9.

THE LIMES, EVESHAM ROAD, STOW-ON-THE-WOLD GL54 1EN (01451 830034/831056). Large Country House. Attractive garden, overlooking fields, 4 minutes town centre. Television lounge. Central heating. Car park. Bed and Breakfast from £25 to £30 pppn. Twin, double or family rooms, all en suite. Children and pets welcome. AA ◆◆◆, Tourist Board Listed. [🐕]
e-mail: thelimes@zoom.co.uk website: cotswolds.info/webpage/thelimes.stow.htm

THE OLD STOCKS HOTEL THE SQUARE, STOW-ON-THE-WOLD GL54 1AF (01451 830666; Fax: 01451 870014). Ideal base for touring this beautiful area. Tasteful guest rooms with modern amenities. Mouth-watering menus. Special bargain breaks also available. HETB/AA ★★ [Pets £5 per stay]
e-mail: fhg@oldstockshotel.co.uk website: www.oldstockshotel.co.uk

Stroud

Cotswold town on River Frome below picturesque Stroudwater Hills, formerly renowned for cloth making. Bristol 32 miles, Bath 29, Chippenham 25, Cheltenham 14, Gloucester 9.

MRS A. RHOTON, HYDE CREST, CIRENCESTER ROAD, MINCHINHAMPTON GL6 8PE (01453 731631). Beautiful country house with enclosed acre garden. All rooms on ground floor opening on to patios and lawns. 500 acres of commons, plus country walks nearby. AA ◆◆◆◆ [pw! 🐕]
e-mail: stay@hydecrest.co.uk website: www.hydecrest.co.uk

DOWNFIELD HOTEL, CAINSCROSS ROAD, STROUD GL5 4HN (01453 764496). Easy to find – just 5 miles from M5 – and easy to park. Ideal location for exploring Cotswolds. Comfortable lounges, home-cooked evening meal, cosy bar – all at sensible prices. Dogs and children most welcome. ETC/AA ◆◆◆. [🐕]
e-mail: info@downfieldhotel.co.uk website: www.downfieldhotel.co.uk

MRS UNA PEACEY, THE WITHYHOLT GUEST HOUSE, PAUL MEAD, EDGE, NEAR STROUD GL6 6PG (01452 813618: Fax: 01452 812375) Modern guesthouse in Gloucestershire close to Gloucester Cathedral, Tetbury, Stroud. Many lovely country walks. En suite bedrooms, large lounge. Large garden. ETC ◆◆◆◆ [🐕]

Symbols

🐕 Indicates that pets are welcome free of charge.
£ Indicates that a charge is made for pets: nightly or weekly.
pw! Shows some special provision for pets; exercise facility, feeding or accommodation arrangement.
⌂ Indicates separate pets accommodation.

The Woodlands Lodge Hotel

Bartley Road, Woodlands, New Forest, Hampshire SO40 7GN
Reservations: (023) 80 292257 • Fax: (023) 80 293090
e-mail: reception@woodlands-lodge.co.uk • www.woodlands-lodge.co.uk

The Woodlands Lodge Hotel is a luxuriously restored Georgian Country House, set within the beautiful New Forest, yet only 15 minutes from Southampton. Our attractive gardens have direct access to the forest and are ideal for romantic walks. Golf, fishing and horse riding are available nearby and the hotel is perfectly situated for touring the area. Come and unwind from the stress of everyday life and enjoy pure luxury without ostentation.

AA ★★★

All bedrooms enjoy full en suite facilities of whirlpool bath and separate shower and have king sized beds and a full range of amenities. The quality four-course menu is changed seasonally to make use of local produce and is complemented by an interesting wine list. The service is friendly, efficient and informal.

Woodlands Lodge – where a warm welcome awaits you.

★★★ HOTEL

Efford Cottage

Everton, Lymington, Hampshire SO41 0JD
Tel: 01590 642315 • Fax: 01590 641030
e-mail: effordcottage@aol.com • www.effordcottage.co.uk

Guests receive a warm and friendly welcome to our home, which is a spacious Georgian cottage. All rooms are en suite with many extra luxury facilities. We offer a four-course multi-choice breakfast with homemade bread and preserves. Patricia is a qualified chef and uses our home-grown produce. An excellent centre for exploring both the New Forest and the South Coast with sports facilities, fishing, bird watching and horse riding in the near vicinity. Private parking. Dogs welcome. Sorry no children. **Bed and Breakfast from £25–£35 pppn.** *Mrs Patricia J. Ellis.*

Winner of " England For Excellence 2000"
AA ◆◆◆◆
FHG Diploma 1997/1999/2000/2003 / Michelin / Welcome Host
Awards Achieved: Gold Award / RAC Sparkling Diamond & Warm Welcome
Nominated Landlady of Year & Best Breakfast Award.

WELCOME HOST

AA ★★

Ormonde House Hotel

ORMONDE HOUSE HOTEL

Southampton Road, Lyndhurst, Hampshire SO43 7BT
Tel: (023) 8028 2806 • Fax: (023) 8028 2004

E-mail: enquiries@ormondehouse.co.uk • Website: www.ormondehouse.co.uk

A relaxed blend of professionalism and warm hospitality awaits you at our elegant, family-run, Two Star Hotel, situated opposite the open forest, ideal for easy walking. 19 pretty, en suite rooms and four luxury self-contained suites, all with CTV, phone and beverage making. 'Superior' and 'Superior Plus' rooms have sofas, with some 'Superior Plus' rooms and all 'Suites' featuring whirlpool baths and super king-sized zip and link beds. In addition all four Suites offer full kitchens with washing/drying machines and dishwashers. Dine with us - our Chefs have an excellent reputation amongst regular guests for freshly prepared dishes, daily changing specials and wickedly tempting puddings. Close to Exbury Gardens and Beaulieu Motor Museum.

Special 4 night midweek breaks from £111pp B&B and from £162pp DB&B.
Daily rate from £43pp B&B and £60pp DB&B.

AA ★★★

The Crown Hotel, New Forest

Tired of the same old walks? Enjoy forest, heath and the beach whilst staying at The Crown Hotel. 38 en suite rooms, all individual and recently refurbished.

Our Chef of thirty years, Stephen Greenhalgh, delights us with his imaginative menus using local produce wherever possible, either in the informal bar or the Restaurant overlooking our water-featured garden.

Dogs are welcome to bring their well-behaved owners!

High Street, Lyndhurst, Hampshire SO43 7NF • Tel: 023 8028 2922 • Fax: 023 8028 2751

E-mail: reception@crownhotel-lyndhurst.co.uk • Web: www.crownhotel-lyndhurst.co.uk

LITTLE THATCH • 15 South Street, Pennington, New Forest

Beautiful Grade II Listed thatched cob cottage in village location. Sleeps 4 in 2 bedrooms. Superbly renovated to offer traditional cottage features, tastefully combined with luxury modern comforts, including washer/dryer, dishwasher, TV, freeview, video, DVD. Secluded secure garden. Pets welcome. **Contact: Mrs Suzannah Nash (01582 842831)**

E-mail: suzannah@littlethatchcottage.com • www.littlethatchcottage.com

GORSE COTTAGE, BALMER LAWN ROAD, BROCKENHURST

Cottage/bungalow on open forest road close to the village in the New Forest. Beautifully decorated and appointed, sleeps 4 in 2 bedrooms. Conservatory, luxury bathroom, log fire, televisions/video, secluded sunny garden. Pets welcome.

Contact: MR J. GILBERT (0870 3210020) or website for details

e-mail: info@gorsecottage.co.uk www.gorsecottage.co.uk

In the heart of the New Forest - THE WATERSPLASH HOTEL

The Rise, Brockenhurst SO42 7ZP • Tel: 01590 622344

Prestigious family-run country house hotel set in large garden. Noted for fine personal service, accommodation and traditional English cuisine at its best. All rooms en suite. Luxury four-poster with double spa bath. Swimming pool. Short walk to open forest. **RAC, AA ★★**. Colour brochure available.

e-mail: bookings@watersplash.co.uk • www.watersplash.co.uk

ST. URSULA ◆◆◆◆

30 Hobart Road, New Milton, Hants. BH25 6EG

Between sea and New Forest, comfortable family home. Excellent facilities & warm welcome for well behaved pets and owners. Ground floor suite suitable for disabled guests plus single and twin rooms.

Mrs Judith Pearce B&B from £27.50 Tel: 01425 613515

LANGRISH HOUSE

Langrish, Petersfield GU32 1RN

Tel: 01730 266941

e-mail: frontdesk@langrishhouse.co.uk • www.langrishhouse.co.uk

17th century house in idyllic country location.
All bedrooms en suite and non-smoking. Small, cosy restaurant; weddings and conferences catered for.

AA ★★

The High Corner Inn is set deep in the heart of The New Forest in seven beautiful acres of woodland, ideal for long forest walks. Seven en suite bedrooms; two oak-beamed bars with views across the patio and garden; outdoor adventure playground for children. Good choice of real ales, wines and spirits, quality home-cooked meals, Sunday carvery. Dogs and well behaved owners welcome throughout the inn and in the letting rooms, but horses must use our stables or paddocks.

Linwood, Ringwood, Hants BH24 3QY • Tel: 01425 473973 • Fax: 01425 483052

Ashurst

Three miles north-east of Lyndhurst.

WOODLANDS LODGE HOTEL, BARTLEY ROAD, ASHURST, WOODLANDS SO40 7GN ((023) 80 292257; Fax: (023) 80 293090). Luxury Hotel offering peace and tranquillity. 16 bedrooms, all en suite with whirlpool bath, TV, hairdryer, telephone etc. Award winning Restaurant. Direct access to Forest. ETC/AA★★★ [🐕]
e-mail: reception@woodlands-lodge.co.uk website: www.woodlands-lodge.co.uk

Lymington

Residential town and yachting centre 15 miles east of Bournemouth.

MRS P. J. ELLIS, EFFORD COTTAGE, EVERTON, LYMINGTON SO41 0JD (01590 642315; Fax: 01590 641030). Outstanding B&B with old world charm in proprietor's own Georgian home. Excellent touring centre for New Forest and South Coast. All rooms en suite with luxury facilities. B&B from £25-£35pppn. No children. AA ◆◆◆◆, Michelin. [PW! Pets from £2 per night]
e-mail: effordcottage@aol.com website: www.effordcottage.co.uk

HONEYSUCKLE HOUSE, 24 CLINTON ROAD, LYMINGTON SO41 9EA (Tel & Fax: 01590 676635). Ground floor double room, en suite, non-smoking. Woodland walk, park, quay and marinas nearby. B&B from £30.00 pppn. [🐕]
e-mail: skyblue@beeb.net

Lyndhurst

Good base for enjoying the fascinating New Forest as well as the Hampshire coastal resorts. Bournemouth 20 miles, Southampton 9.

ORMONDE HOUSE HOTEL, SOUTHAMPTON ROAD, LYNDHURST SO43 7BT (023 8028 2806, Fax: 023 8028 2004). Opposite open forest, easy drive to Exbury Gardens and Beaulieu. Elegant, family-run Two Star Hotel with pretty, en suite rooms with CTV, phone and beverage making. Superior plus rooms and ground floor suites with whirlpool baths and kingsize beds. Bar, lounge and delicious dinners available. AA ★★. [Pets £3.50 per night, max. 2 per room]
e-mail: enquiries@ormondehouse.co.uk website: www.ormondehouse.co.uk

THE CROWN HOTEL, LYNDHURST, NEW FOREST S043 7NF (023 8028 2922; Fax: 023 8028 2751). A mellow, Listed building in the centre of the village, an ideal base for exploring the delights of the New Forest with your canine friend(s). Free parking, quiet garden, three star luxury and animal loving staff. [Pets £5.00 per night].
e-mail: reception@crownhotel-lyndhurst.co.uk website: www.crownhotel-lyndhurst.co.uk

New Forest

Area of heath and woodland of nearly 150 square miles, formerly Royal hunting grounds.

LITTLE THATCH, 15 SOUTH STREET, PENNINGTON (01582 842831) Beautiful Grade II Listed thatched cob cottage, sleeps 4 in 2 bedrooms. Superbly renovated to offer traditional cottage features, tastefully combined with luxury modern comforts. Secluded secure garden. [🐕]
e-mail: suzannah@littlethatchcottage.com website: www.littlethatchcottage.com

GORSE COTTAGE, BALMER LAWN ROAD, BROCKENHURST. Cottage/bungalow on open forest road close to village in New Forest. Sleeps 4 in 2 bedrooms. Conservatory, luxury bathroom, log fire, TV/video, secluded sunny garden. Pets welcome. Contact: MR J. GILBERT (0870 3210020.) ETC ★★★★ [Pets £15 per week]
e-mail: info@gorsecottage.co.uk website: www.gorsecottage.co.uk

MRS E.E. MATTHEWS, THE ACORNS, OGDENS, NEAR FORDINGBRIDGE SP6 2PY (01425 655552). Luxury two bedroomed residential-type caravan. Sleeps 4/6. Maintained to high standard, kitchen, showeroom, sitting/diningroom, outside laundry area, own garden. Lovely New Forest setting. Non-smoking, ample parking. Children over five years. Well-behaved dogs welcome (max. 2). Terms £185 - £335, Easter to mid-October. [Pets £10 each per week].
e-mail: acornshols@btopenworld.com website: www.dogscome2.co.uk

THE WATERSPLASH HOTEL, THE RISE, BROCKENHURST SO42 7ZP (01590 622344). Prestigious New Forest family-run country house hotel set in large garden. Noted for fine personal service, accommodation and traditional English cuisine at its best. All rooms en suite. Luxury four-poster with double spa bath. Swimming pool. Short walk to open forest. RAC, AA ★★ Colour brochure available.[🐕]
e-mail: bookings@watersplash.co.uk website: www.watersplash.co.uk

MRS J. PEARCE, ST. URSULA, 30 HOBART ROAD, NEW MILTON BH25 6EG (01425 613515). Excellent facilities and warm welcome for well behaved pets and owners! Ground floor suite suitable for disabled guests, plus single and twin rooms. Bed & Breakfast from £27.50. ◆◆◆◆ [🐕]

New Forest (Sway)

Area of heath and woodland of nearly 150 square miles, formerly Royal hunting grounds.

MRS THELMA ROWE, TIVERTON, 9 CRUSE CLOSE, SWAY SO41 6AY (Tel & Fax: 01590 683092). Ground floor and first floor suites. Both en suite with sitting room, tea making facilities, fridge, TV and video. Quiet, very comfortable, friendly accommodation. Prices from £28pppn. VB ★★★★ [Pets £2 per night]
e-mail: ronrowe@talk21.com website: www.tivertonnewforest.co.uk

Petersfield

Town 11 miles north east of Portsmouth.

LANGRISH HOUSE, LANGRISH, PETERSFIELD GU32 1RN (01730 266941).17th century house in idyllic country location. All bedrooms en suite and non-smoking. Small, cosy restaurant; weddings and conferences catered for.
e-mail: frontdesk@langrishhouse.co.uk website: www.langrishhouse.co.uk

Portsmouth

Historic port and naval base, with Nelson's flagship HMS Victory in harbour.

Quality 2-star accommodation with a superb sea front location. Good walking! All rooms en suite, etc. Passenger lift, licensed bar/restaurant, car park. Small charge for pets. Contact: MARK & JENNY BRUNNING, THE SEACREST HOTEL, 12 SOUTH PARADE, SOUTHSEA, PORTSMOUTH PO5 2JB (02392 733192; Fax: 02392 832523). AA ★★ 72%.
e-mail: seacrest@boltblue.com website: www.seacresthotel.co.uk

Ringwood

Busy market town, centre for trout fishing, trekking and rambling. Bournemouth 13 miles.

MRS DYSON, THE HIGH CORNER INN, LINWOOD, RINGWOOD, HANTS BH24 3QY (01425 473973, Fax: 01425 483052). Seven en suite bedrooms deep in the heart of The New Forest. Real ales, home-cooked food, Sunday carvery and log fires. Pets welcome.

BASKERVILLE ARMS HOTEL, Clyro, Near Hay-on-Wye HR3 5RZ
Tel: 01497 820670 **AA ★★**
Delightfully placed comfortable retreat 1.2 miles from Hay-on-Wye. Run by resident proprietors, the hotel provides tasty, home-cooked food in bar and restaurant, using the best local produce. This little hotel is a fine holiday base and well-appointed en suite bedrooms serve the purpose excellently. See website for Special Rate Breaks.
e-mail: info@baskervillearms.co.uk • www.baskervillearms.co.uk

The Rock Cottage – Huntington, Kington
Secluded, stone-built, character cottage overlooking picturesque farm and woodlands near Offa's Dyke footpath. Ideal for touring, birdwatching, golf and pony trekking. Hay-on-Wye and Black Mountains 20 minutes. Sleeps 4/6. Two bedrooms, fully equipped kitchen, lounge with wood-burner. Central Heating. Spacious garden with patio area. Children and pets welcome. Details from **Mrs C. Williams, Radnor's End, Huntington, Kington HR5 3NZ**
Tel: 01544 370289 **www.the-rock-cottage.co.uk**

Church Farm
Coddington, Ledbury HR8 1JJ Tel: 01531 640271
Black and White listed farmhouse on working farm in quiet hamlet. Oak-beamed en suite accommodation in two double and one twin. Close to Malvern Hills. Ideal touring being equidistant Ross-on-Wye, Hereford, Worcester and Gloucester. Plenty of space and fields for dogs to run. Warm hospitality assured in quiet, relaxed atmosphere. Excellent pub in next village. Log fires, TV. AA ★★★★

www.dexta.co.uk

Two flats (sleep 4), each superbly equipped, with open plan lounge, fitted kitchen/dining area, bathroom and toilet.The Granary has a wood burner, the Dairy on the ground floor an open fireplace. All linen and towels included. Ideal base for touring; lovely little woodland and riverside walks on the farm itself. Pets welcome under strict control. Terms from £175 per week.
Mrs N. Owens, The Grove, Pembridge, Leominster HR6 9HP
Tel: 01544 388268 • e-mail: nancy@grovedesign.co.uk
ETC ★★★

LEA HOUSE is a former 16th Century Coaching Inn, beautifully refurbished with antiques, an inglenook fireplace and loads of beams. Home-made breads and preserves complement the excellent home-cooked meals. The area is a doggy paradise - The Royal Forest of Dean, Wye Valley and Welsh hills are close by. NO SMOKING. Dogs £6 per stay.
Lea, Ross-on-Wye HR9 7JZ • Tel: 01989 750652
e-mail: enquiries@leahouse.co.uk • www.leahouse.co.uk

THE KING'S HEAD HOTEL, 8 HIGH STREET, ROSS-ON-WYE HR9 5HL
FREEPHONE: 0800 801098 • www.kingshead.co.uk
Small coaching inn dating back to the 14th century with all bedrooms offering en suite bathrooms and a full range of modern amenities. Comprehensive menu offers home-cooked food which is served in a warm and friendly atmosphere. Bargain breaks all year round.

Pet-Friendly
Pubs, Inns & Hotels
on pages 390-405
Please note that these establishments may not feature in the main section of this book

Great Malvern

Fashionable spa town in last century with echoes of that period.

KATE AND DENIS KAVANAGH, WHITEWELLS FARM COTTAGES, RIDGEWAY CROSS, NEAR MALVERN WR13 5JR (01886 880607; Fax: 01886 880360). Charming converted Cottages, sleep 2–6. Fully equipped with colour TV, microwave, barbecue, fridge, iron, etc. Linen, towels also supplied. One cottage suitable for the disabled with full wheelchair access. Short breaks, long lets, large groups. ETC ★★★★ [pw! Pets £10 per week.] Also see Display Advert..
e-mail: info@whitewellsfarm.co.uk website: www.whitewellsfarm.co.uk

Hay-on-Wye

Small market town 15 miles north east of Brecon.

BASKERVILLE ARMS HOTEL, CLYRO, NEAR HAY-ON-WYE HR3 5RZ (01497 820670). Delightfully placed comfortable retreat with well appointed en suite bedrooms. Tasty, home-cooked food in bar and restaurant, using the best local produce. Special break rates. AA ★★
e-mail: info@baskervillearms.co.uk website: www.baskervillearms.co.uk

Hereford

Cathedral town on River Wye, 45 miles south west of Birmingham.

CAREY DEANE AND ROCK HOUSE. Two oak-beamed cottages on working farm overlooking River Wye. Sleep 4/8 + cot. Non-smoking. Pets and children welcome. Open all year. £250-£675 weekly. One dog free. Contact: MRS M. SLATER, RUXTON FARM, KINGS CAPLE, HEREFORD HR1 4TX (Tel & Fax: 01432 840493). [🐕]
e-mail: milly@wyevalleycottages.com website: www.wyevalleycottages.com

Kington

Town on River Arrow, close to Welsh border, 12 miles north of Leominster.

THE ROCK COTTAGE, HUNTINGTON, KINGTON. Secluded, stone-built cottage near Offa's Dyke footpath. Ideal for touring, birdwatching, golf and pony trekking. Sleeps 4/6. Fully equipped kitchen, lounge with wood-burner. Central Heating. Spacious garden. Children and pets welcome. Details from MRS C. WILLIAMS, RADNOR'S END, HUNTINGTON, KINGTON HR5 3NZ (01544 370289). [🐕]
website: www.the-rock-cottage.co.uk

Symbols

- 🐕 Indicates that pets are welcome free of charge.
- £ Indicates that a charge is made for pets: nightly or weekly.
- pw! Shows some special provision for pets; exercise facility, feeding or accommodation arrangement.
- ⌂ Indicates separate pets accommodation.

Ledbury

Town 12 miles east of Hereford with many timbered houses.

CHURCH FARM, CODDINGTON, LEDBURY HR8 IJJ (01531 640271). Black and white 16th-century Farmhouse on a working farm close to the Malvern Hills — ideal for touring and walking. Two double and one twin bedrooms. Excellent home cooking. Warm welcome assured. Open all year. AA ★★★★. [🐕]
website: www.dexta.co.uk

Leominster

Town on the River Lugg, 12 miles north of Hereford.

CLIVE & CYNTHIA PRIOR, MOCKTREE BARNS, LEINTWARDINE, LUDLOW SY7 0LY (01547 540441). Award-winning cottages around sunny courtyard. Sleep 2-6. Comfortable, well-equipped. Friendly owners. Dogs and children welcome. Non-Smoking. Lovely country walks. Ludlow, seven miles. Brochure. Level 1 Accessibility Award. VB ★★★ [🐕] See also colour advertisement page 251.
e-mail: mocktreebarns@care4free.net website: www.mocktreeholidays.co.uk

Pembridge

Tiny medieval village surrounded by meadows and orchards.

MRS N. OWENS, THE GROVE, PEMBRIDGE, LEOMINSTER HR6 9HP (01544 388268). Two flats (sleep 4), each superbly equipped. All linen and towels included. Ideal base for touring; lovely walks on farm. Pets welcome under strict control. Terms from £175 pw. ETC ★★★ [Pets £5 per week, pw!]
e-mail: nancy@grovedesign.co.uk

Ross-on-Wye

An attractive town standing on a hill rising from the left bank on the Wye. Cardiff 47 miles, Gloucester 17.

LEA HOUSE, LEA, ROSS-ON-WYE HR9 7JZ (Tel & Fax: 01989 750652). Double/family en suite; twin/double en suite; twin private bath - all individually styled with TV and beverage tray. Secluded garden. Dogs very welcome. AA ★★★★ [Dogs £6 per stay]. See Display Advert.
e-mail: enquiries@leahouse.co.uk website: www.leahouse.co.uk

THE KING'S HEAD HOTEL, 8 HIGH STREET, ROSS-ON-WYE HR9 5HL (FREEPHONE: 0800 801098). Small coaching inn dating back to the 14th century with all bedrooms offering en suite bathrooms and a full range of modern amenities. Comprehensive menu offers home-cooked food which is served in a warm and friendly atmosphere. Bargain breaks all year round. [🐕]
website: www.kingshead.co.uk

THE INN ON THE WYE, KERNE BRIDGE, GOODRICH, NEAR ROSS-ON-WYE HR9 5QS (01600 890872; Fax: 01600 890594). Beautifully restored 18th century coaching inn, near Goodrich Castle on the banks of the River Wye. All bedrooms en suite. Peaceful country walks, ideal base for touring. RAC ◆◆◆, AA (Awaiting Grading).
e-mail: theinnonthewye@kernebridge.freeserve.co.uk website: www.theinnonthewye.co.uk

THE ARCHES GUEST HOUSE, WALFORD ROAD, ROSS-ON-WYE HR9 5PT (01989 563348). All rooms en suite with colour TV and beverage making facilities. Centrally heated. Bed and Breakfast. Family room available. Pets welcome. ETC ◆◆◆ [🐕]
e-mail: the.arches@which.net

ISLAND COTTAGE HOLIDAYS

ETC ★★★ to ★★★★★

Charming individual cottages in lovely rural surroundings and close to the sea. Over 55 cottages situated throughout the Isle of Wight. Beautiful views, attractive gardens, delightful country walks.

All equipped to a high standard and graded for quality by the Tourist Board.

For a brochure please **Tel: (01929) 480080**

e-mail: enq@islandcottageholidays.com • website: www.islandcottageholidays.com

Open all year (Sleep 1 - 12) £185 – £1495 per week. Short breaks available in low season (3 nights) £155 – £399

Bonchurch, Cowes

ASHCLIFF HOLIDAY APARTMENT

Bonchurch, Isle of Wight PO38 1NT

Idyllic and secluded position in the picturesque seaside village of Bonchurch. Self-contained ground floor apartment (sleeps 2) adjoining Victorian house, set in large south-facing gardens with sea views and sheltered by a thickly wooded cliff. Large, private car park. ETC ★★★. Dogs very welcome. ***For free brochure Tel: (01983) 853919***

LAKE HOTEL Shore Road, Lower Bonchurch PO38 IRF

Tel: 01983 852613 • e-mail: fhg@lakehotel.co.uk

Lovely country house hotel in a beautiful quiet two-acre garden on the seaward side of Bonchurch. The hotel offers first class food and service, all in a relaxed and friendly atmosphere. All rooms are en suite with complimentary tea/coffee facilities and TV. We can offer an Isle of Wight car ferry inclusive price of just £185 for four nights' half board during March/April/May and October

ACTUALLY ON THE BEACH

"The Waterfall", Shore Road, Bonchurch, Ventnor, I.O.W. PO38 1RN

Ground-floor self-contained flat. Sleeps 3 adults. Fully equipped. Parking. Sun verandah and Garden.

Brochure from **Mrs A. Evans** **e-mail: benbrook.charioteer@virgin.net** **Tel: 01983 852246**

MEMBER Isle of Wight TOURISM

SUNNYCOTT CARAVAN PARK
COWES • ISLE OF WIGHT

BRITISH GRADED HOLIDAY PARKS ★★★★

Small, quiet, family-run country park in rural surroundings close to Cowes. All caravans have full cooker, microwave, fridge and colour TV. Shop and laundry room on site. We welcome your pets. Short breaks can be arranged subject to availability.

Phone 01983 292859 for brochure • Proprietors: Jennifer Payne and Jim Payne
www.sunnycottcaravanpark.co.uk • e-mail: info@sunnycottcaravanpark.co.uk

Readers are requested to mention this FHG publication when seeking accommodation

A peaceful and beautiful 19th century rectory set in two-and-a-half acres of lovely gardens, just two minutes' drive from Freshwater Bay. Good area for walking, golfing, sailing, paragliding and bird watching. Close to National Trust areas. Double and family rooms, all en suite. TV lounge, log fires. Children and pets welcome.
B&B pppn: £26 low season, £28 mid season, £30 high season. Children ½ price.

Mr and Mrs B. Moscoff, Seahorses, Victoria Road, Freshwater PO40 9PP
Tel/Fax: 01983 752574 • e-mail: seahorses-iow@tiscali.co.uk • website: www.seahorsesisleofwight.com

HILLGROVE PARK

Field Lane, St Helens, Ryde PO33 1UT

A small, secluded, family-run holiday caravan park. Only minutes from safe sandy beaches, beautiful countryside and places of interest. Try our centrally heated units for that early or late season break.
Heated swimming pool, large play areas for both older and younger children, games room. Car ferries arranged on any route.

For details ring (01983) 872802 *or visit our website www.hillgrove.co.uk*

SENTRY MEAD HOTEL

Sentry Mead Hotel is a beautiful Victorian Country House set in its own spacious gardens in the tranquil surroundings of West Wight. Just 150 yards from the beach and with scenic downland walks on the doorstep, this is the perfect place to relax and unwind. Attentive staff, excellent food and an informal atmosphere all combine for a restful stay. Well-behaved dogs are very welcome. Proprietors: ***Sarah & Jean-Pierre***

Sentry Mead Hotel, Madeira Road, Totland Bay
Isle of Wight PO39 0BJ
Tel: 01983 753212 • Fax: 01983 754710
e-mail: info@sentrymead.co.uk • www.sentrymead.co.uk

"....a jewel in the crown of the West Wight"

The Country Garden Hotel

Church Hill, Totland Bay, Isle of Wight PO39 0ET

A five minute stroll to the Solent, surrounded by lovely walks and hikes including Tennyson Downs and The Needles, and a short drive to the bustling port of Yarmouth. Set in lovely gardens, this quiet and intimate hotel offers the best of all worlds for your holiday, including making your pet feel welcome! Excellent cuisine from our Chef of some thirteen years in our locally popular restaurant overlooking the gardens. Garden, sea view and ground floor rooms available, all en suite with colour TV, fridge, duvets, down pillows, bathrobes, phone, central heating, hairdryer, tea & coffee and ample off-street parking.

ANY DAY TO ANY DAY, B&B or HALF BOARD • **ADULTS ONLY**

Ferry inclusive rates October through April

B&B from £50.00pp/day; DB&B from £69pp/day, £422.50pp/week

For brochure, sample menu, tariff, and testimonials from recent guests, please

Phone/Fax: 01983 754 521

e-mail: countrygardeniow@aol.com

www.thecountrygardenhotel.co.uk

HILLSIDE HOTEL

Mitchell Avenue, Ventnor, Isle of Wight PO38 1DR

Peaceful and relaxed atmosphere • Home cooking • All rooms en suite and individually furnished and decorated • Residential Licence • Dogs very welcome

Tel: 01983 852271 • Fax: 01983 855310 • www.hillside-hotel.co.uk

E-mail: hillside-hotel@btconnect.com AA/ ETC ★★

ISLE OF WIGHT · Nr YARMOUTH

the Orchards

HOLIDAY CARAVAN & CAMPING PARK

AA Premier Park · The Caravan Club Affiliated Site

- Indoor pool (open all year)
- Outdoor pool
- Luxury holiday caravans some with central heating
- Dog excercise areas
- 3/4 Day Mini Breaks
- Excellent facilities for caravanners and campers
- Special Ferry Deals

OPEN CHRISTMAS AND NEW YEAR

www.orchards-holiday-park.co.uk t. 01983 531331

ISLAND COTTAGE HOLIDAYS. Charming individual cottages in lovely rural surroundings and close to the sea. Over 55 cottages situated throughout the Isle of Wight. Beautiful views, attractive gardens, delightful country walks. All equipped to a high standard and graded for quality by the Tourist Board. For a brochure please telephone 01929 480080. ETC ★★★ to ★★★★★.
e-mail: enq@islandcottageholidays.com website: www.islandcottageholidays.com

Bonchurch

One mile north-east of Ventnor.

MRS J. LINES, ASHCLIFF HOLIDAY APARTMENT, BONCHURCH PO38 1NT (01983 853919). Self-contained ground floor apartment (sleeps 2) adjoining Victorian house. Large south-facing gardens. Sea views. Large private car park. Pets welcome to use garden. ETC ★★★★ [🐕]

LAKE HOTEL SHORE ROAD, LOWER BONCHURCH PO38 1RF (01983 852613). Lovely country house hotel in a beautiful quiet two-acre garden. First class food and service, all in a relaxed and friendly atmosphere. All rooms en suite. Car ferry inclusive prices available. ETC ★★★★
e-mail: fhg@lakehotel.co.uk website: www.lakehotel.co.uk

A. EVANS, "THE WATERFALL", SHORE ROAD, BONCHURCH, VENTNOR PO38 1RN (01983 852246). Spacious, self-contained Flat. Sleeps 3 adults. Colour TV. Sun verandah and garden. The beach, the sea and the downs. [🐕]
e-mail: benbrook.charioteer@virgin.net

Cowes

Yachting centre with yearly regatta since 1814. Newport 4 miles.

SUNNYCOTT CARAVAN PARK, COWES PO31 8NN (01983 292859). Small, quiet, family-run park close to Cowes. All caravans have full cooker, microwave, fridge and colour TV. Shop and laundry room on site. We welcome pets. Short breaks arranged. ETC ★★★★ [Pets £10 per week]
e-mail: info@sunnycottcaravanpark.co.uk website: www.sunnycottcaravanpark.co.uk

Freshwater

Two kilometres south of Totland. South-west of Farringford, formerly the home of Tennyson.

MR AND MRS B. MOSCOFF, SEAHORSES, VICTORIA ROAD, FRESHWATER PO40 9PP (Tel & Fax: 01983 752574). Peaceful 19th century rectory set in two-and-a-half acres of lovely gardens. Good area for walking, golfing, sailing, paragliding and bird watching. Double and family rooms, all en suite. TV lounge, log fires. B&B pppn: £26 low season, £28 mid season, £30 high season. Children half price. [🐕]
e-mail: seahorses-iow@tiscali.co.uk website: www.seahorsesisleofwight.com

Ryde

Popular resort and yachting centre, fine sands, pier. Shanklin 9 miles, Newport 7, Sandown 6.

HILLGROVE PARK, FIELD LANE, ST HELENS, NEAR RYDE PO33 1UT (01983 872802). Family-run Caravan Park. Select site 10 minutes sea, 3 minutes bus stop. Many local walks, heated swimming pool. Phone for brochure. Pets welcome (only one per unit). ETC ★★★★★ Holiday Park. [Pets £3.00 per night, £20.00 per week]
website: www.hillgrove.co.uk

Symbols

🐕 Indicates that pets are welcome free of charge.

£ Indicates that a charge is made for pets: nightly or weekly.

pw! Shows some special provision for pets; exercise facility, feeding or accommodation arrangement.

⌂ Indicates separate pets accommodation.

Totland Bay

Small resort 3 miles south-west of Yarmouth Bay.

SENTRY MEAD HOTEL, MADEIRA ROAD, TOTLAND BAY PO39 0BJ (01983 753212; Fax: 01983 754710). This beautiful Victorian villa is set in its own spacious gardens in the tranquil surroundings of West Wight. Just 150 yards from the beach, and with scenic downland walks on the doorstep, this is the perfect place to relax and unwind. All bedrooms en suite. ETC/AA ★★★ Silver Award [Pets £3 per day, £18 per week]
e-mail: info@sentrymead.co.uk website: www.sentrymead.co.uk

COUNTRY GARDEN HOTEL, CHURCH HILL, TOTLAND BAY PO39 OET (Tel & Fax: 01983 754521). All en suite, garden and seaview rooms available; TV, phone, duvets, feather/down pillows, fridge, hairdryer etc. Special winter, spring, autumn rates. [pw! Pets £4 per day]
e-mail: countrygardeniow@aol.com website: www.thecountrygardenhotel.co.uk

Ventnor

Well-known resort with good sands, downs, popular as a winter holiday resort. Nearby is St Boniface Down, the highest point on the island. Ryde 13 miles, Newport 12, Sandown 7, Shanklin 4.

CASTLEHAVEN CARAVAN SITE, NITON, NEAR VENTNOR PO38 2ND (01983 730495). Island's most southerly six-berth, two-bedroomed caravans, all overlooking the Channel. Small, friendly site. Unspoilt seashore/countryside setting. On the shore. Kiosk serving breakfasts/evening meals by arrangement.
website: www.castlehaven.me.uk

MRS B. HART, HILLSIDE HOTEL, MITCHELL AVENUE, VENTNOR PO38 1DR (01983 852271; Fax: 01983 855310). Peaceful and relaxed atmosphere. Home cooking . All rooms en suite and individually furnished and decorated. Residential Licence. Dogs very welcome. Open all year. AA/ ETC ★★ [🐕]
e-mail: hillside-hotel@btconnect.com website: www.hillside-hotel.co.uk

Yarmouth

Coastal resort situated 9 miles west of Newport. Castle built by Henry VIII for coastal defence.

THE ORCHARDS HOLIDAY CARAVAN & CAMPING PARK, NEWBRIDGE, YARMOUTH PO41 0TS (Dial-a-brochure 01983 531331; Fax: 01983 531666). Luxury holiday caravans, some with central heating. Excellent facilities including indoor pool with licensed cafe. Dog exercise areas. Coarse fishing; ideal walking, cycling and golf. Open late February to New Year. [Pets £1/£2 per night]
e-mail: info@orchards-holiday-park.co.uk website:www.orchards-holiday-park.co.uk

Pet-Friendly
Pubs, Inns & Hotels
on pages 390-405
Please note that these establishments may not feature in the main section of this book

Garden of England Cottages
Accommodation for all seasons
www.gardenofenglandcottages.co.uk

BIG PAWS and LITTLE PAWS ARE WELCOME and GO FREE with every well-behaved owner, in many of our holiday homes.

ON-LINE BOOKING & AVAILABILITY Tel: +44 [0] 1892-510117
Email: holidays@gardenofenglandcottages.co.uk
All our properties are VisitBritain quality assessed.

Fairhaven Holiday Cottages

A wide selection of personally inspected accommodation in Kent and Sussex

Tel: 01208 821 255 www.fairhaven-holidays.co.uk

Ashford, Broadstairs, St Margaret's Bay, Sevenoaks

Luxury pine lodges, superior self-catering accommodation overlooking two lakes in beautiful Kent countryside. Rough shooting and coarse fishing on our farms. Weeks or short breaks. Contact:

ASHBY FARMS LTD, PLACE FARM, KENARDINGTON, ASHFORD TN26 2LZ • Tel: 01233 733332 • Fax: 01233 733326
e-mail: info@ashbyfarms.com • www.ashbyfarms.com

HANSON HOTEL (Lic.)

41 Belvedere Road, Broadstairs CT10 1PF • Tel: (01843) 868936.

A small friendly Georgian hotel with relaxed atmosphere, centrally situated for beach, shops and transport. B&B only or with 5-course Evening Dinner. Children and pets welcome.

OPEN ALL YEAR • OVER 25 YEARS WELCOMING GUESTS

Brochure – Trevor and Jean Webb. **www. hansonhotel.co.uk**

REACH COURT FARM COTTAGES

REACH COURT FARM, ST MARGARET'S BAY, DOVER CT15 6AQ
Tel & Fax: 01304 852159

Situated in the heart of the Mitchell family farm, surrounded by open countryside. Five luxury self-contained cottages set around the old farmyard, with open views of the rural valley both front and back.

e-mail: enquiries@reachcourtfarmcottages.co.uk
www.reachcourtfarmcottages.co.uk

GOLDING HOP FARM COTTAGE

Plaxtol, Near Sevenoaks TN15 0PS • Tel: 01732 885432

★★★ Cottage on 13-acre cobnut farm in Bourne Valley. Sleeps 5 plus cot. Children and pets welcome. Open all year. £220-£410 pw.

info@goldinghopfarm.com • www.goldinghopfarm.com

Readers are requested to mention this guidebook when making enquiries about accommodation.

GARDEN OF ENGLAND COTTAGES IN KENT & EAST SUSSEX, CLAYFIELD HOUSE, 50 ST JOHNS ROAD, TUNBRIDGE WELLS, KENT TN4 9NY (01892 510117). Pets welcome in many of our holiday homes, and go free with every well-behaved owner. All properties VisitBritain quality assured. On-line booking and availability. [🐕]
e-mail: holidays@gardenofenglandcottages.co.uk website: www.gardenofenglandcottages.co.uk

FAIRHAVEN HOLIDAY COTTAGES. A wide selection of personally inspected accommodation in Kent and Sussex (01208 821255).
website: www.fairhaven-holidays.co.uk

Ashford

Market town on Great Stour River, 13 miles south-west of Canterbury.

Luxury pine lodges, superior self-catering accommodation overlooking two lakes in beautiful Kent countryside. Rough shooting and coarse fishing on our farms. Weeks or short breaks. Contact: ASHBY FARMS LTD, PLACE FARM, KENARDINGTON, ASHFORD TN26 2LZ (01233 733332; Fax: 01233 733326). [Pets £10 per stay]
e-mail: info@ashbyfarms.com website: www.ashbyfarms.com

Broadstairs

Quiet resort, once a favourite of Charles Dickens. Good sands and promenade.

HANSON HOTEL, 41 BELVEDERE ROAD, BROADSTAIRS CT10 1PF (01843 868936). Small, friendly licensed Georgian Hotel. Home comforts; children and pets welcome. Attractive bar. SAE. [pw! Pets £1 per night, £5 per week]
website: www.hansonhotel.co.uk

St Margaret's Bay

4 miles north-east of Dover

DEREK AND JACQUI MITCHELL, REACH COURT FARM COTTAGES, REACH COURT FARM, ST MARGARET'S BAY, DOVER CT15 6AQ (Tel & Fax: 01304 852159). Situated in the heart of the Mitchell family farm, surrounded by open countryside, these five luxury self-contained cottages are very special. The cottages are set around the old farmyard, which has been attractively set to lawns and shrubs, with open views of the rural valley both front and back. ETC ★★★★
e-mail: enquiries@reachcourtfarmcottages.co.uk website: www.reachcourtfarmcottages.co.uk

Sevenoaks

Town on North Downs, 21 miles south east of London.

GOLDING HOP FARM COTTAGE, PLAXTOL, NEAR SEVENOAKS TN15 0PS (01732 885432). Three Star cottage on 13-acre cobnut farm in Bourne Valley. Sleeps 5 plus cot. Children and pets welcome. Open all year. £220-£410 pw. [Pets £12 per week].
e-mail: info@goldinghopfarm.com website: www.goldinghopfarm.com

Ware (near Sandwich)

Rural location 3 miles from Sandwich, 9 miles from Canterbury.

DOREEN ADY, HAWTHORN FARM COTTAGES, WARE, NEAR SANDWICH (01304 813560). Four converted two-bedroom cottages, sleeping 4-5. Ideally situated for relaxing or exploring the Kent coastline. Children's play field. Ample parking. Pets welcome by arrangement. ETC ★★★/★★★★. [pw! Pets £20 per week]
e-mail: hawthornfarmcottages@dsl.pipex.com www.hawthornfarmcottages.co.uk

Blackburn, Blackpool, Clitheroe, Lancaster, Pilling

THE BROWN LEAVES COUNTRY HOTEL, LONGSIGHT ROAD, COPSTER GREEN, NEAR BLACKBURN BB1 9EU • 01254 249523 • Fax: 01254 245240

Situated on the A59 halfway between Preston and Clitheroe, five miles from Junction 31 on M6 in beautiful Ribble Valley. All rooms ground floor, en suite facilities, satellite TV, tea-making and hairdryer. Guests' lounge and bar lounge. Car parking. Pets by arrangement. All credit cards welcome. **www.brownleavescountryhotel.co.uk**

The Brayton

7-8 Finchley Road, Gynn Square, BLACKPOOL FY1 2LP
www.the-brayton-hotel.com
e-mail: info@the-brayton-hotel.com

- *Quiet and pleasantly located licensed hotel.*
- *Overlooking Gynn gardens and the promenade.*
- *Short drive or tram ride to all the attractions.*
- *Full 'Restaurant Style' menu served every day.*
- *Dogs most welcome and free. Open all year.*

Phone: 01253 351645

The Assheton Arms, Downham, Near Clitheroe BB7 4BJ

A delightful traditional country pub in a picturesque village in the beautiful Ribble Valley. Hosts, David and Wendy Busby offer a range of food to suit all tastes, specialising in seafood. There is a variety of modern and traditional beers; ample parking; patio for summer months. Children and dogs welcome. *Totally non-smoking.* **Tel: 01200 441227 www.assheton-arms.co.uk**

Hill Farm Holiday Home, Tatham, Lancaster

Brand new, 2005 static caravan. Fantastic views and warm welcome.
For further details contact: Janet Staveley 015242 62424
e-mail: janstaveley@tiscali.co.uk • www.yorkshire-dales-holiday.co.uk

Tel: 01253 790324
www.bellfarm.co.uk

BELL FARM

Beryl and Peter welcome you to their 18th century farmhouse in the quiet village of Pilling. The area has many footpaths and is ideal for cycling. Easy access to Blackpool, Lancaster, the Forest of Bowland and the Lake District. One family room, one double and one twin. All en suite. Tea and coffee making facilities. Lounge and dining room. All centrally heated. Full English breakfast.
Children and pets welcome.
Open all year except Christmas and New Year.
Bed and Breakfast from £27.50 - £50.

Peter Richardson, Bell Farm, Bradshaw Lane, Scronkey, Pilling, Preston PR3 6SN

Please note

All the information in this book is given in good faith in the belief that it is correct. However, the publishers cannot guarantee the facts given in these pages, neither are they responsible for changes in policy, ownership or terms that may take place after the date of going to press. Readers should always satisfy themselves that the facilities they require are available and that the terms, if quoted, still apply.

❖ THE GARDEN COURT HOTEL ❖

22 BANK SQUARE, SOUTHPORT PR9 0DG

Recently restored Victorian town house overlooking Central Promenade, Marine Lake, Theatre and Floral Hall Conference Centre. All other amenities within easy walking distance. All bedrooms enjoy en suite/private facilities, central heating, double glazing, CTV etc. Some four-poster rooms. Tea,coffee, mineral water. 24 hour access. Parking. B&B from £25 pppn.

Tel & Fax: 01704 530219

Web: www.gardencourtsouthport.co.uk

www.crimondhotel.com **CRIMOND HOTEL** ETC ★★

Knowsley Road, Southport PR9 0HN

Tel: 01704 536456 • Fax: 01704 548643

The Crimond Hotel is situated close to the promenade and town centre. 16 bedrooms all en suite with colour TV, radio, hairdryer and direct-dial telephone. Large car park. Free use of health club and swimming pool nearby. Open all year.

Blackburn

Industrial town on River Darwen and on Leeds and Liverpool Canal.

THE BROWN LEAVES COUNTRY HOTEL, LONGSIGHT ROAD, COPSTER GREEN, NEAR BLACKBURN BB1 9EU (01254 249523; Fax: 01254 245240). Situated on the A59 halfway between Preston and Clitheroe, five miles from Junction 31 on M6 in beautiful Ribble Valley. All rooms ground floor, en suite facilities, satellite TV, tea-making and hairdryer. Guests' lounge and bar lounge. Car parking. Pets by arrangement. All credit cards welcome. [🐕]
website: www.brownleavescountryhotel.co.uk

Blackpool

Famous resort with fine sands and many attractions and vast variety of entertainments. Blackpool Tower (500ft). Three piers. Manchester 47 miles, Lancaster 26, Preston 17, Fleetwood 8.

THE BRAYTON, 7-8 FINCHLEY ROAD, GYNN SQUARE, BLACKPOOL FY1 2LP (01253 351645). Quiet licensed hotel overlooking Gynn gardens and the promenade. Full 'restaurant style' menu served daily. Dogs most welcome. Open all year. ETC ◆◆◆ [🐕]
e-mail: info@the-brayton-hotel.com website: www.the-brayton-hotel.com

MRS C. MOORE, COTSWOLD, 2A HADDON ROAD, NORBRECK, BLACKPOOL FY2 9AH (01253 352227). Quality flat fully equipped. Cross road to beach and trams. Phone or SAE for brochure. [🐕]

Clitheroe

Town above River Ribble valley, 10 miles north east of Blackburn.

THE ASSHETON ARMS, DOWNHAM, NEAR CLITHEROE BB7 4BJ (01200 441227). A traditional country pub in the beautiful Ribble Valley. Food to suit all tastes, variety of modern and traditional beers. Children and dogs welcome. Totally non-smoking.
website: www.assheton-arms.co.uk

Readers are requested to mention this FHG publication when seeking accommodation

Lancaster

City on River Lune, 20 miles north of Preston.

HILL FARM HOLIDAY HOME, TATHAM, LANCASTER LA2 8PP. Brand new 2005 static caravan. Fantastic views and warm welcome. For further details contact JANET STAVELEY on 015242 62424. [Pets £20 per week]
e-mail: janstaveley@tiscali.co.uk website: www.yorkshire-dales-holiday.co.uk

Pilling

Village 3 miles north east of Pressall.

BERYL AND PETER RICHARDSON, BELL FARM, BRADSHAW LANE, SCRONKEY, PILLING, PRESTON PR3 6SN (01253 790324).18th century farmhouse with one family room, one double and one twin. All en suite, and centrally heated. Full English breakfast is served. Open all year except Christmas and New Year. [🐕]
website: www.bellfarm.co.uk

Southport

Elegant seaside resort with Victorian feel. Amusement park, zoo and Birkdale championship golf course.

THE GARDEN COURT, 22 BANK SQUARE, SOUTHPORT PR9 0DG (Tel & Fax: 01704 530219). Victorian town house overlooking Central Promenade, Theatre, Marine Lake and Floral Hall Conference Centre. All attractions within easy walking distance. En suite bedrooms, some four-poster. Friendly, comfortable accommodation from £25 B&B pppn. [🐕]
website: www.gardencourtsouthport.co.uk

CRIMOND HOTEL & RESTAURANT, KNOWSLEY ROAD, SOUTHPORT PR9 0HN (01704 536456; Fax: 01704 548643). Situated close to the town centre, this hotel can cater for all your needs with free use of indoor swimming pool and health club nearby. Open all year. Table d'hôte service. Full central heating. ETC ★★ [Pets £1 per night].
website: www.crimondhotel.com

Market Harborough

Town on River Welland 14 miles south-east of Leicester.

BROOK MEADOW HOLIDAYS. Three self-catering chalets, farmhouse Bed and Breakfast, Carp fishing, camping and caravan site with electric hookups. Phone for brochure. ETC ★★★ to ★★★★. MRS MARY HART, WELFORD ROAD, SIBBERTOFT, MARKET HARBOROUGH LE16 9UJ (01858 880886). [🐕 camping, £5 per night B&B, £10 Self-catering]
e-mail: brookmeadow@farmline.com website: www.brookmeadow.co.uk

Melton Mowbray

Old market town, centre of hunting country. Large cattle market. Church and Ann of Cleves' House are of interest. Kettering 29 miles, Market Harborough 22, Nottingham 18, Leicester 15.

SYSONBY KNOLL HOTEL, ASFORDBY ROAD, MELTON MOWBRAY LE13 OHP (01664 563563; Fax: 01664 410364.). Family-run hotel on edge of market town. Grounds of five acres with river frontage. Superb food, comfortable accommodation and a genuine welcome for pets. No charge for dogs, please see website for further details. ETC/AA ★★★ [🐕]
website: www.sysonby.com

Three well appointed cottages and riding school situated in the heart of the Lincolnshire Wolds.

GRANGEFARM COTTAGES & RIDING SCHOOL

The tasteful conversion of a spacious, beamed Victorian barn provides stylish and roomy cottages, one sleeping 6, and two sleeping 4 in one double and one twin bedroom, comfy sittingroom and diningroom. Fully equipped kitchen. Bathroom with bath and shower.

The Equestrian Centre offers professional tuition, an all-weather riding surface, stabling for guests' own horses, and an extensive network of bridle paths.

GRANGE FARM COTTAGES & RIDING SCHOOL
Waltham Road, Barnoldby-le-Beck, N.E. Lincs DN37 0AR
For Cottage Reservations Tel: 01472 822216 • Fax: 01472 233550
mobile: 07947 627663 • www.grangefarmcottages.com

English Tourism Council ★★★★ SELF CATERING

Little London Cottages, Tetford, Horncastle ETC ★★★★/★★★★★

Three very well-equipped properties, each standing in own garden, on our small estate. Lovely walks. 'The Garth', a single storey conversion of farm buildings with 3 bedrooms. 'Cornerways', a 19th century, two-bedroomed cottage with log fire. 'Mansion Cottage', a 17th/18th century cottage with two bedrooms, low ceilings and doorways, and steep stairs. Short breaks and special offers. Pets welcome free. Contact: **Mrs S. D. Sutcliffe, The Mansion House, Little London, Tetford, Horncastle LN9 6QL**
Tel: 01507 533697 or 07767 321213 • debbie@sutcliffell.freeserve.co.uk • www.littlelondoncottages.co.uk

Ground floor accommodation in chalet-type house. Central for Wolds, coast, fens, historic Lincoln. Market towns, Louth, Horncastle, Boston, Spilsby, Alford, Woodhall Spa. Two double bedrooms. Washbasin, TV; bathroom, toilet adjoining; lounge with colour TV, separate dining room. Drinks provided. Children welcome reduced rates. Car almost essential, parking. Numerous eating places nearby. B&B from £25 per person (double/single let). Open all year. Tourist Board Listed. *** PETS WELCOME FREE ***
MISS JESSIE SKELLERN, LEA HOLME, LANGTON-BY-WRAGBY, LINCOLN LN8 5PZ (01673 858339)

MRS GRAVES, GRANGE FARM, MALTBY-LE-MARSH, ALFORD LN13 0JP • 01507 450267

Farmhouse B&B and country cottages set in ten idyllic acres of Lincolnshire countryside. Peaceful base for leisure and sightseeing. Private fishing lake • Many farm animals • Brochure available

• •Pets welcome• • **www.grange-farmhouse.co.uk**

Barnoldby-le-Beck

Village 4 miles SW of Grimsby.

GRANGE FARM COTTAGES & RIDING SCHOOL, Waltham Road, Barnoldby-le-Beck DN37 0AR (01472 822216; Fax: 01472 233550; mobile: 07947 627663). Three well appointed cottages and riding school situated in the heart of the Lincolnshire Wolds. Sleep 4/6. ETC ★★★★ Equestrian Centre offers tuition, all-weather riding, stabling. [Pets £10 per week]
website: www.grangefarmcottages.com

Horncastle

Market town once famous for annual horse fairs. 13th century Church is noted for brasses and Civil War relic

LITTLE LONDON COTTAGES, TETFORD, HORNCASTLE. Three very well-equipped properties standing in own gardens on our small estate. Lovely walks. Short breaks and special offers. ETC ★★★★/★★★★★. Contact: MRS S.D. SUTCLIFFE, THE MANSION HOUSE, LITTLE LONDON, TETFORD, HORNCASTLE LN9 6QL (01507 533697; mobile: 07767 321213). [🐕]
e-mail: debbie@sutcliffell.freeserve.co.uk website: www.littlelondoncottages.co.uk

Terms quoted in this publication may be subject to increase if rises in costs necessitate

POACHERS HIDEAWAY HOLIDAY COTTAGES, FLINTWOOD FARM, BELCHFORD, HORNCASTLE LN9 5QN (01507 533555). Sleeps 2-24. Award winning 5-Star self catering cottages set in 150 acres of wildflower meadows, fishing lakes and woodland. Miles of private pathways, direct access onto Viking Way footpath. Sauna, jacuzzi and massages available. Linen and towels provided. Stunning views, peaceful and relaxing. ETC ★★★★★ [Pets £10 per week]
e-mail: sallytuxworth@poachershideaway.com website: www.poachershideaway.coms.

Langton-by-Wragby

Village located south-east of Wragby.

MISS JESSIE SKELLERN, LEA HOLME, LANGTON-BY-WRAGBY, LINCOLN LN8 5PZ (01673 858339). Ground floor accommodation in chalet-type house. Central for Wolds, coast, fens, historic Lincoln. Market towns, Louth, Horncastle, Boston, Spilsby, Alford, Woodhall Spa. Two double bedrooms. Washbasin, TV; bathroom, toilet adjoining; lounge with colour TV, separate dining room. Drinks provided. Children welcome reduced rates. Car almost essential, parking. Numerous eating places nearby. B&B from £25 per person (double/single let). Open all year. Pets welcome free. Tourist Board Listed [🐕]

Mablethorpe

Coastal resort 11 miles from Louth.

MRS GRAVES, GRANGE FARM, MALTBY-LE-MARSH, ALFORD LN13 0JP (01507 450267). Farmhouse B&B and country cottages set in ten idyllic acres of Lincolnshire countryside. Peaceful base for leisure, walking and sightseeing. Private fishing lake. Many farm animals. Brochure available. [Pets £4 per night B&B, £30 per week in cottages] [⌂]
website: www.grange-farmhouse.co.uk

Take a Blue Riband Holiday in beautiful Norfolk and take a pet free*

*One pet stays free when you book through this advert. Extra pet £10

Inexpensive Self Catering Holidays at ●Caister ●Hemsby ●Scratby ●California and ●Great Yarmouth All year round

Quality, Value and Service from a family business, since 1955

Detached Bungalows at Parklands
Hemsby Village, Children's Playground, Satellite TV, Miniature Railway.

Seafront Bungalows
Caister-on-Sea, with enclosed rear gardens leading to the beach.

Seafront Caravans
Caister-on-Sea, FREE gas and electricity.

Detached Chalets on Sea-Dell Park
Quiet location, Beach Road, Hemsby.

Belle Aire Park, Beach Rd, Hemsby
Super Chalets, Free electricity and Clubhouse. Safe children's playground. Pets are allowed on local beaches.

All equipped to very high standard

★ ***Free car parking at all locations***

Open Christmas & New Year

- **Popular low season breaks, bungalows from only £80**
- **Bargain Spring & Autumn breaks, excellent value chalets from £65**

Blue Riband Holidays

Simply the Best

☎ Direct Line for Bookings & Brochures
01493 730445 – Call 8am to 9pm 7 days a week
Debit / Credit Cards Accepted

Or browse our full brochure on our website at: www.BlueRibandHolidays.co.uk

For your free colour brochure phone the above number or write to:
Don Witheridge, Blue Riband House, Parklands, North Road, Hemsby, Great Yarmouth, Norfolk NR29 4HA

FHG Guides

publish a large range of well-known accommodation guides. We will be happy to send you details or you can use the order form at the back of this book.

FHG
K·U·P·E·R·A·R·D

Please note

All the information in this book is given in good faith in the belief that it is correct. However, the publishers cannot guarantee the facts given in these pages, neither are they responsible for changes in policy, ownership or terms that may take place after the date of going to press. Readers should always satisfy themselves that the facilities they require are available and that the terms, if quoted, still apply.

CASTAWAYS HOLIDAY PARK

BH & HPA approved

Set in the quiet, peaceful village of Bacton, with direct access to fine sandy beach, and ideal for beach fishing and discovering Norfolk and The Broads. Modern Caravans, Pine Lodges and Flats with all amenities. Licensed Club. Entertainment. Amusement Arcade. Children's Play Area.

PETS WELCOME

Enquiries and Bookings to:

Castaways Holiday Park, Paston Road, Bacton-on-Sea, Norfolk NR12 0JB • Tel: (01692) 650436 and 650418
website: www.castawaysholidaypark.co.uk

Red House
Chalet & Caravan Park

Small, family-run coastal site with direct access to sandy beach. Caravans, flats and centrally heated chalets. All accommodation has self-contained facilities including colour television. Some accommodation available with sea view. On-site licensed bar. Shop and laundry room. Ideal location for touring the Broads or sightseeing North Norfolk. DOGS VERY WELCOME. Open from March to January.

Red House Chalet and Caravan Park,
Paston Road, Bacton-on-Sea, Norfolk NR12 0JB (01692 650815).

Note

All the information in this guide is given in good faith in the belief that it is correct. However, the publishers cannot guarantee the facts given in these pages, neither are they responsible for changes in ownership or facilities that may take place after the date of going to press.

Readers should always satisfy themselves that the facilities they require are available and that the terms, if quoted, still apply.

NOW OPEN MARCH TO JANUARY

Elm Beach is a small, select, 4-star Caravan Park with unique, uninterrupted views of the Sea and Caister's golden, sandy beaches. We offer a range of 4-6 berth, fully equipped Heated Caravans, many of which overlook the sea or have sea views. We are a quiet, privately-run park with no entertainment facilities, but enjoy, free of charge, entertainment supplied by neighbouring parks, both within easy walking distance.
Pets very welcome.

Elm Beach Caravan Park

Manor Road, Caister-on-Sea, Norfolk NR30 5HG

Freephone: 08000 199 360

www.elmbeachcaravanpark.com e-mail: enquiries@elmbeachcaravanpark.com

Superior brick-built, tiled roof cottages • Adjacent golf course
Lovely walks on dunes and coast • 2-4 night breaks early/late season, Christmas and New Year • Terms from £69 to £345.

SAND DUNE COTTAGES, TAN LANE, CAISTER-ON-SEA, GREAT YARMOUTH NR30 5DT (01493 720352; mobile: 07785 561363)
e-mail: sand.dune.cottages@amserve.net
www.eastcoastlive.co.uk/sites/sanddunecottages.php

★★ SELF CATERING

The Norfolk Mead Hotel

Coltishall • Norfolk • NR12 7DN

Privately owned beautiful Georgian Country House Hotel. Located in 12 tranquil riverside acres, six miles from Norwich and 12 miles from the coast. Recently voted one of the top ten country house hotels in the country, accepting well mannered dogs. Twelve en suite rooms all quite individual. Lake, boating and birdlife. Award-winning restaurant offering superb cuisine and extensive wine list.

Telephone 01603 737531

E-mail: info@norfolkmead.co.uk www.norfolkmead.co.uk

FREE or REDUCED RATE entry to Holiday Visits and Attractions – see our READERS' OFFER VOUCHERS on pages 407-423

KING'S CHALET PARK

Enquiries to: Stenson Guest House, 32 Overstrand Road, Cromer, Norfolk NR27 0AJ

Families Welcome & Pets Free of Charge

Well-equipped Chalets sleeping 2 to 6; shower/ bathroom, microwave, TV. Tourist Board and NNH/GHA Approved. One Twin, one Double bedroom, bed sofa in lounge. Well-equipped kitchenette.

Quiet site adjacent to woods, Golf Club and beach. Local shops nearby or pleasant 10 minutes' walk into town.

Telephone: 01263 511308

Kings Chalet Park Cromer, Norfolk

Sleep 2-4

Open March to October

Pet welcome free of charge

Comfortable, well-equipped chalets situated on beautiful, landscaped, quiet site. Ideally placed for walks to adjacent woods, cliffs and sandy beaches. 10 minutes' walk to town. Golf course and local shops nearby. Plenty of local places of interest to visit. One twin, one double room, bathroom, colour TV, microwave, well-equipped kitchenette. Children welcome.

Short Breaks in Spring/Autumn 2 nights or more from £80
Spring/Autumn £140-£210 per week
June-September £230-£305 per week

DETAILS FROM: MRS I. SCOLTOCK, SHANGRI-LA, LITTLE CAMBRIDGE, DUTON HILL, DUNMOW, ESSEX CM6 3QU • TEL: 01371 870482

CLIFTONVILLE HOTEL

Indulge in Edwardian Elegance

AA ★★★ Grade II Listed

30 en-suite bedrooms all with seaviews
Executive suites - A la carte restaurant
Buttery and Bar - Bolton's Bistro
Specialising in Fresh Fish Dishes
Cromer Crabs - Local Lobsters - Steaks
Pasta and Vegetarian Dishes

www.cliftonvillehotel.co.uk Tel: 01263512543 E-mail reservations@cliftonvillehotel.co.uk

Scarning Dale

Dale Road, Scarning, East Dereham NR19 2QN
Tel: 01362 687269

A warm welcome awaits you. 16th Century house in 25 acres of landscaped gardens, paddocks and woodland. Excellent home cooking (à la carte and table d'hôte). Indoor heated swimming pool and full size snooker table. Good access Norfolk and Suffolk. Self-catering cottages also available. Dogs welcome in self-catering cottages. Grazing and Stables available.

Tariff: Single £50 – £60; Double £90 – £100.

Stay in the peaceful, tranquil heart of Norfolk's most beautiful countryside. All rooms tastefully decorated in country style, with full en suite facilities, TVs, tea/coffee making facilities, etc. Overlooking 12 acres of landscaped meadows with its own private fishing lakes. Bed and Breakfast from £36.

Bartles Lodge, Church Street, Elsing, Dereham NR20 3EA
Tel: 01362 637177

Readers are requested to mention this guidebook when making enquiries about accommodation.

4B&B STRENNETH Country Bed and Breakfast

Airfield Road, Fersfield, Diss, Norfolk IP22 2BP

STRENNETH is well-established and family-run, situated in unspoiled countryside just a short drive from Bressingham Gardens and the picturesque market town of Diss. Offering first-class accommodation, the original 17th Century building has been carefully renovated to a high standard with a wealth of exposed oak beams, with a newer single storey courtyard wing and two converted cottages. There is ample off-road parking and plenty of nice walks nearby. All seven bedrooms, including a Four-Poster and an Executive, are tastefully arranged with period furniture and distinctive beds. Each having remote-control colour television, hospitality trays, central heating and full en suite facilities. The establishment is smoke-free. Dinners are served by arrangement. There is an extensive breakfast menu using local produce. Ideal touring base. Pets most welcome. Outside kennels with runs if required. Bed and Breakfast from £25.00.

Telephone: 01379 688182 • Fax: 01379 688260
E-mail: pdavey@strenneth.co.uk • Website: www.strenneth.co.uk

Holly Farm Cottages, High Common, Cranworth, Norfolk IP25 7SX

Two comfortable, single-storey cottages each sleeping 1-4. Fully equipped, including TV/video, dishwasher, washing machine, central heating. Enclosed garden. Ample car parking. Uninterrupted views of beautiful countryside, peaceful lanes for walking/cycling. Local golf and fishing. Convenient for Norwich, North Norfolk Coast and Broads.

Tel: 01362 821468 **e-mail: jennie.mclaren@btopenworld.com**

Experience the great joy of Norfolk...

Idyllic Cottages @ Vere Lodge

English Tourism Council

We offer your pets 8 acres of lawns, paddock and woodland as a play area with Norfolk's vast beaches within a few minutes drive. We offer the rest of the family a choice of 14 superbly equipped cottages, leisure centre with heated indoor pool, sauna, solarium and games room. Animal farm, children's play area, enchanted wood, grass tennis court and croquet lawn.

Vere Lodge, South Raynham, Fakenham, Norfolk NR21 7HE
Tel: 01328 838261 (24 hour answering service)
Fax: 01328 838300 E-mail: major@verelodge.co.uk

www.idylliccottages.co.uk
for those who demand the very best

Call for FREE colour brochure

Located on a working farm, a courtyard of 2/3 bedroomed converted stables, 3 converted barns and 2 cottages, all fully equipped. Ideally situated for the beautiful North Norfolk coast, Sandringham, Norwich, and The Broads. 365 acres of mature woodland adjoining farm – private fishing in owners' lake. Indoor heated swimming Pool. Pets welcome at a charge of £10.

MOOR FARM STABLE COTTAGES,
FOXLEY, NORFOLK NR20 4QP • Tel or Fax: 01362 688523
e-mail: enquiry@moorfarmstablecottages.co.uk
www.moorfarmstablecottages.co.uk

Short Breaks
available all season, from £25 per person based on 4 sharing. Pets welcome at £10.

SUPERB VALUE FOR 2007 SEASON

Carefree HOLIDAYS

A warm welcome for you and your pets. Inexpensive, 'live-as-you-please' self-catering holidays in beautiful Norfolk. Chalets, Bungalows, Caravans and Cottages near Great Yarmouth & Norfolk Broads.

Booking Hotline
Tel: 01493 732176
All calls personally answered

Colour Brochure : Carefree Holidays, Chapel Briers, Yarmouth Road, Hemsby, Norfolk NR29 4NJ.
Find us on the internet: www.carefree-holidays.co.uk

Jocelyn & David Stroud, The Map House, Smokers Hole, Saxlingham, Holt NR25 7JU (01263 741304). Historic gamekeeper's lodge set in peaceful countryside 4 miles from the North Norfolk coast, with walks directly from the house. B&B with two luxurious, totally private double suites (bedroom, bathroom and sitting room) with own staircase and front door. Well-behaved dogs welcome free of charge.

e-mail: enquiries@maphouse.net • www.maphouse.net

THE OLD STABLES
HOLIDAY COTTAGES

Horningtoft, Dereham, Norfolk NR20 5DX

Attractive, new brick and flint barn conversions, sleeping 4 - 6 people with all the comforts of home.

Situated in a peaceful, rural village, within easy access of pubs, restaurants, shops, sportscentres and the North Norfolk coastline. Also good for fishing, and walking.

Games Room • Cycle Hire Available • Wheel Chair Access • Pets Welcome • Short breaks

For further details please contact: **IVAN on Tel: 01328 700262 • Mobile: 07775 707992**

ETC ★★★

HOLMDENE FARM,
BEESTON, KING'S LYNN PE32 2NJ

17th century farmhouse situated in central Norfolk within easy reach of the coast and Broads. Sporting activities available locally, village pub nearby. One double room, one twin and two singles. Pets welcome. Bed and Breakfast from £22.50 per person; Evening Meal from £15. Weekly terms available and child reductions. Two self-catering cottages. Sleeping 4/8. Terms on request.

MRS G. DAVIDSON • Tel: 01328 701284

e-mail: holmdenefarm@farmersweekly.net
www.northnorfolk.co.uk/holmdenefarm

Pott Row

Detached 2 bedroom bungalow sleeps 4. In quiet rural Norfolk village close to Sandringham and beaches. Facilities include colour TV, video, microwave, fridge/freezer, washing machine, off road parking, dog run. All dogs welcome FREE. Open all year. Please telephone for brochure.

Mrs. J.E. Ford, 129 Leziate Drove, Pott Row, King's Lynn PE32 1DE Tel: 01553 630356

Silver Birches **Fairstead Drive, Shouldham, Kings Lynn, Norfolk PE33 0DL**

Delightful log cabin in beautiful West Norfolk, with direct access to 2,500 acres – heaven for dog walkers and bird watchers. A short drive to Royal Sandringham and half an hour's drive to the lovely beaches of Hunstanton, which also has many family attractions. Norwich is only one hour. The cabin comprises a large kitchen/diner, sitting room, 2 bedrooms plus a "put-you-up". Bathroom. Fully equipped, linen, towels, electricity and heating included in rent.

Telephone for booking forms: 01366 348 106 or 01366 348 107 or 07930147892
www.sdmicro.ukf.net/silverbirches/

A warm welcome to all pets and their owners at "Whincliff" by the sea. Family/en suite, twin or single room available. Tea/coffee facilities, TV in all rooms, private parking, sea views, unspoilt beach and coastal walks to enjoy. ***Mrs Christine Thrower.***

WHINCLIFF Bed & Breakfast

CROMER ROAD, MUNDESLEY NR11 8DU • TEL: 01263 721554
http://whincliff.freeuk.com • e-mail: whincliff@freeuk.com

KILN CLIFFS CARAVAN PARK

Peaceful family-run site with NO clubhouse situated around an historic brick kiln. Luxury six-berth caravans for hire, standing on ten acres of grassy cliff top. Magnificent view out over the sea; private path leads down to extensive stretches of unspoilt sandy beach. All caravans fully equipped (except linen) and price includes all gas and electricity. Caravans always available for sale or for hire. Within easy reach are the Broads, Norwich, the Shire Horse Centre, local markets, nature reserves, bird sanctuaries; nearby golf, riding and fishing. Facilities on site include general store and launderette. Responsible pet owners welcome. **Substantial discounts for off-peak bookings – phone for details. Call for brochure.**

Mr R. Easton, Kiln Cliffs Caravan Park, Cromer Road, Mundesley, Norfolk NR11 8DF • Tel: 01263 720449

47 SEAWARD CREST MUNDESLEY

West-facing brick built chalet on private site with lawns, flowers and parking. Large lounge/dining room, kitchenette, two bedrooms, bathroom. Beach and shops nearby. Pets most welcome. SAE please for further information.

Mrs Doar, 4 Denbury Road, Ravenshead, Notts. NG15 9FQ
Tel: 01623 798032

Dolphin Lodge

ETC ◆◆◆◆

Friendly-run bungalow accommodation. B&B in village setting just two-and-a-half miles from beaches. Many rural walks. Easy reach of all Norfolk attractions including Norfolk Broads. All rooms en suite, tea/coffee facilities, TVs, hairdryers etc.

Mrs G. Faulkner, Dolphin Lodge, 3 Knapton Road, Trunch, North Walsham, Norfolk NR28 0QE • Tel: 01263 720961
E-mail: dolphin.lodge@btopenworld.com • www.dolphinlodges.net

FHG Guides

publish a large range of well-known accommodation guides.

We will be happy to send you details or you can use the order form at the back of this book.

FHG
K·U·P·E·R·A·R·D

The Cobblers Cottage B&B

3 Wodehouse Road • Old Hunstanton • Norfolk • 01485 534036

Quietly situated in 'Old Hunstanton' and about 400 yards from a wide sandy beach, three pubs/restaurants. We offer very well equipped en suite double/twin rooms (one on the ground floor) including a sea glimpse from rooms upstairs. An extensive menu professionally cooked to order. Highly recommended by valued returning guests. Try a Bargain Break. We are open March to October, and your good dog, can come too - FREE, by arrangement.

ST CRISPINS

OLD HUNSTANTON, NORFOLK

Tel: 01485 534036

e-mail: st.crispins@btinternet.com

Quietly tucked away in Old Hunstanton village, near a sandy beach and golf course, but within a few hundred yards of three pubs/restaurants. This ground floor annexe sleeps 1 or 2 adults, and is beautifully decorated to a high standard. Short notice bargain breaks usually available early and late season.

PETS WELCOME

English Tourism Council ★★★ SELF CATERING

The Lifeboat Inn

16th Century Smugglers' Ale House

Ship Lane,Thornham, Norfolk PE36 6LT

Tel: 01485 512236 • Fax: 01485 512323

e-mail: reception@lifeboatinn.co.uk

THE LIFEBOAT INN has been a welcome sight for the weary traveller for centuries – roaring open fires, real ales and a hearty meal awaiting. The Summer brings its own charm – a cool beer, gazing over open meadows to the harbour, and rolling white horses gently breaking upon Thornham's sandy beach.

Dogs are welcome in all our bars and we provide the sort of breakfast that will enable you to keep up with your four-legged friend on the way to the beach!

Guests arriving at reception are greeted by our grand old fireplace in the lounge – ideal for toasting your feet after a day walking the coastal path – if you can coax your sleeping dog out of prime position! The restaurant (AA Rosette) opens every evening offering a varied selection of dishes to suit all tastes. Our extensive bar snack menu is also available if guests wish their pets to join them in the bar.

There are numerous and varied walks along miles of open beaches, across sweeping sand dunes, through pine woods or along chalk and sandstone cliff tops. It is truly a walker's paradise – especially if you're a dog.

We hope you will come and visit us. For our brochure and tariff which includes details of breaks please ring **01485 512236 or visit our website**

www.lifeboatinn.co.uk

★★★★ Poppyland Holiday Cottages & Touring Park Welcomes Dogs

Poppyland is situated on The Green in the middle of the picturesque village of Thorpe Market, in North Norfolk, just 4 miles south of the well known fishing port of Cromer and approximately 16 miles north of the ancient city of Norwich. The location is ideal for guests who want to just relax with their friend away from the daily pressures on a quiet holiday, or use the cottage as a base to visit local places of interest. The two holiday cottages have their own private entrances and gardens. The touring park (adults only) is situated in an acre of landscaped garden surrounded by trees. There is a public house /hotel opposite which serves excellent food.

Tel: 01263 833219 • e-mail: poppylandjc@netscape.net • www.poppyland.com

HOLIDAY IN OUR ENGLISH COUNTRY GARDEN

Two acres in rural Norfolk. Ten spacious family-run bungalows and 7-bedroom farmhouse. Games room, heated pool, children's play area, fishing, boating, riding and golf nearby. Near River Staithe with access to Broads. Parking. Licensed bar. For details/colour brochure contact: **F.G. Delf, Thurne Cottage, The Staithe, Thurne, Norfolk NR29 3BU**
Tel: 01692 670242 or 01493 844568 • www.norfolkbroads.co.uk/hederahouse

Pets very welcome at both sites.

Winterton Valley Holidays

A selection of modern superior fully appointed holiday chalets in a choice of locations near Great Yarmouth. Enjoy panoramic views of the sea from WINTERTON, a quiet and picturesque 35-acre estate minutes from the beach, while CALIFORNIA has all the usual amenities for the more adventurous holidaymaker, with free entry to the pool and clubhouse.

For colour brochure please ring 01493 377175 or write to 15 Kingston Avenue, Caister-on-Sea, Norfolk NR30 5ET
www.wintertonvalleyholidays.co.uk

Go BLUE RIBAND for quality inexpensive self-catering holidays where your dog is welcome – choice of locations all in the borough of Great Yarmouth. Detached 3 bedroom bungalows, seafront bungalows, detached Sea-Dell chalets and modern sea front caravans. Free colour brochure: DON WITHERIDGE, BLUE RIBAND HOUSE, PARKLANDS, HEMSBY, GREAT YARMOUTH NR29 4HA (01493 730445). [pw! First pet free when booking through Pets Welcome!, 2nd pet £10 per week].
website: www.BlueRibandHolidays.co.uk

NORFOLK COUNTRY COTTAGES. Norfolk's leading holiday cottage letting agency. More than 300 cottages to escape to. For brochure tel: 01603 871872; Fax: 01603 870304. CARLTON HOUSE, MARKET PLACE, REEPHAM, NORFOLK NR10 4JJ.
e-mail: info@norfolk.cottages.co.uk website: www.norfolkcottages.co.uk/pw

SOWERBYS HOLIDAY COTTAGES. North Norfolk Coastal Cottages. Over 90 much loved second homes sleeping from 2 to 16, many with sea views. Tailor-made short breaks available. Please call us on 01328 730880
website: www.sowerbysholidaycottages.co.uk

Bacton-on-Sea

Village on coast. 5 miles from North Walsham.

CASTAWAYS HOLIDAY PARK, PASTON ROAD, BACTON-ON-SEA NR12 0JB (01692 650436 and 650418). In peaceful village with direct access to sandy beach. Modern caravans, Pine Lodges and Flats, with all amenities. Licensed club, entertainment, children's play area. Ideal for discovering Norfolk. [Pets £17 per week]
website: www.castawaysholidaypark.co.uk

RED HOUSE CHALET AND CARAVAN PARK, PASTON ROAD, BACTON-ON-SEA NR12 0JB (01692 650815). Small family-run site, ideal for touring Broads. Chalets, caravans and flats all with showers, fridges and colour TV. Some with sea views. Licensed. Open March–January. [Pets £10 weekly.]

Caister-on-Sea

Historic site with Roman ruins and 15th century Caister Castle with 100 foot tower

ELM BEACH CARAVAN PARK, MANOR ROAD, CAISTER-ON-SEA NR30 5HG (Freephone: 08000 199 360). Small, quiet park offering 4-6 berth, fully equipped caravans, most with sea views. Entertainment supplied free of charge by neighbouring parks. Pets very welcome. [Pets £25 per week]
e-mail: enquiries@elmbeachcaravanpark.com website: www.elmbeachcaravanpark.com

Superior brick-built, tiled roof cottages. Adjacent golf course. Lovely walks on dunes and coast. 2-4 night breaks early/late season, Christmas and New Year. Terms from £69 to £345. SAND DUNE COTTAGES, TAN LANE, CAISTER-ON-SEA, GREAT YARMOUTH NR30 5DT (01493 720352; mobile: 07785 561363). ETC ★★ [Pets £15 per week]
e-mail: sand.dune.cottages@amserve.net
website: www.eastcoastlive.co.uk/sites/sanddunecottages.php

Coltishall

Village to the north east of Norwich.

THE NORFOLK MEAD HOTEL, COLTISHALL, NORWICH NR12 7DN (01603 737531). Renowned restaurant offering superb cuisine and a comprehensive wine list. Well mannered dogs welcome. Johansens recommended. ETC ★★ Gold Award. [Pets £8 per night]
e-mail: info@norfolkmead.co.uk website: www.norfolkmead.co.uk

Cromer

Attractive resort built round old fishing village. Norwich 21 miles.

KINGS CHALET PARK, CROMER NR27 0AJ (01263 511308) . Well-equipped chalets sleeping 2 to 6; shower/bathroom, microwave and TV. 1 Twin, 1 Double bedroom, bed sofa in lounge, well-equipped kitchenette. Quiet site adjacent to woods, golf club and beaches. Local shops nearby. Pleasant 10 minutes' walk to town. Tourist Board and NNH/GHA Approved. Families welcome. [ ]

KINGS CHALET PARK, CROMER. Comfortable well-equipped chalets on quiet site; ideally placed for woodland and beach walks. 10 minutes' walk to town, shops nearby. Details from MRS I. SCOLTOCK, SHANGRI-LA, LITTLE CAMBRIDGE, DUTON HILL, DUNMOW, ESSEX (01371 870482). [one pet free]

CLIFTONVILLE HOTEL, SEAFRONT, CROMER NR27 9AS (01263 512543; Fax: 01263 515700). Ideally situated on the Norfolk coast. Beautifully restored Edwardian Hotel. 30 en suite bedrooms all with sea view. Executive suites. Seafood Bistro, à la carte Restaurant. AA ★★★ [pw! pets £4 per night]
e-mail: reservations@cliftonvillehotel.co.uk website: www.cliftonvillehotel.co.uk

Dereham

Situated 16 miles west of Norwich. St Nicholas Church has 16th century bell tower.

SCARNING DALE, SCARNING, EAST DEREHAM NR19 2QN (01362 687269). Self-catering cottages (not commercialised) in grounds of owner's house. On-site indoor heated swimming pool and full-size snooker table. B&B for six also available in house (sorry no pets in house). Grazing and Stables available.

BARTLES LODGE, CHURCH STREET, ELSING, DEREHAM NR20 3EA (01362 637177). Stay in the peaceful, tranquil heart of Norfolk's most beautiful countryside. All rooms en suite, TVs, tea/coffee making facilities, etc. [pw! Pets £2 per night, £10 per week]

FREE or REDUCED RATE entry to Holiday Visits and Attractions – see our READERS' OFFER VOUCHERS on pages 407-423

Diss

Small market town on the River Waveney 19 miles south west of Norwich.

PAUL AND YOLANDA DAVEY, STRENNETH, AIRFIELD ROAD, FERSFIELD, DISS IP22 2BP (01379 688182; Fax 01379 688260). Family-run, fully renovated period property with two cottages. All rooms en suite, colour TVs, hospitality trays. Ground floor rooms. Non-smoking. Extensive breakfast menu. Licensed. Bed and Breakfast from £25. ETC ◆◆◆◆. [🐕]
e-mail: pdavey@strenneth.co.uk website: www.strenneth.co.uk

East Dereham

Site of 7th Century nunnery. Archaeogical Museum at Bishop Banner's Cottages, with distinctive fruit and flower plaster work.

HOLLY FARM COTTAGES, HIGH COMMON, CRANWORTH IP25 7SX (01362 821468). 2 single-storey cottages each sleeping 1-4. TV/video, dishwasher, washing machine, central heating. Enclosed garden. Ample car parking. Peaceful lanes for walking/cycling. Local golf and fishing. Use of field for pony/horse. [🐕]
e-mail: jennie.mclaren@btopenworld.com

Fakenham

Agricultural centre on River Wensum 23 miles north-west of Norwich.

VERE LODGE, SOUTH RAYNHAM, NEAR FAKENHAM NR21 7HE (01328 838261; Fax: 01328 838300). 14 superbly equipped cottages with leisure centre and heated indoor pool. 8 acres of lawns, paddock and woodland, with Norfolk's vast beaches nearby. [pw! Pets £6 per night, £29.50 per week]
e-mail: major@verelodge.co.uk website: www.idylliccottages.co.uk

Foxley

Village 6 miles east of East Dereham.

Self-catering Cottages (2/3 bedrooms) on working farm. All fully equipped, with central heating. 20 miles from coast, 15 from Broads. Mature woodland nearby. Fishing in owner's lake. Indoor heated swimming pool. ETC ★★/★★★★. MOOR FARM STABLE COTTAGES, FOXLEY NR20 4QP (Tel & Fax: 01362 688523). [Pets £10 per week]
e-mail: enquiry@moorfarmstablecottages.co.uk website: www.moorfarmstablecottages.co.uk

Great Yarmouth

Traditional lively seaside resort with a wide range of amusements, including the Marina Centre and Sealife Centre.

CAREFREE HOLIDAYS, CHAPEL BRIERS, YARMOUTH ROAD, HEMSBY, GREAT YARMOUTH NR29 4NJ (01493 732176). A wide selection of superior chalets for live-as-you-please holidays near Great Yarmouth and Norfolk Broads. All amenities on site. Parking. Children and pets welcome. [Pets £10.]

Holt

Small town 10 miles west of Cromer.

JOCELYN & DAVID STROUD, THE MAP HOUSE, SMOKERS HOLE, SAXLINGHAM, HOLT NR25 7JU (01263 741304). Historic gamekeeper's lodge set in peaceful countryside 4 miles from the coast, with walks directly from the house. B&B with two luxurious, totally private double suites (bedroom, bathroom and sitting room). Well-behaved dogs welcome free of charge. [🐕]
e-mail: enquiries@maphouse.net website: www.maphouse.net

Readers are requested to mention this guidebook when making enquiries about accommodation.

Horningtoft

Village 4 miles south east of Fakenham.

MR IVAN BAKER, OLD STABLES HOLIDAY COTTAGES, CHURCH FARM, HORNINGTOFT, DEREHAM NR20 5DX (01328 700262; Mobile: 07775 707992). All the comforts of home in new barn conversions in a peaceful, rural village. Easy access to pubs, restaurants, shops and the north Norfolk coastline. ETC ★★★★ [🐕]

King's Lynn

Ancient market town and port on the Wash with many beautiful medieval and Georgian buildings.

MRS G. DAVIDSON, HOLMDENE FARM, BEESTON, KING'S LYNN PE32 2NJ (01328 701284). 17th century farmhouse situated in central Norfolk within easy reach of the coast and Broads. Sporting activities available locally, village pub nearby. One double room, one twin and one single. Pets welcome. Bed and Breakfast from £22.50pp; Evening Meal from £15. Weekly terms available and child reductions. Two self-catering cottages. Sleeping 4/8. Terms on request. ETC ★★★ [🐕]
e-mail: holmdenefarm@farmersweekly.net website: www.northnorfolk.co.uk/holmdenefarm

MRS J. E. FORD, 129 LEZIATE DROVE, POTT ROW, KING'S LYNN PE32 1DE (01553 630356). Detached bungalow sleeps 4. In quiet village close to Sandringham and beaches. Facilities include colour TV, video, microwave, fridge/freezer, washing machine, off road parking, dog run. [🐕]

MRS KITTLE, SILVER BIRCHES, FAIRSTEAD DRIVE, SHOULDHAM, KINGS LYNN PE33 0DL (01366 348 106 or 01366 348 107 or 07930147892). Delightful log cabin with direct access to 2,500 acres. Half hour's drive to lovely beaches, Norwich one hour. Large kitchen/diner, sitting room, 2 bedrooms plus a "put-you-up". Bathroom. Fully equipped, linen, towels, electricity included in rent. [🐕 ⌂]
website; www.sdmicro.ukf.net/silverbirches/

Mundesley-on-Sea

Small resort backed by low cliffs. Good sands and bathing. Norwich 20 miles, Cromer 7.

MRS CHRISTINE THROWER, WHINCLIFF BED & BREAKFAST, CROMER ROAD, MUNDESLEY NR11 8DU (01263 721554). Clifftop house, sea views and sandy beaches. Rooms with colour TV and tea-making. Families and pets welcome. Open all year round. [🐕]
e-mail: whincliff@freeuk.com website: http://whincliff.freeuk.com

KILN CLIFFS CARAVAN PARK, CROMER ROAD, MUNDESLEY NR11 8DF (01263 720449). Peaceful family-run site situated around an historic brick kiln. Six-berth caravans for hire, standing on ten acres of grassy cliff top. All caravans fully equipped (except linen) and price includes all gas and electricity. [Pets £5 per week].

47 SEAWARD CREST, MUNDESLEY. West-facing brick built chalet on private site with lawns, flowers and parking. Large lounge/dining room, kitchenette, two bedrooms, bathroom. Beach and shops nearby. Pets most welcome. [🐕] SAE please: MRS DOAR, 4 DENBURY ROAD, RAVENSHEAD, NOTTS. NG15 9FQ (01623 798032).

HOLIDAY PROPERTIES (MUNDESLEY) LTD, 6a PASTON ROAD, NORWICH NR11 8BN (01263 720719). Self-catering holiday chalets on three pretty sites in village on North Norfolk coast, close to sandy beach, and village amenities. All chalets are heated with fully equipped kitchens, colour TVs. Sleep 4-6. Pets welcome. Low season short breaks. [Pets £10 per week].
e-mail: info@holidayprops.co.uk website: www.holidayprops.co.uk

Neatishead

Ideal for touring East Anglia. Close to Norwich. Aylsham 14 miles, Norwich 10, Wroxham 3.

ALAN AND SUE WRIGLEY, REGENCY GUEST HOUSE, THE STREET, NEATISHEAD, NORFOLK BROADS NR12 8AD (Tel & Fax: 01692 630233). 18th century three-bedroomed guest house renowned for generous English breakfasts. Ideal East Anglian touring base. Accent on personal service. B&B from £27. ETC/AA ◆◆◆◆ SILVER AWARD. Dogs welcome. [Pets £7 per night.]
e-mail: regencywrigley@btopenworld.com website: www.go2norfolk.co.uk

North Walsham

Market town 14 miles north of Norwich, traditional centre of the Norfolk reed thatching industry.

MRS. G. FAULKNER, DOLPHIN LODGE, 3 KNAPTON ROAD,TRUNCH, NORTH WALSHAM NR28 0QE (01263 720961). Friendly-run bungalow accommodation. B&B in village setting two-and-a-half miles from beaches. Many rural walks. Easy reach of all Norfolk attractions including Norfolk Broads. All rooms en suite, tea/coffee facilities, TVs, hairdryers etc. ETC ◆◆◆◆ [🐕]
e-mail: dolphin.lodge@btopenworld.com website: www.dolphinlodges.net

Old Hunstanton

Coastal resort on the Wash 14 miles north east of King's Lynn.

THE COBBLERS COTTAGE B&B, 3 WODEHOUSE ROAD, OLD HUNSTANTON (01485 534036). Quietly situated B&B 400 yards from wide, sandy beach. Well equipped en suite double/twin rooms. Bargain breaks. Open March to October. Good dogs welcome by arrangement. [🐕]

ST CRISPINS, OLD HUNSTANTON (01485 534036). Ground floor annexe sleeping 1 to 2 adults, near sandy beach and golf course. Beautifully decorated. Bargain breaks early/late season. Pets welcome. ETC ★★★ [One or two dogs £15 per week]
e-mail: st.crispins@btinternet.com

Thornham

Village 4 miles east of Hunstanton. Site of Roman signal station.

THE LIFEBOAT INN, SHIP LANE, THORNHAM PE36 6LT (01485 512236; Fax: 01485 512323). A welcome sight for the weary traveller for centuries. Dogs welcome. Restaurant (one AA rosette). Bird watching and walking along miles of open beaches. Please ring for brochure and tariff. [🐕]
e-mail: reception@lifeboatinn.co.uk website: www.lifeboatinn.co.uk

Thorpe Market

Village 4 miles south of Cromer.

POPPYLAND HOLIDAY COTTAGES & TOURING PARK, THE GREEN, THORPE MARKET NR11 8AJ (01263 833219). Ideal for guests who want to relax. Two holiday cottages with private entrances and gardens. Touring park (adults only) in landscaped gardens surrounded by trees. Excellent food nearby.[🐕]
e-mail: poppylandjc@netscape.net website: www.poppyland.com

Thurne

Idyllic Broadland village. Great Yarmouth 10 miles.

HEDERA HOUSE AND PLANTATION BUNGALOWS, THURNE NR29 3BU (01692 670242 or 01493 844568). Adjacent river, seven bedroomed farmhouse, 10 competitively priced bungalows in peaceful gardens. Outdoor heated pool. Enjoy boating, fishing, walking, touring, nearby golf, horseriding, sandy beaches and popular resorts.
website: www.norfolkbroads.co.uk/hederahouse

Winterton-on-Sea

Good sands and bathing. Great Yarmouth 8 miles.

WINTERTON VALLEY HOLIDAYS. A selection of modern superior fully appointed holiday chalets in a choice of locations near Great Yarmouth. Enjoy panoramic views from WINTERTON, a quiet and picturesque 35-acre estate, while CALIFORNIA has all the usual amenities, with free entry to the pool and clubhouse. Pets are very welcome at both sites. For colour brochure: 15 KINGSTON AVENUE, CAISTER-ON-SEA NR30 5ET (01493 377175).
website: www.wintertonvalleyholidays.co.uk

NORTHUMBERLAND COTTAGES LTD

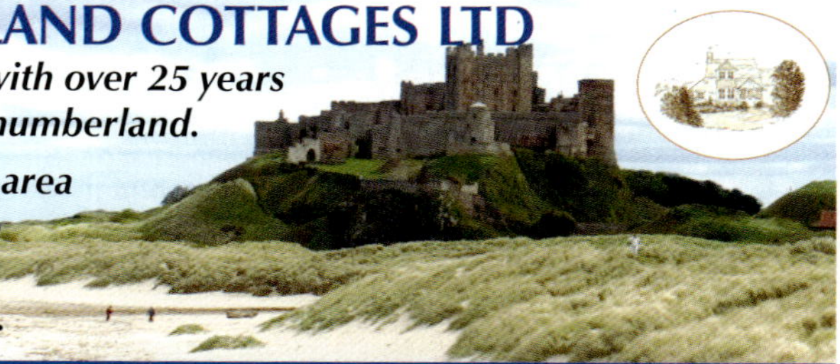

A local booking agency, with over 25 years of living and loving Northumberland.

Based in the heart of the area between Alnwick and the beautiful sandy beaches of the Heritage Coastline.

Choose from our selection of cottages Telephone 01665 589434 or check availability online at www.northumberlandcottages.com

Alnmouth, Bamburgh, Belford

Saddle Hotel & Grill

ETC ★★

24/25 Northumberland Street, Alnmouth NE66 2RA • Tel: 01665 830476

Friendly, family-run hotel situated in Alnmouth, on the Northumberland coast, with miles of white sandy beaches and unspoilt countryside; two golf courses. Fully licensed, home-cooked meals a speciality. All bedrooms en suite. Children and pets most welcome.

The Mizen Head Hotel

Lucker Road, Bamburgh, Northumberland NE69 7BS

En suite bedrooms, a residents' conservatory lounge and non-smoking à la carte restaurant using local produce. Public bar offers good food and real ales, live music, with an open log fire in winter. Children welcome – family rooms are available with cots if required. Car park. Pets welcome in bedrooms and bar. Local attractions include Bamburgh Castle and Holy Isle. Three-and-a-half mile sandy beach five minutes away. Pets welcome. For golfers discounts can be arranged. Short break details on request.

Tel: 01668 214254 • Fax: 01668 214104

website: www.themizenheadhotel.co.uk

e-mail: reception@themizenheadhotel.co.uk

Bluebell Farm enjoys a quiet central position in the village of Belford, three miles from the Heritage Coast and within easy walking distance of all village amenities. Sleep 4-6. Each cottage is equipped with gas cooker, microwave, fridge/freezer or fridge, coffee machine, kettle, toaster and colour television, most with DVD player. All have gas-fired central heating; living/dining/kitchen areas are open plan.

Mrs Phyl Carruthers, Bluebell Farm, Belford, Northumberland NE70 7QE
Tel: 01668 213362• e-mail: phyl.carruthers@virgin.net

Etive Cottage • Warenford, Near Belford NE70 7HZ

Etive is a well-equipped two bedroomed stone cottage with double glazing and central heating. Situated on the outskirts of the hamlet of Warenford with open views to the Bamburgh coast. Fenced garden and secure courtyard parking. Pet and owners welcome pack on arrival - give your pets the holiday they deserve. *Regional Winner - Winalot 'Best Place to Stay' 2004*

*For brochure contact Jan Thompson • **Tel/Fax: 01668 213233***

Please mention PETS WELCOME! when making enquiries about accommodation featured in these pages

Berwick-upon-Tweed, Haltwhislte, Hexham, Morpeth

2, THE COURTYARD, BERWICK-UPON-TWEED

Secluded Self Catering Townhouse in heart of old Berwick. Planted courtyard garden and sunny verandah. Historic ramparts 400 yards, golf course, beaches. Ideal for exercising pets.

Contact: J Morton, 1, The Courtyard, Church Street, Berwick-Upon-Tweed, TD15 1EE (01289 308737)
e-mail: jvm@patmosphere.uklinux.net www.berwickselfcatering.co.uk

The Cobbled Yard Hotel

Situated in centre of town and yet near to scenic walks.
En suite rooms. Own restaurant and Bar. Car park.
Bring this advert for Pets Free of Charge.

Fred and Lynda Miller, Cobbled Yard Hotel,
40 Walkergate, Berwick-upon-Tweed, Northumberland TD15 1DJ
Tel: 01289 308 407 • Fax: 01289 330 623
e-mail: cobbledyardhotel@berwick35.fsnet.co.uk • www.cobbledyardhotel.com

Friendly Hound Cottage, Ford Common, Berwick-upon-Tweed TD15 2QD

Friendly Hound Cottage, set in a quiet country location, one mile from the picturesque village of Ford but only 15 minutes from Holy Island, Berwick and Bamburgh, is ideally situated for you and your pet.
Only 10 minutes from the A1, you can come and enjoy our quality accommodation, excellent breakfasts, friendly hospitality and our warm welcome. Arrive as our guests and leave as our friends.

Tel: 01289 388554 • www.friendlyhoundcottage.co.uk

Close to the best parts of Hadrian's Wall • A warm welcome and good food • All rooms en suite • Parking • TV • Central heating. • Children and pets welcome • Open all year • Prices from £20 pppn.

e-mail: kathandbrad@aol.com • www.saughyrigg.co.uk

KATH AND BRAD DOWLE, SAUGHY RIGG FARM, TWICE BREWED, HALTWHISTLE NE49 9PT (01434 344120)

Scotchcoulthard • Haltwhistle, Northumberland NE49 9NH

01434 344470 • *Props: A.D. & S.M. Saunders*
e-mail: info@scotchcoulthard.co.uk • www.scotchcoulthard.co.uk

Situated in 178 acres within Northumberland National Park, fully equipped self-catering cottages (sleep 2/7). All bedrooms en suite; open fires. Fridge/freezer, colour TV, microwave; all except one have dishwasher and washing machine. Linen, towels, all fuel incl. Heated indoor pool, games room. Rare breed farm animals. Children and dogs welcome.

Battlesteads Hotel & Restaurant

Wark, Hexham, Northumberland
NE48 3LS. TEL: (01434) 230 209
Email: info@battlesteads.com
www.battlesteads.com

Dating from 1747, this 4-star Inn and restaurant features excellent bar meals and a la carte menus, good choice of wines and cask and bottle conditioned beers.

A friendly, family run hotel, with 14 en-suite bedrooms, including ground floor rooms with disabled access, it is ideally placed for exploring Hadrian's Wall, Kielder and Border Reiver country. Pets are very welcome. PPPN £40.00 min £45.00 max

Micklewood Park

Self catering houses set within 75 acres at Longhirst, Morpeth, Micklewood is an ideal base from which to explore historic Northumberland. We cater for groups and families who are explorers and sports enthusiasts or simply enjoy relaxing breaks.

Call: 01670 794 530 or visit: www.micklewoodpark.co.uk

Readers are requested to mention this guidebook when making enquiries about accommodation.

BIRLING VALE, WARKWORTH

Attractive stone built detached house in secluded garden. Fully equipped, two double bedrooms, one twin, cot. Free central heating. Close to sandy beaches, trout and salmon rivers and many places of interest. Well-trained dogs welcome.

Weekly rates: *£130 per week (low season) • £250 (medium price) • £490 (high season)*

SAE to Mrs J. Brewis, Woodhouse Farm, Shilbottle, Near Alnwick, Northumberland NE66 2HR

Tel: 01665 575222

NORTHUMBERLAND COTTAGES LTD. A local booking agency, with over 25 years of living and loving Northumberland. Based in the heart of the area between Alnwick and the beautiful sandy beaches of the Heritage Coastline. Choose from our selection of inland and coastal cottages. Telephone 01665 589434 or check availability online. [Pets £10 per week]
e-mail: enquiries@northumberlandcottages.com website: www.northumberlandcottages.com

Alnmouth

Seaside village situated at the mouth of the River Aln.

SADDLE HOTEL & GRILL, 24/25 NORTHUMBERLAND STREET, ALNMOUTH NE66 2RA (01665 830476). Friendly, family-run hotel, on the Northumberland coast. Fully licensed, home-cooked meals a speciality. All bedrooms en suite. Children and pets most welcome. ETC ★★. [🐕]

Bamburgh

Village on North Sea coast with magnificent castle. Grace Darling buried in churchyard

THE MIZEN HEAD HOTEL, BAMBURGH NE69 7BS (01668 214254; Fax: 01668 214104). A warm welcome awaits owners and pets alike at the Mizen Head. Close to the beautiful Northumbrian coastline and just a short drive from many lovely walks in the Ingram Valley. The hotel boasts log fires, live music, good food and real ales.
e-mail: reception@themizenheadhotel.co.uk website: www.themizenheadhotel.co.uk

Belford

Village 14 miles south-east of Berwick-upon-Tweed.

MRS PHYL CARRUTHERS, BLUEBELL FARM, BELFORD NE70 7QE (01668 213362). In a quiet central position in the village of Belford, three miles from the Heritage Coast and within easy walking distance of all village amenities. Sleep 4-6. Each cottage is very well equipped, with gas-fired central heating; living/dining/kitchen areas are open plan.
e-mail: phyl.carruthers@virgin.net

ETIVE COTTAGE, WARENFORD, NEAR BELFORD NE70 7HZ. Well-equipped two-bedroomed cottage with double glazing, central heating. Open views to coast. Fenced garden; secure parking. Welcome pack. Regional Winner, Winalot Best Place to Stay 2004. Brochure: JAN THOMPSON (Tel & Fax: 01668 213233). [🐕]

Berwick-upon-Tweed

Border town at mouth of River Tweed 58 miles north west of Newcastle and 47 miles south east of Edinburgh. Medieval town walls, remains of a Norman Castle.

2, THE COURTYARD, BERWICK-UPON-TWEED. Secluded Self catering Townhouse in heart of old Berwick. Planted courtyard garden and sunny verandah. Historic ramparts 400 yards, golf course, beaches. Ideal for exercising pets. Contact: J. MORTON, 1, THE COURTYARD, CHURCH STREET, BERWICK -UPON-TWEED, TD15 1EE (01289 308737). ETC ★★★ [pw! 🐕]
e-mail: jvm@patmosphere.uklinux.net website: www.berwickselfcatering.co.uk

FRED AND LYNDA MILLER, COBBLED YARD HOTEL, 40 WALKERGATE, BERWICK-UPON-TWEED TD15 1DJ (01289 308 407; Fax: 01289 330 623) Situated in centre of town and yet near to scenic walks. En suite rooms. Own restaurant and Bar. Car park. Bring this advert for Pets Free of Charge. [🐕]
e-mail:cobbledyardhotel@berwick35.fsnet.co.uk website : www.cobbledyardhotel.com

FRIENDLY HOUND COTTAGE, FORD COMMON, BERWICK-UPON-TWEED TD15 2QD (01289 388554) Set in a quiet country location, one mile from the picturesque village of Ford but only 15 minutes from Holy Island, Berwick and Bamburgh. Come and enjoy our quality accommodation, excellent breakfasts, friendly hospitality and our warm welcome. ETC ◆◆◆◆ [🐕]
website: www.friendlyhoundcottage.co.uk

Corbridge

Small town on north bank of River Tyne, 3 miles west of Hexham. Nearby are remains of Roman military town of Corstopitum.

MR & MRS MATTHEWS, THE HAYES GUEST HOUSE, NEWCASTLE ROAD, CORBRIDGE NE45 5LP (01434 632010). Stone-built stables in grounds of large country house converted into two self-catering cottages, each accommodating 4/5. ETC ★★★ [Pets £12.50 per week]
e-mail: camon@surfree.co.uk website: www.hayes-corbridge.co.uk

Haltwhistle

Small market town about one mile south of Hadrian's Wall.

KATH AND BRAD DOWLE, SAUGHY RIGG FARM, TWICE BREWED, HALTWHISTLE NE49 9PT (01434 344120). Close to the best parts of Hadrian's Wall. A warm welcome and good food. All rooms en suite. Parking. TV. Central heating. Children and pets welcome. Open all year. Prices from £20 pppn. ETC ◆◆◆◆
e-mail: kathandbrad@aol.com website: www.saughyrigg.co.uk

A.D. & S.M. SAUNDERS, SCOTCHCOULTHARD, HALTWHISTLE NE49 9NH (01434 344470). Situated in 178 acres within Northumberland National Park, fully equipped self-catering cottages (sleep 2/7). Linen, towels, all fuel incl. Heated indoor pool, games room. Rare breed farm animals. Children and dogs welcome. [🐕]
e-mail: info@scotchcoulthard.co.uk website: www.scotchcoulthard.co.uk

Hexham

Market town on south bank of the River Tyne, 20 miles west of Newcastle-upon-Tyne.

BATTLESTEADS HOTEL & RESTAURANT, WARK, HEXHAM NE48 3LS (01434 230209). Excellent bar meals and à la carte menus; good choice wines and beers. 14 en suite bedrooms including ground floor with disabled access. Pets very welcome. B&B from £40-£45pppn. ★★★★ Inn.
e-mail: info@battlesteads.com website: www.battlesteads.com

Morpeth

Market town on River Wansbeck, 14 miles north of Newcastle-upon-Tyne.

MICKLEWORTH PARK, LONGHIRST, MORPETH (01670 794530). Self-catering houses set in 75 acres. An ideal base from which to explore historic Northumberland. We cater for groups and families who are explorers and sports enthusiasts, or who simply enjoy relaxing breaks. [🐕]
website: www.micklewoodpark.co.uk

Warkworth

Village on River Coquet near North Sea coast north-west of Amble with several interesting historic remains.

BIRLING VALE is an attractive stone built detached house in secluded garden. Fully equipped, two double bedrooms, one twin, cot. Free central heating. Close to sandy beaches, trout and salmon rivers and many places of interest. Well-trained dogs welcome. Weekly rates from £130 Low Season, £250 Mid Season, £490 High Season. SAE to MRS J. BREWIS, WOODHOUSE FARM, SHILBOTTLE, NEAR ALNWICK NE66 2HR (01665 575222). [🐕]

Terms quoted in this publication may be subject to increase if rises in costs necessitate

Burton Joyce

Residential area 4 miles north-east of Nottingham.

MRS V. BAKER, WILLOW HOUSE, 12 WILLOW WONG, BURTON JOYCE, NOTTINGHAM NG14 5FD (0115 931 2070). Large Victorian house in quiet village location, two minutes walk River Trent, four miles city. Attractive accommodation in bright, clean rooms with tea/coffee making facilities, TV. Parking. From £22 pppn. Good local eating. Please phone first for directions. [🐕]

Edwinstowe

Village 2 miles west of Ollerton.

CROW HOLLOW COTTAGE, NEAR EDWINSTOWE. Recently refurbished farm cottage stands in its own hedged garden. Close to Sherwood Forest and its numerous attractions. Explore the local area on horseback, or by foot, car or bicycle. DIY stabling at adjacent Broomhill Grange. Contact Helen Proctor (01636 677847). ETC ★★★

e-mail: shp18@lineone.net website: www.crowhollow.co.uk

Burford

Small Cotswold Town on River Windrush, 7 miles west of Witney.

THE INN FOR ALL SEASONS, THE BARRINGTONS, NEAR BURFORD OX18 4TN (01451 844324). Family-run and owned Hotel based on traditional 16th century English Coaching Inn. Ideal base for touring, walking and garden visiting. From £65.00pppn DB&B. [pw! Pets £5 per night, £20 per week]
e-mail: sharp@innforallseasons.com website: www.innforallseasons.com

Oxford

City 52 miles from London. University dating from 13th century. Many notable buildings.

MR B. CRONIN, NANFORD GUEST HOUSE, 137 IFFLEY ROAD, OXFORD OX4 1EJ (01865 244743; Fax: 01865 249596). Period guest house located five minutes on foot from the University of Oxford. Wide range and number of rooms, all with private shower and toilet. [🐕]
e-mail: b.cronin@btinternet.com website: www.nanfordguesthouse.com

Tackley/Kidlington

Village 3 miles north-east of Woodstock; approximately 5 miles north of Oxford.

JUNE AND GEORGE COLLIER, 55 NETHERCOTE ROAD, TACKLEY, KIDLINGTON, OXFORD OX5 3AT (01869 331255; mobile: 07790 338225). Bed and Breakfast in Tackley. An ideal base for touring, walking, cycling and riding. Central for Oxford, The Cotswolds, Stratford-on-Avon, Blenheim Palace. Woodstock four miles. There is a regular train and bus service with local Hostelries serving excellent food. ETC ◆◆◆ [🐕⌂]
e-mail: colliers.bnb@virgin.net website: www.colliersbnb.com

Symbols

- 🐕 Indicates that pets are welcome free of charge.
- £ Indicates that a charge is made for pets: nightly or weekly.
- pw! Shows some special provision for pets; exercise facility, feeding or accommodation arrangement.
- ⌂ Indicates separate pets accommodation.

Thame

Old town 8 miles north-west of Oxford. Home to Oxford City and County Museum.

MS. JULIA TANNER, LITTLE ACRE, TETSWORTH, NEAR THAME OX9 7AT (01844 281423; mobile: 07798 625252). A small country house retreat offering every comfort, set in several private acres. Most rooms en suite. Twin en suite £25pppn, king/double en suite £27.50pppn, family room (3 sharing) £75 per night. Prices include a full English breakfast. A perfect place to relax - your dog will love it. Three minutes Junction 6 M40. Also self-catering accommodation. [pw! Bring dog basket with you.]
website: www.little-acre.co.uk

Woodstock

Old town 8 miles north-west of Oxford. Home to Oxford City and County Museum.

GORSELANDS HALL, BODDINGTON LANE, NORTH LEIGH, WITNEY, OXFORD OX29 6PU (01993 882292; Fax: 01993 881895). Stone country house with oak beams and flagstone floors. Large secluded garden, grass tennis court. All rooms en suite, with colour television. VisitBritain ★★★★ *SILVER AWARD*. [🐕]
e-mail: hamilton@gorselandshall.com website: www.gorselandshall.com

Bishop's Castle, Church Stretton, Grinshill, Ludlow

Linen & fuel included. Minimum price £230 p.w Sleep 5 and 2. Open all year.

Broadway House, Churchstoke, Powys SY15 6DU
Tel : 01588 620770 • E-mail: enqs@bordercottages.co.uk
website: www.bordercottages.co.uk WTB ★★★★★ Self Catering

The 17th century Lodge and 18th century Coach House are located in the grounds of a Regency gentleman's residence with picturesque views towards the South Shropshire hills and Clun Forest. Situated on the Wales/England border, steeped in a colourful history, with historic monuments, wonderful wildlife and country sports and pursuits nearby.

The Travellers Rest Inn

Upper Affcot, Church Stretton, SY6 6RL
Tel: 01694 781275 • Fax: 01694 781555
e-mail: reception@travellersrestinn.co.uk
www.travellersrestinn.co.uk

Situated between Church Stretton and Craven Arms, and surrounded by The South Shropshire Hills. We, Fraser and Mauresia Allison, the owners assure you a warm welcome, good food, good beers, good accommodation, and good old fashioned service. For those wishing to stay overnight with us at The Travellers Rest we have 12 very nice en suite guest bedrooms: six of these being on the ground floor with easy access, and two of these are suitable for accompanied wheel chair users. The bedrooms are away from the main area of the Inn and have their own entrance to the car park and garden, ideal if you have brought your pet with you and a midnight walk is needed. Our well stocked Bar can satisfy most thirsts; cask ales, lagers, stouts, spirits, wines and minerals, throughout the day and the Kitchen takes care of your hunger; be it for a snack or a full satisfying meal, vegetarians no problem, food being served until 9pm in the evening.

THE INN AT GRINSHILL

High Street, Grinshill, Shrewsbury SY4 3BL • Tel: 01939 220410
info@theinnatgrinshill.co.uk • www.theinnatgrinshill.co.uk

Situated 7 miles north of Shrewsbury, this warm, friendly inn offers the highest standards of food, refreshment and accommodation. Dogs on leads are welcome in the bar.

Warm, comfortable Georgian coach house, friendly informal atmosphere, good traditional English Breakfast; delightful en suite rooms. Easy walking distance from town centre and local inns. Lots of nice local walks. TV, tea /coffeemaking facilities in all rooms. One double en suite,one twin en suite, one twin, one single with shared bathroom. Bed and Breakfast from £27.50 pppn ETC ◆◆◆ ***Henwick House, Gravel Hill, Ludlow SY8 1QU***
Tel: 01584 873338 • Miss S.J. Cecil

Heart of England Excellence in Tourism Awards 2006. Gold Award • Best Value for Money Accommodation

Mocktree Barns Holiday Cottages

A small group of Gold Award-winning, comfortable self-catering cottages around sunny courtyard. • Well-equipped, sleeping between two and six. • Two cottages with no stairs. • Friendly owners. • Open all year. • Short breaks available • Pets and children welcome. • Lovely views, excellent walks • Direct access to footpaths through farmland and woods. • Hereford, Cider Country, Shropshire Hills, Shrewsbury, Ironbridge and the splendid mid-Wales countryside all an easy drive away. • Beautiful Ludlow seven miles. • Golf, fishing, cycling nearby.

Colour brochure from Clive and Cynthia Prior,
Mocktree Barns, Leintwardine, Ludlow SY7 0LY (01547 540441)
e-mail: mocktreebarns@care4free.net • web: www.mocktreeholidays.co.uk

VisitBritain ★★★

Four delightful cottages thoughtfully converted and equipped to the highest standard. All with en suite facilities and garden or seating area. One cottage with disabled access. Situated in a secluded valley and ideally located to explore the beautiful South Shropshire countryside. Sleep 2-6.
SALLY AND TIM LOFT, GOOSEFOOT BARN, PINSTONES, DIDDLEBURY, CRAVEN ARMS SY7 9LB • 01584 861326 ETC ★★★★
sally@goosefoot.freeserve.co.uk • www.goosefootbarn.co.uk

THE MOOR HALL

Built in 1789, the Moor Hall is a splendid example of Georgian Palladian style and enjoys breathtaking views over miles of unspoilt countryside. The atmosphere is relaxed and friendly. The gardens, which extend to five acres, provide a perfect setting in which to idle away a few hours, whilst the hills beyond offer wonderful discoveries for the more energetic. B&B from £25 pppn.

Near Ludlow, Shropshire SY8 3EG • 01584 823209 • Fax: 08707 443725
e-mail: info@moorhall.co.uk • website: www.moorhall.co.uk

TOP FARM HOUSE Knockin, Near Oswestry SY10 8HN

TELEPHONE: 01691 682582 E-MAIL: *p.a.m@knockin.freeserve.co.uk*

Grade I Listed black and white house. Bedrooms are all en suite, attractively decorated and furnished. All have tea/coffee making facilities, colour TV, etc. Convenient for the Welsh Border, Shrewsbury, Chester and Oswestry. Bed and Breakfast from £24 to £35 per person. AA *'Best Breakfast' nominee for 3 years.*

"WHICH? HOTEL" RECOMMENDED

GOOD HOTEL GUIDE
Country Hotel of the year 2003

ETC
★★★
(Silver Award)

AA ★★★

Food Award

Pen-y-Dyffryn Country Hotel

RHYDYCROESAU, NEAR OSWESTRY, SHROPSHIRE SY10 7JD

This silver stone former Georgian Rectory, set almost a thousand feet up in the Shropshire/Welsh hills, is in a dream situation for both pets and their owners. Informal atmosphere, no traffic, just buzzards, badgers and beautiful country walks, yet Shrewsbury, Chester, Powis Castle & Lake Vyrnwy are all close by. The well-stocked bar and licensed restaurant are always welcoming at the end of another hard day's relaxing. All bedrooms en suite etc; four have private patios, ideal for pets; several have spa baths. Short breaks available from £78 pppd, Dinner, B&B. Pets free.

Tel: 01691 653700
e-mail: stay@peny.co.uk • website: www.peny.co.uk

Bishop's Castle

Small town in the hills on the Welsh Border, 8 miles from Craven Arms.

BROADWAY HOUSE, CHURCHSTOKE, POWYS SY15 6DU (01588 620770). 17th century Lodge and 18th century Coach House in the grounds of a Regency gentleman's residence on Wales/England border. Picturesque views. Linen and fuel included. Open all year. Sleep five and two. WTB ★★★★★ Self-Catering. [🐕]
e-mail: enqs@bordercottages.co.uk website: www.bordercottages.co.uk

Readers are requested to mention this FHG publication when seeking accommodation

Church Stretton

Delightful little town in lee of Shropshire Hills. Walking and riding country. Facilities for tennis, bowls, gliding and golf. Knighton 22 miles, Bridgnorth 19, Ludlow 15, Shrewsbury 12.

F. & M. ALLISON, TRAVELLERS REST INN, UPPER AFFCOT, NEAR CHURCH STRETTON SY6 6RL (01694 781275; Fax: 01694 781555). Fully licensed inn on the main A49. Good base for touring. Ample parking space. Children and dogs welcome. SAE or phone for further details. ETC ◆◆◆ [pw! 🐕]
e-mail: reception@travellersrestinn.co.uk website: www.travellersrestinn.co.uk

Grinshill

Village 7 miles north of Shrewsbury.

THE INN AT GRINSHILL, HIGH STREET, GRINSHILL, NEAR SHREWSBURY SY4 3BL (01939 220410). Situated 7 miles north of Shrewsbury, this warm, friendly inn offers the highest standards of food, refreshment and accommodation. Dogs on leads are welcome in the bar.
info@theinnatgrinshill.co.uk website: www.theinnatgrinshill.co.uk

Ludlow

Lovely and historic town on Rivers Teme and Corve with numerous old half-timbered houses and inns. Worcester 29 miles, Shrewsbury 27, Hereford 24, Bridgnorth 19, Church Stretton 16.

HENWICK HOUSE, GRAVEL HILL, LUDLOW SY8 1QU (01584 873338). Warm, comfortable Georgian coach house, good traditional English Breakfast. Easy walking distance from town centre and local inns. Lots of nice local walks. TV, tea/coffee making facilities. One double/ one twin en suite, one twin, one single with shared bathroom. B&B from £27.50 pppn. ETC ◆◆◆ [🐕]

CLIVE & CYNTHIA PRIOR, MOCKTREE BARNS, LEINTWARDINE, LUDLOW SY7 0LY (01547 540441). Award-winning self-catering cottages around sunny courtyard. Sleep 2-6. Comfortable, well-equipped. Friendly owners. Dogs and children welcome. Non-Smoking. Lovely country walks. Ludlow, seven miles. Brochure. Level 1 Accessibility Award. VB ★★★ [🐕] See also colour advertisement page 251.
e-mail: mocktreebarns@care4free.net website: www.mocktreeholidays.co.uk

SALLY AND TIM LOFT, GOOSEFOOT BARN, PINSTONES, DIDDLEBURY, CRAVEN ARMS, SHROPSHIRE SY7 9LB (01584 861326). Four delightful cottages thoughtfully converted and equipped to the highest standard. All with en suite facilities and garden or seating area. One cottage with disabled access. Situated in a secluded valley and ideally located to explore the beautiful South Shropshire countryside. Sleep 2-6. ETC ★★★★ [🐕]
e-mail: sally@goosefoot.freeserve.co.uk website: www.goosefootbarn.co.uk

THE MOOR HALL, NEAR LUDLOW SY8 3EG (01584 823209; Fax: 08707 443725). Built in 1789, a splendid example of the Georgian Palladian style. Breathtaking views, 5 acre garden. B&B from £25 pppn. AA ◆◆◆◆ [🐕]
e-mail: info@moorhall.co.uk website: www.moorhall.co.uk

Oswestry

Borderland market town. Many old castles and fortifications. Shrewsbury 16, Vyrnwy 18.

TOP FARM HOUSE, KNOCKIN, NEAR OSWESTRY SY10 8HN (01691 682582). Grade 1 Listed black and white house set in flower-filled gardens. En suite bedrooms. Hearty breakfast. Convenient for the Welsh Border, Shrewsbury, Chester and Oswestry. ETC ◆◆◆◆ Silver Award, AA 4 Red Diamonds, AA 'Best Breakfast' nominee.
e-mail: p.a.m@knockin.freeserve.co.uk

PEN-Y-DYFFRYN COUNTRY HOTEL, NEAR RHYDYCROESAU, OSWESTRY SY10 7JD (01691 653700). Picturesque Georgian Rectory quietly set in Shropshire/ Welsh Hills. 12 en suite bedrooms, four with private patios. 5-acre grounds. No passing traffic. Johansens recommended. Dinner, Bed and Breakfast from £78.00 per person per day. AA/ETC ★★★. [🐕 pw!]
e-mail: stay@peny.co.uk website: www.peny.co.uk

Allerford, Bath, Brean, Castle Cary, Cheddar

Exmoor •• The Pack Horse

Allerford, Near Porlock, Somerset TA24 8HW
Tel/Fax: 01643 862475
www.thepackhorse.net • e-mail: holidays@thepackhorse.net

Our self-catering apartments and cottage are situated in this unique location within a picturesque National Trust village which has local amenities. The Pack Horse sits alongside the shallow River Aller, overlooking the famous bridge. Enjoy immediate access from our doorstep to the beautiful surrounding countryside, pretty villages, spectacular coast, and Exmoor.

Terms from £240 to £495 per week

OPEN ALL YEAR • PRIVATE PARKING • SHORT BREAKS

Very warm welcome assured

Bath - Toghill House Farm Cottages and B&B

Luxury barn conversions on working farm just north of Bath. Each cottage is equipped to a very high standard with bed linen provided. You are welcome to roam amongst our many animals and enjoy the outstanding country views. We also provide Bed and Breakfast accommodation in our warm and cosy 17th century farmhouse where all rooms are en suite with TV and tea making facilities. Pets £2 per night, £8 per week.

Brochure - Tel: 01225 891261 • Fax: 01225 892128 • www.toghillhousefarm.co.uk
David and Jackie Bishop, Toghill House Farm, Freezing Hill, Wick, Near Bath BS30 5RT

WESTWARD RISE HOLIDAY PARK

Brean, Near Burnham-on-Sea TA8 2RD Tel & Fax: 01278 751310

Highly Recommended Luxury 2/6 berth Chalet-Bungalows on a small quiet family-owned Park adjoining sandy beach. • 2 Double Bedrooms • Shower • Toilet • Colour TV • Fridge • Cooker • Duvets and Linen • Open all year • Centrally Heated during winter months • Laundry on Park • Caravan Sales Available • Shops • Clubs • Amusements & Restaurants Nearby • Dogs Welcome

Call now for a FREE BROCHURE www.breansands.freeserve.co.uk

Beachside Holiday Park

Coast Road, Brean Sands, Somerset TA8 2QZ
Tel: 01278 751346 • Fax: 01278 751683

• Chalets and Caravan holiday homes on quiet park • Direct access to beach (pets £21 per week) • Full facilities • Colour television • Golf courses nearby • Bars and restaurants nearby •

FREE BROCHURE • FREEPHONE 08000 190322 • www.beachsideholidaypark.co.uk

The Horse Pond Inn and Motel

Tel: 01963 350318
Fax: 01963 351762

Castle Cary is an attractive twelfth century town with easy access to Bath & West Showground, Glastonbury, Yeovil and the Dorset coast. Good walking area. The Horse Pond Inn offers a warm welcome and fresh home cooked meals. Fully en suite rooms, 3 double, 2 family, from £40 to £65. Pets FREE.

The Triangle, Castle Cary BA4 7BD

CHEDDAR - SUNGATE HOLIDAY APARTMENTS

Church Street, Cheddar, Somerset BS27 3RA

Delightful apartments in Cheddar village, each fully equipped. Sleep two/four. Laundry facilities. Private parking. Family, disabled and pet friendly.

For full details contact Mrs M. Fieldhouse. Tel: 01934 842273/742264
enquiries@sungateholidayapartments.co.uk • www.sungateholidayapartments.co.uk

Readers are requested to mention this FHG publication when seeking accommodation

Just 1.1miles (1770metres) Steps
"NOT MILES" from Cheddar Gorge & Village
BROADWAY HOUSE
BROADWAY HOUSE
Holiday Touring Caravan & Camping Park CHEDDAR
HOLIDAY CARAVANS FOR HIRE
PREMIER TOURING AND CAMPING PITCHES
FREE HEATED SWIMMING POOL & PIXIE PLAYGROUND
FREE ADVENTURE PLAYGROUND
DISABLED AND BABIES ROOM
CORNER SHOP WITH FRIENDLY SERVICE
COME AND SEE OUR PET LLAMA AND PARROT
FREE ENTRANCE TO THE BAR-CAFÉ & FAMILY ROOM
LAUNDERETTE, AMUSEMENTS, CRAZY GOLF,
SKATEBOARD PARK, INDOOR TABLE TENNIS
BMX TRACK+ BMX HIRE
ACTIVITY PROGRAM
ARCHERY, CANOEING, RIFLE SHOOTING, ABSEILING, CAVING, NATURE TRAILS.
DAVID BELLAMY CONSERVATION AWARD
HOLIDAY PARK
SOMERSET LAND OF THE SUMMER PEOPLE
AA
BROADWAY HOUSE CHEDDAR, SOMERSET. BS27 3DB
TEL:01934 742610 FAX:01934 744950
email: info@broadwayhouse.uk.com www.broadwayhouse.uk.com

In the centre of quaint English village, an ideal location for walking and exploring Exmoor, the surrounding coastline and the many local attractions. Comfortable, family-run hotel which provides a friendly, relaxed atmosphere, home cooking, en suite rooms with colour TV, tea making facilities and a residents' lounge. Packed lunches and drying facilities available. Non-smoking. Well behaved dogs welcome.

Party bookings and mid-week breaks a speciality • Pets Welcome • B&B From £35 • ETC ★★★

THE YARN MARKET HOTEL High Street, Dunster TA24 6SF • 01643 821425
Fax: 01643 821475 • e-mail: yarnmarket.hotel@virgin.net • www.yarnmarkethotel.co.uk

Tel: 01643 831495
e-mail: enquiries@edgcotthouse.co.uk
www.edgcotthouse.co.uk
Exford on Exmoor • Somerset TA24 7QG

Edgcott House

Marc Watts invites you enter another world.

Edgcott House is a gracious rambling country pile quietly situated in Exford in the centre of Exmoor National Park.

The extensive grounds include a charming secluded garden, ancient woodlands and a small lake.

7 en suite bedrooms and those memorable breakfasts and traditional suppers cooked by Marc.

SELF-CATERING COTTAGE – in the grounds of the house – newly refurbished – sleeps 6.

Children and Pets will be made to feel very welcome.

Riscombe Farm Holiday Cottages – Exmoor National Park

Four charming self-catering stone cottages converted from barns surrounding an attractive courtyard with stables. Very comfortable, with log fires and equipped to a high standard, sleeping 2-6. Peaceful, relaxing location beside the River Exe in the centre of Exmoor National Park. Excellent walking and riding country in the valleys, across the moors or along the spectacular coast.

One and a half miles from Exford Village.

Dogs and horses welcome. Stabling provided.

Leone & Brian Martin,
Riscombe Farm, Exford,
Somerset TA24 7NH
Tel: 01643 831480
www.riscombe.co.uk *(with vacancy info.)*

Open all year. VisitBritain ★★★★

SIMONSBATH HOUSE HOTEL

Simonsbath, Exmoor, Somerset TA24 7SH
Tel: 01643 831259 • Fax: 01643 831557

Overlooking the River Barle the oldest house on Exmoor Forest offers a peaceful and relaxing location to enjoy the magnificent coastal scenery or to explore the splendour of Exmoor and the spectacular coastline. Surrounded by moorland this is an ideal location for long walks both on and off the lead. The hotel offers large, individually decorated, centrally heated rooms, some with four poster beds, and all with en suite facilities, colour TV and hospitality tray. The comfortable lounge and library have log fires, offering the perfect setting to enjoy drinks before sampling our highly commended cuisine.

The house is situated in three acres of grounds and there is ample off road parking.

Dogs are welcome to stay free of charge. Please contact Andrew or Louise for further detail

www.simonsbathhouse.co.uk **B&B / B&B & Evening Dinner**

FREE or REDUCED RATE entry to Holiday Visits and Attractions
– see our READERS' OFFER VOUCHERS on pages 407-423

The Crown Hotel

Exford, Exmoor National Park, Somerset TA24 7PP
e-mail: info@crownhotelexmoor.co.uk
www.crownhotelexmoor.com

Situated in the middle of Exford, one of the prettiest villages on the Moor and known as the Capital of Exmoor, The Crown is very much the centre of village life. After a day out in the open, where better to return than the Comfort of The Crown Hotel, with its log fires, comfortable lounges, en suite bedrooms, ancient bar and elegant restaurant where Head Chef Paul Webber serves some of the most wonderfully exciting food on Exmoor. Dogs are welcome in guests' rooms or can be accommodated in our stable block. Why not bring your horse and enjoy a day's hunting with one of the local hunts. (There is a small charge for dogs and horses).

AA ★★★

RESTAURANT AWARD

Tel: 01643 831554/5 • Fax: 01643 831665 •

ETC ★★★★

WOODCOMBE LODGES

Four self-catering lodges in a tranquil rural setting on the edge of Exmoor National Park, standing in a beautiful 2½ acre garden with wonderful views towards the wooded slopes of Exmoor. Minehead's seafront, harbour, shops etc. 1½ miles. Close to Dunster, Selworthy, Porlock and many local beauty spots.

Bratton, Near Minehead TA24 8SQ (Tel & Fax: 01643 702789).
e-mail: nicola@woodcombelodge.co.uk • www.woodcombelodge.co.uk

Occupying an unique location with breathtaking views within the National Park. A special place for you and man's best friends.

ETC ★★★★ Telephone or write for colour brochure:

Wintershead

Jane Styles, Wintershead Farm,
Simonsbath, Exmoor, Somerset TA24 7LF
Tel: 01643 831222 • www.wintershead.co.uk

Westermill is wonderful for dogs and owners

- Four waymarked walks over 500 acre farm
- Small paddock where dogs can run free
- Stabling and fields for horses.

COTTAGES • In grass paddocks, by stream with views across the river valley. Up to 4 star ETC with woodburners. Ideal for children. Disabled facilities Category 2.

Separate **CAMPSITE** by the river.

EDWARDS FAMILY, Westermill Farm,
Exford, Minehead, Somerset TA24 7NJ
Tel: 01643 831238 Ans/Fax: 01643 831216
e-mail: pw@westermill.com
www.westermill.com

Brochure from resident owners

Val & Mike Warner, Westerclose House, Withypool, Somerset TA24 7QR

Holiday Cottages – Exmoor National Park

Quality cottages, including bungalows in the grounds of an old hunting lodge. Wonderful moorland location.

Totally peaceful with superb views. So much to do locally – beautiful coast and countryside. Shop and pub 300 metres. Excellent walking straight from your cottage.Very cosy with log burners and hand-made furnishings. Dogs & horses welcome. Individual gardens. Sleep 2-6. Internet access. Open all year. Short breaks available.

Tel/Fax: 01643 831302 • www.westerclose.co.uk

MINEHEAD – 16th CENTURY THATCHED COTTAGES

ROSE-ASH – Sleeps 2 ✦ Prettily furnished ✦ All electric. **WILLOW** – Inglenook ✦ Oak panelling ✦ Electricity, Gas, CH ✦ Sleeps 6. **LITTLE THATCH** – Sleeps 5 ✦ Inglenook ✦ Cosy location✦ Electricity. Gas, CH.
SAE please to: Mr T. Stone, Troytes Farmstead, Tivington, Somerset TA24 8SU
Private car park – Enclosed gardens – Pets Welcome **Tel: 01643 704531**

Four quality open-plan apartments, former stables, and one spacious family house. All with sea views, parking, easy access, garden or outside space. Linen provided. Pets most welcome. Open all year. Located in historic village between Moor and sea, ideal base for exploring the beauty of Exmoor National Park. **To find out more view www.shipsmews.co.uk or phone 07979 278466 (mobile) and talk to us.**

Tel & Fax: 01935 891532

WOOD DAIRY, WOOD LANE, NORTH PERROTT TA18 7TA

Three well-appointed stone holiday cottages set around courtyard in two and a half acres of Somerset/Dorset countryside. Adjacent golf course. Close to Lyme Bay and Jurassic Coast, excellent base for walking, trails and historic properties. Pets welcome by arrangement. Wheelchair friendly.
e-mail: liz@acountryretreat.co.uk **www.acountryretreat.co.uk**

Nestled in the midst of the wild and fertile countryside of Somerset, just 3 miles from the M5 and Taunton. An elegant Georgian Hotel situated in the heart of Somerset. Beautiful grounds and gardens, orchards, roses, and our own poultry for your breakfast eggs.

AA ★★

FARTHINGS HOTEL & RESTAURANT Hatch Beauchamp, Taunton TA3 6SG • Tel: 01823 480664 • Fax: 01823 481118
www.farthingshotel.co.uk • e-mail: info@farthingshotel.co.uk

Croft Holiday Cottages • **The Croft, Anchor Street, Watchet TA23 0BY**
Tel: 01984 631121 • ETC ★★★★

Courtyard of six cottages/bungalows situated in a quiet backwater of the small harbour town of Watchet. Parking, central heating. TV, DVD, washing machine, fridge/freezer, microwave. Use of heated indoor pool. Sleep 2-8 persons. £165-£650 per property per week. **Contact: Mrs K. Musgrave • e-mail: croftcottages@talk21.com • www.cottagessomerset.com**

Somerset Court Cottages

Wick St Lawrence, Near Weston-super-Mare BS22 7YR • Tel: 01934 521383
Converted stone cottages in mediaeval village. 1, 2 or 3 beds. Some with four-posters, luxury whirlpool/spa baths. Superb centre for touring West Country.
e-mail: peter@somersetcourtcottages.co.uk • www.somersetcourtcottages.co.uk

Braeside Hotel 2 Victoria Park, Weston-super-Mare BS23 2HZ
Delightful , family-run, 9-bedroom hotel only a two-minute walk from the seafront and sandy beach (dogs allowed all year). All bedrooms en suite.
Tel: 01934 626642 • ETC/AA ◆◆◆◆ (Awarded in 2005)
e-mail: braeside@tesco.net •www.braesidehotel.co.uk

Silver
SILVER AWARD
◆◆◆◆

North Down Farm

Pyncombe Lane, Wiveliscombe, Taunton TA4 2BL Tel/Fax: 01984 623730
Traditional working farm set in 100 acres of natural beauty. All rooms tastefully furnished to high standard include en suite, TV, and tea/coffee facilities. Double, twin or single rooms available. Dining room and lounge with log fires; centrally heated and double glazed. Drying facilities. Dogs welcome. B&B from £29 pppn, 7 nights BB+EM £225pp. North Down Break: three nights BB+EM £109 per person.
e-mail: jennycope@tiscali.co.uk **www.north-down-farm.co.uk**

WESTERCLOSE HOUSE, WITHYPOOL, EXMOOR NATIONAL PARK TA24 7QR (01643 831302). Moorland cosy cottages including two bungalows in grounds of old hunting lodge overlooking Barle Valley. Dogs and horses welcome. Shop and pub 300 metres. [pw! Dogs £12 per week]
website: www.westerclose.co.uk

THE EXMOOR WHITE HORSE INN, EXFORD TA24 7PY (01643 831229; Fax: 01643 831246). A warm welcome awaits at this charming 16th Century Inn. Unique in character, giving you a true flavour of Exmoor. 28 ensuite bedrooms, with colour TV, teamaking, radio and hairdryers. Fully licensed Restaurant with varied menu using local produce. ETC ★★★ [Pets £7.50 per night].
e-mail: user@exmoor-whitehorse.co.uk website: www.exmoor-whitehorse.co.uk

Minehead

Neat and stylish resort on Bristol Channel. Sandy bathing beach, attractive gardens, golf course and good facilities for tennis, bowls and horse riding. Within easy reach of the beauties of Exmoor.

MINEHEAD 16TH CENTURY THATCHED COTTAGES. Rose Ash - Sleeps 2, prettily furnished, all electric. Willow - Inglenook, oak panelling, electricity, gas, CH, Sleeps 6. Little Thatch - Sleeps 5, Inglenook, Cosy location, Electricity. Gas, CH. Private car park. Enclosed gardens. Pets welcome. SAE: MR T. STONE, TROYTES FARMSTEAD, TIVINGTON, MINEHEAD TA24 8SU (01643 704531). [🐕]

Somerset/Dorset (North Perrott)

Village 2 miles east of Crewkerne.

MRS E NEVILLE, WOOD DAIRY, WOOD LANE, NORTH PERROTT TA18 7TA (Tel & Fax: 01935 891532). Three well-appointed stone holiday cottages set around courtyard in two and a half acres of Somerset/Dorset countryside. Adjacent golf course. Close to Lyme Bay and Jurassic Coast, excellent base for walking, trails and historic properties. Wheelchair friendly. Pets welcome by arrangement.
e-mail: liz@acountryretreat.co.uk website: www.acountryretreat.co.uk

Porlock

Small resort near coast at foot of a steep hill.

SHIP'S MEWS, PORLOCK. Four quality open-plan apartments, former stables, and one spacious family house. All with sea views, parking, easy access, garden or outside space. Linen provided. Pets most welcome. Open all year. To find out more view website or phone 07979 278466 (mobile).
website: www.shipsmews.co.uk

Taunton

County capital in Vale of Taunton Deane. Museum, Civic Centre, remains of Norman castle.

FARTHINGS HOTEL & RESTAURANT, HATCH BEAUCHAMP, TAUNTON TA3 6SG (01823 480664; Fax: 01823 481118). Nestled in the midst of the wild and fertile countryside of Somerset, just 3 miles from the M5 and Taunton. An elegant Georgian Hotel with beautiful grounds and gardens, orchards, roses, and our own poultry for your breakfast eggs. AA ★★ Two Rosettes
e-mail: info@farthingshotel.co.uk website: www.farthingshotel.co.uk

Watchet

Small port and resort with rocks and sands. Good centre for Exmoor and the Quantocks. Bathing, boating, fishing, rambling. Tiverton 24 miles, Bridgwater 19, Taunton 17, Dunster 6.

MRS K. MUSGRAVE, CROFT HOLIDAY COTTAGES, THE CROFT, ANCHOR STREET, WATCHET TA23 0BY (01984 631121) Courtyard of six cottages/bungalows situated in a quiet backwater of the small harbour town of Watchet. Parking, central heating. TV, DVD, washing machine, fridge/freezer, microwave. Use of heated indoor pool. Sleeps 2-8 persons. £165-£650 per property per week. ETC ★★★★ [🐕]
e-mail: croftcottages@talk21.com website: www.cottagessomerset.com

Wells

England's smallest city. West front of Cathedral built around 1230, shows superb collection of statuary.

INFIELD HOUSE, 36 PORTWAY, WELLS BA5 2BN (01749 670989; Fax: 01749 679093). Richard and Heather invite you and your dog (if older than one year) to visit England's smallest city. Wonderful walks on Mendip Hills. No smoking. Bountiful breakfasts, dinners by arrangement. AA ◆◆◆◆ [🐕]
website: www.infieldhouse.co.uk

Weston-Super-Mare

Popular resort on the Bristol Channel with a wide range of entertainments and leisure facilities. An ideal base for touring the West Country.

SOMERSET COURT COTTAGES, WICK ST LAWRENCE, NEAR WESTON-SUPER-MARE BS22 7YR (01934 521383). Converted stone cottages in mediaeval village. 1, 2 or 3 beds. Some with four-posters, luxury whirlpool/spa baths. Superb centre for touring West Country. Short Breaks available. £200-£660 per week. [Pets £2 per night]
e-mail: peter@somersetcourtcottages.co.uk website: www.somersetcourtcottages.co.uk

BRAESIDE HOTEL, 2 VICTORIA PARK, WESTON-SUPER-MARE BS23 2HZ (01934 626642). Delightful, family-run Hotel, close to shops, beach and park. Parking available. All rooms en suite, colour TV, tea/coffee making. November to March THIRD NIGHT FREE. ETC/AA ◆◆◆◆ (Awarded in 2005)[🐕]
e-mail: braeside@tesco.net website: www.braesidehotel.co.uk

MR C. G. THOMAS, ARDNAVE HOLIDAY PARK, KEWSTOKE, WESTON-SUPER-MARE BS22 9XJ (01934 622319). Caravans - De luxe. 2-3 bedrooms, shower, toilet, colour TVs, all bedding included. Parking. Dogs welcome. Graded ★★★. [🐕 pw!]

Wiveliscombe

Small town 9 miles west of Taunton.

JENNY COPE, NORTH DOWN FARM, PYNCOMBE LANE, WIVELISCOMBE, TAUNTON TA4 2BL (Tel & Fax: 01984 623730). Traditional working farm. All rooms en suite, furnished to high standard. Log fires. Central heating. B&B £29pppn. BB&EM: 7 nights £225pp, 3-night B&B and evening meal £109pp. Dogs welcome. ETC ◆◆◆◆ Silver Award. [£5 per pet per visit].
e-mail: jennycope@tiscali.co.uk website: www.north-down-farm.co.uk

Symbols

🐕 Indicates that pets are welcome free of charge.
£ Indicates that a charge is made for pets: nightly or weekly.
pw! Shows some special provision for pets; exercise facility, feeding or accommodation arrangement.
⌂ Indicates separate pets accommodation.

Note

All the information in this guide is given in good faith in the belief that it is correct. However, the publishers cannot guarantee the facts given in these pages, neither are they responsible for changes in ownership or facilities that may take place after the date of going to press.
Readers should always satisfy themselves that the facilities they require are available and that the terms, if quoted, still apply.

Leek

Village 10 miles from Stoke-on-Trent.

EDITH & ALWYN MYCOCK, 'ROSEWOOD COTTAGE and ROSEWOOD FLAT', LOWER BERKHAMSYTCH FARM, BOTTOM HOUSE, NEAR LEEK ST13 7QP (Tel & Fax: 01538 308213). Cosy three bedroomed cottage with four-poster, sleeps six; also flat, sleeps up to four. Fully equipped and carpeted. Electricity and linen inclusive, laundry room. Ideal base for Alton Towers, Potteries and Peak District. Terms £180 to £350. [Pets £6.50 per week]
website: www.rosewoodcottage.co.uk

Tutbury

Village 4 miles north west of Burton-upon-Trent. Ruins of 14th century castle.

LITTLE PARK HOLIDAY HOMES, PARK LANE, TUTBURY, NEAR BURTON-ON-TRENT DE13 9JQ (Tel & Fax: 01283 812654; Mobile: 07884 343460). Barn Conversion Units. Full self-catering. Facilities situated near to medieval castle and tourist village. Spectacular views. Near Alton Towers and other theme parks. Ample parking. Please phone for brochure. [🐕]

Publisher's note

While every effort is made to ensure accuracy, we regret that FHG Guides cannot accept responsibility for errors, misrepresentations or omissions in our entries or any consequences thereof. Prices in particular should be checked.
We will follow up complaints but cannot act as arbiters or agents for either party.

More than 100 selected holiday cottages in the finest locations...

Tel: 01502 722717 Fax: 01502 722323
Email: holidays@suffolk-secrets.co.uk
www.suffolk-secrets.co.uk

SUFFOLK *Secrets*...
The Old Water Tower
The Common, Southwold
Suffolk IP18 6TB

SUFFOLK *Secrets*...

Aldeburgh, Bury St Edmunds, Cratfield, Dunwich

WENTWORTH HOTEL

WENTWORTH ROAD, ALDEBURGH, SUFFOLK IP15 5BD

Facing the sea, the Wentworth Hotel has the comfort and style of a country house. 35 bedrooms, many with sea views, two comfortable lounges with open fires and antique furniture, provide ample space to relax. The restaurant serves a variety of fresh produce, including local seafood, and a light lunch can be chosen from the bar menu and eaten "al fresco" in the terrace garden. There are many walks, some commencing from the Hotel. Aldeburgh is the perfect touring centre for East Anglia.

AA ★★★ Two Rosettes 85%

For a reservation, please Telephone 01728 452312 or Fax: 01728 454343
E-mail: stay@wentworth-aldeburgh.co.uk Website: www.wentworth-aldeburgh.com

ETC Silver Award

Rede Hall Farm Park

www.redehallfarmpark.co.uk

Rede Hall Farm, Rede, Bury St Edmunds IP29 4UG • Tel: 01284 850695 • Fax: 01284 850345
Two well equipped cottages with loads of Suffolk character and charm on moated mixed farm. Ideal for touring East Anglia and the Suffolk coast. Superb local pubs with good food. Open all year. Totally non-smoking. Hot Tub Spa available for exclusive use (inclusive). Oil-fired central heating • Electric cooker, microwave, washer/dryer, dishwasher • TV with DVD/VCR, hi-fi • Children's play area • BBQ with patio furniture • Well behaved dogs welcome • Livery for horses on request

ETC ★★★★

AA ★★★

16th century heavily beamed Tudor Hall set in 7 acres of perfect dog walks. Individually furnished en suite bedrooms; renowned restaurant; relaxing inglenook fires.

enquiries@ravenwoodhall.co.uk
www.ravenwoodhall.co.uk

RAVENWOOD HALL
COUNTRY HOUSE HOTEL AND RESTAURANT,
ROUGHAM, BURY ST EDMUNDS IP30 9JA
Tel: 01359 270345
Fax: 01359 270788

Poachers Farm, Holiday Cottage, Cratfield, Suffolk

Light and spacious cottage with views across open farm land. Situated on edge of village, pub nearby. Sleeps up to 6 plus sofa bed. 30 minutes to Southwold and coast. Fully fenced garden. Pets welcome. For brochure phone Jane:
01986 798830 or 07788853884 or e-mail: janebrewer@ukonline.co.uk

A useful index of towns/counties appears on pages 424-429

THE CLOSE MIDDLEGATE BARN, DUNWICH IP17 3DP

Situated in a quiet, private road 200 yards from the sea. Ideal for walking/birdwatching. Furnished and equipped to a high standard. Full linen included. Centrally heated; available all year. Please ask for brochure and availability.

E-mail: middlegate@aol.com **Tel: 01728 648244**

Edge Hall www.edgehall-hotel.co.uk

2 HIGH STREET, HADLEIGH IP7 5AP • 01473 822458 • Fax: 01473 827751

Treacle invites you to stay in her master's comfortable lodge house. Well behaved owners will enjoy the perfect walks and super breakfasts. Double/twin £80 per night, Single £55. Self-catering also available. ETC ◆◆◆◆

DAMERONS FARM HOLIDAYS

Five cottages, each sleeping 1-6, converted from an Old Granary and milking parlour into tasteful, modern accommodation. The owners, Wayne & Sue Leggett, guarantee a warm Suffolk welcome. Step out of your cottage and into beautiful countryside away from the hustle and bustle. The Old Dairy has a high level of accessibility for disabled visitors and three of the other cottages have ground floor bedrooms and bathrooms. Children (and the young at heart) will enjoy the 24' x 15' games room with table tennis, pool and table football and there is a large outdoor grass play area. Short breaks are offered out of high season. Less than 2 hours from London and 1 hour from Stansted Airport.

Henley, Ipswich IP6 0RU • www.dameronsfarmholidays.co.uk

Knights Holiday Homes at Kessingland, on the Suffolk Heritage Coast

CHILDREN AND PETS WELCOME

SELF-CATERING HOLIDAYS

OPEN ALL YEAR

Seaview Bungalows

These bungalows are situated on a quiet, attractive estate set in nine acres of lawns overlooking the sea. There is a made-up roadway round the estate and parking near your door. Your bungalow has three bedrooms, bathroom and toilet, kitchen and lounge with a sun door opening onto the lawns. A walkway leads immediately from the estate to the promenade and the beach.

SHOPS ARE APPROXIMATELY 450 YARDS AND BUS STOP 300 YARDS.

'Kessingland: Most easterly village in the United Kingdom. First to greet the sun. Once known as the richest village in England because of its prolific fishing. Now known for its peaceful, pleasant surroundings, its beautiful spacious beach and its Suffolk countryside, where you can relax in peace and watch the boats sail by on the North Sea's Herring Pond.'

THE BUNGALOWS

- 1-6 persons
- Colour Television
- Bed linen supplied • Fully equipped kitchens
- Full size cookers and refrigerators
- Microwaves, video recorders
- Cots and Highchairs are available
- Electrically heated - no meters • Parking

THE VILLAGE

- Clean Beach Award
- Mother Hubbard's Cupboard
  – Kessingland Art Centre and Gift Shop
- Suffolk Wildlife Park
- Shops • Pubs
- Restaurants • Cafes • Bus Service

BROCHURE • CALENDAR • OFFER LETTER • BOOKING FORM from

Knights Holiday Homes, 198 Church Road, Kessingland, Suffolk NR33 7SF

Freephone 0800 269067 • E-mail: info@knightsholidays.co.uk • www.knightsholidays.co.uk

Lodge Cottage, Laxfield, Suffolk

Pretty 16C thatched cottage retaining some fine period features. Sleeps 4. Pets welcome. Fenced garden. 1 mile from village. 30 minutes to Southwold and coast. Rural, quiet and relaxing. For brochure phone Jane:

01986 798830 or 07788853884 or e-mail: janebrewer@ukonline.co.uk

Broadland Holiday Village

Discover the delights of the Forgotten Norfolk Broad
with your Faithful Friend

Stay in Cosy Brick Bungalows or Pine Lodges
Enjoy all the Countryside, Marsh and Beach Walks

And when you've worn him out, you can relax in
our indoor heated pool

The perfect holiday for the whole family!

Oulton Broad, Lowestoft NR33 9JY • 01502 573033
www.broadlandvillage.co.uk

Gladwins Farm *Cottages in Constable Country*

Set in 22 acres of rolling Suffolk countryside, Gladwins Farm offers a selection of accommodation. Guests staying in any of our 4★ or 5★ self-catering cottages (sleeping 2-8) or the B&B can use the heated indoor pool, sauna, hot tub, the hard tennis court and playground. There is coarse fishing in our lake plus farm animals to entertain the children. Pets welcome in most cottages and loads of dog walking! Riding, golf and beach within easy reach.

If a quiet holiday in a charming area of Olde England is on your agenda, call Pauline or Robert Dossor on 01206 262261 and arrange a memorable stay. See us on the internet at www.gladwinsfarm.co.uk or call for our colour brochure and DVD. Winners, Regional Self-Catering Holiday of the Year 2003 and 2006.

e-mail: gladwinsfarm@aol.com
Gladwins Farm, Harper's Hill, Nayland, Suffolk CO6 4NU

★★★★ SELF CATERING

★★★★★ SELF CATERING

THE CROWN and Castle

Orford, Woodbridge, Suffolk IP12 2LJ
Tel: 01394 450205
e-mail: info@crownandcastle.co.uk
www.crownandcastle.co.uk

Suffolk Heritage Coast

Now owned by the ex-proprietors of Hintlesham Hall, this comfortable and very dog-friendly hotel is situated close to the 12th century castle in this historic and unspoilt village. Honest good food served in the acclaimed award-winning Trinity Restaurant.

SWEFFLING HALL FARM

Sweffling, Saxmundham IP17 2BT
Tel & Fax: 01728 663644

Set well back from the main road in a quiet location • Always a warm welcome • Ideal for walking/cycling • Vintage transport available free for longer stays • One double and one family room with en suite/private bathrooms • Open all year.

e-mail: stephenmann@suffolkonline.net

Situated in small, picturesque village within 15 miles of Sudbury, Newmarket Racecourse and historic Bury St Edmunds. Bungalow well equipped to accommodate 4 people. All facilities. Car essential, parking. Children and pets welcome. Terms from £68 to £135 per week. For further details send SAE to

MRS M. WINCH, PLOUGH HOUSE, STANSFIELD, SUDBURY CO10 8LT • Tel: 01284 789253

SUFFOLK SECRETS (01502 722717). Specialists in self-catering holidays on the beautiful and peaceful Suffolk Heritage Coast. More than 100 selected holiday cottages in the finest locations.
e-mail: holidays@suffolk-secrets.co.uk website: www.suffolk-secrets.co.uk

Aldeburgh

Coastal town 6 miles south-east of Saxmundham. Annual music festival at Snape Maltings.

WENTWORTH HOTEL, ALDEBURGH IP15 5BD (01728 452312). Country House Hotel overlooking the sea. Immediate access to the beach and walks. Two comfortable lounges with log fires and antique furniture. Refurbished bedrooms with all facilities and many with sea views. Restaurant specialises in fresh produce and sea food. ETC Silver Award. AA ★★★ Two Rosettes. [Pets £2 per day]
e-mail: stay@wentworth-aldeburgh.co.uk website: www.wentworth-aldeburgh.com

Bury St Edmunds

This prosperous market town on the River Lark lies 28 miles east of Cambridge.

REDE HALL FARM PARK, REDE, BURY ST EDMUNDS IP29 4UG (01284 850695; Fax: 01284 850345). Two well equipped cottages, ideal for touring East Anglia and the coast. Totally non-smoking. Hot Tub Spa available for exclusive use (inclusive). Well behaved dogs welcome. ETC ★★★★ [🐕 ⌂]
website: www.redehallfarmpark.co.uk

RAVENWOOD HALL COUNTRY HOUSE HOTEL AND RESTAURANT, ROUGHAM, BURY ST EDMUNDS IP30 9JA (01359 270345; Fax: 01359 270788). 16th century heavily beamed Tudor Hall set in seven acres of perfect dog walks. Individually furnished en suite bedrooms; renowned restaurant; relaxing inglenook fires. AA ★★★, AA 2 Rosettes. [🐕 pw!]
e-mail: enquiries@ravenwoodhall.co.uk website: www.ravenwoodhall.co.uk

Cratfield

Village 5 miles West of Halesworth.

POACHERS FARM, HOLIDAY COTTAGE, CRATFIELD. Light and spacious cottage with views across open farm land. Situated on edge of village, pub nearby. Sleeps up to 6 plus sofa bed. 30 minutes to Southwold and coast. Fully fenced garden. Pets welcome. For brochure phone: MRS JANE BREWER, LODGE COTTAGE, LAXFIELD ROAD, CRATFIELD, HALESWORTH IP19 0QG (01986 798830 or 07788853884).[🐕]
e-mail: janebrewer@ukonline.co.uk

Diss

Small market town on the River Waveney 19 miles south west of Norwich.

PAUL AND YOLANDA DAVEY, STRENNETH, AIRFIELD ROAD, FERSFIELD, DISS IP22 2BP (01379 688182; Fax 01379 688260). Family-run, fully renovated period property with two cottages. All rooms en suite, colour TVs, hospitality trays. Ground floor rooms. Non-smoking. Extensive breakfast menu. Licensed. Bed and Breakfast from £25. ETC ◆◆◆◆. [🐕]
e-mail: pdavey@strenneth.co.uk website: www.strenneth.co.uk

Dunwich

Small village on coast, 4 miles south west of Southwold.

MR & MRS COLE, THE CLOSE, MIDDLEGATE BARN, DUNWICH IP17 3DP (01728 648244). Situated in a quiet, private road 200 yards from the sea. Ideal for walking/birdwatching. Furnished and equipped to a high standard. Centrally heated; available all year. Short Breaks available in low season, telephone for availability and brochure. [🐕]
e-mail: middlegate@aol.com

FREE or REDUCED RATE entry to Holiday Visits and Attractions
– see our READERS' OFFER VOUCHERS on pages 407-423

Hadleigh

Historic town on River Brett with several buildings of interest including unusual 14th century church. Bury St Edmunds 20 miles, Colchester 14, Sudbury 11, Ipswich 10.

EDGE HALL, 2 HIGH STREET, HADLEIGH IP7 5AP (01473 822458; Fax: 01473 827751). Treacle invites you to stay in her master's comfortable lodge house. Well behaved owners will enjoy the perfect walks and super breakfasts. Twin/double £80 per night, single £55. Self-catering also available. ETC ◆◆◆◆ [Pets £5 per night, £10 per week]

Henley

Vilage 4 miles north of Ipswich.

WAYNE & SUE LEGGETT, DAMERONS FARM HOLIDAYS, HENLEY, IPSWICH IP6 0RU (01473 832454 or 07881 824083). Five cottages, each sleeping 1-6. The Old Dairy has a high level of accessibility for disabled visitors; three others have ground floor bedrooms and bathrooms. Games room with table tennis, pool and table football. Short Breaks out of season.
www.dameronsfarmholidays.co.uk

Kessingland

Little seaside place with expansive beach, safe bathing, wildlife park, lake fishing. To the south is Benacre Broad, a beauty spot. Norwich 26 miles, Adleburgh 23, Lowestoft 5.

Quality seaside bungalows in lawned surrounds overlooking the sea. Open all year, central heating, colour TV, parking, bed-linen, microwave, video recorder, heat and light included. Sleep 1/6. Direct access to award-winning beach. Pets very welcome. APPLY– KNIGHTS HOLIDAY HOMES, 198 CHURCH ROAD, KESSINGLAND, SUFFOLK NR33 7SF (FREEPHONE 0800 269067).
e-mail: info@knightsholidays.co.uk website: www.knightsholidays.co.uk

Comfortable well-equipped bungalow on lawned site overlooking beach, next to Heritage Coast. Panoramic sea views. Easy beach access. Unspoiled walking area. ETC ★★ MRS L.G. SAUNDERS, 159 THE STREET, ROCKLAND ST MARY, NORWICH NR14 7HL (01508 538340). [Pets £10 per week].

Laxfield

Village 6 miles North of Framlingham.

LODGE COTTAGE, LAXFIELD. Pretty 16C thatched cottage retaining some fine period features. Sleeps 4. Pets welcome. Fenced garden. 1 mile from village. 30 minutes to Southwold and coast. Rural, quiet and relaxing. For brochure phone: MRS JANE BREWER, LODGE COTTAGE, LAXFIELD ROAD, CRATFIELD, HALESWORTH IP19 0QG (01986 798830 or 07788853884).
e-mail: janebrewer@ukonline.co.uk

Lowestoft

Resort town on the North Sea coast, 38 miles north east of Ipswich.

BROADLAND HOLIDAY VILLAGE, OULTON BROAD, LOWESTOFT NR33 9JY (01502 573033). Discover the delights of the Forgotten Norfolk Broad with your faithful friend. Stay in cosy brick bungalows or pine lodges. Indoor heated pool. The perfect holiday for the whole family! [Pets £30 per week].
website: www.broadlandvillage.co.uk

Nayland

Small town on River Stour, 6 miles north of Colchester.

GLADWINS FARM, HARPER'S HILL, NAYLAND CO6 4NU (01206 262261). Self-catering cottages (sleep 2-8) and B&B set in 22 acres of Suffolk countryside. Indoor heated pool, sauna, hot tub, tennis court and playground. Loads of dog walking. [Pets £20 per week] ETC ★★★★/★★★★★.
e-mail: gladwinsfarm@aol.com website: www.gladwinsfarm.co.uk

Chase Lodge Hotel

An Award Winning Hotel

with style & elegance, set in tranquil surroundings at affordable prices.

10 Park Road Hampton Wick Kingston-Upon-Thames KT1 4AS

Tel: 020 8943 1862 . Fax: 020 8943 9363

E-mail: info@chaselodgehotel.com Web: www.chaselodgehotel.com & www.surreyhotels.com

Pets welcome

Quality en suite bedrooms
Close to Bushy Park
Buffet-style Full Continental Breakfast
A la carte menu
Licensed bar
Wedding Receptions
Honeymoon suite
available with jacuzzi & steam area
20 minutes from Heathrow Airport
Close to Kingston town centre & all major transport links.

AA ◆◆◆◆ Les Routiers RAC ★★★★

All Major Credit Cards Accepted

Kingston-upon-Thames

Market town, Royal borough and administrative centre of Surrey. Kingston is ideally placed for London and environs.

CHASE LODGE HOTEL, 10 PARK ROAD, HAMPTON WICK, KINGSTON-UPON-THAMES KT1 4AS (020 8943 1862; Fax: 020 8943 9363). Award-winning hotel offering quality en suite bedrooms. Easy access to town centre and major transport links. A la carte menu, licensed bar. ETC/AA◆◆◆◆, RAC ★★★★ [🐕]

e-mail: info@chaselodgehotel.com websites: www.chaselodgehotel.com & www.surreyhotels.com

Peaslake

Village 4 miles north of Cranleigh.

THE HURTWOOD INN HOTEL, WALKING BOTTOM, PEASLAKE, NEAR GUILDFORD GU5 9RR (01306 730851; Fax: 01306 731390). Privately run hotel with 22 en suite bedrooms, bar, restaurant; weddings and functions catered for. In heart of Surrey Hills, with miles of beautiful walks on the doorstep. ETC ★★★, AA ★★★ and Rosette.
e-mail: sales@hurtwoodinnhotel.com website: www.hurtwoodinnhotel.com

Symbols

- 🐕 Indicates that pets are welcome free of charge.
- £ Indicates that a charge is made for pets: nightly or weekly.
- pw! Shows some special provision for pets; exercise facility, feeding or accommodation arrangement.
- ⌂ Indicates separate pets accommodation.

ARLINGTON, EAST SUSSEX Lakeside Farm Holiday Bungalows

On the edge of Arlington Reservoir, with views of the South Downs. Eastbourne, Brighton and Lewes within 15 miles. Drusillas Zoo two miles, shopping half a mile. Modern comfortable accommodation: two double rooms, lounge, dining room, bathroom, toilet, colour TV. Well equipped kitchen with microwave. Open April to October. Car essential, parking. Suitable for disabled guests. Children welcome, cot and high chair available. Well controlled pets accepted. Weekly terms from £200. Electricity included.

Mrs P. Boniface, Lakeside Farm, Arlington, Polegate BN26 6SB (01323 870111)

Beautiful secluded 18th century woodcutter's cottage, nestling in over 40 acres of its own rolling, lush East Sussex land. Surrounded by Forestry Commission woodland.

FOX HOLE FARM, KANE HYTHE ROAD, BATTLE TN33 9QU
Tel & Fax: 01424 772053

AA ♦♦♦♦ Guest Accommodation

Little Hemingfold Hotel

- Relax and enjoy the friendly and tranquil atmosphere of our part 17th century and early Victorian farmhouse.
- Meander through our 40 acres of farm and woodland with endless walks in the adjoining countryside.
- Treat your pets to one of our courtyard garden rooms, all en suite and some with log-burning stoves.
- Fish, row and swim in our two-acre trout lake or take up a challenge on our grass tennis court.

**Discounts for children 7-14 years old.
and FREE accommodation for pets.
Weekly Dinner, Bed and Breakfast
from £68 per person per night.
Two day breaks from £70 per person per night.**

Please ring or write to Paul and Alison Slater

English Tourism Council ♦♦♦ Guest Accommodation

**Telham, Battle, East Sussex TN33 0TT
Tel: 01424 774338
Fax: 01424 775351
littlehemingfoldhote@tiscali.co.uk
www.littlehemingfoldhotel.co.uk**

BEST OF Brighton & Sussex COTTAGES

AQA Quality Accredited Agency

**+44 (0) 1273 308779
www.bestofbrighton.co.uk**

- Brighton & Hove
- Eastbourne • Lewes
- Worthing • Seaford
- Alfriston • Arundel
- Chichester • Selsey

A very good selection of houses, flats, apartments and cottages.

Town Centre, Seafront & Countryside locations - many taking pets (Pets £15/£20 per week)

FREE or REDUCED RATE entry to Holiday Visits and Attractions – see our READERS' OFFER VOUCHERS on pages 407-423

Chiddingly, East Sussex • *Adorable, small, well-equipped cottage in grounds of Tudor Manor*

• Two bedrooms • Full kitchen and laundry facilities • Telephone • Use of indoor heated swimming pool, sauna/jacuzzi, tennis and badminton court • Large safe garden

From £385 – £730 per week inclusive • Pets and children welcome • Short Breaks £240-£340

Apply: Eva Morris, "Pekes", 124 Elm Park Mansions, Park Walk, London SW10 0AR

Tel: 020-7352 8088 Fax: 020-7352 8125 e-mail: pekes.afa@virgin.net web:www.pekesmanor.com

FAIRLIGHT COTTAGE

English Tourism Council ♦♦♦♦ GUEST ACCOMMODATION

Warren Road (via Coastguard Lane), Fairlight, East Sussex TN35 4AG

Peace, tranquillity and a warm welcome await you at our comfortable country house, adjoining 650 acres of country park in an area of outstanding natural beauty – a paradise for dogs and owners. Panoramic sea views from large balcony. Centrally heated en suite bedrooms with beverage trays and colour TV. Comfortable guest lounge. Delicious breakfasts. No smoking. Ample parking. Pets stay with owners (free of charge). Badgers and foxes dine in the garden every evening.

B&B from £32.50pppn. • Single supplement

Janet & Ray Adams • 01424 812545

Little Oaks Farley Way, Fairlight East Sussex

Luxury bungalow on one level set in quiet coastal village with clifftop parklands, close to ancient towns of Rye, Battle and Hastings. Furnished to a very high standard, the spacious accommodation comprises double bedroom with luxury en suite shower room, twin bedroom, lounge with TV, dining room, fully equipped kitchen/diner, bathroom, conservatory and balcony overlooking beautiful secluded garden and garage. No smoking in bungalow. Pets welcome. Rates on application, which include central heating, electricity, bed linen and towels.

Contact: Ray and Janet Adams, Fairlight Cottage, Warren Road, Fairlight, East Sussex TN35 4AG • Tel: 01424 812545

English Tourism Council ★★★★ SELF CATERING

BEAUPORT PARK HOTEL ETC/AA ★★★

A Georgian Country House Hotel set amid formal gardens and woodland. All rooms are well equipped and have private bath. Outdoor Swimming Pool, Tennis, Squash, Badminton, Outdoor Chess, French Boules, Croquet Lawn, Putting, Golf and Riding School. Indoor pool, Gym, Sauna and Steamroom. Special Country House Breaks available all year. Please telephone for Brochure and Tariff.

Battle Road, Hastings TN38 8EA (01424 851222).

e-mail: reservations@beauportparkhotel.co.uk • www.beauportparkhotel.co.uk

Kilcolgan Premier Bungalows

Rottingdean Coastal Village, Brighton BN2 7DL

Well appointed three bedroom bungalows offering quality accommodation. Sleep 5/6. Tranquil secluded garden, overlooking farmland. Ideal retreat in picturesque conservation village with seafront and promenade. Wheelchair access. Dog-friendly walks over Downs. No smoking. Tariff: £550-£850pw. Pets £35pw.

English Tourism Council ★★★★★ SELF CATERING

Tel: 020 7250 3678

www.holidaybungalowsbrightonuk.com

e-mail: jc.stgeorge@virgin.net

JEAKE'S HOUSE

Mermaid Street, Rye, East Sussex TN31 7ET
Telephone: 01797 222828 Fax: 01797 222623
e-mail: stay@jeakeshouse.com • www.jeakeshouse.com

Dating from 1689, this beautiful Listed Building stands in one of England's most famous streets. Oak-beamed and panelled bedrooms overlook the marsh to the sea. Brass, mahogany, half-tester and four-poster beds; honeymoon suite; TV, radio, telephone. Book-lined bar. Residential licence. Traditional and vegetarian breakfast served. £45–£61pp. Private car park. Visa and Mastercard accepted.

PREMIER SELECTED — **Good Hotel Guide César Award**

BRANDY'S COTTAGE

Mrs Jane Apperly, Cadborough Farm, Rye, East Sussex TN31 6AA
Tel: 01797 225426 • www.cadborough.co.uk • apperly@cadborough.co.uk

Newly converted and sympathetically restored cottage provides luxurious and spacious accommodation for two people. Located one mile from Rye, close to 1066 Country walks. Facilities include TV/Video/Music Centre, full gas C/H, cooker/hob, microwave, washer/dryer, private courtyard with garden furniture and BBQ. Linen and towels incl. We accept one small well behaved dog and children over 12. Weekly rates from £195 low season to £395 high season. Short breaks available. Four other cottages also available. No Smoking.

AA Pet-Friendly Establishment of the Year 2005

THE SILVERDALE

21 Sutton Park Road, Seaford BN25 IRH
Tel: 01323 491849
e-mail silverdale@mistral.co.uk
www.silverdale.mistral.co.uk

We don't just accept dogs, we ***welcome*** them. We have two American Cockers who enjoy the company of our visitors. Our guests are given a list of pubs and restaurants that welcome dogs in the town and details of places where they can walk and exercise them. We are only a few minutes' walk away from the seafront and local parks. We have a delightful small dining room and bar specialising in English wines and single malt whiskies. Our rooms are individually decorated with lots of extra touches.

SEEDA award winner 2003, Clean Catering Award winner for 13 years ETC/AA ★★★★
Runner-up, Considerate Hotel of the Year 2006

BEACH COTTAGES, CLAREMONT ROAD, SEAFORD BN25 2QQ

Well-equipped, three-bedroomed terraced cottage on seafront. CH, open fire and woodburner. South-facing patio overlooking sea. Downland walks (wonderful for dogs), fishing, golf, wind-surfing, etc.

Details from: Julia Lewis, 47 Wandle Bank, London SW19 1DW

Tel: 020 8542 5073 • e-mail: julia@beachcottages.info • website: www.beachcottages.info

Arlington

Village in valley of River Cuckmere below the South Downs. Hailsham 3 miles.

MRS P. BONIFACE, LAKESIDE FARM, ARLINGTON, POLEGATE BN26 6SB (01323 870111). Situated on the edge of Arlington Reservoir. Eastbourne within 15 miles. Accommodation sleeps 4–6 with two double rooms, lounge, dining area, kitchen, bathroom. Open April to October. Weekly terms from £200. [🐕]

Battle

Site of the famous victory of William the Conqueror; remains of an abbey mark the spot where Harold fell.

FOX HOLE FARM, KANE HYTHE ROAD, BATTLE TN33 9QU (Tel & Fax: 01424 772053). Beautiful secluded 18th century woodcutter's cottage, nestling in over 40 acres of its own rolling, lush East Sussex land. Surrounded by Forestry Commission woodland. AA ◆◆◆◆ [🐕]

LITTLE HEMINGFOLD HOTEL, TELHAM, BATTLE TN33 0TT (01424 774338; Fax: 01424 775351). In the heart of 1066 Country, 40 acres of bliss for you and your pets. Farmhouse hotel, all facilities. Fishing, boating, swimming, tennis. Special Breaks all year. Discounts for children 7-14 years old. FREE accommodation for pets. ETC ◆◆◆ [pw! 🐕]
e-mail: littlehemingfoldhote@tiscali.co.uk website: www.littlehemingfoldhotel.co.uk

Brighton

Famous resort with shingle beach and sand at low tide. Varied entertainment and nightlife; excellent shops and restaurants. Portsmouth 48 miles, Hastings 37, Newhaven 9.

BEST OF BRIGHTON & SUSSEX COTTAGES has available a very good selection of houses, flats, apartments and cottages in Brighton and Hove as well as East and West Sussex from Eastbourne to Chichester. Town centre/seaside and countryside locations – many taking pets. (+44 (0) 1273 308779). [Pets £15/£20 per week.]
website: www.bestofbrighton.co.uk

Chiddingly

Charming village, 4 miles north-west of Hailsham. Off the A22 London-Eastbourne road.

Adorable, small, well-equipped cottage in grounds of Tudor Manor. Two bedrooms. Full central heating. Colour TV. Fridge/freezer, laundry facilities. Large safe garden. Use indoor heated swimming pool, sauna/jacuzzi and tennis. From £385 to £730 per week inclusive. ETC ★★★. Contact: EVA MORRIS, "PEKES", 124 ELM PARK MANSIONS, PARK WALK, LONDON SW10 0AR (020 7352 8088; Fax: 020 7352 8125). [2 dogs free, extra dog £7 (max. 4) pw!].
e-mail: pekes.afa@virgin.net website: www.pekesmanor.com

Fairlight

Village 3 miles east of Hastings

JANET & RAY ADAMS, FAIRLIGHT COTTAGE, WARREN ROAD, FAIRLIGHT TN35 4AG (01424 812545). Country house in idyllic location with clifftop walks. Tasteful en suite rooms, comfortable guest lounge. Delicious breakfasts. No smoking. Dogs stay with owners. ETC ◆◆◆◆ [🐕]

LITTLE OAKS, FARLEY WAY, FAIRLIGHT. Luxury bungalow set in quiet coastal village close to Rye, Hastings and Battle. Beautiful secluded garden, balcony and conservatory. No smoking. ETC ★★★★ Contact: RAY & JANET ADAMS, FAIRLIGHT COTTAGE, WARREN ROAD, FAIRLIGHT, EAST SUSSEX TN35 4AG (01424 812545). [Pets welcome at a charge]

Hastings

Seaside resort with a famous past - the ruins of William the Conqueror's castle lie above the Old Town. Many places of historic interest in the area, plus entertainments for all the family.

BEAUPORT PARK HOTEL, BATTLE ROAD, HASTINGS TN38 8EA (01424 851222). Georgian Country House Hotel set amid formal gardens and woodland. All rooms are well equipped and have private bath. Special Country House Breaks available all year.
e-mail: reservations@beauportparkhotel.co.uk website: www.beauportparkhotel.co.uk

Polegate

Quiet position, 5 miles from the popular seaside resort of Eastbourne. London 58 miles, Lewes 12.

MRS M. FIELD, 20 ST JOHN'S ROAD, POLEGATE BN26 5BP (01323 482691). Homely private house. Quiet location; large enclosed garden. Parking space. Ideally situated for walking on South Downs and Forestry Commission land. All rooms, washbasins and tea/coffee making facilities. Bed and Breakfast. Pets very welcome. [pw!]

Readers are requested to mention this FHG guidebook when seeking accommodation

Rottingdean/Brighton

Picturesque seaside resort in historic conservation village 5 km from Brighton city..

KILCOLGAN PREMIER BUNGALOWS (020 7250 3678) Well appointed three-bedroom properties sleeping 5/6. Beautiful secluded garden.Terms from £550 to £850 per week fully inclusive. Location should appeal to those seeking a quality retreat.. ETC ★★★★★ [Pets £35 per week].
e-mail: jc.stgeorge@virgin.net website: www.holidaybungalowsbrightonuk.com

Rye

Picturesque hill town with steep cobbled streets. Many fine buildings of historic interest. Hastings 12 miles, Tunbridge Wells 28.

JEAKE'S HOUSE, MERMAID STREET, RYE TN31 7ET (01797 222828; Fax: 01797 222623). Dating from 1689, this Listed building has oak-beamed and panelled bedrooms overlooking the marsh. TV, radio, telephone. Book-lined bar. £45-£61 per person. ETC/AA★★★★★ [Pets £5 per night]
e-mail: stay@jeakeshouse.com website: www.jeakeshouse.com

MRS JANE APPERLY, BRANDY'S COTTAGE, CADBOROUGH FARM, RYE TN31 6AA (01797 225426; Fax: 01797 224097).Newly converted cottage provides luxurious and spacious accommodation for two people. Private courtyard. One small well-behaved dog and children over 12 welcome. No-smoking. Short breaks available. ETC ★★★★ [🐕]
e-mail: apperly@cadborough.co.uk website: www.cadborough.co.uk

FLACKLEY ASH HOTEL, PEASMARSH, RYE TN31 6YH (01797 230651). Georgian Country House Hotel set in beautiful grounds. Indoor swimming pool and Leisure Centre. Beauty and massage. Visit Rye, castles and the gardens of East Sussex and Kent. AA★★★ [Pets £8.50 per night]
e-mail: enquiries@flackleyashhotel.co.uk website: www.flackleyashhotel.co.uk

Seaford

On the coast midway between Newhaven and Beachy Head.

THE SILVERDALE, 21 SUTTON PARK ROAD, SEAFORD BN25 IRH (01323 491849). We don't just accept dogs, we welcome them. Only a few minutes from seafront and parks. Delightful small diningroom and bar. All rooms individually decorated. SEEDA award winner 2003, Clean Catering Award winner for 13 years. AA Pet Friendly Establishment of the Year 2005. ETC/AA ★★★★ [🐕].
e-mail: silverdale@mistral.co.uk website: www.silverdale.mistral.co.uk

BEACH COTTAGES, CLAREMONT ROAD, SEAFORD. Well-equipped, three-bedroomed terraced cottage on seafront. CH, open fire and woodburner. South-facing patio overlooking sea. Downland walks (wonderful for dogs), fishing, golf, wind-surfing, etc. Details from JULIA LEWIS, 47 WANDLE BANK, LONDON SW19 1DW (020 8542 5073). [pw! 🐕]
e-mail: julia@beachcottages.info website: www.beachcottages.info

Symbols

- 🐕 Indicates that pets are welcome free of charge.
- £ Indicates that a charge is made for pets: nightly or weekly.
- pw! Shows some special provision for pets; exercise facility, feeding or accommodation arrangement.
- ⌂ Indicates separate pets accommodation.

Fairhaven Holiday Cottages

A wide selection of personally inspected accommodation in Kent and Sussex

Tel: 01208 821 255 www.fairhaven-holidays.co.uk

Chichester, Eastergate, Selsey, Worthing

Spire Cottage, built from the old spire of Chichester Cathedral that collapsed in 1861, is a Grade II Listed country cottage offering stylish bed and breakfast accommodation. Friendly, relaxed atmosphere, excellent facilities, village pub and two golf courses. Also available on a self-catering basis(sleeping 8). Please telephone for further details.

Jan & Andy, Spire Cottage, Church Lane, Hunston, Chichester PO20 1AJ
Tel: 01243 778937 • e-mail: jan@spirecottage.co.uk • www.spirecottage.co.uk

Wandleys Caravan Park

Eastergate, West Sussex PO20 6SE
Telephone: 01243 543235
or 01243 543384 (evenings/weekends)

You will find peace, tranquillity and relaxation in one of our comfortable holiday caravans. All have internal WC and shower. Dogs welcome. The Sussex Downs, Chichester, Bognor Regis, Arundel, Littlehampton – all these historic and interesting places are only 15 minutes from our beautiful, small and quiet country park. Telephone for brochure. New and used holiday homes for sale when available.

ETC/AA ★★★★

ST ANDREWS LODGE

Chichester Road, Selsey, West Sussex PO20 0LX
Tel: 01243 606899 • Fax: 01243 607826
e-mail: info@standrewslodge.co.uk
web: www.standrewslodge.co.uk

Welcome to St Andrews Lodge, the perfect place for a relaxing break. Situated in the small seaside town of Selsey and well located for Chichester and the South Downs; close to unspoilt beaches and 5 minutes from Pagham Harbour Nature Reserve. Enjoy our delicious breakfast and stay in one of our individually decorated rooms. All equipped with fridge, hospitality tray and ironing facilities. Rooms open on to our large garden to allow your dog to stretch his legs. No charge for dogs but donation to local nature reserve welcome. Licensed bar, wheelchair accessible room, large car park.

Please apply for brochure and details of our special winter offer.

Cavendish Hotel

115 Marine Parade
Worthing BN11 3QG
Tel: 01903 236767
Fax: 01903 823840

The prime sea front location provides an ideal base for touring Sussex villages and the rolling South Downs. Dogs allowed on the beach 1st October until 30th April and on the beach half a mile away all year. Nearby are Arundel, Chichester and Goodwood House; to the east is Brighton and the Royal Pavilion and the historic town of Lewes.
All rooms at the Cavendish are en suite, have satellite television, direct-dial telephone and tea/coffee making facilities. The friendly bar is a popular rendezvous with the locals and offers real ale with a wide range of beers, lagers, wines and spirits.

Standard double/twin £65-£75 Seaview double/Twin £80-£90 Inclusive of Full English Breakfast

E-mail: reservations@cavendishworthing.co.uk **Website:** www.cavendishworthing.co.uk

No charge for dogs belonging to readers of Pets Welcome! AA/RAC ★★

FAIRHAVEN HOLIDAY COTTAGES. A wide selection of personally inspected accommodation in Kent and Sussex (01208 821255).
website: www.fairhaven-holidays.co.uk

Chichester

County town 9 miles east of Havant. Town has cathedral and 16th century market cross.

SPIRE COTTAGE, CHURCH LANE, HUNSTON, CHICHESTER PO20 1AJ (01243 778937). Stylish bed and breakfast accommodation in a friendly and relaxed atmosphere. Excellent facilities. Village pub and two golf courses. [Dogs £5 per night]
e-mail: jan@spirecottage.co.uk website: www.spirecottage.co.uk

Eastergate

Village between the sea and South Downs. Fontwell Park nearby. Bognor Regis 5 miles south.

WANDLEYS CARAVAN PARK, EASTERGATE PO20 6SE (01243 543235 or 01243 543384 evenings/weekends). You will find peace, tranquillity and relaxation in one of our comfortable holiday caravans. All have internal WC and shower. Dogs welcome. Many historic and interesting places nearby. Telephone for brochure. [🐕]

Pulborough

Popular fishing centre on the River Arun. South Downs Way nearby; Arundel 8 miles.

BEACON LODGE, LONDON ROAD, WATERSFIELD, PULBOROUGH RH20 1NH (Tel & Fax: 01798 831026). Charming self-contained annexe. B&B accommodation, en suite, TV, coffee/tea making facilities. Wonderful countryside views. B&B from £60 per night, family room. No charge for your pets!. Telephone for more details. ETC ◆◆◆◆ [🐕]
e-mail: gbwingfield@yahoo.co.uk website: www.beaconlodge.co.uk

Selsey

Seaside resort 8 miles south of Chichester. Selsey Bill is headland extending into the English Channel.

ST ANDREWS LODGE HOTEL, CHICHESTER ROAD, SELSEY PO20 0LX (01243 606899; Fax: 01243 607826). 10 bedrooms, all en suite, with direct dial telephones and modem point, some on ground floor. Spacious lounges with log fire; licensed bar for residents only. Wheelchair accessible room. Dogs welcome in rooms overlooking large garden. Apply for brochure and prices. ETC/AA ★★★★ [🐕]
e-mail: info@standrewslodge.co.uk website: www.standrewslodge.co.uk

Worthing

Residential town and seaside resort with 5 miles seafront. Situated 10 miles west of Brighton.

CAVENDISH HOTEL, 115 MARINE PARADE, WORTHING BN11 3QG (01903 236767; Fax: 01903 823840). Ideal base for touring Sussex villages and the rolling South Downs. All rooms are en suite, have TV, direct-dial telephone and tea/coffee facilities. No charge for dogs belonging to readers of Pets Welcome! AA/RAC ★★ [🐕].
e-mail: reservations@cavendishworthing.co.uk website: www.cavendishworthing.co.uk

MANOR GUEST HOUSE, 100 BROADWATER ROAD, WORTHING BN14 8AN (01903 236028). Hotel facilities and service at guest house prices. Children 8+ and pet friendly. Fully licensed restaurant open to non-residents. Strictly non smoking. AA ★★★★[🐕]
e-mail: stay@manorworthing.com website: www.manorworthing.com

Stratford-upon-Avon

RIVERSIDE LOCATION - ONLY ONE MILE FROM THE TOWN CENTRE

LUXURY HOLIDAY HOMES FOR HIRE • TOURING CARAVANS AND MOTORHOME PITCHES • RIVERFRONT COTTAGES TO RENT

Short Stay Bookings Welcome & 3-Day Long Weekend Deals

Set in the heart of the lovely Warwickshire countryside and right on the banks of the beautiful River Avon, is Riverside Caravan Park, the perfect location for exploring Shakespeare Country and the Cotswolds. Holiday Home units accommodate 6 persons and Riverfront Cottages 4 persons comfortably.

RIVER TAXIS TO AND FROM TOWN • ADJACENT LOCAL VILLAGE • FREE FISHING RIVERSIDE WALKS • ON SITE SHOP & CAFE • CLUB HOUSE • KIDS PLAYGROUND

Riverside Caravan Park

Tiddington Road,
Stratford-upon-Avon,
Warwickshire CV37 7AB

01789 292312

www.stratfordcaravans.co.uk

Comfortable family Guest House situated at the town end of Evesham Road on the B439 (Bidford). 10 minutes' walk to River Avon, Shakespearean properties, theatre. One hour's drive to Cotswolds. Tea-making facilities and TV in bedrooms; centrally heated. Pets in room. Parking, though car not essential. Lift from bus or train station by arrangement.

Bed and Breakfast: room with shower, washbasin £20pp en suite toilet, shower, washbasin £22.50pp. Weekly terms £130-£150. Evening Meals £10.00 extra. Single person supplement £10 pppn.

Mrs Hazel Mellor, ARRANDALE, 208 Evesham Road, Stratford-upon-Avon CV37 9AS

Tel: (01789) 267112 • www.arrandale.netfirms.com

Overlooking beautiful countryside, near Warwick.
All rooms en suite, TV, tea/coffee making.
Ground floor double room. Non-smoking.
Private car park. Large paddock, ideal for dogs.

DOREEN BROMILOW, "WAVERLEY", WOLVERTON FIELDS, NORTON LINDSEY, WARWICK CV35 8JN • 01926 842446

THE CROFT

ETC/AA ★★★★

Haseley Knob, Warwick CV35 7NL • Tel & Fax: 01926 484447

- Friendly family country guesthouse • non-smoking
- All rooms en suite or private bathroom, TV, hairdryer, tea/coffee
- Central location for Warwick, Stratford, Coventry and NEC.

e-mail: david@croftguesthouse.co.uk **www.croftguesthouse.co.uk**

CLIFTON CRUISERS OF RUGBY, CLIFTON WHARF, VICARAGE HILL, CLIFTON, RUGBY, WARWICKSHIRE CV23 0DG (01788 543570; Fax: 01788 579799). Varied choice of boat layouts and accommodation to satisfy the requirements of most family and holiday groups (sleeping 2-8). Starting base centrally situated on the waterway network. [🐕]
e-mail: info@cliftoncruisers.com website: www.cliftoncruisers.com

Stratford-upon-Avon

Historic town famous as Shakespeare's birthplace and home. Birmingham 24, Warwick 8.

RIVERSIDE CARAVAN PARK, TIDDINGTON ROAD, STRATFORD-UPON-AVON CV37 7BE (01789 292312). Luxury Caravans, sleep 6. Fully equipped kitchens, bathroom/ shower/WC. Also two riverside Cottages, all modern facilities to first-class standards. Private fishing. On banks of River Avon. [Pets £15 weekly.]
website: www.stratfordcaravans.co.uk

MRS H. J. MELLOR, ARRANDALE, 208 EVESHAM ROAD, STRATFORD-UPON-AVON CV37 9AS (01789 267112). Guest House situated near River Avon, theatre, Shakespeare properties. Washbasins, tea making, TV, central heating, en suite available. Children, pets welcome. Parking. Bed and Breakfast £20-£22.50. Weekly terms £130-£150. Evening Meal £10.00. [🐕]
website: www.arrandale.netfirms.com

DOREEN BROMILOW, "WAVERLEY", WOLVERTON FIELDS, NORTON LINDSEY, WARWICK CV35 8JN (01926 842446) Overlooking beautiful countryside, near Warwick. All rooms en suite, TV, tea/coffee making. Ground floor double room. Large paddock, ideal for dogs. Non-smoking. Private car park.

Warwick

Town on the River Avon, 9 miles south-west of Coventry, with medieval castle and many fine old buildings.

DAVID & PATRICIA CLAPP, CROFT GUESTHOUSE, HASELEY KNOB, WARWICK CV35 7NL (Tel & Fax: 01926 484447). All bedrooms en suite or with private bathroom, some ground floor. Non-smoking. Picturesque rural setting. Central for NEC, Warwick, Stratford, Stoneleigh and Coventry. B&B single £36, double/twin £56. ETC/AA ★★★★ [Dogs £3 per night]
e-mail: david@croftguesthouse.co.uk website: www.croftguesthouse.co.uk

Symbols

🐕 Indicates that pets are welcome free of charge.
£ Indicates that a charge is made for pets: nightly or weekly.
pw! Shows some special provision for pets; exercise facility, feeding or accommodation arrangement.
⌂ Indicates separate pets accommodation.

THE NEELD ARMS INN
THE STREET, GRITTLETON SN14 6AP
01249 782470 • Fax: 01249 782358 • e-mail: info@neeldarms.co.uk
17th century inn offering comfortable accommodation and home-cooked food; four-poster available. Children and pets welcome. Convenient for Bath, Stonehenge, Cotswolds. **www.neeldarms.co.uk**

Grittleton

Village 6 miles north west of Chippenham.

THE NEELD ARMS INN, THE STREET, GRITTLETON SN14 6AP (01249 782470; Fax: 01249 782358). 17th century inn offering comfortable accommodation and home-cooked food; four-poster available. Children and pets welcome. Convenient for Bath, Stonehenge, Cotswolds. ETC ◆◆◆
e-mail: info@neeldarms.co.uk website: www.neeldarms.co.uk

Salisbury

13th century cathedral city, with England's highest spire at 404ft. Many fine buildings.

MR A. SHERING, SWAYNES FIRS FARM, GRIMSDYKE, COOMBE BISSETT, SALISBURY SP5 5RF (01725 519240). Small working farm with cattle, poultry, geese and duck ponds. Spacious rooms, all en suite with colour TV. Ideal for visiting the many historic sites in the area. ETC ★★★ [Pets £5 per night]
e-mail: swaynes.firs@virgin.net website: www.swaynesfirs.co.uk

WORCESTERSHIRE

Traditional 18th century country house surrounded by peaceful and picturesque gardens. All rooms en suite with colour TV, generous beverage tray, hairdryer, radio alarm and more. Children welcome. Babysitting service. Dogs and cats by arrangement. Worcester 10 minutes, Stratford-upon-Avon, Warwick, Cotswolds, Birmingham and Wales all within one hour. M5 motorway six minutes. Single from £40, double from £60, family room from £75.

Mrs Salli Harrison, Middleton Grange, Salwarpe, Droitwich Spa WR9 0AH
Tel: 01905 451678 Fax: 01905 453978 ETC ◆◆◆◆ SILVER AWARD
e-mail: salli@middletongrange.com • website: www.middletongrange.com

WHITEWELLS FARM COTTAGES
ETC ★★★★
Silver Award Winners 'Heart of England Excellence in Tourism Awards' Self-Catering Holiday of the Year
Ridgeway Cross, Near Malvern, Worcs WR13 5JR
Tel: 01886 880607 • Fax: 01886 880360 • e-mail: info@whitewellsfarm.co.uk • www.whitewellsfarm.co.uk

Seven well-established cottages converted from old farm buildings and a hop kiln, full of charm and character with original exposed timbering. The cottages are exceptionally clean and comfortable and equipped to the highest standards. One cottage suitable for the disabled with full wheelchair access. Idyllically set around a duckpond with two and a half acres of the property being a fully-fenced woodland plantation, ideal for exercising dogs, on or off the lead.

Set in unspoilt countryside with outstanding views of the **Malvern Hills** on the **Herefordshire/Worcestershire border. Ideal base for touring Worcestershire, Herefordshire, the Malverns, Gloucestershire, Welsh mountains, Cotswolds and Shakespeare country**. Electricity and linen included in price. Short breaks and long lets, suitable for relocation. Children and pets welcome. Open all year.

Colour brochure available from: Kate and Denis Kavanagh.

FREE or REDUCED RATE entry to Holiday Visits and Attractions –
see our READERS' OFFER VOUCHERS on pages 407-423

Droitwich

Town 6 miles north-east of Worcester. Former spa status due to saline springs.

MRS SALLI HARRISON, MIDDLETON GRANGE, SALWARPE, DROITWICH SPA WR9 0AH (01905 451678; Fax: 01905 453978). Traditional 18th century country house surrounded by picturesque gardens. Children welcome. Babysitting service. Dogs and cats by arrangement. All rooms en suite. M5 motorway six minutes. Worcester 10 minutes. ETC ♦♦♦♦ *SILVER AWARD.* [🐕]

Great Malvern

Fashionable spa town in last century with echoes of that period.

KATE AND DENIS KAVANAGH, WHITEWELLS FARM COTTAGES, RIDGEWAY CROSS, NEAR MALVERN WR13 5JR (01886 880607; Fax: 01886 880360). Charming converted Cottages, sleep 2–6. Fully equipped with colour TV, microwave, barbecue, fridge, iron, etc. Linen, towels also supplied. One cottage suitable for the disabled with full wheelchair access. Short breaks, long lets, large groups. ETC ★★★★ [pw! Pets £10 per week.] Also see Display Advert..
e-mail: info@whitewellsfarm.co.uk website: www.whitewellsfarm.co.uk

THE COTTAGE IN THE WOOD (01684 575859). High on Malvern hills. Accommodation over three buildings. 2 AA Restaurant Rosettes, over 600 wines. "Best view in England" - The Daily Mail. Call for brochure. ★★★ [🐕]
website: www.cottageinthewood.co.uk

MALVERN HILLS HOTEL, WYNDS POINT, MALVERN WR13 6DW (01684 540690). Enchanting family-owned and run hotel nestling high in the hills. Direct access to superb walking with magnificent views. Oak-panelled lounge, log fire, real ales, fine food and friendly staff. Great animal lovers. AA ★★ [Pets £5 per night].
website: www.malvernhillshotel.co.uk

ANN AND BRIAN PORTER, CROFT GUEST HOUSE, BRANSFORD, WORCESTER WR6 5JD (01886 832227). 16th-18th century country house. 10 minutes from Worcester, Malvern and M5. Non-smoking house. Family Room. Bedrooms have en suite (3), colour TV, tea and coffee tray, hairdryer, radio alarm. Dinners available. Dogs welcome. AA ◆◆◆ [🐕]
e-mail: hols@crofthousewr6.fsnet.co.uk website: www.croftguesthouse.com

Worcester

Cathedral city on River Severn, 24 miles south-west of Birmingham.

MOSELEY FARM BED & BREAKFAST, MOSELEY ROAD, HALLOW, WORCESTER WR2 6NL (01905 641343; Fax: 01905 641416). Spacious 17th century former farmhouse with countryside views. Two en suite family rooms and two standard rooms, with colour TV, radio alarm clocks and tea/coffee making facilities. Room only weekdays. Full breakfast at weekends.[🐕]
e-mail: r@moseleyfarmbandb.co.uk website: www.moseleyfarmbandb.co.uk

Yorkshire Dales, Coast and Wolds

As you set foot into these breathtaking locations, you will be drawn to many diverse sights. Jagged coastlines, expansive moors and ancient castles to name but a few. That is of course should you wish to leave your wonderful, personally inspected cottage. Each with it s own charm whether catering for couples, families or pet lovers.

Dales Holiday Cottages

For your choice of over 500 cottages
call **0870 909 9505** or visit **www.dalesholcot.com** A66

RECOMMENDED COTTAGE HOLIDAYS. 1st choice for dream cottages at very competitive prices in all holiday regions of beautiful Britain. Pets welcome. All properties inspected. Free brochure - call 01751 475547.
website: www.recommended-cottages.co.uk

DALES HOLIDAY COTTAGES . Personally inspected cottages in breathtaking locations, with jagged coastlines, expansive moors and ancient castles. Each cottage with its own charm, whether catering for couples, families or pet lovers. Call 0870 909 9505 or visit our website.
website: www.dalesholcot.com

EAST YORKSHIRE

Bridlington, Driffield, Flamborough

THE TENNYSON
19 TENNYSON AVENUE,
BRIDLINGTON YO15 2EU
Tel: 01262 604382

Small, non-smoking, family hotel offering all usual amenities. B&B from £26pppn. All rooms en suite. Located within easy walking distance of town centre, North Beach and cliff walks.
Dogs £2.50 per dog per stay. AA ★★★
www.thetennysonhotel.co.uk

KELLEYTHORPE FARM
Driffield, East Yorkshire YO25 9DW • Tel: 01377 252297
Lovely Georgian farmhouse overlooking small lake. Friendly atmosphere, attractive bedrooms. Aberdeen Angus herd with beef sold in own farm shop. Children welcome. B&B from £25.

ETC ★★★★

Set on the spectacular heritage coast with unrivalled coastal scenery. Six-berth caravans and chalets for hire. Tents and tourers welcome. Bars, entertainment, shop, pool and gym on site.

Thornwick & Sea Farm Holiday Centre
Flamborough, East Yorks
Tel 01262 850369
www.thornwickbay.co.uk

Readers are requested to mention this guidebook when making enquiries about accommodation.

Bridlington

Traditional family resort with picturesque harbour and a wide range of entertainments and leisure facilities. Ideal for exploring the Heritage coastline and the Wolds.

THE TENNYSON, 19 TENNYSON AVENUE, BRIDLINGTON YO15 2EU (01262 604382). Small, non-smoking, family hotel offering all usual amenities. B&B from £26pppn. All rooms en suite. Located within easy walking distance of town centre, North Beach and cliff walks. AA ★★★ [Pets £2.50 per night].
website: www.thetennysonhotel.co.uk

Driffield

Town 11 miles south west of Bridlington.

MRS TIFFY HOPPER, KELLEYTHORPE FARM, DRIFFIELD YO25 9DW (01377 252297). Lovely Georgian farmhouse overlooking small lake. Friendly atmosphere, attractive bedrooms. Aberdeen Angus herd with beef sold in own farm shop. Children welcome. B&B from £25. [🐕]

Flamborough

Village 4 miles north-east of Bridlington.

THORNWICK & SEA FARM HOLIDAY CENTRE, NORTH MARINE ROAD, FLAMBOROUGH YO15 1AV (01262 850369; Fax: 01262 851550) Set on the spectacular Heritage Coast with unrivalled coastal scenery. Six-berth caravans and chalets for hire. Tents and tourers welcome. Bars, entertainment, shop, pool and gym on site. [Pets £5 per week.] ETC ★★★★, David Bellamy Silver Award.
e-mail: enquiries@thornwickbay.co.uk website: www.thornwickbay.co.uk

Kilnwick Percy

Located 2 miles east of Pocklington

PAWS-A-WHILE, KILNWICK PERCY, POCKLINGTON YO42 1UF (01759 301168; Mobile: 07711 866869). Small family B & B set in forty acres of parkland twixt York and Beverley. Golf, sauna, walking, riding. Pets and horses most welcome. Brochure available. ETC ◆◆◆◆ [pw! 🐕]
e-mail: paws.a.while@lineone.net website: www.pawsawhile.net

York

Historic cathedral city and former Roman Station on River Ouse. Magnificent Minster and 3 miles of ancient walls. Facilities for a wide range of sports and entertainments. Horse-racing on Knavesmire. Bridlington 41 miles, Filey 41, Leeds 24, Harrogate 22.

ROBEANNE HOUSE, DRIFFIELD LANE, SHIPTONTHORPE, YORK YO43 3PW (01430 873312). Family B&B, country location, 18 miles from historic York. Ideal for coast, Moors, racing, Beverley, Cycle Route 66 and Wolds Way. Beautiful country house and gardens. All rooms en suite. Contact: JEANNE WILSON. AA ★★★ [pw! Pets £5 per night]
e-mail: enquiries@robeannehouse.co.uk website: www.robeannehouse.co.uk

Ingrid Flute Holiday Accommodation Agency Est1970

Over 200 Cottages, Bungalows, Chalets & Apartments Throughout Whitby, Scarborough, North Yorks Moors & Ryedale

For A Free Brochure Contact: www.ingridflute.co.uk or 01723 376 777

Austwick, Bentham, Coverdale, Danby, Filey

WOOD VIEW GUEST HOUSE Austwick, North Yorkshire LA2 8BB

Tel: 015242 51190 • e-mail: woodview@austwick.org

Wood View is a Grade II Listed building overlooking the green in this picturesque village, surrounded by stunning limestone scenery in the Yorkshire Dales National Park. All rooms en suite and non-smoking, with private parking. www.woodviewbandb.com VB ★★★★

HOLMES FARM • Low Bentham, Lancaster LA2 7DE

Attractively converted and well equipped stone cottage adjoining 17th century farm house, sleeping 4. In a secluded position surrounded by 127 acres of beautiful pastureland. Central heating, fridge, TV, washing machine, games room. Ideal base for visiting Dales, Lake District and coast.

Tel: 015242 61198 • www.holmesfarmcottage.co.uk

★★★★ SELF CATERING

Peacefully situated farmhouse away from the madding crowd. B&B with optional Evening Meal. Home cooking. Pets sleep where you prefer. Ideally positioned for exploring the beautiful Yorkshire Dales.

Mrs Julie Clarke,
Middle Farm, Woodale,
Coverdale, Leyburn,
North Yorkshire DL8 4TY
01969 640271
e-mail: j-a-clarke@amserve.com

The Fox & Hounds Inn **Ainthorpe, Danby YO21 2LD**

Residential 16th Century Coaching Inn. Freshly prepared dishes served every day. Superb en suite accommodation available. Ideal centre for the moors and coast. Open all year. Pets: £2.50 per night.

ETC ★★★★ *Situated between Castleton and Danby on the Fryup Road.*

For bookings please Tel: 01287 660218 • orpe.com

Email: info@foxandhounds-ainthorpe.com • www.foxandhounds-ainthorpe.com

"SEA CABIN" 16 Gap Road, Hunmanby Gap, Near Filey YO14 9QP

Warm and friendly hospitality plus good food at our well-appointed twin-bedroomed Granny annexe. En suite, own private lounge. Located on the cliff top, with access to the golden sands of Filey Bay. Private parking, quiet location, five minutes' drive from Filey town. Bookings for B&B only. Pet friendly beach and area.

for brochure & terms:
Leonard & Diane Hunter Tel: 01723 891368 **Dogs come free of charge!**

FHG
·K·U·P·E·R·A·R·D·

Visit the FHG website
www.holidayguides.com
for details of the wide choice of accommodation featured in the full range of FHG titles

JERRY AND BEN'S HOLIDAY COTTAGES

Three comfortable properties on a private estate near Grassington in the Yorkshire Dales National Park, with wooded mountain becks, waterfalls, rocky crags and surrounded by accessible hill and footpath walking. £150 to £950. Brochure from:

Mrs Fiona Hoole, Jerry and Ben's Holiday Cottages, Hebden, Skipton, North Yorkshire BD23 5DL • Tel: 01756 752369
e-mail: Fiona@jerryandbens.co.uk • www.jerryandbens.co.uk

The Foresters Arms

MAIN STREET, GRASSINGTON, SKIPTON
NORTH YORKSHIRE BD23 5AA
Tel: 01756 752349 • Fax: 01756 753633

The Foresters Arms, Grassington, once an old coaching inn, situated in the heart of the Yorkshire Dales. An ideal centre for walking or touring. A family-run business for over 35 years. Serving hand-pulled traditional ales. Home made food served lunchtime and evening. All bedrooms are en suite, having satellite TV and tea/coffee making facilities. Prices £35 single; £70 double. *Proprietor: Rita Richardson*

★★★ GUEST ACCOMMODATION

RELAX IN THE HEART OF YORKSHIRE

RUDDING
HOLIDAY PARK

LUXURY COTTAGES AND **TIMBER LODGES**
IN **BEAUTIFUL SURROUNDINGS**

- Deer House family pub
- Children's adventure playground
- Pets welcome • Games room
- Heated outdoor swimming pool and paddling pool
- 18 hole pay & play golf course plus floodlit driving range

FOLLIFOOT, HARROGATE HG3 1JH
TEL: 01423 870439 | FAX: 01423 870859
e-mail - holiday-park@ruddingpark.com
www.ruddingpark.com

ETC ★★★/★★★★

In glorious Nidderdale, in beautiful surroundings, a group of well-maintained and equipped holiday cottages adjoining Georgian farmhouse. Sleeps two to six; linen, fully equipped kitchens and colour TV. Laundry and payphone, gas barbecue and woodland garden. Riding stables on site. Excellent walking. Pets and children most welcome. B&B now available.

The Courtyard at Duke's Place, Bishop Thornton, Near Harrogate HG3 3JY
01765 620229 • Fax: 01765 620454 • e-mail: jakimoorhouse@aol.com

FREE or REDUCED RATE entry to Holiday Visits and Attractions – see our READERS' OFFER VOUCHERS on pages 407-423

Cocklake House

MALLERSTANG CA17 4JT • 017683 72080

Charming, High Pennine Country House B&B in unique position above Pendragon Castle in Upper Mallerstang Dale offering good food and exceptional comfort to a small number of guests. Two double rooms with large private bathrooms. Three acres riverside grounds. Dogs welcome.

John and Sally Robinson's

HOLIDAY COTTAGES Sleep 2, 4, 6, 10

Spoil yourselves with a stay in beautiful North Yorks •
Working farm • All home comforts • Private parking •
Pets welcome • Dogs free! • Good walking area •
Quiet roads • Tea and cake to welcome you •
Guests' comfort a priority • *Dogs bring your owners!*

Get in touch with Sally Robinson at Valley View Farm, Old Byland, Helmsley YO62 5LG Tel: 01439 798221
email: sally@valleyviewfarm.com or visit www.valleyviewfarm.com

***GALLON HOUSE** 47 Kirkgate, Knaresborough HG5 8BZ • 01423 862102*

e-mail: gallon-house@ntlworld.com • www.gallon-house.co.uk

Overlooking the beautiful Nidd Gorge, Gallon House offers award-winning accommodation and superb, locally sourced fresh food. Two double and one twin bedrooms, all en suite. Licensed. **ETC/AA ◆◆◆◆** *Gold Award*

NEWTON HOUSE, KNARESBOROUGH

Winner of the AA Pet Friendly Award – pets genuinely welcomed and lots of great walks nearby. Spacious and comfortable, newly refurbished ensuite accommodation and great breakfasts. **Tel: 01423 863539**

AA 4 Red Diamonds, VisitBritain Gold Award

www.newtonhouseyorkshire.com •newtonhouse@btinternet.com

THE WHITE ROSE HOTEL, LEEMING BAR, NORTHALLERTON DL7 9AY

Tel: 01677 422707/424941 • Fax: 01677 425123

Ideally situated for touring the spectacular scenery of two National Parks, Yorkshire Dales, coastal resorts, Herriot & Heartbeat Country. 18 rooms, all private bathroom, 10-channel digital TV/radio, tea & coffee, hair dryer, trouser press and telephone. B&B £49 single, £63 double/twin, £69 family room all including breakfast.

e-mail: john@whiterosehotel.co.uk www.whiterosehotel.co.uk

Friendly guest house, near South Bay attractions. We offer quality en suite and four-poster rooms (5 bedrooms). Excellent food. Brochure on request.

B&B £22pppn, BBEM £32pppn. Open all

harmonyguesthouse@hotmail.com
www.theharmonyguesthouse.co.uk

HARMONY GUEST HOUSE

13 PRINCESS ROYAL TERRACE, SOUTH CLIFF, SCARBOROUGH YO11 2RP
01723 373562

Raven Hall COUNTRY HOUSE HOTEL & GOLF COURSE

Ravenscar, Scarborough YO13 0ET • 01723 870353 • Fax: 01723 870072
e-mail: enquiries@ravenhall.co.uk • www.ravenhall.co.uk

High above the cliffs where the North York Moors roll down to the sea , this imposing hotel is full of Georgian splendour, and offers outstanding accommodation, superb, typically Yorkshire cuisine and an impressive range of leisure facilities including a 9-hole golf course. A family holiday paradise. AA ★★★

HARMONY COUNTRY LODGE ETC ★★★★

Limestone Road, Burniston, Scarborough YO13 0DG (Non-Smoking)

Unique octagonal peaceful retreat in own grounds with superb 360º views of National Park and sea. Two miles from Scarborough. Parking facilities and fully licensed. B&B £25 to £36. Five-berth caravan available for self-catering from £110 to £325. Local dog walks. Pets welcome.

Sue & Tony Hewitt • Tel: 0800 2985840 • www.harmonylodge.net

Over 250 super self-catering cottages
IN THE YORKSHIRE DALES, YORK, COAST, MOORS, LANCASHIRE, PEAK and LAKE DISTRICT

Holiday Cottages

Fully illustrated brochure 01756 700872 • e-mail: p@holidaycotts.co.uk
Holiday Cottages Yorkshire Ltd., Water St, Skipton, North Yorkshire BD23 1PB

Situated on the A65 Skipton to Kendal Road, the Hotel provides an ideal base for guests wishing to explore the Yorkshire Dales or just get away from it all. Set in a stunning 1400-acre estate with 24-acre lake. the hotel offers 50 en suite bedrooms, a restaurant, with a bar and orangery for more informal meals.

Ten luxury bedrooms now open!

Clay Pigeon Shooting, Off-Road Driving, Falconry and Fishing available on site. Exceptional location for conferences and weddings. Special rates for Leisure Breaks and family rooms.

THE CONISTON HOTEL

Coniston Cold, Skipton, North Yorkshire BD23 4EB

Tel: 01756 748080 • Fax: 01756 749487 • e-mail: sales@theconistonhotel.com • www.theconistonhotel.com

BECK HALL, MALHAM BD23 4DJ

18th century B&B on the Pennine Way, log fires and huge breakfasts. Midweek and 4-night specials.
Ideal for exploring the Yorkshire Dales. **Tel: 01729 830332**
e-mail: simon@beckhallmalham.com
www.beckhallmalham.com

Pennysteel Cottage **Staithes**

Old fisherman's cottage overlooking picturesque harbour. Ideal for walking and visiting Whitby, Heartbeat Country and the North York Moors. Sleep 5. Electricity, heating, bed linen incl. Wood-burning stove. One well-behaved pet welcome.

01377 217662/217523 • 07801 124264
e-mail: chris.wade@adastra-music.co.uk • www.waterfrontcottages.co.uk

POPLARS HOLIDAY COTTAGES AND BED AND BREAKFAST • THIRSK

The Poplars stands in two acres of lovely gardens with a field for dog walking. We have old brick cottages and new lodges, with bed and breakfast in the Poplars House. Contact

MRS CHILTON, CARLTON MINIOTT, THIRSK YO7 4LX

Tel: 01845 522712 • www.poplars-cottages.co.uk

Foxhills Hideaways • Felixkirk, Thirsk YO7 2DS

Quiet, no hassle holidays in cosy Scandinavian log cabins. Secluded garden setting. Central for the Moors, Dales, York and the coast. Village pub round the corner.

Fully inclusive prices (£230 to £350 per week).

Open all year.

Out of season short breaks from £120 inclusive.

Please write or phone for a brochure

TELEPHONE 01845 537575

Golden Fleece, Market Square, Thirsk YO7 1LL

Tel: 01845 523108 • Fax: 01845 523996

This Characterful old Coaching Inn offers good food and up to date facilities. All rooms are en suite, with satellite TV, phone, trouser press, hairdryer. On site parking. Perfect for Dales and Moors touring and walking or shopping in York or Harrogate.

ETC ★★ Silver Award AA ★★ 75% **www.goldenfleecehotel.com**

Discover historic Whitby, pretty fishing villages, countryside with way-marked walks. Four cottages, one or two bedrooms. Private parking. Children and dogs welcome.

ETC ★★★★

Weekly rates from £195 to £500. Please phone or write for brochure. **MRS JILL McNEIL, SWALLOW HOLIDAY COTTAGES, LONG LEAS FARM, HAWSKER, WHITBY YO22 4LA 01947 603790**

ARCHES GUESTHOUSE

8 Havelock Place, Hudson Street, Whitby YO21 3ER

Pet friendly, family-run guesthouse, where a warm welcome and large breakfast is always assured. The ideal base for experiencing the old world charms of this historic seaside town, exploring the beautiful North Yorkshire Moors, or just relaxing. Strictly Non-Smoking. Tariff: £28 - £35 pppn.

Ruth & Dick Brew (01947 601880 or 0800 9154256)

e-mail: archeswhitby@freeola.com • www.whitbyguesthouses.co.uk

ST GEORGE'S

6 ST GEORGE'S PLACE

YORK YO24 1DR

Family-run guest house in quiet cul-de-sac near racecourse. All rooms en suite with colour TV, tea/coffee making facilities.

Private parking • Pets welcome.

ETC/AA ★★★

e-mail: sixstgeorg@aol.com

web: www.stgeorgesyork.com

01904 625056

FHG Guides

publish a large range of well-known accommodation guides. We will be happy to send you details or you can use the order form at the back of this book.

FHG

K·U·P·E·R·A·R·D

HIGH BELTHORPE

Set on an ancient moated site at the foot of the Yorkshire Wolds, this comfortable Victorian farmhouse offers huge breakfasts, private fishing and fabulous walks. With York only 13 miles away, it is a peaceful rural idyll that both dogs and owners will love. Open all year except Christmas. From £25.

BISHOP WILTON, YORK YO42 1SB
TEL: 01759 368238
MOBILE: 07786 923330

YORK LAKESIDE LODGES

Moor Lane, York YO24 2QU
Tel: 01904 702346 • Fax: 01904 701631
E-mail: neil@yorklakesidelodges.co.uk

Unique in a city! Luxurious Scandinavian lodges, and cottages in mature parkland overlooking large private fishing lake. Nearby superstore with coach to centre every 10 minutes. Easy access to ring road for touring. Open year round.

YORKSHIRE & HUMBERSIDE TOURIST BOARD WHITE ROSE AWARDS FOR TOURISM
WINNER

Award – British Holiday Home Parks Association

4-5 STARS SELF-CATERING **www.yorklakesidelodges.co.uk**

ASCOT HOUSE, 80 East Parade, York YO31 7YH • Tel: 01904 426826
Fax: 01904 431077 • ETC/AA ◆◆◆◆ • ETC SILVER AWARD

An attractive Victorian villa with easy access to the historic city centre by walking or by public transport. Most rooms have four-poster or canopy beds, and family and double rooms are en suite. All rooms have central heating, colour TV and tea/coffee facilities. Sauna available to hire by the hour. Singles from £30 to £60, doubles £60 to £75 including Traditional English Breakfast and VAT.

e-mail: admin@ascothouseyork.com • website: www.ascothouseyork.com

WOLDS VIEW HOLIDAY COTTAGES ~ 12 miles from York

GRANVILLE LODGE (Sleeps 6-8) newly built, 1 twin/double, 1 king-size, bed settee in TV room, lounge, dining room, very modern kitchen. PARLOUR (Sleeps 6) 1 double, 2 twin rooms, large kitchen/diner, lounge, bathroom, 1 en suite. BARN (sleeps 4) kitchen, hall/diner, lounge, 1 king-size and one double bedroom (1 with shower & vanity unit and 1 bathroom) Downstairs wash hand basin and WC. STABLES (Sleeps 3) 1 double, 1 single bedroom, lounge, dining room, bathroom. COURTYARD (Sleeps 4) 2 double bedrooms (1 with shower) 1 bathroom, kitchen/diner/lounge.

Mrs M. S. A. Woodliffe, Mill Farm, Yapham, Pocklington, York YO42 1PH Tel: 01759 302172

INGRID FLUTE HOLIDAY ACCOMMODATION AGENCY. Established 1970. Over 200 cottages, bungalows, chalets and apartments throughout Whitby, Scarborough, North Yorkshire Moors and Ryedale. For a free brochure contact 01723 376777.
website: www.ingridflute.co.uk

Austwick

Village 4 miles north west of Settle.

WOOD VIEW GUEST HOUSE, AUSTWICK LA2 8BB (015242 51190). Grade II Listed building overlooking the green in picturesque village in the Yorkshire Dales National Park. All rooms en suite and non-smoking, with private parking. VB ★★★★ [🐕]
e-mail: woodview@austwick.org website: www.woodviewbandb.com

Bentham

Quiet village amidst the fells. Good centre for rambling and fishing. Ingleton 5 miles north-east.

MRS L. J. STORY, HOLMES FARM, LOW BENTHAM, LANCASTER LA2 7DE (015242 61198). Cottage conversion in easy reach of Dales, Lake District and coast. Central heating, fridge, TV, washer, games room. ★★★★. [🐕]
website: www.holmesfarmcottage.co.uk

Coverdale

Small village set in Yorkshire Dales, in heart of Herriot Country.

MRS JULIE CLARKE, MIDDLE FARM, WOODALE, COVERDALE, LEYBURN DL8 4TY (01969 640271). Peacefully situated farmhouse away from the madding crowd. B&B with optional Evening Meal. Home cooking. Pets sleep where you prefer. Ideally positioned for exploring the beautiful Yorkshire Dales. [🐕 pw!]
e-mail: j-a-clarke@amserve.com

Danby

Village on River Esk 12 miles west of Whitby.

THE FOX & HOUNDS INN, AINTHORPE, DANBY YO21 2LD (01287 660218; Fax: 01287 660030). Residential 16th Century Coaching Inn. Comfortable en suite bedrooms available. Enjoy our real ales or quality wines. Special mid-week breaks available Oct - May. Open all year. ETC ★★★★ [Pets £2.50 per night.]
e-mail: info@foxandhounds-ainthorpe.com website: www.foxandhounds-ainthorpe.com

Filey

Well-known resort with sandy beach. Off-shore is Filey Brig. Hull 40 miles, Bridlington 11, Scarborough 7.

LEONARD & DIANE HUNTER, "SEA CABIN", 16 GAP ROAD, HUNMANBY GAP, NEAR FILEY YO14 9QP (01723 891368). En suite, twin-bedroomed Granny annexe with private lounge. B&B only. Open all year. Pet friendly beach. [🐕 pw!]

Grassington

Wharfedale village in attractive moorland setting. Ripon 22 miles, Skipton 9.

JERRY AND BEN'S HOLIDAY COTTAGES. Three comfortable properties on private estate near Grassington in Yorkshire Dales National Park. Wooded mountain becks, waterfalls, rocky crags and accessible hill and footpath walking. Brochure from: MRS FIONA HOOLE, JERRY AND BEN'S HOLIDAY COTTAGES, HEBDEN, SKIPTON BD23 5DL (01756 752369). [Pets £10 per week]
e-mail: Fiona@jerryandbens.co.uk website: www.jerryandbens.co.uk

FORESTERS ARMS, MAIN STREET, GRASSINGTON, SKIPTON BD23 5AA (01756 752349; Fax: 01756 753633). The Foresters Arms is situated in the heart of the Yorkshire Dales and provides an ideal centre for walking or touring. Within easy reach of York and Harrogate. ETC ★★★ [🐕]

Harrogate

Charming and elegant spa town set amid some of Britain's most scenic countryside. Ideal for exploring Herriot Country and the moors and dales. York 22 miles, Bradford 19, Leeds 16.

RUDDING HOLIDAY PARK, FOLLIFOOT, HARROGATE HG3 1JH (01423 870439; Fax: 01423 870859). Luxury cottages and lodges sleeping two to seven people. All equipped to a high standard. Pool, licensed bar, golf and children's playground in the Parkland. Illustrated brochure available. ETC ★★★ [🐕]
e-mail: holiday-park@ruddingpark.com website: www.ruddingpark.com

THE COURTYARD AT DUKE'S PLACE, BISHOP THORNTON, NEAR HARROGATE HG3 3JY (01765 620229; Fax: 01765 620454). In glorious Nidderdale, group of well maintained and equipped holiday cottages. Sleep 2/6; linen, fully equipped kitchens. Riding stables on site. B&B now available. Pets and children most welcome. ETC ★★★/★★★★ [🐕]
e-mail: jakimoorhouse@aol.com

Hawes (near Mallerstang)

12 miles north-west on the Hawes to Kirkby Stephen road.

COUNTRY COTTAGE HOLIDAYS, DRYDEN HOUSE, MARKET PLACE, HAWES DL8 3RA (01969 667654). 100 cottages in the lovely Yorkshire Dales. Colour TV, central heating, open fires. Gardens, private parking. Many allow pets. Rents from £200 per week. Sleep 1-10.
website: www.countrycottageholidays.co.uk

SIMONSTONE HALL, HAWES, WENSLEYDALE DL8 3LY (01969 667255; Fax: 01969 667741). Facing south across picturesque Wensleydale. All rooms en suite with colour TV. Fine cuisine. Extensive wine list. Friendly personal attention. A relaxing break away from it all. AA ★★. [🐕 ⌂]
e-mail: information@simonstonehall.demon.co.uk website: www.simonstonehall.co.uk

STONE HOUSE HOTEL, SEDBUSK, HAWES DL8 3PT (01969 667571; Fax: 01969 667720). This fine Edwardian country house has spectacular views and serves delicious Yorkshire cooking with fine wines. Comfortable en suite bedrooms, some ground floor. Phone for details. [🐕]
website: www.stonehousehotel.com

COCKLAKE HOUSE, MALLERSTANG CA17 4JT (017683 72080). Charming, High Pennine Country House B&B in unique position above Pendragon Castle in Upper Mallerstang Dale offering good food and exceptional comfort to a small number of guests. Two double rooms with large private bathrooms. Three acres riverside grounds. Dogs welcome. [🐕]

Helmsley

A delightful stone-built town on River Rye with a large cobbled square. Thirsk 12 miles.

JOHN & SALLY ROBINSON'S VALLEY VIEW FARM, OLD BYLAND, HELMSLEY, YORK YO62 5LG (01439 798221). Fully equipped self-catering cottages on working farm in North Yorks moors. Ideal for touring Yorkshire, or just walking the hills and lanes around. Rural peace and tranquillity. Dogs free. Kennel and run available. ETC ★★★★ [🐕]
e-mail: sally@valleyviewfarm.com website: www.valleyviewfarm.com

Knaresborough

Town on escarpment above the River Nidd, 3 miles NE of Harrogate..

GALLON HOUSE 47 KIRKGATE, KNARESBOROUGH HG5 8BZ (01423 862102). Overlooking the beautiful Nidd Gorge, Gallon House offers award-winning accommodation and superb fresh food. Two double and one twin bedrooms, all en suite. Licensed. ETC/AA ◆◆◆◆ Gold Award. [🐕]
e-mail: gallon-house@ntlworld.com website: www.gallon-house.co.uk

FREE or REDUCED RATE entry to Holiday Visits and Attractions – see our READERS' OFFER VOUCHERS on pages 407-423

NEWTON HOUSE, KNARESBOROUGH. Winner of the AA Pet Friendly Award – pets genuinely welcomed and lots of great walks nearby. Spacious and comfortable, newly refurbished ensuite accommodation and great breakfasts. AA Four Red Diamonds, VisitBritain Gold Award. Contact MRS S. EARL, NEWTON HOUSE, 5-7 YORK PLACE, KNARESBOROUGH HG5 OAD (Tel: 01423 863539). [🐕]
e-mail: newtonhouse@btinternet.com website: www.newtonhouseyorkshire.com

Leeming Bar

Small, pretty village two miles north-east of Bedale.

THE WHITE ROSE HOTEL, LEEMING BAR, NORTHALLERTON DL7 9AY (01677 422707/424941; Fax: 01677 425123). Ideally situated for touring National Parks, Dales, coastal resorts, Herriot and Heartbeat Country. 18 rooms, all private bathroom, 10-channel digital TV/radio, tea and coffee, hair dryer, trouser press and telephone. RAC ★★ [🐕]
e-mail: john@whiterosehotel.co.uk website: www.whiterosehotel.co.uk

Leyburn

Small market town, 8 miles south-west of Richmond, standing above the River Ure in Wensleydale.

BARBARA & BARRIE MARTIN, THE OLD STAR, WEST WITTON, LEYBURN DL8 4LU (01969 622949). Former 17th century Coaching Inn now run as a guest house. Oak beams, log fire, home cooking. En suite B&B from £24 pppn. ETC ◆◆◆. [🐕]
e-mail: enquiries@theoldstar.com website: www.theoldstar.com

GOLDEN LION HOTEL, MARKET PLACE, LEYBURN DL8 5AS (01969 622161; Fax: 01969 623836). Excellent accommodation in this splendid hotel at the gateway to Wensleydale. En suite bathrooms, TV, telephone, radio and tea/coffee makers. Lift to all floors. Many rooms adapted for disabled guests. ETC ★. [🐕]
e-mail: info@goldenlionleyburn.co.uk

Malham

Village in upper Airedale, 5 miles east of Settle, across the moors.

MR C. SHARP, MIRESFIELD FARM, MALHAM, SKIPTON BD23 4DA (01729 830414). In beautiful gardens bordering village green and stream. Excellent food. 11 bedrooms, all with private facilities. Full central heating. Two well-furnished lounges and conservatory. B&B from £24pppn. ETC ◆◆◆ [🐕 pw!]

Northallerton

Town 14 miles south of Darlington.

JULIE & JIM GRIFFITH, HILL HOUSE FARM, LITTLE LANGTON, NORTHALLERTON DL7 0PZ (01609 770643). Sleep 2/4. Four well-equipped cottages, cosily heated for year round appeal. Centrally located between Dales and Moors. Weekly rates from £175 incl. Short breaks available. Golf 2 miles, shops 3 miles, pub food 1.5 miles. Pets welcome. ETC ★★★★ [🐕]
e-mail: info@hillhousefarmcottages.com website: www.hillhousefarmcottages.com

North Dalton

Village 6 miles south west of Great Driffield.

OLD COBBLER'S COTTAGE, NORTH DALTON. Pretty cottage with garden looking over village mere with its ducks and fish. Good walking area and easy access to York and coast. Open fire. First-class restaurants and pubs within 20 yards. For details contact (01377 217662/217523/07801 124264). [🐕]
e-mail:chris.wade@adastra-music.co.uk website: www.waterfrontcottages.co.uk

Readers are requested to mention this FHG publication when seeking accommodation

Pateley Bridge

Small town in Nidderdale, 11m north-west of Harrogate.

ROSEMARY HELME, HELME PASTURE LODGES & COTTAGES, OLD SPRING WOOD, HARTWITH BANK, SUMMERBRIDGE, HARROGATE HG3 4DR (01423 780279, Fax: 01423 780994). Country accommodation for owners and dogs and numerous walks in unspoilt Nidderdale. Central for Harrogate, York, Herriot and Bronte country. National Trust area. ETC ★★★★, ETC Category 1 for Disabled Access. [pw! Pets £5 per night, £25 per week.]
e-mail:helmepasture@btinternet.com website: www.helmepasture.co.uk

Pickering

Pleasant market town on southern fringe of North Yorkshire Moors National Park with moated Norman Castle. Bridlington 31 miles, Whitby 20, Scarborough 16, Helmsley 13, Malton 3.

THE WHITE SWAN INN AT PICKERING, YORKSHIRE HOTEL OF THE YEAR 2000 (01751 472288). One of only a handful of inns with the Silver Quality award. Dog friendly with excellent: service, rooms, food and wine. "...consistently brilliant.." Please phone or visit our website for a brochure. ETC ★★ Silver Award. [Pets £12.50 per visit].
website: www.white-swan.co.uk

MRS ELLA BOWES, BANAVIE, ROXBY ROAD, THORNTON-LE-DALE, PICKERING YO18 7SX (01751 474616). Large stone-built semi-detached house set in Thornton-le-Dale. Ideal for touring. One family bedroom and two double bedrooms, all en suite. All with TV, shaver points, central heating and tea-making facilities. Open all year. Car park, cycle shed. B&B from £24-£29pppn. Welcome Host and Hygiene Certificate held. ETC ◆◆◆◆ [🐕]
e-mail: info@banavie.uk.com website: www.banavie.uk.com

Port Mulgrave

Located 1km north of Hinderwell.

NORTH YORK MOORS NATIONAL PARK. Stone Cottage (sleeps) 4 in North York Moors National Park. Sea view, near Cleveland coastal footpath. Log fire, non-smoking. Whitby 9 miles. Brochure available (01642 613888). [🐕]

Ripon

Town 10 miles north of Harrogate. Cathedral in a mixture of styles, Racecourse 2 miles south east.

Five ground floor en suite rooms round a pretty courtyard. All rooms are full of character: oak beams etc., with modern facilities, all with views of the countryside. Private fishing lake. Terms from £60 to £75. AA ★★★★ Details from MRS L. HITCHEN, ST GEORGE'S COURT, OLD HOME FARM, HIGH GRANTLEY, RIPON HG4 3PJ (Tel: 01765 620618). [🐕]

Scalby Nabs (Scarborough)

Small town and suburb 2 miles north west of Scarborough.

EAST FARM COUNTRY COTTAGES, SCALBY NABS, SCALBY, SCARBOROUGH (01723 353635). Single-storey two-bedroom stone cottages (no steps/stairs) in national Park; only 5 minutes from Scarborough. All completely non-smoking. Ideal base for walking or touring. VisitBritain ★★★ [Pets from £10 per week.]
e-mail: joeastfarmcottages@hotmail.co.uk website: www.eastfarmcountrycottages.co.uk

Symbols

- 🐕 Indicates that pets are welcome free of charge.
- £ Indicates that a charge is made for pets: nightly or weekly.
- pw! Shows some special provision for pets; exercise facility, feeding or accommodation arrangement.
- ⌂ Indicates separate pets accommodation.

Scarborough

Very popular family resort with good sands. York 41 miles, Whitby 20, Bridlington 17, Filey 7.

HONEYSUCKLE COTTAGE (01653 698251). Lovely, stone-built cottage, four miles from Scarborough. Sleeps 2-5 + cot in 2 bedrooms. Private parking. Patio/garden with barbecue. Pets welcome. Non-smoking. Open all year. [Pets £10 per week] ETC ★★★★. Contact DAVID AND JANE BEELEY. [🐕]
e-mail: enquiries@forgevalleycottages.co.uk website: www.forgevalleycottages.co.uk

HARMONY GUEST HOUSE, 13 PRINCESS ROYAL TERRACE, SOUTH CLIFF, SCARBOROUGH YO11 2RP (01723 373562). Friendly guest house, near South Bay attractions. We offer quality en suite and four-poster rooms. Excellent food. Brochure on request. Five bedrooms B&B £22pppn, BBEM £32pppn. Open all year. ETC ★★ [🐕].
e-mail: harmonyguesthouse@hotmail.com website: www.theharmonyguesthouse.co.uk

RAVEN HALL COUNTRY HOUSE HOTEL & GOLF COURSE, RAVENSCAR, SCARBOROUGH YO13 0ET (01723 870353; Fax: 01723 870072). This imposing hotel offers oustanding accommodation, superb, typically Yorkshire cuisine and an impressive range of leisure facilities including a 9-hole golf course. A family holiday paradise. AA ★★★ [pw! Pets £5 per night.]
e-mail: enquiries@ravenhall.co.uk website: www.ravenhall.co.uk

SUE AND TONY HEWITT, HARMONY COUNTRY LODGE, LIMESTONE ROAD, BURNISTON, SCARBOROUGH YO13 0DG (0800 2985840). A peaceful retreat set in two acres of private grounds with 360° panoramic views of the National Park and sea. An ideal centre for walking or touring. En suite centrally heated rooms with superb views. Non-smoking, licensed, private parking facilities. B&B from £25 to £36. ETC ★★★★
website: www.harmonylodge.net

Skipton

Airedale market town, centre for picturesque Craven district. Fine Castle (14th cent). York 43 miles, Manchester 42, Leeds 26, Harrogate 22, Settle 16.

Over 250 super self-catering Cottages, throughout the Yorkshire Dales, York, Moors, Lancashire, Peak and Lake District. For our fully illustrated brochure apply: HOLIDAY COTTAGES (YORKSHIRE) LTD, WATER STREET, SKIPTON BD23 1PB (01756 700872). [🐕]
e-mail: p@holidaycotts.co.uk website: www.holidaycotts.co.uk

THE CONISTON HOTEL, CONISTON COLD, SKIPTON BD23 4EB (01756 748080; Fax: 01756 749487). Set in a stunning 1400 acre estate, an ideal base for guests wishing to explore the Yorkshire Dales. 50 en suite bedrooms with full facilities. Special rates for leisure breaks and family rooms. ETC ★★★ Silver Award, AA ★★★ & Rosette. [pw! Pets £10 per stay]
e-mail: sales@theconistonhotel.com website: www.theconistonhotel.com

BECK HALL, MALHAM BD23 4DJ (01729 830332). 18th century B&B on the Pennine Way, log fires and huge breakfasts. Midweek and 4-night specials. Ideal for exploring the Yorkshire Dales. AA ◆◆◆, WELCOME HOST. [🐕]
e-mail: simon@beckhallmalham.com website: www.beckhallmalham.com

Staithes

Fishing village surrounded by high cliffs on North Sea coast, 9 miles north west of Whitby.

PENNYSTEEL COTTAGE, STAITHES. Old fisherman's cottage overlooking picturesque harbour. Ideal for walking and touring. Sleep 3 + 2 children. Electricity, heating, bed linen incl. One well-behaved pet welcome. ETC ★★★ For details contact CHRIS WARD (01377 217662/217523/07801 124264)
e-mail: chris.wade@adastra-music.co.uk website: www.waterfrontcottages.co.uk

Readers are requested to mention this FHG publication when seeking accommodation

Thirsk

Market town with attractive square. Excellent touring area. Northallerton 3 miles.

POPLARS HOLIDAY COTTAGES AND BED AND BREAKFAST, THIRSK. The Poplars stands in two acres of lovely gardens with a field for dog walking. We have old brick cottages and new lodges, with bed and breakfast in the Poplars House. Contact MRS CHILTON, CARLTON MINIOTT, THIRSK YO7 4LX (01845 522712). ETC ★★★★, Silver Award
website: www.poplars-cottages.co.uk

FOXHILLS HIDEAWAYS, FELIXKIRK, THIRSK YO7 2DS (01845 537575). Scandinavian log cabins, heated throughout, linen provided. A supremely relaxed atmosphere on the edge of the North Yorkshire Moors National Park. Open all year. Village pub round the corner. [🐕]

GOLDEN FLEECE HOTEL, MARKET SQUARE, THIRSK YO7 1LL (01845 523108; Fax: 01845 523996). Characterful Coaching Inn offering good food and up to date facilities. All rooms are en suite, with satellite TV, phone, trouser press, hairdryer. ETC/AA ★★, [🐕]
e-mail: reservations@goldenfleecehotel.com website: www.goldenfleecehotel.com

Whitby

Charming resort with harbour and sands. Of note is the 13th century ruined Abbey. Stockton-on-Tees 34 miles, Scarborough 20, Saltburn-by-the-Sea 19.

MRS JILL McNEIL, SWALLOW HOLIDAY COTTAGES, LONG LEAS FARM, HAWSKER, WHITBY YO22 4LA (01947 603790). Discover historic Whitby, pretty fishing villages, way-marked walks. Four cottages, one or two bedrooms. Private parking. Children and dogs welcome. Weekly rates from £195 to £500. Please phone or write for a brochure. ETC ★★★★ [🐕]

ARCHES GUESTHOUSE, 8 HAVELOCK PLACE, HUDSON STREET, WHITBY YO21 3ER. Pet friendly, family-run guesthouse, where a warm welcome and large breakfast is always assured. The ideal base for experiencing the old world charms of this historic seaside town, exploring the beautiful North Yorkshire Moors, or just relaxing. Strictly Non-Smoking. Tariff: £28 - £35 pppn. RUTH & DICK BREW (01947 601880 or 0800 9154256). [🐕]
e-mail: archeswhitby@freeola.com website: www.whitbyguesthouses.co.uk

WHITE ROSE HOLIDAY COTTAGES, NEAR WHITBY. Superior centrally heated village cottages and bungalows, also apartments in Whitby. Available all year. Ideal for coast and country. Up to ETC ★★★★. APPLY: MRS J. ROBERTS (PW), 5 BROOK PARK, SLEIGHTS, NEAR WHITBY YO21 1RT (01947 810763) [£5 per week, pw!]
e-mail: enquiries@whiterosecottages.co.uk website: www.whiterosecottages.co.uk

WHITBY TOWN CENTRE. Six stylish cottages in excellent locations, some with enclosed gardens/patios. Open all year for weeks, midweeks and short breaks. Telephone: 01947 820370.
website: www.directwhitbyaccom.co.uk

THE SEACLIFFE HOTEL, WEST CLIFF, WHITBY Y021 3JX (Freephone 0800 0191747). A very warm-hearted, family-run hotel overlooking the beach. Children and dogs welcome. Enjoy fine ales and delicious "Heartbeat Country" cooking in our own "Aidensfield Arms" traditional licensed bar or sample superb seafoods and fine wines in the Candleight restaurant (booking advised). VisitBritain ◆◆◆◆. [🐕]
e-mail: stay@seacliffehotel.co.uk website: www.seacliffehotel.co.uk

HARDSTRUGGLE COTTAGES, ESK VALLEY Cosy stone cottage with Aga and woodburner. Fantastic walking, stunning scenery, coast and steam railway. Sleeps 6 to 8 adults. Linen and fuel included. One dog only. Contact: MRS MIRIAM DUFFY, 22 EASTHORPE, SOUTHWELL, NOTTINGHAMSHIRE NG25 0HY (01636 815572; mobile: 07967374483).[🐕]
e-mail: jonmiriam@aol.com website: www.esk.org.uk

Terms quoted in this publication may be subject to increase if rises in costs necessitate

York

Historic cathedral city and former Roman Station on River Ouse. Magnificent Minster and 3 miles of ancient walls. Facilities for a wide range of sports and entertainments. Horse-racing on Knavesmire. Bridlington 41 miles, Filey 41, Leeds 24, Harrogate 22.

ST GEORGE'S, 6 ST GEORGE'S PLACE, YORK YO24 1DR (01904 625056). Family-run guest house in quiet cul-de-sac near racecourse. All rooms en suite with colour TV, tea/coffee making facilities. Private parking. Pets welcome. ETC/AA ★★★ [🐕]
e-mail: sixstgeorg@aol.com website: www.stgeorgesyork.com

YORK LAKESIDE LODGES, MOOR LANE, YORK YO24 2QU (01904 702346; Fax: 01904 701631). Self-catering pine lodges. Mature parkland setting. Large fishing lake. Nearby superstore with coach to centre every 10 mins. ETC ★★★★/★★★★★ [pw! Pets £18 per week]
e-mail: neil@yorklakesidelodges.co.uk website: www.lakesidelodges.co.uk

ASCOT HOUSE, 80 EAST PARADE, YORK YO31 7YH (01904 426826; Fax: 01904 431077). Attractive Victorian villa with easy access to city centre. Family and double rooms en suite. Comfortable residents' lounge, dining room. Sauna. Single room £30-£60, double room £60-£75. ETC/AA ◆◆◆◆, ETC Silver Award. [🐕]
e-mail: admin@ascothouseyork.com website: www.ascothouseyork.com

MRS M. S. A. WOODLIFFE, MILL FARM, YAPHAM, POCKLINGTON, YORK YO42 1PH (01759 302172). WOLDS VIEW HOLIDAY COTTAGES. Granville Lodge (sleeps 6-8), Parlour (sleeps 6), Barn (sleeps 4), Stables (sleeps 3) and Courtyard (sleeps 4). Full details on request.

HIGH BELTHORPE, BISHOP WILTON, YORK YO42 1SB (01759 368238; Mobile: 07786 923330). Set on an ancient moated site at the foot of the Yorkshire Wolds, this comfortable Victorian farmhouse offers huge breakfasts, private fishing and fabulous walks. Dogs and owners will love it! Open all year except Christmas. Prices from £25. ETC ◆◆◆ [pw! 🐕]

WEST YORKSHIRE

Bingley

Bingley

Town on River Aire 5 miles north-west of Bradford.

THE FIVE RISE LOCKS HOTEL & RESTAURANT, BECK LANE, BINGLEY BD16 4DD (01274 565296). Large Victorian house in tranquil area, but close main roads, tourist sites. Good views, individual decor, informal style. Historic canal locks and excellent walking (dogs and humans) close by. AA/VisitBritain ★★★★.
e-mail: info@five-rise-locks.co.uk website: www.five-rise-locks.co.uk

A useful index of towns/counties appears on pages 424-429

FHG
KUPERARD

Your guides to Good Holidays 2007

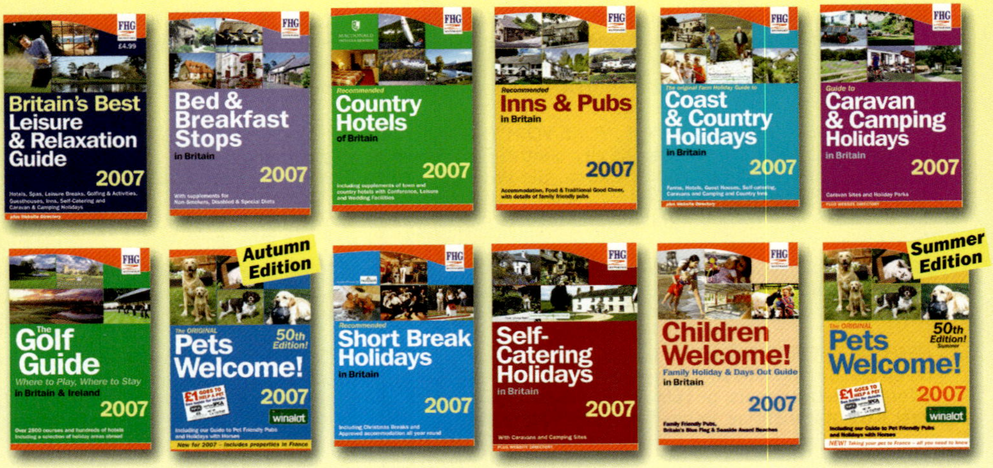

BRITAIN'S BEST LEISURE & RELAXATION GUIDE user-friendly guide to all kinds of holidays **£4.99**

BED & BREAKFAST STOPS ever more popular independent guide with over 1000 entries **£7.99**

Recommended COUNTRY HOTELS a quality selection of Britain's best Country Houses and Hotels **£7.99**

Recommended INNS & PUBS accommodation, food and traditional good cheer **£7.99**

COAST & COUNTRY HOLIDAYS holidays for all the family, from traditional farm houses to inns, guesthouses and small hotels **£7.99**

CARAVAN & CAMPING HOLIDAYS covers every type of caravan and camping facility **£7.99**

THE GOLF GUIDE Where to Play / Where to Staya detailed list covering virtually every club and course in the UK with hotels and other accommodation nearby – recommended by golfers, to golfers **£9.99**

PETS WELCOME! the pet world's version of the ultimate hotel guide, over 1000 properties where pets and their owners are made welcome **£8.99**

Recommended SHORT BREAK HOLIDAYS approved accommodation all year round for short breaks **£7.99**

SELF CATERING HOLIDAYS perhaps the widest selection of self-catering accommodation **£7.99**

CHILDREN WELCOME! Family Holiday and Days Out guide **£7.99**

Available from bookshops or larger newsagents

FHG GUIDES LTD Abbey Mill Business Centre, Seedhill, Paisley, Renfrewshire PAI ITJ

www.holidayguides.com

The best-selling series of UK Holiday Guides

Scotland

otos: Ardoch Lodge, Strathyre, Perthshire *Lagnakeil Highland Lodges, Lerags, Oban* *Invermoriston Chalets, Glenmoriston, Highlands*

Ratings & Awards

For the first time ever the AA, VisitBritain, VisitScotland, and the Wales Tourist Board will use a single method of assessing and rating serviced accommodation. Irrespective of which organisation inspects an establishment the rating awarded will be the same, using a common set of standards, giving a clear guide of what to expect. The RAC is no longer operating an Hotel inspection and accreditation business.

Accommodation Standards: Star Grading Scheme

Using a scale of 1-5 stars the objective quality ratings give a clear indication of accommodation standard, cleanliness, ambience, hospitality, service and food, This shows the full range of standards suitable for every budget and preference, and allows visitors to distinguish between the quality of accommodation and facilities on offer in different establishments.All types of board and self-catering accommodation are covered, including hotels, B & Bs, holiday parks, campus accommodation, hostels, caravans and camping, and boats.

The more stars, the higher level of quality

★★★★★
exceptional quality, with a degree of luxury

★★★★
excellent standard throughout

★★★
very good level of quality and comfort

★★
good quality, well presented and well run

★
acceptable quality; simple, practical, no frills

VisitBritain and the regional tourist boards, **enjoyEngland.com, VisitScotland** and **VisitWales,** and **the AA** have full details of the grading system on their websites

enjoyEngland.com

visitScotland.com

visitWales.com

theAA.com

National Accessible Scheme

If you have particular mobility, visual or hearing needs, look out for the National Accessible Scheme. You can be confident of finding accommodation or attractions that meet your needs by looking for the following symbols.

- Typically suitable for a person with sufficient mobility to climb a flight of steps but would benefit from fixtures and fittings to aid balance
- Typically suitable for a person with restricted walking ability and for those that may need to use a wheelchair some of the time and can negotiate a maximum of three steps
- Typically suitable for a person who depends on the use of a wheelchair and transfers unaided to and from the wheelchair in a seated position. This person may be an independent traveller
- Typically suitable for a person who depends on the use of a wheelchair in a seated position. This person also requires personal or mechanical assistance (eg carer, hoist).

ARDTUR COTTAGES

Two adjacent cottages in secluded surroundings. Ideal for hill walking, climbing, pony trekking, boating and fly fishing. Shop one mile; sea 200 yards; car essential; pets allowed.

MRS J PERY, ARDTUR, APPIN PA38 4DD (01631 730223 or 01626 834172)
e-mail: pery@btinternet.com • www.selfcatering-appin-scotland.com

HOUSE IN THE WOOD HOLIDAYS

Glenachulish, Ballachulish, Argyll PH49 4JZ Telephone: 01855 811379

Cottage and Chalets in Natural Woodland sleeping two to six people.
From £155–£270.

GOOD AREA FOR WALKING – AND NATURE LOVERS

PETS WELCOME *BROCHURE AVAILABLE* *NO VAT* *REGRET NO SMOKERS*

CAIRNDOW STAGECOACH INN

Cairndow, Argyll PA26 8BN
Tel: 01499 600286 • Fax: 01499 600220
www.cairndow.com

HALF PRICE GOLF AT INVERARAY GOLF CLUB (9 MILES), THE MOST INTERESTING AND TESTING 9-HOLE COURSE IN ARGYLL
SPECIAL RATES AT COWAL GOLF CLUB, DUNOON

Historic Coaching Inn on Loch Fyne ★ 14 well-appointed en suite bedrooms ★ Excellent cuisine in Stables Restaurant and lounge meals all day ★ Two de luxe bedrooms with two-person spa baths. ★ Amenities include lochside beer garden, sauna, multi-gym and solarium.

CAIRNDOW, ARGYLL.
AT THE HEAD OF LOCH FYNE

Two comfortable holiday cottages at the head of the longest sea loch in Scotland. **INVERFYNE** (pictured left), a very spacious cottage with 4 twin bedded rooms, overlooks the estuary. There is a piano in the 32 foot living room and a large utility/drying room. **BRIDGE COTTAGE** (pictured right), is a traditional stone cottage and sleeps four, overlooks the bottom pool of the river Fyne. Linen and electricity are included. Achadunan Estate is set amidst lovely walking country. Golden eagles and deer are your neighbours. Achadunan is home to Fyne Ales micro brewery. Brochures available from:

Mrs Delap, Achadunan, Cairndow, Argyll PA26 8BJ
Tel & Fax: +44 (0) 1499 600 238
Web: www.argyllholidaycottages.com

Set in 20 acres of garden woodland on the south shore of spectacular Loch Awe in the heart of Argyll, Ardbrecknish House dates back to the early – seventeenth century. The house has been carefully converted to provide nine delightful self-catering properties accommodating parties from two to twelve with facilities for larger groups. In the grounds are five custom designed holiday cottages, carefully spaced for optimum privacy and outlook, yet easily accessible to the central facilities. The house and grounds command breathtaking panoramic views over loch, mountain and glen. Boat hire, fishing, golf and walking. Close to Oban, Mull and Glencoe. Bar, meals and games room.

3 night breaks from £80 for 2 persons low season, to £1000 weekly high season rental for 12 person apartment

Rockhill Waterside Country House

Est 1960

Ardbrecknish, By Dalmally, Argyll PA33 1BH • Tel: 01866 833218

17th century guest house in spectacular waterside setting on Loch Awe with breathtaking views to Ben Cruachan, where comfort, peace and tranquillity reign supreme.

Small private Highland estate breeding Hanoverian competition horses. 1200 metres free trout fishing. Five delightful rooms with all modern facilities. First-class highly acclaimed home cooking with much home-grown produce. Wonderful area for touring the Western Highlands, Glencoe, the Trossachs and Kintyre. Ideal for climbing, walking, bird and animal watching. Boat trips locally and from Oban (30 miles) to Mull, Iona, Fingal's Cave and other islands.

Dogs' Paradise! ***Also Self-Catering Cottages***

ABBOT'S BRAE HOTEL

West Bay, Dunoon, Argyll PA23 7QJ

Tel: 01369 705021 • Fax: 01369 701191

e-mail: info@abbotsbrae.co.uk • www.abbotsbrae.co.uk

Award-winning, small Country House Hotel set in its own secluded woodland garden with breathtaking views of the sea and hills. Very spacious en suite bedrooms including four-poster, king-size and twin rooms. The welcoming, homely atmosphere, peaceful surroundings and appetising menus will ensure a memorable stay. Special offers in spring and autumn. Pets stay free. Ideal base to explore the Western Highlands, situated at the Gateway to Scotland's first National Park.

For further details contact either Colin or Christine.

Gigha Hotel

THE ISLE OF GIGHA HERITAGE TRUST

Situated in the Inner Hebrides, the community owned Isle of Gigha (God's Island) is surely one of Scotland's most beautiful and tranquil islands. Explore the white sandy bays and lochs. Easy walking, bike hire, birds, wildlife and wild flowers. Home to the famous Achamore Gardens with rhododendrons, azaleas and semi-tropical plants. Grass Airstrip, 9-hole golf course and regular ferry (only 20 minutes from the mainland). We are dog friendly. Holiday Cottages also available.

Call us on 01583 505254 Fax: 01583 505244 www.gigha.org.uk

St Blane's Hotel **Kilchattan Bay, Isle of Bute PA20 9NW**

In one of the most serene and breathtaking locations on Bute, this traditional, family-run, pet-friendly, licensed Hotel offers superior en suite accommodation. It is a perfect base for walking, golf, windsurfing and other water sports. Open to non-residents, and with free moorings for visiting yachts, you can drop by for a meal or drink in the largest beer garden on the island!

01700 831224 • e-mail: info@stblaneshotel.com • www.stblaneshotel.com

Darroch Mhor Chalets

Carrick Castle, Loch Goil, Argyll PA24 8AF

Chill out in Scotland's first national park. Five self catering chalets nestling on the shores of Loch Goil, each with superb lochside views and offering a peaceful and relaxing holiday in the heart of Argyll Forest Park. Each chalet has two bedrooms, living room with colour TV, fitted kitchen with fridge, freezer, microwave, toaster etc. and bathroom with bath and overhead shower. Car parking by each chalet. Great hill walking.

Ideal for pets, genuinely pet-friendly • Open all year – weekly rates £120-£295.
Weekend & short breaks available all year from £70, reductions for 2 persons. One pet free.

Tel: 01301 703249 • Fax: 01301 703348 • chalets@murray-s.fslife.co.uk • www.argyllchalets.com

Self-catering holidays in luxury lodges and new caravans. This immaculate 5-Star park is located on the West Coast of Scotland, near Oban. The wooded surroundings, sandy beach and stunning sea views make Tralee Bay the perfect place for a holiday at any time of year. With a play area, mini golf, fly fishing, woodland walks, boat slipway, and endless supply of RABBITS, the park offers something for everyone. Pets welcome at £15.

TRALEE BAY HOLIDAYS

Tralee Bay Holidays, Benderloch, by Oban, Argyll PA37 1QR

Tel: 01631 720255/217 **e-mail: tralee@easynet.co.uk • www.tralee.com**

Small family-run guest house, 10 minutes' walk from train, boat and bus terminal.
A warm welcome awaits you all year round.

MRS STEWART, GLENVIEW, SOROBA ROAD, OBAN PA34 4JF • Tel: 01631 562267

ELERAIG HIGHLAND LODGES **Near OBAN, ARGYLL**

Gateway to the Highlands and Islands. Well-equipped Norwegian chalets on secluded Eleraig Estate 12 miles from Oban. Available April-Oct. Sleep 4-7. PERFECT FOR PETS.

Anne and Robin Grey, Eleraig Highland Lodges,
Kilninver, by Oban, Argyll PA34 4UX • Tel: 01852 200225
www.scotland2000.com/eleraig • e-mail: robingrey@eleraig.co.uk

FHG Guides

publish a large range of well-known accommodation guides.
We will be happy to send you details or you can use the order form at the back of this book.

FHG
K·U·P·E·R·A·R·D

Seil Island, by Oban, Argyll P34 4TJ
Telephone: 01852 300276
Web page: www.willowburn.co.uk
Personally run and managed by Jan and Chris Wolfe.

Willowburn Hotel and Restaurant

The Willowburn Hotel garden reaches down to the peaceful waters of Clachan Sound. Inside, the lounge, dining room and most of our comfortable en suite bedrooms enjoy this wonderful view – we see otters, seals, deer and a huge variety of birds.

We are informal and relaxed and take pride in what we offer – in particular our food, which is imaginative and varied, as is our wine list. There's some wonderful walking in the area, wildlife, wild flowers, gardens, boat trips, and places and opportunities just to sit and ponder.

We are non-smoking, pet-friendly and we just want you to relax and enjoy yourselves.

Good Food Guide 2004 · Which! Hotel Guide 2004 · AA ★★ Hotel 76% · AA Rosette 2004

Lagnakeil

HIGHLAND LODGES
VisitScotland
★★★/★★★★ Self-Catering

Our timber lodges and four cottages are set in a tranquil, scenic wooded glen overlooking Loch Feochan, only 3 miles from Oban, **'Gateway to the Isles'**. Lodges are fully equipped to a high standard, including linen. Country pub only a short walk up the Glen. OAP discount. Free loch fishing. Special breaks from £44 per lodge per night, weekly from £210. Lodges/houses sleep 2-10 comfortably in 1-4 bedrooms.

Our colour brochure will tell lots more. Please phone or write to:
Colin & Jo Mossman, Lagnakeil Highland Lodges, Lerags, Oban PA34 4SE • 01631 562746 • Fax: 01631 570225 • e-mail: info@lagnakeil.com • website: www.lagnakeil.co.uk •

Loch Melfort Hotel & Restaurant

Enjoy stunning views down the Sound of Jura to the Islands. Located between Inveraray and Oban, beside the famous Arduaine Gardens. Join our regular guests and relax with excellent award-winning cuisine, comfortable accommodation, and friendly and attentive service. The perfect place for a relaxing holiday or short break.

Arduaine, By Oban, Argyll PA34 4XG • Tel: 01852 200233
Fax: 01852 200214 • www.lochmelfort.co.uk

West Loch Hotel

By Tarbert, Loch Fyne, Argyll PA29 6YF
Tel: 01880 820283 • Fax: 01880 820930
www.westlochhotel.co.uk • e-mail: westlochhotel@btinternet.com

Family-run, 18th century coaching inn of character, well situated for a relaxing holiday. It is renowned for outstanding food. Excellent for hill-walking and enjoying the wide variety of wildlife. Attractions include castles, distilleries, gardens and sandy beaches.

Five cottages in architect designed conversion of home farm. Spacious accommodation for 2-8 persons. Stone fireplaces for log fires. Wonderful walks and scenery, peace and quiet. Winter breaks available. Easy access to island ferries. Pets welcome. Open all year. Colour brochure • From £250-£600 • ASSC • STB ★★

Dunmore Court, Near Tarbert, Argyll PA29 6XZ • Tel: 01880 820654
e-mail: bookings@dunmorecourt.com • www.dunmorecourt.com

FREE or REDUCED RATE entry to Holiday Visits and Attractions – see our READERS' OFFER VOUCHERS on pages 407-423

SKIPNESS ESTATE, By Tarbert, Argyll PA29 6XU

Tel: 01880 760207 • Fax: 01880 760208 • e-mail: sophie@skipness.freeserve.co.uk

This unspoilt, peaceful, West Highland estate with its own historic castle, medieval chapel and way-marked walks has traditional cottages to let all year round. Each cottage has an open fire and television; some cottages have a rowing dinghy in summer. Properties sleep 4-10. All cottages have magnificent views and beautiful surrounding countryside and coastline. Safe, sandy beaches can be enjoyed on the estate, with fishing, pony trekking and golf nearby. Skipness village facilities include a shop/post office and the seasonal licensed Seafood Cabin. Local ferries to Arran, Gigha, Islay and Jura.

PETS WELCOME. Apply for rates and further details: Sophie James.

FARM HOLIDAY GUIDE DIPLOMA • STB ★★/★★★ SELF-CATERING

Airdeny Chalets - Taynuilt Situated in 3½ acres of peaceful natural habitat. Three 3-bedroom chalets (STB ★★★★) and four 2-bedroom chalets (STB ★★★), all enjoying spectacular views, own privacy and parking area. Furnished to a very high standard. Ideal for walking, cycling, fishing, bird watching, touring the Western Highlands and Islands, or just relaxing. Dogs welcome. Open all year. Prices from £250 to £675. Contact: **Jenifer Moffat 01866 822648 • e-mail: jenifer@airdenychalets.co.uk • www.airdenychalets.co.uk**

Appin

Mountainous area bounded by Loch Linnhe, Glen Creran and Glencoe.

MRS J PERY, ARDTUR, APPIN PA38 4DD (01631 730223 or 01626 834172). Two adjacent cottages in secluded surroundings. Ideal for hill walking, climbing, pony trekking, boating and fly fishing. Shop one mile; sea 200 yards; car essential; pets allowed.[🐕]
e-mail: pery@btinternet.com website: www.selfcatering-appin-scotland.com

Ballachulish

Impressively placed village at entrance to Glencoe and on Loch Leven. Magnificent mountain scenery including Sgorr Dhearg (3362ft). Good centre for boating, climbing and sailing. Glasgow 89 miles, Oban 38, Fort William 14, Kinlochleven 9.

Cottages and Chalets in Natural Woodland sleeping two to six people. The Glencoe area is lovely for walking and perfect for nature lovers too. Regret no smokers. No VAT. Brochure available. APPLY: HOUSE IN THE WOOD HOLIDAYS, GLENACHULISH, BALLACHULISH PH49 4JZ (01855 811379). Pets welcome. [🐕]

Cairndow

Village at mouth of Kinglas Water on Loch Fyne in Argyll, near head of Loch.

CAIRNDOW STAGECOACH INN, CAIRNDOW PA26 8BN (01499 600286; Fax: 01499 600220). 14 well-appointed en suite bedrooms. Excellent cuisine in Stables Restaurant and lounge meals all day. Amenities include lochside beer garden, sauna, multi-gym and solarium. STB ★★★ Inn.
website: www.cairndow.com

Two comfortable holiday cottages at the head of the longest sea loch in Scotland, in lovely walking country. Sleep four and eight. Linen and electricity included. STB ★★★ Self Catering. MRS DELAP, ACHADUNAN, CAIRNDOW, ARGYLL PA26 8BJ (Tel & Fax: 01499 600238).
website: www.argyllholidaycottages.com

Symbols

- 🐕 Indicates that pets are welcome free of charge.
- £ Indicates that a charge is made for pets: nightly or weekly.
- pw! Shows some special provision for pets; exercise facility, feeding or accommodation arrangement.
- ⌂ Indicates separate pets accommodation.

Dalmally

Small town in Glen Orchy to the south-west of Loch Awe, with romantic Kilchurn Castle (14th century). Edinburgh 98 miles, Glasgow 69, Ardrishaig 42, Oban 25, Inveraray 16.

ARDBRECKNISH HOUSE, SOUTH LOCHAWESIDE, BY DALMALLY, ARGYLL PA33 1BH (01866 833223). Self-catering properties and holiday cottages set in 20 acres of garden woodland on the south shore of Loch Awe. Breathtaking panoramic views over loch, mountain and glen. See our website to view properties. [Pets £15 per week]
e-mail: enquiries@loch-awe.co.uk website: www.loch-awe.co.uk

ROCKHILL WATERSIDE COUNTRY HOUSE, ARDBRECKNISH, BY DALMALLY PA33 1BH (01866 833218). 17th century guest house on waterside with spectacular views over Loch Awe. Five delightful rooms with all modern facilities. First-class home cooking with much home-grown produce.

Dunoon

Town and resort in Argyll, 4 miles west of Gourock across Firth of Clyde.

ABBOTS BRAE HOTEL, WEST BAY, DUNOON PA23 7QJ (01369 705021; Fax: 01369 701191). Small welcoming hotel at the gateway to the Western Highlands with breathtaking views. Comfortable, spacious, en suite bedrooms, quality home cooking and select wines. [🐕]
e-mail: info@abbotsbrae.co.uk website: www.abbotsbrae.co.uk

Isle of Gigha

A tranquil island, one of the Inner Hebrides just of the west coast of Scotland. A haven for birds and wildlife.

GIGHA HOTEL, ISLE OF GIGHA PA41 7AA (01583 505254; Fax: 01583 505244). Beautiful, tranquil island. Explore the white sandy bays and lochs; famous Achamore Gardens. Easy walking, bike hire, birds, wildlife and wild flowers. Dog-friendly. Holiday cottages also available. [🐕]
website: www.gigha.org.uk

Kilchattan Bay

Quiet seaside village with wide bay on the east coast of Bute.

ST BLANE'S HOTEL KILCHATTAN BAY, ISLE OF BUTE PA20 9NW (01700 831224). Traditional, family-run, pet-friendly, licensed Hotel offering superior en suite accommodation. Perfect base for walking, golf, windsurfing and other water sports. Open to non-residents. [🐕]
e-mail: info@stblaneshotel.com website: www.stblaneshotel.com

Loch Goil

Six mile long loch stretching from Lochgoilhead to Loch Long.

DARROCH MHOR, CARRICK CASTLE, LOCH GOIL PA24 8AF (01301 703249; Fax: 01301 703348). Five self-catering Chalets on the shores of Loch Goil in the heart of Argyll Forest Park. Fully equipped except linen. Colour TV, fitted kitchen, carpeted. Pets very welcome. Open all year. [🐕]
e-mail: chalets@murray-s.fslife.co.uk website: www.argyllchalets.com

Oban

Popular Highland resort and port, yachting centre, ferry services to Inner and Outer Hebrides. Sandy bathing beach at Ganavan Bay. McCaig's Tower above town is Colosseum replica built in 1890s.

TRALEE BAY HOLIDAYS, BENDERLOCH, BY OBAN PA37 1QR (01631 720255/217). Overlooking Ardmucknish Bay. The wooded surroundings and sandy beaches make Tralee the ideal destination for a self-catering lodge or caravan holiday anytime of the year. STB ★★★★★ [Pets £15 per week]
e-mail: tralee@easynet.co.uk website: www.tralee.com

Terms quoted in this publication may be subject to increase if rises in costs necessitate

MRS STEWART, GLENVIEW, SOROBA ROAD, OBAN PA34 4JF (01631 562267). Small family-run guest house, 10 minutes' walk from train, boat and bus terminal. A warm welcome awaits you all year round. [🐕]

Well-equipped Scandinavian chalets in breathtaking scenery near Oban. Chalets sleep 4–7, are widely spaced and close to Loch Tralaig. Car parking. From £200 per week per chalet. Available April to October. STB ★★ & ★★★ Self Catering. APPLY – ANNE & ROBIN GREY, ELERAIG HIGHLAND LODGES, KILNINVER, BY OBAN PA34 4UX (01852 200225) [🐕]
e-mail: robingrey@eleraig.co.uk website: www.scotland2000.com/eleraig

WILLOWBURN HOTEL, CLACHAN SEIL, BY OBAN PA34 4TJ (01852 300276). Peaceful, relaxing, informal and addictive. Superb setting overlooking the Sound of Seil. Walk, fish, birdwatch or simply just laze. Completely non-smoking. Tempted? Bring your owners too! STB ★★★★ Small Hotel, AA ★★ [🐕]
website: www.willowburn.co.uk

LAGNAKEIL HIGHLAND LODGES, LERAGS, OBAN, ARGYLL PA34 4SE (01631 562746; Fax: 01631 570225). Our Timber Lodges and four cottages are set in a tranquil, scenic wooded glen overlooking Loch Feochan, only 3 miles from the picturesque harbour town of Oban: "Gateway to the Isles". Fully equipped Lodges to a high standard, including linen and towels, country pub a short walk. OAP. discount. Free loch fishing. Special Breaks from £44 per lodge per night, weekly from £210 Sleep 2-10 comfortably. Our colour brochure will tell lots more. VisitScotland ★★★/★★★★ Self-Catering. [Pets £15 per week].
e-mail: info@lagnakeil.com website: www.lagnakeil.co.uk

LOCH MELFORT HOTEL & RESTAURANT, ARDUAINE, BY OBAN PA34 4XG (01852 200233; Fax: 01852 200214). Stunning views down the Sound of Jura to the Islands. Located between Inveraray and Oban, beside the famous Arduaine Gardens. Excellent award-winning cuisine, comfortable accommodation, and friendly and attentive service. [🐕]
website: www.lochmelfort.co.uk

Tarbert

Fishing port on isthmus connecting Kintyre to the mainland.

WEST LOCH HOTEL, BY TARBERT, LOCH FYNE PA29 6YF (01880 820283; Fax: 01880 820930). Family-run, 18th century coaching inn, well situated for a relaxing holiday. It is renowned for outstanding food. Excellent for hill-walking and enjoying the wide variety of wildlife. Attractions include castles, distilleries, gardens and sandy beaches. STB ★★ Inn. [🐕]
e-mail: westlochhotel@btinternet.com website: www.westlochhotel.co.uk

DUNMORE COURT, KILBERRY ROAD, NEAR TARBERT PA29 6XZ (01880 820654). Five cottages sleeping 2-8. Wonderful walks and scenery, peace and quiet. Winter breaks available. Easy access to island ferries. Terms from £250-£600. Open all year. ASSC member. STB ★★ SELF CATERING. [🐕]
e-mail: bookings@dunmorecourt.com website: www.dunmorecourt.com

Peaceful, unspoilt West Highland estate. Traditional cottages, with open fires; some with a dinghy in summer. Sleep 4–10. Pets welcome. Walks, pony trekking, golf nearby. APPLY SOPHIE JAMES, SKIPNESS CASTLE, BY TARBERT PA29 6XU (01880 760207; Fax: 01880 760208). STB ★★/★★★[🐕]
e-mail: sophie@skipness.freeserve.co.uk

Taynuilt

Village in Argyll 1km south west of Bonawe.

JENIFER MOFFAT, AIRDENY CHALETS, TAYNUILT PA35 1HY (01866 822648). Three 3-bedroom chalets (STB ★★★★) and four 2-bedroom chalets (STB ★★★), furnished to a very high standard. Ideal for walking, cycling, fishing, bird watching, touring, or just relaxing. Dogs welcome. Open all year. [Pets £10 per week].
e-mail: jenifer@airdenychalets.co.uk website www.airdenychalets.co.uk

Terms quoted in this publication may be subject to increase if rises in costs necessitate

Ayr

Popular family holiday resort with sandy beaches. Excellent shopping, theatre, racecourse.

HORIZON HOTEL, ESPLANADE, AYR KA7 1DT (01292 264384; Fax: 01292 264011). Highly recommended for golf breaks; special midweek rates. Coach parties welcome. Lunches, dinners and bar suppers served. Phone now for free colour brochure. [🐕]
e-mail: reception@horizonhotel.com website: www.horizonhotel.com

Ballantrae

Small fishing port 12 miles south-west of Girvan.

ROGER AND MARILYN BOURNE, LAGGAN HOUSE LEISURE PARK, BALLANTRAE KA26 0LL (01465 831229; Fax: 01465 831511). Luxury caravans and chalets for hire. Overlooking secluded countryside and sea. Heated indoor pool, sauna, bar, children's playground. Short Breaks available. STB ★★★★ [£2 per night, £12 per week]
e-mail: lhlp@lagganhouse.co.uk website: www.lagganhouse.co.uk

Catacol (Isle of Arran)

Location on north side of Catacol Bay on north-west coast of Arran.

CATACOL BAY HOTEL, CATACOL, LOCHRANZA KA27 8HN (01770 830231; Fax: 01770 830350). Comfortable, friendly, small country house hotel where good cooking is our speciality. Extensive bar menu, meals are served from noon until 10pm. Centrally heated. Open all year. Details of Special Breaks and brochure on request. Children and pets welcome. [🐕]
e-mail: catbay@tiscali.co.uk website: www.catacol.co.uk

Jedburgh, Kelso, Selkirk, West Linton

Glenbank House Hotel

Castlegate, Jedburgh TD8 6BD

Tel: 01835 862258

e-mail: enquiries@glenbankhotel.co.uk
website: www.glenbankhotel.co.uk

Set in its own grounds with ample private parking and beer garden. Licensed restaurant and bar with an extensive wine list and selection of malt whiskies. All rooms are en suite with TV. Open to non-residents. Reduced rates for children. Pets Welcome.

Ferniehirst Mill Lodge

A chalet style guest house set in grounds of 25 acres. All rooms en suite with tea/coffee making facilities. Licensed for residents. Well behaved pets (including horses) welcome by arrangement. VisitScotland ★, AA ★★ ALAN & CHRISTINE SWANSTON, FERNIEHIRST MILL LODGE, JEDBURGH TD8 6PQ • 01835 863279

e-mail: ferniehirstmill@aol.com • www.ferniehirstmill.co.uk

Westwood House – Kelso

Overlooking Scotland's famous River Tweed

TOTAL "OFF LEAD" FREEDOM FOR DOGS IN ENCLOSED AND SECLUDED GROUNDS

Renovated riverside cottage with 12 acres of paths, through walled gardens and on own private island.
4 bedrooms sleeping 2 - 8 (+ child), 2 bathrooms, period features, cosy log fire and centrally heated.
• ½ mile Kelso town • one hour Edinburgh/Newcastle • ½ hour Berwick (station) and Northumberland coast

DOGS WELCOME FREE

For Brochure and tariff, from £325 per week fully inclusive of all linen and towels, electricity and heating.
2-person discounts available. Trout fishing also included.

Welcome Host

Debbie Crawford,
Pippin Heath Farm, Holt,
Norfolk NR25 6SS
Tel: 07788 134 832

ACHIEVING GOLD IN GREEN TOURISM AND 'HIGHLY COMMENDED' IN SCOTTISH THISTLE AWARDS

❖ Gordon Arms Hotel ❖

Yarrow Valley, Scottish Borders TD7 5LE

Situated in the picturesque Yarrow Valley, the Gordon Arms Hotel offers warm, friendly hospitality, good food, a great atmosphere, real ale and accommodation to suit all tastes.

Tel: 01750 82222

e-mail: info@thegordonarms.com • www.thegordonarms.com

Slipperfield House

West Linton EH46 7AA

America Cottage

Two well-equipped cottages a mile from West Linton at the foot of the Pentland Hills, set in 100 acres of lochs and woodlands. Only 19 miles from Edinburgh City Centre. Both cottages have sittingrooms with central heating and open fires, digital TV, modern bathrooms and kitchens, microwave ovens and telephones etc.

Loch Cottage

Details from Mrs C.M. Kilpatrick

• Dogs welcome • Ample parking
• Car essential • Central Edinburgh 19 miles
• Golf, walking and fishing nearby • Available all year.

This is an ideal dog-friendly location for a family holiday near Edinburgh. (Max 2 dogs per cottage)

Tel and Fax: 01968 660401 e-mail: cottages@slipperfield.com www.slipperfield.com

FREE or REDUCED RATE entry to Holiday Visits and Attractions
– see our READERS' OFFER VOUCHERS on pages 407-423

Bonchester Bridge

Village on Rule Water, 6 miles east of Hawick. To east is Bonchester Hill surmounted by ancient earthworks.

WAUCHOPE COTTAGES, BONCHESTER BRIDGE, HAWICK TD9 9TG (01450 860630). Self-Catering, sleep 2-4. Four detached timber cottages each with enclosed gardens. Secluded location with stunning scenery on the edge of Wauchope forest. All dogs welcome. [🐕]
e-mail: wauchope@btinternet.com website: www.wauchopecottages.co.uk

Jedburgh

Small town on Jed water, 10 miles north-east of Hawick. Ruins of abbey founded in 1138.

GLENBANK HOUSE HOTEL, CASTLEGATE, JEDBURGH TD8 6BD (01835 862258). Set in its own grounds with ample private parking and beer garden. Licensed restaurant and bar. All rooms en suite with TV. Open to non-residents. Reduced rates for children. [🐕]
e-mail: enquiries@glenbankhotel.co.uk website: www.glenbankhotel.co.uk

ALAN & CHRISTINE SWANSTON, FERNIEHIRST MILL LODGE, JEDBURGH TD8 6PQ (01835 863279). A chalet style guest house set in grounds of 25 acres. All rooms en suite with tea/coffee making facilities. Licensed for residents. Well behaved pets (including horses) welcome by arrangement. VisitScotland ★, AA ★★. [🐕]
e-mail: ferniehirstmill@aol.com website: www.ferniehirstmill.co.uk

Kelso

Market town 18 miles north-west of Hawick and 20 miles south-west of Berwick-upon-Tweed.

WESTWOOD HOUSE, OVERLOOKING SCOTLAND'S FAMOUS RIVER TWEED. Enclosed and secluded riverside cottage with walled gardens and own private island. Sleeps 2-8 persons plus child, from £325 per week. 2 person discounts. For brochure contact: DEBBIE CRAWFORD, PIPPIN HEATH FARM, HOLT, NORFOLK NR25 6SS (07788 134832). [🐕]

Selkirk

Town on hill above Ettrick Water, 9 miles north of Hawick.

GORDON ARMS HOTEL, YARROW VALLEY, SELKIRK TD7 5LE. (01750 82222). Situated in the picturesque Yarrow Valley, the Gordon Arms Hotel offers warm, friendly hospitality, good food, a great atmosphere, real ale and accommodation to suit all tastes. [🐕]
e-mail: info@thegordonarms.com website: www.thegordonarms.com

West Linton

Village on east side of Pentland hills, 7 miles south-west of Penicuick. Edinburgh 18 miles.

MRS C. M. KILPATRICK, SLIPPERFIELD HOUSE, WEST LINTON EH46 7AA (Tel & Fax: 01968 660401). Two well-equipped converted cottages set in 100 acres of lochs and woodlands. Sleep 4/6. Available all year. Central Heating. Car essential. Self Catering. Ideal, dog-friendly location. STB ★★★/★★★★ [🐕]
e-mail: cottages@slipperfield.com website: www.slipperfield.com

Please note

All the information in this book is given in good faith in the belief that it is correct. However, the publishers cannot guarantee the facts given in these pages, neither are they responsible for changes in policy, ownership or terms that may take place after the date of going to press. Readers should always satisfy themselves that the facilities they require are available and that the terms, if quoted, still apply.

Castle Douglas, Dalbeattie, Drummore, Dumfries, Gatehouse of Fleet, Moffat

Working organic sheep farm. Family-run 18th century farmhouse. All bedrooms en suite. Billiard room/honesty bar. Lovely oak-panelled dining room offering Cordon Bleu cooking using local produce such as venison, pheasant and salmon. Trout fishing, walking, and golfing available.

Tel & Fax: 01556 650233 • Mrs C. Pickup, Craigadam, Castle Douglas DG7 3HU

www.craigadam.com Winner Macallan Taste of Scotland

STB ★★★★ B&B • **RAC** ◆◆◆◆◆ & Little Gem Award • **AA** ◆◆◆◆◆ Premier Award

No. 4 Silver Birches Close, Dalbeattie DG5 4UQ • Tel: 01556 504030

Newly built house, furnished to a high standard and situated adjacent to the forest for walking and mountain biking . Golf, horse riding and river fishing available nearby; Sandyhills beach 7 miles. Stay for a short break and enjoy all that bonnie Galloway has to offer - visit Castle Douglas or Kirkcudbright, the varied coastline or the lovely rolling hills. Secure cycle storage. Well behaved dogs welcome (bring own bedding).

Quote Ref: S101ST • e-mail: mary.watt@gmthomsoncd.co.uk

Mull of Galloway ••••••• Drummore

Harbour Row Cottages. A few short steps from the beach. STB 3/4-Star cottages. Tranquil and unspoiled village. Logan Botanical Gardens, golf, fishing, birdwatching nearby. Unrestricted beaches. £15 per animal. Contact SALLY COLMAN:

01776 840631 •••••••• www.harbourrow.co.uk

AE FOREST COTTAGES • Modern accommodation in old stone buildings on a traditional farm, overlooking a peaceful valley, surrounded by hills and forests. Beautiful views, plentiful wildlife and endless paths on the doorstep.

A great country retreat between Dumfries, Moffat and Thornhill.

David & Gill Stewart, GUBHILL FARM, Dumfries DG1 1RL (01387 860648)

E-mail: gill@gubhill.co.uk STB ★★★ *SELF CATERING* **CATEGORY ONE DISABILITY**

Spacious, beautiful farmhouse and three charming, cosy cottages set amid stunning Scottish scenery near beaches (dogs allowed), hills, forests, castles, gardens and golf course. Loch and river fishing with tuition, free tennis, wonderful walking, cycling and riding country.

Sleep 2-12 • Rates £216-£1278 • Short breaks available.

Pets, including horses, welcome.

info@ruskoholidays.co.uk • www.ruskoholidays.co.uk

Scottish Tourist Board ★★ Self Catering • Scottish Tourist Board ★★★★ Self Catering • Green Tourism Silver • Walkers Welcome • Cyclists Welcome

Rusko Holidays

Gatehouse of Fleet, Castle Douglas DG7 2BS

Tel: 01557 814215

BARNHILL SPRINGS Country Guest House, Moffat DG10 9QS

Early Victorian country house overlooking some of the finest views of Upper Annandale. Comfortable accommodation, residents' lounge with open fire. Ideal centre for touring South-West Scotland and the Borders, or for an overnight stop. Situated on the Southern Upland Way half-a-mile from A74/M74 Moffat Junction. Pets free of charge. Bed & Breakfast from £27; Evening Meal (optional) from £18. *STB ★★ Guest House AA ◆◆◆*

Readers are requested to mention this guidebook when making enquiries about accommodation.

A warm welcome is offered at the award-winning **ANNANDALE ARMS HOTEL** *to dogs with well-mannered and house-trained owners. There are all the comforts and facilities that owners enjoy such as an excellent restaurant and a relaxing panelled bar. The Hotel has a large private parking area at the rear full of the most exquisite sniffs. £95 per room for dogs travelling with two owners; £50 per room for dogs travelling with one owner. STB ★★★ Hotel*
High Street, Moffat DG10 9HF • Tel: 01683 220013 • Fax: 01683 221395
www.annandalearmshotel.co.uk • pw@annandalearmshotel.co.uk

Hope Cottage, Thornhill, Dumfriesshire DG3 5AZ

Pretty stone cottage in the peaceful conservation village of Durisdeer. Well-equipped self-catering cottage with large secluded garden. Sleeps 6. Towels, linen, heating and electricity included. Pets Welcome.
For brochure telephone: Mrs S Stannett • 01848 331510
Fax: 01848 331810• e-mail: a.stann@btinternet.com
www.hopecottage.co.uk

CRAIGLEMINE COTTAGE B&B Our rural location makes this a wonderful place to unwind. Ideal for touring; your dog will love the nearby beaches. Evening meal available.
MIKE AND HELEN ALEXANDER, CRAIGLEMINE COTTAGE B&B, GLASSERTON, NEAR WHITHORN DG8 8NE (01988 500594)
e-mail: cottage@fireflyuk.net • www.startravel.fireflyinternet.co.uk

HILLCREST HOUSE **Maidland Place, Wigtown DG8 9EU**
Tel: 01988 402018

Beautiful Victorian character villa set on edge of national book town. Fabulous views over nature reserve. Six bedrooms, residents' lounge. Evening meals using fresh local produce.
e-mail: info@hillcrest-wigtown.co.uk • www.hillcrest-wigtown.co.uk

Castle Douglas

Old market town at the northern end of Carlingwalk Loch, good touring centre for Galloway

MRS CELIA PICKUP, "CRAIGADAM", CASTLE DOUGLAS DG7 3HU (Tel & Fax: 01556 650233). Family-run 18th century famhouse. All bedrooms en suite. Billiard room/honesty bar. Lovely oak-panelled dining room offering Cordon Bleu cooking using local produce such as venison, pheasant and salmon. Trout fishing, walking and golfing available. STB ★★★★ B&B, RAC ◆◆◆◆◆ & Little Gem Award, AA ◆◆◆◆◆ Premier Collection. [🐕]
website: www.craigadam.com

Dalbeattie

Small town 13 miles south west of Dumfries.

NO. 4 SILVER BIRCHES CLOSE, DALBEATTIE DG5 4UQ. New build house furnished to a high standard. Golf, horse riding and river fishing available nearby. Sandyhills beach 7 miles. Well behaved dogs welcome. Tel: 01556 504030, Quote S101ST. [Pets £15 per week]
e-mail: mary.watt@gmthomsoncd.co.uk

Drummore

Coastal location, 4 miles north of Mull of Galloway.

MULL OF GALLOWAY, DRUMMORE. A few short steps from the beach. STB 3/4-Star cottages. Tranquil and unspoiled village. Logan Botanical Gardens, golf, fishing, birdwatching nearby. Unrestricted beaches. £15 per animal. ASSC. Contact SALLY COLMAN (01776 840631).
website: www.harbourrow.co.uk

Dumfries

County town of Dumfries-shire and a former seaport. Dumfries contains many interesting buildings including an 18th century windmill containing a camera obscura. Robert Burns lived in the town before his death in 1796.

DAVID & GILL STEWART, AE FOREST COTTAGES, GUBHILL FARM, DUMFRIES DG1 1RL (01387 860648). Modern accommodation in old stone buildings on a traditional farm, overlooking a peaceful valley. Beautiful views, plentiful wildlife and endless paths on the doorstep. Between Dumfries, Moffat and Thornhill. STB ★★★ SELF CATERING, CATEGORY ONE DISABILITY. []
e-mail: gill@gubhill.co.uk

Gatehouse of Fleet

Small town near mouth of Water of Fleet, 6 miles north-west of Kirkcudbright

RUSKO HOLIDAYS, GATEHOUSE OF FLEET, CASTLE DOUGLAS DG7 2BS (01557 814215). Spacious farmhouse and three charming, cosy cottages near beaches, hills, gardens, castles and golf course. Walking, fishing, tennis. Pets, including horses, welcome. Sleep 2-12. Rates £216-£1278. STB ★★ to ★★★★ Self-Catering. Disabled Awards. [First pet free, second pet £20.00 per week]
e-mail: info@ruskoholidays.co.uk website: www.ruskoholidays.co.uk

Moffat

At head of lovely Annandale, grand mountain scenery. Good centre for rambling, climbing, angling and golf. The 'Devil's Beef Tub' is 5 miles, Edinburgh 52, Peebles 33, Dumfries 21.

BARNHILL SPRINGS COUNTRY GUEST HOUSE, MOFFAT DG10 9QS (01683 220580). Early Victorian country house overlooking some of the finest views of Upper Annandale. Comfortable accommodation, residents' lounge with open fire. Situated on the Southern Upland Way half-a-mile from A74/M74 Moffat Junction. Pets free of charge. Bed & Breakfast from £27; Evening Meal (optional) from £18. STB ★★ Guest House. AA ◆◆◆. [pw!]

ANNANDALE ARMS HOTEL, HIGH STREET, MOFFAT DG1O 9HF (01683 220013; Fax: 01683 221395). A warm welcome is offered at the Annandale Arms to dogs with well-mannered and house-trained owners. Excellent restaurant and a relaxing panelled bar. Large private parking area. £95 per room for two; £50 per room for one. STB ★★★ [pw!]
e-mail: pw@annandalearmshotel.co.uk website: www.annandalearmshotel.co.uk

Thornhill

Small town on River Nith 13 miles north-west of Dumfries. Site of Roman signal station lies to the south.

MRS S. STANNETT, HOPE COTTAGE, EAST CARRONHILL, THORNHILL, DUMFRIESSHIRE DG3 5AZ (01848 331510; Fax: 01848 331810). Pretty stone cottage in the peaceful conservation village of Durisdeer. Well-equipped self-catering cottage with large secluded garden. Sleeps 6. Towels, linen, heating and electricity included. Self-catering. Phone for brochure. STB ★★★★ []
e-mail: a.stann@btinternet.com website: www.hopecottage.co.uk

Whithorn (near)

Small town 9 miles south of Wigtown.

MIKE AND HELEN ALEXANDER, CRAIGLEMINE COTTAGE B&B, GLASSERTON, NEAR WHITHORN DG8 8NE (01988 500594). Our rural location makes this a wonderful place to unwind. Ideal for touring, your dog will love the nearby beaches. Evening meal available. STB ★★ []
e-mail: cottage@fireflyuk.net website: www.startravel.fireflyinternet.co.uk

Wigtown

Small town on hill above River Cree estuary.

HILLCREST HOUSE, MAIDLAND PLACE, WIGTOWN DG8 9EU (01988 402018). Beautiful character Victorian villa set on edge of national book town. Fabulous views over nature reserve. Six bedrooms, residents' lounge. Evening meals using fresh local produce. [Pets free in kennels, £1 per night indoors]
e-mail: info@hillcrest-wigtown.co.uk website: www.hillcrest-wigtown.co.uk

DUNBARTONSHIRE

Gartocharn/Loch Lomond

Mardella Farmhouse *Bed & Breakfast*
Old School Road, Gartocharn, Dunbartonshire G83 8SD
This peaceful, scenic location on a quiet country lane in magnificent countryside is ideal for you and your pets. Excellent place for walking and touring.
Tel: 01389 830428

Gartocharn/Loch Lomond

Village 4 miles east of Balloch, near Loch Lomond.

ANGUS & SALLY MACDONELL, MARDELLA FARMHOUSE, OLD SCHOOL ROAD, GARTOCHARN, DUNBARTONSHIRE G83 8SD (01389 830428). This peaceful, scenic location on a quiet country lane in magnificent countryside is ideal for you and your pets. Excellent place for walking and touring. [🐕]

EDINBURGH & LOTHIANS

Rosewell

Hunter Holiday Cottages **Thornton Farm, Rosewell, Edinburgh EH24 9EF**
A range of cottages in beautiful countryside only eight miles from Edinburgh City Centre. Recently renovated, with modern facilities and sleep four to ten plus. The ideal base for the perfect Scottish holiday with easy access to Scotland's capital and the major routes to the rest of Scotland. For more information visit our website.
Contact Margot Crichton. Telephone for availability for Short Breaks
Tel: 0131-448 0888 • Fax: 0131-440 2082 • e-mail: info@edinburghcottages.com • www.edinburghcottages.com

Rosewell

Village 4 miles south west of Dalkeith.

HUNTER HOLIDAY COTTAGES, THORNTON FARM, ROSEWELL, EDINBURGH EH24 9EF (0131 448 0888; Fax: 0131 440 2082). A range of cottages in beautiful countryside only eight miles from Edinburgh city centre. Recently renovated, with modern facilities sleeping four to ten plus. Contact MARGOT CRICHTON.
e-mail: info@edinburghcottages.com website: www.edinburghcottages.com

Symbols

- 🐕 Indicates that pets are welcome free of charge.
- £ Indicates that a charge is made for pets: nightly or weekly.
- **pw!** Shows some special provision for pets; exercise facility, feeding or accommodation arrangement.
- ⌂ Indicates separate pets accommodation.

Lower Largo, St Andrews

Lower Largo

Village on the bay, 2 miles NE of Leven. Birth place of Alexander Selkirk of Robinson Crusoe fame.

THE CRUSOE HOTEL, MAIN STREET, LOWER LARGO, NEAR ST ANDREWS KY8 6BT. (01333 320759; Fax: 01333 320865). Old-world ambience with fine harbour views. En suite accommodation, outstanding cuisine, free house. Excellent centre for sailing, golf, birdwatching, wind surfing, coastal walks. STB ★★★ Hotel. [🐕]
email: relax@crusoehotel.co.uk website: www.crusoehotel.co.uk

St Andrews

Home of golf - British Golf Museum has memorabilia dating back to the origins of the game. Remains of castle and cathedral. Sealife Centre and beach Leisure Centre. Excellent sands. Ideal base for exploring the picturesque East Neuk.

MR & MRS PATRICK WEDDERBURN, ST ANDREWS COUNTRY COTTAGES, MOUNTQUHANIE ESTATE, FREEPOST, CUPAR KY15 4BR (01382 330318; Fax: 01382 330480). Quality self-catering houses and cottages in St Andrews and on a tranquil Country Estate. Central heating, TV, phone. Enclosed gardens. STB ★★★ to ★★★★★ Self Catering. [pw! Dogs £15 per week, Cats F.O.C.].
e-mail: enquiries@standrews-cottages.com website: www.standrews-cottages.com

Aultbea, Aviemore, Beauly, Boat of Garten

COVE VIEW 36 Mellon Charles, Aultbea IV22 2JL

Wester Ross is ideal for a quiet restful holiday. Detached chalet, available all year, has two small bedrooms, sitting area with mini kitchen, bathroom with shower. Ideal for two persons. Terms from £200 to £250 per week. Your dog is welcome free. Contact Mrs P. MacRae. **Tel: 01445 731351**

Cairngorm Highland Bungalows

Glen Einich, 29 Grampian View, Aviemore, Inverness-shire PH22 1TF

Tel: 01479 810653 • Fax: 01479 810262

e-mail: linda.murray@virgin.net
www.cairngorm-bungalows.co.uk

Scottish Tourist Board ★★★ Self Catering

Beautifully furnished and well-equipped bungalows ranging from one to four bedrooms. All have colour TV, video, DVD, microwave, cooker, washer-dryer, fridge and patio furniture. Some have log fires. Leisure facilities nearby include golf, fishing on the River Spey, swimming, sauna, jacuzzi, tennis, skating and skiing. Within walking distance of Aviemore. Ideal touring base. Children and pets welcome. Phone for colour brochure. Open all year.

Scottish Tourist Board ★★★★ Self Catering

For the very best in Highland Holidays

ASSC

AVIEMORE PINE BANK CHALETS

Enjoy the stunning beauty of the Highlands and the Cairngorm Mountains from our choice of superbly appointed log cabins and chalets. Great location – close to Spey River. Peaceful and relaxing setting. Friendly service staff, selected Sky TV, video, barbecue, mountain bikes. Many activities available. Leisure pool and restaurants nearby. Large choice of style and price.

5 log cabins, 6 chalets, 2 Flats, sleeping up to 6
Open all year £375-£699 per week • Pets Welcome

Dalfaber Road, Aviemore, Inverness-shire PH22 1PX
Tel: 01479 810000
e-mail: pinebankchallets@btopenworld.com
website: www.pinebankchalets.co.uk

Scottish Tourist Board ★★★ Self Catering · Scottish Tourist Board ★★★★ Self Catering

CULLIGRAN COTTAGES - GLEN STRATHFARRAR

Pure magic! Come for a spell in a chalet or cottage and this glen will cast one over you! Nature Reserve with native woodlands and wildlife. Fifteen miles of private road. Bikes for hire. Fly fishing (salmon and trout) on the rivers Farrar and Glass. Watch the wild deer from your window. Feed the farm deer. Brochure. Open March - November, prices from £179 - £479

FRANK & JULIET SPENCER-NAIRN : STRUY : NEAR BEAULY : INVERNESS-SHIRE : IV4 7JX
Tel/Fax: 01463 761285 : e-mail:info@culligrancottages.co.uk www.culligrancottages.co.uk

Self-catering Lodge, Boat of Garten

Unique lodge in woodland setting, yet minutes from local amenities. Fully equipped, superb log-burning fire. Perfect for an active or a relaxing break, with woodland walks and cycle tracks nearby. Pets welcome. Sleeps 7.

www.treehouselodge.co.uk • Tel: Anne Mather 0131-337 7167
e-mail: fbg@treehouselodge.plus.com

Readers are requested to mention this FHG publication when seeking accommodation

The Pines COUNTRY GUESTHOUSE

DUTHIL, CARRBRIDGE PH23 3ND • 01479 841220

Relax and enjoy our Highland hospitality, woodland setting; all rooms en suite. Traditional or vegetarian home cooking. B&B from £23 daily; DB&B from £220 weekly. Children and pets welcome.

www.thepines-duthil.co.uk

Privately owned and operated 20-bedroom Country House Hotel with miles of forest walks, many log fires, and great food.

Both you and your dog are made to feel most welcome.

Coul House Hotel, Contin, By Strathpeffer Ross-shire IV14 9ES

Tel: 01997 421487 • Fax: 01997 421945

e-mail: stay@coulhousehotel.com • www.coulhousehotel.com

Scottish Tourist Board ★★ HOTEL

Ideally situated in 4.5 acres of grounds and gardens, a few minutes' walk from the famous Royal Dornoch Golf Course.

- 29 bedrooms, all en suite, with colour TV and tea/coffee making.
- A la carte Restaurant • Bar meals available
- Golf on Royal Dornoch and other local courses can be arranged, as well as loch and river fishing.
- Children and dogs welcome.

BURGHFIELD HOUSE HOTEL

THE BURGHFIELD HOUSE HOTEL, DORNOCH IV25 3HN

TEL: 01862 810212 • FAX: 01862 810404

burghfield@cali.co.uk • www.burghfieldhouse.com

GLENURQUHART LODGES Situated between Loch Ness and Glen Affric in a spectacular setting ideal for walking, touring or just relaxing in this tranquil location. Four spacious chalets all fully equipped for six people, set in wooded grounds. Owner's hotel adjacent where guests are most welcome in the restaurant and bar. **Near Drumnadrochit, Inverness IV3 6TJ • Tel: 01456 476234 • Fax: 01456 476286**

www.glenurquhart-lodges.co.uk • e-mail: carol@glenurquhartlodges.co.uk

Fort William, Inverness-shire PH33 6RW

Tel: (01397) 702341 • Fax: (01397) 706174

www.clanmacduff.co.uk

Small, well behaved pets are always welcome at the Clan MacDuff. This family-run hotel overlooks Loch Linnhe, two miles south of Fort William. Situated in its own grounds in a quiet and peaceful location with a large car park, the hotel is in an excellent location for touring and experiencing the rugged mountains and enchanting coastline of the West Highlands. All bedrooms have colour TV, hair dryer and hospitality tray, all with private facilities. The hotel offers great value hospitality.

Scottish Tourist Board ★★★ HOTEL

Bed and Breakfast in an en suite room from £26.00 per person per night.
Three nights Dinner, Bed & Breakfast from £114.00 • Spring and Autumn Special Offer.
Please phone or write for our colour brochure & tariff.

Please mention PETS WELCOME! when making enquiries about accommodation featured in these pages

An ideal centre from which to explore Lochaber, the Ardnamurchan Peninsula and Glencoe. Traditional home cooking goes hand in hand with homely service, comfortable en suite accommodation and private facilities. The inn stands on the shores of beautiful Loch Linnhe at Corran Ferry, 8 miles south of Fort William.

B&B from £30pppn • Children and pets welcome!

Onich, Fort William, Inverness-shire PH33 6SE

Tel: 01855 821235

www.corraninn.co.uk

e-mail: info@corraninn.co.uk

• TIGH-A-PHUIRT • LOCHYSIDE, FORT WILLIAM PH33 7NX

Two self-catering holiday cottages beside the River Lochy, with beautiful views of the river, Ben Nevis and Aonach Mor. Built to the highest standards with all modern furnishings and equipment; double-glazed and fully insulated. Electric central heating (included in tariff). No smoking. Two pets welcome, more by arrangement. **Tel: 01397 704610**

Great Glen Holidays

Torlundy, Fort William PH33 6SW

Tel/Fax: 01397 703015

Eight spacious, 2-bedroom, timber chalets situated in woodland with spectacular mountain scenery. On working Highland farm. Riding, fishing and walking on farm. Ideal for family holidays, excellent base for touring; four miles from town. Sleep 4-6. Prices from £250 to £510 per week.

e-mail: info@fortwilliam-chalets.co.uk • www.fortwilliam-chalets.co.uk

John & Hilary would like to welcome you to the lovely Loch Leven Hotel, a small, informal, family-run hotel with excellent food and an ideal base to explore this beautiful region. Enjoy the spectacular scenery from the Lochview Restaurant, garden and new decking, or toast yourself by the log fire in the Public Bar, with its inexpensive menu and wonderful selection of malts. Children and pets always welcome. B&B from £40pp with discounts for Short Breaks.

Old Ferry Road, North Ballachulish, Near Fort William PH33 6SA • Tel: 01855 821236
Fax: 01855 821550 • e-mail: reception@lochlevenhotel.co.uk • www.lochlevenhotel.co.uk

Linnhe LOCHSIDE HOLIDAYS

Corpach, Fort William, Inverness-shire PH33 7NL

Almost a botanical garden, Linnhe is unique and one of the most beautiful Lochside parks in Britain. Close to Ben Nevis and Fort William. Excellent facilities including licensed shop, bakery, playgrounds, private beach and free fishing. Pets welcome.

Luxury Holiday Caravans (from £210 per week) • Caravans from £110
Tent & Touring Pitches also available. • Open 31st March-31st October • Colour Brochure

Tel: 01397 772376 • Fax: 01397 772007

www.linnhe-lochside-holidays.co.uk • e-mail: relax@linnhe-lochside-holidays.co.uk

Tel/Fax: 01855 821287
e-mail: reception@inchreecentre.co.uk
www.inchreecentre.co.uk

Onich, Near Fort William PH33 6SE

Eight self-catering chalets situated between Ben Nevis and Glencoe in peaceful and spacious grounds. Fully refurbished within, 4 to 6 berth in size. Each chalet has panoramic mountain and loch views. Enjoy forest and waterfall walks from the door. On-site pub and restaurant serving good food and real ales. Short-stay breaks available most of the year. Discount for couples.

TIGH NA SGIATH COUNTRY HOUSE HOTEL,
Dulnain Bridge, Near Grantown-on-Spey PH26 3PA

Former home of the Lipton Tea Family, this elegant mansion house is set in its own fabulous grounds near Grantown-on-Spey. Romantic open log fires, excellent Scottish cuisine using local and organic produce. Seafood and Highland Game feature daily. Vegetarian/gluten free diets catered for. Pets Welcome.

01479 851345 • e-mail: iain@tigh-na-sgiath.co.uk • www.tigh-na-sgiath.co.uk

INVERGARRY HOTEL

INVERGARRY, INVERNESS-SHIRE PH35 4HJ

Set in a small village amidst the beautiful scenery of the Scottish Highlands, The Invergarry Hotel has ten comfortable en suite rooms in a distinctive Victorian building. The restaurant features fine Scottish produce and the well-stocked bar has a range of over 30 malts.

Telephone: 01809 501206 • Fax: 01809 501400
e-mail: info@invergarryhotel.co.uk • website: www.invergarryhotel.co.uk

Spectacular location by Loch Ness at the heart of the Highlands of Scotland. Comfortable, well equipped self catering chalets in spacious grounds, either in woodland or alongside enchanting River Moriston Falls and bridges. Only a few minutes' walk to the village and amenities. Excellent base to explore, hill walk, fish, cycle and much more. Pets welcome in some chalets. Launderette and children's games areas on site.

Glenmoriston, Highlands IV63 7YF
Tel: 01320 351254 • Fax: 01320 351343
www.invermoriston-holidays.com
e-mail: ihc@ipw.com

Scottish Tourist Board ★★★ Guest House

B&B in 1827 Telford Manse and two timber s/c cottages in superb rural location. Ideal for many outdoor activities and good touring base. Dogs and children welcome.

NICK & PATSY THOMPSON, INSH HOUSE GUESTHOUSE AND SELF-CATERING COTTAGES, KINCRAIG, NEAR KINGUSSIE PH21 1NU • Tel: 01540 651377)
www.kincraig.com/inshhouse • e-mail: inshhouse@btinternet.com

B&B in Cairngorms National Park, central for outdoor activities, places of historic interest and scenic day tours in idyllic Spey Valley location. Well behaved dogs welcome in our unique self-contained suite (one double room, one twin room, lounge, bathroom).
Also large double room with en suite on upper level but no dogs allowed.

Rowan House, Newtonmore Road, Kingussie, Inverness-shire PH21 IHD
Tel: 01540 662153 • www.rowanhousescotland.com
e-mail: rowanhouse.scotland@btopenworld.com

Scottish Tourist Board ★★★★ B&B

COLUMBA HOUSE
HOTEL & GARDEN RESTAURANT

In an area of oustanding natural beauty. An Oasis amidst the magnificent scenery, stunning landscapes and tranquillity, in the foothills of snow-capped peaks of the Cairngorm and Monadhliath mountains. Quiet Highland retreat, nestling among tall Scots Pines and Beech trees, in a secluded, landscaped, walled garden with patio for summer time dining. Offering the highest standards of welcoming hospitality, accommodation and customer care, friendly atmosphere. Rooms with their own front doors, perfect for doggie holidays. Candlelit Garden Restaurant, renowned for excellent cuisine and attentive service. Homely, enchanting lounge and cosy bar, offering modern facilities while retaining their original charm. Wireless internet connection and nearby Leisure Club free.

Bed and Breakfast from £35 • STB ★★★ Small Hotel
Manse Road, Kingussie PH21 1JF • Tel: 01540 661402
e-mail: myra@columbahousehotel.com • www.columbahousehotel.com

An inviting and friendly family-run hotel situated in one of the most stunning areas on the North West coast of Scotland, with views of open seas, surrounding majestic hills and unforgettable sunsets. Supremely comfortable guest rooms from £30 per person for bed & breakfast.

Kinlochbervie, by Lairg, Sutherland IV27 4RP
Tel: 01971 521275 • e-mail: klbhotel@aol.com
Fax: 01971 521438 • www.kinlochberviehotel.com

WILDERNESS COTTAGES, LOCH NESS, WEST COAST & PERTHSHIRE

Open all year • Sleep 2-16 • Pets welcome

ASSC

Escape to the country with Wilderness Cottages and leave behind the hectic lifestyle you lead today. Visit any time of the year, enjoy a romantic winter break, snuggled up by the log fire, or during the summer and experience the natural beauty of Scotland. We have a small selection of quality self catering cottages from rustic appeal to 5-star luxury. Log fires, sea views, countryside to seashore we can provide a cottage to suit you. Walking, Munro bagging, cyclings, golfing, birdwatching, fishing or just chilling, whatever your pastime visit a Wilderness Cottage for your perfect retreat. Pets with responsible owners are very welcome..

Scottish Tourist Board ★★★ Self Catering · Scottish Tourist Board ★★★★ Self Catering · Scottish Tourist Board ★★★★★ Self Catering

CONTACT: Gordon & Corinne Roberts, Roebuck Cottage, Errogie, Stratherrick, Inverness-shire IV2 6UH • TEL 01456 486358
e-mail: corinne@wildernesscottages.co.uk • www.wildernesscottages.co.uk

• LOCH NESS •

Exceptional riverside lodges close to the spectacular Loch Ness. Mountains, lochs, waterfalls and wildlife abound.

Charming riverside lodges with private lawns, log fires and mountain views. Lodges range from 1, 2 & 3 bedrooms, sleeping from 2 to 8 people. All lodges are non-smoking and enjoy magnificent views. Quiet location with excellent walks from your lodge. Heating, linen and towels included. Pets welcome. Free fishing. Country pub and restaurant nearby. Short breaks welcome. Colour brochure and website.

Tel: 01456 486 373 • Fax: 01456 486 371
e-mail: info@wildsidelodges.com • web: www.wildsidelodges.com

ASSC · Scottish Tourist Board ★★★★ Self Catering

Nethy Bridge, Highlands • Balnagowan Mill and Woodlark

Comfortable, modern 3 bedroom cottages in secluded locations in the Cairngorms National Park with extensive network of woodland and riverside walks on the doorstep, which is ideal for pets. Furnished to a high standard with full central heating. £250 - £500 per week inclusive of electricity and bed linen.

Contact Paula Fraser, 33 Argyle Grove, Dunblane, Perthshire FK15 9DT
Tel: 01786 824957 email: paulajfraser@aol.com

MONDHUIE CHALETS & B&B, NETHY BRIDGE, INVERNESS-SHIRE PH25 3DF • Tel & Fax: 01479 821062

Situated in the country between Aviemore and Grantown-on-Spey, two comfortable, self-catering chalets, or you can have Dinner, B&B in the house. A warm welcome awaits you. Pets welcome. Red squirrels seen daily.

e-mail: david@mondhuie.com • www.mondhuie.com

Crubenbeg Highland Holiday Cottages

Newtonmore, Highlands PH20 1BE

Scottish Tourist Board ★★★★ Self Catering

Luxury 4 Star country cottages in idyllic surroundings in the Cairngorms National Park as well as 'Monarch of the Glen' country. Lots of lovely walks, loads of sporting activities or simply relax and spot the wildlife around you. PETS WELCOME. Prices start at £255 per week for a one bedroom cottage.

Tel: 01540 673566
E-mail: enquiry@crubenbeg.com • www.crubenbeg.com

FREE or REDUCED RATE entry to Holiday Visits and Attractions
– see our READERS' OFFER VOUCHERS on pages 407-423

Strathlinnhe Holiday Homes

Onich, near Fort William PH33 6SD

Cottages and static caravans on 15 acre croft running down to the shores of Loch Linnhe, midway between Glencoe and Ben Nevis. Views across the loch to Glencoe and the Ardnamurchan Hills. Near amenities, owner maintained.

Tel: 01855 821 264

Crofter's Cottages

Mr Alexander Urquhart

15 Croft, Poolewe, Ross-shire IV22 2JY
Tel: 01445 781268

Two traditional cottages sleeping 4 and 5 persons. Situated in a scenic and tranquil area, ideal for a "get away from it all" holiday. Crofters Cottages are comfortably furnished, some with antiques and all the essential modern gadgets of today, such as auto-washer/dryer, microwave, fridge, bath and shower. Poolewe is a good base to tour the North West Highlands or for those who enjoy walking, fishing, climbing, golf or maybe just a stroll along one of the many sandy beaches. There are also indoor activities to be enjoyed such as the heated pool and leisure and fitness areas. Close by lie the famous Inverewe Gardens. Pets made welcome.

Low season from £120 – £230 • High season from £250 – £490
Midweek and short breaks available from November – March
e-mail: crofterscottages@btopenworld.com
www.crofterscottages.co.uk

Gull Cottage • The Barn •

Rhiconich, Sutherland

Scottish Tourist Board ★★★ Self Catering

Situated on the wild and unspoilt west coast of Scotland overlooking Loch Inchard, the last sea loch on the north west coast. Superb scenery with excellent walks on mountains, moors, and the many beaches in the area. High quality accommodation with full central heating. Gull Cottage sleeps 4, both bedrooms ensuite. The Barn sleeps 2. Pets welcome; secure dog run accessed from cottage.

All enquiries to: **Lynn and Graham, Gull Cottage, Achriesgill, Rhiconich, Lairg, Sutherland IV27 4RJ**
Telephone: 01971 521717

RHICONICH HOTEL

Rhiconich, Sutherland, N.W. Highlands IV27 4RN • Tel: 01971 521224 • Fax: 01971 521732
e-mail: rhiconichhotel@aol.com • website: www.rhiconichhotel.co.uk

STB ★★★

SHE'S YOUR BEST FRIEND, so why leave her at home, bring her to **RHICONICH HOTEL**, she'll be made equally as welcome as you will. A place where we put service, hospitality and really fresh food as a priority, but why don't you come and see for yourself? For further details contact Ray Fish.

ASSC

RIVERSIDE LODGES

Invergloy, Spean Bridge PH34 4DY • Tel: 01397 712684

The ultimate Highland location, set in 12 acres of grounds, just three uniquely designed lodges sleeping six comfortably. Private beach with free fishing, spectacular river gorge, specimen trees and plants. Ideal for all outdoor pursuits, or for just relaxing.

Scottish Tourist Board ★★★★ Self Catering

Tariff from £365-£675 per week - discounts for small parties/long stay. Proprietors: Steve & Marilyn Dennis. **Pets welcome • Linen included • Open all year**

e-mail: enquiries@riversidelodge.org.uk • www.riversidelodge.org.uk

Family-run hotel overlooking sandy beach • Magnificent views across Dornoch Firth • Watersports, golf close by • Regular live music • Children welcome • Horse riding available for experienced riders.

CALEDONIAN HOTEL, BEACH FRONT, PORTMAHOMACK, BY TAIN, ROSS-SHIRE IV20 IYS
01862 871345 • Fax: 01862 871757
e-mail: info@caleyhotel.co.uk • www.caleyhotel.co.uk

Skerray, Tongue, Sutherland KW14 7TH

Set in a secluded Highland glen by the stunning River Borgie lies Borgie Lodge, where mouthwatering food, fine wine, roaring log fires and a very warm welcome awaits after a day's fishing, hill walking, pony trekking or walking on the beach.Relax after dinner with a good malt and tales of salmon, trout and deer.

Tel: 01641 521 332
www.borgielodgehotel.co.uk
e-mail: info@borgielodgehotel.co.uk

WHITEBRIDGE HOTEL WHITEBRIDGE, SOUTH LOCH NESS IV2 6UN • 01456 486226 • Fax: 01456 486413

Peaceful location with magnificent mountain views and excellent walks. Friendly locals' bar with home-cooked food. 12 en suite rooms. B&B from £30pppn.

e-mail: info@whitebridgehotel.co.uk • www.whitebridgehotel.co.uk

Aultbea (Ross-shire)

Village on east shore of Loch Ewe, 5 miles north of Poolewe.

MRS P. MACRAE, COVE VIEW, 36 MELLON CHARLES, AULTBEA IV22 2JL (01445 731351). Wester Ross is ideal for hill walking or a quiet restful holiday. Detached chalet, available all year, with two small bedrooms, sitting area with mini kitchen, bathroom with shower. From £200 to £250 per week. A warm welcome awaits you and your pet. [🐕]

Aviemore (Inverness-shire)

Scotland's leading ski resort in Spey valley with superb sport and entertainment facilities. All-weather holiday centre.

CAIRNGORM HIGHLAND BUNGALOWS, GLEN EINICH, 29 GRAMPIAN VIEW, AVIEMORE, INVERNESS-SHIRE PH22 1TF. (01479 810653, Fax: 01479 810262). Well equipped bungalows ranging from one to four bedrooms. Open all year. Leisure facilities nearby. Children and pets welcome. Phone for brochure. [🐕]
e-mail: linda.murray@virgin.net website: www.cairngorm-bungalows.co.uk

PINE BANK CHALETS, DALFABER ROAD, AVIEMORE PH22 1PX (01479 810000). Cosy Log Cabins and 6 Quality Chalets, situated near the River Spey. Superb Family/Activity Holidays by mountains. Ideal skiing, walking, fishing and golf. Sky TV. Short breaks available. Pets welcome. Open all year. ASSC Member. Brochure. [Pets £20 per week.]
e-mail: pinebankchallets@btopenworld.com website: www.pinebankchalets.co.uk

Beauly (Inverness-shire)

Town at head of Beauly Firth, 11 miles west of inverness.

FRANK & JULIET SPENCER-NAIRN, CULLIGRAN COTTAGES, GLEN STRATHFARRAR, STRUY, NEAR BEAULY IV4 7JX (Tel & Fax: 01463 761285). Pure magic! Come for a spell in a chalet or cottage and this glen will cast one over on you! Nature Reserve with native woodlands and wildlife. Brochure. (March - November). Terms from £179 to £479. [🐕]
e-mail: info@culligrancottages.co.uk website: www.culligrancottages.co.uk

Boat of Garten (Inverness-shire)

Village on River Spey, 5 miles north east of Aviemore.

ANNE MATHER, THE TREEHOUSE SELF-CATERING LODGE, BOAT OF GARTEN (0131-337 7167). Unique lodge in woodland setting, yet minutes from local amenities. Fully equipped, superb log-burning fire. Sleeps 7. Perfect for an active or a relaxing break. Pets welcome. [🐕]
e-mail: fhg@treehouselodge.plus.com website: www.treehouselodge.co.uk

Carrbridge (Inverness-shire)

Village on River Dulnain, 7 miles north of Aviemore. Landmark Visitor Centre has exhibition explaining history of local environment.

THE PINES COUNTRY GUESTHOUSE, DUTHIL, CARRBRIDGE PH23 3ND (01479 841220). Relax and enjoy our Highland hospitality, woodland setting; all rooms en suite. Traditional or vegetarian home cooking. B&B from £23 daily; DB&B from £220 weekly. Children and pets welcome. AA ◆◆◆ [🐕]
website: www.thepines-duthil.co.uk

Contin (Ross-shire)

Village 2 miles south west of Strathpeffer.

COUL HOUSE HOTEL, CONTIN, BY STRATHPEFFER IV14 9ES (01997 421487; Fax: 01997 421945). Privately owned and operated 20-bedroom Country House Hotel with miles of forest walks, many log fires, and great food. Both you and your dog are made to feel most welcome.
e-mail: stay@coulhousehotel.com website: www.coulhousehotel.com

Dornoch (Sutherland)

Small town 10 miles east of Bonar Bridge.

THE BURGHFIELD HOUSE HOTEL, DORNOCH IV25 3HN (01862 810212; Fax: 01862 810404). In 4.5 acres of grounds, close to Royal Dornoch Golf Course. 29 en suite bedrooms; restaurant and bar meals. Golf and fishing can be arranged. Children and dogs welcome. STB ★★[🐕]
e-mail: burghfield@cali.co.uk website: www.burghfieldhouse.com

Drumnadrochit (Inverness-shire)

Village on the shores of Loch Ness with "Monster" visitor centre. Sonar scanning cruises.

CAROL HUGHES, GLENURQUHART LODGES, BY DRUMNADROCHIT IV3 6TJ (01456 476234; Fax: 01456 476286). Situated between Loch Ness and Glen Affric in a spectacular setting ideal for walking, touring or just relaxing in this tranquil location. Four spacious chalets all fully equipped for six people, set in wooded grounds. Owner's hotel adjacent where guests are most welcome in the restaurant and bar. [Pets £10 per week.]
e-mail: carol@glenurquhartlodges.co.uk website: www.glenurquhart-lodges.co.uk

Fort William (Inverness-shire)

Small town at foot of Ben Nevis, ideal base for climbers and hillwalkers.

THE CLAN MACDUFF HOTEL, FORT WILLIAM PH33 6RW (01397 702341; Fax: 01397 706174). This family-run hotel overlooks Loch Linnhe, two miles south of Fort William, excellent for touring the West Highlands. All rooms have TV, hair dryer and hospitality tray; all with private facilities. B&B from £26.00 pppn. Three nights DB&B from £114.00. STB ★★★ Hotel. Phone or write for colour brochure and tariff. [🐕]
website: www.clanmacduff.co.uk

THE CORRAN INN, ONICH, FORT WILLIAM PH33 6SE (01855 821235). Traditional home cooking goes hand in hand with homely service, comfortable accommodation and private facilities on the shores of beautiful Loch Linnhe. B&B from £30pppn. [🐕]
e-mail: info@corraninn.co.uk website: www.corraninn.co.uk

TIGH-A-PHUIRT, LOCHYSIDE, FORT WILLIAM PH33 7NX (01397 704610). Two self-catering holiday cottages beside the River Lochy, with beautiful views. All modern furnishings and equipment; fully double-glazed and fully insulated. Electric central heating incl. No smoking. Two pets welcome, more by arrangement. STB ★★★★ Self Catering. [🐕]

GREAT GLEN HOLIDAYS, TORLUNDY, FORT WILLIAM PH33 6SW (Tel/Fax: 01397 703015). Sleep 4-6. Eight spacious, two-bedroom, timber chalets on working Highland farm. Riding, fishing and walking on farm. Ideal for family holidays, excellent touring base.
e-mail: info@fortwilliam-chalets.co.uk website: www.fortwilliam-chalets.co.uk

LOCH LEVEN HOTEL, OLD FERRY ROAD, NORTH BALLACHULISH, NEAR FORT WILLIAM PH33 6SA (01855 821236; Fax: 01855 821550). En suite rooms with lovely views. Meals using freshly prepared Scottish produce. Secluded garden. Safe, private parking. Extensive grounds. Great walks. [pw! 🐕]
e-mail: reception@lochlevenhotel.co.uk website: www.lochlevenhotel.co.uk

LINNHE LOCHSIDE HOLIDAYS, CORPACH, FORT WILLIAM PH33 7NL (01397 772376; Fax: 01397 772007). Linnhe is unique and one of the most beautiful lochside parks in Britain. Close to Ben Nevis and Fort William. Excellent facilities. Pets welcome. Open 31 March - 31 October. Colour brochure. (Pets £5 per night, £25 per week).
e-mail: relax@linnhe-lochside-holidays.co.uk website: www.linnhe-lochside-holidays.co.uk

Glencoe (Inverness-shire)

Valley of River Coe, running west to Loch Leven, 3 miles east of Ballachulish. Site of notorious massacre in 1692.

INCHREE CENTRE, NEAR FORT WILLIAM PH33 6SE (Tel & Fax: 01855 821287). Between Ben Nevis and Glencoe. 8 self-catering chalets, 4 or 6 berth. Pub and Restaurant on site. Discount for couples. Short-stay breaks available most of the year. [Pets £2.50 per night, £15 per week]
e-mail: reception@inchreecentre.co.uk website: www.inchreecentre.co.uk

Grantown-on-Spey (Inverness-shire)

Market town and resort 19 miles south of Forres.

TIGH NA SGIATH COUNTRY HOUSE HOTEL, DULNAIN BRIDGE, NEAR GRANTOWN-ON-SPEY PH26 3PA (01479 851345). Former home of the Lipton Tea Family, this elegant mansion house is set in it's own fabulous grounds. Romantic open log fires, excellent Scottish cuisine using local and organic produce. Good Food of Scotland 2005, STB ★★★ Hotel. [Pets £4 per night]
e-mail: iain@tigh-na-sgiath.co.uk website: www.tigh-na-sgiath.co.uk

Invergarry (Inverness-shire)

Village south of Fort Augustus on the shore of Loch Oich.

INVERGARRY HOTEL, INVERGARRY PH35 4HJ (01809 501206; Fax: 01809 501400). Fine Scottish produce and a well-stocked bar in a distinctive Victorian building, amidst the beautiful scenery of the Scottish Highlands. Ten comfortable en suite rooms. [Pets £7.50 per night].
e-mail: info@invergarryhotel.co.uk website: www.invergarryhotel.co.uk

Invermoriston (Inverness-shire)

Village on River Moriston, running from Loch Cluanie to Loch Ness.

INVERMORISTON HOLIDAY CHALETS, Glenmoriston IV63 7YF (01320 351254; Fax: 01320 351343). Spectacular location by Loch Ness. Comfortable, well equipped self catering chalets in spacious grounds. Few minutes' walk to the village. Excellent base for touring, walking, fishing etc. Pets welcome in some chalets. [Pets £20 per week]
e-mail: ihc@ipw.com website: www.invermoriston-holidays.com

Kincraig (Inverness-shire)

Attractive Highland village close to Loch Insh and Glenfeshie, midway between Aviemore and Kingussie.

NICK & PATSY THOMPSON, INSH HOUSE GUESTHOUSE AND SELF-CATERING COTTAGES, KINCRAIG, NEAR KINGUSSIE PH21 1NU (01540 651377). B&B in 1827 Telford Manse and two timber s/c cottages in superb rural location. Ideal for many outdoor activities and good touring base. Dogs and children welcome. STB ★★★ [🐕]
e-mail: inshhouse@btinternet.com website: www.kincraig.com/inshhouse

Kingussie (Inverness-shire)

Tourist centre on the River Spey 48 miles south of Inverness.

ROWAN HOUSE, NEWTONMORE ROAD, KINGUSSIE PH21 1HD (01540 662153) B&B in Cairngorms National Park; well behaved dogs welcome in self-contained suite (one double room, one twin, bathroom, lounge). No dogs in separate double en suite room.
e-mail: rowanhouse.scotland@btopenworld.com website: www.rowanhousescotland.com

COLUMBA HOUSE HOTEL AND GARDEN RESTAURANT, MANSE ROAD, KINGUSSIE PH21 1JF (01540 661402). Quiet Highland retreat offering highest standards of hospitality, care and accommodation. Candlelit Garden Restaurant. Ground-floor rooms with own front doors, perfect for doggie holidays. STB ★★★. [pw! Pets £3 per night, £10 per week]
e-mail: myra@columbahousehotel.com website: www.columbahousehotel.com

Kinlochbervie (Sutherland)

Village on north side of Loch Inchard.

THE KINLOCHBERVIE HOTEL, KINLOCHBERVIE, SUTHERLAND IV27 4RP (01971 521 275; Fax: 01971 521 438). Friendly, family-run hotel in one of the most stunning areas of North West Scotland. Supremely comfortable guest rooms from £30 pp for bed & breakfast.
e-mail: klbhotel@aol.com website: www.kinlochberviehotel.com

Lochcarron (Ross-shire)

Village on north shore of Loch Carron 2 miles below the head of the loch. Known for its ties and tartans.

THE COTTAGE, STROMECARRONACH, LOCHCARRON WEST, STRATHCARRON. Small, stone-built Highland cottage, double bedroom, shower room, open plan kitchen/living room, fully equipped. Panoramic views over Loch Carron and the mountains. For further details please phone. MRS A.G. MACKENZIE, STROMECARRONACH, LOCHCARRON WEST, STRATHCARRON IV54 8YH (01520 722284) [🐕]
website: www.lochcarron.org

Loch Ness (Inverness-shire)

Home of 'Nessie', extending for 23 miles from Fort Augustus to south of Inverness.

Self-catering cottages all around Loch Ness plus small selection of West coast properties. Pets welcome. Please see website for details or for a brochure contact: GORDON & CORINNE ROBERTS, ROEBUCK COTTAGE, ERROGIE, STRATHERRICK, INVERNESS-SHIRE IV2 6UH (01456 486358). [1 dog free, extra dogs £10 each per week] STB★★★/★★★★/★★★★★ SELF CATERING
e-mail: corinne@wildernesscottages.co.uk website: www.wildernesscottages.co.uk

JUSTINE HUDSON, WILDSIDE HIGHLAND LODGES, WILDSIDE, WHITEBRIDGE, INVERNESS IV2 6UN. (01456 486373; Fax: 01456 486371). Charming riverside lodges. Log fires and mountain views. Sleep 2 to 8 people. Heating, linen and towels included. Pets welcome. Free fishing. See our colour brochure or visit our website. STB ★★★★ Self-catering. [Pets £15 per booking].
e-mail: info@wildsidelodges.com website: www.wildsidelodges.com

Nethy Bridge (Inverness-shire)

Popular Strathspey resort on River Nethy with extensive Abernethy Forest to the south. Impressive mountain scenery. Grantown-on-Spey 5 miles.

BALNAGOWAN MILL AND WOODLARK, NETHY BRIDGE. Comfortable, modern 3 bedroom cottages in secluded locations in the Cairngorms National Park. Woodland and riverside walks on the doorstep. Ideal for pets. Furnished to a high standard with full central heating. £250-£500 per week incl. of electricity and bed linen. VisitScotland ★★★/★★★★. ASSC MEMBER. Contact PAULA FRASER, 33 ARGYLE GROVE, DUNBLANE FK15 9DT (01786 824957) [🐕]
e-mail: paulajfraser@aol.com

MONDHUIE CHALETS & B&B, NETHY BRIDGE, INVERNESS-SHIRE PH25 3DF (Tel & Fax: 01479 821062). Situated in the country between Aviemore and Grantown-on-Spey, two comfortable, self-catering chalets, or you can have Dinner, B&B in the house. A warm welcome awaits you. Pets welcome. Red squirrels seen daily. [🐕]
e-mail: david@mondhuie.com website: www.mondhuie.com

Newtonmore (Inverness-shire)

Village on River Spey. 3 miles west of Kingussie. Holiday and walking centre. Clan Macpherson Museum..

CRUBENBEG HIGHLAND HOLIDAY COTTAGES, NEWTONMORE PH20 1BE (01540 673566). Luxury 4 Star country cottages in idyllic surroundings in the Cairngorms National Park. Lots of lovely walks, loads of sporting activities or simply relax and spot the wildlife around you. STB ★★★★ [Pets £15 per week]
e-mail: enquiry@crubenbeg.com website: www.crubenbeg.com

Onich (Inverness-shire)

Village 2 miles west of Ballachulish

STRATHLINNHE HOLIDAY HOMES, ONICH, NEAR FORT WILLIAM PH33 6SD (01855 821264). Cottages and static caravans on 15 acre croft running down to the shores of Loch Linnhe, midway between Glencoe and Ben Nevis.Views across the loch to Glencoe and the Ardnamurchan Hills. Near amenities, owner maintained.

Poolewe (Ross-shire)

Village lying between Lochs Ewe and Maree with the river Ewe flowing through.

MR A. URQUHART, CROFTERS COTTAGES, 15 CROFT, POOLEWE IV22 2JY (01445 781 268). Two traditional cottages situated in a scenic and tranquil area, ideal for a "get away from it all" holiday. Comfortably furnished with all mod cons. [🐕]
e-mail: crofterscottages@btopenworld.com website:www.crofterscottages.co.uk

Rhiconich (Sutherland)

Locality at the head of Loch Inchard on west coast of Sutherland District.

LYNN & GRAHAM, GULL COTTAGE, ACHRIESGILL, RHICONICH, SUTHERLAND IV27 4RJ (01971 521717). High quality accommodation on the wild and unspoilt west coast. Superb scenery and excellent walks on mountains, moors and beaches. Pets welcome; secure dog run. STB ★★★ Self-Catering. [🐕]

RHICONICH HOTEL, SUTHERLAND, N. W. HIGHLANDS IV27 4RN (01971 521224; Fax: 01971 521732). She's your best friend so why leave her at home, bring her to Rhiconich Hotel, she'll be made equally as welcome as you will. A place where we put service, hospitality and really fresh food as a priority, but why don't you come and see for yourself? For further details contact Ray Fish. STB ★★★ [🐕]
e-mail: rhiconichhotel@aol.com website: www.rhiconichhotel.co.uk

Spean Bridge (Inverness-shire)

Village on River Spean at foot of Loch Lochy. Site of WWII Commando Memorial.

CORRIEVIEW LODGES, SPEAN BRIDGE PH34 4DX (01397 712395). Two lodges 10 miles north of Fort William, an ideal base for couples, families (and dogs). Each has two bedrooms, and upstairs open-plan lounge/kitchen/dining area. Balcony with views to Nevis Mountain Range. VisitScotland ★★★★
website: www.corrieviewlodges.com

RIVERSIDE LODGES, INVERGLOY, SPEAN BRIDGE PH34 4DY (01397 712684). The ultimate Highland location. Three lodges, each sleep 6 in 12 acres of woodland garden on Loch Lochy. Free fishing. Open all year. Pets welcome. Brochure on request. [🐕]
e-mail: enquiries@riversidelodge.org.uk website: www.riversidelodge.org.uk

Tain (Ross-shire)

Small town in Ross & Cromarty district on south shore of Dornoch Firth. Invergordon 10 miles.

CALEDONIAN HOTEL, BEACH FRONT, PORTMAHOMACK, BY TAIN, ROSS-SHIRE IV20 1YS (01862 871345; Fax: 01862 871757). Family-run hotel overlooking sandy beach. Magnificent views across Dornoch Firth. Watersports, golf close by. Regular live music. Children welcome. Horse riding available for experienced riders. STB ★★★ Hotel.
e-mail: info@caleyhotel.co.uk website: www.caleyhotel.co.uk

Tongue (Sutherland)

Village near north coast of Caithness District on east side of Kyle of Tongue.

BORGIE LODGE HOTEL, SKERRAY, TONGUE KW14 7TH (Tel & Fax: 01641 521332). Set in a secluded Highland glen lies Borgie Lodge. Try pony trekking, fishing and forest walks. Open fires and fine dining. STB ★★★★ [🐕]
e-mail: info@borgielodgehotel.co.uk website: www.borgielodgehotel.co.uk

Whitebridge (Inverness-shire)

WHITEBRIDGE HOTEL, WHITEBRIDGE, SOUTH LOCH NESS IV2 6UN (01456 486226; Fax: 01456 486413). Peaceful location with magnificent mountain views and excellent walks. Friendly locals' bar with home-cooked food. 12 en suite rooms. B&B from £30pppn. AA ★★[🐕]
e-mail: info@whitebridgehotel.co.uk website: www.whitebridgehotel.co.uk

Pet-Friendly
Pubs, Inns & Hotels
on pages 390-405
Please note that these establishments may not feature in the main section of this book

WALSTON MANSION FARMHOUSE

We offer a real home from home where guests return year after year to enjoy the friendly atmosphere. Situated in the peaceful village of Walston just five miles from Biggar, ideal for touring the Clyde Valley and Scottish Borders; 15 minutes from Roslyn Chapel. Pets by arrangement. Recommended by *Which? Good Bed and Breakfast Guide.* B&B £19pp, en suite £21pp, evening meal £10pp, 7 nights for the price of 6 nights.

For details contact: Margaret Kirby, Walston, Carnwath, By Biggar ML11 8NF
Tel & Fax: 01899 810338 • e-mail: kirby-walstonmansion@talk21.com

CARMICHAEL COUNTRY COTTAGES ★★ – ★★★★ *SELF-CATERING*

CARMICHAEL ESTATE, BY BIGGAR, LANARKSHIRE ML12 6PG
Tel: 01899 308336 • Fax: 01899 308481
website: www.carmichael.co.uk/cottages • e-mail:chiefcarm@aol.com

Our Stone Cottages nestle in the woods and fields of our Historic Family-run Estate. Ideal homes for families, pets and particularly dogs. Walking trails, private tennis, fishing, restaurant/farm shop. 15 cottages, 32 bedrooms. Open all year. Central location. £225 to £595 per week.

Blairmains Farm, Harthill ML7 5TJ Tel: 01501 751278

Attractive farmhouse on small farm of 72 acres. Immediately adjacent to Junction 5 of M8 motorway. Ideal centre for touring, with Edinburgh, Glasgow, Stirling 30 minutes' drive. One double, three twin, one single (three en suite); bathroom; sittingroom, diningroom; sun porch. Central heating. Children welcome. Pets welcome. Ample grounds for walking. Car essential – parking. Bed and Breakfast from £20; weekly rates available. Reduced rates for children. Open all year. **e-mail: heather@blairmains.freeserve.co.uk • www.blairmains.co.uk**

Biggar

Small town set round broad main street. Gasworks museum, puppet theatre seating 100, street museum displaying old shop fronts and interiors. Peebles 13 miles.

WALSTON MANSION FARMHOUSE, WALSTON, CARNWATH, BY BIGGAR ML11 8NF (Tel & Fax: 01899 810338). Situated in the peaceful village of Walston just five miles from Biggar, ideal for touring the Clyde Valley and Scottish Borders. 15 minutes to Roslyn Chapel. Pets by arrangement. STB ★★★ *B&B.*
e-mail: kirby-walstonmansion@talk21.com

CARMICHAEL COUNTRY COTTAGES, CARMICHAEL ESTATE, BY BIGGAR ML12 6PG (01899 308336; Fax: 01899 308481). Our stone cottages nestle in the woods and fields of our historic family-run estate. Ideal homes for families, pets and dogs. 15 cottages, 32 bedrooms. STB ★★/★★★★ Self catering. Open all year. £225 to £595 per week. [pw! 🐕]
e-mail: chiefcarm@aol.com website: www.carmichael.co.uk/cottages

Harthill

Village 5 miles south-west of Bathgate.

MRS STEPHENS, BLAIRMAINS FARM, HARTHILL ML7 5TJ (01501 751278; Fax: 01501 753383). Attractive farmhouse on small farm. Ideal for touring. Children welcome. Bed and Breakfast from £20; weekly rates available. Reduced rates for children. Open all year. [🐕]
e-mail: heather@blairmains.freeserve.co.uk website: www.blairmains.co.uk

LOCH TAY LODGES

Acharn, By Aberfeldy PH15 2HR

Escape the rat race. Enjoy the tranquillity, the grandeur, the beauty and the comfort of Highland Perthshire. Walk around the farm in the woods or up the mountains, play golf, fish, tour or sail. Fully modernised stone building Listed for its architectural interest. Self-catering. Log Fires. Well behaved dogs welcome. Linen provided.

Tel: 01887 830209
Fax: 01887 830802
e-mail: remony@btinternet.com
www.lochtaylodges.co.uk

Scottish Tourist Board ★★★ Self Catering

Nestling under Callander Crags, only a short walk from the village centre, this Victorian villa offers a warm welcome, and quality en suite accommodation at affordable prices. *For the comfort of all guests, this is a non-smoking residence.* The generously equipped bedrooms enjoy some unique touches, and the attention to detail which makes all the difference. Only 100 yards from Callander meadows, beautiful riverside walks and the Rob Roy Way. An excellent range of restaurants can be found nearby.

Dunmor House, Leny Road, Callander FK17 8AL Tel: 01877 330756
e-mail: reservations@dunmorhouse.co.uk • www.dunmorhouse.co.uk

Scottish Tourist Board ★★★★ B&B

Only a few minutes' stroll to the village, park and hills; gateway to the Loch Lomond and Trossachs National Park. One double and one twin with private bathroom or shower room, tea/coffee makers, central heating. Varied Scottish Breakfast. Your dogs can sleep in your room, and are welcome in the sitting room and garden.

B&B from £22.50pppn; single by arrangement
REDUCED RATES for 3+ days

Scottish Tourist Board ★★★ B&B

DOGS ESPECIALLY WELCOME (and stay free) IN GREAT WALKIES AREA

Lynne & Alistair Ferguson, 'Brochanach', 43 Fingal Road, Killin, Perthshire FK21 8XA
Tel: 01567 820028 • e-mail: alifer@msn.com

WESTER LIX

Two cottages sleeping 4 each. Family-run. Remote location set in 9 acres with private Lochan. Excellent base for walking, hill climbing, mountain biking, and water sports, or touring and sightseeing. Sky TV in both cottages, plus sauna in one cottage. Jonna's Cottage was completely refurbished for July 2005.

Gill & Dave Hunt, The Steading, Wester Lix, Killin, Perthshire FK21 8RD
Tel: 01567 820 990 or 07747 862641 • e-mail: gill@westerlix.net • www.westerlix.net

---

STB ★★★

Former farmhouse offers comfortable accommodation and good food. One family room, one twin and one double room, all en suite. All have tea/coffee making facilities and face open country to mountains beyond. Peace and quiet guaranteed. B&B from £22; Dinner if required from £12. Haven for wildlife and dogs. Large paddock for walking.

e-mail: maljac@tulloch83.freeserve.co.uk • www.maljac.com
JACKY & MALCOLM CATTERALL, "TULLOCH", ENOCHDHU, BY KIRKMICHAEL, PITLOCHRY PH10 7PW • 01250 881404

We're just mad about dogs, and we have been known to welcome the occasional human companion, subject to behavioural restrictions, naturally! • Friendly, attentive service • Great food • Beautiful views • Fabulous walks

E-mail: rosemount1@tiscali.co.uk
Seek us out on www.scottishhotels.co.uk

Rosemount Hotel

Pitlochry
PH16 5HT
01796 472302

Balrobin Hotel

STB ★★★ Hotel AA & RAC ★★

Pitlochry PH16 5HT • Tel: 01796 472901 • Fax: 01796 474200
www.balrobin.co.uk • e-mail: info@balrobin.co.uk

Scottish Country House Hotel. 15 en suite rooms, most with panoramic views, yet close to the town centre. Non-smoking. Owned and run by the Hohman family at value-for-money prices. Ideal for short or longer breaks.

The finest lochside setting in the Southern Highlands

Choice of two AA Red Rosette Fine Dining or more informal Bar Meals, both offering imaginative modern European cuisine using only the best fresh Scottish produce.

Well placed in central Scotland to enjoy many day trips to include the scenic West Coast, Stirling Castle, Edinburgh, Blair Atholl and the Trossachs to name a few.

For the energetic there are many scenic walks, or as an alternative how about a Munro?

Individually decorated hotel bedrooms, and four-poster rooms, many with loch view, or secluded hillside chalets.

Hi there fellow four-leggers, *just a quick note to say that the Chef is still very good here. Have been doing lots of wonderful long walks as he is trying to get fit (again), so come and join. YOU are of course most welcome, and as usual I have negotiated that you can stay free of overnight charge, so drop me a an email or come and see me.* ***Sham*** *(Resident Reservations Munsterlander)*

The Four Seasons Hotel

St Fillans, Perthshire PH6 2NF

Tel: 01764 685333 e-mail: sham@thefourseasonshotel.co.uk

AA ★★★ · Scottish Tourist Board ★★★ Hotel · Johansens Recommended · Best Loved Hotels · Which? Hotel Guide

FHG Guides

publish a large range of well-known accommodation guides.
We will be happy to send you details or you can use the order form at the back of this book.

FHG · K·U·P·E·R·A·R·D

Please note

All the information in this book is given in good faith in the belief that it is correct. However, the publishers cannot guarantee the facts given in these pages, neither are they responsible for changes in policy, ownership or terms that may take place after the date of going to press. Readers should always satisfy themselves that the facilities they require are available and that the terms, if quoted, still apply.

Aberfeldy

Small town standing on both sides of Uriar Burn near its confluence with the River Tay. Pitlochry 8 miles.

LOCH TAY LODGES, REMONY, ACHARN, ABERFELDY PH15 2HR (01887 830209). Enjoy hill walking, golf, sailing or touring. Salmon and trout fishing available. Log fires. Pets welcome. Walks along loch shore from house. STB ★★★ SELF CATERING in village close to Loch. For brochure, contact MRS P. W. DUNCAN MILLAR at above address. [🐕]
e-mail: remony@btinternet.com website: www.lochtaylodges.co.uk

Callander

Good base for walks and drives around the Trossachs and Loch Katrine. Stirling 14 miles.

DUNMOR HOUSE, LENY ROAD, CALLANDER FK17 8AL (01877 330756). Set within Scotland's first National park, Dunmor offers a warm welcome, and quality en suite accommodation at affordable prices. Short walk from village centre. STB ★★★★ [🐕]
e-mail: reservations@dunmorhouse.co.uk website: www.dunmorhouse.co.uk

Killin

Village at confluence of Rivers Dochart and Lochay at head of Loch Tay.

LYNNE AND ALISTAIR FERGUSON, 'BROCHANACH' 43 FINGAL ROAD, KILLIN FK21 8XA (01567 820028). Bed and varied Scottish Breakfast in small, tranquil village in the heart of Highland Perthshire. Ideal touring base. "Good walkies area" – dogs are especially welcome and stay free. STB ★★★ *B&B*. [🐕 pw!]
e-mail: alifer@msn.com

A useful index of towns/counties appears on pages 424-429

GILL & DAVE HUNT, THE STEADING, WESTER LIX, KILLIN FK21 8RD (01567 820 990 & 07747 862641). Both cottages decorated and equipped to a high standard, and have washing machines, freezers, oven, Sky TV etc; one with sauna. Well-behaved pets welcome by arrangement. [Pets £15 per week for first pet, then £5 per pet for others]
e-mail: gill@westerlix.net website: www.westerlix.net

Kinloch Rannoch

Village at foot of Loch Rannoch.

KILVRECHT CAMP SITE, KINLOCH RANNOCH, PERTHSHIRE (01350 727284; Fax: 01350 727811). Secluded campsite on a level open area in quiet, secluded woodland setting. Fishing available for brown trout on Loch Rannoch. Several trails begin from campsite. Please write, fax or telephone for further information. [🐕]
e-mail: hamish.murray@forestry.gsi.gov.uk

Kinross

Town and resort on west side of Loch Leven, 9 miles north of Dumfermline.

THE GREEN HOTEL, 2 THE MUIRS, KINROSS, KY13 8AS (0845 241 1310 (local rate); Fax: 01577 863180) Four-star hotel with fantastic facilities for leisure and play. Heated swimming pool; sauna and solarium; squash, tennis, curling rink, croquet, putting, two 18-hole golf courses on site.
e-mail: reservations@green-hotel.com website: www.green-hotel.com

Pitlochry

Popular resort on River Tummel in beautiful Perthshire Highlands. Excellent golf, loch and river fishing. Famous for summer Festival Theatre; distillery, Highland Games.

JACKY & MALCOLM CATTERALL, "TULLOCH", ENOCHDHU, BY KIRKMICHAEL, PITLOCHRY PH10 7PW (01250 881404). Former farmhouse offers comfortable accommodation and good food. Peace and quiet guaranteed. B&B from £22; Dinner if required from £12. Haven for wildlife and dogs. Large paddock for walking. STB ★★★ [🐕]
e-mail: maljac@tulloch83.freeserve.co.uk website: www.maljac.com

ROSEMOUNT HOTEL, PITLOCHRY PH16 5HT (01796 472302). We're just mad about dogs, and we have been known to welcome the occasional human companion, subject to behavioural restrictions, naturally! Friendly, attentive service. Great food. Beautiful views. Fabulous walks. [🐕]
e-mail: rosemount1@tiscali.co.uk website: www.scottishhotels.co.uk

BALROBIN HOTEL, HIGHER OAKFIELD, PITLOCHRY PH16 5HT (01796 472901; Fax: 01796 474200). Scottish Country House Hotel. 15 en suite rooms, most with panoramic views, yet close to the town centre. Non-smoking. Owned and run by the Hohman family at value-for-money prices. [🐕]
e-mail: info@balrobin.co.uk website: www.balrobin.co.uk

St Fillans

Village at foot of Lochearn, 5 miles west of Comrie.

THE FOUR SEASONS HOTEL, ST FILLANS PH6 2NF (01764 685333). Ideal holiday venue for pets and their owners. Spectacular Highland scenery, walking, fishing, watersports. Wonderful food. Full details on request. STB ★★★ Hotel, AA ★★★ and 2 Red Rosettes, Which? Hotel Guide, Johansens, Best Loved Hotels. [🐕]
e-mail: sham@thefourseasonshotel.co.uk website: www.thefourseasonshotel.co.uk

Strathyre

Village set in middle of Strathyre Forest, just off A84 north of Callander. Information centre and picnic area.

YVONNE & JOHN HOWES, ARDOCH LODGE, STRATHYRE FK18 8NF (01877 384666). Two log cabins and cottage in wonderful mountain scenery, excellent touring base. Comfortably furnished and well equipped. Delicious food using local produce. Pets most welcome. STB ★★★★ *B&B*/STB ★★★★ *Self Catering.* [pw! 🐕]
e-mail: ardoch@btinternet.com website: www.ardochlodge.co.uk

SHETLAND ISLANDS

Lerwick

Chief town of Shetland, 22 miles North of Sumburgh Head.

GLEN ORCHY HOUSE, 20 KNAB ROAD, LERWICK ZE1 0AX (Tel & Fax: 01595 692031). Former Convent, renovated and extended in the original style, whilst providing every modern comfort. En suite rooms, air conditioning, satellite TV, bar and evening meals. Reductions for children. Pets welcome. [🐕]
website: www.guesthouselerwick.com

ISLE OF SKYE

Breakish, Staffin

Tigh Holm Cottages, *Sculamus Moss, Breakish IV42 8QB*
Furnished to a very high standard, the location and comfort make these cottages ideal for exploring the Misty Isle. Open plan spacious ground floor with all modern appliances, upper level comprises bathroom with shower, one twin and one double bedroom. Restaurants and bars within walking distance. Terms from £215-£435.
Tel: 01471 822848 • e-mail: info@tigh-holm-cottages.com

GLENVIEW HOTEL
CULNACNOC, STAFFIN IV51 9JH
01470 562248
Traditional island house, ideally situated for exploring North East Skye. Comfortable en suite bedrooms.

Restaurant renowned for fresh seafood and traditional home cooking. Pets most welcome. Which? Best B&B.
IAN STRATTON & DOREEN HARBEN
e-mail: enquiries@glenviewskye.co.uk
www.glenviewskye.co.uk

Breakish

Location 2 miles east of Broadford on the Isle of Skye.

TIGH HOLM COTTAGES, SCULAMUS MOSS, BREAKISH IV42 8QB (01471 822848). Open plan spacious ground floor with all modern appliances. Upper level comprises bathroom with shower, one twin and one double bedroom. All bedding and linen supplied, electricity included. [🐕]
e-mail: info@tigh-holm-cottages.com

Staffin

Crofting and fishing village on rocky coast around Staffin bay, 12 miles north of Portree.

IAN STRATTON & DOREEN HARBEN, GLENVIEW HOTEL, CULNACNOC, STAFFIN IV51 9JH (01470 562248). Traditional island house, ideally situated for exploring North East Skye. Comfortable en suite bedrooms. Restaurant renowned for fresh seafood and traditional home cooking. Pets most welcome. Which? Best B&B. [🐕]
e-mail: enquiries@glenviewskye.co.uk website: www.glenviewskye.co.uk

Ratings & Awards

For the first time ever the AA, VisitBritain, VisitScotland, and the Wales Tourist Board will use a single method of assessing and rating serviced accommodation. Irrespective of which organisation inspects an establishment the rating awarded will be the same, using a common set of standards, giving a clear guide of what to expect. The RAC is no longer operating an Hotel inspection and accreditation business.

Accommodation Standards: Star Grading Scheme

Using a scale of 1-5 stars the objective quality ratings give a clear indication of accommodation standard, cleanliness, ambience, hospitality, service and food, This shows the full range of standards suitable for every budget and preference, and allows visitors to distinguish between the quality of accommodation and facilities on offer in different establishments.All types of board and self-catering accommodation are covered, including hotels, B & Bs, holiday parks, campus accommodation, hostels, caravans and camping, and boats.

The more stars, the higher level of quality

★★★★★
exceptional quality, with a degree of luxury

★★★★
excellent standard throughout

★★★
very good level of quality and comfort

★★
good quality, well presented and well run

★
acceptable quality; simple, practical, no frills

VisitBritain and the regional tourist boards, **enjoyEngland.com, VisitScotland** and **VisitWales,** and **the AA** have full details of the grading system on their websites

enjoyEngland.com

visitScotland.com

visitWales.com

theAA.com

National Accessible Scheme

If you have particular mobility, visual or hearing needs, look out for the National Accessible Scheme. You can be confident of finding accommodation or attractions that meet your needs by looking for the following symbols.

Typically suitable for a person with sufficient mobility to climb a flight of steps but would benefit from fixtures and fittings to aid balance

Typically suitable for a person with restricted walking ability and for those that may need to use a wheelchair some of the time and can negotiate a maximum of three steps

Typically suitable for a person who depends on the use of a wheelchair and transfers unaided to and from the wheelchair in a seated position. This person may be an independent traveller

Typically suitable for a person who depends on the use of a wheelchair in a seated position. This person also requires personal or mechanical assistance (eg carer, hoist).

Around the magnificent coast of Wales
Pembrokeshire, Cardigan Bay, Snowdonia, Anglesey, Lleyn Peninsula, Borders
Choose from over 200 Quality Cottages
Pets Welcome Free
A small specialist agency with 40 years experience letting quality cottages.
Enjoy unashamed luxury in traditional Welsh Cottages. Situated near safe sandy beaches and in the heart of Wales — famed for scenery, walks, wild flowers, birds, badgers and foxes.
Pets welcome FREE at most of our properties
Leonard Rees, Quality Cottages, Cerbid, Solva, Haverfordwest, Pembrokeshire. SA62 6YE
Telephone: (01348) 837871 for our FREE Colour Brochure
QUALITY COTTAGES CERBID
www.qualitycottages.co.uk
100s of pictures of quality cottages and beautiful Wales

MR P.W. REES, "QUALITY COTTAGES', CERBID, SOLVA, HAVERFORDWEST, PEMBROKESHIRE SA62 6YE (01348 837871). Cottages set in all coastal areas, unashamed luxury, highest residential standards. Dishwashers, microwaves, washing machines. Log fires. Linen supplied. Pets welcome. [pw! 🐕]
website: www.qualitycottages.co.uk

CAMPING & CARAVANNING CLUB (0845 130 7632). Visit one of our award-winning UK Club Sites. Our sites have dog walking areas for you and your dog to explore. A friendly welcome will be given to you and your pet on our sites, joining is great value for money. QUOTE REF NO 0716
website: www.campingandcaravanningclub.co.uk

RECOMMENDED COTTAGE HOLIDAYS. 1st choice for dream cottages at very competitive prices in all holiday regions of beautiful Britain. Pets welcome. All properties inspected. Free brochure - call 01751 475547.
website: www.recommended-cottages.co.uk

Please note

All the information in this book is given in good faith in the belief that it is correct. However, the publishers cannot guarantee the facts given in these pages, neither are they responsible for changes in policy, ownership or terms that may take place after the date of going to press. Readers should always satisfy themselves that the facilities they require are available and that the terms, if quoted, still apply.

Around the magnificent coast of Wales
Pembrokeshire, Cardigan Bay, Snowdonia, Anglesey, Lleyn Peninsula, Borders
Choose from over 200 Quality Cottages
Pets Welcome Free
A small specialist agency with 40 years experience letting quality cottages.
Enjoy unashamed luxury in traditional Welsh Cottages. Situated near safe sandy beaches and in the heart of Wales — famed for scenery, walks, wild flowers, birds, badgers and foxes.
Pets welcome FREE at most of our properties
Leonard Rees, Quality Cottages, Cerbid, Solva, Haverfordwest, Pembrokeshire. SA62 6YE
Telephone: (01348) 837871
for our FREE Colour Brochure
QUALITY COTTAGES
CERBID
www.qualitycottages.co.uk
100s of pictures of quality cottages and beautiful Wales

•TALYBONT ISA - Self-catering twin-bedded studio-type annexe with bathroom with shower, colour TV, etc.
•TY GWYN - two-bedroomed luxury caravan in private grounds.
Both situated just two miles from Bala in beautiful country area, ideal for walking, sailing, fishing and canoeing. Only 30 miles from seaside.
Contact: **MRS A. SKINNER, TY GWYN, RHYDUCHAF, BALA LL23 7SD**
Tel: 01678 521267 or 520234

Holiday in the heart of Snowdonia

Relax on a short break or a longer holiday at our quiet, family-run holiday park. Caravan-bungalows and caravans at very affordable prices. Indoor heated pool, sauna etc. Shop, off-licence and launderette. Pets welcome. Sandy beaches, golf courses, scenic walking and climbing. Phone 0800 136892 or 01341 247 236/891
Parc Caerelwan, Talybont, Barmouth LL43 2AX • www.holidaysites.co.uk/parc/

COLWYN GUEST HOUSE, CAERNARFON ROAD,

BEDDGELERT LL55 4UY • TEL: 01766 890276

A charming well appointed 18th century Listed guest house in the heart of Snowdonia National Park. Pets welcome with well behaved owners.

e-mail: colwynguesthouse@tiscali.co.uk • www.beddgelertguesthouse.co.uk

SYGUN FAWR COUNTRY HOUSE • Beddgelert, Gwynedd LL55 4NE

A warm welcome and spectacular scenery await you at this former Welsh Manor House, set in 20 acres of mountainside and gardens. 11 en suite rooms with tea/coffee facilities, hairdryer and radio alarm. De luxe rooms with extra comforts and superb views. Four course dinner using local produce, interesting wine list. Cosy bar, conservatory. Only a short walk from the village.

Tel & Fax: 01766 890258 • e-mail: sygunfawr@aol.com • www.sygunfawr.co.uk

OGWEN VALLEY HOLIDAYS

1 PENGARREG, NANT FFRANCON, BETHESDA, BANGOR LL57 3LX

Spectacular Snowdonia. Welsh cottage flat for two, £169 - £299 per week. Cottage for six £259 - £565 per week. Comfortable and welcoming with spectacular views.

Contact: JILL for brochure. Tel: 01248 600122

e-mail: jilljones@ogwensnowdonia.co.uk www.ogwensnowdonia.co.uk

- Comfortable three-bedroomed house
- Enclosed garden • Near beaches, common, forest
- Fully equipped; bedding and electricity inclusive
- Colour TV/video, microwave • Dogs and children welcome. WTB ★★★★

Croeso

MRS J. GUNDRY, FARMYARD LODGE, BODORGAN, ANGLESEY LL62 5LW • Tel: 01407 840977

Plas-Y-Bryn Chalet Park Bontnewydd, Near Caernarfon LL54 7YE (01286 672811)

Our small park is situated two miles from the historic town of Caernarfon. Set into a walled garden it offers safety, seclusion and beautiful views of Snowdonia. It is ideally positioned for touring the area. Shop and village pub nearby. A selection of chalets and caravans available at prices from £120 (low season) to £430 (high season) per week for the caravans and £120 (low season) to £550 (high season) per week for the chalets. Well behaved pets always welcome.

WTB ★★★★ website: www.plasybrynholidayscaernarfon.co.uk

TYDDYN HEILYN

CHWILOG, CRICCIETH LL53 6SW • Tel: 01766 810441

Comfortably renovated Welsh stone cottage with character. Cosy, is double-glazed, centrally heated and enjoying mild Gulf Stream climate with holiday letting anytime. Two bedrooms with sea views. Ramped entrance from outside to an en suite bedroom. Ample grounds with enclosed garden with doggy walk. Positioned on Llyn Peninsula, 3 miles Criccieth, on edge Snowdonia and having one mile tree lined walk to beach.

Rhos Country Cottages

A superb collection of secluded country cottages with private gardens, surrounded by wildflower meadows. Chill out, relax and listen to birdsong; walk the Lleyn Coastal Path from the garden gate or explore the Snowdonia National Park. Private fishing and rough shooting by arrangement. The cottages are heated and really warm in winter.

Open all year. VisitWales ★★★★★ Quality Award

Rhos Country Cottages, Criccieth, Porthmadog LL52 0PB
Telephone: 0776 986 4642 or 01758 720047
E-mail: Cottages@rhos.freeserve.co.uk Website: www.rhos-cottages.co.uk

---

A warm welcome awaits you in comfortable self-catering cottages. Easily accessible to numerous attractions, or enjoy tranquillity of countryside. Short breaks available. Pets welcome.

MRS M. WILLIAMS,
GAERWEN FARM, YNYS,
CRICCIETH, GWYNEDD LL52 0NU
Tel: 01766 810324
e-mail: gaerwen@btopenworld.com

PARC WERNOL PARK Chwilog, Pwllheli LL53 6SW • 01766 810506

• Panoramic views • Peaceful and quiet • Ideal for touring Lleyn and Snowdonia • 4 miles Criccieth and Pwllheli • 3 miles beach • Cycle route • Free coarse fishing lake • Safe children's play area • Games room • Footpaths • Dog exercise field • Self-catering holidays • 1,2 & 3 bedroom cottages • 2 and 3 bedroom caravans and chalets • Colour brochure • Personal attention at all times • A truly Welsh welcome. **www.wernol.com**

Beautiful Victorian Country House standing in 20 acres of woodland, gardens and fields. High standard of accommodation in two family rooms and one double all en suite. Pets welcome. Stabling/grazing available.

★★★★

MRS G. McCREADIE, DERI ISAF, DULAS BAY LL70 9DX
Tel: 01248 410536 • Mobile: 07721 374471
e-mail: mccreadie@deriisaf.freeserve.co.uk • www.angleseyfarms.com/deri.htm

---

Small Georgian cottage overlooking magnificent beach at Harlech. Central for Portmeirion, Ffestiniog Railway, Snowdonia and Lleyn Peninsula. Good home cooking. Bed and Breakfast with dinner by arrangement at reasonable prices. Pretty bedrooms overlooking sea. Pets welcome.

Fron Deg Guest House, Llanfair, Harlech, Gwynedd LL46 2RB
Tel: 01766 780448 • www.bedandbreakfast-harlech.co.uk

Publisher's note

While every effort is made to ensure accuracy, we regret that FHG Guides cannot accept responsibility for errors, misrepresentations or omissions in our entries or any consequences thereof. Prices in particular should be checked.
We will follow up complaints but cannot act as arbiters or agents for either party.

Boathouse Hotel

Tranquil setting overlooking the harbour • Ferry terminal 4 minutes On the edge of country park and marina • Luxury en suite bedrooms at affordable prices • Seafood a speciality • Bar snacks and chef's specials • Lunches and afternoon teas • Ample free parking

BOATHOUSE HOTEL • NEWRY BEACH • HOLYHEAD • ANGLESEY LL65 1YF
Tel: 01407 762094 • www.holyhead.org/boathouse.html
e-mail: boathousehotel@supanet.com

Bryn Maelog, Rhosneigr, Anglesey LL54 5JE

LARGE DETACHED HOUSE with 10 bedrooms (sleeps up to 20). Large well equipped kitchen with American style fridge/freezer. Games room. Bar with pool table and darts. Two large lounges. TV, video and DVD player. Linen provided. 100 yards to beach and 200 yards to town centre. Pets accommodated in our static caravan, but sorry, not in the house. Non-smoking. Electricity and bed linen included.

For further details please telephone: 07971 164339

Comfortable self-catering holiday bungalows sleeping 2-7 near Trearddur's lovely beaches. Indoor heated swiming pool, licensed club, tennis court. Local, beautiful headland walks, fishing, golf and horse riding.Ideal location to explore Anglesey and the North Wales coast; near Holyhead.

TREARDDUR HOLIDAY BUNGALOWS
LON ISALLT TREARDDUR BAY ANGLESEY LL65 2UP

Tel: 01407 860494 • E-mail: trearholiday@btconnect.com • www.holiday-bungalows.co.uk

Cliff Cottages and Plas Darien Apartments

All year round holidays and short breaks in a choice of centrally heated apartments with wonderful sea views or stone-built cottages in village-like situation very near sea.

Own private indoor heated swimming pools, saunas, snooker, table tennis. Outdoor heated pool, tennis courts, badminton, small golf, bowls. Adjacent 18-hole golf course, horse riding, windsurfing, canoeing, fishing.

Phone or write for brochure:
Plas Darien
The Cliff
Trearddur Bay
Anglesey LL65 2UR

Tel: 01407 860789
Fax: 01407 861150
www.plasdarien.com

FREE or REDUCED RATE entry to Holiday Visits and Attractions – see our READERS' OFFER VOUCHERS on pages 407-423

MR P.W. REES, "QUALITY COTTAGES', CERBID, SOLVA, HAVERFORDWEST, PEMBROKESHIRE SA62 6YE (01348 837871). Cottages set in all coastal areas, unashamed luxury, highest residential standards. Dishwashers, microwaves, washing machines. Log fires. Linen supplied. Pets welcome. [pw!]
website: www.qualitycottages.co.uk

Bala

Natural touring centre for Snowdonia. Narrow gauge railway runs along side of Bala lake, the largest natural lake in Wales. Golf, sailing, fishing, canoeing.

TALYBONT ISA - Self-catering twin-bedded studio-type annexe with bathroom with shower, colour TV, etc. TY GWYN - two-bedroomed luxury caravan in private grounds. Both situated just two miles from Bala in beautiful country area, ideal for walking, sailing, fishing and canoeing. Only 30 miles from seaside. Contact: MRS A. SKINNER, TY GWYN, RHYDUCHAF, BALA LL23 7SD (01678 521267 or 520234). [ ]

Barmouth

Modern seaside resort with two miles of sandy beaches. Surrounding hills full of interesting archaeological remains.

PARC CAERELWAN, TALYBONT, BARMOUTH LL43 2AX (0800 136892 or 01341 247 236/891). Relax at our quiet, family-run holiday park. Caravan-bungalows and caravans at very affordable prices. Indoor heated pool, sauna etc. Shop, off-licence and launderette. Pets welcome. WTB ★★★★ [Pets £9 per week]

LAWRENNY LODGE HOTEL, BARMOUTH LL42 1SU (01341 280466). Eight bedroom hotel (seven en suite) overlooking the harbour and estuary and only five minutes from town centre. All rooms have TV and tea/coffee making facilities. Varied restaurant menu, residential licence and private car park. [ ]
e-mail: enquiries@lawrennylodge.co.uk **website: www.lawrennylodge.co.uk**

Beaumaris

Elegant little town dominated by castle built by Edward I in 13th century. Museum of Childhood has Victorian toys and music boxes.

MR P.W. REES, "QUALITY COTTAGES', CERBID, SOLVA, HAVERFORDWEST, PEMBROKESHIRE SA62 6YE (01348 837871). Cottages set in all coastal areas, unashamed luxury, highest residential standards. Dishwashers, microwaves, washing machines. Log fires. Linen supplied. Pets welcome. [pw!]
website: www.qualitycottages.co.uk

Beddgelert

Village at confluence of Rivers Colwyn and Glaslyn, 12 miles from Caernarfon, 4 miles from Snowdon

COLWYN GUEST HOUSE, CAERNARFON ROAD, BEDDGELERT, GWYNEDD LL55 4UY (01766 890276). A charming well appointed 18th century Listed guest house in the heart of Snowdonia National Park. Pets welcome with well behaved owners. [Pets £2.50 per night]
e-mail: colwynguesthouse@tiscali.co.uk website: www.beddgelertguesthouse.co.uk

SYGUN FAWR COUNTRY HOUSE, BEDDGELERT, GWYNEDD LL55 4NE (Tel & Fax: 01766 890258). All rooms en suite with tea/coffee facilities, hairdryer and radio alarm. Superb views. Four-course dinner using local produce, interesting wine list. Cosy bar, conservatory. Only a short walk from the village. [Pets £4 per night.]
e-mail: sygunfawr@aol.com website: ww.sygunfawr.co.uk

Readers are requested to mention this FHG guidebook when seeking accommodation

Bethesda

Town 5 miles south-east of Bangor.

OGWEN VALLEY HOLIDAYS, 1 PENGARREG, NANT FFRANCON, BETHESDA, BANGOR LL57 3LX (01248 600122). Spectacular Snowdonia. Welsh cottage flat for two, cottage for six. Comfortable and welcoming with spectacular views. Private parking. Superb walking. Near River Ogwen, cycle track and dog-walking lane. WTB ★★★★. Contact: JILL for brochure. [Pets £20 per week].
e-mail: jilljones@ogwensnowdonia.co.uk website: www.ogwensnowdonia.co.uk

Bodorgan

A rural area in South West Anglesey.

MRS J. GUNDRY, FARMYARD LODGE, BODORGAN, ANGLESEY LL62 5LW (01407 840977). Comfortable three-bedroomed house. Enclosed garden. Near beaches, common, forest. Fully equipped, bedding and electricity inclusive. Colour TV/video, microwave. Dogs and children welcome. WTB ★★★★ [🐕]

Caernarfon

Historic walled town and resort, ideal for touring Snowdonia. Museums, Segontium Roman Fort, magnificent 13th century castle. Old harbour, sailing trips.

PLAS-Y-BRYN CHALET PARK, BONTNEWYDD, NEAR CAERNARFON LL54 7YE (01286 672811). Two miles from Caernarfon. It offers safety, seclusion and beautiful views of Snowdonia. Ideally positioned for touring. Well behaved pets always welcome. WTB ★★★★ [Pets £20 per week].
website: www.plasybrynholidayscaernarfon.co.uk

Criccieth

Popular family resort with safe beaches divided by ruins of 13th century castle. Salmon and sea trout fishing. Festival of Music and Arts in the summer.

MRS LENA HUGHES JONES, TYDDYN HEILYN, CHWILOG, CRICCIETH LL53 6SW (01766 810441). Comfortably renovated Welsh stone cottage. Double-glazed, centrally heated and enjoying mild Gulf Stream climate. Ample grounds with enclosed garden with doggy walk. One mile tree lined walk to beach. [🐕]

MRS A. M. JONES, RHOS COUNTRY COTTAGES, CRICCIETH, PORTHMADOG LL52 0PB (01758 720047 or 0776 986 4642). Superb collection of secluded country cottages with private gardens. Private fishing and rough shooting by arrangement. Open all year. VisitWales ★★★★★ [🐕]
e-mail: cottages@rhos.freeserve.co.uk website: www.rhos-cottages.co.uk

A warm welcome awaits you in comfortable self-catering cottages. Easily accessible to numerous attractions, or enjoy tranquillity of countryside. Short breaks available. Pets welcome. MRS M. WILLIAMS, GAERWEN FARM, YNYS, CRICCIETH, GWYNEDD LL52 0NU (01766 810324).[🐕]
e-mail: gaerwen@btopenworld.com

PARC WERNOL PARK, CHWILOG, PWLLHELI LL53 6SW (01766 810506). Peaceful and quiet, ideal for touring. Self-catering holidays – 1,2 & 3 bedroom cottages, 2 and 3 bedroom caravans and chalets. Colour brochure. [Pets £10 per week.]
website: www.wernol.com

MR P.W. REES, "QUALITY COTTAGES', CERBID, SOLVA, HAVERFORDWEST, PEMBROKESHIRE SA62 6YE (01348 837871). Cottages set in all coastal areas, unashamed luxury, highest residential standards. Dishwashers, microwaves, washing machines. Log fires. Linen supplied. Pets welcome. [pw! 🐕]
website: www.qualitycottages.co.uk

Terms quoted in this publication may be subject to increase if rises in costs necessitate

Dulas Bay

On north-east coast of Anglesey, between Amlwch and Moelfre.

MRS G. McCREADIE, DERI ISAF, DULAS BAY LL70 9DX (01248 410536; Mobile: 07721 374471). Victorian Country House in 20 acres of woodland, gardens and fields. Two family rooms and one double, all en suite. Pets welcome. Stabling/grazing available. WTB ★★★★ Country House [Dogs £2.50 per night]
e-mail: mccreadie@deriisaf.freeserve.co.uk website: www.angleseyfarms.com/deri.htm

Harlech

Small stone-built town dominated by remains of 13th century castle. Golf, theatre, swimming pool, fine stretch of sands

FRON DEG GUEST HOUSE, LLANFAIR, HARLECH LL46 2RE (01766 780448). Small Georgian cottage overlooking magnificent beach. Pretty bedrooms. Good home cooking. Central for touring. Reasonable terms for B&B, dinner by arrangement. Pets welcome. [🐕]
website: www.bedandbreakfast-harlech.co.uk

MR P.W. REES, "QUALITY COTTAGES', CERBID, SOLVA, HAVERFORDWEST, PEMBROKESHIRE SA62 6YE (01348 837871). Cottages set in all coastal areas, unashamed luxury, highest residential standards. Dishwashers, microwaves, washing machines. Log fires. Linen supplied. Pets welcome. [pw! 🐕]
website: www.qualitycottages.co.uk

Holyhead

Seaport town on north side of Holyhead Island, 24 miles north-west of Bangor.

BOATHOUSE HOTEL, NEWRY BEACH, HOLYHEAD, ANGLESEY LL65 1YF (01407 762094). Tranquil setting overlooking the harbour; on edge of country park and marina. Luxury en suite bedrooms. Seafood a speciality. Ample free parking. [Pets £5 per night].
e-mail: boathousehotel@supanet.com website: www.holyhead.org/boathouse.html

Llanddona

Village on Anglesey 3 miles north west of Beaumaris.

MR P.W. REES, "QUALITY COTTAGES', CERBID, SOLVA, HAVERFORDWEST, PEMBROKESHIRE SA62 6YE (01348 837871). Cottages set in all coastal areas, unashamed luxury, highest residential standards. Dishwashers, microwaves, washing machines. Log fires. Linen supplied. Pets welcome. [pw! 🐕]
website: www.qualitycottages.co.uk

Morfa Nefyn

Picturesque village 2 miles west of Nefyn.

MR P.W. REES, "QUALITY COTTAGES', CERBID, SOLVA, HAVERFORDWEST, PEMBROKESHIRE SA62 6YE (01348 837871). Cottages set in all coastal areas, unashamed luxury, highest residential standards. Dishwashers, microwaves, washing machines. Log fires. Linen supplied. Pets welcome. [pw! 🐕]
website: www.qualitycottages.co.uk

Porthmadog

Harbour town with mile-long Cob embankment, along which runs Ffestiniog Narrow Gauge Steam Railway to Blaenau Ffestiniog. Pottery, maritime museum, car museum. Good beaches nearby.

MR P.W. REES, "QUALITY COTTAGES', CERBID, SOLVA, HAVERFORDWEST, PEMBROKESHIRE SA62 6YE (01348 837871). Cottages set in all coastal areas, unashamed luxury, highest residential standards. Dishwashers, microwaves, washing machines. Log fires. Linen supplied. Pets welcome. [pw! 🐕]
website: www.qualitycottages.co.uk

Red Wharf Bay

Deep curving bay with vast expanse of sand, very popular for sailing and swimmin

MR P.W. REES, "QUALITY COTTAGES', CERBID, SOLVA, HAVERFORDWEST, PEMBROKESHIRE SA62 6YE (01348 837871). Cottages set in all coastal areas, unashamed luxury, highest residential standards. Dishwashers, microwaves, washing machines. Log fires. Linen supplied. Pets welcome. [pw!]
website: www.qualitycottages.co.uk*g.*

Rhosneigr

Small resort on west coast of Anglesey.

BRYN MAELOG, RHOSNEIGR LL54 5JE. Large detached house (sleeps up to 20). Large kitchen, games room, bar, two large lounges. Linen provided. Close to beach and town centre. Pets accommodated. Non-smoking. For further details please contact: MR T. REGAN, HIGH STREET, BELMONT, BOLTON BL7 8AA (07971 164339).

Trearddur Bay

Attractive holiday spot set amongst low cliffs on Holy Island, near Holyhead. Golf, sailing, fishing and swimming.

TREARDDUR HOLIDAY BUNGALOWS, LON ISALLT,TREARDDUR BAY, ANGLESEY LL65 2UP (01407 860494). Comfortable self-catering holiday bungalows sleeping 2-7 near Trearddur's lovely beaches. Locally, beautiful headland walks, fishing, golf and horse riding. Ideal location to explore Anglesey and the North Wales coast. Terms from £100-£580 per week.
e-mail: trearholiday@btconnect.com website: www.holiday-bungalows.co.uk

CLIFF COTTAGES AND PLAS DARIEN APARTMENTS, TREARDDUR BAY LL65 2UR (01407 860789; Fax: 01407 861150). Fully equipped holiday cottages, sleeping 4/8 plus cot. Near sea. Indoor and outdoor heated pools. Colour television. Choice of centrally heated apartments or stone-built cottages. Own private leisure complex with bowls, saunas, snooker, table tennis; tennis courts. Adjacent golf course. [ ]
website: www.plasdarien.com

Tywyn

Pleasant seaside resort, start of Talyllyn Narrow Gauge Railway. Sea and river fishing, golf.

MR P.W. REES, "QUALITY COTTAGES', CERBID, SOLVA, HAVERFORDWEST, PEMBROKESHIRE SA62 6YE (01348 837871). Cottages set in all coastal areas, unashamed luxury, highest residential standards. Dishwashers, microwaves, washing machines. Log fires. Linen supplied. Pets welcome. [pw!]
website: www.qualitycottages.co.uk

WOODLANDS PARK. Delightful chalet where your pet can join in the fun of a family holiday. Phone us for more details. Mercedes and David Morgan. (01568 780912). [ ]

Around the magnificent coast of Wales
Pembrokeshire, Cardigan Bay, Snowdonia, Anglesey, Lleyn Peninsula, Borders
Choose from over 200
Quality Cottages
Pets Welcome Free
A small specialist agency with
40 years experience letting quality cottages.
Enjoy unashamed luxury in traditional Welsh Cottages. Situated near safe sandy beaches and in the heart of Wales — famed for scenery, walks, wild flowers, birds, badgers and foxes.
Pets welcome FREE at most of our properties
Leonard Rees, Quality Cottages, Cerbid,
Solva, Haverfordwest, Pembrokeshire.
SA62 6YE
Telephone: (01348) 837871
for our FREE Colour Brochure
QUALITY COTTAGES
CERBID
www.qualitycottages.co.uk
100s of pictures of quality cottages
and beautiful Wales

Seaside Cottages

In Idyllic North Wales

We have a large selection of self-catering seaside and country cottages, bungalows, farmhouses, caravans etc. offering superb, reasonably priced accommodation for owners and their pets. Our brochures contain details of all you need for a wonderful holiday - please telephone for your FREE copies now.

Mann's Holidays, Shaw's Holidays & Snowdonia Tourist Services

01758 701 702 (24 hrs)

www.manns-holidays.com www.shaws-holidays.co.uk www.snowdoniatourist.com

Betwys-y-Coed, Colwyn Bay

Summer Hill NON-SMOKERS' GUEST HOUSE

BETWS-Y-COED LL24 0BL • 01690 710306

Quiet location, overlooking river. 150 yards from main road and shops. En suite and standard rooms, tea-making facilities, residents' lounge. Ideal for walkers. B&B from £22-£30.

Hill farm in Wales. TV, teamaking, en suite. Set in National Park/ Snowdonia. Very quiet and well off the beaten track. A great welcome and good food. Many return visits. £20 B&B.

MRS MORRIS, TY COCH FARM-TREKKING CENTRE, PENMACHNO, BETWS-Y-COED LL25 0HJ
01690 760248 • e-mail: cindymorris@tiscali.co.uk

For colour brochures telephone:
01492 512903/ 512282
or visit our website

NORTH WALES HOLIDAYS

Cedarwood Chalets • Cottages • Coach House

High quality chalets, cottages and coach house for 2-9, overlooking sea at Bron-Y-Wendon or in picturesque valley at Nant-Y-Glyn. 16 units in total. Wide range of facilities with many leisure activities nearby. Short breaks all year. Pets welcome. WTB 3-5 Stars.

Bron-Y-Wendon & Nant-Y-Glyn Holiday Parks,
Wern Road, Llanddulas, Colwyn Bay LL22 8HG
e-mail: stay@northwales-holidays.co.uk
www.northwales-holidays.co.uk

Pet-Friendly
Pubs, Inns & Hotels

on pages 390-405

Please note that these establishments may not feature in the main section of this book

Tyn-y-Groes, Near Conwy

Homely Victorian stone cottage in picturesque Conwy valley. Mountain views. Enjoy walking, mountains, beaches, bird watching. Bodnant Gardens, RSPB reserve and Conwy castle, harbour and marina close by. Victorian Llandudno, Betws-y-Coed, Anglesey, Caernarfon and Snowdon easy distance. Good local food and pubs. Enclosed garden, patio, furniture. Roadside parking. Gas fired central heating. Lounge with gas fire, dining room, kitchen, utility.

Brongain

Two double bedded rooms, one small single; blankets/duvet provided. Bathroom with bath, shower, toilet and basin. Colour TV, electric cooker, fridge, microwave, washing machine and tumbler dryer. Terms £195-£315; heating, electricity included. Linen extra. Pets welcome. Open all year. No children under five years..

Mrs G. Simpole, 105 Hay Green Road, Terrington-St-Clement, King's Lynn, Norfolk PE34 4PU
Tel: 01553 828897
Mobile: 0798 9080665

Sychnant Pass House

Sychnant Pass Road, Conwy LL32 8BJ

Tel: 01492 596868 • Fax: 01492 585486
e-mail: bre@sychnant-pass-house.co.uk
www.sychnant-pass-house.co.uk

Nellie and Molly, our lovely collies, would love to welcome your four-legged friends to their home in the hills above Conwy. Sychnant Pass House is a lovely Victorian House set in two acres with a little pond and stream running through it. Step out of our garden and straight onto Snowdonia National Park land where you can walk for miles with your dogs. Just over two miles from the beach and one-and-a-half miles from Conwy, it is an ideal base from which to tour Wales. All our rooms are en suite, our garden rooms have French windows opening into the garden which are ideal for pets. We have a lovely sitting room that you can share with your best friends after dinner which is served in our informal, friendly restaurant, doggie bags are always available. Your four- legged friends and their folk are most welcome here.

RAC 5 Diamonds & Little Gem Award 2001/ 2002/ 2003/ 2004/ 2005/2006
AA 5 Red Diamonds • Bed & Breakfast from £50 per person

Hafod Country House

Trefriw, Llanrwst, Conwy Valley LL27 0RQ

Relax in this centuries-old farmhouse. Exceptional food (top grade in the last three WTB inspections), warm hospitality, and a strong sense of style, combine to create a special stay for guests.

As well as some 2½ acres of grounds, there are walks in the woods, beside waterfalls, or along the banks of the River Conwy, where you can exercise your dog.

WTB ★★★★ Country House • AA ★★ 73%

Tel: 01492 640029 • Fax: 01492 641351
e-mail: hafod@breathemail.net • website: www.hafod-house.co.uk

Secluded cottages, log fire and beams
Dogs will love it – a place of their dreams
Plenty of walks around mountains and lakes
Cosy and tranquil – it's got what it takes.
It's really a perfect holiday let
For up to 2-7 people, plus their pet(s).

Apply: Mrs Williams

Tel: 01724 733990 or 07711 217 448 (week lets only)

Deva is a quiet, detached residence divided into three self-contained flats (accommodating 2-4 adults). Own private car park. Centrally situated, within level walking distance of town centre and both beaches. *For details contact Mrs E. Williams Tel: 01492 581789*

www.llandudnoholidayflats-cottages.co.uk

Pentre Mawr House

Llandyrnog, Denbigh, North Wales LL16 4LA
Tel: 01824 790732
E-mail: bre@sychnant-pass-house.co.uk
www.pentremawrhouse.co.uk

Nellie and Molly, our lovely collies, would love to welcome your four-legged friends to their family's ancestral home of 400 years with woodland, park and riverside meadows, all within easy reach of Chester and the coast. The en suite bedrooms have all the little extras to make your stay special. There is a heated swimming pool in the walled garden and lovely sittingrooms where you can sit with your best friends after dinner. Furry folk and their families are most welcome here. B&B from £45.00

Ted, Fred and Megan are waiting to greet new friends!

The Golden Pheasant is an 18th Century Hotel & Inn ideally situated for pets, especially dogs. The old world charm bar has an open range fire, pews and slate floor and real ale; comfortable lounges and two restaurants which have extensive and imaginative menus, all freshly prepared by our chef.

Accommodation ranges from cosy Inn rooms located in the older part of the building to superior larger bedrooms and four-poster rooms with whirlpool baths, which have wonderful views of the valley.

Situated in the beautiful Ceiriog Valley, which is a heaven for walking, with its unspoilt country lanes, paths with wild flower banks and verges, all with panoramic views of the valley.

2 nights D,B&B from £135 pp. B&B from £90, two sharing. Pets from £5 per night.

AA ★★★

Llwynmawr, Glyn Ceiriog, Near Llangollen LL20 7BB

Tel: 01691 718281 • Fax: 01691 718479

e-mail: goldenpheasant@micro-plus-web.net website: www.goldenpheasanthotel.co.uk

★★★

THE GOLDEN PHEASANT Country Hotel & Inn

Standing in the glorious and hidden Ceiriog Valley, The Hand at Llanarmon radiates charm and character.

The Hand at Llanarmon

With 13 comfortable en suite bedrooms, roaring log fires, and fabulous food served with flair and generosity, this is a wonderful base for most country pursuits, or just relaxing in good company.

Llanarmon D.C., Ceiriog Valley, Near Llangollen, North Wales LL20 7LD
reception@thehandhotel.co.uk • www.TheHandHotel.co.uk • Tel: 01691 600666

Please note

All the information in this book is given in good faith in the belief that it is correct. However, the publishers cannot guarantee the facts given in these pages, neither are they responsible for changes in policy, ownership or terms that may take place after the date of going to press. Readers should always satisfy themselves that the facilities they require are available and that the terms, if quoted, still apply.

Sunnydowns Hotel

★★★ *Quality Hotel*

66 Abbey Road, Rhos-on-Sea, Colwyn Bay, Conwy, North Wales LL28 4NU

Tel: 01492 544256 Fax: 01492 543223

(Proprietor: Mike Willington)

A Non-Smoking Hotel

A 3 star family-run hotel situated in a quiet area and just a two minute level walk to the beach & shops. High standard of comfort and cleanliness, car park, bar, games room with pool table, Nordic sauna, restaurant, TV lounge.

Our restaurant is non-smoking, serving freshly prepared good home cooking. The towns of Llandudno, Colwyn Bay & Conwy are only five minutes' drive away and just ten minutes to the mountains and castles of Snowdonia and the Isle of Anglesey.

OAP discounts, large family rooms & family suites available. All en suite bedrooms have remote control TV (teletext, video & satellite), clock radio, tea/coffee making facilities, hairdyer, mini-bar, refrigerator, telephone and central heating. Available on request are irons, trouser press, room service and laundry service. Broadband internet access available throughout the hotel.

New this year all rooms fitted with personal digital room safe. Microwave available for guests' use. Also a fitness/exercise machine in games room all available free of charge for all our guests.

Dogs are very welcome and can stay at a small charge. They are allowed in your bedroom with you and in the hotel except the restaurant. Meals also served in the bar where dogs are allowed.

For further information, please phone or write for our colour brochure.

e-mail: sunnydowns-hotel@tinyworld.co.uk • www.hotelnorthwales.co.uk

Large Country House on outskirts of Trefriw village. Good touring area with Llanrwst, Betws-y-Coed and Swallow Falls five miles away. Fishing, walking, golf, pony trekking close by. Comfortable bedrooms, lounge with TV, diningroom. Good home cooking. Parking. B&B from £25.

MRS B. COLE, GLANDWR, TREFRIW, NEAR LLANRWST LL27 0JP

01492 640431 ~ www.glandwr-trefriw.co.uk

MR P.W. REES, "QUALITY COTTAGES', CERBID, SOLVA, HAVERFORDWEST, PEMBROKESHIRE SA62 6YE (01348 837871). Cottages set in all coastal areas, unashamed luxury, highest residential standards. Dishwashers, microwaves, washing machines. Log fires. Linen supplied. Pets welcome. [pw!]

website: www.qualitycottages.co.uk

SEASIDE COTTAGES. MANN'S, SHAW'S AND SNOWDONIA TOURIST SERVICES (01758 701 702). Large selection of self-catering seaside and country cottages, bungalows, farmhouses, caravans etc. offering superb, reasonably priced accommodation for owners and their pets. Please telephone for brochure.

websites: www.manns-holidays.com www.shaws-holidays.co.uk www.snowdoniatourist.com

Betws-y-Coed

Popular mountain resort in picturesque setting where three rivers meet. Trout fishing, craft shops, golf, railway and motor museums, Snowdonia National Park Visitor Centre. Nearby Swallow Falls are famous beauty spot.

SUMMER HILL NON-SMOKERS' GUEST HOUSE, BETWS-Y-COED LL24 0BL (01690 710306). Quiet location, overlooking river. 150 yards from main road and shops. En suite and standard rooms, tea-making facilities, residents' lounge. Ideal for walkers. B&B from £22 - £30. [Pets £1.50 per night.]

MRS MORRIS, TY COCH FARM-TREKKING CENTRE, PENMACHNO, BETWS-Y-COED LL25 0HJ (01690 760248). Hill farm in Wales. TV, teamaking, en suite. Set in National Park/Snowdonia. Very quiet and well off the beaten track. A great welcome and good food. Many return visits. £20 B&B. [ ]
e-mail: cindymorris@tiscali.co.uk

Colwyn Bay

Lively seaside resort with promenade amusements. Attractions include Mountain Zoo, Eirias Park; golf, tennis, riding and other sports. Good touring centre for Snowdonia. The quieter resort of Rhos-on-Sea lies at the western end of the bay.

NORTH WALES HOLIDAYS, BRON-Y-WENDON AND NANT-Y-GLYN HOLIDAY PARKS, WERN ROAD, LLANDDULAS, COLWYN BAY LL22 8HG (01492 512903/512282). Cottages with sea views at Bron-Y-Wendon or chalets, cottages and coach house in picturesque valley at Nant-Y-Glyn. 16 units in total. WTB ★★★/★★★★/★★★★★ [Pets £10 per week].
e-mail: stay@northwales-holidays.co.uk website: www.northwales-holidays.co.uk

Conwy

One of the best preserved medieval fortified towns in Britain on dramatic estuary setting. Telford Suspension Bridge, many historic buildings, lively quayside (site of smallest house in Britain). Golf, pony trekking, pleasure cruises.

BRONGAIN, TY'N-Y-GROES, CONWY. Homely Victorian stone cottage, picturesque Conwy Valley. Snowdonia Mountain views. Enjoy lakes, mountains, walking, bird watching, beaches, Bodnant, RSPB, Conwy Castle. £195-£315. Contact: MRS G. M. SIMPOLE, 105 HAYGREEN ROAD, TERRINGTON ST CLEMENT, KINGS LYNN, NORFOLK PE34 4PU (01553 828897; Mobile: 0798 9080 665) [pw!]

SYCHNANT PASS HOUSE, SYCHNANT PASS ROAD, CONWY LL32 8BJ (01492 596868: Fax: 01492 585486). A lovely Victorian House set in two acres with a little pond and stream. Step out of our garden and straight onto Snowdonia National Park land. Walk for miles with your dogs. All rooms en suite. B&B from £50. AA/RAC ◆◆◆◆◆ [ ]
e-mail: bre@sychnant-pass-house.co.uk website: www.sychnant-pass-house.co.uk

TIR-Y-COED COUNTRY HOUSE, ROWEN, CONWY LL32 8TP (Tel & Fax: 01492 650219). Comfortable hotel with Snowdonia, North Wales and Anglesey all within easy reach. All rooms en suite. Drawing room and garden lounge; traditionally cooked fayre. WTB ★★★ Country House, AA/RAC ★★ Dining and Hospitality Awards. [ ]
e-mail: reception@tirycoed.com website: www.tirycoed.com

Conwy Valley

Fertile valley with wood and moor rising on both sides. Many places of interest in the area.

HAFOD COUNTRY HOUSE, TREFRIW, CONWY VALLEY LL27 0RQ (01492 640029; Fax: 01492 641351). Small informal hotel. Over two acres of grounds. Excellent food in restaurant. Short breaks available. Well behaved dogs welcome. Non-smoking. WTB ★★★★ Country House AA ★★ 73% [Pets £5 per night, £30 per week]
e-mail: hafod@breathemail.net website: www.hafod-house.co.uk

Secluded cottages with log fire and beams. Dogs will love it. Plenty of walks around mountains and lakes. For 2 - 7 people plus their pet(s). MRS WILLIAMS (01724 733990 or 07711 217 448) week lets only. [ ]

Llandudno

Premier holiday resort of North Wales coast flanked by Great Orme and Little Orme headlands. Wide promenade, pier, two beaches; water ski-ing, sailing, fishing trips from jetty. Excellent sports facilities: golf, indoor pool, tennis, pony trekking, Leisure Centre. Summer variety shows, Alice In Wonderland Visitor Centre.

DEVA is a quiet, detached residence divided into three self-contained flats (accommodating 2-4 adults). Own private car park. Centrally situated, within level walking distance of town centre and both beaches. For details contact MRS E. WILLIAMS (01492 581789). [Pets £10 per week].
website: www.llandudnoholidayflats-cottages.co.uk

Terms quoted in this publication may be subject to increase if rises in costs necessitate

THE CLIFFBURY, 34 ST DAVID'S ROAD, LLANDUDNO LL30 2UH (Tel & Fax: 01492 877224). Pets and well-behaved owners very welcome at our non-smoking guest house situated in a quiet area close to town centre and both beaches. Car park. En suite rooms with TV and beverage making facilities. Please contact John or Rita for brochure. WTB ★★★ Guest House. [🐕]
e-mail: info@thecliffbury.co.uk website: www.thecliffbury.co.uk

Llandyrnog

Village 4 miles east of Denbigh.

PENTRE MAWR COUNTRY HOUSE, LLANDYRNOG LL16 4LA (01824 790732) Ancestral home of 400 years with woodland, park and riverside meadows, within easy reach of Chester and coast. Heated swimming pool. All rooms en suite. Pets most welcome. [🐕]
e-mail: bre@sychnant-pass-house.co.uk www.pentremawrhouse.co.uk

Llangollen

Famous for International Music Eisteddfod held in July. Plas Newydd, Valle Crucis Abbey nearby. Standard gauge steam railway; canal cruises; ideal for golf and walking.

GOLDEN PHEASANT COUNTRY HOTEL, GLYN CEIROG, NEAR LLANGOLLEN LL20 7BB (01691 718281; Fax: 01691 718479). Situated in the beautiful Ceiriog Valley. All 19 rooms en suite, colour TV and tea/coffee making facilities. Pets welcome in all rooms (except restaurant and lounge). WTB/AA ★★★ [pw! £5 per night per pet, £35 per week]
e-mail: goldenpheasant@micro-plus-web.net website: www.goldenpheasanthotel.co.uk

THE HAND AT LLANARMON, LLANARMON D.C., CEIRIOG VALLEY, NEAR LLANGOLLEN LL20 7LD (01691 600666). Standing in the glorious Ceiriog Valley, The Hand at Llanarmon radiates charm and character. 13 comfortable en suite bedrooms, log fires, and fabulous food, a wonderful base for most country pursuits. [🐕]
e-mail: reception@thehandhotel.co.uk website: www.TheHandHotel.co.uk

Rhos-on-Sea

Popular resort at east end of Penrhyn Bay, adjoining Colwyn Bay to the north-west.

SUNNYDOWNS HOTEL, 66 ABBEY ROAD, RHOS-ON-SEA, CONWY LL28 4NU (01492 544256; Fax: 01492 543223). A 3 star luxury family hotel just two minutes' walk to beach and shops. All rooms en suite with colour TV, video & satellite channels, tea/coffee facilities and central heating. Hotel has bar, pool room and car park. A non-smoking hotel. [pets £4.50 per night]
e-mail: sunnydowns-hotel@tinyworld.co.uk website: www.hotelnorthwales.co.uk

Trefriw

Hillside village, popular as spa in Victorian times. Local beauty spots at Llyn Crafnant and Llyn Geironnydd. Woollen mill demonstrating traditional techniques.

MRS B. COLE, GLANDWR, TREFRIW, NEAR LLANRWST LL27 0JP (01492 640431). Large Country House on outskirts of Trefriw village. Good touring area with Llanrwst, Betws-y-Coed and Swallow Falls five miles away. Fishing, walking, golf, pony trekking close by. Comfortable bedrooms, lounge with TV, diningroom. Good home cooking. Parking. B&B from £25.
website: www.glandwr-trefriw.co.uk

Symbols

🐕 Indicates that pets are welcome free of charge.

£ Indicates that a charge is made for pets: nightly or weekly.

pw! Shows some special provision for pets; exercise facility, feeding or accommodation arrangement.

⌂ Indicates separate pets accommodation.

Laugharne, Llandeilo, Llandysul, Llanelli

SIR JOHN'S HILL FARM HOLIDAY COTTAGES

Laugharne, Carmarthenshire SA33 4TD

Old Stables Cottage • Tel: 01994 427001

Wren Cottage & The Farmhouse • Tel: 01994 427667

In one of the finest locations in West Wales with spectacular views of coast and countryside, the three very comfortable cottages are the perfect place for a relaxing break. Here at Sir Johns Hill Farm we specialise in dog-friendly holidays and aim to make their holiday just as good as yours. They will have a great time at the farm which is well away from the main road, and there are lots of great country walks and long sandy beaches nearby too.

www.sirjohnshillfarm.co.uk

Relax in The Farmhouse, one of six traditional cottages set within two acres of secure gardens at **MAERDY COTTAGES**. From this idyllic centre enjoy local walks and famous gardens and discover the beautiful coast and countryside of Carmarthenshire. Each cottage is equipped to give maximum comfort...two cottages are fully wheelchair accessible, and all are ideal for families of all ages. Home cooked evening meals available. Open all year. Brochure and enquiries:

Maerdy Cottages, Taliaris, Llandeilo, Carmarthenshire SA19 7DA • 01550 777448

WTB ★★★★ - ★★★★★ **e-mail: enquiries@maerdyholidaycottages.co.uk • www.maerdyholidaycottages.co.uk**

Pen Y Banc Cottage, Llanfihangel ar Arth, Llandysul

Lovely isolated, cosy bungalow on owner's organic farm. Ideal for walking and touring Brecon Beacons, Pembrokeshire Coastal Footpath and Black Mountains. Sleeps 4, one double and one twin bedroom. Oil fired, two oven Rayburn cooker in beamed open plan sitting/dining room. All heating/electric costs included in price. Brochure available. Non smoking.

Penny & Graeme Whitaker • Tel: 01559 384515 • Fax: 01559 389034

Gwhit34925@aol.com • www.solutions-factory.co.uk/penybanccottage

The Diplomat Hotel Felinfoel Road, Aelybryn, Llanelli SA15 3PJ

Tel: 01554 756156 • Fax: 01554 751649 • AA/WTB ★★★

The Diplomat Hotel offers a rare combination of charm and character, with excellent well appointed facilities to ensure your comfort. Explore the Gower Peninsula and the breathtaking West Wales coastline. Salmon & trout fishing, horse riding, golf, and motor racing at Pembrey are all within reach.

e-mail: reservations@diplomat-hotel-wales.com • www.diplomat-hotel-wales.com

Laugharne

Village on the River Taf estuary 4 miles south of St Clears, burial place of Dylan Thomas.

SIR JOHN'S HILL FARM HOLIDAY COTTAGES, LAUGHARNE SA33 4TD. OLD STABLES COTTAGE 01994 427001, WREN COTTAGE & THE FARMHOUSE 01994 427667. Specialising in dog-friendly holidays, three very comfortable cottages. In one of the finest locations in West Wales, with spectacular views, lots of great country walks, and long sandy beaches nearby. [pw! £15 per week.]
website: www.sirjohnshillfarm.co.uk

Llandeilo

Town on River Towy, 14 miles east of Carmarthen.

MAERDY COTTAGES, TALIARIS, LLANDEILO, CARMARTHENSHIRE SA19 7DA (01550 777448). Six traditional cottages set within two acres of secure gardens. Each cottage is equipped to give maximum comfort, two cottages are fully wheelchair accessible, and all are ideal for families of all ages. Home cooked evening meals available. Open all year. WTB ★★★★ - ★★★★★. [First pet free, others £5 per night, £20 per week].
e-mail: enquiries@maerdyholidaycottages.co.uk website: www.maerdyholidaycottages.co.uk

Llandysul

Small town on River Teifi, 12 miles north of Carmarthen.

PENNY AND GRAEME WHITAKER, PEN Y BANC COTTAGE, LLANFIHANGEL AR ARTH, LLANDYSUL SA39 9JX (01559 384515; Fax: 01559 389034). Lovely, isolated, cosy cottage sleeping four in one double and one twin bedroom. Ideal for walking/touring Brecon Beacons, Black Mountains and Pembrokeshire's Coastal Path. Non smoking. Brochure available. [🐕]
e-mail: Gwhit34925@aol.com website: www.solutions-factory.co.uk/penybanccottage

Llanelli

Village on the River Taf estuary, 10 mile north-west of Swansea.

THE DIPLOMAT HOTEL, FELINFOEL ROAD, AELYBRYN, LLANELLI SA15 3PJ (01554 756156; Fax: 01554 751649). Privately owned and operated with warmth and generous hospitality. The Diplomat Hotel offers a rare combination of charm and character with excellent well appointed facilities to ensure your comfort and convenience. WTB/AA ★★★ [Pets £5 per night]
e-mail: reservations@diplomat-hotel-wales.com website: www.diplomat-hotel-wales.com

Symbols

- 🐕 Indicates that pets are welcome free of charge.
- £ Indicates that a charge is made for pets: nightly or weekly.
- **pw!** Shows some special provision for pets; exercise facility, feeding or accommodation arrangement.
- ⌂ Indicates separate pets accommodation.

MR P.W. REES, "QUALITY COTTAGES', CERBID, SOLVA, HAVERFORDWEST, PEMBROKESHIRE SA62 6YE (01348 837871). Cottages set in all coastal areas, unashamed luxury, highest residential standards. Dishwashers, microwaves, washing machines. Log fires. Linen supplied. Pets welcome. [pw! 🐕]
website: www.qualitycottages.co.uk

Aberaeron

Attractive little town on Cardigan Bay, good touring centre for coast and inland. The Aeron Express Aerial ferry offers an exciting trip across the harbour. Marine aquarium; Aberarth Leisure Park nearby.

GILFACH HOLIDAY VILLAGE, LLWYNCELYN, NEAR ABERAERON SA46 0HN (01545 580288). Choice of modern Bungalows (up to 6 persons) or luxury 2/3 person apartments. Fully equipped, linen available, colour TV. Horse and pony riding. Tennis. Write or phone for brochure pack to the Manager. [Pets £15 per week.]
e-mail: info@stratfordcaravans.co.uk website: www.selfcateringinwales.com or www.stratfordcaravans.co.uk

FREE or REDUCED RATE entry to Holiday Visits and Attractions – see our READERS' OFFER VOUCHERS on pages 407-423

Aberporth

Popular seaside village offering safe swimming and good sea fishing. Good base for exploring Cardigan Bay coastline.

MR P.W. REES, "QUALITY COTTAGES', CERBID, SOLVA, HAVERFORDWEST, PEMBROKESHIRE SA62 6YE (01348 837871). Cottages set in all coastal areas, unashamed luxury, highest residential standards. Dishwashers, microwaves, washing machines. Log fires. Linen supplied. Pets welcome. [pw! 🐕]
website: www.qualitycottages.co.uk

Aberystwyth

Resort at mouth of Rivers Rheidol and Ystwyth on Cardigan Bay, 82 miles from Cardiff.

THE HAFOD HOTEL, Devil's Bridge, Aberystwyth SY23 3JL (01970 890232; Fax: 01970 890394). At the head of the Mynach Falls, perfect for exploring some of Wales' most spectacular scenery. Most bedrooms enjoy superb views. Restaurant and a delightful Victorian Tea Room. WTB ★★, AA ★★★ [🐕] pw!
e-mail: hafodhotel@btconnect.com website: www.thehafodhotel.co.uk

Ciliau Aeron

Village in undulating country just inland from the charming Cardigan Bay resorts of New Quay and Aberaeron. New Quay 12 miles, Aberaeron 6.

MR P.W. REES, "QUALITY COTTAGES', CERBID, SOLVA, HAVERFORDWEST, PEMBROKESHIRE SA62 6YE (01348 837871). Cottages set in all coastal areas, unashamed luxury, highest residential standards. Dishwashers, microwaves, washing machines. Log fires. Linen supplied. Pets welcome. [pw! 🐕]
website: www.qualitycottages.co.uk

Lampeter

Small market town on River Teifi, 20 miles north east of Carmarthen.

JEFF & SUE RICE, GAER COTTAGES, CRIBYN, LAMPETER SA48 7LZ (Tel & Fax: 01570 470275). Nine cottages sleeping 3/9, some suitable for wheelchair users. Very well equipped; bed linen incl. Indoor heated pool, games room and adventure playground. Ideal for walking, cycling, fishing holidays.
e-mail: gaer@bigfoot.com website: www.selfcateringinwales.co.uk

Llangrannog

Pretty little seaside village overlooking a sandy beach. Superb cliff walk to NT Ynys Lochtyn, a secluded promonto

MR P.W. REES, "QUALITY COTTAGES', CERBID, SOLVA, HAVERFORDWEST, PEMBROKESHIRE SA62 6YE (01348 837871). Cottages set in all coastal areas, unashamed luxury, highest residential standards. Dishwashers, microwaves, washing machines. Log fires. Linen supplied. Pets welcome. [pw! 🐕]
website: www.qualitycottages.co.uk*ry.*

Pets Welcome Free

A small specialist agency with
40 years experience letting quality cottages.

Enjoy unashamed luxury in traditional Welsh Cottages. Situated near safe sandy beaches and in the heart of Wales — famed for scenery, walks, wild flowers, birds, badgers and foxes.

Pets welcome FREE at most of our properties

Leonard Rees, Quality Cottages, Cerbid,
Solva, Haverfordwest, Pembrokeshire.
SA62 6YE

Telephone: (01348) 837871
for our FREE Colour Brochure

QUALITY COTTAGES
CERBID

www.qualitycottages.co.uk

100s of pictures of quality cottages
and beautiful Wales

Pembrokeshire Coast • Newport to St Davids

Charming, individual cottages situated near sandy beaches, rocky bays and spectacular cliff walks. All furnished to high residential standards, fully equipped and personally supervised. Pets and children welcome. Sleep 2-10.

Jane Stiles, Cil-y-Cwm, Nant-y-Ffynnon, Letterston, Haverfordwest SA62 5SX
Tel: 01348 840879 • e-mail: cj.stiles@btinternet.com
www.cottageretreats.net

Abermawr, Broad Haven, Fishguard, Haverfordwest

PEMBROKESHIRE NATIONAL PARK. Three-bedroom fully furnished holiday house, within easy walking distance of sandy beaches and the Coastal Footpath. Ideal centre for family holidays, walking, birdwatching. Sleeps 6 + cot. From £120 to £350 per week.

MRS L.P. ASHTON, 10 ST LEONARDS ROAD, THAMES DITTON, SURREY KT7 0RJ
020-8398 6349 • e-mail: lejash@aol.com • www.33timberhill.com

Welcome to Ivybridge, where your pet is as welcome as you are!

Situated down a leafy lane, Ivybridge is a modern guesthouse waiting to welcome you. All rooms en suite with TV/hot drinks tray. Swim in our indoor pool, relax in our lounge/bar. Good home cooking. Ample off-road parking. Close by are quiet walks to the sea which you and your pet will enjoy.

Ivybridge, Drim Mill, Dyffryn, Goodwick SA64 0JT • 01348 875366
Fax: 01348 872338 • e-mail: ivybridge@boltblue.com • www.ivybridgeleisure.co.uk

WTB ★★★-★★★★★

NOLTON HAVEN QUALITY COTTAGES

Ideal for out of season breaks. Most with sea views, some 30 yards from safe, sandy beach. Central heating, open fires. Sleep 2 to 14. Farmhouse B&B also available.

Contact: Jim & Joyce Canton, Nolton Haven Farmhouse, Nolton Haven, Haverfordwest SA62 6NH (01437 710263)
e-mail: PW5@noltonhaven.com • www.noltonhaven.com

Nolton Haven Farm Cottages

We are the only cottages situated on the beachfront side of the main road in Nolton Haven, enjoying direct access to the beach and coastal path. Important if you have children and pets to consider. Cottages sleep 2-8 people.

Nolton Haven, Haverfordwest, Pembrokeshire SA62 3NH
• Tel: 01437 710200 •
e-mail: info@havencottages.co.uk • www.havencottages.co.uk

Scamford Caravan Park • Peaceful family-run park

Close to the Coastal Path and lovely sandy beaches. 25 luxurious caravans with Four Star Tourist Board grading. Five touring pitches. Super playground. Pets welcome. Richard & Christine White

Tel/Fax: 01437 710304 • www.scamford.com
e-mail: holidays@scamford.com

SCAMFORD CARAVAN PARK, KEESTON, HAVERFORDWEST SA62 6HN

FREE or REDUCED RATE entry to Holiday Visits and Attractions – see our READERS' OFFER VOUCHERS on pages 407-423

LLANTEGLOS ESTATE •• 01834 831677/831371

Charming self-contained Woodland Lodges in quiet estate. Wonderful views of coast and country. Safe children's play area. Fully licensed clubhouse. Miles of sandy beaches. Attractions for all ages and interests. For further details/colour brochure: **TONY & JANE BARON, LLANTEGLOS ESTATE, LLANTEG, NEAR AMROTH, PEMBROKESHIRE SA67 8PU**
e-mail: llanteglosestate@supanet.com • www.llanteglos-estate.com

Scamford Holidays

Richard & Christine White
Scamford Holidays Keeston
Haverfordwest Pembrokeshire SA62 6HN
Tel: 01437 710304
Email:holidays@scamford.com
Web Page www.stdavids.co.uk/folkeston/

Folkeston Hill Holiday Bungalows

A small group of bungalows in a sheltered valley which winds down to the sea at Nolton Haven. WTB Graded. Pets welcome.

SELECT QUALITY SELF-CATERING HOLIDAYS IN NORTH PEMBROKESHIRE
WTB Graded. Pets Welcome.
Sleeping 2-11 Short Breaks available

St BRIDES BAY COTTAGES
Pembrokeshire

01437 720027 www.sbbc.uk.com

www.ffynnonddofn.co.uk

FFYNNON DDOFN

Delightful cottage in quiet lane between St Davids and Fishguard, with panoramic views over spectacular coastline. Ideal for walking; rocky coves and safe, sandy beaches nearby. The cottage is fully carpeted, warm, comfortable and very well-equipped, sleeping six in three bedrooms, plus cot. Washing machine, tumble dryer, freezer, microwave, DVD/video. Large games room, children's toys, pleasant secure garden. Perfect for early or late holidays, with central heating and double glazing. Parking. Shop one mile. Footpath to beach. Open all year. Terms from £300, including heating and electricity. Brochure on request.

Mrs B. Rees White, Brickhouse Farm, Burnham Road,Woodham Mortimer, Maldon, Essex CM9 6SR (01245 224611)

Vine Cottage Guesthouse

Saundersfoot SA69 9LA
(Non-smoking)

AA ★★★★ Guest House

Coastal village outskirts. Sandy beaches and coast path nearby. Award-winning garden for guests' and dogs' relaxation and exercise.

01834 814422 www.vinecottageguesthouse.co.uk

★★★

Readers are requested to mention this FHG publication when seeking accommodation

Lochmeyler Farm Guesthouse

Tel: 01348 837724
Fax: 01348 837622
e-mail: stay@lochmeyler.co.uk
www.lochmeyler.co.uk

Mrs Morfydd Jones
Llandeloy,
Pen-y-Cwm,
Near Solva,
St Davids,
Pembrokeshire
SA62 6LL

A warm welcome awaits you at Lochmeyler, a 220 acre dairy farm in the centre of the St Davids Peninsula.
It is an ideal location for exploring the beauty of the coast and countryside.
There are 11 bedrooms, four of them in the adjacent cottage suites. All are en suite, non-smoking, luxury rooms with colour TV, video and refreshment facilities. Rooms serviced daily. Children 14 years and over are welcomed. Well behaved dogs are welcome in some of our rooms. Dogs are not permitted to be left unattended in the rooms. There are kennel facilities for owners wishing to leave their dogs during the day. We do not charge for dogs or the kennel facilities.

Closed Christmas & New Year
Credit cards accepted.
Colour brochure on request.

AWARD AA ◆◆◆◆◆ WTB ★★★★★ FARM GOLD

DAILY RATES

Bed & Breakfast per person per night £27.50 - £40
Optional Dinner every night @ £15 per person
10% discount on Bed & Breakfast and
Evening Meal bookings of 7 nights or more

A country estate of over 450 acres, including 2 miles of riverbank. See a real farm in action, the hustle and bustle of harvest, newborn calves and lambs. Choose from 6 character stone cottages, lovingly converted traditional farm buildings, some over 200 years old.

Farm holidays at Gwarmacwydd

Each cottage is fully furnished and equipped, electricity and linen included, with all year round heating. Children welcome. Brochure available. Contact: **Mrs Angela Colledge, Llanfallteg, Whitland, Pembrokeshire SA34 0XH.** **SELF CATERING ★★★★ COTTAGES**
t 01437 563 260 f 01437 563 839 w www.gwarmacwydd.co.uk

MR P.W. REES, "QUALITY COTTAGES', CERBID, SOLVA, HAVERFORDWEST, PEMBROKESHIRE SA62 6YE (01348 837871). Cottages set in all coastal areas, unashamed luxury, highest residential standards. Dishwashers, microwaves, washing machines. Log fires. Linen supplied. Pets welcome. [pw! 🐕]
website: www.qualitycottages.co.uk

Pembrokeshire Coast - Newport to St Davids. Charming, individual cottages situated near sandy beaches, rocky bays and spectacular cliff walks. All furnished to high residential standards and fully equipped. Pets and children welcome. Sleep 2-10. Details from JANE STILES, CIL-Y-CWM, NANT-Y-FFYNNON, LETTERSTON, HAVERFORDWEST SA62 5SX (01348 840879).
e-mail: cj.stiles@btinternet.com website: www.pembrokeshireholidays.co.uk

Bosherton

Village 4 miles south of Pembroke, bordered by 3 man-made lakes, a haven for wildlife and covered in water lilies in early summer.

MR P.W. REES, "QUALITY COTTAGES', CERBID, SOLVA, HAVERFORDWEST, PEMBROKESHIRE SA62 6YE (01348 837871). Cottages set in all coastal areas, unashamed luxury, highest residential standards. Dishwashers, microwaves, washing machines. Log fires. Linen supplied. Pets welcome. [pw! 🐕]
website: www.qualitycottages.co.uk

Broad Haven

Inlet one mile north of St Govan's Head..

PEMBROKESHIRE NATIONAL PARK. Sleeps 6 + cot. Three-bedroom fully furnished Holiday House. Walking distance sandy beaches and coastal footpath. £120 to £350 per week. MRS L.P. ASHTON, 10 ST LEONARDS ROAD, THAMES DITTON, SURREY KT7 0RJ (020-8398 6349). [🐕]
e-mail: lejash@aol.com website: www.33timberhill.com

Croes Goch

Hamlet 6 miles north east of St Davids

MR P.W. REES, "QUALITY COTTAGES', CERBID, SOLVA, HAVERFORDWEST, PEMBROKESHIRE SA62 6YE (01348 837871). Cottages set in all coastal areas, unashamed luxury, highest residential standards. Dishwashers, microwaves, washing machines. Log fires. Linen supplied. Pets welcome. [pw! 🐕]
website: www.qualitycottages.co.uk

Fishguard

Small town at end of Fishguard Bay

IVYBRIDGE, DRIM MILL, DYFFRYN, GOODWICK SA64 0FT (01348 875366, Fax: 01348 872338). Stay at Ivybridge, swim in our heated pool or relax in our comfortable guest lounge. En suite rooms, home cooking, large off road carpark. Pets welcome! [Pets £5 per stay].
e-mail: ivybridge@boltblue.com website: www.ivybridgeleisure.co.uk

Haverfordwest

Administrative and shopping centre for the area; ideal base for explorlng National Park. Historic town of narrow streets; museum in castle grounds; many fine buildings.

NOLTON HAVEN QUALITY COTTAGES. Sleep 2 to 14. 3,4 & 5 star cottages, some with sea view, some just 30 yards from the beach. Children and pets welcome. Farmhouse B&B also available - seven bedrooms, some en suite. WTB ★★★/★★★★/★★★★★ Self-Catering. Contact: JIM & JOYCE CANTON, NOLTON HAVEN FARMHOUSE, NOLTON HAVEN, HAVERFORDWEST SA62 6NH (01437 710263).
e-mail: PW5@noltonhaven.com website: www.noltonhaven.com

NOLTON HAVEN FARM COTTAGES, NOLTON HAVEN, HAVERFORDWEST SA62 3NH (01437 710200). Quality beachfront cottages, sleep 2-6, adjacent sandy beach. Well equipped. Open all year. Winter breaks. [Pets £10 per week].
e-mail: info@havencottages.co.uk website: www.havencottages.co.uk

SCAMFORD CARAVAN PARK, KEESTON, HAVERFORDWEST SA62 6HN (Tel & Fax: 01437 710304). 25 luxurious caravans (shower, fridge, microwave, colour TV). Peaceful park near lovely sandy beaches. Super playground. Launderette. Five touring pitches, hook-ups. Modern shower block. Pets welcome.WTB ★★★★ Holiday Park.
e-mail: holidays@scamford.com website: www.scamford.com

Lawrenny

Village near River Cresswell estuary, 8 miles south-west of Narberth

MRS VIRGINIA LORT PHILLIPS, KNOWLES FARM, LAWRENNY SA68 0PX (01834 891221). Come and relax with us in our lovely south-facing farmhouse. Listen to the silence and spoil yourselves and your dogs whilst discovering the delights of hidden Pembrokeshire. Walk along the shores of the Estuary which surrounds our organic farm. B&B from £28 to £34 pppn, Dinner on request. WTB ★★★ [First pet free, others £2 per pet per night.]
e-mail: ginilp@lawrenny.org.uk website: www.lawrenny.org.uk

Llanteg

Hamlet 4 miles south of Whitland.

TONY & JANE BARON, LLANTEGLOS ESTATE, LLANTEG, NEAR AMROTH SA67 8PU (01834 831677 /831371). Self-contained Woodland Lodges. Sleep 6. Children's play area. Licensed bar & entertainment. Visitor attractions. Call for brochure. WTB ★★★★ Self Catering [Pets £5 per night, £30 per week.]
e-mail: llanteglosestate@supanet.com website: www.llanteglos-estate.com

Newgale

On St Bride's Bay 3 miles east of Solva. Long beach where at exceptionally low tide the stumps of a submerged forest may be seen.

MR P.W. REES, "QUALITY COTTAGES', CERBID, SOLVA, HAVERFORDWEST, PEMBROKESHIRE SA62 6YE (01348 837871). Cottages set in all coastal areas, unashamed luxury, highest residential standards. Dishwashers, microwaves, washing machines. Log fires. Linen supplied. Pets welcome. [pw! 🐕]
website: www.qualitycottages.co.uk

Newport

Small town at mouth of the River Nyfer, 9 miles south west of Cardigan. Remains of 13th-century castle.

MR P.W. REES, "QUALITY COTTAGES', CERBID, SOLVA, HAVERFORDWEST, PEMBROKESHIRE SA62 6YE (01348 837871). Cottages set in all coastal areas, unashamed luxury, highest residential standards. Dishwashers, microwaves, washing machines. Log fires. Linen supplied. Pets welcome. [pw!]
website: www.qualitycottages.co.uk

Nolton Haven

Hamlet at head of inlet on St Bride's Bay. Fine coastal views.

FOLKESTON HILL HOLIDAY BUNGALOWS. A small group of bungalows in a sheltered valley which winds down to the sea. WTB Graded. Pets welcome. Brochure from RICHARD & CHRISTINE WHITE, SCAMFORD HOLIDAYS, KEESTON, HAVERFORDWEST SA62 6HN (01437 710304). [Pets £10 per week]
e-mail: holidays@scamford.com website: www.stdavids.co.uk/folkeston

St Brides

Located on St Bride's Bay 7 miles north west of Milford Haven.

ST BRIDE'S BAY COTTAGES (0870 7572270). Select quality self-catering holidays in North Pembrokeshire. Sleep 2-11. Short Breaks available. Pets welcome. WTB graded.
website: www.sbbc.uk.com

St David's

Smallest cathedral city in Britain, shrine of Wales' patron saint. Magnificent ruins of Bishop's Palace. Craft shops, farm parks and museums; boat trips to Ramsey Island.

FFYNNON DDOFN, LLANON, LLANRHIAN, NEAR ST DAVID'S. Comfortable, well-equipped cottage with panoramic coastal views. Sleeps 6. Fully carpeted with central heating. Large games room. Open all year. Pets welcome free of charge. Brochure on request from: MRS B. REES WHITE, BRICKHOUSE FARM, BURNHAM RD, WOODHAM MORTIMER, MALDON, ESSEX CM9 6SR (01245 224611). [ ]
website: www.ffynnonddofn.co.uk

ST NONS BAY COTTAGES, ST DAVID'S. Sleep 2-16. Beautifully restored stone and slate cottages. Panoramic views. Near coastal path and sandy beaches. Dishwashers, TV, games rooms, log fire, central heating. Open all year. WTB ★★★★★. [ ] Correspondence: T. M. HARDMAN, HIGH VIEW, CATHERINE STREET, ST DAVID'S, PEMBROKESHIRE SA62 6RJ. Telephone: THELMA HARDMAN (01437 720616). [ ]
e-mail: enquiries@stnbc.co.uk website: www.stnbc.co.uk

FELINDRE COTTAGES, PORTHGAIN, ST DAVID'S, PEMBROKESHIRE SA62 5BH (01348 831220). Self-catering cottages with panoramic sea and country views. Five minutes' walk from Coastal Path, picturesque fishing village of Porthgain and a great pub! Peaceful location. Short breaks available. One well-behaved dog welcome, except August. WTB graded. [pw! £10 per week]
e-mail: steve@felindrecottages.co.uk website: www.felindrecottages.co.uk

MARION LOVERING, TREMYNYDD FACH, ST DAVID'S SA62 6DB (01437 721677; Fax: 01437 720308). A working sheep farm, whose fields extend down to the sea. Farm B&B (in cosy cottages) and Self-catering (in farmhouse and chalet) available. Spectacular and unspoilt stretch of coastal path abounding with rare species of plants and wildlife. [Pets £10 per week]
e-mail: sheepdog_training@lineone.net website: www.sheepdogtraining.co.uk

Terms quoted in this publication may be subject to increase if rises in costs necessitate

MR P.W. REES, "QUALITY COTTAGES', CERBID, SOLVA, HAVERFORDWEST, PEMBROKESHIRE SA62 6YE (01348 837871). Cottages set in all coastal areas, unashamed luxury, highest residential standards. Dishwashers, microwaves, washing machines. Log fires. Linen supplied. Pets welcome. [pw!]
website: www.qualitycottages.co.uk

Saundersfoot

Popular resort and sailing centre with picturesque harbour and sandy beach. Tenby 3 miles

VINE COTTAGE, THE RIDGEWAY, SAUNDERSFOOT SA69 9LA (01834 814422). Coastal village outskirts. Sandy beaches and coast path nearby. Award-winning garden for guests' and dogs' relaxation and exercise. Non-smoking throughout. AA ★★★★. WTB ★★★ Guest House [pw! Pets £5 per stay.]
e-mail: enquiries@vinecottageguesthouse.co.uk website: www.vinecottageguesthouse.co.uk

Solva

Picturesque coastal village with sheltered harbour and excellent craft shops. Sailing and watersports; sea fishing, long sandy beach.

MRS M. JONES, LOCHMEYLER FARM GUEST HOUSE, LLANDELOY, PEN-Y-CWM, NEAR SOLVA, ST DAVIDS, PEMBROKESHIRE SA62 6LL (01348 837724; Fax: 01348 837622). Welcome Host Gold Award. 11 en suite luxury bedrooms, four in the cottage suites adjacent to the house. All bedrooms non-smoking, with TV, video and refreshment facilities. Children 14 years and over welcomed. WTB ★★★★★ *FARM*, AA◆◆◆◆◆ [pw!]

MR P.W. REES, "QUALITY COTTAGES', CERBID, SOLVA, HAVERFORDWEST, PEMBROKESHIRE SA62 6YE (01348 837871). Cottages set in all coastal areas, unashamed luxury, highest residential standards. Dishwashers, microwaves, washing machines. Log fires. Linen supplied. Pets welcome. [pw!]
website: www.qualitycottages.co.uk

Tenby

Popular resort with two wide beaches. Fishing trips, craft shops, museum. Medieval castle ruins, 13th-century church. Golf, fishing and watersports; boat trips to nearby Caldy Island with monastery and medieval church.

MR P.W. REES, "QUALITY COTTAGES', CERBID, SOLVA, HAVERFORDWEST, PEMBROKESHIRE SA62 6YE (01348 837871). Cottages set in all coastal areas, unashamed luxury, highest residential standards. Dishwashers, microwaves, washing machines. Log fires. Linen supplied. Pets welcome. [pw!]
website: www.qualitycottages.co.uk

Whitland

Village 6 miles east of Narberth. Whitland Abbey 2 km.

MRS ANGELA COLLEDGE, GWARMACWYDD FARM, LLANFALLTEG, WHITLAND SA34 0XH (01437 563260; Fax: 01437 563839). Country estate with six character stone cottages, fully furnished and equipped. All linen and electricity included; heated for year-round use. WTB ★★★★ [pw! Pets £10 per week]
e-mail: fhg@gwarmacwydd.co.uk website: www.gwarmacwydd.co.uk

Symbols

- Indicates that pets are welcome free of charge.
- **£** Indicates that a charge is made for pets: nightly or weekly.
- **pw!** Shows some special provision for pets; exercise facility, feeding or accommodation arrangement.
- ☖ Indicates separate pets accommodation.

Darnley Cottage — Pencelli • Brecon • Powys

Character cottage in peaceful Brecon Beacons canalside village. Sleeps 4. One double and one twin bedroom. Secure private garden, ideal for well behaved pets. Non-smoking. Weekly breaks all year, short breaks (min. 3 nights) outside peak season.

Caron & Dave Wise • Tel: 01873 810811 or 07790 907155
E-mail: sage@wiseinwales.co.uk • www.wiseinwales.co.uk

AA ★★★

Caer Beris Manor

GWESTY ★★★ HOTEL

Family-owned three star Country House Hotel set in 27 acres of parkland. Free salmon and trout fishing on River Wye (two rods) and on River Irfon. Superb walking and touring. 18 hole Golf Course nearby. Excellent cuisine.
All rooms en suite with telephone, TV and tea making.

DOGS WELCOME!

DB&B £64.50pppn; £387 weekly; B&B £54.50pppn.

Mrs Katharine Smith, Caer Beris Manor, Builth Wells
Powys LD2 3NP • Tel: 01982 552601 • Fax: 01982 552586
e-mail: caerberis@btconnect.com • www.caerberis.co.uk

• ERWOOD, BUILTH WELLS LD2 3SZ • Tel: 01982 560680 •

Situated in secluded grounds with glorious views of the beautiful Wye Valley. Attractive spacious rooms (one en suite, two sharing guests' own bathroom), have TV, drinks tray, fridge, wash basin. Bacon and sausage from locally reared pigs, free range eggs and home made preserves for breakfast. Two bedrooms with double aspect. FHG Diploma Winner 2004.

e-mail: linda@oldvicwyevalley.co.uk • www.oldvicwyevalley.co.uk WTB ★★ Farm

---

Set in a 30 acre woodland, all our lodges are individually designed and fully fitted throughout, including colour TV, microwave, full kitchen, bath/shower room, and include all bedding. 19 lodges sleeping 2 – 8 people and one cottage which sleeps six. Fishing on the Montgomery canal, River Severn and our own private lake. Quad trekking and pony trekking nearby.
Pets welcome in certain cabins,
From £175 to £675 per cabin per week inc. VAT.
Short Breaks. Open all year round.

Tel/Fax 01686 640269 for a colour brochure
Penllwyn Lodges, Garthmyl, Powys SY15 6SB
e-mail: daphne.jones@onetel.net
www.penllwynlodges.co.uk

17th century farm in rural Radnorshire, five miles Hay-on-Wye. Wonderful walking country. Self-catering apartments and Bed and Breakfast accommodation. A warm welcome for you and your pet(s). WTB ★★★

MRS E. BALLY, LANE FARM, PAINSCASTLE, BUILTH WELLS LD2 3JS

Tel & Fax: 01497 851605 • e-mail: lanefarm@onetel.com

Situated 3 miles from the market town of Knighton - self-contained, fully furnished, ground floor accommodation. One twin bedroom + sofa bed in lounge. Towels, linen and electricity incl. Fully equipped kitchen; washing machine and tumble dryer. Private patio area with BBQ. No smoking. Pets welcome. Open all year - short breaks available. B&B also available. **Apply: Roger & Sue Morris, Graig Cottage, Llanfairwaterdine, Knighton LD7 1TS (01547 529542)**

www.thegardenlodgeatgraigcottage.co.uk

The Park House Motel

Crossgates, Llandrindod Wells
Powys LD1 6RF
Tel: (01597) 851201

Set in 3 acres of beautiful Welsh countryside and close to the famous Elan Valley. Accommodation includes static caravans, touring pitches and fully equipped motel units which have either a twin or double bedroom, shower room, and kitchen with a dinette that converts to a double bed. Sleeping up to 4, they can be booked for either self-catering or B&B. On-site facilities include restaurant, bar and snug. Well behaved pets are very welcome.

barr560@btinternet.com • www.parkmotel.co.uk

MADOG'S WELLS Llanfair Caereinion, Welshpool, Powys SY21 0DE

Beautiful, peaceful valley with lots of wildlife. Three bungalows, wheelchair accessible. Free gas, electricity and linen. Cot/highchair available on request. Games room and children's play area. Daily rates available out of main school holidays. Two three-bedroom bungalows (**WTB** ★★★★★) from £140 to £480. Two bedroom bungalow (**WTB ★★★**) £100 to £300. Open all year. Farmhouse B&B at £23 pppn. **Contact Michael & Ann Reed for further details • Tel/Fax: 01938 810446 • e-mail: info@madogswells.co.uk • www.madogswells.co.uk**

Cosy cottage in lovely Border countryside. 2 miles from Offa's Dyke • Central heating, washing machine, microwave, colour TV, inglenook, woodburner, linen included • Sleeps 4 plus cot • Ample parking • Sun-trap garden • On working farm in peaceful hamlet • Children and pets welcome • WTB Grade 4.

MRS R. L. JONES, UPPER HOUSE, KINNERTON, NEAR PRESTEIGNE LD8 2PE

Tel: 01547 560207

Oak Wood Lodges

Llwynbaedd, Rhayader, Powys LD6 5NT

Luxurious Self Catering Log Cabins situated at approximately 1000ft above sea level with spectacular views of the Elan Valley and Cambrian mountains. Enjoy pursuits such as walking, pony trekking, mountain biking, fishing, and bird watching in the most idyllic of surroundings. Excellent touring centre. Dogs welcome. Short breaks as well as full weeks. Open all year round

For more information and brochure call:

01597 811422

www.oakwoodlodges.co.uk

HUNAN DDARPAR ★★★★ SELF CATERING

FREE or REDUCED RATE entry to Holiday Visits and Attractions – see our READERS' OFFER VOUCHERS on page 407-423

Brecon

Main touring centre for National Park. Busy market; Jazz Festival in summer. Brecknock Museum, ruined castle, cathedral of interest. Golf, walking, fishing, canal cruising, pony trekking.

CARON & DAVE WISE, DARNLEY COTTAGE, PENCELLI, BRECON (01873 810811 or 07790 907155). Character cottage in peaceful Brecon Beacons canalside village. Sleeps 4. One double and one twin bedroom. Secure private garden, ideal for well behaved pets. Non-smoking. Weekly breaks all year, short breaks (min. 3 nights) outside peak season. WTB★★★★ Self-catering.
e-mail: sage@wiseinwales.co.uk website: www.wiseinwales.co.uk

Well-equipped, tastefully decorated and personally supervised, offering the highest standard of cleanliness. Three-bedroomed bungalow, plus two apartments sleeping 2/4 or 8 combined in quiet, accessible rural location in heart of Brecon Beacons National Park. Lawns. Play area. Parking. Short Breaks. Superb walking. Excellent pub food locally. Ideal touring base. WTB ★★★★ / ★★★★★ Brochure: MRS ANN PHILLIPS, OWL BARN, WERNYMARCHOG, CANTREF, BRECON LD3 8LW (Tel & Fax: 01874 665329; mobile: 07977 337523). [pw! £20 per week]
e-mail: enquiries@wernymarchog.co.uk website: www.wernymarchog.co.uk

Builth Wells

Old country town in lovely setting on River Wye amid beautiful hills. Lively markets; host to Royal Welsh Agricultural Show

MRS KATHARINE SMITH, CAER BERIS MANOR, BUILTH WELLS LD2 3NP (01982 552601; Fax: 01982 552586). Family-owned country house hotel set in 27 acres of parkland. Free salmon and trout fishing; golf nearby, superb walking and touring. All rooms en suite. WTB/AA ★★★. [Pets £5 per night, £30 per week].
e-mail: caerberis@btconnect.com website: www.caerberis.co.uk

MRS LINDA WILLIAMS, OLD VICARAGE, ERWOOD, BUILTH WELLS LD2 3SZ (01982 560680). Situated in secluded grounds with glorious views of the beautiful Wye Valley. Attractive spacious rooms (one en suite, two sharing guests' own bathroom), have TV, drinks tray, fridge, wash basin. Bacon and sausage from locally reared pigs, free range eggs and home made preserves for breakfast. Two bedrooms with double aspect. WTB ★★ Farm, FHG Diploma Winner 2004.[🐕]
e-mail: linda@oldvicwyevalley.co.uk website: www.oldvicwyevalley.co.uk

Garthmyl

Situated on A483 between Welshpool and Newtown in unspoilt countryside.

Self-catering log cabins set in 30 acres of unspoilt woodland teeming with wildlife. Central heating, colour TV, microwave etc. Pets welcome in certain cabins. From £175-£675 per cabin per week breaks. Apply PENLLWYN LODGES, GARTHMYL, POWYS SY15 6SB (Tel & Fax: 01686 640269) for colour brochure. [Pets £15 per stay]
e-mail: daphne.jones@onetel.net website: www.penllwynlodges.co.uk

Hay-on-Wye

Small market town at north end of Black Mountains, 15 miles north-east of Brecon.

MRS E. BALLY, LANE FARM, PAINSCASTLE, BUILTH WELLS LD2 3JS (Tel & Fax: 01497 851605). 17th century farm in rural Radnorshire, five miles Hay-on-Wye. Wonderful walking country. Self-catering apartments and Bed and Breakfast accommodation. A warm welcome for you and your pet(s). WTB ★★★ [🐕]
e-mail: lanefarm@onetel.com

Knighton

Town on River TEme, 14 miles west of Ludlow.

Situated three miles from Knighton - self-contained, fully furnished, ground floor accommodation. One twin bedroom + sofa bed in lounge. No smoking. Pets welcome. Open all year - short breaks available. B&B also available. Apply: ROGER & SUE MORRIS, GRAIG COTTAGE, LLANFAIRWATERDINE, KNIGHTON LD7 1TS (01547 529542). VisitWales ★★★. [🐕]
website: thegardenlodgeatgraigcottage.co.uk

Llandrindod Wells

Popular inland resort, Victorian spa town, excellent touring centre. Golf, fishing, bowling, boating and tennis. Visitors can still take the waters at Rock Park Gardens.

THE PARK HOUSE MOTEL, CROSSGATES, LLANDRINDOD WELLS LD1 6RF (01597 851201). In three acres, amidst beautiful countryside near Elan Valley. Static caravans, touring pitches and fully equipped motel units. Licensed restaurant, bar. Pets welcome. [Pets £3 per night, £20 per week. Guide dogs free). [🐕]
e-mail: barr560@btinternet.com website: www.parkmotel.co.uk

Llanfair Caereinion

Small town on River Banwy, 8 miles west of Welshpool.

MRS ANN REED, MADOG'S WELLS, LLANFAIR CAEREINION, WELSHPOOL SY21 0DE (Tel & Fax: 01938 810446). Three self-catering bungalows, wheelchair accessible; farmhouse B&B. Open all year. WTB ★★★/★★★★★ *SELF-CATERING*. [🐕]
e-mail: info@madogswells.co.uk website: www.madogswells.co.uk

Llangurig

Village on River Wye, 4 miles south-west of Llanidloes. Ideal walking countryside.

MRS J. BAILEY, GLANGWY, LLANGURIG, LLANIDLOES SY18 6RS (01686 440697). Bed, breakfast and evening meals in the countryside. Plenty of walking locally. Also caravan and campsite. Prices on request. [🐕]

Machynlleth

Attractive old town with half timbered houses. Ideal for hillside rambles and pony trekking.

PETS WELCOME at The Wynnstay Hotel. Award-winning food, wine and beer. Glorious countryside and miles of sandy beaches. Masses to do and see. WTB/AA ★★★. Good Food Guide & Good Beer Guide Recommended, Les Routiers "Best Wine List in Britain". (01654 702941). [Pets free in kennels, £5 one-off charge in rooms]
e-mail: info@wynnstay-hotel.com website: www.wynnstay-hotel.com

Presteigne

Attractive old town with half timbered houses. Ideal for hillside rambles and pony trekking.

MRS R. L. JONES, UPPER HOUSE, KINNERTON, NEAR PRESTEIGNE LD8 2PE (01547 560207). Cosy cottage two miles from Offa's Dyke. Central heating, washing machine, microwave, colour TV, inglenook, woodburner, linen included. Sleeps 4 plus cot. Children and pets welcome. WTB Grade 4. [🐕].

Rhayader

Small market town on River Wye north of Builth Wells. Popular for angling and pony trekking

OAK WOOD LODGES, LLWYNBAEDD, RHAYADER LD6 5NT (01597 811422). Luxurious self-catering log cabins with spectacular views of the Elan Valley and Cambrian Mountains. Walking, pony trekking, mountain biking, fishing and bird watching in idyllic surroundings. WTB ★★★★ Self-catering. [Pets £20 per week, £13 per short break; additional dogs half price].
website: www.oakwoodlodges.co.uk

Symbols

- 🐕 Indicates that pets are welcome free of charge.
- £ Indicates that a charge is made for pets: nightly or weekly.
- pw! Shows some special provision for pets; exercise facility, feeding or accommodation arrangement.
- ⌂ Indicates separate pets accommodation.

Cardiff, Monmouth, Redbrook-on-Wye, Swansea, Tintern, Wye Valley

Egerton Grey

Porthkerry, Vale of Glamorgan, Near Cardiff CF62 3BZ
Tel: 01446 711666 • Fax: 01446 711690
e-mail: info@egertongrey.co.uk • www.egertongrey.co.uk

AA ★★★

A recommended centre from which to explore the lovely and uncrowded Gower Peninsula and the Brecon Beacons, this stylish and distinguished country house was opened as a small and luxurious hotel in 1988. Only 10 miles from Cardiff, it is set in a secluded, wooded valley in seven acres of gardens, with views down to Porthkerry Park and the sea. The excellent facilities accorded guests include exquisitely furnished bedrooms (all with private bathrooms), two dining rooms, library and magnificent Edwardian drawing room. Only a short stroll away is a well-maintained country park with an 18-hole pitch and putt course. The cuisine is outstanding and dining here by candlelight is a memorable experience. Recommended by many national and international hotel and restaurant guides. ***Taste of Wales Cuisine Award***

A spacious and homely 16th century (Grade II Listed) former farmhouse with oak beams and inglenook fireplaces, set in large garden with stream. Easy access to A40. All nine bedrooms are en suite or have private facilities. B&B from £24 to £28 per person. Evening meals by arrangement • Non-smoking • WTB ★★ Guest House, AA ◆◆◆

ROSEMARY AND DEREK RINGER, CHURCH FARM GUEST HOUSE, MITCHEL TROY, MONMOUTH NP25 4HZ • 01600 712176
e-mail: info@churchfarmguesthouse.eclipse.co.uk • www.churchfarmmitcheltroy.co.uk

OLD BREWERY HOUSE, BREWERY YARD, REDBROOK ON WYE, MONMOUTHSHIRE NP25 4LU • 01600 713819
e-mail: enquiries@oldbreweryhouse.com • www.oldbreweryhouse.com

Welcoming en suite accommodation with courtyard garden and private parking. Scenic riverside off-road walks. Two village pubs serve meals. B&B £75 per room per night. 10% discount 2 or more nights. Dogs free.

BEST WESTERN ABERAVON BEACH HOTEL

Modern seafront hotel. A warm Welsh welcome awaits you and your pets. 2 miles of flat promenade and a pet friendly beach. Pets Paradise!! And for you..... comfortable rooms, fine cuisine, leisure centre and many local attractions.

AA ★★★

Neath Port Talbot, Swansea Bay SA12 6QP TEL 01639 884949

The Wye Valley Hotel • www.wyevalleyhotel.co.uk

Tintern, Near Chepstow, South Wales NP16 6SQ

Homely hotel in the heart of the Wye Valley, just a short stroll from historic Tintern Abbey. Splendid base for touring. Well furnished en suite rooms. Dogs welcome by arrangement.

Tel: 01291 689441 • Fax: 01291 689440 • E-mail: info@wyevalleyhotel.co.uk

Cwrt-y-Gaer in the Vale of Usk and Wye Valley

One, four or more dogs welcome FREE. Three self-catering units in well converted stone Welsh Longhouse, set in old hilltop fort in 20 acres with fine views across to mountains. Quiet area with good access to many places of interest. Good walking. Open all year. Brochure from **Sue & John Llewellyn, Cwrt-y-Gaer, Wolvesnewton, Chepstow, Monmouthshire NP16 6PR**
Tel: (01291) 650700 • E-mail: john.llewellyn11@btinternet.com
All units are WTB ★★★. One unit is Grade 1 access for the disabled.

CASTLE NARROWBOATS CHURCH ROAD WHARF, GILWERN NP7 0EP (01873 830001). The Monmouthshire & Brecon Canal in South Wales. Discover the beauty of Wales onboard one of our excellent narrowboats. 2-8 berth boats, short breaks available. Pets welcome.For a free colour brochure call Castle Narrowboats:
website: www.castlenarrowboats.co.uk

Abergavenny

Historic market town at south-eastern gateway to Brecon Beacons National Park. Pony trekking, leisure centre; excellent touring base for Vale of Usk.

THE HALF MOON INN, LLANTHONY, NEAR ABERGAVENNY NP7 7NN (01873 890611). Friendly 17th-Century Hotel. Serves good food and real ale. Enjoy wonderful scenery of Black Mountains. Good base. Walking, pony trekking. Next to Offa's Dyke and Beacon's Way. B&B accommodation. Dogs welcome. [🐕] e-mail: halfmoon@llanthony.wanadoo.co.uk

Cardiff

City and port at mouth of River Taff. Capital of Wales.

EGERTON GREY COUNTRY HOUSE HOTEL, PORTHKERRY, BARRY, NEAR CARDIFF, VALE OF GLAMORGAN CF62 3BZ (01446 711666; Fax: 01446 711690). Magnificently preserved country house set in seven acres in a secluded valley 10 miles from Cardiff. Ideal for touring South Wales. WTB ★★★★ Hotel, AA ★★★ [🐕]
e-mail: info@egertongrey.co.uk website: www.egertongrey.co.uk

Gower

Britain's first designated Area of Outstanding Natural Beauty with numerous sandy beaches and lovely countryside to explore.

CULVER HOUSE HOTEL, PORT EYNON, GOWER SA3 1NN (01792 390755). Small, friendly Hotel with fabulous breakfast and quality service. Peacefully situated, with superb coast and countryside. En suite, sea views. WTB ★★ Country Hotel. [Pets £2 per night.]
website: www.culverhousehotel.co.uk

Monmouth

Market town at confluence of Rivers Wye and Monnow 20 miles north-east of Newport.

ROSEMARY AND DEREK RINGER, CHURCH FARM GUEST HOUSE, MITCHEL TROY, MONMOUTH NP25 4HZ (01600 712176). A spacious 16th century (Grade II Listed) former farmhouse set in large garden with stream. Easy access to A40. All bedrooms en suite or with private facilities. B&B from £24 to £28 per person. Evening meals by arrangement. Non-smoking. WTB ★★ Guest House, AA ◆◆◆ [🐕].
e-mail: info@churchfarmguesthouse.eclipse.co.uk website: www.churchfarmmitcheltroy.co.uk

Mumbles

Seaside resort of Swansea to west and north west of Mumbles Head.

MUMBLES & SWANSEA. Seafront ground floor flat. Well-equipped modern conveniences. Ideal for beaches, countryside and local amenities. Personally supervised. Plenty of dog walks! WTB ★★★★. MRS JEAN GRIERSON, 112 MUMBLES ROAD, BLACKPILL, SWANSEA SA3 5AS (01792 402278). [🐕]

Swansea

*Second largest city in Wales with a wide variety of leisure activities and excellent shopping.*e

BEST WESTERN ABERAVON BEACH HOTEL, NEATH PORT TALBOT, SWANSEA BAY SA12 6QP (01639 884949). Modern seafront hotel. A warm Welsh welcome awaits you and your pets. 2 miles of flat promenade and a pet friendly beach. Pets Paradise!! And for you..... comfortable rooms, fine cuisine, leisure centre and many local attractions. AA ★★★.[🐕]

Tintern

Village on River Wye, 4 miles North of Chepstow.

BARRY & SUE COOKE, THE WYE VALLEY HOTEL, TINTERN, NEAR CHEPSTOW NP16 6SQ (01291 689441; Fax: 01291 689440). Homely hotel in the heart of the Wye Valley, just a short stroll from historic Tintern Abbey. Splendid base for touring. Well furnished en suite rooms. Dogs welcome by arrangement. WTB ★★.
e-mail: info@wyevalleyhotel.co.uk website: www.wyevalleyhotel.co.uk

Wye Valley

Scenic area, ideal for relaxation.

MR & MRS J. LLEWELLYN, CWRT-Y-GAER, WOLVESNEWTON, CHEPSTOW NP16 6PR (01291 650700). 1, 4 or more dogs welcome free. Self-catering, attractively converted stone buildings of Welsh Longhouse. 20 acres, super views of Usk Vale. Brochure. Three units (one suitable for disabled). WTB ★★★, Welcome Host Gold Award. [pw! 🐕]
e-mail: john.llewellyn11@btinternet.com website: www.cwrt-y-gaer.co.uk

IRELAND

IMAGINE IRELAND, COASTAL HOLIDAY COTTAGES. 700 inspected coastal Holiday Cottages. From £13 per person per night, inc. ferry. Pets go free. Low ferry inclusive prices. Car hire and smaller party prices. Free 100 page brochure. (0870 066 3352).
website: www.petswelcomeholidaycottages.co.uk

NARROWBOATS

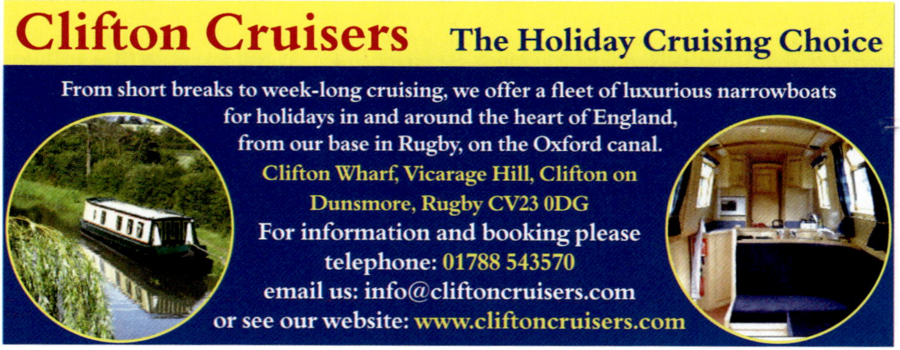

A selection of accommodation where horse and owner/rider can be put up at the same address – if not actually under the same roof!
We would be grateful if readers making enquiries and/or bookings from this supplement would mention
Pets Welcome!

Spike and friends

Holidays with Horses

England

Buckinghamshire

SWAN REVIVED HOTEL,
HIGH STREET, NEWPORT PAGNELL, MILTON KEYNES MK16 8AR
(01908 610565; Fax: 01908 210995)
e-mail: swanrevived@btclick.com website: www.swanrevived.co.uk
Delightful 16thC former coaching inn, extensively modernised to provide 40 comfortable guest rooms, two bars, à la carte restaurant, meeting rooms and banqueting facilities. Pets very welcome.

Cornwall

B. WRIGHT,
TREWORGEY COTTAGES, DULOE, LISKEARD PL14 4PP
(01503 262730)
website: www.cornishdreamcottages.co.uk

Idyllic 18th century country cottages for romantics and animal lovers. Looe three miles. Wonderful walks from your gate. Riding, heated swimming pool and tennis court. Cottages warm and cosy in winter. VisitBritain Quality Assurance Scheme ★★★★★ Quality Award.

Cumbria

FARLAM HALL HOTEL
BRAMPTON CA8 2NG.
(016977 46234; Fax: 016977 46683)
e-mail: farlam@relaischateaux.com • website: www.farlamhall.co.uk

Standing in four acres of gardens, with its own lake, Farlam Hall offers fine quality cuisine and individually decorated guest rooms. Ideal touring centre for the Lakes, Borders and hadrian's Wall. AA Three Stars Inspectors' Choice and Two Rosettes, Relais & Chateaux.

Devon

JAYE JONES & HELEN ASHER,
TWITCHEN FARM, CHALLACOMBE, BARNSTAPLE EX31 4TT
(01598 763568)
e-mail: holidays@twitchen.co.uk • website: www.twitchen.co.uk

Comfort for country lovers in Exmoor National Park. All rooms en suite with TV. Meals prepared with local and some organic produce. Stabling £50 per week. Dogs no charge. B&B £26-£36, DB&B £46-£56. ETC ◆◆◆◆

COLLACOTT FARM, KING'S NYMPTON, UMBERLEIGH EX37 9TP
(01769 572491)
e-mail: info@collacott.co.uk • website: www.collacott.co.uk

Eight Country Cottages sleeping from 2 to 12 in rural area. Well furnished and equipped. Open all year. BHS Approved riding school.

COLIN & JILL HARMAN
DOONE VALLEY HOLIDAYS, CLOUD FARM, OARE, LYNTON EX35 6NU
(01598 741234; Fax: 01598 741154).
e-mail: doonevalleyholidays@hotmail.com
website: www.doonevalleyholidays.co.uk www.doonevalleytrekking.co.uk

Why not bring your horse on holiday...? We have ample stabling and grazing available and specialise in horse riding holidays, weekends and short breaks. VisitBritain ★★★★

SPIRIT OF EXMOOR
(01598 753318).
e-mail: stephany@spiritofexmoor.fsnet.co.uk website: www.spiritofexmoor.com

Exhilarating riding across miles of untamed moorland in small groups. Fit, friendly, forward going well schooled horses. Non-riders, own horses and pets welcome. Delicious home cooked cuisine, vegetarians welcome. Special winter breaks available. Colour brochure. Contact: Stephany Pettinger.

STEVE AND LORY JENDEN
LYDFORD HOUSE, LYDFORD, OKEHAMPTON EX20 4AU
(01822 820347; Fax: 01822 820539)
e-mail: info@lydfordhouse.com website: www.lydfordhouse.com

Superb riding in Dartmoor National Park. Warm relaxed atmosphere self-catering and nine luxury rooms in eight acres of grounds. In-house Italian restaurant. Your horse comes free. Stables, sand-school, grazing, parking for lorries. B&B from £35. ETC ◆◆◆◆

Durham

MRS P A BOOTH,
IVESLEY EQUESTRIAN CENTRE, IVESLEY, WATERHOUSES DH7 9HB.
(0191 373 4324; Fax: 0191 373 4757)
e-mail: ivesley@msn.com • website: www.ridingholidays-ivesley.co.uk

Beautifully furnished comfortable country house set in 220 acres in Durham but very quiet and rural. Excellent dog exercising facilities. En suite bedrooms. Excellent food. Licensed. Fully equipped Equestrian Centre adjacent.

Readers are requested to mention this FHG guidebook when seeking accommodation

Gloucestershire

CAROLINE MANN
HARTWELL FARM COTTAGES, NEAR BIBURY, CIRENCESTER GL7 5SY
(01285 740210)
e-mail: ec.mann@btinternet.com website: www.selfcateringcotswolds.com

Two comfortable cottages in Cotswolds with country views. Ideally located for touring, horse riding. Stabling available. Children and well-behaved dogs welcome. ETC ★★★★

Lincolnshire

POACHERS HIDEAWAY HOLIDAY COTTAGES
FLINTWOOD FARM, BELCHFORD, HORNCASTLE LN9 5QN
(01507 533555)
e-mail: sallytuxworth@poachershideaway.com website: www.poachershideaway.com

Set in 150 acres of wildflower meadows, fishing lakes and moorland. Miles of private pathways, direct access onto the Viking Way footpath. Stunning views, peaceful and relaxing. ETC ★★★★★

Oxfordshire

JUNE AND GEORGE COLLIER
55 NETHERCOTE ROAD, TACKLEY, KIDLINGTON, OXFORD OX5 3AT
(01869 331255; mobile: 07790 338225)
e-mail: colliers.bnb@virgin.net website: www.colliersbnb.com

An ideal base for riding - superb network of Bridleways. Stop-over for Claude Duval route. Close to Blenheim. Regular train and bus service. Local Hostelries serve excellent food. ETC ◆◆◆

Somerset

LEONE & BRIAN MARTIN,
RISCOMBE FARM HOLIDAY COTTAGES, EXFORD,
EXMOOR NATIONAL PARK TA24 7NH
(01643 831480)
website: www.riscombe.co.uk (with up-to-date vacancy info.)

Four self-catering stone cottages in the centre of Exmoor National Park. Excellent walking and riding country. Dogs and horses welcome. Open all year. VB ★★★★

WESTERCLOSE HOUSE,
WITHYPOOL, EXMOOR NATIONAL PARK TA24 7QR
(01643 831302)
website: www.westerclose.co.uk

Moorland cottages including two bungalows in grounds of old hunting lodge overlooking Barle Valley. Dogs and horses welcome. Shop and pub 300 metres. Cosy, quality and peaceful accommodation with wonderful riding, and superb stables and paddocks.

East Yorkshire

PAWS-A-WHILE
KILNWICK PERCY, POCKLINGTON YO42 1UF
(01759 301168; Mobile: 07711 866869)
e-mail: paws.a.while@lineone.net • website: www.pawsawhile.net

Small family B & B set in forty acres of parkland twixt York and Beverley. Golf, sauna, walking, riding. Pets and horses most welcome. Brochure available. ETC ◆◆◆◆

North Yorkshire

MEG ABU HAMDAN,
HIGH BELTHORPE, BISHOP WILTON, YORK YO42 1SB
(01759 368238; Mobile: 07786 923330)

BHS Approved Livery yard in lovely surroundings. Bring your horse to enjoy the most fabulous hacking over the Yorkshire Wolds, still unspoilt and quiet. Farmhouse B&B. ETC ◆◆◆

Scotland

Dumfries & Galloway

RUSKO HOLIDAYS,
GATEHOUSE OF FLEET, CASTLE DOUGLAS DG7 2BS
(01557 814215)
e-mail: info@ruskoholidays.co.uk • website: www.ruskoholidays.co.uk

Spacious, traditional farmhouse and three charming, cosy cottages near beaches, hills and forest park. Lots of off-road riding amid stunning scenery. Stabling and grazing available for your own horse. Beautiful walking and riding country, fishing and tennis. Rates £216-£1278. STB ★★ to ★★★★

Wales

Powys

MRS E. BALLY
LANE FARM, PAINSCASTLE, BUILTH WELLS LD2 3JS
(Tel & Fax: 01497 851605)
e-mail: lanefarm@onetel.com

Self-Catering and Bed and Breakfast accommodation. Nine good stables and ample grazing in the heart of rural Radnorshire with wonderful open riding. Some cross-country jumps. WTB ★★★★

Note

All the information in this guide is given in good faith in the belief that it is correct. However, the publishers cannot guarantee the facts given in these pages, neither are they responsible for changes in ownership or facilities that may take place after the date of going to press.
Readers should always satisfy themselves that the facilities they require are available and that the terms, if quoted, still apply.

Ratings & Awards

For the first time ever the AA, VisitBritain, VisitScotland, and the Wales Tourist Board will use a single method of assessing and rating serviced accommodation. Irrespective of which organisation inspects an establishment the rating awarded will be the same, using a common set of standards, giving a clear guide of what to expect. The RAC is no longer operating an Hotel inspection and accreditation business.

Accommodation Standards: Star Grading Scheme

Using a scale of 1-5 stars the objective quality ratings give a clear indication of accommodation standard, cleanliness, ambience, hospitality, service and food, This shows the full range of standards suitable for every budget and preference, and allows visitors to distinguish between the quality of accommodation and facilities on offer in different establishments.All types of board and self-catering accommodation are covered, including hotels, B & Bs, holiday parks, campus accommodation, hostels, caravans and camping, and boats.

The more stars, the higher level of quality

★★★★★
exceptional quality, with a degree of luxury

★★★★
excellent standard throughout

★★★
very good level of quality and comfort

★★
good quality, well presented and well run

★
acceptable quality; simple, practical, no frills

VisitBritain and the regional tourist boards, **enjoyEngland.com, VisitScotland** and **VisitWales,** and **the AA** have full details of the grading system on their websites

enjoy**England**.com

★★★★ FARMHOUSE

Scottish TOURIST BOARD ★★★ HOTEL

visit**Scotland**.com

visit**Wales**.com

BWRDD CROESO CYMRU WALES TOURIST BOARD GWESTY ★★★ HOTEL

AA ★★★ Guest Accommodation

the AA .com

National Accessible Scheme

If you have particular mobility, visual or hearing needs, look out for the National Accessible Scheme. You can be confident of finding accommodation or attractions that meet your needs by looking for the following symbols.

- Typically suitable for a person with sufficient mobility to climb a flight of steps but would benefit from fixtures and fittings to aid balance
- Typically suitable for a person with restricted walking ability and for those that may need to use a wheelchair some of the time and can negotiate a maximum of three steps
- Typically suitable for a person who depends on the use of a wheelchair and transfers unaided to and from the wheelchair in a seated position. This person may be an independent traveller
- Typically suitable for a person who depends on the use of a wheelchair in a seated position. This person also requires personal or mechanical assistance (eg carer, hoist).

Ap-paws Top Dog Spots

Winalot Approved Most Dog Friendly Place to Eat & Drink
Hollybush Inn, Staffordshire

And the other 2005 category winners were...

Winalot Approved Most Dog Friendly Place to GO

Chatsworth House, Derbyshire

Chatsworth House prides itself on being a great location for families, and its dog friendly policies mean that no one has to be left at home! Visitors can enjoy many miles of free walks and there are also water bowls to keep dogs refreshed after exercising in the beautiful surroundings. The Duchess of Devonshire takes great pleasure in walking her dogs around the grounds and she is thrilled that others share her passion for Chatsworth House and enjoy exploring the grounds with their dogs.

Winalot Approved Most Dog Friendly Place To EAT & DRINK

Hollybush Inn, Denford, Staffordshire

Regulars are raising a glass in celebration to the popular public house and restaurant whose welcoming attitude made them the clear category winner. The Inn works hard to make sure that all its customers feel welcome, including its four-legged friends! It has an open door policy for dogs and wants visitors to know that their pets are always welcome.

Winalot Approved Most Dog Friendly Place to PLAY

Daymer Bay Beach, Cornwall

Daymer Bay Beach's consistently welcoming and friendly attitude to dogs made it the clear winner of this category. A spokesperson from North Cornwall district council comments: "We always make sure that dogs and their owners are welcome to visit the beach all year round. The beach boasts wonderful long stretches of sand, which are perfect for both playing and walking."

Winalot Approved Most Dog Friendly Place to SHOP

Bark 'n' Bite, Ripley, Derbyshire

Bark 'n' Bite beat other stores due to its enormously personal service, always making sure that the dog's best interests and comfort are given priority. As well as offering water bowls and treats, the shop also has a personal fitting service for dogs. Every dog is individually fitted for its coat, harness or collar.

Winalot Approved Most Dog Friendly CELEBRITY

Paul O'Grady

Paul is rarely without his beloved dog Buster, a nine year-old shih tzu/ bichon frise cross that Paul first met on the set of The Big Breakfast. Paul instantly fell in love with the three week-old puppy and from that day Buster has been a permanent fixture in both Paul's and Lily Savages's acts, regularly stealing the limelight!

Winalot Approved Most Dog Friendly SERVICE STATION

Moto Service Station, Medway

Medway service station provides a Moto Pets feeding station which is a dedicated place for visitors to feed and water their dogs, with disposable bowls available from the Fresh Express Restaurant, as well as leaflets offering top tips for travelling with your dog.

Pet-Friendly Pubs and Inns

Please note that these establishments may not feature in the man section of this book

ENGLAND

BERKSHIRE

UNCLE TOM'S CABIN
Hills Lane, Cookham Dean, Berkshire (01628 483339).
Dogs allowed throughout.
Pet Regulars: Flossie and Ollie (Old English Sheepdog). Free dog biscuit pub.

THE GREYHOUND (known locally as 'The Dog')
The Walk, Eton Wick, Berkshire (01753 863925).
Dogs allowed throughout the pub.
Pet Regulars: Harvey (Retriever), retrieves anything, including Beer mats. Tully - German Shepherd.

THE OLD BOOT
Stanford Bingley, Berkshire (01189 744292).
Pets welcome in bar area.
Pet Regulars: Resident dog Skip - Black Labrador.

THE TWO BREWERS
Park Street, Windsor, Berkshire (01753 855426).
Dogs allowed, public and saloon bars.
Pet Regulars: Molly (Newfoundland), Bear (Black Labrador), Rufus (Springer Spaniel), Mr Darcy (Poodle), Rosie (Chocolate Labrador), Lilly (English Bulldog), Molly (Fox Terrier), McIntosh (Highland Terrier) and Lulu & Paddy (Cocker Spaniels).

BUCKINGHAMSHIRE

WHITE HORSE
Village Lane, Hedgerley, Buckinghamshire SL2 3UY (01753 643225).
Dogs allowed at tables on pub frontage, beer garden (on leads), public bar.

FROG AT SKIRMETT
Skirmett, Henley-on-Thames, Buckinghamshire RG9 6TG (01491 638996)
Dogs welcome, pet friendly.

GEORGE AND DRAGON
High Street, West Wycombe, Buckinghamshire HP14 3AB (01494 464414)
Pet friendly.

CAMBRIDGESHIRE

YE OLD WHITE HART
Main Street, Ufford, Peterborough, Cambridgeshire (01780 740250).
Dogs allowed in non-food areas.

CHESHIRE

THE GROSVENOR ARMS
Chester Road, Aldford, Cheshire CH3 6HJ (01244 620228)
Pet friendly.
Pet Regulars: resident dog "Sadie" (Labrador).

CORNWALL

DRIFTWOOD SPARS HOTEL
Trevaunance Cove, St Agnes, Cornwall (01872 552428).
Dogs allowed everywhere except the restaurant.
Pet Regulars: Buster (Cornish Labrador cross with a Seal) - devours anything.

JUBILEE INN
Pelynt, Near Looe, Cornwall PL13 2JZ (01503 220312).
Dogs allowed in all areas except restaurant; accommodation for guests with dogs.

THE MILL HOUSE INN
Trebarwith Strand, Tintagel, Cornwall PL34 0HD (01840 770200).
Pet friendly.

THE MOLESWORTH ARMS HOTEL
Molesworth Street, Wadebridge, Cornwall PL27 7DP (01208 812055).
Dogs allowed in all public areas and in hotel rooms.
Pet Regulars: Thomson Cassidy (Black Lab), Ruby Cassidy and Lola (Black Lab).

CUMBRIA

THE BRITANNIA INN
Elterwater, Ambleside, Cumbria LA22 9HP (015394 37210).
Dogs allowed in all areas except dining room and residents' lounge.
Pet Friendly.

STAG INN
Dufton, Appleby, Cumbria (017683 51608).
Dogs allowed in non-food bar, beer garden, village green plus cottage.
Pet Regulars: Sofie (Labrador) and Jeanie (Terrier).

WATERMILL INN
School Lane, Ings, Near Staveley, Kendal, Cumbria (01539 821309).
Dogs allowed in beer garden, Wrynose bottom bar.
Pet Regulars: Blot (sheepdog), Finn (mongrel) and Pub dog Shelley (German Shepherd). Owners cannot walk dogs past pub, without being dragged in! Biscuits and water provided.

DERBYSHIRE

THE GEORGE HOTEL
Commercial Road, Tideswell, Near Buxton, Derbyshire SK17 8NU (01298 871382).
Dogs allowed in snug and around the bar, water bowls provided.

DOG AND PARTRIDGE COUNTRY INN & MOTEL
Swinscoe, Ashbourne, Derbyshire (01335 343183).
Dogs allowed throughout, except restaurant.
Pet Regulars: Include Mitsy (57); Rusty (Cairn); Spider (Collie/GSD) and Rex (GSD).

DEVONSHIRE ARMS
Peak Forest, Near Buxton, Derbyshire SK17 8EJ (01298 23875)
Pet friendly.

DEVON

THE SHIP INN
Axmouth, Devon EX12 4AF (01297 21838).
A predominantly catering pub, so dogs on a lead please.
Pet Regulars: Kym (Boxer), Soxy (cat). Also 2 Japanese Quail, 2 Cockatiels and 2 Kaki Riki (New Zealand Lovebirds).

BRENDON HOUSE
Brendon, Lynton, North Devon EX35 6PS (01598 741206).
Dogs very welcome and allowed in tea gardens, guest bedrooms by arrangement.
Owner's dogs - Drummer, Piper and Angus (Labradors).

THE BULLERS ARMS
Chagford, Newton Abbot, Devon (01647 432348).
Dogs allowed throughout pub, except dining room/kitchen. "More than welcome".

CROWN AND SCEPTRE
2 Petitor Road, Torquay, Devon TQ1 4QA (01803 328290).
Dogs allowed in non-food bar, family room, lounge. All dogs welcome.
Pet Regulars: Two Jack Russells - Scrappy Doo and Minnie Mouse.

THE JOURNEY'S END INN
Ringmore, Near Kingsbridge, South Devon TQ7 4HL (01548 810205).
Dogs allowed throughout the pub.

PALK ARMS INN
Hennock, Bovey Tracey, Devon TQ13 9QS (01626 836584).
Pets welcome.

THE ROYAL OAK INN
Dunsford, Near Exeter, Devon EX6 7DA (01647 252256).
Dogs allowed in bars, beer garden, accommodation for guests with dogs.
Pet Regulars: Kizi. Resident Dogs - Connie and Posie.

THE POLSHAM ARMS
Lower Polsham Road, Paignton, Devon (01803 558360).
Dogs allowed throughout the pub.
Pet Regulars: Patch, owner brings his supply of dog biscuits, and Bracken (German Shepherd).

THE SEA TROUT INN
Staverton, Near Totnes, Devon TQ9 6PA (01803 762274).
Dogs welcome in lounge and public bar, beer garden, owners' rooms (but not on beds).
Pet Regulars: Buster (resident dog) partial to Guiness.

THE DEVONSHIRE INN
Sticklepath, Okehampton, Devon EX20 2NW (01837 840626).
Dogs allowed in non-food bar, car park, beer garden, family room and guest rooms.
Pet Regulars: Clarrie and Rosie (Terriers).

THE TROUT & TIPPLE
(A386 - Tavistock to Okehampton Road), Parkwood Road, Tavistock,
Devon PL10 0JS (01822 618886)
Dogs welcome at all times in bar, games room and patio.
Pet regulars include: Connor and Fenrhys (Black Labradors) - sometimes misbehave. Casey (Bronze Springer) - always after food. Border, Chaos and Mischief (Border Collies), Snoopy (Rhodesian Ridgeback) likes his beef dinners. Also, our own dog - Dave (Lurcher).

DORSET

THE ANVIL HOTEL
Sailsbury Road, Pimperne, Blandford, Dorset DT11 8UQ (01258 453431).
Pets allowed in bar, lounge and bedrooms.

THE SQUARE AND COMPASS
Swanage, Dorset BH19 3LF (01929 439229).
Well-behaved dogs allowed - but beware of the chickens!

DRUSILLA'S INN
Wigbeth, Horton, Dorset (01258 840297).
Well-behaved dogs welcome.

DURHAM

MOORCOCK INN
Hill Top, Eggleston, Teesdale, County Durham DL12 9AU (01833 650395).
Pet Regulars: Thor, the in-house hound dog, and Raymond, the resident hack, welcome all equine travellers; Gem (Jack Russell); Arnie (Ginger Tom); Poppy (Jack Russell); Haflinger - the horse.

TAP AND SPILE
27 Front Street, Framwellgate Moor, Durham DH1 5EE (0191 386 5451).
Dogs allowed throughout the pub.

THE ROSE TREE
Low Road West, Shincliff, Durham DH1 2LY (0191-386 8512).
Pets allowed in bar area and garden.
Pet Regulars: "Benson" (Boxer), "Ben" (Miniature White Poodle) and "Oliver" (King Charles).

THE SEVEN STARS
High Street North, Shincliff, Durham (0191-384 8454).
Dogs welcome in bar area only.

ESSEX

WHITE HARTE
The Quay, Burnham-on-Crouch, Essex CM0 8AS (01621 782106).
Pets welcome.
Pet Regulars: Resident dog "Tilly" (Collie).

THE OLD SHIP
Heybridge Basin, Heybridge, Maldon, Essex (01621 854150).
Dogs allowed downstairs only, on lead.

GLOUCESTERSHIRE

THE OLD STOCKS HOTEL
The Square, Stow on the Wold, Gloucestershire GL54 1AF (01451 830666).
Dogs allowed in the beer garden, accommodation for dogs and their owners also available.
Pet Regulars: Ben (Labrador) enjoys bitter from the drip trays and Casey (Doberman) often gets carried out as he refuses to leave.

GREATER LONDON

THE PHOENIX
28 Thames Street, Sunbury on Thames, Middlesex (01932 785358).
Dogs allowed on lead in beer garden, family room. Capability 2 Grading.
Pet Regulars: Sammy (Black Labrador).

THE TIDE END COTTAGE
Ferry Road, Teddington, Middlesex (0208 977 7762).
Dogs allowed throughout the pub, except dining area.
Pet Regulars: Mimi (Labrador), Toffee (Terrier), Gracie (Guide Dog) and Fiona.

HAMPSHIRE

THE SUN
Sun Hill, Bentworth, Alton, Hampshire GU34 5JT (01420 562338)
Pets welcome throughout the pub.
Pet Regulars: Willow (Collie), Hazel and Purdey (Jack Russells) and "Dilweed" the cat.

HIGH CORNER INN
Linwood, Near Ringwood, Hampshire BH24 3QY (01425 473973).
Dogs, and even horses, are catered for here.

THE CHEQUERS
Ridgeway Lane, Lower Pennington, Lymington, Hants (01590 673415).
Dogs allowed in non-food bar, outdoor barbecue area (away from food).
Pet Regulars: Rusty Boyd - parties held for him. Resident pet - D'for (Labrador).

THE VICTORY
High Street, Hamble-le-Rice, Southampton, Hampshire (023 80 453105).
Dogs allowed.
Pet Regulars: Chester (Boxer).

HERTFORDSHIRE

THE BLACK HORSE
Chorley Wood Common, Dog Kennel Lane, Rickmansworth, Herts (01923 282252).
Dogs very welcome and allowed throughout the pub, on a lead.

THE RED LION
Chenies Village, Rickmansworth, Hertfordshire WD3 6ED (01923 282722).
Pets welcome in bar area only.
Pet Regulars: Resident dog Bobby (Collie mixture), Paddy and Mollie (Boxers).

THE ROBIN HOOD AND LITTLE JOHN
Rabley Heath, near Codicote, Hertfordshire (01438 812361).
Dogs allowed in non-food bar, car park tables, beer garden.
Pet Regulars: Pongo (Dalmation) and Eailey (Labrador). The locals of the pub have close to 50 dogs between them, most of which visit from time to time. The team includes a two Labrador search squad dispatched by one regular's wife to indicate time's up. When they arrive he has five minutes' drinking up time before all three leave together.

FREE or REDUCED RATE entry to Holiday Visits and Attractions – see our READERS' OFFER VOUCHERS on pages 407-423

KENT

KENTISH HORSE

Cow Lane, Mark Beech, Edenbridge, Kent (01342 850493).
Dogs allowed in reserved area on lead, outside included.

THE SWANN INN

Little Chart, Kent TN27 0QB (01233 840702).
Dogs allowed - everywhere except restaurant.

LANCASHIRE

MALT'N HOPS

50 Friday Street, Chorley, Lancashire PR6 0AH (01257 260967).
Dogs allowed throughout pub if kept under control.

LINCOLNSHIRE

THE BLUE DOG INN

Main Street, Sewstern, Grantham, Lincs NG33 5QR (01476 860097).
Dogs allowed.
Pet Regulars: Cassie (Scottie) shares biscuits with Beth (pub cat); Nelson (Terrier), Diesel (Springer Spaniel) and Ted (Spaniel).

Note

All the information in this guide is given in good faith in the belief that it is correct. However, the publishers cannot guarantee the facts given in these pages, neither are they responsible for changes in ownership or facilities that may take place after the date of going to press.
Readers should always satisfy themselves that the facilities they require are available and that the terms, if quoted, still apply.

MERSEYSIDE

THE SCOTCH PIPER
Southport Road, Lydiate, Merseyside (0151 526 0503).
Dogs allowed throughout the pub.

NORFOLK

THE OLD RAILWAY TAVERN
Eccles Road, Quidenham, Norwich, Norfolk NR16 2JG (01953 888223).
Dogs allowed, must be on lead.
Pet Regulars: Pub dogs Flo (German Shepherd) and Benji (Jack Russell).

THE HOSTE ARMS
The Green, Burnham Market, King's Lynn, Norfolk PE31 8HD (01328 738777).
Dogs allowed throughout the pub, except restaurant.
Pet Regulars: "Augustus" and "Sweep" (Black Labradors).

THE ROSE AND CROWN
Nethergate Street, Harpley, King's Lynn, Norfolk (01485 520577).
Well behaved dogs welcome.

OXFORDSHIRE

THE BELL
Shenington, Banbury, Oxfordshire OX15 6NQ (01295 670274).
Pets allowed throughout.
Pet Regulars: Resident pub dogs "Oliver" (Great Dane) and "Daisy" (Labrador).

THE PLOUGH INN
High Street, Finstock, Chipping Norton, Oxfordshire (01993 868333).
Dogs more than welcome.
Pet Regulars: Zac (Sheepdog), Strumpet and Trollop (Labradors).

THE BELL INN
High Street, Adderbury, Oxon (01295 810338).
Dogs allowed throughout the pub.
Owner's dogs: Murphy and Dizzy (Lancashire Heelers) and Rika (Rottweiler).

SHROPSHIRE

THE TRAVELLERS REST INN
Church Stretton, Shropshire (01694 781275).
Well-mannered pets welcome - but beware of the cats!

LONGMYND HOTEL
Cunnery Road, Church Stretton, Shropshire SY6 6AG (01694 722244).
Dogs allowed in owners' hotel bedrooms but not in public areas.
Pet Regulars: Bruno and Frenzie; and owner's dogs, Sam and Sailor.

SOMERSET

CASTLE OF COMFORT HOTEL
Dodington, Nether Stowey, Bridgwater, Somerset TA5 1LE (01278 741264).
Pet friendly.

THE SPARKFORD INN
High Street, Sparkford, Somerset BA22 7JN (01963 440218).
Dogs allowed in bar areas but not in restaurant; safe garden and car park.

THE BUTCHERS ARMS
Carhampton, Somerset (01643 821333).
Dogs allowed in bar. B&B accommodation available.

HOOD ARMS
Kilve, Somerset TA5 1EA (01278 741210)
Pets welcome.

THE SHIP INN
High Street, Porlock, Somerset (01643 862507).
Dogs allowed throughout and in guests' rooms.
Pet Regulars: Include Silver (Jack Russell); Sam (Black Lab) and Max (Staffordshire). Resident Pets include Brit (Spaniel) and Holly (Belgian Shepherd).

STAFFORDSHIRE

The Hollybush Inn

Denford Road, Denford, Leek, Staffordshire ST13 7JT

Dating back to the 17th century, this former corn mill is a favourite with people cruising the Caldon Canal. Features include quarry-tiled floors, open fires, copper and brass ornaments, and old oak beams. Open all day, the Inn has a good selection of beers, wines, ales and other refreshments. Food is also available seven days a week, all dishes prepared in the inn's own kitchens, using fresh, locally sourced produce whenever possible.

The Inn works hard to make sure that all its customers feel welcome, including its four-legged friends.

Tel: 01538 371819

SUFFOLK

THE KINGS HEAD
High Street, Southwold, Suffolk IP18 6AD (01502 724517).
Well-behaved dogs welcome.

SIX BELLS AT BARDWELL
The Green, Bardwell, Bury St Edmunds, Suffolk IP31 1AW (01359 250820).
Dogs allowed in guest bedrooms by arrnagement but not allowed in bar and restaurant.

SURREY

THE PLOUGH
South Road, Woking, Surrey GU21 4JL (01483 714105).
Pets welcome in restricted areas.

THE SPORTSMAN
Mogador Road, Mogador, Surrey (01737 246655).
Adopted dogs congregate at this pub.
Pet Regulars: Meesha (Border Collie) and Max (German Shepherd).

THE CRICKETERS
12 Oxenden Road, Tongham, Farnham, Surrey (01252 333262).
Dogs allowed in beer garden on lead.

SUSSEX

THE FORESTERS ARMS
High Street, Fairwarp, Near Uckfield, East Sussex TN22 3BP (01825 712808).
Dogs allowed in the beer garden and at car park tables, also inside.
Dog biscuits always available.

THE PLOUGH
Crowhurst, Near Battle, East Sussex TN33 9AY (01424 830310).
Dogs allowed in non-food bar, car park tables, beer garden.

QUEENS HEAD
Village Green, Sedlescombe, East Sussex (01424 870228).
Dogs allowed throughout the pub.

THE SLOOP INN
Freshfield Lock, Haywards Heath, West Sussex RH17 7NP (01444 831219).

Dogs allowed in public bar and garden.

THE SPORTSMAN'S ARMS
Rackham Road, Amberley, Near Arundel, West Sussex BN18 9NR (01798 831787).
Dogs allowed in the bar area.

WILTSHIRE

THE HORSE AND GROOM
The Street, Charlton, Near Malmesbury, Wiltshire (01666 823904).
Dogs welcome in bar.
Pet Regulars: Troy and Gio (Labradors).

THE PETERBOROUGH ARMS
Dauntsey Lock, Near Chippenham, Wiltshire SN15 4HD (01249 890409).
All pets welcome in bar.
Resident pets - Poppy, Holly, Lilly and Dotty (4 generations of Jack Russell).

THE THREE HORSESHOES
High Street, Chapmanslade, Near Westbury, Wiltshire (01373 832280).
Dogs allowed in non-food bar and beer garden.
Three horses overlooking the beer garden.

YORKSHIRE

BARNES WALLIS INN
North Howden, Howden, East Yorkshire (01430 430639).
Guide dogs only

KINGS HEAD INN
Barmby on the Marsh, East Yorkshire DN14 7HL (01757 630705).
Dogs allowed in non-food bar.
Pet Regulars: Many and varied!

THE FORESTERS ARMS
Kilburn, North Yorkshire YO6 4AH (01347 868386).
Dogs allowed throughout, except restaurant.
Pet Regulars: Ainsley (Black Labrador).

NEW INN HOTEL
Clapham, Near Settle, North Yorkshire LA2 8HH (015242 51203).
Dogs allowed in bar, beer garden, bedrooms.

SIMONSTONE HALL
Hawes, North Yorkshire DL8 3LY (01969 667255).
Dogs allowed except dining area.
Dogs of all shapes, sizes and breeds welcome.

THE SPINNEY
Forest Rise, Balby, Doncaster, South Yorkshire DN4 9HQ (01302 852033).
Dogs allowed throughout the pub.
Pet Regulars: Wyn (Labrador) a guide dog and Buster (Staff). Resident dog Paddy (Irish Setter).

THE ROCKINGHAM ARMS
8 Main Street, Wentworth, Rotherham, South Yorkshire S62 7LO (01226 742075).
Pets welcome.
Pet Regulars: Sheeba (Springer Spaniel), Charlie and Gypsy (Black Labradors), Sally (Alsatian) and Rosie (Jack Russell).

THE GOLDEN FLEECE
Lindley Road, Blackley, near Huddersfield, West Yorkshire (01422 372704).
Guide Dogs only.

WALES

ANGLESEY & GWYNEDD

THE GRAPES HOTEL
Maentwrog, Blaenau Ffestiniog, Gwynedd LL41 4HN (01766 590365).
Pets allowed in bar area only.

THE BUCKLEY HOTEL
Castle Street, Beaumaris, Isle of Anglesey LL58 8AW (01248 810415).
Dogs allowed throughout the pub, except in the dining room and bistro.
Pet Regulars: Cassie (Springer Spaniel) and Rex (mongrel), dedicated 'companion' dogs, also Charlie (Spaniel).

NORTH WALES

THE WEST ARMS HOTEL
Llanarmon Dyffryn Ceiriog, Llangollen, North Wales LL20 7LD (01691 600665).
Welcome pets.

PEMBROKESHIRE

THE FARMERS
14-16 Goat Street, St David's, Pembrokeshire (01437 721666).
Pets welcome in the pub area.

SEVERN ARMS HOTEL
Penybont, Llandrindod Wells, Powys LD1 5UA (01597 851224).
Dogs allowed in the bar, but not the restaurant, and in the rooms - but not on the beds.

SCOTLAND

ABERDEEN, BANFF & MORAY

THE CLIFTON BAR
Clifton Road, Lossiemouth, Moray (01343 812100).
Dogs allowed in beer garden only.

ROYAL OAK
Station Road, Urquhart, Elgin, Moray (01343 842607).
Dogs allowed throughout pub.
Pet Regulars: Jack (Collie).

ARGYLL & BUTE

CAIRNDOW STAGECOACH INN
Cairndow, Argyll PA26 8BN (01499 600286).
Pets welcome.

THE BALLACHULISH HOTEL
Ballachulish, Argyll PA39 4JY (01855 811606).
Dogs allowed in the lounge and guests' bedrooms, excluding food areas.

EDINBURGH & LOTHIANS

JOHNSBURN HOUSE
Johnsburn Road, Balerno, Lothians EH14 7BB (0131-449 3847).
Pets welcome in bar area only.
Pet Regulars: Resident dog "Topaz" (Great Dane).

LAIRD & DOG
Lasswade, Midlothian (0131-663 9219).
Dogs allowed in bar.
Pet Regulars: Fleetwood (cat). Many pet regulars. Drinking bowls .

PERTH & KINROSS

FOUR SEASONS HOTEL
St Fillans, Perthshire (01764 685333).
Dogs allowed in all non-food areas.

THE MUNRO INN
Main Street, Strathyre, Perthshire FK18 8NA (01877 384333).
Dogs allowed throughout pub, lounge, games room, beer garden and bedrooms (except restaurant).
Pet Regulars: Residents Jess (black mongrel with brown eyes) and Jules (white lurcher with blue eyes). Bring your dog to visit! Water and dog biscuits always available.

A 70-minute journey into the lost world of the English narrow gauge light railway. Features historic steam locomotives from many countries.

PETS MUST BE KEPT UNDER CONTROL AND NOT ALLOWED ON TRACKS

Open: Sundays and Bank Holiday weekends 11 March to 28 October. Additional days in summer.

Directions: on A4146 towards Hemel Hempstead, close to roundabout junction with A505.

FHG GUIDES, ABBEY MILL BUSINESS CENTRE, PAISLEY PA1 1TJ • www.holidayguides.com

A working steam railway centre. Steam train rides, miniature railway rides, large collection of historic preserved steam locomotives, carriages and wagons.

Open: Sundays and Bank Holidays April to October, plus Wednesdays in school holidays 10.30am to 5.30pm.

Directions: off A41 Aylesbury to Bicester Road, 6 miles north west of Aylesbury.

FHG GUIDES, ABBEY MILL BUSINESS CENTRE, PAISLEY PA1 1TJ • www.holidayguides.com

Farm animals, 18th century watermill and farmhouse, farm artifacts, caravan and camping, children's play areas. Restaurant and gift shop.

Open: all year.
9.30am to 5pm 1st March -30th Sept
10am-4pm 1st Oct to 28th Feb

Directions: signposted off both A47 and A1.

FHG GUIDES, ABBEY MILL BUSINESS CENTRE, PAISLEY PA1 1TJ • www.holidayguides.com

Britain's leading grey seal rescue centre

Open: daily (except Christmas Day) from 10am

Directions: from A30 follow signs to Helston, then brown tourist signs to Seal Sanctuary.

FHG GUIDES, ABBEY MILL BUSINESS CENTRE, PAISLEY PA1 1TJ • www.holidayguides.com

SCOTLAND

ABERDEEN, BANFF & MORAY

THE CLIFTON BAR

Clifton Road, Lossiemouth, Moray (01343 812100).
Dogs allowed in beer garden only.

ROYAL OAK

Station Road, Urquhart, Elgin, Moray (01343 842607).
Dogs allowed throughout pub.
Pet Regulars: Jack (Collie).

ARGYLL & BUTE

CAIRNDOW STAGECOACH INN

Cairndow, Argyll PA26 8BN (01499 600286).
Pets welcome.

THE BALLACHULISH HOTEL

Ballachulish, Argyll PA39 4JY (01855 811606).
Dogs allowed in the lounge and guests' bedrooms, excluding food areas.

EDINBURGH & LOTHIANS

JOHNSBURN HOUSE

Johnsburn Road, Balerno, Lothians EH14 7BB (0131-449 3847).
Pets welcome in bar area only.
Pet Regulars: Resident dog "Topaz" (Great Dane).

LAIRD & DOG

Lasswade, Midlothian (0131-663 9219).
Dogs allowed in bar.
Pet Regulars: Fleetwood (cat). Many pet regulars. Drinking bowls .

PERTH & KINROSS

FOUR SEASONS HOTEL

St Fillans, Perthshire (01764 685333).
Dogs allowed in all non-food areas.

THE MUNRO INN

Main Street, Strathyre, Perthshire FK18 8NA (01877 384333).
Dogs allowed throughout pub, lounge, games room, beer garden and bedrooms (except restaurant).
Pet Regulars: Residents Jess (black mongrel with brown eyes) and Jules (white lurcher with blue eyes). Bring your dog to visit! Water and dog biscuits always available.

ISBN 10: 981-4155-01-2
ISBN 13: 978-9-81415-501-4

Mexico Chic is the definitive guide to Mexico's most luxurious and alluring hotels. The properties featured—whether a city hotel, a beachside resort or a rustic hacienda—have been chosen for their individuality and chic appeal.

Over 40 hotels are featured in detail. Insights into the essence of each property help readers decide on the one that best suits their needs and preferences. A fact-packed panel summarises each hotel's facilities and nearby attractions.Seven regional chapters—Mexican Caribbean, Mayan Region, Central East and South Highlands, Pacific Coast, Mexico City, Central Western Highlands and Sea of Cortez—introduce major tourist destinations and attractions, giving readers a headstart in their exploration of Mexico.

thechicseries

Extraordinary destinations. Incomparable accommodations. Exceptional advice. Join discerning travellers who have found everything they desire in the chic series travel guides: hot properties, stunning photography and brilliant tips on where to go and how to do it in some of the world's chicest locations. Now jetting off to Mexico, Bali, South Africa, Shanghai, Morocco, Thailand, India and Spain.

ISBN 10: 1-85733-415-9
ISBN 13: 978-1-85733-415-9

ISBN 10: 1-85733-410-8
ISBN 13: 978-1-85733-410-4

ISBN 10: 1-85733-408-6
ISBN 13: 978-1-85733-408-1

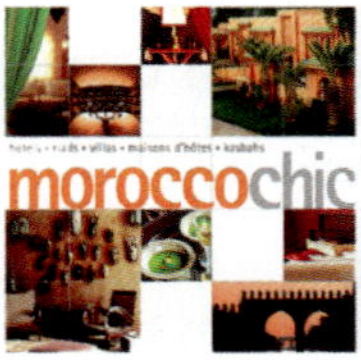

ISBN 10: 1-85733-406-X
ISBN 13: 978-1-85733-406-7

ISBN 10: 1-85733-414-0
ISBN 13: 978-1-85733-414-2

ISBN 10: 1-85733-411-6
ISBN 13: 978-185733-411-1

ISBN 10: 1-85733-405-1
ISBN 13: 978-1-85733-405-0

ISBN 10: 1-85733-409-4
ISBN 13: 978-1-85733-409-8

ISBN 10: 1-85733-416-7
ISBN 13: 978-1-85733-416-6

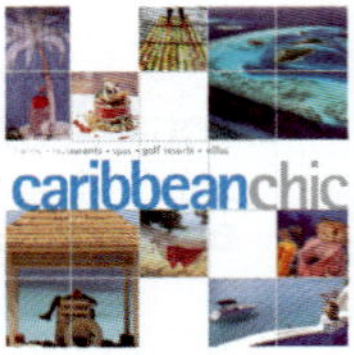

ISBN 10: 185-7334-132
ISBN 13: 978-1857-334-135

The guides are available to purchase via our website: www.kuperard.co.uk
and for trade purchases via your wholesaler or Orca Book Services.

Price £16.95

'Order any chic! guide via the Kuperard website and receive free postage on any quantity of guides. Visit www.kuperard.co.uk to see the full range in the series and type in the following promotional code on the payment page chic01.

Or call us on 0208 446 2440 and quote the same code'

FHG
K·U·P·E·R·A·R·D
READERS' OFFER 2007

LEIGHTON BUZZARD RAILWAY

Page's Park Station, Billington Road,
Leighton Buzzard, Bedfordshire LU7 4TN
Tel: 01525 373888
e-mail: info@buzzrail.co.uk
www.buzzrail.co.uk

One FREE adult/child with full-fare adult ticket
Valid 11/3/2007 - 28/10/2007

NOT TO BE USED IN CONJUNCTION WITH ANY OTHER OFFER

FHG
K·U·P·E·R·A·R·D
READERS' OFFER 2007

BUCKINGHAMSHIRE RAILWAY CENTRE

Quainton Road Station, Quainton,
Aylesbury HP22 4BY
Tel & Fax: 01296 655720
e-mail: bucksrailcentre@btopenworld.com
www.bucksrailcentre.org

One child FREE with each full-paying adult
Not valid for Special Events

NOT TO BE USED IN CONJUNCTION WITH ANY OTHER OFFER

FHG
K·U·P·E·R·A·R·D
READERS' OFFER 2007

SACREWELL FARM & COUNTRY CENTRE

Sacrewell, Thornhaugh,
Peterborough PE8 6HJ
Tel: 01780 782254
e-mail: info@sacrewell.fsnet.co.uk
www.sacrewell.org.uk

One child FREE with one full paying adult
Valid from March 1st to October 1st 2007

NOT TO BE USED IN CONJUNCTION WITH ANY OTHER OFFER

FHG
K·U·P·E·R·A·R·D
READERS' OFFER 2007

NATIONAL SEAL SANCTUARY

Gweek, Helston,
Cornwall TR12 6UG
Tel: 01326 221361
e-mail: seals@sealsanctuary.co.uk
www.sealsanctuary.co.uk

TWO for ONE - on purchase of another ticket of equal or greater value. Valid until December 2007.

NOT TO BE USED IN CONJUNCTION WITH ANY OTHER OFFER

A 70-minute journey into the lost world of the English narrow gauge light railway. Features historic steam locomotives from many countries. **PETS MUST BE KEPT UNDER CONTROL AND NOT ALLOWED ON TRACKS**	**Open:** Sundays and Bank Holiday weekends 11 March to 28 October. Additional days in summer. **Directions:** on A4146 towards Hemel Hempstead, close to roundabout junction with A505.

A working steam railway centre. Steam train rides, miniature railway rides, large collection of historic preserved steam locomotives, carriages and wagons.	**Open:** Sundays and Bank Holidays April to October, plus Wednesdays in school holidays 10.30am to 5.30pm. **Directions:** off A41 Aylesbury to Bicester Road, 6 miles north west of Aylesbury.

Farm animals, 18th century watermill and farmhouse, farm artifacts, caravan and camping, children's play areas. Restaurant and gift shop.	**Open:** all year. 9.30am to 5pm 1st March -30th Sept 10am-4pm 1st Oct to 28th Feb **Directions:** signposted off both A47 and A1.

Britain's leading grey seal rescue centre	**Open:** daily (except Christmas Day) from 10am **Directions:** from A30 follow signs to Helston, then brown tourist signs to Seal Sanctuary.

FHG
K·U·P·E·R·A·R·D
READERS' OFFER 2007

CARS OF THE STARS MOTOR MUSEUM

Standish Street, Keswick,
Cumbria CA12 5HH
Tel: 017687 73757
e-mail: cotsmm@aol.com
www.carsofthestars.com

One child free with two paying adults
Valid during 2007

NOT TO BE USED IN CONJUNCTION WITH ANY OTHER OFFER

FHG
K·U·P·E·R·A·R·D
READERS' OFFER 2007

ESKDALE HISTORIC WATER MILL

Mill Cottage, Boot, Eskdale,
Cumbria CA19 1TG
Tel: 019467 23335
e-mail: david.king403@tesco.net
www.eskdale.info

Two children FREE with two adults
Valid during 2007

NOT TO BE USED IN CONJUNCTION WITH ANY OTHER OFFER

FHG
K·U·P·E·R·A·R·D
READERS' OFFER 2007

CRICH TRAMWAY VILLAGE

Crich, Matlock
Derbyshire DE4 5DP
Tel: 01773 854321 • Fax: 01773 854320
e-mail: enquiry@tramway.co.uk
www.tramway.co.uk

One child FREE with every full-paying adult
Valid during 2007

NOT TO BE USED IN CONJUNCTION WITH ANY OTHER OFFER

FHG
K·U·P·E·R·A·R·D
READERS' OFFER 2007

THE BIG SHEEP

Abbotsham, Bideford,
Devon EX39 5AP
Tel: 01237 472366
e-mail: info@thebigsheep.co.uk
www.thebigsheep.co.uk

Admit one child FREE with each paying adult
Valid during 2007

NOT TO BE USED IN CONJUNCTION WITH ANY OTHER OFFER

A collection of cars from film and TV, including Chitty Chitty Bang Bang, James Bond's Aston Martin, Del Boy's van, Fab1 and many more. **PETS MUST BE KEPT ON LEAD**	**Open:** daily 10am-5pm. Open February half term, Ist April to end November, also weekends in December. **Directions:** in centre of Keswick close to car park.

FHG GUIDES, ABBEY MILL BUSINESS CENTRE, PAISLEY PA1 1TJ • www.holidayguides.com

The oldest working mill in England with 18th century oatmeal machinery running daily. **DOGS ON LEADS**	**Open:** 11am to 5pm April to Sept. (may be closed Saturdays). **Directions:** near inland terminus of Ravenglass & Eskdale Railway or over Hardknott Pass.

FHG GUIDES, ABBEY MILL BUSINESS CENTRE, PAISLEY PA1 1TJ • www.holidayguides.com

A superb family day out in the atmosphere of a bygone era. Explore the recreated period street and fascinating exhibitions. Unlimited tram rides are free with entry. Play areas, woodland walk and sculpture trail, shops, tea rooms, pub, restaurant and lots more.	**Open:** daily April to October 10 am to 5.30pm, weekends in winter. **Directions:** eight miles from M1 Junction 28, follow brown and white signs for "Tramway Museum".

FHG GUIDES, ABBEY MILL BUSINESS CENTRE, PAISLEY PA1 1TJ • www.holidayguides.com

"England for Excellence" award-winning family entertainment park. Highlights: hilarious shows including the famous sheep-racing and the duck trials; the awesome Ewetopia indoor adventure playground for adults and children; brewery; mountain boarding; great local food.	**Open:** daily, 10am to 6pm April - Oct Phone for Winter opening times and details. **Directions:** on A39 North Devon link road, two miles west of Bideford Bridge.

FHG GUIDES, ABBEY MILL BUSINESS CENTRE, PAISLEY PA1 1TJ • www.holidayguides.com

FHG
·K·U·P·E·R·A·R·D·
READERS' OFFER 2007

CREALY ADVENTURE PARK

Sidmouth Road, Clyst St Mary, Exeter,
Devon EX5 1DR
Tel: 0870 116 3333 • Fax: 01395 233211
e-mail: fun@crealy.co.uk
www.crealy.co.uk

FREE superkart race or panning for gold.
Height restrictions apply. Valid until 31/10/07.
Photocopies not accepted. One voucher per person.

NOT TO BE USED IN CONJUNCTION WITH ANY OTHER OFFER

FHG
·K·U·P·E·R·A·R·D·
READERS' OFFER 2007

KILLHOPE LEAD MINING MUSEUM

Cowshill, Upper Weardale,
Co. Durham DL13 1AR
Tel: 01388 537505
e-mail: killhope@durham.gov.uk
www.durham.gov.uk/killhope

One child FREE with full-paying adult
Valid April to October 2007 (not Park Level Mine)

NOT TO BE USED IN CONJUNCTION WITH ANY OTHER OFFER

FHG
·K·U·P·E·R·A·R·D·
READERS' OFFER 2007

AVON VALLEY RAILWAY

Bitton Station, Bath Road, Bitton,
Bristol BS30 6HD
Tel: 0117 932 5538
e-mail: info@avonvalleyrailway.org
www.avonvalleyrailway.org

One FREE child with every fare-paying adult
Valid May - Oct 2007 (not 'Day Out with Thomas' events)

NOT TO BE USED IN CONJUNCTION WITH ANY OTHER OFFER

FHG
·K·U·P·E·R·A·R·D·
READERS' OFFER 2007

DOCKER PARK FARM

Arkholme, Carnforth,
Lancashire LA6 1AR
Tel & Fax: 015242 21331
e-mail: info@dockerparkfarm.co.uk
www.dockerparkfarm.co.uk

One FREE child per one paying adult (one voucher per child)
Valid from January to December 2007

NOT TO BE USED IN CONJUNCTION WITH ANY OTHER OFFER

Maximum fun, magic and adventure. An unforgettable family experience, with Tidal Wave log flume, rollercoaster, Queen Bess pirate ship, techno race karts, bumper boats, Vicorian carousel, animal handling, and huge indoor and outdoor play areas. The South-West's favourite family attraction!

Open: Summer: daily 10am to 5pm
High season: daily 10am to 7pm
Winter (Nov-March): Wed-Sun 10am -5pm

Directions: minutes from M5 J30 on the A3052 Sidmouth road, near Exeter

FHG GUIDES, ABBEY MILL BUSINESS CENTRE, PAISLEY PA1 1TJ • www.holidayguides.com

Voted 'Most Family-Friendly Museum 2004' and 'Most Welcome Experience 2005', Killhope is Britain's best preserved lead mining site, with lots to see and do. Underground Experience is something not to be missed.

Open: April 1st to October 31st 10.30am to 5pm daily.

Directions: alongside A689, midway between Stanhope and Alston in the heart of the North Pennines.

FHG GUIDES, ABBEY MILL BUSINESS CENTRE, PAISLEY PA1 1TJ • www.holidayguides.com

The Avon Valley Railway offers a whole new experience for some, and a nostalgic memory for others.

PETS MUST BE KEPT ON LEADS AND OFF TRAIN SEATS

Open: Steam trains operate every Sunday, Easter to October, plus Bank Holidays and Christmas.

Directions: on the A431 midway between Bristol and Bath at Bitton.

FHG GUIDES, ABBEY MILL BUSINESS CENTRE, PAISLEY PA1 1TJ • www.holidayguides.com

We are a working farm, with lots of animals to see and touch. Enjoy a walk round the Nature Trail or refreshments in the tearoom. Lots of activities during school holidays.

Open: Summer: daily 10.30am- 5pm. Winter: weekends only 10.30am-4pm.

Directions: Junction 35 off M6, take B6254 towards Kirkby Lonsdale, then follow the brown signs.

FHG GUIDES, ABBEY MILL BUSINESS CENTRE, PAISLEY PA1 1TJ • www.holidayguides.com

FHG
K·U·P·E·R·A·R·D
READERS' OFFER 2007

SKEGNESS NATURELAND SEAL SANCTUARY

North Parade, Skegness,
Lincolnshire PE25 1DB
Tel: 01754 764345
e-mail: natureland@fsbdial.co.uk
www.skegnessnatureland.co.uk

Free entry for one child when accompanied by full-paying adult. Valid during 2007.

NOT TO BE USED IN CONJUNCTION WITH ANY OTHER OFFER

FHG
K·U·P·E·R·A·R·D
READERS' OFFER 2007

THE COLLECTORS WORLD OF ERIC ST JOHN-FOTI

Hermitage Hall, Downham Market,
Norfolk PE38 0AU
Tel: 01366 383185 • Fax: 01366 386519
www.collectors-world.org

50p off adult admission - 25p off child admission
Valid during 2007

NOT TO BE USED IN CONJUNCTION WITH ANY OTHER OFFER

FHG
K·U·P·E·R·A·R·D
READERS' OFFER 2007

NEWARK AIR MUSEUM

The Airfield, Winthorpe, Newark,
Nottinghamshire NG24 2NY
Tel: 01636 707170
e-mail: newarkair@onetel.com
www.newarkairmuseum.co.uk

Party rate discount for every voucher (50p per person off normal admission). Valid during 2007.

NOT TO BE USED IN CONJUNCTION WITH ANY OTHER OFFER

FHG
K·U·P·E·R·A·R·D
READERS' OFFER 2007

DIDCOT RAILWAY CENTRE

Didcot,
Oxfordshire OX11 7NJ
Tel: 01235 817200 • Fax: 01235 510621
e-mail: didrlyc@globalnet.co.uk
www.didcotrailwaycentre.org.uk

One child FREE when accompanied by full-paying adult
Valid until end 2007 except during Day Out With Thomas events

NOT TO BE USED IN CONJUNCTION WITH ANY OTHER OFFER

Well known for rescuing and rehabilitating orphaned and injured seal pups found washed ashore on Lincolnshire beaches. Also: penguins, aquarium, pets' corner, reptiles, Floral Palace (tropical birds and butterflies etc).

Open: daily from 10am. Closed Christmas/Boxing/New Year's Days.

Directions: at the north end of Skegness seafront.

FHG GUIDES, ABBEY MILL BUSINESS CENTRE, PAISLEY PA1 1TJ • www.holidayguides.com

The collections of local eccentric Eric St John-Foti (Mr Norfolk Punch himself!) on view and the Magical Dickens Experience. Two amazing attractions for the price of one. Somewhere totally different, unique and interesting.

Open: 11am to 5pm (last entry 4pm) Open all year.

Directions: one mile from town centre on the A1122 Downham/ Wisbech Road.

FHG GUIDES, ABBEY MILL BUSINESS CENTRE, PAISLEY PA1 1TJ • www.holidayguides.com

A collection of 70 aircraft and cockpit sections from across the history of aviation. Extensive aero engine and artefact displays.

Open: daily from 10am (closed Christmas period and New Year's Day).

Directions: follow brown and white signs from A1, A46, A17 and A1133.

FHG GUIDES, ABBEY MILL BUSINESS CENTRE, PAISLEY PA1 1TJ • www.holidayguides.com

See the steam trains from the golden age of the Great Western Railway. Steam locomotives in the original engine shed, a reconstructed country branch line, and a re-creation of Brunel's original broad gauge railway. On Steam Days there are rides in the 1930s carriages.

Open: Sat/Sun all year; daily 23 June to 2 Sept + school holidays. 10am-5pm weekends and Steam Days, 10am-4pm other days and in winter.

Directions: at Didcot Parkway rail station; on A4130, signposted from M4 (Junction 13) and A34

FHG GUIDES, ABBEY MILL BUSINESS CENTRE, PAISLEY PA1 1TJ • www.holidayguides.com

FHG
KUPERARD
READERS' OFFER 2007

THE HELICOPTER MUSEUM

The Heliport, Locking Moor Road,
Weston-Super-Mare BS24 8PP
Tel: 01934 635227• Fax: 01934 645230
e-mail: office@helimuseum.fsnet.co.uk
www.helicoptermuseum.co.uk

One child FREE with two full-paying adults
Valid from April to October 2007

NOT TO BE USED IN CONJUNCTION WITH ANY OTHER OFFER

FHG
KUPERARD
READERS' OFFER 2007

AMERICAN ADVENTURE GOLF

Fort Fun, Royal Parade,
Eastbourne, East Sussex BN22 7LU
Tel: 01323 642833
e-mail: fortfuneb@aol.com
www.fortfun.co.uk

One FREE game of golf with every full-paying customer (value £3). Valid April-Oct 2007 before 12 noon only

NOT TO BE USED IN CONJUNCTION WITH ANY OTHER OFFER

FHG
KUPERARD
READERS' OFFER 2007

WILDERNESS WOOD

Hadlow Down, Near Uckfield,
East Sussex TN22 4HJ
Tel: 01825 830509• Fax: 01825 830977
e-mail: enquiries@wildernesswood.co.uk
www.wildernesswood.co.uk

one FREE admission with a full-paying adult
Valid during 2007 (not for Special Events)

NOT TO BE USED IN CONJUNCTION WITH ANY OTHER OFFER

FHG
KUPERARD
READERS' OFFER 2007

HATTON COUNTRY WORLD FARM VILLAGE

Dark Lane, Hatton, Near Warwick,
Warwickshire CV35 8XA
Tel: 01926 843411
e-mail: hatton@hattonworld.com
www.hattonworld.com

Admit one child FREE with one full-paying adult day ticket. Admission into Shopping Village free. Valid during 2007

NOT TO BE USED IN CONJUNCTION WITH ANY OTHER OFFER

The world's largest helicopter collection - over 70 exhibits, includes two royal helicopters, Russian Gunship and Vietnam veterans plus many award-winning exhibits. Cafe, shop. Flights. **PETS MUST BE KEPT UNDER CONTROL**	**Open:** Wednesday to Sunday 10am to 5.30pm. Daily during school Easter and Summer holidays and Bank Holiday Mondays. November to March: 10am to 4.30pm **Directions:** Junction 21 off M5 then follow the propellor signs.

FHG GUIDES, ABBEY MILL BUSINESS CENTRE, PAISLEY PA1 1TJ • www.holidayguides.com

18-hole American Adventure Golf set in ⅓ acre landscaped surroundings. Played on different levels including water features.	**Open:** April until end October 10am until dusk. **Directions:** on the seafront ¼ mile east of Eastbourne Pier.

FHG GUIDES, ABBEY MILL BUSINESS CENTRE, PAISLEY PA1 1TJ • www.holidayguides.com

Wilderness Wood is a unique family-run working woodland in the Sussex High Weald. Explore trails and footpaths, enjoy local cakes and ices, try the adventure playground. Many special events and activities. Parties catered for.	**Open:** daily 10am to 5.30pm or dusk if earlier. **Directions:** on the south side of the A272 in the village of Hadlow Down. Signposted with a brown tourist sign.

FHG GUIDES, ABBEY MILL BUSINESS CENTRE, PAISLEY PA1 1TJ • www.holidayguides.com

Two attractions side-by-side. Hatton Farm Village has fun for the whole family, with animals, demonstrations and adventure play. Hatton Shopping Village has 25 craft and gift shops, an antiques centre, a factory-style store, and two restaurants. Free parking.	**Open:** daily 10am to 5pm. Open until 4pm Christmas Eve; 11am-4pm 27 Dec-1st Jan incl; closed Christmas Day & Boxing Day. **Directions:** 5 minutes from M40 (J15), A46 towards Coventry, then just off A4177 (follow brown tourist signs).

FHG GUIDES, ABBEY MILL BUSINESS CENTRE, PAISLEY PA1 1TJ • www.holidayguides.com

FHG
K·U·P·E·R·A·R·D
READERS' OFFER 2007

AVONCROFT MUSEUM

AVONCROFT MUSEUM OF HISTORIC BUILDINGS

Stoke Heath,
Bromsgrove,
Worcestershire B60 4JR
Tel: 01527 831363 • Fax: 01527 876934
www.avoncroft.org.uk

One FREE child with one full-paying adult
Valid from March to November 2007

NOT TO BE USED IN CONJUNCTION WITH ANY OTHER OFFER

FHG
K·U·P·E·R·A·R·D
READERS' OFFER 2007

EMBSAY & BOLTON ABBEY STEAM RAILWAY

EMBSAY & BOLTON ABBEY STEAM RAILWAY

Bolton Abbey Station, Skipton,
North Yorkshire BD23 6AF
Tel: 01756 710614
e-mail: embsay.steam@btinternet.com
www.embsayboltonabbeyrailway.org.uk

One adult travels FREE when accompanied by a full fare paying adult (does not include Special Event days). Valid during 2007.

NOT TO BE USED IN CONJUNCTION WITH ANY OTHER OFFER

FHG
K·U·P·E·R·A·R·D
READERS' OFFER 2007

MUSEUM OF RAIL TRAVEL

Ingrow Railway Centre, Near Keighley,
West Yorkshire BD22 8NJ
Tel: 01535 680425
e-mail: admin@vintagecarriagestrust.org
www.vintagecarriagestrust.org • www.museumofrailtravel.co.uk

"ONE for ONE" free admission
Valid during 2007 except during special events (ring to check)

NOT TO BE USED IN CONJUNCTION WITH ANY OTHER OFFER

FHG
K·U·P·E·R·A·R·D
READERS' OFFER 2007

THE GRASSIC GIBBON CENTRE

The Grassic Gibbon Centre

Arbuthnott, Laurencekirk,
Aberdeenshire AB30 1PB
Tel: 01561 361668
e-mail: lgginfo@grassicgibbon.com
www.grassicgibbon.com

TWO for the price of ONE entry to exhibition (based on full adult rate only). Valid during 2007 (not groups)

NOT TO BE USED IN CONJUNCTION WITH ANY OTHER OFFER

A fascinating world of historic buildings covering 7 centuries, rescued and rebuilt on an open-air site in the heart of the Worcestershire countryside.

PETS ON LEADS ONLY

Open: July and August all week. March to November varying times, please telephone for details.

Directions: A38 south of Bromsgrove, near Junction 1 of M42, Junction 5 of M5.

FHG GUIDES, ABBEY MILL BUSINESS CENTRE, PAISLEY PA1 1TJ • www.holidayguides.com

Steam trains operate over a 4½ mile line from Bolton Abbey Station to Embsay Station. Many family events including Thomas the Tank Engine take place during major Bank Holidays.

Open: steam trains run every Sunday throughout the year and up to 7 days a week in summer. 10.30am to 4.30pm

Directions: Embsay Station signposted from the A59 Skipton by-pass; Bolton Abbey Station signposted from the A59 at Bolton Abbey.

FHG GUIDES, ABBEY MILL BUSINESS CENTRE, PAISLEY PA1 1TJ • www.holidayguides.com

A fascinating display of railway carriages and a wide range of railway items telling the story of rail travel over the years.

ALL PETS MUST BE KEPT ON LEADS

Open: daily 11am to 4.30pm

Directions: approximately one mile from Keighley on A629 Halifax road. Follow brown tourist signs

FHG GUIDES, ABBEY MILL BUSINESS CENTRE, PAISLEY PA1 1TJ • www.holidayguides.com

Visitor Centre dedicated to the much-loved Scottish writer Lewis Grassic Gibbon. Exhibition, cafe, gift shop. Outdoor children's play area. Disabled access throughout.

Open: daily April to October 10am to 4.30pm. Groups by appointment including evenings.

Directions: on the B967, accessible and signposted from both A90 and A92.

FHG GUIDES, ABBEY MILL BUSINESS CENTRE, PAISLEY PA1 1TJ • www.holidayguides.com

FHG
K·U·P·E·R·A·R·D
READERS' OFFER 2007

STORYBOOK GLEN

Maryculter,
Aberdeen
Aberdeenshire AB12 5FT
Tel: 01224 732941
www.storybookglenaberdeen.co.uk

10% discount on all admissions
Valid until end 2007

NOT TO BE USED IN CONJUNCTION WITH ANY OTHER OFFER

FHG
K·U·P·E·R·A·R·D
READERS' OFFER 2007

INVERARAY JAIL

Church Square, Inveraray,
Argyll PA32 8TX
Tel: 01499 302381 • Fax: 01499 302195
e-mail: info@inverarayjail.co.uk
www.inverarayjail.co.uk

One child FREE with one full-paying adult
Valid until end 2007

NOT TO BE USED IN CONJUNCTION WITH ANY OTHER OFFER

FHG
K·U·P·E·R·A·R·D
READERS' OFFER 2007

SCOTTISH MARITIME MUSEUM

Harbourside, Irvine,
Ayrshire KA12 8QE
Tel: 01294 278283
Fax: 01294 313211
www.scottishmaritimemuseum.org

TWO for the price of ONE
Valid from April to October 2007

NOT TO BE USED IN CONJUNCTION WITH ANY OTHER OFFER

FHG
K·U·P·E·R·A·R·D
READERS' OFFER 2007

JEDFOREST DEER & FARM PARK

Mervinslaw Estate, Camptown, Jedburgh,
Borders TD8 6PL
Tel: 01835 840364
e-mail: mervinslaw@ecosse.net
www.aboutscotland.com/jedforest

One FREE child with two full-paying adults
Valid May/June and Sept/Oct 2007

NOT TO BE USED IN CONJUNCTION WITH ANY OTHER OFFER

28-acre theme park with over 100 nursery rhyme characters, set in beautifully landscaped gardens. Shop and restaurant on site.	**Open:** 1st March to 31st October: daily 10am to 6pm; 1st Nov to end Feb: Sat/Sun only 11am to 4pm **Directions:** 6 miles west of Aberdeen off B9077

FHG GUIDES, ABBEY MILL BUSINESS CENTRE, PAISLEY PA1 1TJ • www.holidayguides.com

19th century prison with fully restored 1820 courtroom and two prisons. Guides in uniform as warders, prisoners and matron. Remember your camera!	**Open:** April to October 9.30am-6pm (last admission 5pm); November to March 10am-5pm (last admission 4pm) **Directions:** A83 to Campbeltown

FHG GUIDES, ABBEY MILL BUSINESS CENTRE, PAISLEY PA1 1TJ • www.holidayguides.com

Scotland's seafaring heritage is among the world's richest and you can relive the heyday of Scottish shipping at the Maritime Museum.	**Open:** 1st April to 31st October - 10am-5pm **Directions:** situated on Irvine harbourside and only a 10 minute walk from Irvine train station.

FHG GUIDES, ABBEY MILL BUSINESS CENTRE, PAISLEY PA1 1TJ • www.holidayguides.com

Working farm with visitor centre showing rare breeds, deer herds, ranger-led activities, and walks. Birds of prey displays and tuition. Corporate activities. Shop and cafe.	**Open:** daily Easter to August 10am to 5.30pm; Sept/Oct 11am to 4.30pm. **Directions:** 5 miles south of Jedburgh on A68.

FHG GUIDES, ABBEY MILL BUSINESS CENTRE, PAISLEY PA1 1TJ • www.holidayguides.com

FHG
·K·U·P·E·R·A·R·D·
READERS' OFFER 2007

BO'NESS & KINNEIL RAILWAY

Bo'ness Station, Union Street,
Bo'ness, West Lothian EH51 9AQ
Tel: 01506 822298
e-mail: enquiries.railway@srps.org.uk
www.srps.org.uk

FREE child train fare with one paying adult/concession. Valid 31st March-31st Oct 2007. Not Thomas events or Santa Steam trains

NOT TO BE USED IN CONJUNCTION WITH ANY OTHER OFFER

FHG
·K·U·P·E·R·A·R·D·
READERS' OFFER 2007

MYRETON MOTOR MUSEUM

Aberlady,
East Lothian
EH32 0PZ
Tel: 01875 870288

One child FREE with each paying adult
Valid during 2007

NOT TO BE USED IN CONJUNCTION WITH ANY OTHER OFFER

FHG
·K·U·P·E·R·A·R·D·
READERS' OFFER 2007

LLANBERIS LAKE RAILWAY

Gilfach Ddu, Llanberis,
Gwynedd LL55 4TY
Tel: 01286 870549
e-mail: info@lake-railway.co.uk
www.lake-railway.co.uk

One pet travels FREE with each full fare paying adult
Valid Easter to October 2007

NOT TO BE USED IN CONJUNCTION WITH ANY OTHER OFFER

FHG
·K·U·P·E·R·A·R·D·
READERS' OFFER 2007

NATIONAL CYCLE COLLECTION

Automobile Palace, Temple Street,
Llandrindod Wells, Powys LD1 5DL
Tel: 01597 825531
e-mail: cycle.museum@powys.org.uk
www.cyclemuseum.org.uk

TWO for the price of ONE
Valid during 2007 except Special Event days

NOT TO BE USED IN CONJUNCTION WITH ANY OTHER OFFER

Steam and heritage diesel passenger trains from Bo'ness to Birkhill for guided tours of Birkhill fireclay mines. Explore the history of Scotland's railways in the Scottish Railway Exhibition. Coffee shop and souvenir shop.

Open: weekends April to October, daily July and August.

Directions: in the town of Bo'ness. Leave M9 at Junction 3 or 5, then follow brown tourist signs.

On show is a large collection, from 1899, of cars, bicycles, motor cycles and commercials. There is also a large collection of period advertising, posters and enamel signs.

Open: March-November - open daily 11am to 4pm. December-February - weekends 11am to 3pm or by special appointment.

Directions: off A198 near Aberlady. Two miles from A1.

FHG GUIDES, ABBEY MILL BUSINESS CENTRE, PAISLEY PA1 1TJ • www.holidayguides.com

A 60-minute ride along the shores of beautiful Padarn Lake behind a quaint historic steam engine. Magnificent views of the mountains from lakeside picnic spots.

DOGS MUST BE KEPT ON LEAD AT ALL TIMES ON TRAIN

Open: most days Easter to October. Free timetable leaflet on request.

Directions: just off A4086 Caernarfon to Capel Curig road at Llanberis; follow 'Country Park' signs.

FHG GUIDES, ABBEY MILL BUSINESS CENTRE, PAISLEY PA1 1TJ • www.holidayguides.com

Journey through the lanes of cycle history and see bicycles from Boneshakers and Penny Farthings up to modern Raleigh cycles. Over 250 machines on display

PETS MUST BE KEPT ON LEADS

Open: 1st March to 1st November daily 10am onwards.

Directions: brown signs to car park. Town centre attraction.

FHG GUIDES, ABBEY MILL BUSINESS CENTRE, PAISLEY PA1 1TJ • www.holidayguides.com

Index of Towns and Counties

Aberaeron	CEREDIGION
Aberfeldy	PERTH & KINROSS
Abergavenny	SOUTH WALES
Abermawr	PEMBROKESHIRE
Aberporth	CEREDIGION
Aberystwyth	CEREDIGION
Aldeburgh	SUFFOLK
Allerford	SOMERSET
Allonby	CUMBRIA
Alnmouth	NORTHUMBERLAND
Ambleside	CUMBRIA
Appin	ARGYLL & BUTE
Appleby-in-Westmorland	CUMBRIA
Arlington	EAST SUSSEX
Ashbourne	DERBYSHIRE
Ashburton	DEVON
Ashford	KENT
Ashurst	HAMPSHIRE
Ashwater	DEVON
Aultbea	HIGHLANDS
Austwick	NORTH YORKSHIRE
Aviemore	HIGHLANDS
Axminster	DEVON
Ayr	AYRSHIRE & ARRAN
Bacton-on-Sea	NORFOLK
Bala	ANGLESEY & GWYNEDD
Ballachulish	ARGYLL & BUTE
Ballantrae	AYRSHIRE & ARRAN
Balterley	CHESHIRE
Bamburgh	NORTHUMBERLAND
Bamford	DERBYSHIRE
Barlow	DERBYSHIRE
Barmouth	ANGLESEY & GWYNEDD
Barnoldby-Le-Beck	LINCOLNSHIRE
Barnstaple	DEVON
Bassenthwaite	CUMBRIA
Bath	SOMERSET
Battle	EAST SUSSEX
Beauly	HIGHLANDS
Beaumaris	ANGLESEY& GWYNEDD
Beddgelert	ANGLESEY & GWYNEDD
Belford	NORTHUMBERLAND
Bentham	NORTH YORKSHIRE
Berrynarbor	DEVON
Berwick-upon-Tweed	NORTHUMBERLAND
Bethesda	ANGLESEY & GWYNEDD
Betws-y-Coed	NORTH WALES
Bibury	GLOUCESTERSHIRE
Bideford	DEVON
Bigbury-on-Sea	DEVON
Biggar	LANARKSHIRE
Bingley	WEST YORKSHIRE
Bishop Auckland	DURHAM
Bishop's Castle	SHROPSHIRE
Blackburn	LANCASHIRE
Blackpool	LANCASHIRE
Blandford	DORSET
Boat of Garten	HIGHLANDS
Bodmin	CORNWALL
Bodmin Moor	CORNWALL
Bodorgan	ANGLESEY & GWYNEDD
Bonchester Bridge	BORDERS
Bonchurch	ISLE OF WIGHT
Borrowdale	CUMBRIA
Boscastle	CORNWALL
Bosherton	PEMBROKESHIRE
Bournemouth	DORSET
Bourton-on-the-Water	GLOUCESTERSHIRE
Bradworthy	DEVON
Brampton	CUMBRIA
Braunton	DEVON
Breakish	ISLE OF SKYE
Brean	SOMERSET
Brecon	POWYS
Bridlington	EAST YORKSHIRE
Bridport	DORSET
Brighton	EAST SUSSEX
Brixham	DEVON
Broad Haven	PEMBROKESHIRE
Broadstairs	KENT
Broadwell	GLOUCESTERSHIRE
Broadwoodwidger	DEVON
Broughton-in-Furness	CUMBRIA
Bude	CORNWALL
Builth Wells	POWYS
Burford	OXFORDSHIRE
Burton Bradstock	DORSET
Burton Joyce	NOTTINGHAMSHIRE

Bury St Edmunds	SUFFOLK
Buttermere	CUMBRIA
Buxton	DERBYSHIRE
Caernarfon	ANGLESEY & GWYNEDD
Cairndow	ARGYLL & BUTE
Caister-on-Sea	NORFOLK
Callander	PERTH & KINROSS
Cardiff	SOUTH WALES
Carlisle	CUMBRIA
Carrbridge	HIGHLANDS
Cartmel	CUMBRIA
Castle Cary	SOMERSET
Castle Douglas	DUMFRIES & GALLOWAY
Castleside	DURHAM
Catacol	AYRSHIRE & ARRAN
Cattistock	DORSET
Cawsand	CORNWALL
Chalford	GLOUCESTERSHIRE
Charmouth	DORSET
Cheddar	SOMERSET
Chesham	BUCKINGHAMSHIRE
Chester	CHESHIRE
Chichester	WEST SUSSEX
Chiddingly	EAST SUSSEX
Chittlehamholt	DEVON
Christchurch	DORSET
Chudleigh	DEVON
Chulmleigh	DEVON
Church Stretton	SHROPSHIRE
Clitheroe	LANCASHIRE
Ciliau Aeron	CEREDIGION
Cockermouth	CUMBRIA
Colebrooke	DEVON
Coltishall	NORFOLK
Colwyn Bay	NORTH WALES
Combe Martin	DEVON
Coniston	CUMBRIA
Contin	HIGHLANDS
Conwy	NORTH WALES
Conwy Valley	NORTH WALES
Corbridge	NORTHUMBERLAND
Coverdale	NORTH YORKSHIRE
Cowes	ISLE OF WIGHT
Crackington Haven	CORNWALL
Crantock	CORNWALL
Cratfield	SUFFOLK
Criccieth	ANGLESEY & GWYNEDD
Croes Goch	PEMBROKESHIRE
Cromer	NORFOLK
Cullompton	DEVON
Cusgarne	CORNWALL
Dalbeattie	DUMFRIES & GALLOWAY
Dalmally	ARGYLL & BUTE
Danby	NORTH YORKSHIRE
Dartmoor	DEVON
Dartmouth	DEVON
Dereham	NORFOLK
Diss	NORFOLK
Diss	SUFFOLK
Doddiscombsleigh	DEVON
Dorchester	DORSET
Dornoch	HIGHLANDS
Driffield	EAST YORKSHIRE
Droitwich	WORCESTERSHIRE
Drummore	DUMFRIES & GALLOWAY
Drumnadrochit	HIGHLANDS
Dulas Bay	ANGLESEY & GWYNEDD
Duloe	CORNWALL
Dumfries	DUMFRIES & GALLOWAY
Dunoon	ARGYLL & BUTE
Dunsford	DEVON
Dunster	SOMERSET
Dunwich	SUFFOLK
East Dereham	NORFOLK
Eastergate	WEST SUSSEX
Edwinstowe	NOTTINGHAMSHIRE
Ely	CAMBRIDGESHIRE
Eskdale	CUMBRIA
Exeter	DEVON
Exford	SOMERSET
Exmoor	SOMERSET
Exmoor	DEVON
Fairford	GLOUCESTERSHIRE
Fairlight	EAST SUSSEX
Fakenham	NORFOLK
Falmouth	CORNWALL
Filey	NORTH YORKSHIRE
Fishguard	PEMBROKESHIRE
Flamborough	EAST YORKSHIRE
Fochabers	ABERDEEN, BANFF & MORAY
Forest of Dean	GLOUCESTERSHIRE
Fort William	HIGHLANDS
Fowey	CORNWALL
Foxley	NORFOLK

Freshwater	ISLE OF WIGHT
Garthmyl	POWYS
Gartocharn/Loch Lomond	DUNBARTONSHIRE
Gatehouse of Fleet	DUMFRIES & GALLOWAY
Glencoe	HIGHLANDS
Glenlivet	ABERDEEN, BANFF & MORAY
Gorran Haven	CORNWALL
Gower	SOUTH WALES
Grange-over-Sands	CUMBRIA
Grantown-on-Spey	HIGHLANDS
Grantown-on-Spey	ABERDEEN, BANFF & MORAY
Grasmere	CUMBRIA
Grassington	NORTH YORKSHIRE
Great Malvern	WORCESTERSHIRE
Great Yarmouth	NORFOLK
Grinshill	SHROPSHIRE
Grittleton	WILTSHIRE
Hadleigh	SUFFOLK
Haltwhistle	NORTHUMBERLAND
Harlech	ANGLESEY & GWYNEDD
Harrogate	NORTH YORKSHIRE
Harthill	LANARKSHIRE
Hartland	DEVON
Hastings	EAST SUSSEX
Haverfordwest	PEMBROKESHIRE
Hawes (Near Mallerstang)	NORTH YORKSHIRE
Hawkshead	CUMBRIA
Hay-on-Wye	HEREFORDSHIRE
Helmsley	NORTH YORKSHIRE
Helston	CORNWALL
Henley	SUFFOLK
Hereford	HEREFORDSHIRE
Hexham	NORTHUMBERLAND
Hexworthy	DEVON
Holsworthy	DEVON
Holt	NORFOLK
Holyhead	ANGLESEY & GWYNEDD
Hope Cove	DEVON
Horncastle	LINCOLNSHIRE
Horningtoft	NORFOLK
Ilfracombe	DEVON
Instow	DEVON
Invergarry	HIGHLANDS
Invermoriston	HIGHLANDS
Ireby	CUMBRIA
Isle of Gigha	ARGYLL & BUTE
Jedburgh	BORDERS
Kelso	BORDERS
Kendal	CUMBRIA
Kessingland	SUFFOLK
Keswick	CUMBRIA
Kilchattan Bay	ARGYLL & BUTE
Killin	PERTH & KINROSS
Kilnwick Percy	EAST YORKSHIRE
Kincraig	HIGHLANDS
Kings Lynn	NORFOLK
Kings Nympton	DEVON
Kingsbridge	DEVON
Kingston-upon-Thames	SURREY
Kington	HEREFORDSHIRE
Kingussie	HIGHLANDS
Kinloch Rannoch	PERTH & KINROSS
Kinlochbervie	HIGHLANDS
Kinross	PERTH & KINROSS
Kirkby Lonsdale	CUMBRIA
Kirkby Stephen	CUMBRIA
Kirkby-in-Furness	CUMBRIA
Kirkoswald	CUMBRIA
Knaresborough	NORTH YORKSHIRE
Knighton	POWYS
Lake District	CUMBRIA
Lake District / Hawkshead	CUMBRIA
Lampeter	CEREDIGION
Lamplugh	CUMBRIA
Lancaster	LANCASHIRE
Langdale	CUMBRIA
Langton-by-Wragby	LINCOLNSHIRE
Laugharne	CARMARTHENSHIRE
Launceston	CORNWALL
Lawrenny	PEMBROKESHIRE
Laxfield	SUFFOLK
Ledbury	HEREFORDSHIRE
Leek	STAFFORDSHIRE
Leeming Bar	NORTH YORKSHIRE
Leominster	HEREFORDSHIRE
Lerwick	SHETLAND ISLANDS
Leyburn	NORTH YORKSHIRE
Liskeard	CORNWALL
Little Langdale	CUMBRIA
Lizard	CORNWALL
Llanddona	ANGLESEY & GWYNEDD
Llandeilo	CARMARTHENSHIRE
Llandrindod Wells	POWYS
Llandudno	NORTH WALES

Llandyrnog	NORTH WALES
Llandysul	CARMARTHENSHIRE
Llanelli	CARMARTHENSHIRE
Llanfair Caereinion	POWYS
Llangollen	NORTH WALES
Llangrannog	CEREDIGION
Llangurig	POWYS
Llanteg	PEMBROKESHIRE
Loch Goil	ARGYLL & BUTE
Loch Ness	HIGHLANDS
Lochcarron	HIGHLANDS
Longrock	CORNWALL
Looe	CORNWALL
Lower Largo	FIFE
Lowestoft	SUFFOLK
Ludlow	SHROPSHIRE
Lulworth	DORSET
Lyme Regis	DORSET
Lymington	HAMPSHIRE
Lyndhurst	HAMPSHIRE
Lynmouth	DEVON
Lynton/Lynmouth	DEVON
Mablethorpe	LINCOLNSHIRE
Machynlleth	POWYS
Malham	NORTH YORKSHIRE
Manaccan	CORNWALL
Marazion	CORNWALL
Market Harborough	LEICESTERSHIRE
Mawgan Porth	CORNWALL
Melton Mowbray	LEICESTERSHIRE
Mevagissey	CORNWALL
Meysey Hampton	GLOUCESTERSHIRE
Milton Abbas	DORSET
Milton Keynes	BUCKINGHAMSHIRE
Minehead	SOMERSET
Moffat	DUMFRIES & GALLOWAY
Monmouth	SOUTH WALES
Morfa Nefyn	ANGLESEY & GWYNEDD
Morpeth	NORTHUMBERLAND
Mortehoe	DEVON
Mousehole	CORNWALL
Mumbles	SOUTH WALES
Mundesley-on-Sea	NORFOLK
Nailsworth	GLOUCESTERSHIRE
Nayland	SUFFOLK
Neatishead	NORFOLK
Nethy Bridge	HIGHLANDS
New Forest	HAMPSHIRE
Newgale	PEMBROKESHIRE
Newnham-on-Severn	GLOUCESTERSHIRE
Newport	PEMBROKESHIRE
Newquay	CORNWALL
Newtonmore	HIGHLANDS
Nolton Haven	PEMBROKESHIRE
North Dalton	NORTH YORKSHIRE
North Perrott	SOMERSET
North Walsham	NORFOLK
Northallerton	NORTH YORKSHIRE
Noss Mayo	DEVON
Oban	ARGYLL & BUTE
Okehampton	DEVON
Old Hunstanton	NORFOLK
Onich	HIGHLANDS
Orford	SUFFOLK
Oswestry	SHROPSHIRE
Ottery St Mary	DEVON
Oxford	OXFORDSHIRE
Padstow	CORNWALL
Paignton	DEVON
Painswick	GLOUCESTERSHIRE
Pateley Bridge	NORTH YORKSHIRE
Peak District National Park	DERBYSHIRE
Peaslake	SURREY
Pembridge	HEREFORDSHIRE
Penrith	CUMBRIA
Penzance	CORNWALL
Perranporth	CORNWALL
Petersfield	HAMPSHIRE
Pickering	NORTH YORKSHIRE
Pilling	LANCASHIRE
Pitlochry	PERTH & KINROSS
Plymouth	DEVON
Polegate	EAST SUSSEX
Polperro	CORNWALL
Poole	DORSET
Poolewe	HIGHLANDS
Porlock	SOMERSET
Port Gaverne	CORNWALL
Port Isaac	CORNWALL
Port Mulgrave	NORTH YORKSHIRE
Porthleven	CORNWALL
Porthmadog	ANGLESEY & GWYNEDD
Portreath	CORNWALL
Portscatho	CORNWALL

Portsmouth	HAMPSHIRE
Portwrinkle	CORNWALL
Powerstock	DORSET
Praa Sands	CORNWALL
Presteigne	POWYS
Pulborough	WEST SUSSEX
Ravenstonedale	CUMBRIA
Rattray Head	ABERDEEN, BANFF & MORAY
Red Wharf Bay	ANGLESEY & GWYNEDD
Redbrook-on-Wye	SOUTH WALES
Rhayader	POWYS
Rhiconich	HIGHLANDS
Rhosneigr	ANGLESEY & GWYNEDD
Rhos-on-Sea	NORTH WALES
Ringwood	HAMPSHIRE
Ripon	NORTH YORKSHIRE
Rosewell	EDINBURGH & LOTHIANS
Ross-on-Wye	HEREFORDSHIRE
Rottingdean/Brighton	EAST SUSSEX
Ryde	ISLE OF WIGHT
Rye	EAST SUSSEX
St Agnes	CORNWALL
St Andrews	FIFE
St Austell	CORNWALL
St Breward	CORNWALL
St Brides	PEMBROKESHIRE
St Davids	PEMBROKESHIRE
St Ives	CORNWALL
St Margaret's Bay	KENT
St Mary's	ISLES OF SCILLY
St Mawes	CORNWALL
St Mawgan	CORNWALL
St Tudy	CORNWALL
St Wenn	CORNWALL
Salcombe	DEVON
Salisbury	WILTSHIRE
Saundersfoot	PEMBROKESHIRE
Saxmundham	SUFFOLK
Scalby Nabs (Scarborough)	NORTH YORKSHIRE
Scarborough	NORTH YORKSHIRE
Seaford	EAST SUSSEX
Seaton	DEVON
Selkirk	BORDERS
Selsey	WEST SUSSEX
Sevenoaks	KENT
Sherborne	DORSET
Sidmouth	DEVON
Silloth-on-Solway	CUMBRIA
Skipton	NORTH YORKSHIRE
Solva	PEMBROKESHIRE
Southport	LANCASHIRE
Spean Bridge	HIGHLANDS
Staffin	ISLE OF SKYE
Staithes	NORTH YORKSHIRE
Sonehaven	ABERDEEN, BANFF & MORAY
Stow-on-the-Wold	GLOUCESTERSHIRE
Stratford-upon-Avon	WARWICKSHIRE
Strathyre	PERTH & KINROSS
Stroud	GLOUCESTERSHIRE
Studland Bay	DORSET
Sudbury	SUFFOLK
Swanage	DORSET
Swansea	SOUTH WALES
Tackley/Kidlington	OXFORDSHIRE
Tain	HIGHLANDS
Tarbert	ARGYLL & BUTE
Taunton	SOMERSET
Tavistock	DEVON
Taynuilt	ARGYLL & BUTE
Teesdale	DURHAM
Tenby	PEMBROKESHIRE
Thame	OXFORDSHIRE
Thirsk	NORTH YORKSHIRE
Thornham	NORFOLK
Thornhill	DUMFRIES & GALLOWAY
Thorpe Market	NORFOLK
Thurlestone	DEVON
Thurne	NORFOLK
Tintagel	CORNWALL
Tintern	SOUTH WALES
Tiverton	DEVON
Tolpuddle	DORSET
Tongue	HIGHLANDS
Torquay	DEVON
Torrington	DEVON
Totland Bay	ISLE OF WIGHT
Totnes	DEVON
Trearddur Bay	ANGLESEY & GWYNEDD
Trefriw	NORTH WALES
Truro	CORNWALL
Turriff	ABERDEEN, BANFF & MORAY
Tutbury	STAFFORDSHIRE
Tywyn	ANGLESEY & GWYNEDD
Ullswater	CUMBRIA

Ulverston	CUMBRIA
Ventnor	ISLE OF WIGHT
Wadebridge	CORNWALL
Ware	KENT
Wareham	DORSET
Warkworth	NORTHUMBERLAND
Warwick	WARWICKSHIRE
Wasdale	CUMBRIA
Watchet	SOMERSET
Waterhouses	DURHAM
Weardale	DURHAM
Wells	SOMERSET
West Bexington	DORSET
West Linton	BORDERS
Weston-super-Mare	SOMERSET
Westward Ho!	DEVON
Weymouth	DORSET
Whitby	NORTH YORKSHIRE
Whitebridge	HIGHLANDS
Whithorn	DUMFRIES & GALLOWAY
Whitland	PEMBROKESHIRE
Wigtown	DUMFRIES & GALLOWAY
Windermere	CUMBRIA
Winterton-on-Sea	NORFOLK
Witheridge	DEVON
Wiveliscombe	SOMERSET
Woodbridge	SUFFOLK
Woodstock	OXFORDSHIRE
Woolacombe	DEVON
Worcester	WORCESTERSHIRE
Worthing	WEST SUSSEX
Wye Valley	SOUTH WALES
Yarmouth	ISLE OF WIGHT
Yelverton	DEVON
York	EAST YORKSHIRE
York	NORTH YORKSHIRE

FRANCE

Argentat (Correze)	Limousin
Arlanc (Puy-de-Dome)	Auvergne
Bayac (Dordogne)	Aquitaine
Collorec (Finistere)	Brittany
Estivals (Haute Vienne)	Limousin
Fontenay le Comte (Vendee)	Western Loire
La Ferte-Mace (Orne)	Lower Normandy
Le Bugue (Dordogne)	Aquitaine
Le Gast (Calvados)	Lower Normandy
Malestroit (Morbihan)	Brittany
Montagnac (Herault)	Languedoc-Roussillon
Pleine Fougeres (Rennes)	Brittany
St Georges de Reintembault (Ille-et-Villaine)	Brittany
St Malo de la Lande (Manche)	Lower Normandy
St marcel du Perigord (Dordogne)	Aquitaine
St Nicolas du Pelem (Rostrenen)	Brittany
Vernet-les-Bains (Pyrenees-Orientales)	Languedoc-Roussillon

Note

All the information in this guide is given in good faith in the belief that it is correct. However, the publishers cannot guarantee the facts given in these pages, neither are they responsible for changes in ownership or facilities that may take place after the date of going to press. Readers should always satisfy themselves that the facilities they require are available and that the terms, if quoted, still apply.